THE LOEB CLASSICAL LIBRARY

FOUNDED BY JAMES LOEB, LL.D.

DIODORUS OF SICILY

X

DIODORUS OF SICILY

WITH AN ENGLISH TRANSLATION BY

RUSSEL M. GEER, Ph.D.

TULANE UNIVERSITY, NEW ORLEANS, LA.

IN TWELVE VOLUMES

X

BOOKS XIX. 66–110 AND XX

CAMBRIDGE, MASSACHUSETTS
HARVARD UNIVERSITY PRESS
LONDON
WILLIAM HEINEMANN LTD
MCMLIV

Printed in Great Britain

CONTENTS

1. SICILY WITH THE PART OF THE AFRICAN COAST OPPOSITE TO IT

2. THE HELLENISTIC KINGDOMS

3. GREECE AND THE AEGEAN

THE LIBRARY OF HISTORY

OF

DIODORUS OF SICILY

BOOK XIX

Τάδε ἔνεστιν ἐν τῇ ἐννεακαιδεκάτῃ τῶν
Διοδώρου βύβλων

Τὰ πραχθέντα τοῖς Ἀντιγόνου καὶ Κασάνδρου στρατηγοῖς περὶ τὴν Ἑλλάδα.

Κασάνδρου στρατεία εἰς τὴν Αἰτωλίαν καὶ τοὺς κατὰ
τὸν Ἀδρίαν τόπους.

Ἅλωσις περὶ Καρίαν τῆς ἀποσταλείσης ὑπὸ Κασάνδρου δυνάμεως.

Ὡς οἱ φυγάδες τῶν Συρακουσίων Ἀκραγαντίνους
πείσαντες πολεμεῖν Ἀγαθοκλεῖ στρατηγὸν ἐκ Λακεδαί-
μονος Ἀκρότατον μετεπέμψαντο.

Ὡς οὗτος μὲν παραλαβὼν τὴν ἡγεμονίαν τυραννικῶς[1]
ἄρχων διεγένετο, οἱ δ' Ἀκραγαντῖνοι τὴν εἰρήνην ἐποιήσαντο πρὸς τὸν δυνάστην.

Τὰ πραχθέντα Ῥωμαίοις περὶ τὴν Ἰαπυγίαν.

Καλλαντιανῶν ἀπόστασις ἀπὸ Λυσιμάχου καὶ τὰ
συμβάντα τοῖς ἐπὶ τὴν βοήθειαν ἀποσταλεῖσιν ὑπ'
Ἀντιγόνου.

Ὡς Φίλιππος ἀποσταλεὶς ὑπὸ Κασάνδρου στρατηγὸς
εἰς τὴν Αἰτωλίαν ἐνίκησεν Αἰτωλοὺς ἅμα καὶ τοὺς
Ἠπειρώτας.

Ὡς Ῥωμαῖοι μάχῃ νικήσαντες Σαμνίτας μετ' ὀλίγον
Καμπανοὺς ἀποστάντας προσηγάγοντο.

---

[1] τυραννικῶς Rhodoman: καὶ εἰρηνικῶς.

2

CONTENTS OF THE NINETEENTH BOOK
OF DIODORUS

The operations of the generals of Antigonus and of Cassander in Greece (chap. 66).

Cassander's campaign in Aetolia and the country about the Adriatic (chaps. 67-68).

The capture in Caria of the army sent out by Cassander (chap. 68).[1]

How the Syracusan exiles, after persuading the people of Acragas to fight against Agathocles, sent for a general from Lacedaemon, Acrotatus (chap. 70).

How Acrotatus accepted the generalship and ruled as a tyrant; and how the Acragantines made peace with the dynast (chap. 71).

The Roman operations in Iapygia (chap. 72).

The revolt of the Callantians from Lysimachus, and what befell those who were dispatched to their aid by Antigonus (chap. 73).

How Philip, who had been sent as general into Aetolia by Cassander, defeated at one time the peoples of Aetolia and Epirus (chap. 74).[2]

How the Romans defeated the Samnites in battle, and a little later won back the Campanians who had revolted (chap. 76).

[1] The table of contents omits chap. 69: Antigonus' preparations against Ptolemy.
[2] Chap. 75 is omitted: operations of Antigonus in Asia Minor, and of Cassander in Greece.

DIODORUS OF SICILY

Ὡς Ἀντίγονος Πτολεμαῖον[1] στρατηγὸν ἐξαπέστειλε μετὰ δυνάμεως ἐλευθερώσοντα τοὺς Ἕλληνας καὶ τὰ πραχθέντα περὶ τὴν Ἑλλάδα.

Ἀπόστασις Κυρηναίων καὶ ἅλωσις, ἔτι δὲ Πτολεμαίου στρατεία εἰς Κύπρον καὶ Συρίαν.

Μάχη Δημητρίου πρὸς Πτολεμαῖον καὶ νίκη Πτολεμαίου.

Ἀπόστασις Τελεσφόρου τοῦ στρατηγοῦ ἀπὸ Ἀντιγόνου.

Τὰ περὶ τὴν Ἤπειρον καὶ τὸν Ἀδρίαν πραχθέντα Κασάνδρῳ.

Ὡς Σέλευκος παρὰ Πτολεμαίου λαβὼν δύναμιν ὀλίγην ἐκράτησε Βαβυλῶνος καὶ τὴν προϋπάρχουσαν αὐτῷ σατραπείαν ἀνεσώσατο.

Ὡς Ἀντίγονος ἀκινδύνως παραλαβὼν Κοίλην Συρίαν δύναμιν ἐξέπεμψεν εἰς τὴν Ἀραβίαν.

Περὶ τῶν νομίμων οἷς χρῆται τὰ ἔθνη τῶν Ἀράβων.

Περὶ τῆς καλουμένης Ἀσφαλτίτιδος λίμνης.

Ὡς Ἀντίγονος τὸν υἱὸν Δημήτριον ἐξαπέστειλε μετὰ τῆς δυνάμεως εἰς τὴν Βαβυλωνίαν.

Περὶ τῶν πραχθέντων Ῥωμαίοις καὶ Σαμνίταις.

Ὡς Ἀγαθοκλῆς Μεσσηνίους παρακρουσάμενος τῆς πόλεως ἐκυρίευσεν.

Ὡς τοὺς ἀντιταξαμένους Μεσσηνίων καὶ Ταυρομενιτῶν, ἔτι δὲ Κεντοριπίνων ἀπέσφαξεν.

Ὡς Ἀγαθοκλῆς Δεινοκράτη καὶ τοὺς φυγάδας περὶ Γαλαρίαν ἐνίκησεν.

---

[1] Πτολεμαῖον Geer : Πολέμωνα (cp. chap. 77. 2 ; also chaps. 57. 4, 68. 5 and notes).

4

CONTENTS OF THE NINETEENTH BOOK

Ῥωξάνης καὶ Ἀλεξάνδρου τοῦ βασιλέως θάνατος.

Τὰ πραχθέντα Ῥωμαίοις κατὰ τὴν Ἰταλίαν.

Περὶ τῆς γενομένης τοῖς Καρχηδονίοις ναυαγίας.

Ὡς Καρχηδόνιοι περὶ τὸν Ἱμέραν Ἀγαθοκλέα παρατάξει νικήσαντες συνέκλεισαν εἰς τὰς Συρακούσσας.

CONTENTS OF THE NINETEENTH BOOK

ΔΙΟΔΩΡΟΥ

ΤΟΥ ΣΙΚΕΛΙΩΤΟΥ
ΒΙΒΛΙΟΘΗΚΗΣ ΙΣΤΟΡΙΚΗΣ

ΒΙΒΛΟΣ ΕΝΝΕΑΚΑΙΔΕΚΑΤΗ

66. Τοῦ δ' ἔτους τούτου διελθόντος Ἀθήνησι μὲν
ἦρχε Νικόδωρος, ἐν Ῥώμῃ δ' ἦσαν ὕπατοι
Λεύκιος Παπείριος τὸ τέταρτον καὶ Κόιντος Πό-
2 πλιος τὸ δεύτερον. ἐπὶ δὲ τούτων Ἀριστόδημος
μὲν ὁ κατασταθεὶς ὑπ' Ἀντιγόνου στρατηγὸς ὡς
ἐπύθετο τὴν Ἀλεξάνδρου τοῦ Πολυπέρχοντος ἀπόστασιν, ἐπὶ τοῦ κοινοῦ τῶν Αἰτωλῶν δικαιο-
λογησάμενος προετρέψατο τὰ πλήθη βοηθεῖν τοῖς
Ἀντιγόνου πράγμασιν, αὐτὸς δὲ μετὰ τῶν μισθοφόρων διαβὰς ἐκ τῆς Αἰτωλίας εἰς Πελοπόννησον
κατέλαβεν Ἀλέξανδρόν τε καὶ τοὺς Ἠλείους
πολιορκοῦντας τὴν Κυλλήνην, εὐκαίρως δὲ τοῖς
3 κινδυνεύουσιν ἐπιφανεὶς ἔλυσε τὴν πολιορκίαν.
καταλιπὼν δ' ἐνταῦθα τοὺς παρεξομένους τῷ φρουρίῳ τὴν ἀσφάλειαν ἀνέζευξεν εἰς τὴν Ἀχαΐαν καὶ
Πάτρας μὲν ἠλευθέρωσε φρουρουμένας ὑπὸ τοῦ

8

THE LIBRARY OF HISTORY

OF

DIODORUS OF SICILY

BOOK XIX

66. After this year had passed, Nicodorus was 314 B.C.
archon at Athens, and at Rome Lucius Papirius was
consul for the fourth time and Quintus Publius for
the second.[1] While these held office, Aristodemus,
who had been made general by Antigonus, on learning of the defection of Polyperchon's son Alexander,
presented his own side of the matter to the common
assembly of the Aetolians and persuaded the majority
to support the fortunes of Antigonus. He himself,
however, with his mercenaries crossed from Aetolia
to the Peloponnesus, where he found Alexander
and the Eleans laying siege to Cyllenê, and, arriving
at a moment opportune for the endangered people,
raised the siege. Leaving troops there to insure the
safety of the stronghold, he advanced into Achaia
and freed Patrae, which was subject to a garri-

---

[1] Nicodorus was archon in 314/13 B.C. The consuls of
315 B.C. are given by the Fasti Capitolini as L. Papirius
Cursor and Q. Poblilius Philo, each for the fourth time
(*CIL*, 1, p. 130). The names of the consuls of this year have
been lost from Livy, 9. 22.

9

Κασάνδρου στρατιωτῶν, Αἴγιον δὲ ἐκπολιορκήσας
τῆς τε φρουρᾶς ἐκυρίευσε καὶ τοῖς Αἰγιεῦσι κατὰ
δόγμα τὴν ἐλευθερίαν βουλόμενος ἀποκαταστῆσαι
διὰ ταύτην τὴν περίστασιν ἐκωλύθη· τῶν γὰρ
στρατιωτῶν τραπέντων πρὸς ἁρπαγὴν πολλοὶ μὲν
ἀπεσφάγησαν τῶν Αἰγιέων πλεῖσται δὲ τῶν οἰκιῶν
4 διεφθάρησαν. μετὰ δὲ ταῦτα διαπλεύσαντος εἰς
Αἰτωλίαν αὐτοῦ Δυμαῖοι, φρουρὰν ἔχοντες παρὰ
Κασάνδρου, διετείχισαν τὴν πόλιν, ὥστε κατ' ἰδίαν
οὖσαν ἀπὸ τῆς ἀκροπόλεως διεζεῦχθαι. παρα-
καλέσαντες δ' ἀλλήλους ἀντέχεσθαι τῆς αὐτονομίας
περιεστρατοπέδευσαν τὴν ἄκραν καὶ συνεχεῖς προσ-
5 βολὰς ἐποιοῦντο. ἃ δὴ πυθόμενος ὁ Ἀλέξανδρος
ἧκεν μετὰ δυνάμεως καὶ βιασάμενος ἐντὸς τοῦ
τείχους ἐκυρίευσε τῆς πόλεως, τῶν δὲ Δυμαίων
τοὺς μὲν ἀπέσφαξεν, τοὺς δ' εἰς φυλακὴν ἀπέθετο,
6 πολλοὺς δὲ ἐφυγάδευσεν. οἱ δὲ περιλειφθέντες
ἀπαλλαγέντος ἐκ τῆς πόλεως Ἀλεξάνδρου χρόνον
μέν τινα τὴν ἡσυχίαν ἦγον, καταπεπληγμένοι τὸ
μέγεθος τῆς συμφορᾶς ἅμα δὲ καὶ συμμάχων ὄντες
ἔρημοι· μετὰ δέ τινα χρόνον ἐξ Αἰγίου τοὺς Ἀρι-
στοδήμου μισθοφόρους μεταπεμψάμενοι πάλιν ἐπέθεντο τῇ φρουρᾷ καὶ κυριεύσαντες τῆς ἄκρας τὴν
μὲν πόλιν ἠλευθέρωσαν, τῶν δὲ καταλειφθέντων[1]
τοὺς πλείστους ἀποσφάξαντες συνανεῖλαν καὶ τῶν
ἰδίων πολιτῶν ὅσοι πρὸς Ἀλέξανδρον εἶχον φιλίαν.
67. Ἅμα δὲ τούτοις πρασσομένοις Ἀλέξανδρος
μὲν ὁ Πολυπέρχοντος ἐκ Σικυῶνος ἀναζευγνύων
μετὰ τῆς δυνάμεως ὑπ' Ἀλεξίωνος τοῦ Σικυ-
ωνίου καί τινων ἄλλων προσποιουμένων εἶναι

---

[1] So the MSS., but with η added above ει by second hands.

son of Cassander's troops. After a successful siege of Aegium he became master of its garrison; but, although he wished to establish freedom for the people of Aegium according to the decree,[1] he was blocked by the following incident: for while the soldiers were engaged in pillaging, many of the Aegienses were killed and very many of their buildings were destroyed. Thereafter, when Aristodemus had sailed to Aetolia, the Dymaeans,[2] who were subject to a garrison sent by Cassander, cut off their city by a dividing wall in such a way that it was isolated and separated from the citadel. Then, after encouraging each other to assert their freedom, they invested the citadel and made unremitting attacks upon it. But Alexander on learning of this came with his army, forced his way within the wall, and became master of the city, slaying some of the Dymaeans, imprisoning others, and sending many into exile. When Alexander had departed from the city, the survivors remained quiet for some time, stunned by the magnitude of the disaster and also bereft of allies. After a little while, however, they summoned from Aegium the mercenaries of Aristodemus and once more made an attack on the garrison. Taking the citadel, they freed the city; and when they had massacred most of those who had been left there,[3] they likewise slew all those of their own citizens who maintained friendship with Alexander.

67. While this was taking place, Polyperchon's son Alexander, as he was setting out from Sicyon with his army, was killed by Alexion of Sicyon and certain others who pretended to be friends. His

---

[1] Cp. chap. 61. 3.   [2] Dymê is a town in western Achaia.
[3] Or, reading καταληφθέντων: "who had been captured."

11

φίλων ἀνῃρέθη, ἡ δὲ γυνὴ Κρατησίπολις διαδεξα-
μένη τὰ πράγματα συνεῖχε τὸ στρατόπεδον,
ἀγαπωμένη διαφερόντως ὑπὸ τῶν στρατιωτῶν διὰ
τὰς εὐεργεσίας· διετέλει γὰρ βοηθοῦσα τοῖς ἀτυ-
χοῦσι καὶ πολλοὺς τῶν ἀπόρων ὑπολαμβάνουσα.

2 ἦν δὲ περὶ αὐτὴν καὶ σύνεσις πραγματικὴ καὶ τόλμα
μείζων ἢ κατὰ γυναῖκα· τῶν γὰρ Σικυωνίων κατα-
φρονησάντων αὐτῆς διὰ τὴν τοῦ ἀνδρὸς τελευτὴν
καὶ συνδραμόντων μετὰ τῶν ὅπλων ἐπὶ τὴν ἐλευθερίαν, παραταξαμένη καὶ νικήσασα πολλοὺς μὲν
ἀνεῖλε, συλλαβοῦσα δὲ περὶ τριάκοντα τὸν ἀριθμὸν
ἀνεσταύρωσεν. ἀσφαλισαμένη δὲ τὰ κατὰ τὴν
πόλιν ἐδυνάστευε τῶν Σικυωνίων, ἔχουσα πολλοὺς
στρατιώτας ἑτοίμους εἰς πάντα κίνδυνον.

Καὶ τὰ μὲν περὶ Πελοπόννησον ἐν τούτοις ἦν.

3 Κάσανδρος δ᾽ ὁρῶν τοὺς Αἰτωλοὺς συναγωνιζομένους μὲν Ἀντιγόνῳ πόλεμον δ᾽ ἔχοντας ὅμορον
πρὸς Ἀκαρνᾶνας ἔκρινε συμφέρειν ἅμα συμμάχους
μὲν Ἀκαρνᾶνας ποιήσασθαι ταπεινῶσαι δὲ τοὺς
Αἰτωλούς. διόπερ ἀναζεύξας ἐκ Μακεδονίας μετὰ
δυνάμεως μεγάλης ἧκεν εἰς Αἰτωλίαν καὶ κατεστρατοπέδευσεν περὶ τὸν καλούμενον Καμπύλον

4 ποταμόν· συναγαγὼν δὲ τοὺς Ἀκαρνᾶνας εἰς κοινὴν
ἐκκλησίαν καὶ διελθὼν ὅτι πόλεμον ἔχουσιν ὅμορον
ἐκ παλαιῶν χρόνων, συνεβούλευσεν ἐκ τῶν ἀνοχύρων[1]
καὶ μικρῶν χωρίων εἰς ὀλίγας πόλεις μετοικῆσαι,
ὅπως μὴ διεσπαρμένης τῆς οἰκήσεως ἀδυνατῶσιν

---

[1] ἀνοχύρων Reiske, ἀνωχύρων Dindorf : ὀχυρῶν.

---

[1] It is probable that this name (literally, "conqueror of
the city," cp. such a poetic word as κρατησίμαχος, Pindar,

12

wife, Cratesipolis,[1] however, succeeded to his power and held his army together, since she was most highly esteemed by the soldiers for her acts of kindness ; for it was her habit to aid those who were in misfortune and to assist many of those who were without resources. She possessed, too, skill in practical matters and more daring than one would expect in a woman. Indeed, when the people of Sicyon scorned her because of her husband's death and assembled under arms in an effort to gain their freedom, she drew up her forces against them and defeated them with great slaughter, but arrested and crucified about thirty. When she had a firm hold on the city, she governed the Sicyonians, maintaining many soldiers, who were ready for any emergency.

Such, then, was the situation in the Peloponnesus.

When Cassander saw that the Aetolians were supporting Antigonus and were also engaged in a border war with the Acarnanians, he decided that it was to his advantage at a single stroke to make the Acarnanians his allies and to humble the Aetolians. For this reason, setting out from Macedonia with a large army, he moved into Aetolia and camped beside the river called the Campylus.[2] When he had summoned the Acarnanians to a common assembly and had related to them in detail how they had been engaged in border warfare from ancient days, he advised them to move from their villages, which were small and unfortified, into a few cities so that they would no longer, because their homes

Pythian Odes, 9. 150), which is not found elsewhere, was conferred upon the princess after the episode here related. She held Sicyon for Polyperchon for some years, surrendering it to Ptolemy in 308 B.C., cp. Book 20. 37. 1.

[2] A tributary of the Acheloüs.

ἀλλήλοις βοηθεῖν καὶ πρὸς τὰς ἀπροσδοκήτους τῶν
πολεμίων ἐπιθέσεις δυσχερῶς[1] ἀθροίζωνται. πει-
σθέντων δὲ τῶν Ἀκαρνάνων οἱ πλεῖστοι μὲν εἰς
Στράτον πόλιν συνῴκησαν, ὀχυρωτάτην οὖσαν καὶ
μεγίστην, Οἰνιάδαι δὲ καί τινες ἄλλοι συνῆλθον ἐπὶ
5 Σαυρίαν, Δεριεῖς δὲ μεθ᾽ ἑτέρων εἰς Ἀγρίνιον. ὁ
δὲ Κάσανδρος ἀπολιπὼν στρατηγὸν Λυκίσκον μετὰ
τῶν ἱκανῶν στρατιωτῶν τούτῳ μὲν παρήγγειλε
βοηθεῖν Ἀκαρνᾶσιν, αὐτὸς δὲ μετὰ δυνάμεως παρελθὼν ἐπὶ Λευκάδος τὴν πόλιν διὰ πρεσβείας
6 προσηγάγετο. μετὰ δὲ ταῦτα τὴν ὁρμὴν ἐπὶ τὸν
Ἀδρίαν ποιησάμενος Ἀπολλωνίαν ἐξ ἐφόδου παρέλαβεν. εἰς δὲ τὴν Ἰλλυρίδα προελθὼν καὶ διαβὰς
τὸν Ἕβρον ποταμὸν παρετάξατο πρὸς Γλαυκίαν
7 τὸν Ἰλλυριῶν βασιλέα. περιγενόμενος δὲ τῇ μάχῃ
πρὸς μὲν τοῦτον συνθήκας ἐποιήσατο, καθ᾽ ἃς οὐκ
ἐξῆν τῷ Γλαυκίᾳ στρατεύειν ἐπὶ τοὺς Κασάνδρου
συμμάχους, τὴν δὲ τῶν Ἐπιδαμνίων πόλιν προσαγαγόμενος καὶ φρουρὰν ἐγκαταστήσας ἐπανῆλθεν
εἰς Μακεδονίαν.

68. Ἀπαλλαγέντος δὲ ἐκ τῆς Αἰτωλίας τοῦ
Κασάνδρου συστραφέντες τῶν Αἰτωλῶν εἰς τρισχιλίους καὶ περιχαρακώσαντες Ἀγρίνιον ἐπολιόρκουν,
τῶν δὲ κατοικούντων τὸ χωρίον ὁμολογίας ποιησα-
μένων ὥστε τὴν μὲν πόλιν παραδοῦναι, τῆς δ᾽
ἀσφαλείας τυχόντας αὐτοὺς ἀπαλλαγῆναι, οὗτοι μὲν
πιστεύοντες ταῖς σπονδαῖς ἀπῄεσαν, οἱ δ᾽ Αἰτωλοὶ
παραβάντες τὰς συνθήκας καὶ καταδιώξαντες τοὺς
οὐδὲν ἐλπίζοντας πείσεσθαι δεινὸν πλὴν ὀλίγων
2 πάντας ἀπέσφαξαν. ὁ δὲ Κάσανδρος παραγενόμενος εἰς Μακεδονίαν καὶ πυθόμενος πολεμεῖσθαι

---

[1] εὐχερῶς or μὴ δυσχερῶς Reiske.

were scattered, be powerless to aid each other and 314 B.C. find difficulty in assembling to meet the unexpected raids of their enemies. The Acarnanians were persuaded, and most of them came to live together in Stratus, since this was their strongest and largest city ; but the Oeniadae and some others gathered at Sauria, and the Derians and the rest settled at Agrinium. Cassander left Lyciscus in command with adequate troops, ordering him to aid the Acarnanians ; but he himself moved upon Leucas with an army and secured the allegiance of the city through an embassy. Thereafter, directing his campaign to the Adriatic, he took Apollonia at the first assault. Advancing into Illyria and crossing the Hebrus River, he drew up his army against Glaucias, the king of the Illyrians.[1] Being successful in the battle, he made a treaty with the king according to which Glaucias was not to wage war on Cassander's allies ; then he himself, after securing the city of Epidamnus and establishing a garrison therein, returned to Macedonia.[2]

68. When Cassander had departed from Aetolia, the Aetolians, gathering together to the number of three thousand, invested Agrinium and began a siege. The inhabitants of the place came to terms with them, agreeing to surrender the city and depart under safe conduct ; but when, trusting in the treaty, they were leaving, the Aetolians violated the terms, pursued hotly after these men while they were anticipating no danger, and slaughtered all but a few of them. When Cassander had arrived in Macedonia and heard that war was being waged on

---

[1] Justin, 15. 2. 1-2, gives a different account of this campaign. The Hebrus River in Illyria seems otherwise unknown.
[2] Continued in chap. 78.

τὰς ἐν Καρίᾳ πόλεις ὅσαι συνεμάχουν τοῖς περὶ
Πτολεμαῖον καὶ Σέλευκον, ἐξέπεμψε δύναμιν εἰς
τὴν Καρίαν, ἅμα μὲν βουλόμενος βοηθεῖν τοῖς συμμάχοις, ἅμα δὲ σπεύδων εἰς περισπασμοὺς ἐμβαλεῖν Ἀντίγονον ἵνα μὴ σχολὴν ἔχῃ διαβαίνειν εἰς
3 τὴν Εὐρώπην. ἔγραψε δὲ καὶ πρὸς Δημήτριον
τὸν Φαληρέα καὶ Διονύσιον τὸν φρουροῦντα τὴν
Μουνυχίαν, προστάττων εἴκοσι ναῦς εἰς Λῆμνον
ἐκπέμψαι. ἀποστειλάντων δ' αὐτῶν εὐθὺς τὰ
σκάφη καὶ ναύαρχον ἐπ' αὐτῶν Ἀριστοτέλη οὗτος
μὲν καταπλεύσας εἰς Λῆμνον καὶ μεταπεμψάμενος
Σέλευκον μετὰ στόλου τοὺς Λημνίους ἔπειθεν ἀποστῆναι τῶν περὶ Ἀντίγονον· οὐ προσεχόντων δ'
αὐτῶν τήν τε χώραν ἐδήωσε καὶ τὴν πόλιν περι-
4 χαρακώσας ἐπολιόρκει. μετὰ δὲ ταῦτα Σέλευκος
μὲν ἀπέπλευσεν εἰς Κῶν, Διοσκουρίδης δὲ κατασταθεὶς ναύαρχος ὑπ' Ἀντιγόνου, πυθόμενος τὸν
πλοῦν Σελεύκου, κατῆρεν εἰς Λῆμνον καὶ τὸν μὲν
Ἀριστοτέλη ἐξέβαλεν ἐκ τῆς νήσου, τῶν δὲ νεῶν
τὰς πλείους αὐτάνδρους εἷλε.
5 Ἄσανδρος[1] δὲ καὶ Πρεπέλαος ἀφηγοῦντο μὲν τῆς
ὑπὸ Κασάνδρου πεμφθείσης δυνάμεως εἰς τὴν
Καρίαν, πυθόμενοι δὲ Πτολεμαῖον τὸν Ἀντιγόνου
στρατηγὸν τὴν δύναμιν εἰς παραχειμασίαν διῃρη-

---

[1] Ἄσανδρος Wesseling (cp. Book 18. 3. 1) ; Κάσανδρος.

[1] A nephew of Antigonus (chap. 62. 9).
[2] Cp. the critical note. Asander became governor of
Caria in 323 B.C., continued in power in 321 B.C., and was
still satrap of Caria (Books 18. 3. 1, 39. 6 ; 19. 62. 2, 75. 1).
In the MSS. his name is often confused with that of Cassander, as here.

all the cities in Caria that were allied to Ptolemy
and Seleucus, he sent an army into Caria, for he
both wished to aid his allies and at the same time
was eager to force Antigonus into distracting undertakings so that he might not have leisure for crossing
over into Europe. He also wrote to Demetrius of
Phalerum and to Dionysius, who commanded the
garrison on Munychia, bidding them dispatch twenty
ships to Lemnos. They at once sent the boats with
Aristotle in command of them. After the latter had
sailed to Lemnos and had summoned Seleucus and
a fleet, he undertook to persuade the Lemnians to
revolt from Antigonus ; but as they did not assent,
he ravaged their land, invested the city, and began
a siege. Afterwards, however, Seleucus sailed off to
Cos ; and Dioscurides,[1] who had been made admiral
by Antigonus, on learning of Seleucus' departure,
swooped down upon Lemnos, drove Aristotle himself from the island, and captured most of his ships
together with their crews.

Asander [2] and Prepelaüs [3] were in command of
the expedition sent by Cassander into Caria ; and,
on being informed that Ptolemaeus,[4] the general
of Antigonus, had divided his army for wintering [5]

[3] Prepelaüs had been sent by Cassander to Polyperchon's
son, Alexander, in a successful effort to win him away from
Antigonus (chap. 64. 3). We hear no more of him until the
present campaign until 303 B.C., when he commanded the
garrison at Corinth for Cassander (Book 20. 103. 1).

[4] Ptolemaeus (or Polemaeus, cp. IG, 2². 1. 469), a nephew
of Antigonus, had accompanied his uncle at the siege of
Nora and had been accepted by Eumenes as a hostage
(Plutarch, Eumenes, 10. 3). In 315 B.C. he conducted a
successful campaign in Asia Minor against the generals of
Cassander (chaps. 57. 4 ; 60. 2).

[5] The winter of 314/13.

κέναι καὶ αὐτὸν ἀσχολεῖσθαι περὶ τὴν ταφὴν τοῦ
πατρός, Εὐπόλεμον ἀπέστειλαν ἐνεδρεῦσαι τοῖς πολεμίοις περὶ Κάπριμα τῆς Καρίας· συνεξέπεμψαν
δ' αὐτῷ πεζοὺς μὲν ὀκτακισχιλίους, ἱππεῖς δὲ
6 διακοσίους. καθ' ὃν δὴ χρόνον Πτολεμαῖος παρά
τινων αὐτομόλων ἀκούσας τὴν προαίρεσιν τῶν πολεμίων ἤθροισε μὲν τῶν πλησίον χειμαζόντων στρατιωτῶν πεζοὺς μὲν ὀκτακισχιλίους τριακοσίους,
7 ἱππεῖς δ' ἑξακοσίους. ἀνελπίστως δὲ περὶ μέσας
νύκτας ἐπιβαλὼν τῷ χάρακι τῶν ἐναντίων καὶ
καταλαβὼν ἀφυλάκτους καὶ κοιμωμένους αὐτόν τε
τὸν Εὐπόλεμον ἐζώγρησε καὶ τοὺς στρατιώτας
συνηνάγκασε παραδοῦναι σφᾶς αὐτούς.

Τὰ μὲν οὖν συμβάντα περὶ τοὺς ἀποσταλέντας
ὑπὸ Κασάνδρου στρατηγοὺς εἰς τὴν Ἀσίαν τοιαῦτ'
ἦν.

69. Ἀντίγονος δ' ὁρῶν τὸν Κάσανδρον ἀντεχό-
μενον τῆς Ἀσίας Δημήτριον μὲν τὸν υἱὸν ἀπέλιπεν
ἐν τῇ Συρίᾳ, προστάξας ἐνεδρεύειν τοὺς περὶ
Πτολεμαῖον, οὓς ὑπώπτευεν ἐκ τῆς Αἰγύπτου
προάξειν μετὰ δυνάμεως ἐπὶ Συρίας, συναπέλιπε δ'
αὐτῷ πεζοὺς μὲν ξένους μυρίους, Μακεδόνας δὲ
δισχιλίους, Λυκίους δὲ καὶ Παμφυλίους πεντακοσίους, Πέρσας δὲ τοξότας καὶ σφενδονήτας τετρακοσίους, ἱππεῖς δὲ πεντακισχιλίους, ἐλέφαντας δὲ
τρεῖς[1] πλείους τῶν τεσσαράκοντα. παρακατέστησε
δ' αὐτῷ καὶ συμβούλους τέσσαρας, Νέαρχόν τε τὸν
Κρῆτα καὶ Πίθωνα τὸν Ἀγήνορος, ὃς καταβεβήκει

---

[1] τρεῖς omitted by Fischer.

[1] Caprima in Caria is otherwise unknown.
[2] Cp. Plutarch, *Demetrius*, 5. 2 ; Appian, *Syrian Wars*, 54.
[3] Nearchus was a boyhood friend of Alexander (Arrian,

and was himself engaged in burying his father, they _{314 B.C.} dispatched Eupolemus to lie in wait for the enemy near Caprima [1] in Caria, sending with him eight thousand foot soldiers and two hundred horse. But at this time Ptolemaeus, who had heard from some deserters of the plan of the enemy, gathered from the troops who were wintering near by eight thousand three hundred foot soldiers and six hundred horse. Falling unexpectedly upon the fortified camp of the enemy about midnight and catching them off guard and asleep, he captured Eupolemus himself alive and forced the soldiers to give themselves up.

This, then, is what befell the generals who were sent by Cassander into Asia.

69. When Antigonus perceived that Cassander was trying to win Asia for himself, he left his son Demetrius in Syria,[2] ordering him to lie in wait for Ptolemy, whom he suspected of intending to advance from Egypt with an army against Syria; with Demetrius he left an infantry force consisting of ten thousand mercenaries, two thousand Macedonians, five hundred Lycians and Pamphylians, and four hundred Persian archers and slingers, a cavalry force of five thousand, and forty-three elephants. He assigned to him four counsellors: Nearchus of Crete,[3] Pithon, son of Agenor,[4] who had returned

Anabasis, 3. 6. 5 ; Plutarch, *Alexander*, 10. 3), who had accompanied him on the march eastward and commanded the fleet on the return. In 323 B.C. he was appointed to command a voyage of exploration around Arabia, but this was abandoned on Alexander's death (Arrian, *Anabasis*, 7. 25. 4 ; Plutarch, *Alexander*, 68). He served under Antigonus in 317 B.C. (chap. 19. 4) and joined Demetrius in urging that Eumenes be spared (Plutarch, *Eumenes*, 18. 3).

[4] This Pithon had been left by Alexander as satrap of lower India (Arrian, *Anabasis*, 6. 15. 4) and had remained

πρότερον ὀλίγαις ἡμέραις ἐκ Βαβυλῶνος, πρὸς δὲ
τούτοις Ἀνδρόνικόν τε τὸν Ὀλύνθιον καὶ Φίλιππον,
ἄνδρας πρεσβυτέρους καὶ συνεστρατευκότας Ἀλεξάνδρῳ πᾶσαν τὴν στρατείαν· ἦν γὰρ Δημήτριος
ἔτι νέος τὴν ἡλικίαν, ὡς ἂν γεγονὼς ἔτη δύο πρὸς
2 τοῖς εἴκοσιν. αὐτὸς δὲ τὴν ἄλλην δύναμιν ἀνέλαβε[1]
καὶ τὸ μὲν πρῶτον ὑπερβάλλων τὸν Ταῦρον καὶ
περιπεσὼν χιόνι πολλῇ συχνοὺς ἀπέβαλε τῶν
στρατιωτῶν. διὸ καὶ πάλιν ἀναστρέψας εἰς τὴν
Κιλικίαν καὶ μεταλαβὼν ἕτερον καιρὸν διεξῆλθε
μὲν ἀσφαλέστερον τὸ προειρημένον ὄρος, παραγενόμενος δ' εἰς Κελαινὰς τῆς Φρυγίας διεῖλε τὸ
3 στρατόπεδον εἰς χειμασίαν. μετὰ δὲ ταῦτα τὸν
στόλον ἐκ Φοινίκης μετεπέμψατο Μηδίου ναυ-
αρχοῦντος, ὃς περιτυχὼν ταῖς Πυδναίων[2] ναυσίν,
οὔσαις τριάκοντα ἕξ, καὶ καταναυμαχήσας αὐτάνδρων τῶν σκαφῶν ἐκυρίευσεν.

Καὶ τὰ μὲν περὶ τὴν Ἑλλάδα καὶ τὴν Ἀσίαν ἐν
τούτοις ἦν.

70. Κατὰ δὲ τὴν Σικελίαν οἱ τῶν Συρακοσίων
φυγάδες διατρίβοντες ἐν Ἀκράγαντι παρεκάλουν
τοὺς προεστηκότας τῆς πόλεως μὴ περιορᾶν Ἀγα-

---

[1] ἀνέλαβε Fischer : ἔλαβε.
[2] For the meaningless Πυδναίων Fischer suggests Πτολεμαίου or Πολυκλείτου, cp. chap. 64. 4.

---

there (Book 18. 3. 3 ; 39. 6) until recalled by Antigonus in
316 B.C. to become satrap of Babylonia (chap. 56. 4). He
is not to be confused with Pithon of the Bodyguard, who
had been put to death by Antigonus in 316 B.C. (chap. 46. 3-4),
or with the Pithon who was satrap of Media (Book 18. 3. 1 ;
39. 6).

[1] Nothing is known of his service under Alexander. He
served under Antigonus at the siege of Tyre in 315 B.C. (chap.
59. 2).

a few days before from Babylon, also Andronicus 314 B.C. of Olynthus [1] and Philip,[2] men advanced in years who had accompanied Alexander on his whole campaign ; for Demetrius was still youthful, being twenty-two years of age. Antigonus himself, taking the rest of the army, first tried to cross the Taurus Range, where he encountered deep snow and lost large numbers of his soldiers. Turning back therefore into Cilicia and seizing another opportunity, he crossed the aforesaid range in greater safety ; and, on reaching Celaenae in Phrygia, he divided his army for wintering.[3] Thereafter he summoned from Phoenicia his fleet under the command of Medius,[4] who fell in with the ships of the Pydnaeans,[5] thirty-six in number, defeated them in an engagement, and captured the vessels together with their crews.

This was the situation in Greece and in Asia.[6]

70. In Sicily [7] those of the Syracusan exiles who were tarrying in Acragas urged the rulers of that city not to watch complacently while Agatocles

[2] Nothing is known of his earlier career, but he may be the Philip who received Bactrianê and Sogdianê in 323 B.C. (Book 18. 3. 3). Ten years later he is still faithfully serving Antigonus (Book 20. 107. 5).

[3] This is the winter of 314/13 B.C.

[4] Medius served under Alexander, playing a more important part after the death of Hephaestion (Book 17. 117. 1). He was accused of poisoning Alexander (Arrian, *Anabasis*, 7. 27. 2), and after Alexander's death served Perdiccas (Arrian, *Successors*, 24. 6) and then joined Antigonus.

[5] " Pydnaeans " is certainly wrong. Possibly we should read " of Ptolemy," or " of Polyclitus," who was an admiral of Ptolemy.

[6] Continued in chap. 73.

[7] Continued from chap. 65. 6. The invitation to Acrotatus is probably to be dated in the preceding year.

θοκλέα συσκευαζόμενον τὰς πόλεις· αἱρετώτερον
γὰρ εἶναι πρὸ τοῦ τὸν τύραννον ἰσχυρὸν γενέσθαι
διαπολεμεῖν ἑκουσίως ἢ περιμείναντας αὐτοῦ τὴν
αὔξησιν ἐξ ἀνάγκης πρὸς ἰσχυρότερον διαγωνίζε-
2 σθαι. δοξάντων δ' αὐτῶν ἀληθῆ λέγειν ὁ μὲν δῆμος
τῶν Ἀκραγαντίνων ἐψηφίσατο τὸν πόλεμον καὶ
Γελῴους μὲν καὶ Μεσσηνίους εἰς τὴν συμμαχίαν
προσελάβοντο, εἰς δὲ τὴν Λακεδαιμονίαν τῶν φυγάδων τινὰς ἐξέπεμψαν, ἐντειλάμενοι πειρᾶσθαι
στρατηγὸν ἄγειν τὸν δυνάμενον πραγμάτων ἀφηγή-
3 σασθαι· τοὺς γὰρ πολιτικοὺς ὑπώπτευον ὡς ὄντας
οἰκείους τυραννίδος, τοὺς δ' ἔξωθεν ὑπελάμβανον
δικαίως ποιήσεσθαι τὴν τῶν ὅλων ἐπιμέλειαν,
ἀναμιμνησκόμενοι τῆς Τιμολέοντος τοῦ Κορινθίου
4 στρατηγίας. οἱ δὲ πεμφθέντες ὥς ποθ' ἧκον εἰς
τὴν Λακωνικήν, εὗρον Ἀκρότατον τὸν Κλεομένους
τοῦ βασιλέως υἱὸν προσκεκοφότα πολλοῖς τῶν
νέων καὶ διὰ τοῦτο ξενικῶν πραγμάτων ὀρεγόμενον.
5 τῶν γὰρ Λακεδαιμονίων μετὰ τὴν πρὸς Ἀντίπατρον
μάχην ἀπολυόντων τῆς ἀτιμίας τοὺς ἐκ τῆς ἥττης
διασωθέντας μόνος ἐνέστη τῷ δόγματι. διόπερ
αὐτὸν συνέβη καὶ τῶν ἄλλων οὐκ ὀλίγοις προσ-
κόψαι, μάλιστα δ' οἷς ἦν τῶν νόμων τὰ πρόστιμα·
οὗτοι γὰρ συστραφέντες πληγάς τε ἐνεφόρησαν[1]
6 αὐτῷ καὶ διετέλουν ἐπιβουλεύοντες. διὰ ταῦτα δὴ
ξενικῆς ἡγεμονίας ἐπιθυμῶν ἀσμένως ὑπήκουσε
τοῖς Ἀκραγαντίνοις. τὴν δ' ἀποδημίαν ποιησάμενος ἄνευ τῆς τῶν ἐφόρων γνώμης ἀνήχθη ναυσὶν

---

[1] πληγάς τε ἐνεφόρησαν editors : πληγάς τε ἐνεφορήθησαν RX,
πληγὰς συνεφόρησαν F.

---

[1] Cp. the action of the Syracusans who, after the death
of Timoleon, passed a law that henceforth they would always

organized the cities ; for it was better, they said, to 314 B.C. fight it out of their own free will before the tyrant became strong than to await the increase of his power and then be forced to struggle against him when he had grown stronger. Since they seemed to speak the truth, the popular assembly of the Acragantines voted for the war, added the people of Gela and Messenê to the alliance, and sent some of the exiles to Lacedaemon, instructing them to try to bring back a general capable of taking charge of affairs ; for they were suspicious of their own statesmen as being inclined toward tyranny, but, remembering the generalship of Timoleon the Corinthian,[1] assumed that leaders from abroad would honestly devote themselves to the common cause. The envoys, when they arrived in Laconia, found that Acrotatus, the son of King Cleomenes, had given offence to many of the younger men and for this reason was eager for activity away from home. This was because, when the Lacedaemonians after the battle against Antipater relieved from ignominy those who had survived the defeat,[2] he alone opposed the decree. He thus gave offence to many others and in particular to those who were subject to the penalties of the laws ; indeed, these persons gathered together and gave him a beating, and they were constantly plotting against him. Being therefore anxious for a foreign command, he gladly accepted the invitation of the men from Acragas. Taking his departure from the state without the consent of the ephors, he set sail

---

elect a Corinthian to lead them in foreign wars (Plutarch, *Timoleon*, 38. 2).

[2] The battle at Megalopolis in 331 B.C., in which King Agis III of Sparta was defeated and lost his life (Book 17. 62-63).

7 ὀλίγαις, ὡς διαρῶν¹ ἐπ' Ἀκράγαντος. ἀπενεχθεὶς
δ' ὑπ' ἀνέμων εἰς τὸν Ἀδρίαν κατῆρε μὲν εἰς τὴν
τῶν Ἀπολλωνιατῶν χώραν, καταλαβὼν δὲ τὴν
πόλιν πολιορκουμένην ὑπὸ Γλαυκίου τοῦ βασιλέως
τῶν Ἰλλυριῶν ἔλυσε τὴν πολιορκίαν, πείσας τὸν
βασιλέα συνθήκας ποιήσασθαι πρὸς τοὺς Ἀπολ-
8 λωνιάτας. ἐντεῦθεν δὲ πλεύσας εἰς Τάραντα καὶ
παρακαλέσας τὸν δῆμον συνελευθεροῦν Συρακοσίους, ἔπεισε ψηφίσασθαι ναυσὶν εἴκοσι βοηθεῖν·
διὰ γὰρ τὴν συγγένειαν καὶ τὸ τῆς οἰκίας σχῆμα
προσένεμον² τοῖς λόγοις αὐτοῦ πίστιν τε μεγάλην
καὶ βάρος.

71. Τῶν δὲ Ταραντίνων περὶ τὴν παρασκευὴν
ὄντων αὐτὸς αὐτόθεν ἐκπλεύσας³ εἰς τὸν Ἀκράγαντα παρέλαβε τὴν στρατηγίαν καὶ τὸ μὲν πρῶτον
μετεωρήσας τὰ πλήθη μεγάλαις ἐλπίσι παρεστή-
σατο πάντας προσδοκᾶν σύντομον κατάλυσιν τοῦ
2 τυράννου, τοῦ δὲ χρόνου προϊόντος πρᾶξιν μὲν οὐδεμίαν οὔτε τῆς πατρίδος οὔτε τῆς περὶ τὸ γένος
ἐπιφανείας ἀξίαν διεπράξατο, τοὐναντίον δὲ φονι-
κὸς ὢν καὶ τῶν τυράννων ὠμότερος προσέκοπτε
3 τοῖς πλήθεσι. πρὸς δὲ τούτοις τὴν πάτριον δίαιταν
μετέβαλεν καὶ ταῖς ἡδοναῖς ἐνετρύφησεν οὕτως
ἀσελγῶς ὥστε Πέρσην εἶναι δοκεῖν καὶ οὐ Σπαρ-
4 τιάτην. ἐπεὶ δὲ τῶν προσόδων τὸ πλεῖον μέρος
ἀνήλωσεν τὰ μὲν πολιτευόμενος, τὰ δὲ διανοσφιζό-
μενος τέλος Σωσίστρατον, ἐπιφανέστατον τῶν φυ-

---

¹ διαρῶν Dindorf : διαίρων MSS. followed by Fischer.
² προσένεμον Dindorf : προσενόουν RX, προσέπεσθαι F.
³ αὐτόθεν ἐκπλεύσας Capps : συνεκπλεύσας.

---

¹ Almost certainly identical with the Sostratus of chaps.
3–5. He was leader of the oligarchical party in Syracuse

with a few ships as if to cross to **Acragas**. He was, 314 B.C. however, carried by the winds into the Adriatic and landed in the territory of Apollonia. Finding that city besieged by Glaucias, the king of the Illyrians, he brought the siege to an end, persuading the king to make a treaty with the people of Apollonia. Thence he sailed to Tarentum, where he urged the people to join in freeing the Syracusans; and he persuaded them to vote to assist with twenty ships; for because of ties of kinship and on account of the dignity of his family, they ascribed to his words a high degree of sincerity and great importance.

71. While the Tarentines were engaged in their preparations, Acrotatus immediately sailed to Acragas where he assumed the office of general. At first he buoyed up the common people with great expectations and caused all to anticipate a speedy overthrow of the tyrant; however, as time advanced, he accomplished nothing worthy either of his fatherland or of the distinction of his family, but on the contrary, being bloodthirsty and more cruel than the tyrants, he continually gave offence to the common people. Moreover, he abandoned his native manner of living and devoted himself so unrestrainedly to pleasure that he seemed to be a Persian and not a Spartan. When he had squandered the larger part of the revenue, partly by his public activity, partly by private peculation, he finally invited to dinner Sosistratus,[1] who was the most distinguished of the

and one of the Six Hundred at the time when Agathocles became tyrant, escaping death by flight. In chap. 3. 3, Diodorus, following some democratic source, describes him as one who " had spent the greater part of his life in plots, murders, and great impieties," in sharp contrast to the praise given him in this passage, probably based on Timaeus.

γάδων, πολλάκις δυνάμεων ἀφηγησάμενον, ἐπὶ τὸ
δεῖπνον παραλαβὼν ἐδολοφόνησεν, ἐγκαλέσαι μὲν
ἁπλῶς οὐδ᾽ ὁτιοῦν ἔχων, ἐκ ποδῶν δὲ ποιήσασθαι
σπεύδων[1] δραστικὸν ἄνδρα καὶ δυνάμενον ἐφεδρεῦσαι
5 τοῖς κακῶς προϊσταμένοις τῆς ἡγεμονίας. διαβοηθείσης δὲ τῆς πράξεως εὐθὺς οἵ τε φυγάδες συνέτρεχον ἐπ᾽ αὐτὸν καὶ πάντες οἱ λοιποὶ διετέθησαν
ἀλλοτρίως καὶ τὸ μὲν πρῶτον ἀπέστησαν αὐτὸν τῆς
στρατηγίας, μετ᾽ ὀλίγον δὲ καὶ βάλλειν τοῖς λίθοις
ἐπεχείρησαν· διόπερ φοβηθεὶς τὴν τοῦ πλήθους
ὁρμὴν νυκτὸς ἔφυγε καὶ λαθὼν διῆρεν εἰς τὴν
6 Λακωνικήν. τούτου δ᾽ ἀπαλλαγέντος Ταραντῖνοι
μὲν ἀπεσταλκότες εἰς Σικελίαν τὸν στόλον μετεπέμψαντο, Ἀκραγαντῖνοι δὲ καὶ Γελῷοι καὶ Μεσσήνιοι κατέλυσαν τὸν πρὸς Ἀγαθοκλέα πόλεμον,
μεσιτεύσαντος τὰς συνθήκας Ἀμίλκου τοῦ Καρχη-
7 δονίου. ἦσαν δὲ τὰ κεφάλαια τῶν συντεθέντων
τοιάδε, τῶν Ἑλληνίδων πόλεων τῶν κατὰ Σικελίαν
Ἡράκλειαν μὲν καὶ Σελινοῦντα καὶ πρὸς ταύταις
Ἱμέραν ὑπὸ Καρχηδονίοις τετάχθαι, καθὰ καὶ
προϋπῆρχον, τὰς δ᾽ ἄλλας πάσας αὐτονόμους εἶναι,
τὴν ἡγεμονίαν ἐχόντων Συρακοσίων.

72. Μετὰ δὲ ταῦτα Ἀγαθοκλῆς ὁρῶν ἔρημον
οὖσαν τὴν Σικελίαν στρατοπέδων πολεμίων ἀδεῶς
προσήγετο τὰς πόλεις καὶ τὰ χωρία. ταχὺ δὲ πολλῶν ἐγκρατὴς γενόμενος ἰσχυρὰν κατεσκευάσατο
τὴν δυναστείαν· καὶ γὰρ συμμάχων πλῆθος καὶ
προσόδους ἁδρὰς καὶ στρατόπεδον ἀξιόλογον περι-

---

[1] σπεύδων added by Fischer, cp. chap. 55. 4.

---

[1] But in chap. 102. 1 we are told that Messenê was
excluded from the peace.

exiles and had often commanded armies, and treacher- 314 B.C.
ously killed him, not having any charge whatever
to bring against him and yet being eager to put out
of the way a man who was accustomed to act and
who was capable of keeping under surveillance those
who misused positions of leadership. When this
deed became known, the exiles at once began to
join forces against Acrotatus, and all the rest were
alienated from him. First they removed him from
his generalship, and soon afterwards they attempted
to stone him, whereupon, terrified by the popular
uprising, he took flight by night and sailed secretly
to Laconia. After his departure the Tarentines,
who had sent their fleet to Sicily, recalled it ; and
the peoples of Acragas, Gela, and Messenê [1] brought
their war against Agathocles to an end, Hamilcar [2]
the Carthaginian acting as mediator in making the
treaty. The chief points of the agreement were as
follows : of the Greek towns in Sicily, Heraclea,
Selinus, and Himera were to be subject to the Carthaginians as they had been before, and all the others were
to be autonomous under the hegemony of Syracuse.

72. Afterwards,[3] however, when Agathocles perceived that Sicily was clear of hostile armies, he
began unhampered to subject the cities and strongholds to himself. Mastering many of them quickly,
he made his power secure ; in fact, he built up
for himself a host of allies, ample revenues, and a

[2] He had previously shown himself favourable to Agathocles (Justin, 22. 2. 6). He is possibly to be identified
with the Hamilcar who had fought against Timoleon (Plutarch, *Timoleon*, 25).
[3] It is probable that the events narrated in this paragraph
belong, at least in part, to the following year, in the account
of which Sicily is not mentioned.

2 ἐποιήσατο. χωρὶς γὰρ τῶν συμμάχων καὶ τῶν ἐκ
Συρακουσσῶν καταγραφέντων εἰς τὴν στρατείαν
μισθοφόρους ἐπιλέκτους εἶχε πεζοὺς μὲν μυρίους,
ἱππεῖς δὲ τρισχιλίους πεντήκοντα. ἐποιήσατο δὲ
καὶ παρασκευὴν ὅπλων καὶ βελῶν παντοδαπῶν,
εἰδὼς τοὺς Καρχηδονίους ἐπιτετιμηκότας τῷ
Ἀμίλκᾳ περὶ τῶν συνθηκῶν συντόμως δὲ πρὸς
αὐτὸν τὸν πόλεμον ἐξοίσοντας.

Καὶ τὰ μὲν περὶ Σικελίαν ἐν τούτοις τοῖς χρόνοις
τοιαύτην ἔσχε τὴν κατάστασιν.

3 Κατὰ δὲ τὴν Ἰταλίαν Σαμνῖται διαπολεμοῦντες
Ῥωμαίοις ἔτη πλείονα περὶ τῆς ἡγεμονίας Πλη-
στικὴν μὲν φρουρὰν ἔχουσαν Ῥωμαϊκὴν ἐξεπολιόρκησαν, Σωρανοὺς δ' ἔπεισαν κατασφάξαι μὲν τοὺς
παρ' αὐτοῖς Ῥωμαίους, συμμαχίαν δὲ πρὸς Σαμνί-
4 τας συνθέσθαι. μετὰ δὲ ταῦτα Ῥωμαίων Σατι-
κόλαν πολιορκούντων ἐπεφάνησαν μετὰ δυνάμεως
ἁδρᾶς, σπεύδοντες λῦσαι τὴν πολιορκίαν· γενομένης
οὖν μάχης ἰσχυρᾶς πολλοὶ μὲν παρ' ἀμφοτέρων
ἀνῃρέθησαν, τέλος δὲ ἐπὶ τοῦ προτερήματος ἐγένοντο Ῥωμαῖοι. μετὰ δὲ τὴν μάχην ἐκπολιορκήσαντες τὴν πόλιν ἐπῄεσαν ἀδεῶς τὰ πλησίον
5 πολίσματα καὶ χωρία προσαγόμενοι. τοῦ δὲ
πολέμου περὶ τὰς ἐν Ἀπουλίᾳ πόλεις συνεστῶτος
οἱ μὲν Σαμνῖται πάντας τοὺς ἐν ἡλικίᾳ[1] στρατείας
ὄντας καταγράψαντες ἐστρατοπέδευσαν πλησίον τῶν
6 πολεμίων, ὡς περὶ τῶν ὅλων κριθησόμενοι. ἃ δὴ
πυθόμενος ὁ δῆμος τῶν Ῥωμαίων καὶ διαγωνιάσας

[1] ἡλικίᾳ Hertlein : ἡλικίαις.

---

[1] Hamilcar was accused of treason but died before the
trial was completed (Justin, 22. 3. 2-7).
[2] Continued in chap. 102.

considerable army. Indeed, without counting the 314 B.C. allies and those of the Syracusans who had enlisted for military service, he had a picked mercenary force comprising ten thousand foot soldiers and thirty-five hundred horse. Moreover, he prepared a store of weapons and of missiles of all kinds, since he knew that the Carthaginians, who had censured Hamilcar for the terms of peace,[1] would shortly wage war against him.

This was the situation of Sicilian affairs at this time.[2]

In Italy[3] the Samnites, fighting bitterly against the Romans for supremacy in a struggle lasting many years, took by siege Plesticê,[4] which had a Roman garrison, and persuaded the people of Sora to slay the Romans who were among them and to make an alliance with themselves. Next, as the Romans were besieging Saticula, the Samnites suddenly appeared with a strong army intent on raising the siege. A great battle then took place in which many were slain on both sides, but eventually the Romans gained the upper hand. After the battle the Romans carried the siege of the city to completion and then advanced at will, subjecting the near-by towns and strongholds. Now that the struggle for the cities of Apulia[5] had been joined, the Samnites enrolled all who were of age for military service and encamped near the enemy as if intending to decide the whole issue. When the Roman people learned

---

[3] Continued from chap. 65. 7 ; cp. Livy, 9. 21-23.

[4] The location of this town, called Plistica or Postia in the MSS. of Livy, is not known.

[5] So the MSS., but Sora is in south-eastern Latium, Saticula on the frontier between Campania and Samnium, and Laustolae covers the shore road from Latium to Campania. Perhaps we should read " Campania."

περὶ τοῦ μέλλοντος δύναμιν προέπεμψε πολλήν.
εἰωθότες δ' ἐν τοῖς ἐπικινδύνοις καιροῖς αὐτοκράτορα τοῦ πολέμου καθιστᾶν τινὰ τῶν ἀξιολόγων
ἀνδρῶν προεχειρίσαντο τότε Κόιντον Φάβιον καὶ
7 μετ' αὐτοῦ Κόιντον Αὔλιον[1] ἵππαρχον. οὗτοι δὲ
τὰς δυνάμεις παραλαβόντες παρετάξαντο πρὸς τοὺς
Σαμνίτας περὶ τὰς καλουμένας Λαυστόλας καὶ πολλοὺς τῶν στρατιωτῶν ἀπέβαλον. τροπῆς δὲ γενομένης καθ' ἅπαν τὸ στρατόπεδον ὁ μὲν Αὔλιος
καταισχυνθεὶς ἐπὶ τῇ φυγῇ μόνος ὑπέστη τῷ[2]
πλήθει τῶν πολεμίων, οὐ κρατήσειν ἐλπίζων, ἀλλ'
ἀήττητον τὴν πατρίδα τὸ καθ' αὑτὸν μέρος ἀπο-
8 δεικνύων. οὗτος μὲν οὖν οὐ μετασχὼν τοῖς
πολίταις τῆς κατὰ τὴν φυγὴν αἰσχύνης ἰδίᾳ περι-
εποιήσατο θάνατον ἔνδοξον· οἱ δὲ Ῥωμαῖοι
φοβηθέντες μὴ τὰ κατὰ τὴν Ἀπουλίαν πράγματα
τελέως ἀποβάλωσιν, ἀποικίαν ἐξέπεμψαν εἰς Λουκερίαν[3] πόλιν ἐπιφανεστάτην τῶν ἐν τοῖς τόποις. ἐκ
ταύτης δὲ ὁρμώμενοι διεπολέμουν τοῖς Σαμνίταις,
9 οὐ κακῶς τῆς ἀσφαλείας προνοησάμενοι· διὰ γὰρ
ταύτην τὴν πόλιν οὐ μόνον ἐν τούτῳ τῷ πολέμῳ
προετέρησαν, ἀλλὰ καὶ κατὰ[4] τοὺς μετὰ ταῦτα
γενομένους ἕως τῶν καθ' ἡμᾶς χρόνων διετέλεσαν
ὁρμητηρίῳ χρώμενοι κατὰ τῶν πλησίον ἐθνῶν.

---

[1] Αὔλιον Rhodoman, cp. Livy, 9. 22 : Ὥλιον RX, Αἴλιον F.
[2] τε after τῷ omitted by Rhodoman.
[3] Λουκερίαν Stephanus : Λοκρίαν RX, Λουκρίαν F.
[4] κατὰ added by Stephanus.

---

[1] Called Lautulae by Livy (9. 23. 4-5), who says that this
was a drawn battle, but admits that some of his sources
called it a defeat in which Aulius lost his life. According
to Livy, Fabius a few days later won a great victory, but
this second battle is unknown to our other historians.

this, they became anxious about what was impending 314 B.C.
and sent out a large army. As it was their custom
in a dangerous crisis to appoint as military dictator
one of their eminent men, they now elected Quintus
Fabius and with him Quintus Aulius as master-of-
horse. These, after assuming command of the army,
took the field and fought against the Samnites at
Laustolae,[1] as it is called, losing many of their
soldiers. As panic spread through the whole army,
Aulius, in shame at the flight, stood alone against the
mass of the enemy, not that he hoped to prevail, but
he was maintaining his fatherland undefeated as far
as he was concerned. Thus he, by not sharing with
his fellow citizens in the disgrace of flight, gained a
glorious death for himself alone ; but the Romans,
fearing that they might completely lose control
throughout Apulia, sent a colony to Luceria, which
was the most noteworthy of the cities of that region.
Using it as a base, they continued the war against
the Samnites, having made no mean provision for
their future security ; for not only were the Romans
victorious in this war because of this city, but also in
the wars that have subsequently taken place down to
our own time they have continued to use Luceria as a
base of operations against the neighbouring peoples.[2]

[2] Livy (9. 26. 1-5) places the establishment of this colony
under the next consuls, that is in 314 B.C. by the conventional
Roman chronology, 313 B.C. according to Diodorus. Luceria
served as a Roman base in the Second Punic War, remaining
loyal in the darkest days of the conflict (Livy, 22. 9. 5 ; 23.
37. 13 ; 24. 3. 16, etc.) ; and in the Civil War Pompey used
it for a time as his headquarters (Caesar, *Civil War*, 1. 24).
For the possible bearing of this passage on the date of Diodorus' source for Roman history, see the Introduction to
Vol. IX, page ix. The account of Italian affairs is continued
in chap. 76.

73. Τῶν δὲ κατὰ τοῦτον τὸν ἐνιαυτὸν πράξεων τέλος ἐχουσῶν Ἀθήνησι μὲν παρέλαβε τὴν ἀρχὴν Θεόφραστος, ἐν Ῥώμῃ δ' ὕπατοι κατεστάθησαν Μάρκος Πόπλιος καὶ Γάιος Σουλπίκιος. ἐπὶ δὲ τούτων Καλλαντιανοὶ κατοικοῦντες ἐν τοῖς ἐν ἀριστερᾷ μέρεσι τοῦ Πόντου καὶ φρουρὰν ἔχοντες παρὰ Λυσιμάχου ταύτην ἐξέβαλον καὶ τῆς αὐτονομίας

2 ἀντείχοντο. ὡσαύτως δὲ τήν τε τῶν Ἰστριανῶν πόλιν καὶ τὰς ἄλλας τὰς πλησιοχώρους ἐλευθερώσαντες συνέθεντο συμμαχίαν ὡς κοινῇ πολεμεῖν τῷ δυνάστῃ· προσελάβοντο δ' εἰς τὴν φιλίαν τῶν τε Θρακῶν καὶ Σκυθῶν τοὺς ὁμοροῦντας, ὥστε τὸ πᾶν εἶναι σύστημα βάρος ἔχον καὶ δυνάμενον ἁδραῖς

3 δυνάμεσιν ἀντιτάσσεσθαι. ὁ δὲ Λυσίμαχος πυθόμενος τὰ πεπραγμένα μετὰ τῆς δυνάμεως ὥρμησεν ἐπὶ τοὺς ἀφεστηκότας. ποιούμενος δὲ τὴν πορείαν διὰ τῆς Θρᾴκης καὶ τὸν Αἷμον ὑπερβαλὼν κατεστρατοπέδευσε πλησίον τῆς Ὀδησσοῦ. πολιορκίαν δὲ συστησάμενος ταχὺ τοὺς ἔνδον κατεπλήξατο καὶ

4 δι' ὁμολογίας παρέλαβε τὴν πόλιν. μετὰ δὲ ταῦτα τῷ παραπλησίῳ τρόπῳ τοὺς Ἰστριανοὺς ἀνακτησάμενος ἀνέζευξεν ἐπὶ Καλλαντιανούς. καθ' ὃν δὴ χρόνον ἧκον οἵ τε Σκύθαι καὶ Θρᾷκες σὺν πολλῇ δυνάμει βοηθήσοντες τοῖς συμμάχοις κατὰ τὰς

5 συνθήκας. οἷς ἀπαντήσας Λυσίμαχος καὶ συμβαλὼν ἐξ ἐφόδου τοὺς μὲν Θρᾷκας καταπληξάμενος ἔπεισε μεταθέσθαι, τοὺς δὲ Σκύθας ἐκ παρατάξεως νικήσας καὶ πολλοὺς ἀνελὼν τούτων μὲν τοὺς ὑπολειφθέντας ἐδίωξεν ἐκτὸς τῶν ὅρων, τὴν δὲ τῶν

---

[1] Theophrastus was archon in 313/12 B.C. In the Fasti Capitolini the consuls for 314 B.C. are M. Poetelius Libo

73. When the activities of this year had come to 313 B.C.
an end, Theophrastus obtained the archonship in
Athens, and Marcus Publius and Gaius Sulpicius
became consuls in Rome.[1] While these were in office,
the people of Callantia, who lived on the left side of
the Pontus [2] and who were subject to a garrison
that had been sent by Lysimachus, drove out this
garrison and made an effort to gain autonomy. In
like manner they freed the city of the Istrians and
the other neighbouring cities, and formed an alliance
with them binding them to fight together against
the prince. They also brought into the alliance
those of the Thracians and Scythians whose lands
bordered upon their own, so that the whole was a
union that had weight and could offer battle with
strong forces. As soon, however, as Lysimachus
learned what had taken place, he set out with his
army against the rebels. After marching through
Thrace and crossing the Haemus Mountains, he
encamped near Odessus. Beginning a siege, he
quickly frightened the inhabitants and took the city
by capitulation. Next, after recovering the Istrians
in a similar way, he set out against the Callantians.
At this very time the Scythians and the Thracians
arrived with large forces to aid their allies in accordance with the treaty. Lysimachus, meeting them
and engaging them at once, terrified the Thracians
and induced them to change sides ; but the Scythians
he defeated in a pitched battle, slaying many of
them and pursuing the survivors beyond the frontiers.

and C. Sulpicius Longus for the third time (*CIL*, 1, p. 130 ;
cp. Livy, 9. 24. 1).

[2] *i.e.* on the left as one enters the Euxine from the Bosporus. The city is called Callatis by Strabo, 7. 5. 12. The
narrative is continued from chap. 69.

Καλλαντιανῶν πόλιν περιστρατοπεδεύσας συνεστήσατο πολιορκίαν, φιλοτιμούμενος ἐκ παντὸς τρόπου
6 κολάσαι τοὺς αἰτίους τῆς ἀποστάσεως. περὶ
ταῦτα δ' ὄντος αὐτοῦ παρῆσάν τινες ἀπαγγέλλοντες
ὅτι δύο δυνάμεις ἀπέσταλκεν Ἀντίγονος ἐπὶ βοήθειαν τοῖς Καλλαντιανοῖς, τὴν μὲν πεζῇ, τὴν δὲ
κατὰ θάλασσαν, καὶ διότι τῷ μὲν στόλῳ Λύκων ὁ
στρατηγὸς παραπέπλευκεν εἰς τὸν Πόντον, Παυ-
σανίας δ' ἔχων οὐκ ὀλίγους στρατιώτας περὶ τὸ
7 καλούμενον Ἱερὸν κατεστρατοπέδευσεν. ἐφ' οἷς ὁ
Λυσίμαχος διαταραχθεὶς ἐπὶ μὲν τῆς πολιορκίας
ἀπέλιπεν τοὺς ἱκανοὺς στρατιώτας, τὸ δὲ κράτιστον
τῆς δυνάμεως ἀναλαβὼν αὐτὸς ἠπείγετο, σπεύδων
8 συνάψαι τοῖς πολεμίοις. παραγενόμενος δὲ ἐπὶ τὴν
κατὰ τὸν Αἷμον ὑπερβολὴν εὗρε Σεύθην τὸν βασιλέα
τῶν Θρᾳκῶν ἀφεστηκότα πρὸς Ἀντίγονον μετὰ
πολλῶν στρατιωτῶν φυλάσσοντα τὰς παρόδους.
9 συνάψας δ' αὐτῷ μάχην ἐφ' ἱκανὸν χρόνον τῶν τε
ἰδίων ἀπέβαλεν οὐκ ὀλίγους καὶ τῶν πολεμίων
10 ἀνελὼν παμπληθεῖς ἐβιάσατο τοὺς βαρβάρους. ἐπιφανεὶς δὲ καὶ τοῖς περὶ τὸν Παυσανίαν καὶ καταλαβὼν αὐτοὺς εἰς δυσχωρίας συμπεφευγότας ταύτας
τ' ἐξεπολιόρκησε καὶ Παυσανίαν ἀνελὼν τῶν στρατιωτῶν οὓς μὲν ἐλύτρωσεν, οὓς δὲ εἰς τὰς ἰδίας
τάξεις διένειμεν.

Τὰ μὲν οὖν περὶ Λυσίμαχον ἐν τούτοις ἦν.

74. Ὁ δ' Ἀντίγονος ἀποτυχὼν ταύτης τῆς ἐπιβολῆς ἐξέπεμψε Τελεσφόρον εἰς Πελοπόννησον,
δοὺς αὐτῷ πεντήκοντα ναῦς καὶ στρατιώτας τοὺς

---

[1] i.e. the Temple, or Sacred Place. The exact location
is not known.

Then, encamping about the city of the Callantians, 313 B.C. he laid siege to it, since he was very eager to chastise in every way those who were responsible for the revolt. While he was thus engaged, there came certain men bringing word that Antigonus had sent two expeditions to the support of the Callantians, one by land and one by sea, that the general Lycon with the fleet had sailed through into the Pontus, and that Pausanias with a considerable number of soldiers was in camp at a place called Hieron.[1] Perturbed at this, Lysimachus left an adequate body of soldiers to carry on the siege[2]; but with the strongest part of the army he himself pushed on, intent on making contact with the enemy. When, however, he reached the pass over the Haemus, he found Seuthes, the Thracian king, who had gone over to Antigonus, guarding the crossing with many soldiers. Engaging him in a battle that lasted a considerable time, Lysimachus lost not a few of his own men; but he destroyed a vast number of the enemy and overpowered the barbarians. He also came suddenly upon the forces of Pausanias, catching them after they had taken refuge in a place difficult of access. This he captured; and, after slaying Pausanias, he dismissed some of the soldiers on receiving ransom and enrolled others in his own army. This was the situation of Lysimachus.

74. Antigonus, after he had failed in this undertaking, dispatched Telesphorus[3] into the Peloponnesus, giving him fifty ships and a suitable force of

---

[2] We do not know the outcome of the siege. In 310 B.C. the Callantians are still resisting Lysimachus although hard pressed (Book 20. 25. 1).

[3] Probably a nephew of Antigonus (Diogenes Laertius, 5. 79; cp. Beloch, *Griechische Geschichte²*, 4. 1. 122, note 3).

ἱκανούς, καὶ τὰς πόλεις ἐλευθεροῦν ἐνετείλατο·
τοῦτο γὰρ πράξας ἤλπιζε πίστιν κατασκευάζειν
παρὰ τοῖς Ἕλλησιν ὅτι πρὸς ἀλήθειαν φροντίζει
τῆς αὐτονομίας αὐτῶν· καὶ ἅμα γινώσκειν ὑπ-
2 έβαλε[1] τὰ Κασάνδρου πρά γματα. ὁ δὲ Τελεσφόρος
ἐπειδὴ τάχιστα κατέπλευσεν εἰς τὴν Πελοπόννησον,
ἐπῆλθε τὰς ὑπ' Ἀλεξάνδρου φρουρουμένας πόλεις
καὶ πάσας ἠλευθέρωσε πλὴν Σικυῶνος καὶ Κορίν-
θου· ἐν ταύταις γὰρ Πολυπέρχων διέτριβεν δυνάμεις
ἁδρὰς ἔχων καὶ πιστεύων ταύταις τε καὶ ταῖς τῶν
3 τόπων ὀχυρότησιν. ἅμα δὲ τούτοις πραττομένοις
Φίλιππος ὑπὸ Κασάνδρου πεμφθεὶς στρατηγὸς εἰς
τὸν πρὸς Αἰτωλοὺς πόλεμον, ὡς τάχισθ' ἧκεν εἰς
τὴν Ἀκαρνανίαν μετὰ τῆς δυνάμεως, τὸ μὲν πρῶτον
ἐπεχείρει λεηλατεῖν τὴν Αἰτωλίαν, μετ' ὀλίγον δὲ
πυθόμενος Αἰακίδην τὸν Ἠπειρώτην εἰς τὴν βασιλείαν κατεληλυθότα[2] καὶ δύναμιν ἁδρὰν συνηθροικότα ταχέως ὥρμησεν ἐπ' αὐτόν· ἔσπευδε γὰρ
κατ' ἰδίαν διαγωνίσασθαι πρὶν ἢ συμμῖξαι τὴν τῶν
4 Αἰτωλῶν δύναμιν. εὑρὼν δὲ τοὺς Ἠπειρώτας
ἑτοίμους εἰς μάχην ἐξ ἐφόδου συνῆψεν εἰς χεῖρας
καὶ πολλοὺς μὲν ἀνεῖλεν, οὐκ ὀλίγους δ' ἐζώγρησεν,
ἐν οἷς συνέβαινεν εἶναι καὶ τῶν αἰτίων τῆς τοῦ

---

[1] ὑπέβαλε Post : ὑπέλαβε.
[2] κατεληλυθότα Reiske : διεληλυθότα.

---

[1] Alexander, son of Polyperchon, was dead, but his wife
still held certain cities, cp. chap. 67. 1-2.

infantry, and he ordered him to free the cities, for 313 B.C.
he hoped by doing this to establish among the Greeks
the belief that he truly was concerned for their
independence ; and at the same time he gave him
a hint to note the activities of Cassander. As soon
as Telesphorus had reached port in the Peloponnesus,
he advanced upon the cities that were occupied by
Alexander's garrisons [1] and freed all of them except
Sicyon and Corinth ; for in these cities Polyperchon
had his quarters, maintaining strong forces and
trusting in these and in the strength of the positions.
While this was being done, Philip,[2] who had been
sent by Cassander to the war against the Aetolians
as commander, immediately on arriving in Acarnania
with his army undertook to plunder Aetolia, but
soon, hearing that Aeacides [3] the Epirote had returned to his kingdom and had collected a strong
army, he set out very quickly against him, for he was
eager to bring this struggle to an end separately
before the army of the Aetolians joined forces with
the king. Although he found the Epirotes ready
for battle, he attacked them at once, slaying many
and taking captive no small number, among whom
there chanced to be about fifty of those responsible

[2] This is probably the younger brother of Cassander,
who, as one of Alexander's cupbearers, was charged by
Olympias with having given him poison (Justin, 12. 14. 6).
After this campaign he returns to obscurity ; a son, Anti-
pater, was king of Macedonia for 45 days in 281-280 B.C.
(Porphyrius, *FGrH*, 260. 3. 10).

[3] He was exiled with his father by Philip but returned
to power by aid of Olympias. After Alexander's death he
supported Olympias and Polyperchon (chap. 11. 2), his zeal
finally turning his own people against him and leading to
a second exile (chap. 36. 2-4). He appears to have returned
to Aetolia with Polyperchon in 316 B.C. (chap. 52. 6).

βασιλέως καθόδου περὶ πεντήκοντα τὸν ἀριθμόν,
5 οὓς δήσας ἀπέστειλε πρὸς Κάσανδρον. τῶν δὲ περὶ
τὸν Αἰακίδην ἀθροισθέντων ἐκ τῆς φυγῆς καὶ τοῖς
Αἰτωλοῖς συμμιξάντων πάλιν ἐπελθὼν ὁ Φίλιππος
μάχῃ ἐκράτησεν καὶ πολλοὺς ἀνεῖλεν, ἐν οἷς ἦν καὶ
6 Αἰακίδης ὁ βασιλεύς. ἐν ὀλίγαις δ' ἡμέραις τηλι-
καῦτα ποιήσας προτερήματα κατεπλήξατο πολλοὺς
τῶν Αἰτωλῶν ἐπὶ τοσοῦτον ὥστε τὰς ἀνοχύρους
πόλεις ἐκλιπεῖν, εἰς δὲ τὰ δυσβατώτατα τῶν ὀρῶν
συμφυγεῖν μετὰ τέκνων καὶ γυναικῶν.

Καὶ τὰ μὲν περὶ τὴν Ἑλλάδα πραχθέντα τοιοῦτον
ἔσχε τὸ τέλος.

75. Κατὰ δὲ τὴν Ἀσίαν Ἄσανδρος[1] ὁ τῆς Καρίας
κυριεύων πιεζούμενος τῷ πολέμῳ διελύσατο πρὸς
Ἀντίγονον ἐφ' ᾧ τοὺς μὲν στρατιώτας παραδώσει
πάντας Ἀντιγόνῳ, τὰς δ' Ἑλληνίδας πόλεις αὐτονόμους ἀφήσει, τὴν δὲ σατραπείαν ἣν πρότερον
εἶχε δωρεὰν καθέξει,[2] βέβαιος ὢν φίλος Ἀντιγόνῳ.
2 δοὺς δὲ περὶ τούτων ὅμηρον Ἀγάθωνα τὸν ἀδελφὸν
καὶ μετ' ὀλίγας ἡμέρας μεταμεληθεὶς ἐπὶ ταῖς
συνθήκαις τὸν μὲν ἀδελφὸν ἐξέκλεψεν ἐκ τῆς ὁμη-
ρίας πρὸς δὲ Πτολεμαῖον καὶ Σέλευκον διαπρεσ-
3 βευσάμενος ἠξίου βοηθεῖν τὴν ταχίστην. ἐφ' οἷς
Ἀντίγονος δεινοπαθήσας δύναμιν ἀπέστειλεν ἐπὶ
τὴν ἐλευθέρωσιν τῶν πόλεων καὶ κατὰ γῆν καὶ
κατὰ θάλασσαν, τοῦ μὲν στόλου ναύαρχον ἀποδείξας

---

[1] Ἄσανδρος Wesseling (cp. Book 18. 3. 1): Κάσανδρος
MSS., Fischer.
[2] τὴν δὲ σατραπείαν ἣν πρότερον εἶχε δωρεὰν καθέξει F 2d

for the return of the king ; these he bound and sent ^{313 B.C.} to Cassander.[1] As Aeacides and his men rallied from the fight and joined the Aetolians, Philip again advanced and overpowered them in battle, slaying many, among whom was King Aeacides [2] himself. By gaining such victories in a few days Philip so terrified many of the Aetolians that they abandoned their unfortified cities and fled to the most inaccessible of their mountains with their children and their women.

Such was the outcome of the campaign in Greece.[3]

75. In Asia, Asander,[4] the ruler of Caria, being hard pressed by the war, came to terms with Antigonus, agreeing to transfer to him all his soldiers, to relinquish the Greek cities and leave them autonomous, and to hold as a grant the satrapy that he had formerly had, remaining a steadfast friend of Antigonus. Having given his brother Agathon as a hostage for the fulfilment of these terms and then after a few days having repented of the agreement, he secretly removed his brother from custody and sent emissaries to Ptolemy and Seleucus, begging them to aid him as soon as possible. Antigonus, enraged at this, dispatched a force both by sea and by land to liberate the cities, appointing Medius

---

[1] Pausanias (1. 11. 4) tells us that this battle was fought at Oeniadae.

[2] His son Pyrrhus, the later king of Epirus, was adopted and reared by Glaucias, king of Illyria, who seems to have been related to him in some way (Plutarch, *Pyrrhus*, 3 ; Justin, 17. 3. 16-19).   [3] Continued in chap. 75. 6.

[4] He had been sent to Caria in the preceding year by Cassander (chap. 68. 4-7).

---

hand : τὰς δὲ σατραπείας ἃς πρότερον εἶχε δωρεὰν καθέξειν F, τὰς δὲ σατραπείας δωρεὰς ἃς πρότερον εἶχε καθέξει RX.

Μήδιον, τοῦ δὲ στρατοπέδου καταστήσας στρατη-
4 γὸν Δόκιμον. οὗτοι δὲ παραγενόμενοι πρὸς τὴν
πόλιν τῶν Μιλησίων τούς τε πολίτας ἐκάλουν ἐπὶ
τὴν ἐλευθερίαν καὶ τὴν φρουρουμένην ἄκραν ἐκπολιορκήσαντες εἰς αὐτονομίαν ἀποκατέστησαν τὸ
5 πολίτευμα. περὶ ταῦτα δ' ὄντων τούτων 'Αντί-
γονος Τράλλεις ἐξεπολιόρκησεν· εἰς δὲ Καῦνον
παρελθὼν καὶ τὸν στόλον μεταπεμψάμενος εἷλε καὶ
ταύτην τὴν πόλιν πλὴν τῆς ἄκρας· ταύτην δὲ περι-
χαρακώσας, καθ' ὃ μέρος ἦν προσμάχεσθαι, συνεχεῖς προσβολὰς ἐποιεῖτο. ἐπὶ δὲ τὴν 'Ιασὸν πόλιν
ἐκπεμφθεὶς Πτολεμαῖος μετὰ δυνάμεως ἱκανῆς
6 ἠνάγκασε[1] προσθέσθαι τοῖς περὶ 'Αντίγονον. αὗται
μὲν οὖν τῆς Καρίας οὖσαι τοῦτον τὸν τρόπον ὑπ-
ετάγησαν 'Αντιγόνῳ. μετ' ὀλίγας δ' ἡμέρας
ἐλθόντων πρὸς αὐτὸν πρεσβευτῶν παρ' Αἰτωλῶν
καὶ Βοιωτῶν πρὸς μὲν τούτους συμμαχίαν συνέθετο, τῷ δὲ Κασάνδρῳ συνελθὼν εἰς λόγους ὑπὲρ
εἰρήνης περὶ τὸν 'Ελλήσποντον ἀπῆλθεν ἄπρακτος,
οὐ δυναμένων αὐτῶν οὐδαμῶς συμφωνῆσαι. διόπερ
ὁ Κάσανδρος ἀπογνοὺς τὰς διαλύσεις διέγνω τῶν
κατὰ τὴν 'Ελλάδα πάλιν πραγμάτων ἀντέχεσθαι.
7 ἀναζεύξας οὖν μετὰ τριάκοντα νεῶν εἰς 'Ωρεὸν
ἐπολιόρκει τὴν πόλιν. ἐνεργῶς δ' αὐτοῦ ταῖς
προσβολαῖς χρωμένου καὶ τοῦ πολίσματος ἤδη
κατὰ κράτος ἁλισκομένου παρεγένετο βοηθήσων
τοῖς 'Ωρείταις Τελεσφόρος μὲν ἐκ Πελοποννήσου
μετὰ νεῶν εἴκοσι καὶ στρατιωτῶν χιλίων, Μήδιος
8 δ' ἐκ τῆς 'Ασίας ἔχων ναῦς ἑκατόν. οὗτοι δ'
ὁρῶντες ἐφορμούσας τῷ λιμένι τὰς τοῦ Κασάνδρου

---

[1] ἠνάγκασε Wesseling : ἠναγκάσθη.

admiral of the fleet and making Docimus general 313 B.C. of the army.[1] These men, coming to the city of the Milesians, encouraged the citizens to assert their freedom ; and, after taking by siege the citadel, which was held by a garrison, they restored the independence of the government. While they were thus engaged, Antigonus besieged and took Tralles ; then, proceeding to Caunus and summoning the fleet, he captured that city also except for its citadel. Investing this, he kept making continuous attacks on the side where it was most easily assailed. Ptolemaeus,[2] who had been sent to Iasus with an adequate force, compelled that city to support Antigonus. In this way, then, these cities, which were in Caria, were made subject to Antigonus. A few days later, when ambassadors came to the latter from the Aetolians and the Boeotians, he made an alliance with them ; but, when he entered into negotiations with Cassander about peace in the Hellespontine region, he accomplished nothing since they could in no way agree. For this reason Cassander gave up hope of settlement and decided to play a part once more in the affairs of Greece. Setting out for Oreüs,[3] therefore, with thirty ships, he laid siege to the city. While he was vigorously attacking and was already at the point of taking the city by storm, reinforcements appeared for the people of Oreüs : Telesphorus from the Peloponnesus with twenty ships and a thousand soldiers, and Medius from Asia with a hundred ships. They saw the ships of Cassander blockading the harbour and threw fire

---

[1] For Medius cp. chap. 69. 3 and note. Nothing is known of the earlier career of Docimus.

[2] The nephew of Antigonus, cp. chap. 68. 5.

[3] At the northern end of Euboea.

ναῦς πῦρ ἐνῆκαν καὶ τέσσαρας μὲν κατέκαυσαν,
παρ' ὀλίγον δὲ καὶ πάσας διέφθειραν· τοῖς δ'
ἐλαττουμένοις παραγενομένης βοηθείας ἐξ 'Αθηνῶν
ἐπέπλευσαν οἱ περὶ Κάσανδρον καταφρονοῦσι τοῖς
πολεμίοις. συμβαλόντες δ' αὐτοῖς μίαν μὲν κατέδυσαν, τρεῖς δ' αὐτάνδρους ἔλαβον.

Καὶ τὰ μὲν πραχθέντα περὶ τὴν Ἑλλάδα καὶ τὸν
Πόντον τοιαῦτ' ἦν.

76. Κατὰ δὲ τὴν Ἰταλίαν Σαμνῖται μὲν μετὰ
πολλῆς δυνάμεως ἐπῄεσαν πορθοῦντες τῶν κατὰ
Καμπανίαν[1] πόλεων ὅσαι τοῖς ἐναντίοις συνηγωνί-
ζοντο, οἱ δ' ὕπατοι τῶν Ῥωμαίων μετὰ στρατοπέδου παραγενόμενοι παραβοηθεῖν ἐπειρῶντο τοῖς
2 κινδυνεύουσιν τῶν συμμάχων. ἀντεστρατοπεδεύ-
σαντο δὲ τοῖς πολεμίοις περὶ Ταρακίναν[2] πόλιν καὶ
ταύτην μὲν εὐθὺς ἐρύσαντο τῶν ἐπικειμένων φόβων,
μετ' ὀλίγας δ' ἡμέρας ἐκταξάντων ἀμφοτέρων τὰς
δυνάμεις ἐγένετο μάχη καρτερὰ καὶ συχνοὶ παρ'
ἀμφοτέροις ἔπεσον. τὸ δὲ τέλος οἱ Ῥωμαῖοι βιασάμενοι κατὰ κράτος περιεγένοντο τῶν πολεμίων,
ἐπὶ πολὺν δὲ χρόνον χρησάμενοι τῷ διωγμῷ πλείους
3 τῶν μυρίων ἀνεῖλον. καὶ τῆς μάχης ἀγνοουμένης
ἔτι Καμπανοὶ μὲν καταφρονήσαντες τῶν Ῥωμαίων
ἀπέστησαν, ὁ δὲ δῆμος εὐθὺς δύναμίν τε τὴν ἱκανὴν
ἐξέπεμψεν ἐπ' αὐτοὺς καὶ στρατηγὸν αὐτοκράτορα
Γάιον Μάνιον καὶ μετ' αὐτοῦ κατὰ τὸ πάτριον ἔθος
4 Μάνιον Φούλβιον ἵππαρχον.[3] τούτων δὲ πλησίον
τῆς Καπύης καταστρατοπεδευσάντων οἱ Καμπανοὶ

---

[1] Καμπανίαν Binneboessel : Ἰταλίαν MSS., Fischer (who
calls the reading *certe mendosum*).

into them, burning four and almost destroying them 313 B.C.
all; but when reinforcements for the defeated came
from Athens, Cassander sailed out against the enemy,
who were off their guard. When they met, he sank
one ship and seized three with their crews.[1]

Such were the activities in Greece and the Pontus.[2]

76. In Italy,[3] the Samnites were advancing with
a large army, destroying whatever cities in Campania[4]
were supporting their enemies; and the Roman
consuls, coming up with an army, were trying to aid
those of their allies who were in danger. They took
the field against the enemy near Tarracina[5] and at
once relieved that city from its immediate fears;
then a few days later, when both sides had drawn
up their armies, a hard-fought battle took place and
very many fell on both sides. Finally the Romans,
pressing on with all their strength, got the better of
their enemies and, pushing the pursuit for a long
time, slew more than ten thousand. While this battle
was still unknown to them, the Campanians, scorning
the Romans, rose in rebellion; but the people at
once sent an adequate force against them with the
dictator Gaius Manius as commander and accompany-
ing him, according to the national custom, Manius
Fulvius as master-of-horse. When these were in
position near Capua, the Campanians at first en-

---

[1] The fleet from Athens was commanded by Thymochares
(IG^2, 2. 1. 682).   [2] The narrative is continued in chap. 77.
[3] Continued from chap. 72. 9. Cp. Livy, 9. 26-27.
[4] But cp. the critical note.
[5] But cp. the critical note. No such battle as the one here
described is recorded by Livy among the events of this year
(Livy, 9. 26-27).

---

[2] Ταρακίναν Burger : Κίνναν MSS., Fischer.
[3] ἵππαρχον added by editors.

τὸ μὲν πρῶτον ἐπεχείρουν ἀγωνίζεσθαι, μετὰ δὲ
ταῦτα πυθόμενοι τὴν τῶν Σαμνιτῶν ἧτταν καὶ
νομίσαντες πάσας τὰς δυνάμεις ἥξειν ἐπ' αὐτοὺς
5 διελύσαντο πρὸς Ῥωμαίους· τοὺς γὰρ αἰτίους τῆς
ταραχῆς ἐξέδωκαν, οἳ προτεθείσης κρίσεως οὐ περι-
μείναντες τὴν ἀπόφασιν αὐτοὺς ἀνεῖλαν. αἱ δὲ
πόλεις τυχοῦσαι συγγνώμης εἰς τὴν προϋπάρχουσαν
συμμαχίαν ἀποκατέστησαν.

77. Τοῦ δ' ἔτους τούτου διελθόντος Ἀθήνησι μὲν
ἦρχε Πολέμων, ἐν Ῥώμῃ δ' ὑπῆρχον ὕπατοι Λεύκιος Παπείριος τὸ πέμπτον καὶ Γάιος Ἰούνιος,
ἤχθη δὲ καὶ Ὀλυμπιὰς κατὰ τοῦτον τὸν ἐνιαυτὸν
ἑβδόμη πρὸς ταῖς ἑκατὸν καὶ δέκα, καθ' ἣν ἐνίκα
2 στάδιον Παρμενίων Μιτυληναῖος. ἐπὶ δὲ τούτων
τῶν χρόνων Ἀντίγονος ἀπέστειλεν εἰς τὴν Ἑλλάδα
στρατηγὸν Πτολεμαῖον[1] τοὺς Ἕλληνας ἐλευθερώσοντα, συνέπεμψε δ' αὐτῷ ναῦς μὲν μακρὰς ἑκατὸν
καὶ πεντήκοντα, Μήδιον ἐπιστήσας ναύαρχον, στρατιώτας δὲ πεζοὺς μὲν πεντακισχιλίους, ἱππεῖς δὲ
3 πεντακοσίους. ἐποιήσατο δὲ καὶ πρὸς Ῥοδίους
συμμαχίαν καὶ προσελάβετο παρ' αὐτῶν ναῦς
ἐξηρτισμένας πρὸς τὸν πόλεμον δέκα πρὸς τὴν τῶν
4 Ἑλλήνων ἐλευθέρωσιν. ὁ δὲ Πτολεμαῖος μετὰ
παντὸς τοῦ στόλου καταπλεύσας τῆς Βοιωτίας εἰς
τὸν Βαθὺν καλούμενον λιμένα παρὰ μὲν τοῦ κοινοῦ
τῶν Βοιωτῶν προσελάβετο στρατιώτας πεζοὺς μὲν
δισχιλίους διακοσίους, ἱππεῖς δὲ χιλίους τριακοσίους. μετεπέμψατο δὲ καὶ τὰς ἐξ Ὠρεοῦ ναῦς καὶ

---

[1] Πτολεμαῖον Palmer : Πολέμωνα.

[1] For this revolt cp. Livy, 9. 26. 5-7, where, however,

deavoured to fight ; but afterwards, hearing of the defeat of the Samnites and believing that all the forces would come against themselves, they made terms with the Romans. They surrendered those guilty of the uprising, who without awaiting the judgement of the trial that was instituted killed themselves. But the cities gained pardon and were reinstated in their former alliance.[1]

77. When this year had passed, Polemon was archon in Athens, and in Rome the consuls were Lucius Papirius for the fifth time and Gaius Iunius [2] ; and in this year the Olympic Games were celebrated for the one hundred and seventeenth time, Parmenion of Mitylenê winning the footrace. In this year [3] Antigonus ordered his general Ptolemaeus into Greece to set the Greeks free and sent with him one hundred and fifty warships, placing Medius in command of them as admiral, and an army of five thousand foot and five hundred horse. Antigonus also made an alliance with the Rhodians and received from them for the liberation of the Greeks ten ships fully equipped for war. Ptolemaeus, putting in with the entire fleet at the harbour of Boeotia known as Bathys,[4] received from the Boeotian League two thousand two hundred foot soldiers and one thousand three hundred horse. He also summoned his ships

the dictator and master-of-horse are called respectively C. Maenius and M. Folius. The account of Roman affairs is continued in chap. 101.

[2] Polemon was archon in 312/11 B.C. In the Fasti Capitolini the consuls for 313 B.C. are L. Papirius Cursor for the fifth time and C. Iunius Bubulcus Brutus for the second time (*CIL*, 1, p. 130 ; cp. Livy, 9. 28. 2). The events related in chaps. 77-80. 2 still belong to the year 313 B.C.

[3] The narrative is continued from chap. 75. 8.

[4] *i.e.* " Deep," on the Euripus near Aulis.

τειχίσας τὸν Σαλγανέα[1] συνήγαγεν ἐνταῦθα πᾶσαν
τὴν δύναμιν· ἤλπιζε γὰρ προσδέξασθαι τοὺς Χαλκιδεῖς, οἵπερ μόνοι τῶν Εὐβοέων ὑπὸ τῶν πολε-
5 μίων ἐφρουροῦντο. ὁ δὲ Κάσανδρος ἀγωνιῶν ὑπὲρ
τῆς Χαλκίδος τὴν Ὠρεοῦ πολιορκίαν ἔλυσεν, εἰς
δὲ τὴν Χαλκίδα παρῆλθεν καὶ τὰς δυνάμεις μετεπέμπετο. Ἀντίγονος δὲ πυθόμενος περὶ τὴν
Εὔβοιαν ἐφεδρεύειν ἀλλήλοις τὰ στρατόπεδα, μετεπέμψατο τὸν Μήδιον εἰς τὴν Ἀσίαν μετὰ τοῦ
στόλου, εὐθὺς δὲ καὶ τὰς δυνάμεις ἀναλαβὼν προῆγεν ἐφ' Ἑλλησπόντῳ κατὰ τάχος, ὡς διαβησόμε-
νος εἰς Μακεδονίαν, ὅπως ἢ μένοντος Κασάνδρου
περὶ τὴν Εὔβοιαν αὐτὸς ἔρημον καταλάβῃ Μακεδονίαν τῶν ἀμυνομένων ἢ τῇ βασιλείᾳ βοηθῶν ἀποβάλῃ
6 τὰ κατὰ τὴν Ἑλλάδα πράγματα. ὁ δὲ Κάσανδρος
συνιδὼν τὴν ἐπίνοιαν αὐτοῦ Πλείσταρχον μὲν ἀπέλιπεν ἐπὶ τῆς ἐν Χαλκίδι φρουρᾶς, αὐτὸς δὲ μετὰ
πάσης τῆς δυνάμεως ἀναζεύξας Ὠρωπὸν μὲν κατὰ
κράτος εἷλε, Θηβαίους δ' εἰς τὴν αὑτοῦ συμμαχίαν
κατέστησεν· πρὸς δὲ τοὺς ἄλλους Βοιωτοὺς ἀνοχὰς
ποιησάμενος καὶ καταλιπὼν ἐπὶ τῆς Ἑλλάδος
στρατηγὸν Εὐπόλεμον ἀπῆλθεν εἰς Μακεδονίαν,
7 ἀγωνιῶν περὶ τῆς τῶν πολεμίων διαβάσεως. ὁ δ'
Ἀντίγονος ἐπειδὴ κατήντησεν εἰς τὴν Προποντίδα,
διεπρεσβεύσατο πρὸς Βυζαντίους ἀξιῶν μετέχειν
τῆς συμμαχίας. παραγενομένων δὲ καὶ παρὰ
Λυσιμάχου πρεσβευτῶν καὶ παρακαλούντων μηδὲν
ποιεῖν μήτε κατ' αὐτοῦ μήτε κατὰ Κασάνδρου τοῖς
μὲν Βυζαντίοις ἔδοξε μένειν ἐφ' ἡσυχίας καὶ τηρεῖν
τὴν πρὸς ἀμφοτέρους εἰρήνην ἅμα καὶ φιλίαν. ὁ
δ' Ἀντίγονος δυσχρηστούμενος ἐπὶ τούτοις, ἅμα

---

[1] Σαλγανέα Palmer : Σαλγονέα RX, Σαλμονέα F.

from Oreüs, fortified Salganeus,[1] and gathered there 313 B.C. his entire force ; for he hoped to be admitted by the Chalcidians, who alone of the Euboeans were garrisoned by the enemy. But Cassander, in his anxiety for Chalcis, gave up the siege of Oreüs, moved to Chalcis, and summoned his forces. When Antigonus heard that in Euboea the armed forces were watching each other, he recalled Medius to Asia with the fleet, and at once with his armies set out at top speed for the Hellespont as if intending to cross over into Macedonia, in order that, if Cassander remained in Euboea, he might himself occupy Macedonia while it was stripped of defenders, or that Cassander, going to the defence of his kingdom, might lose his supremacy in Greece. But Cassander, perceiving Antigonus' plan, left Pleistarchus[2] in command of the garrison in Chalcis and setting out himself with all his forces took Oropus by storm and brought the Thebans into his alliance. Then, after making a truce with the other Boeotians and leaving Eupolemus as general for Greece, he went into Macedonia, for he was apprehensive of the enemy's crossing. As for Antigonus, when he came to the Propontis, he sent an embassy to the Byzantines, asking them to enter the alliance. But there had arrived envoys from Lysimachus also who were urging them to do nothing against either Lysimachus or Cassander ; and the Byzantines decided to remain neutral and to maintain peace and friendship toward both parties. Antigonus, because he had been foiled in these undertakings and also because the winter season

[1] A town on the east coast of Boeotia, commanding the northern entrance of the Euripus (Strabo, 9. 2. 9).

[2] A son of Antipater and brother of Cassander (Plutarch, *Demetrius*, 31, 5 ; cp. Book 20. 112 ; Pausanias, 1. 15. 1).

δὲ καὶ τῆς χειμερινῆς ὥρας συγκλειούσης διέδωκε
τοὺς στρατιώτας κατὰ πόλιν εἰς τὴν χειμασίαν.

78. Ἅμα δὲ τούτοις πραττομένοις Κορκυραῖοι
μὲν βοηθήσαντες Ἀπολλωνιάταις καὶ τοῖς Ἐπι-
δαμνίοις τοὺς μὲν στρατιώτας Κασάνδρου ὑποσπόνδους ἀφῆκαν, τῶν δὲ πόλεων Ἀπολλωνίαν μὲν
ἠλευθέρωσαν, Ἐπίδαμνον δὲ Γλαυκίᾳ τῷ τῶν
2 Ἰλλυριῶν βασιλεῖ παρέδωκαν. ὁ δ' Ἀντιγόνου
στρατηγὸς Πτολεμαῖος χωρισθέντος εἰς Μακεδονίαν
Κασάνδρου καταπληξάμενος τοὺς φρουροῦντας τὴν
Χαλκίδα παρέλαβε τὴν πόλιν καὶ τοὺς Χαλκιδεῖς
ἀφῆκεν ἀφρουρήτους, ὥστε γενέσθαι φανερὸν ὡς
πρὸς ἀλήθειαν Ἀντίγονος ἐλευθεροῦν προήρηται
τοὺς Ἕλληνας· ἐπίκαιρος γὰρ ἡ πόλις ἐστὶ τοῖς
βουλομένοις ἔχειν ὁρμητήριον πρὸς τὸ[1] διαπολεμεῖν
3 περὶ τῶν ὅλων. ὁ δ' οὖν Πτολεμαῖος[2] ἐκπολιορκήσας Ὠρωπὸν παρέδωκε τοῖς Βοιωτοῖς καὶ τοὺς
Κασάνδρου στρατιώτας ὑποχειρίους ἔλαβε. μετὰ
δὲ ταῦτα Ἐρετριεῖς καὶ Καρυστίους εἰς τὴν συμμαχίαν προσλαβόμενος ἐστράτευσεν εἰς τὴν Ἀτ-
τικήν, Δημητρίου τοῦ Φαληρέως ἐπιστατοῦντος τῆς
4 πόλεως. οἱ δ' Ἀθηναῖοι τὸ μὲν πρῶτον λάθρᾳ
διεπέμποντο πρὸς Ἀντίγονον ἀξιοῦντες ἐλευθερῶσαι
τὴν πόλιν· τότε δὲ τοῦ Πτολεμαίου παραγενηθέντος
πλησίον τῆς πόλεως θαρρήσαντες ἠνάγκασαν τὸν
Δημήτριον ἀνοχὰς ποιήσασθαι καὶ πρεσβείας ἀπο-
5 στέλλειν πρὸς Ἀντίγονον περὶ συμμαχίας. ὁ δὲ
Πτολεμαῖος ἀναζεύξας ἐκ τῆς Ἀττικῆς εἰς τὴν
Βοιωτίαν τήν τε Καδμείαν εἷλε καὶ τὴν φρουρὰν
ἐκβαλὼν ἠλευθέρωσε τὰς Θήβας. μετὰ δὲ ταῦτα

---

[1] πρὸς τὸ added by Kallenberg.
[2] Πτολεμαῖος Palmer : Πολέμων.

was closing in upon him, distributed his soldiers 313 B.C. among the cities for the winter.[1]

78. While these things were going on, the Corcyraeans,[2] who had gone to the aid of the people of Apollonia and Epidamnus, dismissed Cassander's soldiers under a truce ; and of these cities they freed Apollonia, but Epidamnus they gave over to Glaucias, the king of the Illyrians. After Cassander had departed for Macedonia, Antigonus' general Ptolemaeus, striking fear into the garrison that was holding Chalcis, took the city ; and he left the Chalcidians without a garrison in order to make it evident that Antigonus in very truth proposed to free the Greeks, for the city is well placed for any who wish to have a base from which to carry through a war for supremacy.[3] However that may be, when Ptolemaeus had taken Oropus by siege, he gave it back to the Boeotians and made captive the troops of Cassander.[4] Thereafter, having received the people of Eretria and Carystus into the alliance, he moved into Attica, where Demetrius of Phalerum was governing the city. At first the Athenians kept sending secretly to Antigonus, begging him to free the city ; but then, taking courage when Ptolemaeus drew near the city, they forced Demetrius to make a truce and to send envoys to Antigonus about an alliance. Ptolemaeus, moving from Attica into Boeotia, took the Cadmea, drove out the garrison, and freed Thebes. After this he advanced into Phocis

---

[1] The winter of 313/12 B.C.

[2] Cp. chaps. 67. 6 ; 70. 7.

[3] Philip V of Macedonia named Chalcis one of the " three fetters of Greece " (Polybius, 18. 11 ; Livy, 32. 37. 3).

[4] *i.e.* the troops left in Oropus by Cassander as a garrison, cp. chap. 77. 6.

πορευθεὶς εἰς τὴν Φωκίδα καὶ τὰς μὲν πλείους τῶν πόλεων προσαγόμενος ἐξέβαλε πανταχόθεν τὰς Κασάνδρου φρουράς· ἐπῆλθε δὲ καὶ τὴν Λοκρίδα καὶ τῶν Ὀπουντίων τὰ Κασάνδρου φρονούντων συνεστήσατο πολιορκίαν καὶ συνεχεῖς προσβολὰς ἐποιεῖτο.

79. Τῆς δ᾽ αὐτῆς θερίας οἱ[1] Κυρηναῖοι μὲν ἀποστάντες Πτολεμαίου τὴν ἄκραν περιεστρατοπέδευσαν, ὡς αὐτίκα μάλα τὴν φρουρὰν ἐκβαλοῦντες, παραγενομένων δὲ πρεσβευτῶν ἐκ τῆς Ἀλεξανδρείας καὶ παρακαλούντων παύσασθαι τῆς φιλοτιμίας τούτους μὲν ἀπέκτειναν, τὴν δ᾽ ἄκραν 2 ἐνεργέστερον ἐπολιόρκουν. ἐφ᾽ οἷς παροξυνθεὶς ὁ Πτολεμαῖος ἀπέστειλεν Ἅγιν στρατηγὸν μετὰ δυνάμεως πεζῆς, ἐξέπεμψε δὲ καὶ στόλον τὸν συλληψόμενον τοῦ πολέμου, ναύαρχον ἐπιστήσας Ἐπαι- 3 νετόν. ὁ δὲ Ἅγις ἐνεργῶς διαπολεμήσας τοῖς ἀφεστηκόσιν ἐκυρίευσε κατὰ κράτος τῆς πόλεως καὶ τοὺς μὲν αἰτίους τῆς ἀποστάσεως δήσας ἀπέστειλεν εἰς τὴν Ἀλεξάνδρειαν καὶ τῶν ἄλλων τὰ ὅπλα παρελόμενος καὶ τὰ κατὰ τὴν πόλι διοικήσας ὥς ποτ᾽ ἔδοξεν αὐτῷ συμφέρειν ἐπανῆλθεν εἰς τὴν Αἴγυπτον.

4 Πτολεμαῖος δέ, τῶν περὶ Κυρήνην αὐτῷ κατὰ νοῦν ἀπηντηκότων, διῆρεν ἐκ τῆς Αἰγύπτου μετὰ δυνάμεως εἰς τὴν Κύπρον ἐπὶ τοὺς ἀπειθοῦντας τῶν βασιλέων. Πυγμαλίωνα δὲ εὑρὼν διαπρεσβευόμενον πρὸς Ἀντίγονον ἀνεῖλε, Πράξιππον δὲ τὸν τῆς Λαπιθίας βασιλέα καὶ[2] τὸν τῆς Κερυνίας δυ-

---

[1] οἱ added by Capps.

where he won over most of the cities and from all 313 B.C.
of these expelled the garrisons of Cassander. He
also marched against Locris ; and, since the Opuntians
belonged to the party of Cassander, he began a siege
and made continuous attacks.[1]

79. In that same summer [2] the people of Cyrenê
revolted from Ptolemy, invested the citadel, and
seemed on the point of immediately casting out the
garrison ; and, when envoys came from Alexandria
and bade them cease from their sedition, they killed
them and continued the attack on the citadel with
greater vigour. Enraged at them, Ptolemy dispatched Agis as general with a land army and also
sent a fleet to take part in the war, placing Epaenetus
in command. Agis attacked the rebels with vigour
and took the city by storm. Those who were guilty
of the sedition he bound and sent to Alexandria ;
and then, after depriving the others of their arms
and arranging the affairs of the city in whatever way
seemed best to himself, he returned to Egypt.

But Ptolemy, now that the matter of Cyrenê had
been disposed of according to his wishes, crossed over
with an army from Egypt into Cyprus against those
of the kings who refused to obey him. Finding that
Pygmalion was negotiating with Antigonus, he put
him to death ; and he arrested Praxippus, king of
Lapithia and ruler of Cerynia,[3] whom he suspected of

---

[1] Opus was probably taken, but no statement to the effect
survives in our sources. Diodorus returns to Greek affairs
in chap. 87. [2] The summer of 313 B.C.
[3] It is quite probable that the name of the ruler of Cerynia
has been lost from the MSS. Lapithia and Cerynia are
near the middle of the north coast of Cyprus.

---

[2] Fischer suspects the loss of a proper name after καὶ.

51

νάστην ὑποπτεύσας ἀλλοτρίως ἔχειν συνέλαβε, καὶ
Στασίοικον τὸν τῶν Μαριέων[1]· καὶ τὴν μὲν πόλιν
κατέσκαψε, τοὺς δ᾽ ἐνοικοῦντας[2] μετήγαγεν εἰς
5 Πάφον. ταῦτα δὲ διαπραξάμενος τῆς μὲν Κύπρου
κατέστησε στρατηγὸν Νικοκρέοντα, παραδοὺς τάς
τε πόλεις καὶ τὰς προσόδους τῶν ἐκπεπτωκότων
6 βασιλέων, αὐτὸς δὲ μετὰ τῆς δυνάμεως ἐκπλεύσας
ἐπὶ Συρίας τῆς ἄνω καλουμένης Ποσείδιον καὶ
Ποταμοὺς Καρῶν ἐκπολιορκήσας διήρπασεν. ἑτοίμως δὲ πλεύσας ἐπὶ Κιλικίας Μάλον εἷλε καὶ τοὺς
ἐγκαταληφθέντας ἐλαφυροπώλησεν. ἐπόρθησε δὲ
καὶ τὴν ἐγγὺς χώραν καὶ τὸ στρατόπεδον ὠφελείας
7 ἐμπλήσας ἀπέπλευσεν εἰς τὴν Κύπρον. ἐπολιτεύετο δὲ πρὸς τοὺς στρατιώτας οὕτως, ἐκκαλούμενος αὐτῶν τὰς προθυμίας εἰς τοὺς ἐπιφερομένους
κινδύνους.

80. Δημήτριος δὲ ὁ Ἀντιγόνου διέτριβεν ἀεὶ
περὶ Κοίλην Συρίαν, ἐφεδρεύων ταῖς τῶν Αἰγυπτίων δυνάμεσιν. ὡς δ᾽ ἤκουσε τὰς τῶν πόλεων
ἁλώσεις Πίθωνα μὲν ἐπὶ τῶν τόπων κατέλιπε
στρατηγόν, δοὺς αὐτῷ τοὺς ἐλέφαντας καὶ τὰ βαρέα
τῶν ταγμάτων, αὐτὸς δ᾽ ἀναλαβὼν τούς τε ἱππεῖς
καὶ τὰ ψιλικὰ τάγματα προῆγεν ἐπὶ Κιλικίας συν-
2 τόμως, βοηθήσων τοῖς κινδυνεύουσιν. ὑστερήσας
δὲ τῶν καιρῶν καὶ καταλαβὼν ἀποπεπλευκότας
τοὺς πολεμίους ἐπανῆλθε συντόμως ἐπὶ τὸ στρατό-

---

[1] καὶ Στασίοικον τὸν τῶν Μαριέων Rhodoman, cp. chap.
62. 6 : Στασιοίκου τοῦ Μαλιέως RX, καὶ Στασίοικον τὸν τοῦ
Μαλιέως F.   [2] ἐνοικοῦντας Dindorf : οἰκοῦντες.

---

[1] Stasioecus, king of Marion on the west coast of Cyprus,
had first supported Antigonus and then Ptolemy (chap. 62. 6),
and now seems to have turned against Ptolemy.

being ill disposed toward himself, and also Stasioecus,[1] 313 B.C. ruler of Marion, destroying the city and transporting the inhabitants to Paphos.[2] After accomplishing these things, he appointed Nicocreon[3] as general of Cyprus, giving him both the cities and the revenues of the kings who had been driven out ; but he himself with his army, sailing toward Upper Syria, as it is called, captured and sacked Poseidium and Potami Caron.[4] Sailing without delay to Cilicia, he took Malus and sold as booty those who were captured there. He also plundered the neighbouring territory and, after sating his army with spoil, sailed back to Cyprus. His playing up to the soldiers in this way was designed to evoke enthusiasm in face of the encounters that were approaching.

80. Now Antigonus' son Demetrius was staying on in Coelê Syria lying in wait for the Egyptian armies.[5] But when he heard of the capture of the cities, he left Pithon as general in charge of the region, giving him the elephants and the heavy-armed units of the army ; and he himself, taking the cavalry and the light-armed units, moved rapidly toward Cilicia to give aid to those who were in danger. Arriving after the opportunity had passed and finding that the enemy had sailed away, he went rapidly

[2] The text of this sentence is unsatisfactory, and a lacuna is suspected. Paphos is on the south-west coast of Cyprus.

[3] Nicocreon, king of Salamis on the south coast of Cyprus, had been with Alexander at Tyre in 332/31 B.C. (Arrian, *Anabasis*, 2. 22. 2 ; Plutarch, *Alexander*, 29. 2). After Alexander's death he supported Ptolemy (chap. 59. 1). For his treachery and death in 310 B.C. cp. Book 20. 21.

[4] There is a promontory called Poseidium on the coast of Cilicia. No city by the name of Potami Caron (Rivers of the Carians) is known.

[5] Cp. chap. 69.

πεδον, ἀποβεβληκὼς τῶν ἵππων τοὺς πλείους κατὰ
τὴν ὁδοιπορίαν· διέτεινε γὰρ ἐξ ἡμέραις ἐπὶ[1]
Μάλου σταθμοὺς εἴκοσι καὶ τέσσαρας, ὥστε διὰ
τὴν ὑπερβολὴν τῆς κακοπαθίας μήτε σκευοφόρον
ἀκολουθῆσαι μηδένα μήτε τοὺς ἱπποκόμους.

3   Ὁ δὲ Πτολεμαῖος, κατὰ νοῦν αὐτῷ τῶν πραγμάτων ἀπηντηκότων, τότε μὲν ἀπῆρεν εἰς Αἴγυπτον, μετ᾽ ὀλίγον δὲ χρόνον παροξυνόμενος ὑπὸ
Σελεύκου διὰ τὴν πρὸς Ἀντίγονον ἀλλοτριότητα
διέγνω στρατεύειν ἐπὶ Κοίλην Συρίαν καὶ παρα-
4 τάττεσθαι τοῖς περὶ τὸν Δημήτριον. συναγαγὼν
οὖν πανταχόθεν τὰς δυνάμεις ἀνέζευξεν ἀπὸ Ἀλεξανδρείας εἰς Πηλούσιον, ἔχων πεζοὺς μὲν μυρίους
ὀκτακισχιλίους, ἱππεῖς δὲ τετρακισχιλίους, ὧν ἦσαν
οἱ μὲν Μακεδόνες, οἱ δὲ μισθοφόροι, Αἰγυπτίων δὲ
πλῆθος, τὸ μὲν κομίζον βέλη καὶ τὴν ἄλλην παρασκευήν, τὸ δὲ καθωπλισμένον καὶ πρὸς μάχην
5 χρήσιμον. ἀπὸ δὲ Πηλουσίου διὰ τῆς ἐρήμου διελθὼν κατεστρατοπέδευσε πλησίον τῶν πολεμίων
περὶ τὴν παλαιὰν Γάζαν τῆς Συρίας. ὁμοίως δὲ
καὶ Δημήτριος μεταπεμψάμενος πανταχόθεν τοὺς
ἐκ τῆς χειμασίας στρατιώτας εἰς τὴν παλαιὰν
Γάζαν ὑπέμεινε τὴν τῶν ἐναντίων ἔφοδον.

81. Τῶν δὲ φίλων αὐτῷ συμβουλευόντων μὴ
παρατάττεσθαι πρὸς ἡγεμόνα τηλικοῦτον καὶ δύναμιν μείζω, τούτοις μὲν οὐ προσεῖχεν, εἰς δὲ τὸν
κίνδυνον παρεσκευάζετο τεθαρρηκώς, καίπερ[2] νέος
ὢν παντελῶς καὶ τηλικαύτην μάχην μέλλων ἀγ-

---

[1] ἐπί Geer : ἀπό.   [2] καίπερ Fischer : καὶ γάρ.

[1] Cp. the critical note. The forced march must have
been the one from his base in Coelê Syria toward Malus in Cilicia.
The length of the stage or distance between posting stations

back to his camp, having lost most of his horses 313 B.C.
during the march ; for in six days' march towards
Malus [1] he covered twenty-four stages, with the
result that on account of the excessive hardship not
one of his sutlers or of his grooms kept up the pace.

Ptolemy, since his undertakings had turned out 312 B.C.
as he wished, now sailed away to Egypt ; but after
a little while, spurred on by Seleucus because of his
hostility toward Antigonus, he decided to make a
campaign into Coelê Syria and take the field against
the army of Demetrius. He therefore gathered
together his forces from all sides and marched from
Alexandria to Pelusium with eighteen thousand foot
and four thousand horse. Of his army some were
Macedonians and some were mercenaries, but a great
number were Egyptians, of whom some carried
the missiles and the other baggage but some were
armed and serviceable for battle. Marching through
the desert from Pelusium, he camped near the enemy
at Old Gaza in Syria.[2] Demetrius, who had likewise summoned his soldiers to Old Gaza from their
winter quarters [3] on all sides, awaited the approach
of his opponents.

81. Although his friends were urging him not to
take the field against so great a general and a superior
force, Demetrius paid no heed to them but confidently
prepared for the conflict even though he was very
young and was about to engage in so great a battle

on the Persian roads was not uniform. If we take 17 miles
as an average, the army covered some 400 miles in 6 days,
but the distance seems actually to have been very much less.

[2] According to Strabo (16. 2. 30), Alexander had destroyed
Gaza ; but the city clearly retained its importance at least
as a fortress (Arrian, *Anabasis*, 2. 26-27).

[3] The winter of 313/12 B.C.

2 ωνίζεσθαι χωρὶς τοῦ πατρός. συναγαγόντος δ' ἐν
τοῖς ὅπλοις ἐκκλησίαν αὐτοῦ καὶ στάντος ἐπί τινος
ἀναστήματος μετὰ ἀγωνίας καὶ διατροπῆς ὁ μὲν
ὄχλος ἀνεβόησε μιᾷ φωνῇ θαρρεῖν καὶ πρὸ τοῦ τὸν
κήρυκα καταπαῦσαι τοὺς θορυβοῦντας ἅπαντες σιω-
3 πὴν παρείχοντο. οὔτε γὰρ στρατιωτικὸν ἔγκλημα
ὑπῆρχε περὶ αὐτὸν οὔτε πολιτικόν, ἅτε προσφάτως
ἐφ' ἡγεμονίας τεταγμένον· ὅπερ εἴωθε γίγνεσθαι
τοῖς παλαιοῖς στρατηγοῖς ὅταν ἐκ πολλῶν προφά-
σεων ἓν ἔγκλημα πρὸς ἕνα καιρὸν ἀθροίζηται· τὸ
γὰρ πλῆθος ἀεὶ δυσάρεστον ἐπὶ τῶν αὐτῶν μένον
καὶ πᾶν τὸ μὴ πλεονάζον κεχαρισμένην ἔχει τὴν
μεταβολήν· τοῦ τε πατρὸς ἤδη γεγηρακότος αἱ τῆς
βασιλείας ἐλπίδες εἰς τὴν τούτου διαδοχὴν ἦγον
4 ἅμα τὴν ἀρχὴν καὶ τὴν τῶν ὄχλων εὔνοιαν. ἦν δὲ
καὶ τῷ κάλλει καὶ τῷ μεγέθει διάφορος, ἔτι δὲ κε-
κοσμημένος ὅπλοις βασιλικοῖς εἶχε πολλὴν ὑπεροχὴν καὶ κατάπληξιν, δι' ἧς εἰς ἐλπίδας ἁδρὰς
ἦγε τοὺς πολλούς· πρὸς δὲ τούτοις πρᾳότης τις ἦν
περὶ αὐτόν, ἁρμόζουσα νέῳ βασιλεῖ, δι' ἧς εἰς προ-
θυμίαν ἐξεκαλεῖτο πάντας, ὥστε καὶ τοὺς ἐκτὸς
τάξεως συνδραμεῖν ἐπὶ τὴν ἀκρόασιν, συναγωνιῶντας τῇ νεότητι καὶ τῇ μελλούσῃ γίνεσθαι κρίσει
5 διὰ τῆς παρατάξεως. οὐ μόνον γὰρ πρὸς πλείονας
ἤμελλε διακινδυνεύειν, ἀλλὰ καὶ πρὸς ἡγεμόνας
σχεδὸν μεγίστους, Πτολεμαῖον καὶ Σέλευκον· οὗτοι
γὰρ πάντας τοὺς πολέμους Ἀλεξάνδρῳ συστρα-
τευσάμενοι καὶ πολλάκις καθ' αὑτοὺς δυνάμεων

---

¹ In the late summer of 314 B.C., when he was sent to
Syria, he was 22 years old (chap. 69. 1). For the following
56

apart from his father.[1] When he had called together
an assembly under arms and, anxious and agitated,
had taken his position on a raised platform, the
crowd shouted with a single voice, bidding him be
of good courage ; and then, before the herald bade
the shouting men cease their tumult, they all became
silent.   For, because he had just been placed in
command, neither soldiers nor civilians had for
him any ill will such as usually develops against
generals of long standing when at a particular time
many minor irritations are combined in a single
mass grievance ; for the multitude becomes exacting
when it remains under the same authority, and
every group that is not preferred welcomes change.
Since his father was already an old man, the hopes
of the kingdom, centring upon his succession, were
bringing him the command and at the same time
the goodwill of the multitude.   Moreover, he was
outstanding both in beauty and in stature, and
also when clad in royal armour he had great distinction and struck men with awe, whereby he created
great expectations in the multitude.   Furthermore,
there was in him a certain gentleness becoming
to a youthful king, which won for him the devotion
of all, so that even those outside the ranks ran
together to hear him, feeling sympathetic anxiety on
account of his youth and the critical struggle that
impended.   For he was about to fight a decisive
battle not only against more numerous forces, but
also against generals who were almost the greatest,
Ptolemy and Seleucus.   Indeed, these generals, who
had taken part with Alexander in all his wars and had

battle cp. the brief accounts in Justin, 15. 1. 6-9, and Plutarch,
Demetrius, 5.

ἡγησάμενοι μέχρι τῶν καιρῶν τούτων ὑπῆρχον
6 ἀνίκητοι. ὁ δ' οὖν Δημήτριος παρακαλέσας τὰ
πλήθη τοῖς οἰκείοις λόγοις καὶ δωρεάς τε δώσειν
κατὰ τὴν ἀξίαν καὶ τὰ λάφυρα συγχωρήσειν ἐπαγγειλάμενος ἐξέταξε τὴν δύναμιν εἰς τὴν μάχην.

82. Ἐπὶ μὲν οὖν τὸ λαιὸν κέρας ἔταξε,[1] καθ' ὃ
τὸν κίνδυνον αὐτὸς ἤμελλε ποιεῖσθαι, πρώτους μὲν
τοὺς περὶ αὐτὸν ἱππεῖς ἐπιλέκτους διακοσίους, ἐν
οἷς ἦσαν οἵ τε ἄλλοι φίλοι πάντες καὶ Πίθων
ὁ συνεστρατευμένος μὲν Ἀλεξάνδρῳ, συγκαθιστά-
μενος δὲ ὑπ' Ἀντιγόνου στρατηγὸς καὶ τῶν ὅλων
2 μέτοχος. πρόταγμα δὲ τρεῖς εἴλας ἱππέων ἔταξεν
καὶ πλαγιοφυλάκους τὰς ἴσας καὶ χωρὶς ἔξω τοῦ
κέρατος ἀπολελυμένας τρεῖς Ταραντίνων, ὥστ' εἶναι τοὺς περὶ τὸ σῶμα τεταγμένους ἱππεῖς ξυστο-
φόρους μὲν πεντακοσίους Ταραντίνους δὲ ἑκατόν.
3 ἑξῆς δ' ἔταξε τῶν ἱππέων τοὺς καλουμένους
μὲν ἑταίρους, ὄντας δὲ τὸν ἀριθμὸν ὀκτακοσίους,
μετὰ δὲ τούτους παντοδαποὺς ἱππεῖς οὐκ ἐλάττους
τῶν χιλίων πεντακοσίων. πρὸ παντὸς δὲ τοῦ κέρατος ἔστησε τῶν ἐλεφάντων τριάκοντα καὶ τὰ
διαστήματα αὐτῶν ἐπλήρωσε τοῖς ψιλικοῖς τάγ-
μασιν, ὧν ἦσαν ἀκοντισταὶ μὲν καὶ τοξόται χίλιοι,
4 σφενδονῆται δὲ Πέρσαι πεντακόσιοι. τὸ μὲν οὖν
εὐώνυμον κέρας οὕτω κατασκευάσας διενοεῖτο
τούτῳ κρίνειν[2] τὴν μάχην. ἐχομένην δ' ἔστησε τὴν
τῶν πεζῶν φάλαγγα, συνεστῶσαν ἐξ ἀνδρῶν μυρίων χιλίων· τούτων δὲ ἦσαν Μακεδόνες μὲν δισχί-

---

[1] ἔταξε editors : ἐξέταξε.
[2] κρίνειν Sintenis : κρινεῖν, κινεῖν.

often led armies independently, were unconquered up to this time. At all events, Demetrius, after encouraging the crowd with words suitable to the occasion and promising to give gifts to them as they were deserved and to yield the booty to the soldiers, drew up his army for the battle.

82. On the left wing, where he himself was going to take part in the battle, he placed first the two hundred selected horsemen of his guard, among whom were all his other friends and, in particular, Pithon, who had campaigned with Alexander and had been made by Antigonus co-general and partner in the whole undertaking.[1] As an advanced guard he drew up three troops of cavalry and the same number as guards on the flank, and in addition to these and stationed separately outside the wing, three troops of Tarentines[2]; thus those that were drawn up about his person amounted to five hundred horsemen armed with the lance and one hundred Tarentines. Next he posted those of the cavalry who were called the Companions, eight hundred in number, and after them no less than fifteen hundred horsemen of all kinds. In front of the whole wing he stationed thirty of his elephants, and he filled the intervals between them with units of light-armed men, of whom a thousand were javelin-throwers and archers and five hundred were Persian slingers. In this fashion then he formed the left wing, with which he intended to decide the battle. Next to it he drew up the infantry phalanx composed of eleven thousand men, of whom two thousand were Macedonians,

[1] Cp. chap. 69. 1 and note.
[2] Light cavalry armed with javelins. The origin of the name and the connection, if any, with Tarentum, are unknown. Cp. chap. 29. 2.

λιοι, Λύκιοι δὲ καὶ Παμφύλιοι χίλιοι, μισθοφόροι
δ᾽ ὀκτακισχίλιοι. ἐπὶ δὲ τὸ δεξιὸν κέρας ἔταξε
τοὺς λοιποὺς ἱππεῖς χιλίους πεντακοσίους, ὧν ᾽Αν-
δρόνικος ἡγεῖτο. τούτῳ δ᾽ ἦν συντεταγμένον λοξὴν
φυλάττειν τὴν στάσιν καὶ φυγομαχεῖν, καραδο-
κοῦντα τὴν δι᾽ αὐτοῦ γινομένην κρίσιν. τοὺς δὲ
λοιποὺς τῶν ἐλεφάντων τρεισκαίδεκα ἔστησε πρὸ
τῆς τῶν πεζῶν φάλαγγος, μίξας εἰς τὰ¹ διαστήματα
τῶν ψιλῶν τοὺς ἱκανούς. Δημήτριος μὲν οὖν δι-
εκόσμησε τὴν ἰδίαν δύναμιν τὸν τρόπον τοῦτον.

83. Οἱ δὲ περὶ τὸν Πτολεμαῖον καὶ Σέλευκον τὸ
μὲν πρῶτον ἔταξαν ἰσχυρὰν τὴν εὐώνυμον τάξιν,
ἀγνοοῦντες τῶν ἐναντίων τὴν ἐπιβολήν· μαθόντες
δὲ παρὰ τῶν κατασκόπων τὸ γεγονὸς ταχέως ἐξέ-
ταξαν τὴν δύναμιν ὅπως τὸ δεξιὸν κέρας ἰσχὺν ἔχον
καὶ δύναμιν τὴν κρατίστην διαγωνίσηται πρὸς τοὺς
μετὰ Δημητρίου τεταγμένους ἐν τοῖς εὐωνύμοις
μέρεσιν. ἔταξαν δὲ ἐπὶ τοῦ κέρατος τούτου² τῶν
ἱππέων τοὺς κρατίστους τρισχιλίους, ἐν οἷς καὶ
2 αὐτοὶ διεγνώκεισαν ἀγωνίσασθαι. προέταξαν δὲ
τῆς στάσεως ταύτης τοὺς κομίζοντας χάρακα σεσιδηρωμένον καὶ δεδεμένον ἁλύσεσιν, ὃν παρε-
σκευάσαντο πρὸς τὴν τῶν ἐλεφάντων ἔφοδον·
ταθέντος γὰρ τούτου ῥᾴδιον ἦν εἴργειν τὰ θηρία

---

¹ εἰς τὰ Dindorf : εἴς τινα.
² τούτου second hand in R : τοῦ.

---

¹ As a military term χάραξ elsewhere means either a pointed
stake to be used in making a palisade or the palisade itself,
and this passage is cited in L.S.J. as an example of the latter
meaning. However, here it is certainly a device with upright
spikes on which the elephants step (chap. 84). In the defence
of Megalopolis, knowing that Polyperchon would send his

one thousand were Lycians and Pamphylians, and 312 B.C. eight thousand were mercenaries. On the right wing he drew up the rest of his cavalry, fifteen hundred men commanded by Andronicus. This officer was ordered to hold his line back at an angle and avoid fighting, awaiting the outcome of the conflict fought by Demetrius. The thirteen other elephants he stationed in front of the phalanx of the infantry with the normal complement of light troops in the intervals. In this manner, then, Demetrius arrayed his army.

83. Ptolemy and Seleucus at first made strong the left part of their line, not knowing the intention of the enemy ; but when they learned from scouts the formation he had adopted, they quickly reformed their army in such a way that their right wing should have the greatest strength and power and be matched against those arrayed with Demetrius on his left. They drew up on this wing the three thousand strongest of their cavalry, along with whom they themselves had decided to fight. In front of this position they placed the men who were to handle the spiked devices [1] made of iron and connected by chains that they had prepared against the onset of the elephants ; for when this contrivance had been stretched out, it was easy to prevent the beasts

elephants through a breach in the wall, Damis (who had served with Alexander and knew the nature of the elephant) studded many frames with sharp nails and, after placing them with their points upwards in the way the elephants would necessarily follow, covered them with loose earth (Book 18. 71. 2-6). In the present battle, since the point of attack would not be known long in advance, a portable device was needed. Perhaps we should think of planks with spikes driven through them, connected by chains. Kromayer, referring to our passages, speaks of " Fuszangeln," *i.e.* caltrops or crowfeet (Kromayer and Veith, *Heerwesen u. Kriegsführung*, 141).

3 τῆς εἰς τοὔμπροσθεν πορείας. προέταξαν δὲ τοῦ κέρατος τούτου καὶ τὰ ψιλικὰ τάγματα, παραγγείλαντες τοῖς τε ἀκοντισταῖς καὶ τοξόταις συνεχῶς κατατιτρώσκειν τὰ θηρία καὶ τοὺς ἐπ' αὐτοῖς ἀναβεβηκότας. τοῦτον δὲ τὸν τρόπον ὀχυρωσάμενοι τὸ δεξιὸν κέρας καὶ τὴν ἄλλην δύναμιν ἐκτάξαντες ἐνδεχομένως ἐπῆγον τοῖς πολεμίοις μετὰ πολλῆς κραυγῆς.

Ἀντεπαγόντων δὲ καὶ τῶν ἐναντίων τὸ μὲν πρῶτον ἐπ' ἄκρων τῶν κεράτων ἱππομαχία συνέστη τῶν προτεταγμένων ἱππέων, ἐν οἷς πολὺ προ-
4 ετέρουν οἱ περὶ τὸν Δημήτριον. μετ' ὀλίγον δὲ τῶν περὶ Πτολεμαῖον καὶ Σέλευκον περιιππευσάντων τὸ κέρας καὶ βιαιότερον ἐπενεχθέντων ὀρθίαις[1] ταῖς εἴλαις συνέστη καρτερὰ μάχη διὰ τὰς ἑκατέρων
5 προθυμίας. κατὰ μὲν οὖν τὴν πρώτην ἔφοδον τοῖς ξυστοῖς ἀγωνισάμενοι τούτων τε τὰ πλεῖστα συνέτριψαν καὶ τῶν ἀγωνιζομένων οὐκ ὀλίγους κατετραυμάτισαν· κατὰ δὲ τὴν δευτέραν ἀναστροφὴν[2] εἰς τὴν ἀπὸ τοῦ ξίφους μάχην ὥρμησαν καὶ συμπλεκόμενοι πολλοὺς ἀλλήλων ἀνῄρουν, οἵ τε ἡγεμόνες αὐτοὶ πρὸ πάντων κινδυνεύοντες προετρέποντο τοὺς ὑποτεταγμένους εὐρώστως ὑπομένειν τὸ δεινόν, οἵ τ' ἐπὶ τῶν κεράτων ἱππεῖς, ἅπαντες ἐπιλελεγμένοι κατ' ἀρετήν, ἡμιλλῶντο πρὸς ἀλλήλους, θεατὰς ἔχοντες τῆς ἀνδρείας τοὺς συναγωνιζομένους στρατηγούς.

84. Ἐπὶ πολὺν δὲ χρόνον τῆς ἱππομαχίας οὔσης ἐφαμίλλου τὰ θηρία διὰ τῶν Ἰνδῶν εἰς τὸν ἀγῶνα παρορμηθέντα μέχρι μέν τινος προῆγεν καταπληκτικῶς, ὡς οὐδενὸς ὑποστησομένου· ὡς δ' ἐπὶ τὸν

---

[1] ὀρθίαις Kromayer (cp. Suidas s.v. ὀρθία): ὀρθαῖς.

from moving forward. In front of this wing they also stationed their light-armed units, ordering the javelin-men and archers to shoot without ceasing at the elephants and at those who were mounted upon them. When they had made their right wing strong in this manner and had drawn up the rest of their army as circumstances permitted, they advanced upon the enemy with a great shout.

Their opponents also advanced; and first there was a cavalry action on the extreme wings between the troops of the advance guards in which the men of Demetrius had much the better of it. But after a little, when Ptolemy and Seleucus had ridden around the wing and charged upon them more heavily with cavalry drawn up in depth, there was severe fighting because of the zeal of both sides. In the first charge, indeed, the fighting was with spears, most of which were shattered, and many of the antagonists were wounded; then, rallying again, the men rushed into battle at sword's point, and, as they were locked in close combat, many were slain on each side. The very commanders, endangering themselves in front of all, encouraged those under their command to withstand the danger stoutly; and the horsemen upon the wings, all of whom had been selected for bravery, vied with each other since as witnesses of their valour they had their generals, who were sharing the struggle with them.

84. After the cavalry battle had continued for a long time on equal terms, the elephants, urged on into the combat by their Indian mahouts, advanced for a certain distance in a way to inspire terror, just as if no one were going to withstand them. When,

---

[2] ἐπιστροφὴν editors except Fischer.

σεσιδηρωμένον χάρακα κατήντησε, τὸ μὲν πλῆθος
τῶν ἀκοντιστῶν καὶ τοξοτῶν συνεχῶς βαλλόντων
κατετίτρωσκε τὰ σώματα τῶν ἐλεφάντων καὶ τοὺς
2 ἐπ᾽ αὐτοῖς ἀναβεβηκότας· βιαζομένων δὲ τῶν
Ἰνδῶν καὶ κολαζόντων τὰ θηρία τινὰ μὲν αὐτῶν
περιεπείροντο τῷ φιλοτεχνηθέντι χάρακι, καὶ ταῖς
πληγαῖς καὶ πυκνότησι τῶν τιτρωσκόντων περιώ-
3 δυνα γινόμενα ἐποίει θόρυβον. τὸ γὰρ γένος τοῦτο
κατὰ μὲν τοὺς ὁμαλοὺς καὶ μαλακοὺς τόπους ἀν-
υπόστατον παρέχεται κατὰ στόμα τὴν ῥώμην, ἐν δὲ
τοῖς τραχέσι καὶ δυσβάτοις τελέως ἄπρακτον ἔχει
4 τὴν ἀλκὴν διὰ τὴν τῶν ποδῶν μαλακότητα. διὸ καὶ
τότε, τῶν περὶ Πτολεμαῖον συνετῶς προεωραμένων
τὸ μέλλον ἐκ τοῦ χάρακος τῆς πήξεως,[1] ἄπρακτον
ἐποίει τὴν βίαν αὐτῶν. τέλος δὲ τῶν πλείστων
Ἰνδῶν κατακοντισθέντων ὑποχειρίους συνέβη γενέ-
5 σθαι πάντας τοὺς ἐλέφαντας. οὗ τελεσθέντος οἱ
πολλοὶ τῶν περὶ τὸν Δημήτριον ἱππέων καταπλαγέντες πρὸς φυγὴν ὥρμησαν· αὐτὸς δὲ μετ᾽ ὀλίγων
ἀπολειφθεὶς καὶ δεόμενος ἑκάστου στῆναι καὶ μὴ
καταλιπεῖν αὐτόν, ὡς οὐδεὶς προσεῖχε, συναποχω-
6 ρεῖν ἠναγκάζετο. μέχρι μὲν οὖν Γάζης οἱ πολλοὶ
τῶν ἱππέων συνακολουθοῦντες ὑπήκουον καὶ κατέστησαν εἰς τάξεις, ὥστε μηδένα ῥᾳδίως τολμᾶν
προσάγειν τῶν εἰκῇ διωκόντων· τὸ γὰρ πεδίον εὐ-
ρύχωρον ὂν καὶ μαλακὸν συνήργει τοῖς βουλομένοις
7 ἐν τάξει ποιεῖσθαι τὴν ἀποχώρησιν. συνείποντο δὲ
καὶ πεζῶν οἱ βουληθέντες λιπεῖν τὰς τάξεις καὶ

---

[1] For τῆς πήξεως Fischer in his apparatus suggests ἡ πήρωσις.

[1] Cp. Book 18. 71. 6, where πληγή is clearly used of the wounds caused by the spikes.

however, they came up to the barrier of spikes, the 312 B.C. host of javelin-throwers and archers, who were sending their missiles unremittingly, began to wound severely the elephants themselves and those who were mounted upon them ; and while the mahouts were forcing the beasts forward and were using their goads, some of the elephants were pierced by the cleverly devised spikes and, tormented by their wounds[1] and by the concentrated efforts of the attackers, began to cause disorder. For on smooth and yielding ground these beasts display in direct onset a might that is irresistible, but on terrain that is rough and difficult their strength is completely useless because of the tenderness of their feet. Thus, too, on this occasion, since Ptolemy shrewdly foresaw what would result from the setting up of the spikes, he rendered the power of the elephants unavailing.[2] The final outcome was that, after most of the mahouts had been shot down, all the elephants were captured. When this happened, most of Demetrius' horsemen were panic-stricken and rushed into flight ; and he himself was left with a few and then, since no one heeded him when he begged them each to stand and not desert him, was forced to leave the field with the rest. Now as far as Gaza most of the cavalry who were following with him listened to orders and remained in formation, so that no one of those who were pursuing at random lightly risked attacking ; for the plain was open and yielding, and favourable to men who wished to withdraw in formation. There followed also those of the infantry who preferred to

---

[2] Or, reading ἡ πήρωσις ; "Thus on this occasion also, as Ptolemy shrewdly foresaw would happen, the wounds caused by the spikes rendered, etc."

χωρὶς τῶν ὅπλων διασῴζειν ἑαυτοὺς ἐλαφρούς.
παραλλάσσοντος δὲ αὐτοῦ Γάζαν περὶ ἡλίου δύσιν
ἀπολιπόντες τῶν ἱππέων τινὲς παρῆλθον εἰς τὴν
8 πόλιν, ἐκκομίσαι βουλόμενοι τὰς ἀποσκευάς. ἀνοι-
χθεισῶν οὖν τῶν πυλῶν καὶ πλήθους ὑποζυγίων
ἀθροισθέντος, ἔτι δ' ἑκάστου πρώτου σπεύδοντος
ἐξαγαγεῖν τὰ σκευοφόρα τοσοῦτον θόρυβον γενέσθαι
συνέβη περὶ τὰς πύλας ὥστε τῶν περὶ Πτολεμαῖον
ἐπιόντων μηδένα δύνασθαι φθάσαι συγκλείσαντα.
διόπερ εἰσπεσόντων τῶν πολεμίων ἐντὸς τοῦ τείχους ἡ πόλις ὑποχείριος ἐγένετο τοῖς περὶ Πτολεμαῖον.

85. Τῆς δὲ μάχης τοιοῦτο τὸ τέλος λαβούσης
Δημήτριος μὲν διέτεινεν εἰς Ἄζωτον περὶ μέσας
νύκτας, διελθὼν σταδίους ἑβδομήκοντα καὶ διακοσίους. ἐντεῦθεν δὲ κήρυκα περὶ τῆς τῶν νεκρῶν
ἀναιρέσεως ἐξέπεμψεν, σπεύδων ἐκ παντὸς τρόπου τῆς ἐπιβαλλούσης κηδείας ἀξιῶσαι τοὺς τε-
2 τελευτηκότας· ἐτύγχανον γὰρ οἱ πλεῖστοι τῶν
φίλων πεπτωκότες, ὧν ἦσαν ἐπιφανέστατοι Πίθων
τε ὁ μετέχων τῆς στρατηγίας ἐπ' ἴσης αὐτῷ καὶ
Βοιωτὸς πολὺν χρόνον συνεζηκὼς Ἀντιγόνῳ τῷ
3 πατρὶ καὶ μετεσχηκὼς παντὸς ἀπορρήτου· κατὰ δὲ
τὴν παράταξιν ἔπεσον μὲν πλείους τῶν πεντακοσίων, ὧν ἦσαν οἱ πλείους ἱππεῖς τῶν ἐπιφανῶν ἀνδρῶν, ἑάλωσαν δ' ὑπὲρ ὀκτακισχιλίους. οἱ δὲ περὶ
Πτολεμαῖον καὶ Σέλευκον δόντες τὴν ἀναίρεσιν τῶν
νεκρῶν τήν τε ἁλοῦσαν βασιλικὴν ἀποσκευὴν καὶ
τῶν αἰχμαλώτων τοὺς περὶ τὴν αὐλὴν εἰωθότας δια-
τρίβειν χωρὶς λύτρων ἀπέστειλαν πρὸς Δημήτριον·

leave their lines and, abandoning their heavy arms, 312 B.C. save themselves by travelling light. But as Demetrius was passing Gaza at about sunset, some of the cavalry dropped out and entered the city since they wished to carry away their baggage. Then, when the gates were opened and a large number of pack animals were gathered together and when each man tried to lead out his own beasts first, there arose such confusion around the gates that when the troops of Ptolemy came up no one was able to close the gates in time. Hence the enemy dashed within the walls, and the city came into the possession of Ptolemy.

85. After the battle had ended in this fashion, Demetrius reached Azotus about the middle of the night, covering two hundred and seventy stades.[1] Thence he sent a herald about the burial of the dead since he was very anxious at any cost to honour those who had perished with the funeral that was their due ; for it happened that most of his friends had fallen, the most distinguished of whom were Pithon, who had shared the command on equal terms with himself, and Boeotus, who for a long time had lived with his father Antigonus and had shared in all his state secrets. In the battle there had fallen more than five hundred men,[2] the majority of whom were cavalry and men of distinction ; and more than eight thousand had been captured. Ptolemy and Seleucus permitted the recovery of the dead, and they returned to Demetrius without ransom the royal baggage, which had been captured, and those of the prisoners who had been accustomed to be in attendance at the

---

[1] About 31 miles.

[2] Plutarch, *Demetrius*, 5. 2, says that 5000 men were slain.

οὐ γὰρ περὶ τούτων ἔφασαν διαφέρεσθαι πρὸς
Ἀντίγονον, ἀλλ᾽ ὅτι τοῦ πολέμου γενομένου κοινοῦ πρότερον μὲν πρὸς Περδίκκαν, ὕστερον δὲ πρὸς
Εὐμενῆ τὰ μέρη τῆς δορικτήτου χώρας οὐκ ἀποδοίη
τοῖς φίλοις καὶ συνθέμενος φιλίαν[1] πρὸς αὐτὸν τοὐναντίον ἀφέλοιτο τὴν σατραπείαν τῆς Βαβυλωνίας
4 Σελεύκου παρὰ πάντα τὰ δίκαια. ὁ δὲ Πτολεμαῖος
τοὺς μὲν ἁλόντας στρατιώτας ἀποστείλας εἰς Αἴγυπτον προσέταξεν ἐπὶ τὰς νομαρχίας[2] διελεῖν, αὐτὸς
δὲ θάψας τῶν ἰδίων τοὺς ἐν τῇ μάχῃ τελευτήσαντας
ἅπαντας μεγαλοπρεπῶς μετὰ τῆς δυνάμεως ἐπῄει
τῶν κατὰ Φοινίκην πόλεων τὰς μὲν πολιορκῶν, τὰς
5 δὲ πειθοῖ προσαγόμενος. Δημήτριος δὲ δύναμιν
οὐκ ἔχων ἀξιόχρεων πρὸς μὲν τὸν πατέρα βυβλια-
φόρον ἀπέστειλεν, ἀξιῶν βοηθεῖν τὴν ταχίστην·
αὐτὸς δὲ παρελθὼν εἰς Τρίπολιν τῆς Φοινίκης μετ-
επέμπετό τε τοὺς ἐκ Κιλικίας στρατιώτας καὶ τῶν
ἄλλων ὅσοι παρεφύλαττον ἢ πόλεις ἢ φρούρια μακρὰν ἀφεστῶτα τῶν πολεμίων.

86. Πτολεμαῖος δὲ κρατῶν τῶν ὑπαίθρων Σιδῶνα μὲν προσηγάγετο, τῆς δὲ Τύρου πλησίον
στρατοπεδεύσας παρεκάλεσεν Ἀνδρόνικον τὸν
φρούραρχον παραδοῦναι τὴν πόλιν καὶ δωρεάς τε
2 καὶ τιμὰς ἁδρὰς ἐπηγγείλατο δοῦναι. ὁ δὲ φήσας
μηδενὶ τρόπῳ προδώσειν τὴν δεδομένην ὑπ᾽ Ἀντιγόνου καὶ Δημητρίου πίστιν, ἐλοιδόρησε φορτικῶς
τὸν Πτολεμαῖον. ὕστερον δὲ στασιασάντων τῶν
στρατιωτῶν ἐκπεσὼν ἐκ Τύρου καὶ γενόμενος ὑποχείριος προσεδόκα μὲν τιμωρίας τεύξεσθαι διά τε

---

[1] φιλίαν Hertlein : πάλιν.
[2] νομαρχίας Wesseling : ναυαρχίας.

court ; for, they said, it was not about these that 312 B.C.
they were at variance with Antigonus but because,
although he and they had made war in common,
first against Perdiccas and later against Eumenes, he
had not turned over to his companions their share
of the captured territory, and again because, after
making a compact of friendship with Seleucus, he
had nevertheless taken away from him his satrapy
of Babylonia contrary to all right. Ptolemy sent
the captured soldiers off into Egypt, ordering them
to be distributed among the nomes ; but he himself,
after giving a magnificent burial to all those of his
own men who had died in the battle, went with his
forces against the cities of Phoenicia, besieging some
of them and winning others by persuasion. But
Demetrius, since he did not have a sufficiently
strong army, sent a messenger to his father, asking
him to aid him as quickly as possible. He himself,
moving to Tripolis in Phoenicia, summoned the
soldiers from Cilicia and also those of his other men
who were guarding cities or strongholds far removed
from the enemy.

86. Ptolemy, after he had gained control of the
open country, first won Sidon to his side ; and then,
camping near Tyre, he summoned Andronicus,[1] the
commander of the garrison, to surrender the city,
and he promised to give him gifts and abundant
honours. Andronicus, however, said that he would
in no wise betray the trust that had been placed in
him by Antigonus and Demetrius, and he vilely insulted Ptolemy. Later, when his soldiers mutinied and
he was expelled from the city and fell into the hands
of Ptolemy, he expected to receive punishment both

---

[1] Cp. chap. 69. 1.

τὴν γενομένην λοιδορίαν καὶ διὰ τὸ μὴ βεβουλῆσθαι
τὴν Τύρον παραδοῦναι· οὐ μὴν ὅ γε Πτολεμαῖος
ἐμνησικάκησεν, ἀλλὰ τοὐναντίον δοὺς δωρεὰς εἶχε
περὶ αὑτόν, ἕνα τῶν φίλων ποιησάμενος καὶ προ-
3 άγων ἐντίμως. ἦν γὰρ ὁ δυνάστης οὗτος καθ᾽
ὑπερβολὴν ἐπιεικὴς καὶ συγγνωμονικός, ἔτι δ᾽
εὐεργετικός. ὅπερ καὶ μάλιστ᾽ αὐτὸν ηὔξησε καὶ
4 πολλοὺς ἐποίησεν ἐπιθυμεῖν κοινωνῆσαι τῆς φιλίας.
καὶ γὰρ τὸν Σέλευκον ἐκ τῆς Βαβυλωνίας ἐκπε-
σόντα φιλοτίμως ὑπεδέξατο καὶ κοινὴν παρείχετο
τούτῳ τε καὶ τοῖς ἄλλοις φίλοις τὴν περὶ αὑτὸν[1]
5 εὐδαιμονίαν. διὸ καὶ τότε παρακαλοῦντος αὐτὸν
Σελεύκου δοῦναι στρατιώτας τοὺς ἀναβησομένους
εἰς Βαβυλῶνα προθύμως ὡμολόγησε καὶ προσεπηγγείλατο πάντα συμπράξειν μέχρι ἀνακτήσαιτο
τὴν προϋπάρχουσαν σατραπείαν.

Καὶ τὰ μὲν κατὰ τὴν Ἀσίαν ἐν τούτοις ἦν.

87. Κατὰ δὲ τὴν Εὐρώπην Τελεσφόρος μὲν ὁ
Ἀντιγόνου ναύαρχος διατρίβων περὶ Κόρινθον,
ἐπειδὴ Πτολεμαῖον ἑώρα μᾶλλον ἑαυτοῦ προαγό-
μενον καὶ τῶν κατὰ τὴν Ἑλλάδα πραγμάτων πι-
στευόμενον ἁπάντων, ἐγκαλέσας Ἀντιγόνῳ περὶ
τούτων τὰς μὲν ναῦς ἃς εἶχεν ἀπέδοτο, τῶν δὲ
στρατιωτῶν τοὺς βουλομένους κοινωνεῖν τῆς προ-
2 αιρέσεως ἀναλαβὼν ἴδια πράγματα συνίστατο. παρελθὼν γὰρ εἰς Ἦλιν ὡς ἔτι φυλάττων τὴν
πρὸς Ἀντίγονον φιλίαν, τὴν ἀκρόπολιν ἐνετείχισε
καὶ τὴν πόλιν κατεδουλώσατο. ἐσύλησεν δὲ καὶ τὸ
ἱερὸν τὸ κατὰ τὴν Ὀλυμπίαν καὶ συναγαγὼν ἀργυρίου πλείω τῶν πεντήκοντα ταλάντων ξένους
3 ἐμισθοῦτο. Τελεσφόρος μὲν οὖν ζηλοτυπήσας τὴν

---

[1] αὑτόν editors : αὐτὸν Fischer, MSS.

for the insults and for his unwillingness to surrender 312 B.C.
Tyre. But in truth Ptolemy bore no malice ; on
the contrary, he gave him gifts and kept him in his
court, making him one of his friends and advancing
him in honour. For indeed, that prince was exceptionally gentle and forgiving and inclined toward
deeds of kindness. It was this very thing that most
increased his power and made many men desire to
share his friendship.[1] For example, when Seleucus
had been driven from Babylonia, he received him with
friendship[2] ; and he used to share his own prosperity
with him and with his other friends. Therefore on
this occasion also, when Seleucus asked him to give
him soldiers for an expedition into Babylonia, he
readily consented ; and in addition, he promised to
aid him in every way until he should regain the
satrapy that had formerly been his.

Such was the situation of affairs in Asia.[3]

87. In Europe,[4] Antigonus' admiral Telesphorus,
who was tarrying near Corinth, when he saw Ptolemaeus preferred to himself and entrusted with all
affairs throughout Greece, charged Antigonus with
this, sold what ships he had, enlisted such of the
soldiers as volunteered to join his cause, and organized
an enterprise of his own. Entering Elis as if still pre-
serving his friendship for Antigonus, he fortified the
citadel and enslaved the city. He even plundered
the sacred precinct at Olympia and, after collecting
more than five hundred talents of silver, began hiring
mercenaries. In this manner then, Telesphorus,

[1] Cp. Book 18. 28. 5-6.   [2] Cp. chap. 55. 5.
[3] Continued in chap. 90. 1.
[4] Continued from chap. 78. Telesphorus was probably
a nephew of Antigonus (chap. 74. 1), and Ptolemaeus certainly was (chap. 68. 5).

προαγωγὴν Πτολεμαίου τοῦτον τὸν τρόπον ἐγένετο
προδότης τῆς πρὸς Ἀντίγονον φιλίας. Πτολεμαῖος
δ' ὁ Ἀντιγόνου στρατηγὸς ἦν μὲν τεταγμένος ἐπὶ
τῶν κατὰ τὴν Ἑλλάδα πραγμάτων, πυθόμενος δὲ
τὴν ἀπόστασιν τὴν Τελεσφόρου καὶ τὴν κατάληψιν
τῆς Ἠλείων πόλεως, ἔτι δὲ τὴν σύλησιν τῶν κατὰ
τὴν Ὀλυμπίαν χρημάτων παρῆλθεν εἰς Πελοπόννησον μετὰ δυνάμεως. καταντήσας δ' εἰς Ἦλιν
καὶ τὴν ἐντετειχισμένην ἀκρόπολιν κατασκάψας τήν
τε ἐλευθερίαν ἀπέδωκε τοῖς Ἠλείοις καὶ τὰ χρήματα ἀποκατέστησεν τῷ θεῷ. μετὰ δὲ ταῦτα τὸν
Τελεσφόρον πείσας παρέλαβεν τὴν Κυλλήνην, φρουρουμένην ὑπ' αὐτοῦ, καὶ τοῖς Ἠλείοις ἀποκατέστησεν.

88. Ἅμα δὲ τούτοις πρασσομένοις Ἠπειρῶται
τελευτήσαντος Αἰακίδου τοῦ βασιλέως αὐτῶν Ἀλ-
κέτᾳ τὴν βασιλείαν παρέδωκαν, ὃς ἦν πεφυγαδευ-
μένος μὲν ὑπὸ Ἀρύμβου[1] τοῦ πατρός, ἀλλοτρίως δὲ
2 διακείμενος πρὸς Κάσανδρον. διὸ καὶ Λυκίσκος
ὁ τεταγμένος ἐπὶ τῆς Ἀκαρνανίας στρατηγὸς ὑπὸ
Κασάνδρου παρῆλθε μετὰ δυνάμεως εἰς τὴν Ἤπειρον, ἐλπίδας ἔχων ῥᾳδίως τὸν Ἀλκέταν ἀποστήσειν
τῆς ἀρχῆς ἀσυντάκτων ἔτι τῶν κατὰ τὴν βασιλείαν
3 ὄντων. καταστρατοπεδεύσαντος δ' αὐτοῦ περὶ
Κασσωπίαν πόλιν Ἀλκέτας τοὺς μὲν υἱοὺς Ἀλέξανδρον καὶ Τεῦκρον ἀπέστειλεν ἐπὶ τὰς πόλεις,
διακελευσάμενος στρατολογεῖν ὡς πλείστους, αὐτὸς
δὲ μεθ' ἧς εἶχε δυνάμεως ἀναζεύξας, ἐπειδὴ πλησίον
ἐγένετο τῶν πολεμίων, ἀνέμενε τὴν τῶν υἱῶν

because he was jealous of the advancement of Ptolemaeus, betrayed the friendship of Antigonus.
Ptolemaeus, the general of Antigonus, had been
placed in charge of affairs throughout Greece ; and
he, on hearing of the revolt of Telesphorus, the capture of the city of the Eleans, and the plundering of
the wealth of Olympia, moved into the Peloponnesus with an army. When he had come into Elis
and levelled the citadel that had been fortified, he
gave the Eleans back their freedom and restored
the treasure to the god. Then by winning Telesphorus' consent he recovered Cyllenê, which the
latter had garrisoned, and restored it to the Eleans.

88. While this was happening, the Epirotes, their
king Aeacides being dead, gave the kingship to
Alcetas,[1] who had been banished by his father
Arymbus and who was hostile to Cassander. For
this reason, Lyciscus,[2] who had been placed as
general over Acarnania by Cassander, entered
Epirus with an army, hoping to remove Alcetas
easily from his throne while the affairs of the kingdom
were still in disorder. While Lyciscus was in camp
before Cassopia, Alcetas sent his sons Alexander and
Teucer to the cities, ordering them to levy as many
soldiers as possible ; and he himself, taking the
field with what force he had, came near the enemy
and awaited the return of his sons. However, since

[1] Alcetas, an older brother of Aeacides, had been banished
because of his unbridled passions (Pausanias, 1. 11. 5).

[2] Lyciscus was placed in command of Epirus by Cassander
in 316 B.C. (chap. 36. 5), and of Acarnania in 314 B.C. (chap. 67.
5) ; but in 313 B.C. he seems to have been replaced for a time
by Philip (chap. 74. 3).

[1] Ἀρύμβου Palmer : Ἀρρυβίλου RX, Ἀριβήλου F.

4 παρουσίαν. τῶν δὲ περὶ Λυκίσκον ἐπικειμένων καὶ
πολὺ τοῖς πλήθεσιν ὑπερεχόντων οἱ μὲν Ἠπειρῶται
καταπλαγέντες προσεχώρησαν τοῖς πολεμίοις, ὁ δʼ
Ἀλκέτας καταλειφθεὶς κατέφυγεν εἰς Εὐρυμενὰς
5 πόλιν Ἠπειρωτικήν. ἐνταῦθα δʼ αὐτοῦ πολιορκου-
μένου παρεγενήθησαν οἱ περὶ τὸν Ἀλέξανδρον βοήθειαν φέροντες τῷ πατρί. γενομένης οὖν μάχης
ἰσχυρᾶς ἀνηρέθησαν πολλοὶ τῶν στρατιωτῶν, ἐν οἷς
ἦσαν ἄλλοι τέ τινες τῶν¹ ἀνδρῶν καὶ Μίκυθος ὁ
στρατηγὸς καὶ Λύσανδρος Ἀθηναῖος ὁ κατασταθεὶς
6 ἐπὶ τῆς Λευκάδος ὑπὸ Κασάνδρου. μετὰ δὲ ταῦτα
Δεινίου βοηθήσαντος τοῖς ἐλαττουμένοις ἐγένετο
δευτέρα μάχη, καθʼ ἣν οἱ μὲν περὶ Ἀλέξανδρον καὶ
Τεῦκρον ἡττηθέντες ἔφυγον εἴς τι χωρίον ἐρυμνὸν
μετὰ τοῦ πατρός, ὁ δὲ Λυκίσκος Εὐρυμενὰς ἐκπολιορκήσας καὶ διαρπάσας κατέσκαψε.

89. Καθʼ ὃν δὴ χρόνον Κάσανδρος ἀκηκοὼς μὲν
τὴν τῶν ἰδίων ἧτταν, ἀγνοῶν δὲ τὸ μετὰ ταῦτα
γεγονὸς εὐτύχημα κατὰ σπουδὴν ἧκεν εἰς τὴν
Ἤπειρον βοηθήσων τοῖς περὶ Λυκίσκον. καταλαβὼν δʼ αὐτοὺς ἐπὶ τοῦ προτερήματος γεγονότας
πρὸς μὲν Ἀλκέταν διαλυσάμενος φιλίαν συνέθετο,
τῆς δὲ δυνάμεως μέρος ἀναλαβὼν ἀνέζευξεν εἰς τὸν
Ἀδρίαν πολιορκήσων Ἀπολλωνιάτας, ὅτι τὴν
φρουρὰν ἐκβαλόντες τὴν αὐτοῦ προσέθεντο τοῖς Ἰλ-
2 λυριοῖς. οὐ μὴν οἵ γε ἐν τῇ πόλει κατεπλάγησαν,
ἀλλὰ βοήθειαν μεταπεμψάμενοι παρὰ τῶν ἄλλων
συμμάχων πρὸ τῶν τειχῶν παρετάξαντο. γενομένης δὲ καρτερᾶς μάχης ἐπὶ πολὺν χρόνον οἱ μὲν
Ἀπολλωνιᾶται τοῖς πλήθεσιν ὑπερέχοντες τοὺς

¹ Fischer adds ἀξιολόγων after τῶν, cp. chap. 47. 4.

the forces of Lyciscus were at hand and were far 312 B.C. superior in number, the Epirotes were frightened and went over to the enemy [1]; and Alcetas, deserted, fled for refuge to Eurymenae, a city of Epirus. While he was being besieged there, Alexander came up bringing reinforcements to his father. A violent battle took place in which many of the soldiers were slain, among whom were certain others of the followers of Lyciscus and in particular the general Micythus and Lysander, an Athenian who had been put in charge of Leucas by Cassander. But afterwards, when Deinias [2] brought reinforcements to the defeated army, there was another battle, in which Alexander and Teucer were defeated and fled with their father to a certain stronghold, while Lyciscus took Eurymenae, plundered it, and destroyed it.

89. At this time Cassander, who had heard of the defeat of his forces but did not know of the victory that had followed, moved into Epirus in haste to assist Lyciscus. On finding that the latter had gained the upper hand, he made terms and established friendship with Alcetas; and then, taking a part of his army, he moved to the Adriatic to lay siege to Apollonia because the people of that city had driven out his garrison and gone over to the Illyrians. Those in the city, however, were not frightened, but summoned aid from their other allies and drew up their army before the walls. In a battle, which was hard fought and long, the people of Apollonia, who were superior in number, forced their opponents

---

[1] According to Pausanias (1. 11. 5), Alcetas so angered the Epirotes by his cruelty that, immediately after his return, they rose against him and slew him.

[2] Deinias, a general of Cassander, had taken Tempê in 317 B.C. (chap. 35. 3).

ἀντιτεταγμένους φυγεῖν ἠνάγκασαν, ὁ δὲ Κάσανδρος
πολλοὺς στρατιώτας ἀποβαλὼν καὶ δύναμιν μὲν οὐκ
ἔχων περὶ αὑτὸν ἀξιόχρεω τὴν δὲ χειμερινὴν ὥραν
3 θεωρῶν ἐπανῆλθεν εἰς Μακεδονίαν.   τούτου δὲ
χωρισθέντος Λευκάδιοι προσλαβόμενοι βοήθειαν
παρὰ Κορκυραίων ἐξέβαλον τὴν φρουρὰν τοῦ
Κασάνδρου. οἱ δ' Ἠπειρῶται χρόνον μέν τινα
διέμενον ὑπ' Ἀλκέτου βασιλευόμενοι, χρωμένου
δ' αὐτοῦ χαλεπώτερον τοῖς πλήθεσιν αὐτόν τε
κατέσφαξαν καὶ δύο τῶν υἱῶν παῖδας ὄντας τὴν
ἡλικίαν Ἡσιονέα καὶ Νίσον.

90. Κατὰ δὲ τὴν Ἀσίαν Σέλευκος μετὰ τὴν γενομένην ἧτταν Δημητρίῳ περὶ Γάζαν τῆς Συρίας
ἀναλαβὼν παρὰ Πτολεμαίου πεζοὺς μὲν οὐ πλείους
τῶν ὀκτακοσίων ἱππεῖς δὲ περὶ διακοσίους ἀνέζευξεν ἐπὶ Βαβυλῶνος, ἐπὶ τοσοῦτον μεμετεωρισμένος
ταῖς ἐλπίσιν ὥστ' εἰ καὶ μηδεμίαν εἶχε δύναμιν τὸ
παράπαν, μετὰ τῶν φίλων καὶ τῶν ἰδίων παίδων
τὴν εἰς τοὺς ἄνω τόπους ἀνάβασιν ποιεῖσθαι· ὑπελάμβανε γὰρ τοὺς μὲν Βαβυλωνίους διὰ τὴν προϋπάρχουσαν εὔνοιαν ἑτοίμως αὐτῷ προσθήσεσθαι,
τοὺς δὲ περὶ Ἀντίγονον μετὰ τῆς δυνάμεως μακρὰν
ἀπεσπασμένους παραδεδωκέναι καιρὸν οἰκεῖον ταῖς
2 ἰδίαις ἐπιβολαῖς.   τοιαύτης δ' οὔσης τῆς περὶ αὑτὸν
ὁρμῆς οἱ συνόντες φίλοι θεωροῦντες ὅτι μετ' αὐτῶν
μέν εἰσι παντελῶς ὀλίγοι συστρατεύοντες, τοῖς δὲ
πολεμίοις ἐφ' οὓς προάγουσι καὶ δυνάμεις ὑπάρ-
χουσιν ἕτοιμοι μεγάλαι καὶ χορηγίαι λαμπραὶ καὶ
3 συμμάχων πλῆθος, οὐ μετρίως ἠθύμουν.   οὓς ὁρῶν
καταπεπληγμένους ὁ Σέλευκος παρεκάλει, διδάσ-

to flee ; and Cassander, who had lost many soldiers, 312 B.C. since he did not have an adequate army with him and saw that the winter was at hand,[1] returned into Macedonia.   After his departure, the Leucadians, receiving help from the Corcyraeans, drove out Cassander's garrison.   For some time the Epirotes continued to be ruled by Alcetas ; but then, since he was treating the common people too harshly, they murdered him and two of his sons, Esioneus and Nisus, who were children.[2]

90. In Asia,[3] after the defeat of Demetrius at Gaza in Syria, Seleucus, receiving from Ptolemy no more than eight hundred foot soldiers and about two hundred horse,[4] set out for Babylon. He was so puffed up with great expectations that, even if he had had no army whatever, he would have made the expedition into the interior with his friends and his own slaves ; for he assumed that the Babylonians, on account of the goodwill that had previously existed, would promptly join him, and that Antigonus, by withdrawing to a great distance with his army, had given him a suitable opportunity for his own enterprises.   While such was his own enthusiasm, those of his friends who accompanied him were no little disheartened when they saw that the men who were making the campaign with them were very few and that the enemy against whom they were going possessed large armies ready for service, magnificent resources, and a host of allies. When Seleucus saw that they were terror-stricken, he encouraged

---

[1] The winter of 312/11 B.C.

[2] But compare the note on chap. 88. 4.   The narrative is continued in chap. 105.

[3] Continued from chap. 86. 5.

[4] Appian, *Syrian Wars*, 9. 54, says 1000 foot and 300 horse.

κων ὅτι τοὺς Ἀλεξάνδρῳ συνεστρατευκότας καὶ δι᾿
ἀρετὴν ὑπ᾿ ἐκείνου προηγμένους προσήκει μὴ πάντως δυνάμει καὶ χρήμασι πεποιθότας ἀντέχεσθαι
πραγμάτων, ἀλλ᾿ ἐμπειρίᾳ καὶ συνέσει, δι᾿ ὧν
κἀκεῖνος τὰ μεγάλα καὶ παρὰ πᾶσι θαυμαζόμενα
κατειργάσατο. πιστεύειν δὲ δεῖν καὶ ταῖς τῶν
θεῶν προρρήσεσι τὸ τέλος ἔσεσθαι τῆς στρατείας
4 ἄξιον τῆς ἐπιβολῆς· ἐν μὲν γὰρ Βραγχίδαις αὐτοῦ
χρηστηριαζομένου τὸν θεὸν προσαγορεῦσαι Σέλευκον βασιλέα, τὸν δὲ Ἀλέξανδρον καθ᾿ ὕπνον ἐπι-
στάντα φανερῶς διασημᾶναι περὶ τῆς ἐσομένης
ἡγεμονίας, ἧς δεῖ τυχεῖν αὐτὸν προϊόντος τοῦ χρό-
5 νου. πρὸς δὲ τούτοις ἀπεφαίνετο διότι πάντα
γίνεται τὰ καλὰ καὶ παρ᾿ ἀνθρώποις θαυμαζόμενα
διὰ πόνων καὶ κινδύνων. ἐπολιτεύετο δὲ καὶ πρὸς
τοὺς συστρατεύοντας καὶ κατεσκεύαζεν αὐτὸν ἴσον
ἅπασιν, ὥσθ᾿ ἕκαστον αἰδεῖσθαι καὶ τὸ παράβολον
τῆς τόλμης ἑκουσίως ὑπομένειν.

91. Ἐπεὶ δὲ προάγων κατήντησεν εἰς Μεσοποταμίαν, τῶν ἐν Κάραις κατῳκισμένων Μακεδόνων
οὓς μὲν ἔπεισεν, οὓς δ᾿ ἐβιάσατο συστρατεύειν
αὐτῷ. ὡς δ᾿ εἰς τὴν Βαβυλωνίαν ἐνέβαλεν, οἱ
πλείους τῶν ἐγχωρίων ἀπήντων καὶ προστιθέμενοι
2 πᾶν ἔφασαν αὐτῷ τὸ δοκοῦν συμπράξειν· τετραετῆ
γὰρ χρόνον γεγονὼς σατράπης τῆς χώρας ταύτης
πᾶσι προσενήνεκτο καλῶς, ἐκκαλούμενος τὴν εὔνοιαν τοῦ πλήθους καὶ πόρρωθεν προπαρασκευαζό-
μενος· τοὺς συμπράξοντας, ἐὰν αὐτῷ δοθῇ καιρὸς

---

[1] Cp. also chap. 55. 7, where we are told that the astrologers
warned Antigonus to expect danger from Seleucus. Other
signs and omens of Seleucus' future greatness are given by
Appian, *Syrian Wars*, 9. 56.

them, saying that men who had campaigned with
Alexander and had been advanced by him because
of their prowess ought not to rely solely on armed
force and wealth when confronting difficult situations, but upon experience and skill, the means
whereby Alexander himself had accomplished his
great and universally admired deeds. He added
that they ought also to believe the oracles of the
gods which had foretold that the end of his campaign
would be worthy of his purpose ; for, when he had
consulted the oracle in Branchidae, the god had
greeted him as King Seleucus, and Alexander standing
beside him in a dream had given him a clear sign
of the future leadership that was destined to fall
to him in the course of time.[1] Moreover, he pointed
out that everything that is good and admired among
men is gained through toil and danger. But he also
sought the favour of his fellow soldiers and put
himself on an equality with them all in such a way
that each man respected him and willingly accepted
the risk of the daring venture.

91. When in his advance he entered Mesopotamia,
he persuaded some of the Macedonians who were
settled at Carae [2] to join his forces, and compelled
the rest. When he pushed into Babylonia, most of
the inhabitants came to meet him, and, declaring
themselves on his side, promised to aid him as he
saw fit ; for, when he had been for four years satrap
of that country, he had shown himself generous to
all, winning the goodwill of the common people and
long in advance securing men who would assist him
if an opportunity should ever be given him to make

[2] Probably the same as Carrhae, and not to be identified
with the Carae of Book 17. 110. 3 ; 19. 12. 1.

3 ἀμφισβητεῖν ἡγεμονίας. προσεχώρησε δ' αὐτῷ
καὶ Πολύαρχος, τεταγμένος ἐπί τινος διοικήσεως,
μετὰ στρατιωτῶν πλειόνων ἢ χιλίων. οἱ δὲ δια-
φυλάττοντες τὴν πρὸς Ἀντίγονον φιλίαν, ὁρῶντες ἀκατάσχετον οὖσαν τὴν τοῦ πλήθους ὁρμήν,
συνέφευγον εἰς τὴν ἄκραν, ἧς φύλαξ ἀπεδέδεικτο
4 Δίφιλος. ὁ δὲ Σέλευκος συστησάμενος πολιορκίαν
καὶ κατὰ κράτος ἑλὼν τὴν ἄκραν ἐκομίσατο τὰ
φυλαττόμενα σώματα τῶν φίλων καὶ τῶν παίδων,
ὅσοι παρεδόθησαν εἰς φυλακὴν παρ' Ἀντιγόνου
μετὰ τὴν ἐκ Βαβυλῶνος εἰς Αἴγυπτον ἀποχώρησιν.
5 ἀπὸ δὲ τούτων γενόμενος στρατιώτας συνήγαγεν
καὶ συναγοράσας ἵππους ἀνεδίδου τοῖς δυναμένοις
χρᾶσθαι. πᾶσι δὲ φιλανθρώπως ὁμιλῶν καὶ καθ-
ιστὰς εἰς ἀγαθὰς ἐλπίδας ἑτοίμους εἶχε καὶ προθύμους ἐν πάσῃ περιστάσει τοὺς συγκινδυνεύοντας.
Σέλευκος μὲν οὖν τοῦτον τὸν τρόπον ἀνεκτήσατο
τὴν Βαβυλωνίαν.

92. Νικάνορος δὲ τοῦ περὶ Μηδίαν στρατηγοῦ
συναγαγόντος ἐπ' αὐτὸν ἔκ τε Μηδίας καὶ Περσίδος
καὶ τῶν σύνεγγυς τόπων στρατιώτας πεζοὺς μὲν
πλείους τῶν μυρίων ἱππεῖς δὲ περὶ ἑπτακισχιλίους
ὥρμησεν κατὰ σπουδὴν ἀπαντήσων τοῖς πολεμίοις.
2 εἶχε δὲ τοὺς σύμπαντας πεζοὺς μὲν πλείους τῶν
τρισχιλίων, ἱππεῖς δὲ τετρακοσίους. διαβὰς δὲ
τὸν Τίγριν ποταμὸν καὶ πυνθανόμενος ὀλίγων ἡμερῶν ὁδὸν ἀπέχειν τοὺς πολεμίους, ἔκρυψε τοὺς
στρατιώτας ἐν τοῖς πλησίον ἕλεσι, διανοούμενος
3 ἀπροσδόκητον ποιήσασθαι τὴν ἐπίθεσιν. ὁ δὲ
Νικάνωρ ἐπειδὴ παραγενηθεὶς ἐπὶ τὸν Τίγριν ποταμὸν οὐχ ηὕρισκε τοὺς πολεμίους, κατεστρατοπέδευσε πρός τινι βασιλικῷ σταθμῷ, νομίζων αὐτοὺς

a bid for supreme power. He was joined also by
Polyarchus, who had been placed in command of a
certain district, with more than a thousand soldiers.
When those who remained loyal to Antigonus saw
that the impulse of the people could not be checked,
they took refuge together in the citadel, of which
Diphilus had been appointed commander. But
Seleucus, by laying siege to the citadel and taking
it by storm, recovered the persons of all those of
his friends and slaves who had been placed there
under guard by the order of Antigonus after Seleucus'
own departure from Babylon into Egypt. When he
had finished this, he enlisted soldiers, and, having
bought up horses, he distributed them to those who
were able to handle them. Associating with all on
friendly terms and raising high hopes in all, he kept
his fellow adventurers ready and eager under every
condition. In this way, then, Seleucus regained
Babylonia.

92. But when Nicanor, the general in Media,
gathered against him from Media and Persia and
the neighbouring lands more than ten thousand foot
soldiers and about seven thousand horse, Seleucus set
out at full speed to oppose the enemy. He himself
had in all more than three thousand foot and four
hundred horse. He crossed the Tigris River ; and,
on hearing that the enemy were a few days' march
distant, he hid his soldiers in the adjacent marshes,
intending to make his attack a surprise. When
Nicanor arrived at the Tigris River and did not find
the enemy, he camped at one of the royal stations,

πεφευγέναι μακρότερον. ἐπιγενομένης δὲ νυκτὸς
καὶ τῶν περὶ Νικάνορα καταπεφρονηκότως[1] καὶ
ῥᾳθύμως ἐχόντων τὰ περὶ τὰς φυλακὰς ἐπιπεσὼν ὁ
Σέλευκος ἄφνω πολλὴν ταραχὴν καὶ κατάπληξιν
4 κατεσκεύασε· συναψάντων γὰρ μάχην τῶν Περσῶν
συνέβη τόν τε σατράπην αὐτῶν Εὔαγρον πεσεῖν καὶ
τινας τῶν ἄλλων ἡγεμόνων. οὗ συμβάντος οἱ
πλείους τῶν στρατιωτῶν τὰ μὲν τὸν κίνδυνον καταπεπληγμένοι, τὰ δὲ προσκόπτοντες τοῖς ὑπ' Ἀντιγόνου πραττομένοις μετεβάλοντο πρὸς Σέλευκον.
5 ὁ δὲ Νικάνωρ μετ' ὀλίγων ἀπολειφθεὶς καὶ δεδιὼς
μὴ παραδοθῇ τοῖς πολεμίοις, ἔφυγε μετὰ τῶν φίλων
διὰ τῆς ἐρήμου. Σέλευκος δὲ δυνάμεως ἁδρᾶς
κυριεύσας καὶ φιλανθρώπως πᾶσι προσφερόμενος
ῥᾳδίως προσηγάγετο τήν τε Σουσιανὴν καὶ Μηδίαν
καί τινας τῶν σύνεγγυς τόπων· περί τε τῶν διῳκη-
μένων ἔγραψε πρὸς Πτολεμαῖον καὶ τοὺς ἄλλους
φίλους, ἔχων ἤδη βασιλικὸν ἀνάστημα καὶ δόξαν
ἀξίαν ἡγεμονίας.

93. Ἅμα δὲ τούτοις πραττομένοις Πτολεμαῖος
μὲν διέτριβε περὶ Κοίλην Συρίαν, νενικηκὼς Δημήτριον τὸν Ἀντιγόνου παρατάξει μεγάλῃ. ὃν
πυνθανόμενος ἐκ Κιλικίας ἀνεστραφέναι καὶ στρατοπεδεύειν περὶ τὴν ἄνω Συρίαν, προεχειρίσατο
2 τῶν περὶ αὐτὸν φίλων Κίλλην τὸν Μακεδόνα· τούτῳ
δὲ δοὺς δύναμιν ἱκανὴν προσέταξεν ἐκδιῶξαι τὸν
Δημήτριον τὸ παράπαν ἐκ τῆς Συρίας ἢ περικατα-
λαβόντα συντρῖψαι. τούτου δ' ὄντος κατὰ πορείαν
Δημήτριος διὰ τῶν σκοπῶν ἀκούσας τὸν Κίλλην

believing that they had fled to a greater distance 312 B.C. than was the case. When night was come and the army of Nicanor was keeping a perfunctory and negligent guard, Seleucus fell on them suddenly, causing great confusion and panic ; for it happened that when the Persians had joined battle, their satrap Evager [1] fell together with some of the other leaders. When this occurred, most of the soldiers went over to Seleucus, in part because they were frightened at the danger but in part because they were offended by the conduct of Antigonus. Nicanor, who was left with only a few men and feared lest he be delivered over to the enemy, took flight with his friends through the desert. But Seleucus, now that he had gained control of a large army and was comporting himself in a way gracious to all, easily won over Susianê, Media, and some of the adjacent lands ; and he wrote to Ptolemy and his other friends about his achievements, already possessing a king's stature and a reputation worthy of royal power.

93. Meanwhile Ptolemy remained in Coelê Syria after having conquered Antigonus' son Demetrius in a great battle.[2] On hearing that Demetrius had returned from Cilicia and was encamped in Upper Syria, he chose from the friends who were with him Cilles the Macedonian; and, giving him an adequate army, he ordered him to drive Demetrius completely out of Syria or to entrap and crush him.[3] While Cilles was on the way, Demetrius, hearing from spies that he

[1] Possibly to be identified with the Evagoras who is mentioned in chap. 48. 2 as satrap of Aria.

[2] For the victory of Ptolemy at Gaza cp. chaps. 83 ff.

[3] Cp. Plutarch, *Demetrius*, 6. 1-2.

---

[1] καταπεφρονηκότως Stephanus : καταπεφρονηκότων.

στρατοπεδεύειν καταπεφρονηκότως περὶ Μυοῦντα,
τὴν μὲν ἀποσκευὴν ἀπέλιπε, τοὺς δὲ στρατιώτας
εὐζώνους παραλαβὼν νυκτὸς πορείαν σύντομον
ἐποιήσατο, προσπεσὼν δὲ τοῖς πολεμίοις ἑωθινῆς
φυλακῆς ἄφνω τῆς τε δυνάμεως ἄνευ μάχης ἐκυρίευσεν καὶ αὐτὸν τὸν στρατηγὸν ἐζώγρησε. τη-
λικούτου δ' εὐτυχήματος γεγενημένου τὴν ἧτταν
3 ἀναμαχήσασθαι διειλήφει. οὐ μὴν ἀλλὰ τὸν Πτολεμαῖον ὑπολαμβάνων ἥξειν ἐπ' αὐτὸν μετὰ πάσης
τῆς δυνάμεως, ἐστρατοπέδευσε προβλήματα τῆς
παρεμβολῆς ποιησάμενος ἕλη καὶ λίμνας. ἔγραψε
δὲ καὶ πρὸς τὸν πατέρα περὶ τοῦ γενομένου κατορ-
θώματος, παρακαλῶν¹ αὐτὸν ἢ δύναμιν ἀποστεῖλαι
τὴν ταχίστην ἢ καὶ αὐτὸν παραβαλεῖν εἰς τὴν
4 Συρίαν. ὁ δ' Ἀντίγονος ἐτύγχανε μὲν ὢν ἐν Κε-
λαιναῖς τῆς Φρυγίας, κομισάμενος δὲ τὴν ἐπιστολὴν
ἐχάρη διαφερόντως ἐπὶ τῷ δοκεῖν τὸν υἱὸν νέον
ὄντα κατωρθωκέναι δι' αὐτοῦ καὶ φαίνεσθαι βασιλείας ἄξιον. αὐτὸς δὲ τὴν δύναμιν ἀναλαβὼν
ἀνέζευξεν ἐκ τῆς Φρυγίας καὶ τὸν Ταῦρον ὑπερβαλὼν ὀλίγαις ἡμέραις συνέμιξε τοῖς περὶ τὸν
5 Δημήτριον. Πτολεμαῖος δὲ πυθόμενος τὴν Ἀντιγόνου παρουσίαν καὶ συναγαγὼν τοὺς ἡγεμόνας καὶ
φίλους ἐβουλεύετο πότερον συμφέρει μένειν καὶ
ἀγωνίζεσθαι περὶ τῶν ὅλων κατὰ Συρίαν ἢ προάγειν εἰς Αἴγυπτον καὶ πολεμεῖν ἐκεῖθεν, καθάπερ
6 καὶ πρότερον Περδίκκᾳ. πάντες οὖν συνεβούλευον
μὴ διακινδυνεύειν πρὸς δύναμιν πολλαπλασίονα
καὶ θηρίων πλῆθος, ἔτι δὲ στρατηγὸν ἀήττητον·

---

¹ καὶ before παρακαλῶν omitted by Dindorf.

---

¹ Myus in Syria is otherwise unknown.

was carelessly encamped at Myus,[1] left his baggage 312 B.C.
behind and with his soldiers in light equipment made
a forced march ; then, falling suddenly upon the
enemy during the early morning watch,[2] he captured
the army without a battle and took the general
himself prisoner.[3] By achieving such a success he
believed that he had wiped out the defeat. Nevertheless, assuming that Ptolemy would march against
him with all his army, he went into camp, using as
the outworks of his defence swamps and marshes.
He also wrote to his father about the success that
had been gained, urging him either to send an army
as soon as possible or to cross over into Syria himself.
Antigonus chanced to be in Celaenae in Phrygia ;
and, on receiving the letter, he rejoiced greatly that
his son, young as he was, seemed to have got out
of his difficulties by himself and to have shown himself worthy to be a king. He himself with his army
set out from Phrygia, crossed the Taurus, and within
a few days joined Demetrius. Ptolemy, however,
on hearing of the arrival of Antigonus, called together
his leaders and friends and took counsel with them
whether it was better to remain and reach a final
decision in Syria or to withdraw to Egypt and carry
on the war from there as he had formerly done
against Perdiccas.[4] Now all advised him not to risk
a battle against an army that was many times stronger
and had a larger number of elephants as well as against
an unconquered general ; for, they said, it would

[2] *i.e.* the last watch of the night.
[3] This victory is minimized by Pausanias, 1. 6. 5. According to Plutarch (*Demetrius*, 6. 3), Demetrius restored Cilles
and his staff to Ptolemy alive, thus repaying Ptolemy for
his generosity after Gaza (chap. 85. 3).
[4] Cp. Book 18. 33–35.

εὐχερέστερον γὰρ πολλῷ διαγωνιεῖσθαι κατὰ τὴν
Αἴγυπτον, ταῖς τε χορηγίαις ὑπερέχοντα καὶ τόπων
7 ὀχυρότητι πιστεύοντα. διὸ καὶ κρίνας ἐκλιπεῖν τὴν
Συρίαν κατέσκαψε τὰς ἀξιολογωτάτας τῶν κε-
κρατημένων πόλεων, Ἄκην μὲν τῆς Φοινίκης Συρίας, Ἰόππην δὲ καὶ Σαμάρειαν καὶ Γάζαν τῆς
Συρίας, αὐτὸς δὲ τὴν δύναμιν ἀναλαβὼν καὶ τῶν
χρημάτων ὅσα δυνατὸν ἦν ἄγειν ἢ φέρειν ἐπανῆλθεν
εἰς Αἴγυπτον.

94. Ἀντίγονος δ᾽ ἀκινδύνως ἀνακτησάμενος τήν
τε Συρίαν πᾶσαν καὶ Φοινίκην ἐπεβάλετο στρατεύειν ἐπὶ τὴν χώραν τῶν Ἀράβων τῶν καλουμένων
Ναβαταίων. κρίνας γὰρ τὸ ἔθνος τοῦτο τῶν ἑαυτοῦ
πραγμάτων ἀλλότριον εἶναι, προεχειρίσατο τῶν
αὐτοῦ φίλων Ἀθήναιον, δοὺς δ᾽[1] αὐτῷ πεζοὺς μὲν
εὐζώνους τετρακισχιλίους, ἱππεῖς δὲ τοὺς ἐπιτη-
δείους εἰς δρόμον ἑξακοσίους συνέταξεν ἐπιθέσθαι
τοῖς βαρβάροις ἄφνω καὶ τὴν λείαν πᾶσαν ἀπο-
τεμέσθαι.

2 Χρήσιμον δ᾽ ἐστὶ τῶν ἀγνοούντων ἕνεκα διελθεῖν
τὰ νόμιμα τῶν Ἀράβων τούτων, οἷς χρώμενοι
δοκοῦσι τὴν ἐλευθερίαν διαφυλάττειν. ἔχουσι τοί-
νυν τὸν βίον ὑπαίθριον, πατρίδα καλοῦντες τὴν
ἀοίκητον τὴν μήτε ποταμοὺς ἔχουσαν μήτε κρήνας
δαψιλεῖς ἐξ ὧν δυνατὸν στρατόπεδον πολέμιον
3 ὑδρεύσασθαι. νόμος δ᾽ ἐστὶν αὐτοῖς μήτε σῖτον
σπείρειν μήτε φυτεύειν μηδὲν φυτὸν καρποφόρον
μήτε οἴνῳ χρῆσθαι μήτε οἰκίαν κατασκευάζειν· ὃς
δ᾽ ἂν παρὰ ταῦτα ποιῶν εὑρίσκηται, θάνατον αὐτῷ

[1] δ᾽ added by Dindorf.

be much easier for him to settle the war in Egypt 312 B.C. where he had plenty of supplies and could trust to the difficulty of the terrain. Deciding, therefore, to leave Syria, he razed the most noteworthy of the cities that he had captured : Akê in Phoenician Syria, and Ioppê, Samaria, and Gaza in Syria ; then he himself, taking the army and what of the booty it was possible to drive or carry, returned into Egypt.[1]

94. Now that Antigonus without a fight had gained possession of all Syria and Phoenicia, he desired to make a campaign against the land of the Arabs who are called Nabataeans.[2] Deciding that this people was hostile to his interests, he selected one of his friends, Athenaeus, gave him four thousand light foot-soldiers and six hundred horsemen fitted for speed, and ordered him to set upon the barbarians suddenly and cut off all their cattle as booty.

For the sake of those who do not know, it will be useful to state in some detail the customs of these Arabs, by following which, it is believed, they preserve their liberty. They live in the open air, claiming as native land a wilderness that has neither rivers nor abundant springs from which it is possible for a hostile army to obtain water. It is their custom neither to plant grain, set out any fruit-bearing tree, use wine, nor construct any house ; and if anyone is found acting contrary to this, death is his penalty.[3]

[1] Cp. Pausanias, 1. 6. 5.

[2] This was clearly a preliminary step to the invasion of Egypt itself which he already had in mind. Cambyses before invading Egypt made terms with the Arabs (Herodotus, 3. 4-9). For these Arabs cp. Strabo, 16. 4 *passim* (particularly § 26) ; and also Diodorus' own earlier description of them (Book 2. 48).

[3] Cp. the description of the Rechabites in Jeremiah, 35. 6-10.

4 πρόστιμον εἶναι. χρῶνται δὲ τῷ νόμῳ τούτῳ διαλαμβάνοντες τοὺς ταῦτα κτωμένους ἀναγκασθήσεσθαι ῥᾳδίως ὑπὸ τῶν δυνατῶν ἕνεκα τῆς τούτων
χρείας ποιεῖν τὸ προστασσόμενον. τρέφουσι δ'
αὐτῶν οἱ μὲν καμήλους, οἱ δὲ πρόβατα, τὴν ἔρημον
ἐπινέμοντες. οὐκ ὀλίγων δ' ὄντων Ἀραβικῶν ἐθνῶν τῶν τὴν ἔρημον ἐπινεμόντων οὗτοι πολὺ τῶν
ἄλλων προέχουσι ταῖς εὐπορίαις, τὸν ἀριθμὸν ὄντες
5 οὐ πολὺ πλείους τῶν μυρίων· εἰώθασι γὰρ αὐτῶν
οὐκ ὀλίγοι κατάγειν ἐπὶ θάλασσαν λιβανωτόν τε
καὶ σμύρναν καὶ τὰ πολυτελέστατα τῶν ἀρωμάτων,
διαδεχόμενοι παρὰ τῶν κομιζόντων ἐκ τῆς Εὐδαί-
6 μονος καλουμένης Ἀραβίας. φιλελεύθεροι δέ εἰσι
διαφερόντως καὶ ὅταν πολεμίων δύναμις ἁδρὰ
προσίῃ, φεύγουσιν εἰς τὴν ἔρημον, ταύτῃ χρώμενοι
ὀχυρώματι· ἄνυδρος γὰρ οὖσα τοῖς μὲν ἄλλοις
ἀνεπίβατός ἐστι, τούτοις δὲ κατεσκευακόσιν ἀγγεῖα
κατὰ γῆς ὀρυκτὰ κεκονιαμένα μόνοις παρέχεται τὴν
7 ἀσφάλειαν. τῆς γὰρ γῆς οὔσης τῆς μὲν ἀργιλ-
λώδους, τῆς δὲ πέτραν ἐχούσης μαλακὴν ὀρύγματα
μεγάλα ποιοῦσιν ἐν αὐτῇ, ὧν τὰ μὲν στόμια μικρὰ
παντελῶς κατασκευάζουσι, κατὰ βάθους δ' ἀεὶ
μᾶλλον εὐρυχωρῆ ποιοῦντες τὸ τελευταῖον τηλικοῦτ'
ἀποτελοῦσι τὸ μέγεθος ὥστε γίνεσθαι πλευρὰν ἑκά-
8 στην πλέθρου. ταῦτα δὲ τὰ ἀγγεῖα πληροῦντες
ὕδατος ὀμβρίου τὰ στόματ' ἐμφράττουσι καὶ ποιοῦντες ἰσόπεδον τῇ λοιπῇ χώρᾳ σημεῖα καταλείπουσιν
ἑαυτοῖς μὲν γιγνωσκόμενα, τοῖς δ' ἄλλοις ἀνεπι-
9 νόητα. ποτίζουσι δὲ καὶ τὴν λείαν δι' ἡμερῶν
τριῶν, ὅπως ἐν ταῖς ἀνυδρίαις καὶ φυγαῖς μὴ προσ-

---

[1] *i.e.* Arabia the Fortunate (Arabia Felix), the south-
western part of the peninsula (cp. Book 2. 49).

They follow this custom because they believe that 312 b.c. those who possess these things are, in order to retain the use of them, easily compelled by the powerful to do their bidding. Some of them raise camels, others sheep, pasturing them in the desert. While there are many Arabian tribes who use the desert as pasture, the Nabataeans far surpass the others in wealth although they are not much more than ten thousand in number ; for not a few of them are accustomed to bring down to the sea frankincense and myrrh and the most valuable kinds of spices, which they procure from those who convey them from what is called Arabia Eudaemon.[1] They are exceptionally fond of freedom ; and, whenever a strong force of enemies comes near, they take refuge in the desert, using this as a fortress[2]; for it lacks water and cannot be crossed by others, but to them alone, since they have prepared subterranean reservoirs lined with stucco, it furnishes safety. As the earth in some places is clayey and in others is of soft stone, they make great excavations in it, the mouths of which they make very small, but by constantly increasing the width as they dig deeper, they finally make them of such size that each side has a length of one plethrum.[3] After filling these reservoirs with rain water, they close the openings, making them even with the rest of the ground, and they leave signs that are known to themselves but are unrecognizable by others. They water their cattle every other day, so that, if they flee through waterless places, they may not need a continuous

[2] In Book 2. 48. 5 Diodorus states that the kings of the Assyrians and of the Medes and Persians vainly sent large forces against these Arabs.

[3] About 100 feet.

δέωνται συνεχῶν ὑδάτων. αὐτοὶ δὲ χρῶνται
τροφῇ κρέασι καὶ γάλακτι καὶ τῶν ἐκ τῆς γῆς
10 φυομένων τοῖς ἐπιτηδείοις· φύεται γὰρ παρ' αὐτοῖς
τὸ πέπερι καὶ ἀπὸ τῶν δένδρων[1] μέλι πολὺ τὸ
καλούμενον ἄγριον, ᾧ χρῶνται ποτῷ μεθ' ὕδατος.
ἔστι δὲ καὶ ἄλλα γένη τῶν Ἀράβων, ὧν ἔνια καὶ
γεωργεῖ μιγνύμενα τοῖς φορολογουμένοις καὶ μετ-
έχει τῶν αὐτῶν τοῖς Σύροις πλὴν τοῦ κατασκηνοῦν
ἐν οἰκίαις.

95. Τὰ μὲν οὖν νόμιμα τῶν Ἀράβων τοιαῦτ'
εἶναι συμβέβηκεν. ὑπογύου δ' αὐτοῖς οὔσης πανη-
γύρεως, εἰς ἣν εἰώθασιν οἱ περίοικοι καταντᾶν οἱ
μὲν ἀποδωσόμενοι τῶν φορτίων, οἱ δ' ἀγοράσοντές
τι τῶν αὐτοῖς χρησίμων, εἰς ταύτην ἐπορεύθησαν,
ἀπολιπόντες ἐπί τινος πέτρας τὰς κτήσεις καὶ τοὺς
2 πρεσβυτάτους, ἔτι δὲ τέκνα καὶ γυναῖκας. τὸ δὲ
χωρίον ὑπῆρχεν ὀχυρὸν μὲν καθ' ὑπερβολὴν ἀτεί-
χιστον δέ, καὶ τῆς οἰκουμένης ἀπέχον δυεῖν
ἡμερῶν ὁδόν.

Οἱ δὲ περὶ τὸν Ἀθήναιον παρατηρήσαντες τοῦτον
τὸν καιρὸν ὥρμησαν ἐπὶ τὴν πέτραν εὔζωνον
ἔχοντες τὴν δύναμιν· διανύσαντες δ' ἀπὸ τῆς Ἰδουμαίας ἐπαρχίας ἐν ἡμέραις τρισὶ καὶ νυξὶ ταῖς ἴσαις
σταδίους δισχιλίους καὶ διακοσίους ἔλαθον τοὺς
Ἄραβας περὶ μέσας νύκτας καταλαβόμενοι τὴν
3 πέτραν. εὐθὺς δὲ τῶν ἐγκατειλημμένων οὓς μὲν
ἀνῄρουν, οὓς δ' ἐζώγρουν, ἐνίους δὲ τραυματίας

---

[1] καὶ ἀπὸ τῶν δένδρων Wesseling : ἀπὸ τῶν δένδρων καί.

---

[1] Perhaps the so-called tamarisk-manna, a sweet gum
which exudes from the slender branches of *Tamarix gallica*
when these have been punctured by a certain insect. This

supply of water. They themselves use as food flesh 312 B.C.
and milk and those of the plants that grow from
the ground which are suitable for this purpose ; for
among them there grow the pepper and plenty of
the so-called wild honey from trees,[1] which they
drink mixed with water. There are also other tribes
of Arabs, some of whom even till the soil, mingling
with the tribute-paying peoples, and have the same
customs as the Syrians, except that they do not
dwell in houses.

95. It appears that such are the customs of the
Arabs. But when the time draws near for the national
gathering at which those who dwell round about are
accustomed to meet, some to sell goods and others
to purchase things that are needful to them, they
travel to this meeting, leaving on a certain rock [2]
their possessions and their old men, also their women
and their children. This place is exceedingly strong
but unwalled, and it is distant two days' journey
from the settled country.

After waiting for this season, Athenaeus set out
for the rock with his army in light marching order.
Covering the twenty-two hundred stades [3] from the
district of Idumaea in three days and the same
number of nights, he escaped the attention of the
Arabs and seized the rock at about midnight. Of
those that were caught there, some he slew at once,
some he took as prisoners, and others who were

is thought by some to be the manna of Exodus 16. Cp.
Herodotus, 7. 31.

[2] This natural stronghold may be the later Petra.

[3] About 250 miles ; but the number must be corrupt. In
chap. 98. 1 the distance from the rock to the Dead Sea,
" which lies along the middle of Idumaea," is given as
300 stades, about 34 miles.

ἀπέλιπον καὶ τοῦ μὲν λιβανωτοῦ καὶ τῆς σμύρνης
συνεσκευάσαντο τὸ πλεῖον μέρος, ἀργυρίου δὲ περὶ
πεντακόσια τάλαντα. ἐνδιατρίψαντες δ᾽ οὐ πλείω
χρόνον φυλακῆς ἑωθινῆς[1] εὐθὺς ἀνέστρεψαν κατὰ
σπουδήν, διαλαμβάνοντες ὑπὸ τῶν βαρβάρων διωχ-
θήσεσθαι. διατείναντες δὲ σταδίους διακοσίους
κατεστρατοπέδευσαν, ὄντες κατάκοποι καὶ ῥαθύμως
ἔχοντες τὰ περὶ τὰς φυλακάς, ὡς ἂν νομίζοντες μὴ
πρότερον δύνασθαι τοὺς πολεμίους ἐλθεῖν δυεῖν ἢ
4 τριῶν ἡμερῶν. οἱ δ᾽ Ἄραβες πυθόμενοι παρὰ τῶν
ἑωρακότων τὸ στρατόπεδον παραχρῆμα ἠθροίσθησαν καὶ τὴν πανήγυριν ἀπολιπόντες ἧκον ἐπὶ τὴν
πέτραν· παρὰ δὲ τῶν τραυματιῶν μαθόντες τὰ γε-
5 γονότα κατὰ σπουδὴν ἐδίωκον τοὺς Ἕλληνας. τῶν
δὲ περὶ τὸν Ἀθήναιον στρατοπεδευσάντων καταπεφρονηκότως καὶ διὰ τὸν κόπον ἐν ὕπνῳ καθεστώ-
των ἔλαθόν τινες τῶν αἰχμαλώτων διαδράντες, παρ᾽
ὧν οἱ Ναβαταῖοι μαθόντες τὰ κατὰ τοὺς πολεμίους
ἐπέθεντο τῇ στρατοπεδείᾳ περὶ τρίτην φυλακήν,
ὄντες οὐκ ἐλάσσω ὀκτακισχιλίων. καὶ τοὺς πλείους μὲν ἐν ταῖς κοίταις ὄντας ἔτι κατέσφαξαν,
τοὺς δὲ διεγειρομένους καὶ χωροῦντας εἰς ὅπλα
κατηκόντιζον· καὶ πέρας οἱ μὲν πεζοὶ πάντες ἀνηρέθησαν, τῶν δὲ ἱππέων διεσώθησαν εἰς πεντήκοντα καὶ τούτων οἱ πλείους τραυματίαι.
6 Οἱ μὲν οὖν περὶ τὸν Ἀθήναιον ἐν ἀρχῇ κατορθώ-
σαντες ἐξ ὑστέρου διὰ τὴν ἑαυτῶν ἀβουλίαν τοῦτον
τὸν τρόπον ἐσφάλησαν· ταῖς γὰρ εὐτυχίαις εἴωθεν
ὡς ἐπίπαν ἀκολουθεῖν ῥαθυμία καὶ καταφρόνησις.

wounded he left behind ; and of the frankincense and 312 B.C.
myrrh he gathered together the larger part, and about
five hundred talents of silver. Delaying no longer than
the early morning watch,[1] he at once departed at top
speed, expecting to be pursued by the barbarians.
When he and his men had marched without pause for
two hundred stades,[2] they made camp, being tired
and keeping a careless watch as if they believed that
the enemy could not come before two or three days.
But when the Arabs heard from those who had seen
the expedition, they at once gathered together and,
leaving the place of assembly, came to the rock :
then, being informed by the wounded of what had
taken place, they pursued the Greeks at top speed.
While the men of Athenaeus were encamped with
little thought of the enemy and because of their
weariness were deep in sleep, some of their prisoners
escaped secretly ; and the Nabataeans, learning from
them the condition of the enemy, attacked the camp
at about the third watch, being no less than eight
thousand in number. Most of the hostile troops they
slaughtered where they lay ; the rest they slew with
their javelins as they awoke and sprang to arms. In
the end all the foot-soldiers were slain, but of the
horsemen about fifty escaped, and of these the larger
part were wounded.

And so Athenaeus, after being successful at first,
later because of his own folly failed in this manner ;
for carelessness and indifference are, in general,

---

[1] *i.e.* the last watch of the night. If we follow the MSS.
and omit ἑωθινῆς, we may translate : " Delaying no longer
than a single watch, he departed at top speed . . ."
[2] About 22½ miles.

---

[1] ἑωθινῆς added by Kallenberg.

7 διόπερ ἔνιοι προσηκόντως ὑπολαμβάνουσιν εὐχερέστερον ὑπάρχειν συμφορὰς ἐνεγκεῖν ἐπιδεξίως ἢ
τὰς εὐμεγέθεις εὐημερίας ἐμφρόνως· αἱ μὲν γὰρ
διὰ τὸν περὶ τοῦ μέλλοντος φόβον ἐπαναγκάζουσιν
ἐπιμελεῖσθαι, αἱ δὲ διὰ τὸ προγεγονὸς εὐτύχημα
προτρέπονται καταφρονεῖν πάντων.

96. Οἱ δὲ Ναβαταῖοι τοὺς πολεμίους κολάσαντες
ἀνδρωδῶς αὐτοὶ μὲν ἐπανῆλθον εἰς τὴν πέτραν τὰ
σφέτερα κεκομισμένοι, πρὸς δ' Ἀντίγονον ἐπιστολὴν γράψαντες Συρίοις γράμμασι τῶν μὲν περὶ
Ἀθήναιον κατηγόρουν ὑπὲρ ἑαυτῶν δὲ ἀπελο-
2 γοῦντο. ὁ δ' Ἀντίγονος ἀντέγραψεν αὐτοῖς, προσ-
μαρτυρῶν ὡς δικαίως μὲν ἠμύναντο, τῶν δὲ περὶ
Ἀθήναιον κατήγορει, φάσκων παρὰ τὰς δεδομένας
ἐντολὰς ὑπ' αὐτοῦ πεποιῆσθαι τὴν ἐπίθεσιν. τοῦτο
δ' ἔπραττε κρύπτων τὴν ἑαυτοῦ προαίρεσιν καὶ
βουλόμενος ὑπαγαγέσθαι τοὺς βαρβάρους εἰς ῥαθυ-
μίαν, ὅπως ἀνελπίστως ἐπιθέμενος κρατήσῃ τῆς
ἐπιβολῆς· οὐ γὰρ ῥάδιον ἦν ἄνευ δόλου τινὸς ἀνδρῶν περιγενέσθαι νομάδα βίον ἐζηλωκότων καὶ
3 καταφυγὴν ἀπρόσιτον ἐχόντων τὴν ἔρημον. οἱ δ'
Ἄραβες περιχαρεῖς μὲν ἦσαν ἐπὶ τῷ δοκεῖν ἀπο-
λελύσθαι μεγάλων φόβων, οὐ μὴν παντελῶς ἐπί-
στευόν γε τοῖς Ἀντιγόνου λόγοις, ἀλλὰ τὰς ἐλπίδας
ἔχοντες ἀμφιδοξουμένας σκοποὺς μὲν κατέστησαν
ἐπὶ τῶν λόφων, ἀφ' ὧν ἦν ῥάδιον συνορᾶν πόρρωθεν
τὰς εἰς τὴν Ἀραβίαν ἐμβολάς, αὐτοὶ δὲ συνταξάμενοι τὰ περὶ ἑαυτοὺς προσηκόντως ἐκαραδόκουν
4 τὸ ἀποβησόμενον. ὁ δ' Ἀντίγονος φιλοποιησά-
μενος χρόνον τινὰ τοὺς βαρβάρους καὶ νομίσας
αὐτοὺς ἐξηπατημένους παραδεδωκέναι τὸν καθ'

wont to follow success. For this reason some rightly
believe that it is easier to meet disaster with skill
than very great success with discretion ; for disaster,
because of the fear of what is to follow, forces men
to be careful, but success, because of the previous
good fortune, tempts men to be careless about
everything.

96. When the Nabataeans had manfully punished
the enemy they themselves returned to the rock
with the property that they had recovered ; but
to Antigonus they wrote a letter in Syrian characters
in which they accused Athenaeus and vindicated
themselves. Antigonus replied to them, agreeing
that they had been justified in defending themselves ;
but he found fault with Athenaeus, saying that he
had made the attack contrary to the instructions
that had been given. He did this, hiding his own
intentions and desiring to delude the barbarians into
a sense of security so that, by making an unexpected attack, he might accomplish his desire ; for it
was not easy without some deception to get the
better of men who zealously pursued a nomadic
life and possessed the desert as an inaccessible
refuge. The Arabs were highly pleased because they
seemed to have been relieved of great fears ; yet
they did not altogether trust the words of Antigonus, but, regarding their prospects as uncertain,
they placed watchmen upon the hills from which it was
easy to see from a distance the passes into Arabia,
and they themselves, after having arranged their
affairs in proper fashion, anxiously awaited the issue.
But Antigonus, when he had treated the barbarians
as friends for some time and believed that they had
been thoroughly deceived and thus had given him

αὐτῶν καιρόν, ἐξέλεξεν ἐξ ἁπάσης τῆς δυνάμεως
πεζοὺς μὲν ψιλοὺς καὶ πρὸς δρόμον εὖ πεφυκότας
τετρακισχιλίους, ἱππεῖς δὲ πλείους τῶν τετρακισχιλίων καὶ τούτοις μὲν παρήγγειλε φέρειν ἄπυρα
σῖτα πλειόνων ἡμερῶν, Δημήτριον δὲ τὸν υἱὸν
καταστήσας ἡγεμόνα πρώτης φυλακῆς ἐξέπεμψε,
προστάξας κολάσαι τοὺς Ἄραβας καθ᾽ ὃν ἂν δύνηται τρόπον.

97. Οὗτος μὲν οὖν ἐφ᾽ ἡμέρας τρεῖς ἀνοδίᾳ πορευόμενος ἔσπευδε λαθεῖν τοὺς βαρβάρους, οἱ δὲ
σκοποὶ κατανοήσαντες πολεμίαν δύναμιν εἰσβεβληκυῖαν[1] ἐσήμηναν τοῖς Ναβαταίοις διὰ τῶν συγκειμένων πυρσῶν· διόπερ οἱ βάρβαροι νομίσαντες
συντόμως ἥκειν τοὺς Ἕλληνας, εἰς μὲν τὴν πέτραν
ἀπέθεντο τὰς ἀποσκευὰς καὶ φυλακὴν τὴν ἱκανὴν
ἐπέστησαν, οὔσης μιᾶς ἀναβάσεως χειροποιήτου,
αὐτοὶ δὲ διελόμενοι τὴν λείαν ἄλλοι κατ᾽ ἄλλους
2 τόπους ἀπήλαυνον εἰς τὴν ἔρημον. Δημήτριος δὲ
παραγενόμενος εἰς τὴν πέτραν καὶ τὴν λείαν
καταλαβὼν ἀπηλλαγμένην προσβολὰς συνεχεῖς
ἐποιεῖτο τῷ χωρίῳ. ἀμυνομένων δὲ τῶν ἔνδον
εὐρώστως καὶ περιγιγνομένων ῥᾳδίως διὰ τὴν
ὑπεροχὴν τῶν τόπων τότε μὲν μέχρι δείλης ἀγωνισάμενος ἀνεκαλέσατο τῇ σάλπιγγι τοὺς στρατιώτας.
3 Τῇ δ᾽ ὑστεραίᾳ προσαγαγόντος αὐτοῦ τῇ πέτρᾳ
τῶν βαρβάρων τις ἀνεβόησεν '' Βασιλεῦ Δημήτριε,
τί βουλόμενος ἢ τίνος ἀναγκάζοντος πολεμεῖς ἡμᾶς,
οἰκοῦντας ἐν ἐρημίᾳ καὶ τόποις οὔθ᾽ ὕδωρ ἔχουσιν
οὔτε σῖτον οὔτε οἶνον οὔτ᾽ ἄλλο τι ἁπλῶς οὐδὲν

his opportunity against themselves, selected from
his whole force four thousand foot-soldiers, who were
lightly armed and well fitted by nature for rapid
marching, and more than four thousand mounted
men. He ordered them to carry several days' supply
of food that would not require cooking, and, after
placing his son Demetrius in command, he sent them
off during the first watch, ordering him to punish the
Arabs in whatever way he could.

97. Demetrius, therefore, advanced for three days
through regions with no roads, striving not to be
observed by the barbarians ; but the lookouts, having
seen that a hostile force had entered, informed the
Nabataeans by means of prearranged fire signals.
The barbarians, having thus learned at once that the
Greeks had come, sent their property to the rock
and posted there a garrison that was strong enough
since there was a single artificial approach ; and
they themselves divided their flocks and drove them
into the desert, some into one place and some into
another. Demetrius, on arriving at the rock and
finding that the flocks had been removed, made repeated assaults upon the stronghold. Those within
resisted stoutly, and easily had the upper hand
because of the height of the place ; and so on this
day, after he had continued the struggle until evening,
he recalled his soldiers by a trumpet call.

On the next day, however, when he had advanced
upon the rock, one of the barbarians called to him,
saying : " King Demetrius, with what desire or under
what compulsion do you war against us who live
in the desert and in a land that has neither water nor
grain nor wine nor any other thing whatever of those

---

¹ εἰσβεβληκυῖαν Dindorf : εἰσβεβηκυῖαν.

4 τῶν παρ' ὑμῖν εἰς τὴν χρείαν ἀνηκόντων; ἡμεῖς
γὰρ οὐδενὶ τρόπῳ προσιέμενοι δουλεύειν συμπε-
φεύγαμεν εἰς χώραν σπανίζουσαν πάντων τῶν ἐν
τοῖς ἄλλοις χρησίμων καὶ βίον εἱλόμεθα ζῆν ἔρημον
καὶ θηριώδη παντελῶς, οὐδὲν ὑμᾶς βλάπτοντες.
ἀξιοῦμεν οὖν καὶ σὲ καὶ τὸν πατέρα μὴ ἀδικεῖν
ἡμᾶς, ἀλλὰ λαβόντας δωρεὰς παρ' ἡμῶν ἀπαγαγεῖν
τὸ στρατόπεδον καὶ φίλους νομίζειν Ναβαταίους εἰς
5 τὸν λοιπὸν χρόνον. οὔτε γὰρ βουλόμενος δύνασαι
μένειν ἐνταῦθα πλείους ἡμέρας, ἀπορούμενος
ὕδατος καὶ τῶν ἄλλων ἐπιτηδείων ἁπάντων, οὔθ'
ἡμᾶς δύνασαι συναναγκάσαι βίον ζῆν ἕτερον, ἀλλά
τινας αἰχμαλώτους ἕξεις δούλους ἀθύμους καὶ ζῆν
6 οὐκ ἂν ὑπομείναντας ἐν ἄλλοις νομίμοις." ῥηθέντων δὲ τοιούτων λόγων Δημήτριος μὲν ἀπαγαγὼν τὴν στρατιὰν ἐκέλευσεν αὐτοὺς πρέσβεις
ἀποστέλλειν περὶ τούτων· οἱ δὲ Ἄραβες ἐξέπεμψαν τοὺς πρεσβυτάτους, οἳ παραπλήσια τοῖς
προειρημένοις διελθόντες ἔπεισαν δεξάμενον δῶρα
τὰ[1] πολυτελέστατα τῶν παρ' αὐτοῖς διαλύσασθαι.

98. Ὁ μὲν οὖν Δημήτριος λαβὼν ὁμήρους καὶ
τὰς ὁμολογηθείσας δωρεὰς ἀνέζευξεν ἀπὸ τῆς πέ-
τρας· διατείνας δὲ σταδίους τριακοσίους κατεστρατοπέδευσε πλησίον τῆς Ἀσφαλτίτιδος λίμνης, ἧς
τὴν φύσιν οὐκ ἄξιον παραδραμεῖν ἀνεπισήμαν-
τον. κεῖται γὰρ κατὰ μέσην τὴν σατραπείαν τῆς
Ἰδουμαίας, τῷ μὲν μήκει παρεκτείνουσα σταδίους μάλιστά που πεντακοσίους, τῷ δὲ πλάτει
περὶ ἑξήκοντα. τὸ δ' ὕδωρ ἔχει διάπικρον καὶ

[1] τὰ added by Hertlein.

that pertain to the necessities of life among you. 312 B.C.
For we, since we are in no way willing to be slaves,
have all taken refuge in a land that lacks all the
things that are valued among other peoples and have
chosen to live a life in the desert and one altogether
like that of wild beasts, harming you not at all. We
therefore beg both you and your father to do us no
injury but, after receiving gifts from us, to withdraw
your army and henceforth regard the Nabataeans
as your friends. For neither can you, if you wish,
remain here many days since you lack water and
all the other necessary supplies, nor can you force
us to live a different life ; but you will have a few
captives, disheartened slaves who would not consent
to live among strange ways." When words such
as these had been spoken, Demetrius withdrew his
army and ordered the Arabs to send an embassy
about these matters. They sent their oldest men,
who, repeating arguments similar to those previously
uttered, persuaded him to receive as gifts the most
precious of their products and to make terms with
them.[1]

98. Demetrius received hostages and the gifts that
had been agreed upon and departed from the rock.
After marching for three hundred stades,[2] he camped
near the Dead Sea,[3] the nature of which ought not
to be passed over without remark. It lies along the
middle of the satrapy of Idumaea, extending in
length about five hundred stades and in width about
sixty.[4] Its water is very bitter and of exceedingly

[2] About 34 miles, but cp. chap. 95. 2, and note.
[3] Literally, the Asphaltic Lake. The rest of this chapter
repeats Book 2. 48. 6-9, almost verbally.
[4] About 57½ and 7 miles respectively. The actual length
to-day is about 47 miles.

καθ᾽ ὑπερβολὴν δυσῶδες, ὥστε μήτ᾽ ἰχθὺν δύνασθαι τρέφειν μήτ᾽ ἄλλο τῶν καθ᾽ ὕδατος εἰωθότων
ζῴων εἶναι.¹ ἐμβαλλόντων δ᾽ εἰς αὐτὴν ποταμῶν
μεγάλων τῇ γλυκύτητι διαφόρων τούτων μὲν περι-
γίνεται κατὰ τὴν δυσωδίαν, ἐξ αὐτῆς δὲ μέσης
ἐκφυσᾷ κατ᾽ ἐνιαυτὸν ἀσφάλτου στερεᾶς μέγεθος
ποτὲ μὲν μεῖζον ἢ τρίπλεθρον, ἔστι δ᾽ ὅτ᾽ οὐ πολὺ
λειπόμενον πλέθρου· ἐφ᾽ ᾧ δὴ συνήθως οἱ περι-
οικοῦντες βάρβαροι τὸ μὲν μεῖζον καλοῦσι ταῦρον,
τὸ δὲ ἔλασσον μόσχον. ἐπιπλεούσης δὲ τῆς ἀσφάλτου πελαγίας ὁ τόπος φαίνεται τοῖς ἐξ ἀποστή-
ματος θεωροῦσιν οἱονεί τις νῆσος. τὴν δ᾽ ἔκπτωσιν
φανερὰν συμβαίνει γίνεσθαι πρὸ ἡμερῶν εἴκοσι·
κύκλῳ γὰρ τῆς λίμνης ἐπὶ πολλοὺς σταδίους ὀσμὴ
τῆς ἀσφάλτου προσπίπτει μετὰ² πνεύματος μοχθη-
ροῦ καὶ πᾶς ὁ περὶ τὸν τόπον ἄργυρος καὶ χρυσὸς
καὶ χαλκὸς ἀποβάλλει τὴν ἰδιότητα τοῦ χρώματος.
ἀλλ᾽ αὕτη μὲν ἀποκαθίσταται πάλιν ἐπειδὰν ἀνα-
φυσηθῆναι συμβῇ πᾶσαν τὴν ἄσφαλτον· ὁ δὲ
πλησίον τόπος ἔμπυρος ὢν καὶ δυσώδης ποιεῖ τὰ
σώματα τῶν περιοικούντων ἐπίνοσα καὶ παντελῶς
ὀλιγοχρόνια. ἀγαθὴ δ᾽ ἐστὶ φοινικόφυτος ὅσην
αὐτῆς συμβαίνει διειλῆφθαι ποταμοῖς χρησίμοις ἢ
πηγαῖς δυναμέναις ἀρδεύειν. γίνεται δὲ περὶ τοὺς
τόπους τούτους ἐν αὐλῶνί τινι καὶ τὸ καλούμενον
βάλσαμον, ἐξ οὗ πρόσοδον ἁδρὰν εἶναι συμβαίνει,
οὐδαμοῦ μὲν τῆς ἄλλης οἰκουμένης εὑρισκομένου

¹ εἶναι added by Stephanus from Book 2. 48. 7.
² μετὰ added by Wesseling from Book 2. 48. 8.

---

¹ Here the plethrum is a surface measure of about 10,000
square feet. For such asphalt from lakes cp. Vitruvius,
8. 3. 8.

foul odour, so that it can support neither fish nor any 312 B.C.
of the other creatures usually found in water. Although great rivers whose waters are of exceptional
sweetness flow into it, it prevails over these by reason
of its foulness ; and from its centre each year it
sends forth a mass of solid asphalt, sometimes more
than three plethra in area, sometimes a little less
than one plethrum.[1] When this happens the barbarians who live near habitually call the larger mass
a bull and the smaller one a calf. When the asphalt
is floating on the sea, its surface seems to those who
see it from a distance just like an island. It appears
that the ejection of the asphalt is indicated twenty
days in advance,[2] for on every side about the sea for
a distance of many stades the odour of the asphalt
spreads with a noisome exhalation, and all the silver,
gold, and bronze in the region lose their proper
colours. These, however, are restored as soon as
all the asphalt has been ejected ; but the neighbouring region is very torrid and ill smelling, which makes
the inhabitants sickly in body and exceedingly short-
lived. Yet the land is good for raising palm trees
in whatever part it is crossed by serviceable rivers [3]
or is supplied with springs that can irrigate it. In
a certain valley in this region there grows what is
called balsam,[4] from which there is a great income
since nowhere else in the inhabited world is this plant

[2] Twenty-two days in Book 2. 48. 8.
[3] *i.e.* rivers that flow during the dry season. To-day the
Jordan is the only perennial stream of any size entering the
sea. There are, however, a number of oases about springs
near the sea.
[4] For the balsam cp. Theophrastus, *Enquiry into Plants*,
9. 6. 1-4 ; Pliny, *Natural History*, 12. 111-123 ; Strabo,
16. 2. 41.

τοῦ φυτοῦ, τῆς δ' ἐξ αὐτοῦ χρείας εἰς φάρμακα
τοῖς ἰατροῖς καθ' ὑπερβολὴν εὐθετούσης.

99. Τὴν δ' ἐκπίπτουσαν ἄσφαλτον οἱ περιοικοῦν-
τες ἐξ ἀμφοτέρων τῶν μερῶν τὴν λίμνην διαρπά-
ζουσι πολεμικῶς διακείμενοι πρὸς ἀλλήλους, ἄνευ
πλοίων ἰδιαζόντως τὴν κομιδὴν ποιούμενοι. παρα-
σκευασάμενοι γὰρ δέσμας καλάμων εὐμεγέθεις
ἐμβάλλουσιν εἰς τὴν λίμνην· ἐπὶ δὲ τούτων ἐπι-
κάθηνται οὐ πλείω τριῶν, ὧν[1] δύο μὲν ἔχοντες
προσδεδεμένας πλάτας κωπηλατοῦσιν, εἷς δὲ φορῶν
τόξα τοὺς προσπλέοντας ἐκ τοῦ πέραν ἢ βιάζεσθαι
2 τολμῶντας ἀμύνεται. ὅταν δὲ πλησίον γένωνται
τῆς ἀσφάλτου, πελέκεις ἔχοντες ἐπιπηδῶσι καὶ καθάπερ μαλακῆς πέτρας ἀποκόπτοντες γεμίζουσι
τὴν δέσμην, εἶτα ἀποπλέουσιν εἰς τοὐπίσω. ἂν δέ
τις αὐτῶν ἀποπέσῃ τῆς δέσμης διαλυθείσης μὴ
δυνάμενος νεῖν, οὐ καταδύεται καθάπερ ἐν τοῖς ἄλλοις ὕδασιν, ἀλλὰ ἐπινήχεται τοῖς ἐπισταμένοις
3 ὁμοίως. φύσει γὰρ τοῦτο τὸ ὑγρὸν παραδέχεται
βάρος ὃ συμβαίνει μετέχειν αὐξήσεως ἢ πνεύματος,
ἔξω τῶν στερεῶν, ἃ τὴν πυκνότητα δοκεῖ παραπλησίαν ἔχειν ἀργύρῳ καὶ χρυσῷ καὶ μολύβδῳ καὶ
τοῖς ὁμοίοις· καὶ ταῦτα μὲν πολὺ βραδύτερον
καταφέρεται τῶν αὐτῶν[2] ἐν ταῖς ἄλλαις λίμναις
ῥιπτουμένων. ταύτην δ' ἔχοντες οἱ βάρβαροι πρόσοδον ἀπάγουσι τὴν ἄσφαλτον εἰς τὴν Αἴγυπτον
καὶ πωλοῦσιν εἰς τὰς ταριχείας τῶν νεκρῶν· μὴ
μιγνυμένης γὰρ ταύτης τοῖς λοιποῖς ἀρώμασιν οὐ
δυνατὸν γενέσθαι τὴν τῶν σωμάτων φυλακὴν
πολυχρόνιον.

100. Ὁ δ' Ἀντίγονος, ἐπανελθόντος τοῦ Δημητρίου καὶ τὰ κατὰ μέρος τῶν πεπραγμένων

found, and its use as a drug is very important to 312 B.C. physicians.

99. When the asphalt has been ejected, the people who live about the sea on both sides carry it off like plunder of war since they are hostile to each other, making the collection without boats in a peculiar fashion. They make ready large bundles of reeds and cast them into the sea. On these not more than three men take their places, two of whom row with oars, which are lashed on, but one carries a bow and repels any who sail against them from the other shore or who venture to interfere with them. When they have come near the asphalt they jump upon it with axes and, just as if it were soft stone, they cut out pieces and load them on the raft, after which they sail back. If the raft comes to pieces and one of them who does not know how to swim falls off, he does not sink as he would in other waters, but stays afloat as well as do those who do know. For this liquid by its nature supports heavy bodies that have the power of growth or of breathing, except for solid ones that seem to have a density like that of silver, gold, lead, and the like ; and even these sink much more slowly than do these same bodies if they are cast into other lakes. The barbarians who enjoy this source of income take the asphalt to Egypt and sell it for the embalming of the dead ; for unless this is mixed with the other aromatic ingredients, the preservation of the bodies cannot be permanent.

100. Antigonus, when Demetrius returned and made a detailed report of what he had done, rebuked

---

¹ ὧν added by Schaefer.   ² αὐτῶν added by Capps.

ἀπαγγείλαντος, ἐπὶ μὲν τῇ συνθέσει τῇ πρὸς
τοὺς Ναβαταίους ἐπετίμησεν αὐτῷ, λέγων ὅτι
πολλῷ θρασυτέρους πεποίηκε τοὺς βαρβάρους ἐάσας
ἀτιμωρήτους· δόξειν γὰρ αὐτοὺς τετευχέναι συγγνώμης οὐ δι' ἐπιείκειαν ἀλλὰ δι' ἀδυναμίαν τοῦ
κρατῆσαι· ἐπὶ δὲ τῷ κατασκέψασθαι τὴν λίμνην καὶ
δοκεῖν εὑρηκέναι τινὰ τῇ βασιλείᾳ πρόσοδον ἐπαι-
νέσας ἐπὶ μὲν ταύτης ἐπιμελητὴν ἔταξεν Ἱερώνυμον
2 τὸν τὰς ἱστορίας συγγράψαντα, τούτῳ δὲ συνετέτακτο πλοῖα παρασκευάσασθαι καὶ πᾶσαν τὴν
ἄσφαλτον ἀναλαβόντα συνάγειν εἴς τινα τόπον. οὐ
μὴν ἀπέβη γε καὶ τὸ τέλος κατὰ τὴν ἐλπίδα τοῖς
περὶ τὸν Ἀντίγονον· οἱ γὰρ Ἄραβες συστραφέντες
εἰς ἑξακισχιλίους, ἐπιπλεύσαντες ἐν ταῖς δέσμαις
ἐπὶ τοὺς ἐν τοῖς πλοίοις, σχεδὸν ἅπαντας κατ-
3 ετόξευσαν. ἐξ οὗ δὴ συνέβη τὸν Ἀντίγονον ἀπο-
γνῶναι τὰς προσόδους ταύτας διὰ τὸ γεγονὸς
παράπτωμα καὶ διὰ τὸ τὸν νοῦν ἔχειν πρὸς ἑτέροις
μείζοσι. παρεγένετο γὰρ κατὰ τούτους τοὺς καιροὺς βυβλιαφόρος ἔχων ἐπιστολὴν παρὰ Νικάνορος
τοῦ στρατηγοῦ τῆς τε Μηδίας καὶ τῶν ἄνω[1] σατρα-
πειῶν· ἐν ταύτῃ δ' ἦν γεγραμμένον περί τε τῆς
ἀναβάσεως τῆς Σελεύκου καὶ τῶν γεγονότων περὶ
4 αὐτὸν ἀτυχημάτων. διόπερ ἀγωνιῶν ὁ Ἀντίγονος
περὶ[2] τῶν ἄνω σατραπειῶν ἐξέπεμψε Δημήτριον
τὸν υἱὸν ἔχοντα πεζοὺς Μακεδόνας μὲν πεντακισχιλίους, μισθοφόρους δὲ μυρίους, ἱππεῖς δὲ τετρα-
κισχιλίους· συνετέτακτο δ' αὐτῷ μέχρι Βαβυλῶνος

---

[1] ἄνω Dindorf : ἄλλων.
[2] καὶ before περὶ in all MSS., deleted by first hand in R
and by editors. Perhaps we should read καὶ <περὶ τῆς Μηδίας
καὶ> περὶ τῶν etc.

him for the treaty with the Nabataeans, saying that 312 B.C.
he had made the barbarians much bolder by leaving
them unpunished, since it would seem to them that
they had gained pardon not through his kindness
but through his inability to overcome them ; but he
praised him for examining the lake and apparently
having found a source of revenue for the kingdom.
In charge of this he placed Hieronymus,[1] the writer
of the history, and instructed him to prepare boats,
collect all the asphalt, and bring it together in a
certain place. But the result was not in accord
with the expectations of Antigonus ; for the Arabs,
collecting to the number of six thousand and sailing
up on their rafts of reeds against those on the boats,
killed almost all of them with their arrows. As a
result, Antigonus gave up this source of revenue
because of the defeat he had suffered and because
his mind was engaged with other and weightier
matters. For there came to him at this time a dis-
patch-bearer with a letter from Nicanor, the general
of Media and the upper satrapies. In this letter was
written an account of Seleucus' march inland and
of the disasters that had been suffered in connection
with him.[2] Therefore Antigonus, worried about the
upper satrapies,[3] sent his son Demetrius with five
thousand Macedonian and ten thousand mercenary
foot-soldiers and four thousand horse ; and he ordered
him to go up as far as Babylon and then, after

---

[1] For Hieronymus cp. the Introduction to Vol. IX.

[2] Cp. chaps. 90-92. For the campaign that follows cp.
Plutarch, *Demetrius*, 7. 2-3. It should, perhaps, be placed
in 311 B.C.

[3] Or, reading καὶ περὶ τῆς Μηδίας καὶ περὶ τῶν . . . :
" worried both about Media and about the upper satrapies."

105

ἀναβῆναι καὶ τὴν σατραπείαν ἀνακτησάμενον κατα-
βαίνειν συντόμως ἐπὶ θάλασσαν.

5 Ὁ μὲν οὖν Δημήτριος ὁρμήσας ἐκ Δαμασκοῦ τῆς
Συρίας τὸ συνταχθὲν ὑπὸ τοῦ πατρὸς ἐπετέλει μετὰ
σπουδῆς· ὁ δὲ καθεσταμένος ὑπὸ Σελεύκου τῆς
Βαβυλωνίας στρατηγὸς Πατροκλῆς πυθόμενος περὶ
Μεσοποταμίαν εἶναι τοὺς πολεμίους, ὑπομεῖναι μὲν
τὴν ἔφοδον αὐτῶν οὐκ ἐτόλμησεν, ὀλίγους ἔχων
περὶ αὐτόν, ἀλλὰ τοῖς μὲν ἄλλοις προσέταξεν ἐκλιπεῖν τὴν πόλιν καὶ τοὺς μὲν αὐτῶν διαβάντας[1] τὸν
Εὐφράτην φυγεῖν εἰς τὴν ἔρημον, τοὺς δὲ περά-
σαντας τὸν Τίγριν ἀπελθεῖν εἰς τὴν Σουσιανὴν πρὸς
6 Εὐτελῆ[2] καὶ τὴν Ἐρυθρὰν θάλατταν, αὐτὸς δὲ μεθ'
ὧν εἶχε στρατιωτῶν προβολαῖς χρώμενος ῥεύμασι[3]
ποταμῶν καὶ διώρυξιν ἀνεστρέφετο περὶ τὴν σατραπείαν, ἅμα μὲν ἐφεδρεύων τοῖς πολεμίοις, ἅμα δὲ
πέμπων πρὸς Σέλευκον εἰς Μηδίαν περὶ τῶν ἀεὶ
συντελουμένων καὶ παρακαλῶν βοηθεῖν τὴν ταχί-
7 στην. ὁ δὲ Δημήτριος ἐπειδὴ παραγενόμενος εἰς
Βαβυλῶνα τὴν πόλιν ἐκλελειμμένην εὗρεν, πολιορκεῖν ἐπεχείρει τὰς ἀκροπόλεις. ὧν τὴν ἑτέραν
ἑλὼν ἔδωκε τοῖς ἰδίοις στρατιώταις εἰς διαρ-
παγήν· τὴν δ' ἑτέραν πολιορκήσας ἡμέρας τινάς,
ἐπειδὴ χρόνου προσεδεῖτο, Ἀρχέλαον μὲν ἕνα τῶν
φίλων ἀπέλιπε στρατηγὸν ἐπὶ τῆς πολιορκίας, δοὺς
αὐτῷ πεζοὺς μὲν πεντακισχιλίους, ἱππεῖς δὲ χιλίους, αὐτὸς δέ, τοῦ χρόνου συντρέχοντος ἐν ᾧ
συντεταγμένον ἦν τὴν ἄφοδον αὐτῷ ποιήσασθαι,

[1] διαβάντας Rhodoman : ἐκλιπόντας.

recovering the satrapy, to come down to the sea at _{312 B.C.} full speed.

So Demetrius, having set out from Damascus in Syria, carried out his father's orders with zeal. Patrocles, who had been established as general of Babylonia by Seleucus, hearing that the enemy was on the frontiers of Mesopotamia, did not dare await their arrival since he had few men at hand ; but he gave orders to the civilians to leave the city, bidding some of them cross the Euphrates and take refuge in the desert and some of them pass over the Tigris and go into Susianê to Euteles [1] and to the Red Sea [2] ; and he himself with what soldiers he had, using river courses and canals as defences, kept moving about in the satrapy, watching the enemy and at the same time sending word into Media to Seleucus about what was taking place from time to time and urging him to send aid as soon as possible. When Demetrius on his arrival at Babylon found the city abandoned, he began to besiege the citadels. He took one of these and delivered it to his own soldiers for plundering ; the other he besieged for a few days and then, since the capture required time, left Archelaüs, one of his friends, as general for the siege, giving him five thousand infantry and one thousand cavalry, while he himself, the time being close at hand at which he had been ordered to return,

---

[1] If the proper name is retained (cp. the critical note) we must suppose Euteles to be the commander established in Susianê by Seleucus (chap. 92. 5).

[2] *i.e.* the Persian Gulf.

---

[2] πρὸς Εὐτελῆ deleted by earlier editors, restored by Fischer.

[3] ῥεύμασι added by Fischer, cp. Book 17. 55. 1.

μετὰ τῆς λοιπῆς δυνάμεως τὴν ἐπὶ θάλασσαν
κατάβασιν ἐποιεῖτο.

101. Ἅμα δὲ τούτοις πραττομένοις κατὰ μὲν τὴν
Ἰταλίαν Ῥωμαίων διαπολεμούντων τὸν πρὸς Σαμνίτας πόλεμον συνεχεῖς ἐγίνοντο προνομαὶ τῆς
χώρας καὶ πολιορκίαι πόλεων καὶ δυνάμεων ἐν
ὑπαίθρῳ στρατοπεδεῖαι· τὰ γὰρ μαχιμώτατα τῶν
κατὰ τὴν Ἰταλίαν ἐθνῶν περὶ ἡγεμονίας φιλοτιμού-
2 μενα παντοίους συνίσταντο κινδύνους. οἱ μὲν οὖν
τῶν Ῥωμαίων ὕπατοι μέρος τῆς δυνάμεως ἀναλα-
βόντες ἀντεστρατοπέδευσαν[1] ταῖς τῶν πολεμίων[2]
παρεμβολαῖς καὶ πρὸς μὲν μάχην καιρὸν ἐπετήρουν
οἰκεῖον, ταῖς δὲ συμμαχίσι πόλεσι παρείχοντο τὴν
3 ἀσφάλειαν. τὸ δὲ λοιπὸν στρατόπεδον ἀναλαβὼν
Κόιντος Φάβιος, ὃς ἦν αὐτοκράτωρ ἡρημένος, τήν
τε Φρεγελλανῶν[3] πόλιν εἷλε καὶ τῶν ἀλλοτρίως
διακειμένων πρὸς τὴν Ῥώμην τοὺς ἐπιφανεστάτους ἐζώγρησεν. τούτους δὲ τὸν ἀριθμὸν ὄντας
πλείους τῶν διακοσίων ἀπήγαγεν εἰς Ῥώμην καὶ
προαγαγὼν εἰς τὴν ἀγορὰν ῥαβδίσας ἐπελέκησε
κατὰ τὸ πάτριον ἔθος. μετ' ὀλίγον δὲ ἐμβαλὼν εἰς
τὴν τῶν πολεμίων χώραν Καλατίαν[4] καὶ τὴν
Νωλάνων ἀκρόπολιν ἐξεπολιόρκησεν καὶ λαφύρων
μὲν πλῆθος ἀπέδοτο, τοῖς δὲ στρατιώταις πολλὴν
τῆς χώρας κατεκληρούχησεν. ὁ δὲ δῆμος, κατὰ νοῦν

---

[1] ἀντεστρατοπέδευσαν Dindorf : κατεστρατοπέδευσαν RX,
κατεστρατοπέδευον F.

[2] τῶν πολεμίων Rhodoman : τῶν Ῥωμαίων.

[3] Φρεγελλανῶν Scaliger, Φρέγελλαν ⟨ἀνεκτήσατο καὶ τὴν
Σωρ⟩ανῶν Burger : Φρετομανῶν RX, Φρετεμανῶν F.

made the march down to the sea with the rest of his 312 B.C. army.[1]

101. While this was taking place, in Italy [2] the Romans were carrying on their war with the Samnites, and there were repeated raids through the country, sieges of cities, and encampments of armies in the field, for the two most war-like of the peoples of Italy were struggling as rivals for the supremacy and meeting in conflicts of every sort. Now the Roman consuls with part of the army had taken a position in the face of the encampments of the enemy and were awaiting an opportune time for battle while at the same time furnishing protection to the allied cities. With the rest of the army Quintus Fabius,[3] who had been chosen dictator, captured the city of the Fregellani and made prisoners the chief men among those who were hostile to the Romans. These to the number of more than two hundred he took to Rome; and, bringing them into the Forum, he beat them with rods and beheaded them according to the ancestral custom.[4] Soon afterwards, entering the hostile territory, he took by siege Calatia and the citadel of Nola; and he sold a large amount of spoil but allotted much of the land to his soldiers. The

[1] Continued in chap. 105.
[2] Continued from chap. 76. 5. Cp. Livy, 9. 28.
[3] In Livy (9. 28. 1-6) it is a dictator named C. Poetilius who captured Fregellae, and either the same dictator or C. Junius Bubulcus, one of the consuls, who took Nola. For the dictatorship of Fabius two years earlier cp. chap. 72. 6-7, and Livy, 9. 24. 1.
[4] For punishment *more maiorum* cp. Suetonius, *Nero*, 49. 2.

---

[4] Καλατίαν Cluverius (cp. Livy, 9. 28. 6): καὶ λείαν RX, κελίαν F.

τῶν πραγμάτων αὐτῷ προχωρούντων, ἀποικίαν
ἀπέστειλεν εἰς τὴν νῆσον τὴν Ποντίαν καλουμένην.

102. Ἐν δὲ τῇ Σικελίᾳ τῆς εἰρήνης ἄρτι γεγενημένης Ἀγαθοκλεῖ πρὸς τοὺς Σικελιώτας πλὴν
Μεσσηνίων οἱ μὲν φυγάδες τῶν Συρακοσίων ἠθροίσθησαν εἰς τὴν Μεσσήνην, ταύτην ὁρῶντες λοιπὴν
οὖσαν τῶν ἀλλοτρίως ἐχουσῶν πρὸς τὸν δυνάστην,
2 ὁ δ' Ἀγαθοκλῆς σπεύδων αὐτῶν καταλῦσαι τὸ
σύστημα Πασίφιλον στρατηγὸν ἐξαπέστειλε μετὰ
δυνάμεως εἰς τὴν Μεσσήνην, ἐντειλάμενος ἐν ἀπορ-
3 ρήτοις ἃ χρὴ πράττειν. οὗτος δὲ ἀπροσδοκήτως
ἐμβαλὼν εἰς τὴν χώραν καὶ πολλῶν αἰχμαλώτων
καὶ τῆς ἄλλης λείας ἐγκρατὴς γενόμενος ἠξίου τοὺς
Μεσσηνίους βούλεσθαι τὴν φιλίαν καὶ μὴ συναν-
4 αγκάζεσθαι τοῖς πολεμιωτάτοις αὐτοῦ διαλύεσθαι.[1]
οἱ δὲ Μεσσήνιοι λαβόντες ἐλπίδας τοῦ χωρὶς κινδύνων ἀπολυθήσεσθαι τοῦ πολέμου τούς τε φυγάδας
τοὺς ἐκ Συρακουσσῶν ἐξέβαλον καὶ τὸν Ἀγαθοκλέα
5 παραγενόμενον μετὰ δυνάμεως προσεδέξαντο. ὁ
δὲ τὸ μὲν πρῶτον φιλανθρώπως αὐτοῖς προσεφέ-
ρετο καὶ τοὺς φυγάδας ἔπεισεν καταδέξασθαι τοὺς
συστρατευομένους[2] μὲν αὐτῷ, πεφυγαδευμένους δὲ
6 νόμῳ ὑπὸ τῶν Μεσσηνίων. μετὰ δὲ ταῦτα τοὺς
ἐναντιουμένους ἐν τοῖς ἔμπροσθεν χρόνοις τῇ δυ-
ναστείᾳ μεταπεμψάμενος ἔκ τε Ταυρομενίου καὶ
τῆς Μεσσήνης ἅπαντας ἀπέσφαξεν, οὐκ ἐλάττους
7 ὄντας ἑξακοσίων· διανοούμενος γὰρ πόλεμον ἐκφέ-

---

[1] βούλεσθαι . . . διαλύεσθαι. Madvig suggests διαλύεσθαι
τὴν φιλίαν καὶ μὴ συνεξετάζεσθαι τοῖς πολεμιωτάτοις αὐτοῦ.
[2] συστρατευομένους Dindorf : στρατευομένους.

---

[1] The modern Ponza, one of the group of small islands
off the west coast of Italy opposite the Circeian promontory.

people, since matters were progressing according 312 B.C. to their will, sent a colony to the island that is called Pontia.[1]

102. In Sicily,[2] where peace had just been established between Agathocles and the Sicilians except the Messenians,[3] the exiles of Syracuse gathered in Messenê since they saw that this was the only city remaining of those that were hostile to the dynast; but Agathocles, who was eager to break up their group, sent Pasiphilus with an army to Messenê as general, telling him in secret instructions what he should do. Pasiphilus, entering the region unexpectedly and gaining possession of many prisoners and much other booty, urged the Messenians to choose friendship with him and not be forced to seek terms in common with his bitterest foes.[4] The Messenians, gaining hope of a bloodless termination of the war, expelled the Syracusan exiles and welcomed Agathocles when he came near with his army. At first he treated them in a friendly manner and persuaded them to receive back the exiles who were in his army, men who had been legally banished by the Messenians. But then he brought together from Tauromenium and Messenê those who had previously been opposed to his rule and put them all to death, being no less than six hundred in number; for his intention was to wage war on the Carthaginians,

Cp. Livy, 9. 28. 7-8. Italian affairs are continued in chap. 105. 5.

[2] Continued from chap. 72. 2.

[3] In chap. 71. 6 Messenê is included among the cities that made peace with Agathocles.

[4] Or, following Madvig's reading: "urged the Messenians to dissolve their friendship and not not be counted among his bitterest foes."

ρειν τοῖς Καρχηδονίοις πᾶν τὸ διακείμενον ἀλλοτρίως κατὰ τὴν Σικελίαν ἐκ ποδῶν ἐποιεῖτο. οἱ δὲ
Μεσσήνιοι τῶν ξένων τοὺς εὐνουστάτους αὐτοῖς
καὶ δυναμένους ἀμύνασθαι τὸν τύραννον ἐκβεβλη-
κότες ἐκ τῆς πόλεως καὶ τῶν πολιτῶν τοὺς
ἀλλοτρίως ἔχοντας πρὸς τὸν δυνάστην ὁρῶντες
ἀνηρημένους, ἔτι δὲ τοὺς ἐπὶ κακουργίᾳ κατα-
δεδικασμένους ἠναγκασμένοι καταδέξασθαι μετε-
μέλοντο μὲν ἐπὶ τοῖς πεπραγμένοις, ἠναγκάζοντο
δὲ καρτερεῖν, καταπεπληγμένοι τὴν ὑπεροχὴν τῶν
8 κρατούντων. ὁ δ' Ἀγαθοκλῆς τὸ μὲν πρῶτον
ἀνέζευξεν ἐπ' Ἀκράγαντος, διανοούμενος καὶ ταύτην τὴν πόλιν συσκευάσασθαι· τῶν δὲ Καρχηδονίων καταπλευσάντων ναυσὶν ἑξήκοντα ταύτης
μὲν τῆς προθέσεως ἀπέστη, τὴν δὲ χώραν τὴν ὑπὸ
Καρχηδονίους ἐπιὼν ἐλεηλάτει καὶ τῶν φρουρίων
ἃ μὲν ᾕρει κατὰ κράτος, ἃ δὲ δι' ὁμολογίας προσήγετο.

103. Ἅμα δὲ τούτοις πρασσομένοις Δεινοκράτης
ὁ τῶν Συρακοσίων φυγάδων ἡγούμενος πρὸς μὲν
τοὺς Καρχηδονίους διεπέμπετο, βοηθεῖν ἀξιῶν πρὶν
ἢ τὸν Ἀγαθοκλέα πᾶσαν ὑφ' ἑαυτὸν ποιήσασθαι
2 Σικελίαν, αὐτὸς δὲ προσδεξάμενος τοὺς ἐκ Μεσσήνης ἐκβεβλημένους φυγάδας, ἔχων ἁδρὰν δύναμιν,
ἀπέστειλέν τινα τῶν περὶ αὐτὸν Νυμφόδωρον, δοὺς
μέρος τῶν στρατιωτῶν, ἐπὶ τὴν Κεντοριπίνων
3 πόλιν· ταύτην γὰρ φρουρουμένην ὑπ' Ἀγαθοκλέους
τῶν πολιτικῶν τινες ἐπηγγείλαντο παραδώσειν, ἐφ'
ὅτῳ τὴν αὐτονομίαν δοθῆναι τῷ δήμῳ. παρεισπε-

and he was getting rid of all opposition throughout 312 B.C. Sicily. When the Messenians had driven out of the city those non-citizens who were most favourably disposed to them and best able to protect them from the tyrant, and saw that those of their own citizens who were opposed to the dynast had been put to death, and when, moreover, they had been forced to receive back men who had been convicted of crime, they regretted what they had done ; but they were forced to submit, since they were completely cowed by the superior power of those who had become their masters. Agathocles first set out for Acragas, intending to organize that city also in his own interest ; when, however, the Carthaginians sailed in with sixty ships, he abandoned that purpose ; but he entered the territory subject to the Carthaginians and plundered it, taking some of the fortified places by force and winning others by negotiation.

103. While this was taking place, Deinocrates,[1] the leader of the Syracusan exiles, sent a message to the Carthaginians, asking them to send aid before Agathocles should bring all Sicily under his sway ; and he himself, since he had a strong army after receiving those exiles who had been driven out of Messenê, dispatched one of his friends, Nymphodorus, with part of the soldiers to the city of the Centoripini.[2] Although this city was garrisoned by Agathocles, some of its chief men had promised to betray it on condition that the people be given autonomy. But when Nymphodorus broke into the

---

[1] An old friend of Agathocles, he had been spared when the tyrant first established himself in power (chap. 8. 6) ; we do not hear of the occasion of his exile.

[2] Centoripa is a city in the interior of Sicily, south-west of Aetna and north-west of Catana.

σόντος δ' εἰς τὴν πόλιν αὐτοῦ νυκτὸς οἱ προεστῶτες τῆς φρουρᾶς αἰσθόμενοι τὸ γεγονὸς αὐτόν τε τὸν Νυμφόδωρον ἀνεῖλον καὶ τοὺς βιαζομένους ἐντὸς 4 τοῦ τείχους. ταύτης δὲ τῆς ἀφορμῆς λαβόμενος Ἀγαθοκλῆς ἐνεκάλεσέ τε τοῖς Κεντοριπίνοις καὶ τοὺς δόξαντας αἰτίους γεγονέναι τοῦ νεωτερισμοῦ πάντας ἀπέσφαξε. περὶ ταῦτα δ' ὄντος τοῦ δυνάστου Καρχηδόνιοι καταπλεύσαντες εἰς τὸν μέγαν λιμένα τῶν Συρακοσίων πεντήκοντα σκάφεσιν ἄλλο μὲν οὐδὲν ἠδυνήθησαν πρᾶξαι, δυσὶ δὲ περιπεσόντες φορτηγοῖς πλοίοις ἐξ Ἀθηνῶν, τὰ μὲν[1] κατέδυσαν, τῶν δ' ἐπιπλεόντων τὰς χεῖρας ἀπέ- 5 κοψαν. δοξάντων δ' αὐτῶν ὠμῶς κεχρῆσθαι μηδ' ὁτιοῦν ἀδικοῦσι ταχὺ τὸ δαιμόνιον αὐτοῖς ἐπεσήμαινεν· εὐθὺ γὰρ τοῦ στόλου τινὲς νῆες ἀποσχισθεῖσαι περὶ τὴν Βρεττίαν ἑάλωσαν ὑπὸ τῶν Ἀγαθοκλέους στρατηγῶν καὶ τὸ παραπλήσιον οἱ ζωγρηθέντες τῶν Φοινίκων ἔπαθον οἷς[2] ἔπραξαν εἰς τοὺς ἁλόντας.

104. Οἱ δὲ περὶ τὸν Δεινοκράτην φυγάδες, ἔχοντες πεζοὺς μὲν ὑπὲρ τοὺς τρισχιλίους, ἱππεῖς δὲ οὐκ ἐλάττους δισχιλίων, τὴν καλουμένην Γαλερίαν κατελάβοντο, τῶν πολιτῶν ἑκουσίως ἐπικαλεσαμένων, καὶ τοὺς μὲν Ἀγαθοκλέους ἐξέβαλον, 2 αὐτοὶ δὲ πρὸ τῆς πόλεως ἐστρατοπέδευσαν. Ἀγαθοκλέους δὲ ταχέως ἀποστείλαντος ἐπ' αὐτοὺς Πασίφιλον καὶ Δημόφιλον μετὰ στρατιωτῶν πεντακισχιλίων ἐγένετο μάχη πρὸς τοὺς φυγάδας, ὧν ἡγεῖτο Δεινοκράτης καὶ Φιλωνίδης, τὰ κέρατα

---

[1] ἐξ Ἀθηνῶν, τὰ μὲν Geer, τὴν μὲν ⟨ἀγορὰν κομίζουσιν⟩ ἐξ Ἀθηνῶν Fischer in apparatus : τὴν μὲν ἐξ Ἀθηνῶν.
[2] οἷς Hertlein : οἷα.

city by night, the commanders of the garrison, perceiving what had taken place, slew both the man
himself and those who pressed fiercely on within
the walls. Seizing upon this opportunity, Agathocles
brought accusations against the Centoripini and
slaughtered all who were thought to have been guilty
of the sedition. While the dynast was thus engaged,
the Carthaginians sailed into the great harbour of
Syracuse with fifty light boats. They were able to
do nothing more, but falling upon two merchant ships
from Athens, they sank the ships themselves and cut
off the hands of the crews. They had clearly treated
with cruelty men who had done them no harm at
all, and the gods quickly gave them a sign of this ;
for immediately, when some of the ships were
separated from the fleet in the vicinity of Brettia,
they were captured by the generals of Agathocles,
and those of the Phoenicians who were taken alive
suffered a fate similar to that which they had inflicted
upon their captives.

104. The exiles who were with Deinocrates, having
more than three thousand foot-soldiers and not less
than two thousand mounted men, occupied the place
called Galeria,[1] the citizens of their own free will
inviting them ; and they exiled the followers of
Agathocles, but they themselves encamped before
the city. When, however, Agathocles quickly dispatched against them Pasiphilus [2] and Demophilus
with five thousand soldiers, a battle was fought with
the exiles, who were led by Deinocrates and Philo-

---

[1] The exact location is not known.
[2] For his later treachery and death cp. Book 20. 77. 2 ; 90. 2.

διειληφότες. ἐφ᾽ ἱκανὸν μὲν οὖν χρόνον ἰσόρροπος ἦν ὁ κίνδυνος, φιλοτίμως ἀμφοτέρων τῶν στρατοπέδων ἀγωνιζομένων· τοῦ δ᾽ ἑτέρου τῶν στρατηγῶν Φιλωνίδου πεσόντος καὶ τοῦ κατὰ τοῦτον μέρους τραπέντος ἠναγκάσθη καὶ Δεινοκράτης ἀποχωρῆσαι. οἱ δὲ περὶ τὸν Πασίφιλον τούτων τε πολλοὺς κατὰ τὴν φυγὴν ἀνεῖλον καὶ τὴν Γαλερίαν ἀνακτησάμενοι τοὺς αἰτίους τῆς ἀποστάσεως ἐκό-3 λασαν. Ἀγαθοκλῆς δὲ πυνθανόμενος τοὺς Καρχηδονίους τὸν Ἔκνομον καλούμενον λόφον ἐν τῇ Γελῴα κατειληφέναι, διέγνω πάσῃ τῇ δυνάμει διαγωνίσασθαι. ὁρμήσας δ᾽ ἐπ᾽ αὐτοὺς καὶ πλησίον γενόμενος προεκαλεῖτο εἰς μάχην, ἐπηρμένος τῇ 4 προγεγενημένῃ νίκῃ. οὐ τολμώντων δὲ τῶν βαρβάρων παρατάξασθαι νομίσας ἀκονιτὶ κρατεῖν τῶν ὑπαίθρων ἐπανῆλθεν εἰς τὰς Συρακούσσας καὶ τῶν ναῶν τοὺς ἐπιφανεστάτους τοῖς σκύλοις ἐκόσμησεν.

Ταῦτα μὲν οὖν ἐπράχθη κατὰ τοῦτον τὸν ἐνιαυτὸν ὧν ἡμεῖς ἐδυνήθημεν ἐφικέσθαι.

105. Ἐπ᾽ ἄρχοντος δ᾽ Ἀθήνησι Σιμωνίδου Ῥωμαῖοι μὲν ὑπάτους κατέστησαν Μάρκον Οὐαλλέριον καὶ Πόπλιον Δέκιον. ἐπὶ δὲ τούτων οἱ περὶ Κάσανδρον καὶ Πτολεμαῖον καὶ Λυσίμαχον διαλύσεις ἐποιήσαντο πρὸς Ἀντίγονον καὶ συνθήκας ἔγραψαν. ἐν δὲ ταύταις ἦν Κάσανδρον μὲν εἶναι στρατηγὸν τῆς Εὐρώπης μέχρι ἂν Ἀλέξανδρος ὁ ἐκ Ῥωξάνης εἰς ἡλικίαν ἔλθῃ, καὶ Λυσίμαχον μὲν τῆς Θρᾴκης κυριεύειν, Πτολεμαῖον δὲ τῆς Αἰγύπτου καὶ τῶν συνοριζουσῶν ταύτῃ πόλεων κατά τε τὴν Λιβύην καὶ τὴν Ἀραβίαν, Ἀντίγονον δὲ ἀφηγεῖ-

nides, each in command of a wing. For some time 312 B.C.
the conflict was evenly balanced, both of the armies
fighting with zest ; but when one of the generals,
Philonides, fell and his part of the army was put
to flight, Deinocrates also was forced to withdraw.
Pasiphilus killed many of his opponents during
the flight and, after gaining possession of Galeria,
punished those guilty of the uprising. Agathocles,
on hearing that the Carthaginians had seized the
hill called Ecnomus in the territory of Gela, decided
to fight them to a finish with his whole army. When
he had set out against them and had drawn near,
he challenged them to battle since he was elated
by his previous victory. But the barbarians not
venturing to meet him in battle, he assumed that he
now completely dominated the open country without
a fight and went off to Syracuse, where he decorated
the chief temples with the spoils.[1]

These are the events of this year that we have
been able to discover.

105. When Simonides was archon in Athens, the 311 B.C.
Romans elected to the consulship Marcus Valerius
and Publius Decius.[2] While these held office, Cassander, Ptolemy, and Lysimachus came to terms
with Antigonus and made a treaty. In this it was
provided that Cassander be general of Europe until
Alexander, the son of Roxanê, should come of age ;
that Lysimachus rule Thrace, and that Ptolemy rule
Egypt and the cities adjacent thereto in Libya and
Arabia ; that Antigonus have first place in all Asia ;

---

[1] Continued in chap. 106.
[2] Simonides was archon in 311/10 B.C. In the Fasti the
consuls of 312 B.C. are M. Valerius Maximus and P. Decius
Mus (*CIL*, 1, p. 130 ; cp. Livy, 9. 28. 8). The narrative is
continued from chap. 100. 7.

σθαι τῆς Ἀσίας πάσης, τοὺς δὲ Ἕλληνας αὐτονόμους εἶναι. οὐ μὴν ἐνέμεινάν γε ταῖς ὁμολογίαις
ταύταις, ἀλλ' ἕκαστος αὐτῶν προφάσεις εὐλόγους
2 ποριζόμενος πλεονεκτεῖν ἐπειρᾶτο. Κάσανδρος δὲ
ὁρῶν Ἀλέξανδρον τὸν ἐκ Ῥωξάνης αὐξόμενον καὶ
κατὰ τὴν Μακεδονίαν λόγους ὑπό τινων διαδιδο-
μένους ὅτι καθήκει προάγειν ἐκ τῆς φυλακῆς τὸν
παῖδα καὶ τὴν πατρῴαν βασιλείαν παραδοῦναι,
φοβηθεὶς ὑπὲρ ἑαυτοῦ προσέταξε Γλαυκίᾳ τῷ προε-
στηκότι τῆς τοῦ παιδὸς φυλακῆς τὴν μὲν Ῥωξάνην
καὶ τὸν βασιλέα κατασφάξαι καὶ κρύψαι τὰ σώματα, τὸ δὲ γεγονὸς μηδενὶ τῶν ἄλλων ἀπαγγεῖλαι.
3 ποιήσαντος δ' αὐτοῦ τὸ προσταχθὲν οἱ περὶ Κάσανδρον καὶ Λυσίμαχον καὶ Πτολεμαῖον, ἔτι δ'
Ἀντίγονον ἀπηλλάγησαν τῶν ἀπὸ τοῦ βασιλέως
4 προσδοκωμένων φόβων· οὐκέτι γὰρ ὄντος οὐδενὸς
τοῦ διαδεξομένου τὴν ἀρχὴν τὸ λοιπὸν ἕκαστος
τῶν κρατούντων ἐθνῶν ἢ πόλεων βασιλικὰς εἶχεν
ἐλπίδας καὶ τὴν ὑφ' ἑαυτὸν τεταγμένην χώραν
εἶχεν ὡσανεί τινα βασιλείαν δορίκτητον.

Τὰ μὲν οὖν κατὰ τὴν Ἀσίαν[1] καὶ τὰ περὶ τὴν
Ἑλλάδα καὶ Μακεδονίαν ἐν τούτοις ἦν.

5 Κατὰ δὲ τὴν Ἰταλίαν Ῥωμαῖοι δυνάμεσιν ἁδραῖς
πεζῶν τε καὶ ἱππέων ἐστράτευσαν ἐπὶ Πολλίτιον,
Μαρρουκίνων οὖσαν πόλιν. ἀπέστειλαν δὲ καὶ τῶν
πολιτῶν εἰς ἀποικίαν καὶ κατῴκισαν τὴν προσαγο-
ρευομένην Ἰντέραμναν.

---

[1] καὶ τὴν Εὐρώπην after Ἀσίαν omitted by Geer.

and that the Greeks be autonomous.   However, they _{311 B.C.} did not abide by these agreements but each of them, putting forward plausible excuses, kept seeking to increase his own power.   Now Cassander perceived that Alexander, the son of Roxanê, was growing up and that word was being spread throughout Macedonia by certain men that it was fitting to release the boy from custody and give him his father's kingdom ; and, fearing for himself, he instructed Glaucias,[1] who was in command of the guard over the child, to murder Roxanê and the king and conceal their bodies, but to disclose to no one else what had been done.   When Glaucias had carried out the instructions, Cassander, Lysimachus, and Ptolemy, and Antigonus as well, were relieved of their anticipated danger from the king ; for henceforth, there being no longer anyone to inherit the realm, each of those who had rule over nations or cities entertained hopes of royal power and held the territory that had been placed under his authority as if it were a kingdom won by the spear.

This was the situation in Asia and in Greece and Macedonia.[2]

In Italy [3] the Romans with strong forces of foot and horse took the field against Pollitium, a city of the Marrucini.   They also sent some of their citizens as a colony and settled the place called Interamna.

---

[1] This Glaucias, who is not to be identified with the Glaucias of chaps. 67. 6 and 70. 7, had been placed in charge of the guard by Cassander (chap. 52. 4).   For the murder of Alexander and Roxanê cp. Justin, 15. 2. 5 ; Pausanias, 9. 7. 2.

[2] Continued in Book 20. 19.

[3] Continued from chap. 101. 3.   Cp. Livy, 9. 28. 8.   Diodorus returns to Roman affairs in Book 20. 26. 3.

106. Κατὰ δὲ τὴν Σικελίαν ἀεὶ μᾶλλον αὐξομένου Ἀγαθοκλέους καὶ δυνάμεις ἁδροτέρας ἀθροίζοντος Καρχηδόνιοι πυνθανόμενοι τὸν δυνάστην συσκευαζόμενον τὰς ἐν τῇ νήσῳ πόλεις ταῖς δὲ δυνάμεσιν ὑπερέχοντα τῶν σφετέρων στρατιωτῶν

2 ἔδοξαν ἐνεργέστερον ἅψασθαι τοῦ πολέμου. εὐθὺς οὖν τριήρεις μὲν κατήρτησαν τριάκοντα πρὸς ταῖς ἑκατόν, στρατηγὸν δὲ προχειρισάμενοι τῶν παρ' αὐτοῖς ἐπιφανεστάτων Ἀμίλκαν ἔδωκαν αὐτῷ τῶν μὲν πολιτικῶν στρατιωτῶν δισχιλίους, ἐν οἷς ἦσαν πολλοὶ καὶ τῶν ἐπιφανῶν, τῶν δ' ἀπὸ τῆς Λιβύης μυρίους, ἐκ δὲ τῆς Τυρρηνίας μισθοφόρους χιλίους καὶ ζευγίππας[1] διακοσίους, ἔτι δὲ Βαλιάρας σφενδονήτας χιλίους, ὁμοίως δὲ χρημάτων πλῆθος καὶ βελῶν καὶ σίτου καὶ τῶν ἄλλων τῶν εἰς πόλεμον

3 χρησίμων τὴν καθήκουσαν παρασκευήν. ἀναχθέντος δ' ἐκ τῆς Καρχηδόνος τοῦ στόλου παντὸς καὶ γενομένου πελαγίου χειμὼν ἐξαίφνης ἐπιπεσὼν ἑξήκοντα μὲν τριήρεις ἠφάνισε, διακόσια δὲ τῶν σιτηγῶν πλοίων διέφθειρεν· ὁ δὲ λοιπὸς στόλος μεγάλοις περιπεσὼν χειμῶσι μόλις διεσώθη πρὸς

4 τὴν Σικελίαν. ἀπώλοντο δὲ καὶ τῶν ἐπιφανῶν Καρχηδονίων οὐκ ὀλίγοι, δι' οὓς συνέβη τὴν πόλιν δημόσιον ἄρασθαι πένθος· εἰώθασι γάρ, ἐπειδὰν μείζων τις ἀτυχία γένηται περὶ τὴν πόλιν, μέλασι

5 σακκίοις κατακαλύπτειν τὰ τείχη. Ἀμίλκας δ' ὁ στρατηγὸς ἀναλαβὼν τοὺς διασωθέντας ἐκ τοῦ χειμῶνος μισθοφόρους συνῆγε καὶ τῶν κατὰ Σικελίαν συμμάχων ἐστρατολόγει τοὺς εὐθέτους.

---

[1] ζευγίτας Reiske.

---

[1] Continued from chap. 104. 4. Cp. Justin, 22. 3. 9.

106. In Sicily,[1] where Agathocles was constantly
increasing in power and collecting stronger forces, the
Carthaginians, since they heard that the dynast was
organizing the cities of the island for his own ends and
that with his armed forces he surpassed their own
soldiers, decided to wage the war with more energy.
Accordingly they at once made ready one hundred
and thirty triremes, chose as general Hamilcar,[2] one of
their most distinguished men, gave him two thousand
citizen soldiers among whom were many of the nobles,
ten thousand men from Libya, a thousand mercenaries
and two hundred zeugippae[3] from Etruria, a thousand
Baliaric slingers, and also a large sum of money and
the proper provision of missiles, food, and the other
things necessary for war. After the whole fleet had
sailed from Carthage and was at sea, a storm fell
suddenly upon it, sank sixty triremes, and completely
destroyed two hundred of the ships that were carrying
supplies. The rest of the fleet, after encountering
severe storms, with difficulty reached Sicily in safety.
Not a few of the Carthaginian nobles were lost, for
whom the city instituted public mourning ; for it
is their custom whenever any major disaster has
befallen the city, to cover the walls with black sack-
cloth. Hamilcar, the general, gathered together the
men who had survived the storm, enrolled mercenaries, and enlisted those troops of the Sicilian allies

Beloch, *Griechische Geschichte*, 4². 1. 189, places this campaign in the early summer of 310 B.C.
  [2] The son of Gisco, not to be confused with the Hamilcar
of chaps. 71. 6, 72. 2, who was now dead.
  [3] If the text is sound, we must suppose the otherwise
unknown zeugippae to be horsemen who had each an extra
horse, like the ἀμφιπποι of chap. 29. 2 ; but perhaps we
should read ζευγίτας, heavy armed infantry.

παρέλαβε δὲ καὶ τὰς προϋπαρχούσας δυνάμεις καὶ
πάντων τῶν εἰς πόλεμον εὐθέτων ἐπιμέλειαν ποιησάμενος ἐν ὑπαίθρῳ συνεῖχε τὰ στρατόπεδα, πεζοὺς
μὲν ἔχων περὶ τοὺς τετρακισμυρίους ἱππεῖς δὲ
σχεδὸν πεντακισχιλίους. ταχὺ δὲ τὴν γεγενημένην
ἀτυχίαν διορθωσάμενος καὶ δόξας ἀγαθὸς στρατηγὸς[1] εἶναι τῶν μὲν συμμάχων τὰς ψυχὰς προκατα-
πεπληγμένας ἀνεκτήσατο, τοῖς δὲ πολεμίοις οὐ τὴν
τυχοῦσαν ἀγωνίαν ἐπέστησεν.

107. Ἀγαθοκλῆς δὲ τὰς τῶν Καρχηδονίων δυνάμεις ὁρῶν ὑπερεχούσας τῶν ἑαυτοῦ διέλαβε τῶν
τε φρουρίων οὐκ ὀλίγα μεταθήσεσθαι πρὸς τοὺς
Φοίνικας καὶ τῶν πόλεων ὅσαι προσέκοπτον αὐτῷ.
2 μάλιστα δ' εὐλαβεῖτο περὶ τῆς τῶν Γελῴων, πυνθανόμενος ἐν τῇ τούτων χώρᾳ πάσας εἶναι τὰς τῶν
πολεμίων δυνάμεις. ἐγένετο δ' αὐτῷ περὶ τοῦτον
τὸν χρόνον καὶ περὶ τὸν στόλον οὐ μικρὸν ἐλάσ-
σωμα· τῶν γὰρ νεῶν εἴκοσιν ἐπὶ τὸν πορθμὸν
ὑποχείριοι τοῖς Καρχηδονίοις κατέστησαν σὺν αὐ-
3 τοῖς ἀνδράσιν. οὐ μὴν ἀλλὰ κρίνας τὴν τῶν
Γελῴων πόλιν ἀσφαλίσασθαι φρουρᾷ, φανερῶς οὐκ
ἐτόλμα δύναμιν εἰσαγαγεῖν, ἵνα μὴ φθάσαι συμβῇ
τοὺς Γελῴους προφάσεως δεομένους καὶ τὴν πόλιν
ἀποβάλῃ μεγάλας ἀφορμὰς αὐτῷ παρεχομένην.
4 ἀπέστειλεν οὖν κατ' ὀλίγους τῶν στρατιωτῶν ὡς
ἐπί τινας χρείας, ἕως ὅτου συνέβη τῷ πλήθει πολὺ
προτερῆσαι τῶν πολιτικῶν. μετ' ὀλίγον δὲ καὶ
αὐτὸς παραγενόμενος προδοσίαν ἐνεκάλεσε καὶ
μετάθεσιν τοῖς Γελῴοις, εἴτε καὶ κατ' ἀλήθειαν
αὐτῶν διανοηθέντων τι πρᾶξαι τοιοῦτον, εἴτε καὶ

who were fit for service.   He also took over the forces
that were already in Sicily and, having attended to
all things expedient for war, mustered his armies in
the open country, about forty thousand foot-soldiers
and nearly five thousand mounted men. Since he had
quickly rectified the misfortune that he had suffered
and won the reputation of being a good general, he
revived the shattered spirits of his allies and presented
no ordinary problem to his enemies.

107. As Agathocles saw that the forces of the
Carthaginians were superior to his own, he surmised
that not a few of the strongholds would go over to
the Phoenicians, and also those of the cities that were
offended with him.   He was particularly concerned
for the city of the Geloans since he learned that
all the forces of the enemy were in their land.   At
about this time he also suffered a considerable naval
loss, for at the straits twenty of his ships with their
crews fell into the hands of the Carthaginians.   Deciding nevertheless to make the city of Gela secure
with a garrison, he did not venture to lead an army
in openly lest the result be that the Geloans, who
were looking for an excuse, forestall him and he lose
the city, which provided him with great resources.[1]
He therefore sent in his soldiers a few at a time as
if for particular needs until his troops far surpassed
those of the city in number.   Soon he himself also
arrived and charged the Geloans with treason and
desertion, either because they were actually planning
to do something of this sort, or because he was

[1] Cp. chap. 71. 6 for the treaty between Agathocles and
Gela.

---

[1] στρατηγὸς added by Reiske.

ψευδέσι διαβολαῖς φυγάδων πεισθεὶς ἢ καὶ χρημάτων βουλόμενος εὐπορῆσαι, καὶ[1] ἀπέσφαξε τῶν
Γελῴων πλείους τῶν τετρακισχιλίων καὶ τὰς οὐσίας αὐτῶν ἀνέλαβε. προσέταξε δὲ καὶ τοῖς
ἄλλοις Γελῴοις πᾶσι τά τε νομίσματα καὶ τὸν
ἄσημον ἄργυρόν τε καὶ χρυσὸν ἀνενεγκεῖν, διαπειλη-
5 σάμενος τιμωρήσασθαι τοὺς ἀπειθήσαντας. ταχὺ
δὲ πάντων πραξάντων τὸ προσταχθὲν διὰ τὸν φόβον
χρημάτων τε πλῆθος ἤθροισε καὶ πᾶσι τοῖς ταττο-
μένοις ὑφ' ἑαυτὸν δεινὴν ἐνεποίησε κατάπληξιν.
δόξας δ' ὠμότερον κεχρῆσθαι τοῦ καθήκοντος τοῖς
Γελῴοις τοὺς μὲν ἀποσφαγέντας εἰς τὰς ἐκτὸς τῶν
τειχῶν τάφρους συνέχωσεν, ἐν δὲ τῇ πόλει τὴν
ἱκανὴν φρουρὰν ἀπολιπὼν ἀντεστρατοπέδευσε τοῖς
πολεμίοις.

108. Κατεῖχον δὲ Καρχηδόνιοι μὲν τὸν Ἔκνομον λόφον, ὅν φασι φρούριον γεγενῆσθαι Φαλάριδος. ἐν τούτῳ δὲ λέγεται κατεσκευακέναι τὸν
τύραννον ταῦρον χαλκοῦν τὸν διαβεβοημένον, πρὸς
τὰς τῶν βεβασανισμένων τιμωρίας ὑποκαιομένου
τοῦ κατασκευάσματος· διὸ καὶ τὸν τόπον Ἔκνομον
ἀπὸ τῆς εἰς τοὺς ἀτυχοῦντας ἀσεβείας προσηγορεύ-
2 σθαι. ἐκ δὲ θατέρου μέρους Ἀγαθοκλῆς ἕτερον
τῶν Φαλάριδος γεγενημένων φρουρίων κατεῖχε, τὸ
προσαγορευθὲν ἀπ' ἐκείνου Φαλάριον. καὶ διὰ
μέσων μὲν τῶν παρεμβολῶν ἦν ποταμός, ὃν ἀμφότεροι πρόβλημα τῶν πολεμίων ἐπεποίηντο, φῆ-
μαι δὲ κατεῖχον ἀπὸ[2] τῶν προτέρων χρόνων ὅτι δεῖ
περὶ τὸν τόπον τοῦτον πλῆθος ἀνθρώπων ἐν μάχῃ

---

[1] καὶ added by Bekker.   [2] ἀπὸ Hertlein : ἐπί.

---

[1] Literally, "Lawless." In Book 13. 90. 4-7, Diodorus

persuaded by false charges made by exiles, or again 311 B.C.
because he wished to gain possession of wealth ; and
he slew more than four thousand of the Geloans
and confiscated their property. He also ordered all
the other Geloans to turn over to him their money
and their uncoined silver and gold, threatening to
punish those who disobeyed. Since all quickly carried out the command because of fear, he gathered
together a large amount of money and caused a
dreadful panic among all who were subject to him.
Being thought to have treated the Geloans more
cruelly than was proper, he heaped together in the
ditches outside the walls those who had been slain ;
and, leaving behind in the city an adequate garrison,
he took the field against the enemy.

108. The Carthaginians held the hill Ecnomus,
which men say had been a stronghold of Phalaris.
Here it is reported that the tyrant had constructed
the bronze bull that has become famous, the device
being heated by a fire beneath for the torment
of those subjected to the ordeal ; and so the place
has been called Ecnomus [1] because of the impiety
practised upon his victims. On the other side
Agathocles held another of the strongholds that had
belonged to Phalaris, the one which was called
Phalarium after him. In the space between the
encamped armies was a river,[2] which each of them
used as a defence against the enemy ; and sayings
from earlier times were current that near this place
a great number of men were destined to perish in

claims that he himself had seen the brazen bull, which
Hamilcar had taken to Carthage (about 480 B.C.) and Scipio
Aemilianus had brought back to Acragas after the sack
of Carthage. Cp. also Book 20. 71. 3.
  [2] The Himeras.

διαφθαρῆναι. οὐκ ὄντος δὲ φανεροῦ παρ᾽ ὁποτέροις
γενήσεται τὸ ἀτύχημα, συνέβαινε δεισιδαιμονεῖν τὰ
στρατόπεδα καὶ πρὸς μάχην ὀκνηρῶς ἔχειν.
3 διόπερ ἐπὶ πολὺν χρόνον οὐδέτεροι τὸν ποταμὸν
ἐτόλμων διαβαίνειν ἀθρόοις στρατιώταις ἕως ὅτου
παράλογός τις αἰτία προεκαλέσατο αὐτοὺς εἰς τὸν
ὁλοσχερῆ κίνδυνον. τῶν γὰρ Λιβύων κατατρεχόν-
των τὴν πολεμίαν Ἀγαθοκλῆς παρωξύνθη τὸ παραπλήσιον ποιῆσαι. ἀγόντων δὲ λείαν τῶν Ἑλλήνων
καί τινα τῶν ἀπὸ τῆς παρεμβολῆς ὑποζυγίων ἀπα-
γαγόντων ἐπεξῆλθον ἐκ τοῦ Καρχηδονίων χάρακος
4 οἱ τούτους διώξοντες. ὁ δ᾽ Ἀγαθοκλῆς προϊδό-
μενος τὸ μέλλον ἔσεσθαι παρὰ τὸν ποταμὸν ἔθηκεν
ἐνέδραν ἀνδρῶν ἐπιλέκτων ταῖς ἀρεταῖς. οὗτοι δέ,
τῶν Καρχηδονίων τοὺς τὴν λείαν ἄγοντας ἐπιδιω-
κόντων καὶ διαβάντων τὸν ποταμόν, ἐξανέστησαν
ἐκ τῆς ἐνέδρας ἄφνω καὶ προσπεσόντες ἀτάκτοις
5 ῥᾳδίως ἐτρέψαντο. φονευομένων δὲ τῶν βαρβάρων
καὶ πρὸς τὴν ἰδίαν παρεμβολὴν φευγόντων Ἀγαθοκλῆς, νομίσας ἥκειν τὸν καιρὸν τοῦ διαγωνίσασθαι, πᾶσαν ἤγαγε τὴν δύναμιν ἐπὶ τὴν τῶν
πολεμίων στρατοπεδείαν. προσπεσὼν δ᾽ αὐτοῖς
ἀπροσδοκήτως καὶ ταχὺ μέρος τῆς τάφρου χώσας
ἀνέσπασε τὸν χάρακα καὶ βιαζόμενος εἰς τὴν παρ-
6 εμβολὴν παρεισέπεσεν. οἱ δὲ Καρχηδόνιοι διά τε
τὸ παράδοξον καταπεπληγμένοι καὶ πρὸς ἔκταξιν
οὐ δυνάμενοι λαβεῖν ἀναστροφήν, ὡς ἔτυχε τοῖς
πολεμίοις ἀπήντων καὶ ἠγωνίζοντο. περὶ δὲ τὴν
τάφρον ἀμφοτέρων ἐρρωμένως κινδυνευόντων ταχὺ
πᾶς ὁ πλησίον τόπος νεκρῶν κατεστρώθη· οἵ τε
γὰρ τῶν Καρχηδονίων ἐπιφανέστατοι τὴν παρεμβολὴν ὁρῶντες ἁλισκομένην ἐβοήθουν, οἵ τε περὶ

battle. Since, however, it was not clear to which 311 B.C. of the two sides the misfortune would happen, the armies were filled with superstitious fear and shrank from battle. Therefore for a long time neither dared to cross the river in force, until an unexpected cause brought them into general battle. The raids made by the Libyans through the enemy's country aroused Agathocles into doing the same ; and while the Greeks were engaged in plundering and were driving away some beasts of burden taken from the Carthaginian camp, soldiers issued from that encampment to pursue them. Agathocles, foreseeing what was about to happen, placed beside the river an ambush of men selected for courage. These, as the Carthaginians crossed the river in their pursuit of those who were driving the beasts, sprang suddenly from the ambush, fell upon the disordered soldiers, and easily drove them back. While the barbarians were being slaughtered and were fleeing to their own camp, Agathocles, thinking that the time had come to fight to a finish, led his whole army against the camp of the enemy. Falling on them unexpectedly and quickly filling up a part of the moat, he overthrew the palisade and forced an entrance into the camp. The Carthaginians, who had been thrown into a panic by the unexpected attack and could find no opportunity for forming their lines, faced the enemy and fought against them at random. Both sides fought fiercely for the moat, and the whole place round about was quickly covered with dead ; for the most notable of the Carthaginians rushed up to give aid when they saw the camp being taken,

127

τὸν Ἀγαθοκλέα τῷ προτερήματι τεθαρρηκότες
καὶ νομίζοντες ἑνὶ κινδύνῳ καταλύσειν πάντα τὸν
πόλεμον ἐνέκειντο τοῖς βαρβάροις.

109. Ὁ δ᾽ Ἀμίλκας ὁρῶν κατισχυομένους τοὺς
ἑαυτοῦ καὶ τῶν Ἑλλήνων ἀεὶ πλείους παρεισπί-
πτοντας εἰς τὴν παρεμβολὴν ἐπέστησε τοὺς σφενδονήτας τοὺς ἐκ τῶν Βαλιαρίδων νήσων, ὄντας οὐκ
2 ἐλάττους τῶν χιλίων. οὗτοι δὲ συνεχεῖς καὶ μεγάλους λίθους ἀφιέντες πολλοὺς μὲν ἐτραυμάτιζον οὐκ
ὀλίγους δὲ καὶ τῶν βιαζομένων ἀπέκτεινον, τῶν δὲ
πλείστων τὰ σκεπάζοντα τῶν ὅπλων συνέτριβον· οἱ
γὰρ ἄνδρες οὗτοι μναιαίους λίθους βάλλειν εἰωθότες μεγάλα συμβάλλονται πρὸς νίκην ἐν τοῖς κινδύνοις, ὡς ἂν ἐκ παίδων παρ᾽ αὐτοῖς τῆς ἐν ταῖς
3 σφενδόναις γυμνασίας διαπονουμένης. τούτῳ δὲ τῷ
τρόπῳ τοὺς Ἕλληνας ἐκ τῆς παρεμβολῆς ἐκβαλόντες ἐκράτησαν. πάλιν δὲ οἱ περὶ τὸν Ἀγαθοκλέα κατ᾽ ἄλλους τόπους προσβολὰς ἐποιοῦντο
καὶ δὴ τῆς παρεμβολῆς ἤδη κατὰ κράτος ἁλισκομένης κατέπλευσε τοῖς Καρχηδονίοις δύναμις ἐκ
4 Λιβύης ἀνέλπιστος. διὸ καὶ ταῖς ψυχαῖς πάλιν
θαρρήσαντες οἱ μὲν ἐκ τῆς παρεμβολῆς κατὰ στόμα
ἐκινδύνευον, οἱ δὲ παρόντες ἐπὶ τὴν βοήθειαν κύκλῳ
περιίσταντο τοὺς Ἕλληνας. ὧν τιτρωσκομένων
παραδόξως ἡ μὲν μάχη ταχὺ παλίντροπος ἐγένετο,
ἔφευγον δ᾽ οἱ μὲν εἰς τὸν Ἱμέραν ποταμόν, οἱ δ᾽ εἰς
τὴν παρεμβολήν. τεσσαράκοντα σταδίους δ᾽¹ ἐχούσης τῆς ἀποχωρήσεως καὶ ταῦτα σχεδὸν πάσης
πεδινῆς οὔσης ἐπεδίωκον οἱ τῶν βαρβάρων ἱππεῖς,
οὐκ ἔλασσον ὄντες πεντακισχιλίων. διὸ καὶ συνέβη

and the forces of Agathocles, encouraged by the 311 B.C. advantage gained and believing that they would end the whole war by a single battle, pressed hard upon the barbarians.

109. But when Hamilcar saw that his men were being overpowered and that the Greeks in constantly increasing numbers were making their way into the camp, he brought up his slingers, who came from the Baliaric Islands and numbered at least a thousand. By hurling a shower of great stones, they wounded many and even killed not a few of those who were attacking, and they shattered the defensive armour of most of them. For these men, who are accustomed to sling stones weighing a mina,[1] contribute a great deal toward victory in battle, since from childhood they practise constantly with the sling. In this way they drove the Greeks from the camp and defeated them. But Agathocles continued to attack at other points, and indeed the camp was already being taken by storm when unexpected reinforcements from Libya arrived by water for the Carthaginians. Thus again gaining heart, those from the camp fought against the Greeks in front, and the reinforcements surrounded them on all sides. Since the Greeks were now receiving wounds from an unexpected quarter, the battle quickly reversed itself; and some of them fled into the Himeras River, others into the camp. The withdrawal was for a distance of forty stades[2]; and since it was almost entirely over level country, they were hotly pursued by the barbarian cavalry, numbering not less than five thousand.

---

[1] Not quite a pound.   [2] About 4½ miles.

---

[1] δ' added by Dindorf.

τὸν μεταξὺ τόπον νεκρῶν πληρωθῆναι, πολλὰ
συμβαλλομένου καὶ τοῦ ποταμοῦ πρὸς τὴν τῶν
5 Ἑλλήνων ἀπώλειαν· ὑπὸ κύνα γὰρ οὔσης τῆς ὥρας
καὶ τοῦ διωγμοῦ περὶ μέσον ἡμέρας γινομένου οἱ
πολλοὶ τῶν φευγόντων διά τε τὸ καῦμα καὶ τὴν ἐκ
τῆς φυγῆς κακοπάθειαν ἔκδιψοι γιγνόμενοι λάβρως
ἔπινον, καὶ ταῦθ' ἁλυκοῦ τοῦ ῥεύματος ὄντος. διόπερ οὐκ ἐλάττους τῶν ἐν τῷ διωγμῷ σφαγέντων
εὑρέθησαν παρὰ τὸν ποταμὸν τετελευτηκότες ἄτρω-
τοι. ἔπεσον δ' ἐν τῇ μάχῃ ταύτῃ τῶν μὲν βαρβάρων περὶ πεντακοσίους, τῶν δ' Ἑλλήνων οὐκ
ἐλάττους ἑπτακισχιλίων.

110. Ἀγαθοκλῆς δὲ τηλικαύτῃ συμφορᾷ περιπεσὼν τοὺς ἐκ τῆς τροπῆς διασωθέντας ἀνέλαβεν καὶ
τὴν παρεμβολὴν ἐμπρήσας εἰς Γέλαν ἀπεχώρησε.
διαδόντος δ' αὐτοῦ λόγον ὡς κατὰ σπουδὴν εἰς
Συρακούσσας ἀναζευγνύειν διέγνωκε, τριακόσιοι
τῶν ἐκ Λιβύης ἱππέων κατὰ τὴν χώραν περιέπεσόν
τισι τῶν Ἀγαθοκλέους στρατιωτῶν. ὧν εἰπόντων
ὡς Ἀγαθοκλῆς εἰς Συρακούσσας ἀποκεχώρηκεν,
εἰσῆλθον εἰς Γέλαν ὡς φίλοι καὶ διαψευσθέντες τῆς
2 ἐλπίδος κατηκοντίσθησαν. ὁ δ' Ἀγαθοκλῆς συν-
έκλεισεν αὐτὸν εἰς τὴν Γέλαν, οὐκ ἀδυνατῶν εἰς
Συρακούσσας διασωθῆναι, βουλόμενος δὲ περισπά-
σαι τοὺς Καρχηδονίους πρὸς τὴν πολιορκίαν τῆς
Γέλας, ἵν' οἱ Συρακόσιοι πολλὴν ἄδειαν σχῶσι
συγκομίσαι τοὺς καρπούς, ἀναγκάζοντος τοῦ και-
3 ροῦ. ὁ δ' Ἀμίλκας τὸ μὲν πρῶτον ἐπεχείρει πολιορκεῖν τὴν Γέλαν, πυνθανόμενος δὲ ἐν ταύτῃ καὶ
δύναμιν εἶναι τὴν ἀμυνομένην καὶ πάντων εὐπορεῖν
τὸν Ἀγαθοκλέα ταύτης μὲν ἀπέστη τῆς ἐπιβολῆς,
τὰ δὲ φρούρια καὶ τὰς πόλεις ἐπιπορευόμενος

As a result the space between was filled with dead ; and the river itself contributed greatly to the destruction of the Greeks. Since it was the season of the Dog Star and since the pursuit took place in the middle of the day, most of the fugitives became very thirsty because of the heat and the distress caused by the flight and drank greedily, and that too although the stream was salt.[1] Therefore no fewer men than those killed in the pursuit itself were found dead beside the river without a wound. In this battle about five hundred of the barbarians fell, but of the Greeks no less than seven thousand.

110. Agathocles, having met with such a disaster, collected those who had survived the rout and after burning his camp withdrew into Gela. After he had given it out that he had decided to set out quickly for Syracuse, three hundred of the Libyan cavalry fell in with some of the soldiers of Agathocles in the open country. Since these said that Agathocles had departed for Syracuse, the Libyans entered Gela as friends, but they were cheated of their expectations and shot down. Agathocles, however, shut himself up in Gela, not because he was unable to go safely to Syracuse, but because he wished to divert the Carthaginians to the siege of Gela in order that the Syracusans might quite fearlessly gather in their crops as the season demanded. Hamilcar at first attempted to besiege Gela, but discovering that there were troops in the city defending it and that Agathocles had ample supplies of all kinds, he gave up the attempt ; instead, by visiting the fortresses and cities, he won them over and treated all

[1] Cp. Vitruvius, 8. 3. 7. From its natural saltiness, the river gets its modern name, " Salso."

προσήγετο καὶ πᾶσιν ἐχρῆτο φιλανθρώπως, ἐκκαλούμενος τοὺς Σικελιώτας πρὸς εὔνοιαν. καὶ
Καμαριναῖοι μὲν καὶ Λεοντῖνοι, πρὸς δὲ τούτοις
Καταναῖοι καὶ Ταυρομενῖται παραχρῆμα πρέσβεις
4 ἐκπέμψαντες προσέθεντο Καρχηδονίοις· μετ᾽ ὀλίγας
δ᾽ ἡμέρας οἵ τε Μεσσήνιοι καὶ ᾽Αβακαινῖνοι[1] καὶ
συχναὶ τῶν πόλεων ἀλλήλας φθάνουσαι πρὸς ᾽Αμίλ-
καν ἀφίσταντο· τοσαύτη τοῖς ὄχλοις ἐνέπεσεν ὁρμὴ
μετὰ τὴν ἧτταν διὰ τὸ πρὸς τὸν τύραννον μῖσος.
5 ὁ δ᾽ ᾽Αγαθοκλῆς ἀπαγαγὼν[2] τὴν ὑπολελειμμένην
δύναμιν εἰς Συρακούσσας τὰ πεπονηκότα τῶν τειχῶν ἐπεσκεύαζε καὶ τὸν ἀπὸ τῆς χώρας σῖτον ἀπε-
κόμιζε, διανοούμενος τῆς μὲν πόλεως τὴν ἱκανὴν
ἀπολιπεῖν φυλακήν, τῆς δὲ δυνάμεως τὴν κρατίστην
μετάγειν εἰς Λιβύην καὶ μετατιθέναι τὸν πόλεμον
εἰς τὴν ἤπειρον ἐκ τῆς νήσου.

῾Ημεῖς δὲ κατὰ τὴν ἐν ἀρχῇ πρόθεσιν τὴν εἰς
Λιβύην ᾽Αγαθοκλέους διάβασιν ἀρχὴν ποιησόμεθα
τῆς ἐπομένης βίβλου.

[1] ᾽Αβακαινῖνοι Cluver : ᾽Αβακηνῖνοι RX, Βακίνειοι F.
[2] ἀπαγαγὼν Rhodoman : ἀπολιπῶν.

the people with kindness, seeking to win the goodwill of the Sicilians. And the people of Camarina and Leontini, also those of Catana and Tauromenium, at once sent embassies and went over to the Carthaginian ; and within a few days Messenê and Abacaenum and very many of the other cities vied with each other in deserting to Hamilcar, for such was the desire that came upon the common people after the defeat because of their hatred of the tyrant. But Agathocles conducted what survived of his army to Syracuse, repaired the ruined parts of the walls, and carried off the grain from the countryside, intending to leave an adequate garrison for the city, but with the strongest part of his army to cross to Libya and transfer the war from the island to the continent.

But we, following the plan laid down at the beginning,[1] will make Agathocles' expedition into Libya the beginning of the following book.

[1] Cp. chap. 1. 10.

BOOK XX

Τάδε ἔνεστιν ἐν τῇ εἰκοστῇ τῶν
Διοδώρου βίβλων

Ὡς Ἀγαθοκλῆς διαβὰς εἰς Λιβύην ἐνίκησεν παρατάξει
Καρχηδονίους καὶ πολλῶν πόλεων ἐκυρίευσεν.

Ὡς Κάσανδρος Αὐδολέοντι μὲν ἐβοήθησε, πρὸς δὲ
Πτολεμαῖον τὸν Ἀντιγόνου στρατηγὸν ἀποστάτην γενόμενον συμμαχίαν ἐποιήσατο.

Ὡς Πτολεμαῖος μὲν τῶν περὶ Κιλικίαν πόλεών τινας
εἷλε, Δημήτριος δ' ὁ Ἀντιγόνου ταύτας ἀνεκτήσατο.

Ὡς Πολυπέρχων μὲν Ἡρακλέα τὸν ἐκ Βαρσίνης ἐπεχείρησε κατάγειν ἐπὶ τὴν πατρῴαν βασιλείαν, Πτολεμαῖος
δὲ Νικοκρέοντα τὸν βασιλέα τῶν Παφίων ἐπανείλατο.

Περὶ τῶν πραχθέντων ἐν μὲν τῷ Βοσπόρῳ τοῖς βασιλεῦσιν, κατὰ δὲ τὴν Ἰταλίαν Ῥωμαίοις καὶ Σαμνίταις.

Πτολεμαίου στρατεία ἐπὶ Κιλικίαν καὶ τὴν ἑξῆς παραθαλάττιον.

Ἡρακλέους ἀναίρεσις ὑπὸ Πολυπέρχοντος.

Ἀμίλκου τοῦ στρατηγοῦ τῶν Καρχηδονίων ἅλωσις
ὑπὸ Συρακοσίων.

Ὡς Ἀκραγαντῖνοι τοὺς Σικελιώτας ἐλευθεροῦν ἐπεχείρησαν.

Ὡς τῶν Συρακοσίων εἴκοσι ναῦς ἥλωσαν.

---

[1] In chap. 21 this king is called Nicocles, probably
incorrectly.

[2] In chap. 32. 5 only ten ships are captured.

CONTENTS OF THE TWENTIETH BOOK
OF DIODORUS

How Agathocles crossed into Libya, defeated the Carthaginians in a battle, and became master of many cities (chaps. 3-18).

How Cassander went to the aid of Audoleon ; and how he made an alliance with Ptolemaeus, Antigonus' general, who had become a rebel (chap. 19).

How Ptolemy took some of the cities of Cilicia, and how Antigonus' son Demetrius recovered them (chap. 19).

How Polyperchon attempted to bring Heracles, the son of Barsinê, back to his ancestral kingdom ; and how Ptolemy made away with Nicocreon,[1] the king of Paphos (chaps. 20-21).

Concerning the actions of the kings in the Bosporus, and of the Romans and Samnites in Italy (chaps. 22-26).

The campaign of Ptolemy against Cilicia and the adjacent coast (chap. 27).

Assassination of Heracles by Polyperchon (chap. 28).

Capture of Hamilcar, the general of the Carthaginians, by the Syracusans (chaps. 29-30).

How the people of Acragas attempted to liberate the Sicilians (chap. 31).

How they captured twenty [2] ships of the Syracusans (chap. 32).

Περὶ τῆς ἐν Λιβύῃ γενομένης στάσεως καὶ τοῦ κινδύνου τοῦ περὶ τὸν Ἀγαθοκλέα.

Περὶ τῶν πραχθέντων Ἀππίῳ Κλαυδίῳ κατὰ τὴν τιμητικὴν ἀρχήν.

Παράδοσις Κορίνθου καὶ Σικυῶνος Πτολεμαίῳ.

Κλεοπάτρας ἐν Σάρδεσιν ἀναίρεσις.

Ὡς Ἀγαθοκλῆς Καρχηδονίους μὲν ἐνίκησεν μάχῃ, τὸν δὲ δυνάστην τῆς Κυρήνης Ὀφέλλαν μεταπεμψάμενος ἐπὶ κοινοπραγίαν κατέσφαξεν, καὶ τὴν μετὰ τούτου δύναμιν παρέλαβεν.

Ὡς Καρχηδόνιοι Βορμίλκαν ἐπιθέμενον τυραννίδι κατέλυσαν.

Ὡς Ἀγαθοκλέους ἀποπέμψαντος εἰς Σικελίαν τὰ λάφυρα τινὰ τῶν πλοίων ἐναυάγησεν.

Ὡς Ῥωμαῖοι Μαρσοῖς μὲν πολεμουμένοις ὑπὸ Σαμνιτῶν ἐβοήθησαν, ἐν δὲ τῇ Τυρρηνίᾳ Κάπριον ἐξεπολιόρκησαν.

Δημητρίου τοῦ πολιορκητοῦ κατάπλους εἰς τὸν Πειραιᾶ καὶ τῆς Μουνυχίας ἅλωσις.

Ἐλευθέρωσις Ἀθηναίων καὶ Μεγαρέων.

Πλοῦς ἐπὶ Κύπρον Δημητρίου καὶ μάχη πρὸς Μενέλαον τὸν στρατηγὸν καὶ Σαλαμῖνος πολιορκία.

Ναυμαχία Δημητρίου πρὸς Πτολεμαῖον καὶ νίκη Δημητρίου.

Παράληψις Κύπρου τε πάσης καὶ τῆς Πτολεμαίου δυνάμεως.

Ὡς μετὰ τὴν νίκην ταύτην Ἀντιγόνου καὶ Δημητρίου περιθεμένων διάδημα ζηλοτυπήσαντες οἱ λοιποὶ δυνάσται βασιλεῖς ἑαυτοὺς ἀνηγόρευσαν.

---

[1] Chap. 35 is omitted : campaigns of the Romans in Etruria and Samnium.

[2] Called Caerium in chap. 44. 9.

CONTENTS OF THE TWENTIETH BOOK

Ὡς Ἀγαθοκλῆς Ἰτύκην ἐκπολιορκήσας διεβίβασε μέρος τῆς δυνάμεως εἰς τὴν Σικελίαν.

Ὡς Ἀκραγαντῖνοι παραταξάμενοι πρὸς τοὺς Ἀγαθοκλέους στρατηγοὺς ἡττήθησαν.

Ὡς Ἀγαθοκλῆς Ἡράκλειαν μὲν καὶ Θέρμα καὶ Κεφαλοίδιον προσηγάγετο, τὴν δὲ τῶν Ἀπολλωνιατῶν χώραν καὶ πόλιν ἐξηνδραποδίσατο.

Ὡς Ἀγαθοκλῆς ἐν Σικελίᾳ ναυμαχίᾳ μὲν ἐνίκησε Καρχηδονίους, μάχῃ δ᾽ Ἀκραγαντίνους.

Διάβασις εἰς Λιβύην Ἀγαθοκλέους τὸ δεύτερον καὶ ἧττα.

Αἱ γενόμεναι ταραχαὶ κατὰ τὰ ἑκατέρων στρατόπεδα.

Ἀγαθοκλέους δρασμὸς εἰς Σικελίαν.

Αἱ γενόμεναι σφαγαὶ τῶν Σικελιωτῶν ὑπὸ Ἀγαθοκλέους.

Στρατεία Ἀντιγόνου βασιλέως μεγάλαις δυνάμεσιν ἐπ᾽ Αἴγυπτον.

Ἀπόστασις Πασιφίλου στρατηγοῦ ἀπὸ Ἀγαθοκλέους.

Ὡς Καρχηδόνιοι συνέθεντο τὴν εἰρήνην πρὸς Ἀγαθοκλέα.

Ὡς Ῥόδον πολιορκήσας Δημήτριος διελύσατο τὴν πολιορκίαν.

Ὡς Ῥωμαῖοι Σαμνίτας δυσὶ μάχαις ἐνίκησαν.

Ὡς Δημήτριος ἀπὸ τῆς Ῥόδου πλεύσας εἰς τὴν Ἑλλάδα τὰς πλείστας πόλεις ἠλευθέρωσεν.

Ὡς Ἀγαθοκλῆς Λιπαραίους χρήματα ἀδίκως εἰσπραξάμενος ἀπέβαλε τὰς ναῦς ἐν αἷς ἦν τὰ χρήματα.

---

[1] Chap. 78 omitted: comparison of Agathocles with Dionysius.

[2] The Greek Table of Contents makes no mention of the events related in chap. 80, the Roman raids on Samnium, and in chap. 89, Agathocles' defeat of Deinocrates in Sicily.

CONTENTS OF THE TWENTIETH BOOK

Ὡς Ῥωμαῖοι τὸ μὲν ἔθνος τῶν Αἴκλων[1] κατεπολέμησαν, πρὸς δὲ τοὺς Σαμνίτας συνέθεντο τὴν εἰρήνην.

Τὰ πραχθέντα Κλεωνύμῳ περὶ τὴν Ἰταλίαν.

Δι' ἃς αἰτίας οἱ περὶ Κάσανδρον καὶ Λυσίμαχον, ἔτι δὲ Σέλευκον καὶ Πτολεμαῖον συνδραμόντες ἐνεστήσαντο τὸν πόλεμον πρὸς Ἀντίγονον.

Στρατεία Κασάνδρου μὲν ἐπὶ Δημήτριον εἰς Θεσσαλίαν, Λυσιμάχου δ' εἰς τὴν Ἀσίαν.

Ἀπόστασις Δοκίμου καὶ Φοίνικος τῶν στρατηγῶν ἀπ' Ἀντιγόνου.

Ὡς Ἀντίγονος ἀντιστρατοπεδεύσας Λυσιμάχῳ πολὺ προεῖχε ταῖς δυνάμεσιν.

Ὡς Δημήτριον τὸν υἱὸν ἐκ τῆς Ἑλλάδος μετεπέμψατο.

Ὡς Πτολεμαῖος μὲν ἐχειρώσατο τὰς πόλεις τὰς ἐν τῇ Κοίλῃ Συρίᾳ, Σέλευκος δ' ἐκ τῶν ἄνω σατραπειῶν τὴν κατάβασιν ἐποιήσατο μέχρι Καππαδοκίας.

Διάλυσις ἁπασῶν τῶν δυνάμεων εἰς χειμασίαν.

[1] Αἴκλων Rhodoman : Ἄσκλων RX, Ἀσκλῶν F, cp. chap. 101. 5.

CONTENTS OF THE TWENTIETH BOOK

[1] Chap. 110 is omitted: the initiation of Demetrius and his campaign against Cassander.

[2] Chap. 112 is omitted: the adventures of Pleistarchus.

ΒΙΒΛΟΣ ΕΙΚΟΣΤΗ

1. Τοῖς εἰς τὰς ἱστορίας ὑπερμήκεις δημηγορίας παρεμβάλλουσιν ἢ πυκναῖς χρωμένοις ῥητορείαις δικαίως ἄν τις ἐπιτιμήσειεν· οὐ μόνον γὰρ τὸ συνεχὲς τῆς διηγήσεως διὰ τὴν ἀκαιρίαν τῶν ἐπεισαγομένων λόγων διασπῶσιν, ἀλλὰ καὶ τῶν φιλοτίμως ἐχόντων πρὸς τὴν τῶν πράξεων ἐπίγνωσιν μεσο-
2 λαβοῦσι τὴν ἐπιθυμίαν.[1] καίτοι γε τοὺς ἐπιδείκνυσθαι βουλομένους λόγου δύναμιν ἔξεστι κατ' ἰδίαν δημηγορίας καὶ πρεσβευτικοὺς λόγους, ἔτι δὲ ἐγκώμια καὶ ψόγους καὶ τἄλλα τὰ τοιαῦτα συντάττεσθαι· τῇ γὰρ οἰκονομίᾳ τῶν λόγων χρησάμενοι καὶ τὰς ὑποθέσεις χωρὶς ἑκατέρας ἐξεργασάμενοι κατὰ λόγον ἂν ἐν ἀμφοτέραις ταῖς πραγματείαις
3 εὐδοκιμοῖεν. νῦν δ' ἔνιοι πλεονάσαντες ἐν τοῖς ῥητορικοῖς λόγοις προσθήκην ἐποιήσαντο τὴν ὅλην ἱστορίαν τῆς δημηγορίας. λυπεῖ δ' οὐ μόνον τὸ κακῶς γραφέν,[2] ἀλλὰ καὶ τὸ δοκοῦν ἐν τοῖς ἄλλοις ἐπιτετεῦχθαι, τόπων καὶ καιρῶν τῆς οἰκείας τάξεως
4 διημαρτηκός. διὸ καὶ τῶν ἀναγινωσκόντων τὰς τοιαύτας πραγματείας οἱ μὲν ὑπερβαίνουσι τὰς ῥητορείας, κἂν ὅλως ἐπιτετεῦχθαι δόξωσιν, οἱ δὲ διὰ τὸ μῆκος καὶ τὴν ἀκαιρίαν τοῦ συγγραφέως ἐκλυθέντες τὰς ψυχὰς τὸ παράπαν ἀφίστανται τῆς

144

BOOK XX

1. One might justly censure those who in their histories insert over-long orations or employ frequent speeches ; for not only do they rend asunder the continuity of the narrative by the ill-timed insertion of speeches, but also they interrupt the interest of those who are eagerly pressing on toward a full knowledge of the events. Yet surely there is opportunity for those who wish to display rhetorical prowess to compose by themselves public discourses and speeches for ambassadors, likewise orations of praise and blame and the like ; for by recognizing the classification of literary types and by elaborating each of the two by itself, they might reasonably expect to gain a reputation in both fields of activity. But as it is, some writers by excessive use of rhetorical passages have made the whole art of history into an appendage of oratory. Not only does that which is poorly composed give offence, but also that which seems to have hit the mark in other respects yet has gone far astray from the themes and occasions that belong to its peculiar type. Therefore, even of those who read such works, some skip over the orations although they appear to be entirely successful, and others, wearied in spirit by the historian's wordiness and lack of taste, abandon

---

¹ μεσολαβοῦσι τὴν ἐπιθυμίαν added by Wesseling.
² γραφέν Dindorf : γράφειν.

145

5 ἀναγνώσεως, οὐκ ἀλόγως τοῦτο πάσχοντες· τὸ γὰρ
τῆς ἱστορίας γένος ἁπλοῦν ἐστι καὶ συμφυὲς αὑτῷ
καὶ τὸ σύνολον ἐμψύχῳ σώματι παραπλήσιον, οὗ τὸ
μὲν ἐσπαραγμένον ἐστέρηται τῆς ψυχικῆς χάριτος,
τὸ δὲ τὴν ἀναγκαίαν σύνθεσιν ἔχον εὐκαίρως τετή-
ρηται καὶ τῷ συμφυεῖ τῆς ὅλης περιγραφῆς ἐπι-
τερπῆ καὶ σαφῆ παρίστησι τὴν ἀνάγνωσιν.

2. Οὐ μὴν παντελῶς γε τοὺς ῥητορικοὺς λόγους
ἀποδοκιμάζοντες ἐκβάλλομεν ἐκ τῆς ἱστορικῆς
πραγματείας τὸ παράπαν· ὀφειλούσης γὰρ τῆς ἱστορίας τῇ ποικιλίᾳ κεκοσμῆσθαι κατ' ἐνίους τόπους
ἀνάγκη προσλαμβάνεσθαι καὶ τοὺς τοιούτους λόγους
—καὶ ταύτης τῆς εὐκαιρίας οὐδ' ἂν ἐμαυτὸν ἀπο-
στερῆσαι βουληθείην—ὥσθ' ὅταν τὰ τῆς περιστάσεως ἀπαιτῇ πρεσβευτοῦ ἢ συμβούλου δημηγορίαν
ἢ τῶν ἄλλων τι τοιοῦτον, ὁ μὴ τεθαρρηκότως
συγκαταβαίνων πρὸς τοὺς ἐν τοῖς λόγοις ἀγῶνας
2 καὶ αὐτὸς ὑπαίτιος ἂν εἴη. οὐκ ὀλίγας γὰρ ἄν τις
αἰτίας εὕροι, καθ' ἃς κατὰ πολλὰ ἀναγκαίως παρα-
ληφθήσεται τὰ τῆς ῥητορείας· ἢ γὰρ πολλῶν εἰρη-
μένων εὐστόχως καὶ καλῶς οὐ παραλειπτέον δι'
ὀλιγωρίαν τὰ μνήμης ἄξια καὶ τῇ ἱστορίᾳ κεκρα-
μένην ἔχοντα τὴν ὠφέλειαν, ἢ μεγάλων καὶ λαμπρῶν
τῶν ὑποθέσεων οὐσῶν οὐ περιορατέον ἐλάττονα
τῶν ἔργων φανῆναι τὸν λόγον· ἔστι δ' ὅτε παρὰ
προσδοκίαν τοῦ τέλους ἐκβάντος ἀναγκασθησόμεθα
τοῖς οἰκείοις[1] τῆς ὑποθέσεως λόγοις χρήσασθαι
χάριν τοῦ λῦσαι τὴν ἀλογίαν.

3 Ἀλλὰ περὶ μὲν τούτων ἅλις ἡμῖν ἐχέτω, περὶ
δὲ τῶν ὑποκειμένων πράξεων ῥητέον, παραθέντας
πρότερον τοὺς οἰκείους τῇ γραφῇ χρόνους. ἐν
μὲν οὖν ταῖς προηγουμέναις βύβλοις ἀναγεγράφαμεν

the reading entirely ; and this attitude is not without reason, for the genius of history is simple and self-consistent and as a whole is like a living organism. If it is mangled, it is stripped of its living charm ; but if it retains its necessary unity, it is duly preserved and, by the harmony of the whole composition, renders the reading pleasant and clear.

2. Nevertheless, in disapproving rhetorical speeches, we do not ban them wholly from historical works ; for, since history needs to be adorned with variety, in certain places it is necessary to call to our aid even such passages—and of this opportunity I should not wish to deprive myself—so that, whenever the situation requires either a public address from an ambassador or a statesman, or some such thing from the other characters, whoever does not boldly enter the contest of words would himself be blameworthy. For one would find no small number of reasons for which on many occasions the aid of rhetoric will necessarily be enlisted ; for when many things have been said well and to the point, one should not in contempt pass over what is worthy of memory and possesses a utility¹ not alien to history, nor when the subject matter is great and glorious should one allow the language to appear inferior to the deeds ; and there are times when, an event turning out contrary to expectation, we shall be forced to use words suitable to the subject in order to explain the seeming paradox.

But let this suffice on this subject ; we must now write about the events that belong to my theme, first setting forth the chronological scheme of our narrative. In the preceding Books we have written of the

---

¹ οἰκείοις added by Fischer, cp. Book 19. 34. 3.

ἀπὸ τῶν ἀρχαιοτάτων χρόνων τὰς πράξεις τάς τε
τῶν Ἑλλήνων καὶ βαρβάρων ἕως ἐπὶ τὸν προη-
γούμενον ἐνιαυτὸν τῆς Ἀγαθοκλέους στρατείας εἰς
τὴν Λιβύην, εἰς ἣν ἀπὸ Τροίας ἁλώσεως ἔτη συν-
άγεται τρισὶ πλείω τῶν ὀκτακοσίων ὀγδοήκοντα·
ἐν ταύτῃ δὲ τὸ συνεχὲς προστιθέντες τῆς ἱστορίας
ἀρξόμεθα μὲν ἀπὸ τῆς εἰς Λιβύην διαβάσεως Ἀγαθοκλέους, καταλήξομεν δ' εἰς τὸν ἐνιαυτὸν καθ'
ὃν οἱ βασιλεῖς συμφρονήσαντες κοινῇ διαπολεμεῖν
ἤρξαντο πρὸς Ἀντίγονον τὸν Φιλίππου, περιλα-
βόντες ἔτη ἐννέα.

3. Ἐπ' ἄρχοντος γὰρ Ἀθήνησιν Ἱερομνήμονος
Ῥωμαῖοι μὲν ὑπάτους κατέστησαν Γάιον Ἰούλιον
καὶ Κόιντον Αἰμίλιον, κατὰ δὲ τὴν Σικελίαν
Ἀγαθοκλῆς ἡττημένος ὑπὸ Καρχηδονίων τῇ περὶ
τὸν Ἱμέραν μάχῃ καὶ τὸ πλεῖστον καὶ κράτιστον
τῆς δυνάμεως ἀποβεβληκὼς συνέφυγεν εἰς τὰς
2 Συρακούσσας. ὁρῶν δὲ τούς τε συμμάχους ἅπαντας
μεταβεβλημένους καὶ τοὺς βαρβάρους πλὴν Συρακουσσῶν ἁπάσης σχεδὸν Σικελίας κυριεύοντας καὶ
πολὺ προέχοντας ταῖς τε πεζικαῖς καὶ ναυτικαῖς
δυνάμεσιν ἐπετελέσατο πρᾶξιν ἀνέλπιστον καὶ παρα-
3 βολωτάτην. πάντων γὰρ διειληφότων μηδ' ἐγχειρήσειν αὐτὸν τοῖς Καρχηδονίοις ἀντιταχθῆναι,
διενοήσατο τῆς μὲν πόλεως ἀπολιπεῖν τὴν ἱκανὴν
φυλακήν, τῶν δὲ στρατιωτῶν τοὺς εὐθέτους ἐπι-
λέξαι καὶ μετὰ τούτων εἰς τὴν Λιβύην διακο-
μισθῆναι· τοῦτο γὰρ πράξας ἤλπιζε τοὺς μὲν ἐν τῇ
Καρχηδόνι τετρυφηκότας ἐν εἰρήνῃ πολυχρονίῳ καὶ
διὰ τοῦτ' ἀπείρους ὄντας τῶν ἐν ταῖς μάχαις

---

[1] An error for 873. Cp. Book 19. 1. 10.

deeds of both the Greeks and the barbarians from the earliest times down to the year before Agathocles' Libyan campaign ; the years from the sack of Troy to that event total eight hundred and eighty-three.[1] In this Book, adding what comes next in the account, we shall begin with Agathocles' crossing into Libya, and end with the year in which the kings, after reaching an agreement with each other, began joint operations against Antigonus, son of Philip, embracing a period of nine years.

3. When Hieromnemon was archon in Athens, the Romans elected to the consulship Gaius Julius and Quintus Aemilius[2] ; and in Sicily Agathocles, who had been defeated by the Carthaginians in the battle at the Himeras River and had lost the largest and strongest part of his army, took refuge in Syracuse. When he saw that all his allies had changed sides and that the barbarians were masters of almost all Sicily except Syracuse and were far superior in both land and sea forces, he carried out an undertaking that was unexpected and most reckless. For when all had concluded that he would not even try to take the field against the Carthaginians, he determined to leave an adequate garrison for the city, to select those of the soldiers who were fit, and with these to cross over into Libya. For he hoped that, if he did this, those in Carthage, who had been living luxuriously in long-continued peace and were therefore without experience in the dangers of battle, would

[2] Hieromnemon was archon in 310/09 B.C. In the Fasti the consuls of 311 B.C. are C. Iunius Bubulcus Brutus for the third time and Q. Aemilius Barbula for the second (*CIL*, 1, p. 130 ; cp. Livy, 9. 30. 1). The narrative is continued from Book 19. 110. 5. For the first part of the African campaign, cp. Justin, 22. 4-6 ; Orosius, 4. 6. 23-29.

κινδύνων ὑπὸ τῶν ἐνηθληκότων τοῖς δεινοῖς ῥᾳδίως
ἡττηθήσεσθαι, τοὺς δὲ κατὰ Λιβύην συμμάχους,
βαρυνομένους τοῖς προστάγμασιν ἐκ πολλῶν χρόνων, λήψεσθαι καιρὸν τῆς ἀποστάσεως, τὸ δὲ
μέγιστον, διαρπάσειν ἀπροσδοκήτως ἐπιφανεὶς
χώραν ἀπόρθητον καὶ διὰ τὴν τῶν Καρχηδονίων
εὐδαιμονίαν πεπληρωμένην παντοίων ἀγαθῶν, τὸ
δ' ὅλον ἀπὸ τῆς πατρίδος καὶ πάσης Σικελίας
περισπάσειν τοὺς βαρβάρους καὶ πάντα τὸν πόλεμον
μετάξειν εἰς τὴν Λιβύην· ὅπερ καὶ συνετελέσθη.

4. Τὴν γὰρ ἐπίνοιαν ταύτην οὐδενὶ τῶν φίλων
δηλώσας τῆς μὲν πόλεως ἐπιμελητὴν Ἄντανδρον
τὸν ἀδελφὸν κατέστησε μετὰ τῆς ἱκανῆς φυλακῆς,
αὐτὸς δὲ τῶν στρατιωτῶν ἐπιλέγων τοὺς εὐθέτους
κατέγραφε, τοῖς μὲν πεζοῖς παραγγέλλων ἑτοίμους
εἶναι μετὰ τῶν ὅπλων, τοῖς δ' ἱππεῦσι διακελευό-
μενος ἔχειν μεθ' ἑαυτῶν χωρὶς τῆς πανοπλίας
ὑπηρέσιον καὶ χαλινόν, ὅπως, ὅταν ἵππων κυριεύσῃ,
τοὺς ἀναβησομένους ἑτοίμους ἔχειν, τὰ πρὸς τὴν
2 χρείαν ἐξηρτυμένους· κατὰ γὰρ τὴν προγεγενημένην
ἧτταν τῶν μὲν πεζῶν ἀπωλώλεισαν οἱ πλείους, οἱ
δ' ἱππεῖς ὑπῆρχον διασεσωσμένοι σχεδὸν ἅπαντες,
ὧν τοὺς ἵππους οὐκ ἠδύνατο διακομίζειν εἰς τὴν
3 Λιβύην. ἵνα δὲ χωρισθέντος αὐτοῦ μὴ νεωτερί-
ζωσιν οἱ Συρακόσιοι, διεζεύγνυε τὰς συγγενείας
ἀπ' ἀλλήλων καὶ μάλιστα ἀδελφοὺς ἀπ' ἀδελφῶν
καὶ πατέρας ἀπὸ παίδων, τοὺς μὲν ἐπὶ τῆς πόλεως

---

[1] He was probably an older brother : in 317 B.C. he was

easily be defeated by men who had been trained in 310 B.C.
the school of danger ; that the Libyan allies of the
Carthaginians, who had for a long time resented their
exactions, would grasp an opportunity for revolt ;
most important of all, that by appearing unexpectedly, he would plunder a land which had not been
ravaged and which, because of the prosperity of the
Carthaginians, abounded in wealth of every kind ;
and in general, that he would divert the barbarians
from his native city and from all Sicily and transfer
the whole war to Libya. And this last, indeed, was
accomplished.

4. Disclosing this intention to none of his friends,
he set up his brother Antander [1] as curator of the
city with an adequate garrison ; and he himself
selected and enrolled those of the soldiers who were
fit for service, bidding the infantry be ready with
their arms, and giving special orders to the cavalry
that, in addition to their full armour, they should have
with them saddle-pads and bridles, in order that,
when he got possession of horses, he might have men
ready to mount them, equipped with what was needed
for the service ; for in the earlier defeat the greater
part of the foot-soldiers had been killed, but almost
all the horsemen had survived uninjured,[2] whose
horses he was not able to transport to Libya. In
order that the Syracusans might not attempt a
revolution after he had left them, he separated
relatives from each other, particularly brothers from
brothers and fathers from sons, leaving the one group

one of the Syracusan generals in the war with the Bruttii, and
Agathocles was only a chiliarch (Book 19. 3. 3). He later
wrote a biography of Agathocles (Book 21. 16. 5).

[2] Agathocles' losses in the battle at the Himeras River are
given in Book 19. 109. 5 as not less than 7000 men.

4 ἀπολείπων, τοὺς δὲ μεθ᾽ ἑαυτοῦ διακομίζων· πρό-
δηλον γὰρ ἦν ὡς οἱ μένοντες ἐν ταῖς Συρακούσσαις,
κἂν ἀλλοτριώτατα τυγχάνωσι πρὸς τὸν δυνάστην
διακείμενοι,¹ διὰ τὴν πρὸς τοὺς ἀπογόνους εὔνοιαν
οὐδὲν ἂν πράξειαν ἄτοπον κατὰ Ἀγαθοκλέους.
5 ἀπορούμενος δὲ χρημάτων τά τε τῶν ὀρφανῶν παρὰ
τῶν ἐπιτροπευόντων εἰσεπράξατο, φάσκων πολὺ
βέλτιον ἐκείνων ἐπιτροπεύσειν καὶ τοῖς παισὶν εἰς
ἡλικίαν ἐλθοῦσι πιστότερον ἀποδώσειν, ἐδανείσατο
δὲ καὶ παρὰ τῶν ἐμπόρων καί τινα τῶν ἐν τοῖς
ἱεροῖς ἀναθημάτων ἔλαβεν καὶ τῶν γυναικῶν τὸν
6 κόσμον περιείλετο. ἔπειθ᾽ ὁρῶν² τῶν εὐπορωτάτων
τοὺς πλείστους δυσχεραίνοντας τοῖς πραττομένοις
καὶ πρὸς αὐτὸν ἀλλοτριώτατα διακειμένους συνήγαγεν ἐκκλησίαν, ἐν ᾗ περί τε τῆς προγεγενημένης
συμφορᾶς καὶ τῶν προσδοκωμένων δεινῶν κατ-
οδυρόμενος αὐτὸς μὲν ῥᾳδίως ὑπομενεῖν³ ἔφησε τὴν
πολιορκίαν συνήθης ὢν πάσῃ κακοπαθείᾳ, ἐλεεῖν δὲ
τοὺς πολίτας, εἰ συγκλεισθέντες ἀναγκασθήσονται
7 πολιορκίαν ὑπομένειν. διεκελεύετο οὖν σώζειν
ἑαυτοὺς μετὰ τῶν ἰδίων κτήσεων τοὺς μὴ βουλομένους ὑπομένειν ὅ τι ποτ᾽ ἂν δοκῇ τῇ τύχῃ πάσχειν.
ἐξορμησάντων δ᾽ ἐκ τῆς πόλεως τῶν μάλιστ᾽ εὐπόρων καὶ μισούντων τὸν δυνάστην τούτους μὲν
ἐπαποστείλας τινὰς τῶν μισθοφόρων ἀνεῖλε καὶ τὰς
8 οὐσίας εἰς αὑτὸν ἀνέλαβε, διὰ δὲ μιᾶς ἀνοσίου πράξεως χρημάτων εὐπορήσας καὶ τῶν ἀλλοτρίως διακειμένων πρὸς αὐτὸν καθαρὰν ποιήσας τὴν πόλιν
ἠλευθέρωσε τῶν οἰκετῶν τοὺς εὐθέτους εἰς στρατείαν.

in the city and taking the others across with him ; 310 B.C.
for it was clear that those who remained in Syracuse,
even if they were most ill disposed toward the tyrant,
because of their affection for their relatives would
do nothing unbecoming against Agathocles. Since
he was in need of money he exacted the property
of the orphans from those who were their guardians,
saying that he would guard it much better than they
and return it more faithfully to the children when they
became of age ; and he also borrowed from the merchants, took some of the dedications in the temples,
and stripped the women of their jewels. Then, seeing
that the majority of the very wealthy were vexed by
his measures and were very hostile to him, he summoned an assembly in which, deploring both the past
disaster and the expected hardships, he said that he
himself would endure the siege easily because he was
accustomed to every manner of hardship, but that
he pitied the citizens if they should be shut in and
forced to endure a siege. He therefore ordered those
to save themselves and their own possessions who
were unwilling to endure whatever fortune might
see fit that they should suffer. But when those who
were wealthiest and most bitter against the tyrant
had set out from the city, sending after them some
of his mercenaries, he killed the men themselves and
confiscated their property. When, through a single
unholy act, he had gained an abundance of wealth
and had cleared the city of those who were opposed
to him, he freed those of their slaves who were fit
for military service.

---

[1] διακείμενοι added by Dindorf, cp. § 6.
[2] καὶ after ὁρῶν omitted by Fischer.
[3] ὑπομενεῖν Dindorf : ὑπομένειν MSS. followed by Fischer.

153

5. Ὡς δ' εὐτρεπῆ πάντ' ἦν, πληρώσας ἑξήκοντα ναῦς ἐπετήρει καιρὸν οἰκεῖον πρὸς τὸν ἔκπλουν. ἀγνοουμένης δὲ τῆς ἐπινοίας αὐτοῦ τινες μὲν εἰς τὴν Ἰταλίαν ὑπελάμβανον αὐτὸν στρατεύειν, τινὲς δὲ πορθήσειν τῆς Σικελίας τὴν ὑπὸ Καρχηδονίους, πάντες δὲ ἀπεγίνωσκον τῶν ἐκπλεῖν μελλόντων τὴν σωτηρίαν καὶ τοῦ δυνάστου τὴν μανίαν κατεγί-
2 νωσκον. ἐφορμούντων δὲ τῶν πολεμίων πολλα-πλασίαις τριήρεσι τὸ μὲν πρῶτον ἐφ' ἡμέρας τινὰς ἠναγκάζετο συνέχειν[1] ἐν ταῖς ναυσὶ τοὺς στρα-τιώτας, οὐ δυναμένους ἐκπλεῦσαι· ἔπειτα δὲ σιτηγῶν πλοίων τῇ πόλει προσθεόντων οἱ μὲν Καρχηδόνιοι παντὶ τῷ στόλῳ πρὸς τὰς ναῦς ἀνήχθησαν, ὁ δ' Ἀγαθοκλῆς ἀπελπίζων ἤδη τὴν ἐπιβολήν, ὡς ἴδεν τὸ στόμα τοῦ λιμένος ἔρημον τῶν ἐφορμούντων,
3 ἐξέπλευσεν ὀξείαις ταῖς εἰρεσίαις χρώμενος. εἶθ' οἱ μὲν Καρχηδόνιοι πλησίον ἤδη τῶν φορτηγῶν ὄντες, ὡς ἴδον τοὺς πολεμίους ἀθρόαις ταῖς ναυσὶ πλέοντας, τὸ μὲν πρῶτον ὑπολαβόντες αὐτὸν ὡρμη-κέναι πρὸς τὴν τῶν σιτηγῶν βοήθειαν, ἀνέστρεφον καὶ τὸν στόλον ἐξήρτυον εἰς ναυμαχίαν· ὡς δ' ἐπ' εὐθείας ἑώρων παραθέοντας καὶ πολὺ τοῦ πλοῦ
4 προλαμβάνοντας, ἐποιοῦντο τὸν διωγμόν. ἔνθα δὴ τούτων πρὸς ἀλλήλους φιλοτιμουμένων τὰ μὲν τὴν ἀγορὰν κομίζοντα πλοῖα παραδόξως ἐκφυγόντα τὸν κίνδυνον πολλὴν εὐπορίαν ἐποίησεν ἐν ταῖς Συρα-κούσσαις τῶν ἐπιτηδείων, σιτοδείας ἤδη τὴν πόλιν ἐχούσης, ὁ δ' Ἀγαθοκλῆς περικατάληπτος ἤδη γινόμενος ἐπιλαβούσης τῆς νυκτὸς ἀνελπίστου σω-
5 τηρίας ἔτυχεν. τῇ δ' ὑστεραίᾳ τηλικαύτην ἔκλειψιν

---

[1] ἠναγκάζετο συνέχειν Wesseling, ἠνάγκαζε σ. ἑαυτοὺς Fischer: ἠνάγκαζε συνέχειν.

5. When everything was ready, Agathocles manned 310 B.C. sixty ships and awaited a suitable time for the voyage. Since his purpose was unknown, some supposed that he was making an expedition into Italy, and others that he was going to plunder the part of Sicily that was under Carthaginian control; but all despaired of the safety of those who were about to sail away and condemned the prince for his mad folly. But since the enemy was blockading the port with triremes many times more numerous than his own, Agathocles at first for some days was compelled to detain his soldiers in the ships since they could not sail out; but later, when some grain ships were putting in to the city, the Carthaginians with their whole fleet made for these ships, and Agathocles, who already despaired of his enterprise, as he saw the mouth of the harbour freed of the blockading ships, sailed out, his men rowing at top speed. Then when the Carthaginians, who were already close to the cargo vessels, saw the enemy sailing with their ships in close order, assuming at first that Agathocles was hastening to the rescue of the grain ships, they turned and made their fleet ready for battle; but when they saw the ships sailing straight past and getting a long start of them, they began to pursue. Thereupon, while these were contending with each other, the ships that were bringing grain, unexpectedly escaping the danger, brought about a great abundance of provisions in Syracuse, when a scarcity of food was already gripping the city; and Agathocles, who was already at the point of being overtaken and surrounded, gained unhoped-for safety as night closed in. On the next day there occurred such an eclipse of the

ἡλίου συνέβη γενέσθαι ὥστε ὁλοσχερῶς φανῆναι
νύκτα, θεωρουμένων τῶν ἀστέρων πανταχοῦ· διόπερ
οἱ περὶ τὸν Ἀγαθοκλέα, νομίσαντες καὶ τὸ θεῖον
αὐτοῖς προσημαίνειν τὸ δυσχερές, ἔτι μᾶλλον ὑπὲρ
τοῦ μέλλοντος ἐν ἀγωνίᾳ καθειστήκεισαν.

6. Ἒξ δ' ἡμέρας καὶ τὰς ἴσας νύκτας αὐτῶν
πλευσάντων ὑποφαινούσης τῆς ἕω παραδόξως ὁ
στόλος τῶν Καρχηδονίων οὐκ ἄπωθεν ὢν ἑωράθη.
διόπερ[1] ἀμφοτέροις ἐμπεσούσης σπουδῆς ἡμιλλῶντο
πρὸς ἀλλήλους ταῖς εἰρεσίαις, οἱ μὲν Φοίνικες νομίζοντες ἅμα τῇ τῶν νεῶν ἁλώσει Συρακούσσας μὲν
ὑποχειρίους ἕξειν, τὴν δὲ πατρίδα μεγάλων ἐλευ-
θερώσειν κινδύνων· οἱ δ' Ἕλληνες, εἰ μὴ φθάσειαν
2 τῆς χώρας ἁψάμενοι, προκειμένην ἑώρων αὐτοῖς
μὲν τιμωρίαν, τοῖς δὲ καταλειφθεῖσιν ἐν οἴκῳ τὰ
τῆς δουλείας δεινά. καθορωμένης δὲ τῆς Λιβύης
παρακελευσμὸς ἐγίνετο τοῖς πληρώμασι καὶ φιλοτιμίας ὑπερβολή· καὶ τάχιον μὲν ἔπλεον αἱ τῶν
βαρβάρων, ἐν πολυχρονίῳ μελέτῃ τῶν ἐρετῶν δια-
πεπονημένων, ἱκανὸν δὲ διάστημα προεῖχον αἱ τῶν
Ἑλλήνων. ὀξύτατα δὲ τοῦ πλοῦ διανυσθέντος,
ἐπειδὴ πλησίον ἐγενήθησαν τῆς γῆς, συνεξέπιπτον
ἀλλήλοις εἰς τὸν αἰγιαλὸν ὡσπερεί τινες ἀγωνισταί·
3 ταῖς γὰρ ἐσχάταις τῶν Ἀγαθοκλέους αἱ πρῶται
τῶν Καρχηδονίων ἐνέβαλλον ἐντὸς βέλους οὖσαι.
διόπερ ἐπ' ὀλίγον χρόνον τοῖς τε τόξοις καὶ σφενδόναις διαγωνισαμένων αὐτῶν καὶ ναυσὶν ὀλίγαις τῶν

―――――――――

[1] διόπερ Dindorf : διὸ παρ'.

―――――――――――――――――――――――――

sun that utter darkness set in and the stars were seen 310 B.C. everywhere [1]; wherefore Agathocles' men, believing that the prodigy portended misfortune for them, fell into even greater anxiety about the future.[2]

6. After they had sailed for six days and the same number of nights, just as day was breaking, the fleet of the Carthaginians was unexpectedly seen not far away. At this both fleets were filled with zeal and vied with each other in rowing, the Carthaginians believing that as soon as they destroyed the Greek ships they would have Syracuse in their hands and at the same time free their fatherland from great dangers ; and the Greeks foreseeing that, if they did not get to land first, punishment was in store for themselves and the perils of slavery for those who had been left at home. When Libya came into sight, the men on board began to cheer and the rivalry became very keen ; the ships of the barbarians sailed faster since their crews had undergone very long training, but those of the Greeks had sufficient lead. The distance was covered very quickly, and when the ships drew near the land they rushed side by side for the beach like men in a race ; indeed, since they were within range, the first of the Carthaginian ships were sending missiles at the last of those of Agathocles. Consequently, when they had fought for a short time with bows and slings and the barbarians had come to close quarters with a few of the Greek

that Agathocles must have sailed north around Sicily (Cary in *Cambridge Ancient History*, 7. 625).

[2] According to Justin, 22. 6. 2, he explained away the omen to his men, saying that if it had happened before the expedition started it would have portended evil to them, but since it took place after the sailing it foretold misfortune for their enemies.

βαρβάρων συμπλακέντων οἱ περὶ τὸν Ἀγαθοκλέα
προετέρουν, τὸ τῶν στρατιωτῶν ἔχοντες πλῆθος.
εἶθ' οἱ μὲν Καρχηδόνιοι πρύμναν ἀνακρουσάμενοι
μικρὸν ἔξω βέλους ἐφώρμουν, ὁ δ' Ἀγαθοκλῆς
ἀποβιβάσας τὴν δύναμιν πρὸς τὰς καλουμένας
Λατομίας καὶ χάρακα βαλόμενος ἐκ θαλάττης εἰς
θάλατταν ἐνεώλκησε τὰς ναῦς.

7. Οὕτω δὲ παράβολον ἐπιτελεσάμενος πρᾶξιν,
ἄλλην ἐτόλμησε ταύτης μᾶλλον κεκινδυνευμένην.
παραστησάμενος γὰρ τοὺς ἐν ἡγεμονίαις ὄντας
εὐπειθεῖς πρὸς τὴν ἰδίαν ἐπιβολὴν καὶ θυσίαν ποιησάμενος Δήμητρι καὶ Κόρῃ συνήγαγεν ἐκκλησίαν·
2 κἄπειτα προελθὼν ἐπὶ τὴν δημηγορίαν ἐστεφανω-
μένος ἐν ἱματίῳ λαμπρῷ καὶ προδιαλεχθεὶς οἰκείως
τοῖς ἐγχειρουμένοις ἔφησε ταῖς κατεχούσαις Σικελίαν θεαῖς Δήμητρι καὶ Κόρῃ πεποιῆσθαι, καθ' ὃν
καιρὸν ἐδιώχθησαν ὑπὸ Καρχηδονίων, εὐχὰς λαμπα-
3 δεύσειν ἁπάσας τὰς ναῦς. καλῶς οὖν ἔχειν
τετευχότας τῆς σωτηρίας ἀποδιδόναι τὰς εὐχάς.
ἀντὶ δὲ τούτων ἐπηγγέλλετο πολλαπλασίους ἀποδώσειν προθύμως αὐτῶν ἀγωνισαμένων· καὶ γὰρ
τὰς θεὰς διὰ τῶν ἱερῶν προσημαίνειν νίκην τοῦ
4 σύμπαντος πολέμου. ἅμα δὲ ταῦτα λέγοντος αὐτοῦ
τῶν ὑπηρετῶν τις προσήνεγκεν ἡμμένην δᾷδα· ἣν
δεξάμενος καὶ τοῖς τριηράρχοις ὁμοίως ἅπασι
προστάξας ἀναδοῦναι τάς τε θεὰς ἐπεκαλέσατο καὶ
πρῶτος ὥρμησεν ἐπὶ τὴν ναυαρχίδα τριήρη· στὰς
δ' ἐπὶ τὴν πρύμναν καὶ τοῖς ἄλλοις τὸ παραπλήσιον
ποιεῖν παρεκελεύετο. ἔνθα δὴ τῶν τριηράρχων

---

ships, Agathocles got the upper hand since he had 310 B.C.
his complement of soldiers. At this the Carthaginians withdrew and lay offshore a little beyond
bowshot ; but Agathocles, having disembarked his
soldiers at the place called Latomiae [1] and constructed
a palisade from sea to sea, beached his ships.

7. When he had thus carried through a perilous
enterprise, Agathocles ventured upon another even
more hazardous. For after surrounding himself with
those among the leaders who were ready to follow
his proposal and after making sacrifice to Demeter
and Corê, he summoned an assembly ; next he came
forward to speak, crowned and clad in a splendid
himation, and when he had made prefatory remarks
of a nature appropriate to the undertaking,[2] he
declared that to Demeter and Corê, the goddesses
who protected Sicily, he had at the very moment
when they were pursued by the Carthaginians vowed
to offer all the ships as a burnt offering. Therefore
it was well, since they had succeeded in gaining
safety, that they should pay the vow. In place of
these ships he promised to restore many times the
number if they would but fight boldly ; and in truth,
he added, the goddesses by omens from the victims
had foretold victory in the entire war. While he was
saying this, one of his attendants brought forward a
lighted torch. When he had taken this and had given
orders to distribute torches likewise to all the ship
captains, he invoked the goddesses and himself first
set out to the trireme of the commander. Standing
by the stern, he bade the others also to follow his
example. Then as all the captains threw in the fire

[2] Justin, 22. 5-6, gives the substance of a long oration,
which he ascribes to Agathocles on this occasion.

ἁπάντων ἐνέντων τὸ πῦρ καὶ ταχὺ τῆς φλογὸς εἰς
ὕψος ἀρθείσης οἱ μὲν σαλπιγκταὶ τὸ πολεμικὸν
ἐσήμαινον, τὸ δὲ στρατόπεδον ἐπηλάλαξε, συνευ-
χομένων ἁπάντων ὑπὲρ τῆς εἰς οἶκον σωτηρίας.
5 τοῦτο δ' ἔπραξεν Ἀγαθοκλῆς μάλιστα μὲν ἕνεκα
τοῦ συναναγκάσαι τοὺς στρατιώτας ἐν τοῖς κινδύνοις ἐπιλαθέσθαι τὸ παράπαν τῆς φυγῆς· δῆλον
γὰρ ὅτι τῆς ἐπὶ τὰς ναῦς καταφυγῆς ἀποκοπείσης
ἐν μόνῳ τῷ νικᾶν ἕξουσι τὰς ἐλπίδας τῆς σωτηρίας·
ἔπειτα καὶ δύναμιν ὀλίγην ἔχων ἐθεώρει διότι φυ-
λάσσων μὲν τὰς ναῦς ἀναγκασθήσεται μερίζειν τὸ
στρατόπεδον καὶ μηδαμῶς ἀξιόμαχος εἶναι, καταλιπὼν δ' ἐρήμους ὑποχειρίους ποιήσει γενέσθαι
Καρχηδονίοις.

8. Οὐ μὴν ἀλλὰ τῶν νεῶν ἁπασῶν φλεγομένων
καὶ τοῦ πυρὸς πολὺν ἐπέχοντος τόπον ἔκπληξις
κατεῖχε τοὺς Σικελιώτας. ἐν ἀρχῇ μὲν γὰρ ὑπὸ
τῆς Ἀγαθοκλέους γοητείας παραλογισθέντες καὶ
τῆς τῶν ἐγχειρουμένων ὀξύτητος ἀναθεώρησιν οὐ
διδούσης πάντες συγκατετίθεντο τοῖς πραττομένοις·
τοῦ δὲ χρόνου τὸν περὶ ἑκάστων ἀναλογισμὸν παρ-
ιστάντος εἰς μεταμέλειαν ἐνέπιπτον καὶ τὸ μέγεθος
τοῦ διείργοντος πελάγους ἀναλογιζόμενοι τὴν
2 σωτηρίαν ἀπεγίνωσκον. ὁ δ' Ἀγαθοκλῆς σπεύδων
ἀπαλλάξαι τῆς ἀθυμίας τοὺς στρατιώτας ἦγε τὴν
δύναμιν ἐπὶ τὴν ὀνομαζομένην Μεγάλην πόλιν,
3 οὖσαν Καρχηδονίων. ἡ δ' ἀνὰ μέσον χώρα, δι'
ἧς ἦν ἀναγκαῖον πορευθῆναι, διείληπτο κηπείαις
καὶ παντοίαις φυτουργίαις, πολλῶν ὑδάτων διωχε-
τευμένων καὶ πάντα τόπον ἀρδευόντων. ἀγροικίαι
τε συνεχεῖς ὑπῆρχον, οἰκοδομαῖς πολυτελέσι καὶ
κονιάμασι διαπεπονημέναι καὶ τὸν τῶν κεκτημένων

and the flames quickly blazed high, the trumpeters 310 B.C. sounded the signal for battle and the army raised the war-cry, while all together prayed for a safe return home. This Agathocles did primarily to compel his soldiers in the midst of dangers to have no thought at all of flight ; for it was clear that, if the retreat to the ships was cut off, in victory alone would they have hope of safety. Moreover, since he had a small army, he reasoned that if he guarded the ships he would be compelled to divide his forces and so be by no means strong enough to meet the enemy in battle, and if he left the ships without defenders, he would put them into the hands of the Carthaginians.

8. Nevertheless, when all the ships were aflame and the fire was spreading widely, terror laid hold upon the Sicilians. Carried away at first by the wiles of Agathocles and by the rapidity of his undertakings, which gave no time for reflection, all acquiesced in what was being done ; but when time made possible detailed consideration, they were plunged into regret, and as they considered the vastness of the sea that separated them from home, they abandoned hope of safety. Agathocles, however, in an effort to rid his soldiers of their despondency, led his army against the place called Megalepolis, a city of the Carthaginians.[1] The intervening country through which it was necessary for them to march was divided into gardens and plantations of every kind, since many streams of water were led in small channels and irrigated every part. There were also country houses one after another, constructed in luxurious fashion and covered with stucco, which gave evidence of the

---

[1] The exact situation of this city is not known.

4 αὐτὰς διασημαίνουσαι πλοῦτον. ἔγεμον δ᾿ αἱ μὲν
ἐπαύλεις πάντων τῶν πρὸς ἀπόλαυσιν, ὡς ἂν τῶν
ἐγχωρίων ἐν εἰρήνῃ πολυχρονίῳ τεθησαυρικότων
γεννημάτων ἀφθονίαν· ἡ δὲ χώρα ἡ μὲν ἦν ἀμπε-
λόφυτος, ἡ δὲ ἐλαιοφόρος καὶ τῶν ἄλλων τῶν
καρπίμων δένδρων ἀνάπλεως. ἐπὶ θάτερα δὲ μέρη
τὸ πεδίον ἐνέμοντο βοῶν ἀγέλαι καὶ ποῖμναι καὶ
τὰ πλησίον ἕλη φορβάδων ἵππων ἔγεμε. καθόλου
δὲ παντοία τις ἦν ἐν τοῖς τόποις εὐδαιμονία, τῶν
ἐπιφανεστάτων Καρχηδονίων διειληφότων τὰς κτήσεις καὶ τοῖς πλούτοις πεφιλοκαληκότων πρὸς
5 ἀπόλαυσιν. διόπερ οἱ Σικελιῶται τό τε τῆς χώρας
κάλλος καὶ τὴν εὐδαιμονίαν τὴν ἐν αὐτῇ θαυμά-
ζοντες μετέωροι ταῖς ἐλπίσιν ἐγένοντο, θεωροῦντες
ἄξια τῶν κινδύνων ἔπαθλα τοῖς νικῶσι προκείμενα.
6 ὁ δ᾿ Ἀγαθοκλῆς ὁρῶν τοὺς στρατιώτας ἀναλαμβά-
νοντας αὑτοὺς ἐκ τῆς ἀθυμίας καὶ προθύμους ὄντας
εἰς τοὺς κινδύνους ἐξ ἐφόδου προσέβαλλε τοῖς τείχεσιν. ἀπροσδοκήτου δὲ τῆς ἐπιθέσεως γενομένης
καὶ τῶν ἔνδον διὰ τὴν ἄγνοιαν καὶ τὴν τῶν πολέμων[1] ἀπειρίαν ὀλίγον ὑποστάντων χρόνον εἷλε
τὴν πόλιν κατὰ κράτος· δοὺς δὲ τοῖς στρατιώταις
εἰς ἁρπαγὴν ἐνέπλησε τὴν δύναμιν ὠφελείας ἅμα
7 καὶ θάρσους. εὐθὺ δὲ καὶ πρὸς τὸν Λευκὸν Τύνητα
καλούμενον ἀναζεύξας ἐχειρώσατο τὴν πόλιν, ἀπ-
έχουσαν Καρχηδόνος δισχιλίους σταδίους. ἀμφο-

---

[1] πολεμικῶν Fischer.

---

[1] Of Megalepolis.
[2] The city cannot be certainly identified. If it is Tunis, as

wealth of the people who possessed them. The farm 310 B.C. buildings were filled with everything that was needful for enjoyment, seeing that the inhabitants in a long period of peace had stored up an abundant variety of products. Part of the land was planted with vines, and part yielded olives and was also planted thickly with other varieties of fruit-bearing trees. On each side herds of cattle and flocks of sheep pastured on the plain, and the neighbouring meadows were filled with grazing horses. In general there was a manifold prosperity in the region, since the leading Carthaginians had laid out there their private estates and with their wealth had beautified them for their enjoyment. Therefore the Sicilians, amazed at the beauty of the land and at its prosperity, were buoyed up by expectation, for they beheld prizes commensurate with their dangers ready at hand for the victors ; and Agathocles, seeing that the soldiers were recovering from their discouragement and had become eager for battle, attacked the city walls [1] by direct assault. Since the onset was unforeseen and the inhabitants, because they did not know what was happening and because they had had no experience in the wars, resisted only a short time, he took the city by storm ; and giving it over to his soldiers for pillage, he at a single stroke loaded his army with booty and filled it with confidence. Then, setting out immediately for White Tunis,[2] as it is called, he subdued this city, which lies about two thousand stades from Carthage.

seems probable, it is distant from Carthage only about 12 miles. In any case, since the city in question must lie between Cape Bon and Carthage, the 2000 stades (about 240 miles) is certainly wrong (cp. Beloch, *Griechische Geschichte*[2], 3. 2. 206).

τέρας δὲ τὰς ἁλούσας πόλεις οἱ μὲν στρατιῶται
διαφυλάττειν ἠβούλοντο καὶ τὰς ὠφελείας εἰς αὐτὰς
ἀπετίθεντο· ὁ δ' Ἀγαθοκλῆς ἀκόλουθα τοῖς προ-
πεπραγμένοις διανοηθεὶς καὶ διδάξας τὸ πλῆθος ὡς
οὐδεμίαν συμφέρει καταφυγὴν ἀπολιπεῖν ἕως ἂν
παρατάξει νικήσωσι, κατέστρεψέ τε τὰς πόλεις
καὶ κατεστρατοπέδευσεν ἐν ὑπαίθρῳ.

9. Οἱ δ' ἐφορμοῦντες[1] Καρχηδόνιοι τῷ ναυ-
στάθμῳ τῶν Σικελιωτῶν τὸ μὲν πρῶτον ὁρῶντες
καομένας τὰς ναῦς περιχαρεῖς ἦσαν, ὡς διὰ τὸν
ἀπ' αὐτῶν φόβον ἠναγκασμένων τῶν πολεμίων
διαφθεῖραι τὰ σκάφη· ὡς δ' ἴδον εἰς τὴν χώραν
προάγουσαν[2] τὴν τῶν ἐναντίων δύναμιν, συλλογι-
ζόμενοι περὶ τῶν ἀποβησομένων συμφορὰν ἰδίαν
ἡγοῦντο τὴν τῶν νεῶν ἀπώλειαν. διὸ καὶ ταῖς
πρῴραις δέρρεις κατεπέτασαν, ὅπερ ἀεὶ ποιεῖν εἰώθασιν ὅταν τι κακὸν δημοσίᾳ συμβεβηκέναι δόξῃ
2 τῇ Καρχηδονίων πόλει,[3] ἔλαβόν τε καὶ τὰ χαλκώματα τῶν Ἀγαθοκλέους νεῶν εἰς τὰς ἰδίας τριήρεις
καὶ τοὺς ἀπαγγελοῦντας ὑπὲρ τῶν συμβεβηκότων
τἀκριβὲς ἐξαπέστειλαν εἰς τὴν Καρχηδόνα. πρὶν
δὲ τούτους δηλῶσαι τὸ γεγονός, ἀπὸ τῆς χώρας
τινὲς αἰσθόμενοι τὸν κατάπλουν τὸν Ἀγαθοκλέους
3 ἀπήγγειλαν κατὰ σπουδὴν τοῖς Καρχηδονίοις. οἱ
δ' ἐκπλαγέντες διὰ τὸ παράδοξον ὑπέλαβον ἀπολωλέναι τὰς ἰδίας δυνάμεις ἐν Σικελίᾳ καὶ τὰς
πεζικὰς καὶ τὰς ναυτικάς· οὐ γὰρ ἄν ποτε τὸν
Ἀγαθοκλέα μὴ νενικηκότα τολμῆσαι καταλιπεῖν
ἐρήμους βοηθείας τὰς Συρακούσσας οὐδ' ἂν ἐπι-
βαλέσθαι περαιοῦν δύναμιν θαλαττοκρατούντων[4]

[1] ἐφορμοῦντες editors : ἐφορμῶντες.
[2] προάγουσαν Rhodoman : προσάγουσαν.

The soldiers wished to garrison both of the captured 310 B.C. cities and deposit the booty in them ; but Agathocles, meditating actions conforming to those that had already been accomplished and telling the crowd that it was advantageous to leave behind them no places of refuge until they should have been victorious in battle, destroyed the cities and camped in the open.

9. When the Carthaginians who lay at anchor off the station where the Sicilian fleet was beached saw the ships burning, they were delighted, thinking that it was through fear of themselves that the enemy had been forced to destroy his ships ; but when they saw that the army of their opponents was moving into the country, as they reckoned up the consequences, they concluded that the destruction of the fleet was their own misfortune. Therefore they spread hides over the prows of their ships as they were in the habit of doing whenever it seemed that any public misfortune had befallen the city of Carthage ; and, after taking the bronze beaks of the ships of Agathocles on board their own triremes, they sent to Carthage messengers to report exactly what had happened. But before these had explained the situation, the country folk who had seen the landing of Agathocles, reported it quickly to the Carthaginians. Panic-stricken at the unexpected event, they supposed that their own forces in Sicily, both army and navy, had been destroyed ; for Agathocles, they believed, would never have ventured to leave Syracuse stripped of defenders unless he had been victorious, nor to transport an army across the straits

---

³ πόλει added by editors.   ⁴ θαλασσοκρατούντων MSS.

4 τῶν πολεμίων. διόπερ θόρυβος καὶ πολλὴ ταραχὴ
κατεῖχε τὴν πόλιν καὶ συνδρομὴ τῶν ὄχλων εἰς τὴν
ἀγορὰν ἐγίνετο καὶ βουλὴ τῆς γερουσίας ὅ τι δέοι
πράττειν. στρατόπεδον μὲν γὰρ οὐκ ἦν ἕτοιμον
τὸ δυνάμενον ἀντιτάξασθαι, τὸ δὲ πολιτικὸν πλῆθος
ἄπειρον ὂν πολέμου προκαταπεπτώκει ταῖς ψυχαῖς,
οἱ πολέμιοι δὲ πλησίον εἶναι τῶν τειχῶν προσεδο-
5 κῶντο. ἔνιοι μὲν οὖν ἔφασαν πρεσβευτὰς ὑπὲρ
εἰρήνης ἀποστέλλειν πρὸς Ἀγαθοκλέα, τοὺς αὐτοὺς
ἅμα καὶ κατασκόπους ἐσομένους τῶν παρὰ τοῖς
πολεμίοις, τινὲς δὲ ἀναμεῖναι μέχρι ἂν γνῶσιν
ἀκριβῶς ἕκαστον τῶν πεπραγμένων. τοιαύτης δὲ
συγχύσεως τὴν πόλιν ἐχούσης κατέπλευσαν οἱ
πεμφθέντες ὑπὸ τοῦ ναυάρχου καὶ τὰς αἰτίας τῶν
πεπραγμένων ἐδήλωσαν.

10. Ἀναθαρσησάντων οὖν πάντων πάλιν ταῖς
ψυχαῖς ἡ γερουσία τοὺς μὲν ναυάρχους ἅπαντας
κατεμέμψατο ὅτι θαλαττοκρατοῦντες εἴασαν πολεμίαν δύναμιν ἐπιβῆναι τῆς Λιβύης, στρατηγοὺς
δὲ ἀπέδειξαν τῶν δυνάμεων Ἄννωνα καὶ Βορ-
2 μίλκαν, πατρῴαν ἔχθραν ἔχοντας· ἡγοῦντο γὰρ διὰ
τὴν ἰδίαν τούτοις ἀπιστίαν καὶ διαφορὰν κοινὴν ἔσεσθαι τῆς πόλεως ἀσφάλειαν. πολὺ δὲ διεσφάλησαν
τῆς ἀληθείας. ὁ γὰρ Βορμίλκας πάλαι μὲν ἦν ἐπιθυμητὴς τυραννίδος, οὐκ ἔχων δ' ἐξουσίαν οὐδὲ
καιρὸν οἰκεῖον ταῖς ἐπιβολαῖς τότε ἔλαβεν ἀφορμὰς
3 ἀξιολόγους, τυχὼν τῆς στρατηγίας. αἰτία δὲ
μάλιστα τούτων ἡ πρὸς τὰς τιμωρίας πικρία τῶν

---

[1] This Hanno is otherwise unknown. Bormilcar (or
Bomilcar according to the more usual spelling) was the son
of a brother of the Hamilcar who had negotiated a treaty
between Agathocles and certain Sicilian cities (Book 19. 71. 6)

while the enemy controlled the sea. Therefore panic 310 B.C.
and great confusion seized upon the city ; the crowds
rushed to the market place, and the council of elders
consulted what should be done. In fact there was
no army at hand that could take the field against the
enemy ; the mass of the citizens, who had had no
experience in warfare, were already in despair ; and
the enemy was thought to be near the walls. Accordingly, some proposed to send envoys to Agathocles to sue for peace, these same men serving also
as spies to observe the situation of the enemy ; but
some urged that they should delay until they had
learned precisely what had taken place. However,
while such confusion prevailed in the city, the messengers sent by the commander of the fleet sailed in
and made clear the true explanation of what had
happened.

10. Now that all had regained their courage, the
council reprimanded all the commanders of the fleet
because, although controlling the sea, they had
allowed a hostile army to set foot on Libya ; and
it appointed as generals of the armies Hanno and
Bormilcar,[1] men who had an inherited feud. The
councillors thought, indeed, that because of the
private mistrust and enmity of the generals the safety
of the city as a whole would be secured ; but they
completely missed the truth. For Bormilcar, who
had long had his heart set on tyranny but had lacked
authority and a proper occasion for his attempt, now
gained an excellent starting point by getting the
command as general. The basic cause in this matter
was the Carthaginians' severity in inflicting punish-

and was recalled because of his supposed friendship with
Agathocles (Justin, 22. 2. 6, 7. 10) ; cp. p. 28, note 1.

Καρχηδονίων· τοὺς γὰρ ἐπιφανεστάτους τῶν ἀνδρῶν ἐν μὲν τοῖς πολέμοις προάγουσιν ἐπὶ τὰς ἡγεμονίας, νομίζοντες δεῖν αὐτοὺς τῶν ὅλων προκινδυνεύειν· ὅταν δὲ τύχωσι τῆς εἰρήνης, τοὺς αὐτοὺς τούτους συκοφαντοῦσι καὶ κρίσεις ἀδίκους ἐπιφέροντες διὰ 4 τὸν φθόνον τιμωρίαις περιβάλλουσι. διὸ καὶ τῶν ἐπὶ τὰς ἡγεμονίας ταττομένων τινὲς μὲν φοβού- μενοι τὰς ἐν τῷ δικαστηρίῳ κρίσεις ἀποστάται γίνονται τῆς ἡγεμονίας,[1] τινὲς δ' ἐπιτίθενται τυραν- νίσιν· ὅπερ καὶ τότε Βορμίλκας ὁ ἕτερος τῶν στρατηγῶν ἐποίησε· περὶ οὗ μικρὸν ὕστερον ἐροῦ- μεν.

5 Οἱ δ'[2] οὖν στρατηγοὶ τῶν Καρχηδονίων ὁρῶντες τὸν καιρὸν οὐδαμῶς ἀναβολῆς οἰκεῖον τοὺς μὲν ἀπὸ τῆς χώρας καὶ τῶν συμμαχίδων πόλεων στρα- τιώτας οὐκ ἀνέμειναν, αὐτοὺς δὲ τοὺς πολιτικοὺς ἐξήγαγον εἰς ὕπαιθρον, ὄντας πεζοὺς μὲν οὐκ ἐλάττους τετρακισμυρίων, ἱππεῖς δὲ χιλίους, ἅρματα 6 δὲ δισχίλια. καταλαβόμενοι δέ τινα γεώλοφον οὐ μακρὰν τῶν πολεμίων ἐξέταττον τὴν δύναμιν εἰς μάχην· καὶ τοῦ μὲν δεξιοῦ κέρατος Ἅννων εἶχε τὴν ἡγεμονίαν, συναγωνιζομένων αὐτῷ τῶν εἰς τὸν ἱερὸν λόχον συντεταγμένων, τοῦ δ' εὐωνύμου Βορ- μίλκας ἡγούμενος βαθεῖαν ἐποίει τὴν φάλαγγα, κωλύοντος τοῦ τόπου παρεκτείνειν ἐπὶ πλεῖον· τὰ δ' ἅρματα καὶ τοὺς ἱππεῖς πρὸ τῆς φάλαγγος ἔστησαν, διεγνωκότες τούτοις πρῶτον ἐμβαλεῖν καὶ τῶν Ἑλλήνων ἀποπειραθῆναι.

11. Ὁ δ' Ἀγαθοκλῆς κατασκεψάμενος τὰς τῶν βαρβάρων τάξεις τὸ μὲν δεξιὸν κέρας ἔδωκεν Ἀρχα-

[1] τῆς ἡγεμονίας omitted by Madvig.
[2] δ' F, Dindorf: γ' RX, Fischer.

ments. In their wars they advance their leading men 310 B.C.
to commands, taking it for granted that these should
be first to brave danger for the whole state ; but when
they gain peace, they plague these same men with
suits, bring false charges against them through envy,
and load them down with penalties. Therefore some
of those who are placed in positions of command,
fearing the trials in the courts, desert their posts, but
others attempt to become tyrants ; and this is what
Bormilcar, one of the two generals, did on this occasion ; about him we shall speak a little later.[1]

But to resume, the generals of the Carthaginians,
seeing that the situation was not at all consistent with
delay, did not await soldiers from the country and
from the allied cities ; but they led the citizen
soldiers themselves into the field, in number not less
than forty thousand foot-soldiers, one thousand horsemen, and two thousand chariots.[2] Occupying a slight
elevation not far from the enemy, they drew up their
army for battle. Hanno had command of the right
wing, those enrolled in the Sacred Band [3] fighting
beside him ; and Bormilcar, commanding the left,
made his phalanx deep since the terrain prevented
him from extending it on a broader front. The
chariots and the cavalry they stationed in front of the
phalanx, having determined to strike with these first
and test the temper of the Greeks.

11. After Agathocles had viewed the array of the
barbarians, he entrusted the right wing to his son

[1] Cp. chaps. 12. 5 ; 43-44.
[2] According to Justin, 22. 6. 5, the army consisted of
30,000 men from the country districts (*pagani*) under the
leadership of Hanno alone, cp. Orosius, 4. 6. 25.
[3] In Book 16. 80. 4 we are told that the Sacred Band consisted of 2500 men, outstanding for valour and wealth.

γάθῳ τῷ υἱῷ, παραδοὺς αὐτῷ πεζοὺς δισχιλίους καὶ πεντακοσίους, ἐξῆς δ' ἔταξε τοὺς Συρακοσίους, ὄντας τρισχιλίους πεντακοσίους, εἶτα μισθοφόρους Ἕλληνας τρισχιλίους, τελευταίους δὲ Σαμνίτας καὶ Τυρρηνοὺς καὶ Κελτοὺς τρισχιλίους. μετὰ δὲ τῆς θεραπείας αὐτὸς τοῦ λαιοῦ[1] κέρατος προηγωνίζετο, χιλίοις ὁπλίταις πρὸς τὸν ἱερὸν λόχον τῶν Καρχηδονίων ἀντιτεταγμένος· τοὺς δὲ τοξότας καὶ σφενδονήτας πεντακοσίους ὄντας ἐπὶ τὰ κέρατα διεῖλεν.

2 ὅπλα μὲν οὖν οἱ στρατιῶται μόγις εἶχον ἱκανά· τοὺς δ' ἐκ τῶν ἀφράκτων[2] ὁρῶν ἀνόπλους ὄντας τὰ τῶν ἀσπίδων ἔλυτρα ῥάβδοις διέτεινε καὶ τῇ φαντασίᾳ τὸν τῆς ἀσπίδος κύκλον μιμησάμενος ἀνέδωκεν αὐτοῖς πρὸς μὲν τὴν χρείαν οὐδαμῶς ἐπιτήδεια, πρὸς δὲ τὴν πόρρωθεν ὁρωμένην ὄψιν δυνάμενα δόξαν ὅπλων ἐμποιῆσαι τοῖς ἀγνοοῦσι

3 τἀληθές. ὁρῶν δὲ τοὺς στρατιώτας καταπεπληγμένους τὸ πλῆθος τῆς βαρβαρικῆς ἵππου καὶ πεζῆς[3] δυνάμεως ἀφῆκεν εἰς τὸ στρατόπεδον κατὰ πλείονας τόπους γλαῦκας, ἃς ἐκ χρόνου παρεσκεύαστο πρὸς

4 τὰς ἀθυμίας τῶν πολλῶν· αὗται δὲ διὰ τῆς φάλαγγος πετόμεναι καὶ προσκαθίζουσαι ταῖς ἀσπίσι καὶ τοῖς κράνεσιν εὐθαρσεῖς ἐποίουν τοὺς στρατιώτας, ἑκάστων οἰωνιζομένων διὰ τὸ δοκεῖν ἱερὸν εἶναι τὸ

5 ζῷον τῆς Ἀθηνᾶς. τοιαῦτα[4] δέ, καίπερ ἄν τισι δόξαντα κενὴν ἔχειν ἐπίνοιαν, πολλάκις αἴτια γίνεται

---

[1] λαιοῦ Dindorf : ἡμίσους.
[2] ἀτάκτων Madvig, cp. Book 17. 80. 7.
[3] πεζῆς added by Dindorf and doubtfully approved by Fischer in apparatus.
[4] τοιαῦτα Hertlein : ταῦτα MSS., Fischer.

Archagathus,[1] giving him twenty-five hundred foot-
soldiers ; next he drew up the Syracusans, who were
thirty-five hundred in number, then three thousand
Greek mercenaries, and finally three thousand Samnites, Etruscans, and Celts. He himself with his
bodyguard fought in front of the left wing, opposing
with one thousand hoplites the Sacred Band of the
Carthaginians. The five hundred archers and slingers
he divided between the wings. There was hardly
enough equipment for the soldiers ; and when he
saw the men of the crews [2] unarmed he had the shield
covers stretched with sticks, thus making them
similar in appearance to the round shields, and distributed them to these men, of no use at all for real
service but when seen from a distance capable of
creating the impression of arms in the minds of men
who did not know the truth. Seeing that his soldiers
were frightened by the great numbers of barbarian
cavalry and infantry, he let loose into the army in
many places owls, which he had long since prepared
as a means of relieving the discouragement of the
common soldiers. The owls, flying through the
phalanx and settling on the shields and helmets, encouraged the soldiers, each man regarding this as an
omen because the bird is held sacred to Athena.[3]
Such things as this, although they might seem to
some an inane device, have often been responsible

---

[1] He is called Agatharchus in chap. 55. 5 and in Book
21. 3. 2 ; also by Polybius, 7. 2. 4.

[2] Or, reading ἀτάκτων, " the camp followers."

[3] For the owls that gave an omen of victory before the
battle of Salamis cp. Plutarch, *Themistocles*, 12. 1, and
Aristophanes, *Wasps*, 1086, together with scholia on the
passage.

μεγάλων προτερημάτων. ὃ καὶ τότε συνέβη γε-
νέσθαι· ἐμπεσόντος γὰρ εἰς τὰ πλήθη θάρσους καὶ
διαδοθέντων λόγων ὡς τὸ θεῖον αὐτοῖς φανερῶς
προσημαίνει νίκην, παραστατικώτερον τὸν κίνδυνον
ὑπέμειναν.

12. Προεμβαλόντων γὰρ εἰς αὐτοὺς τῶν ἁρμάτων
ἃ μὲν κατηκόντισαν, ἃ δ' εἴασαν διεκπεσεῖν, τὰ δὲ
πλεῖστα συνηνάγκασαν στρέψαι πρὸς τὴν τῶν πεζῶν
2 τάξιν. παραπλησίως δὲ καὶ τὴν τῶν ἱππέων[1]
ἐπιφορὰν ὑποστάντες καὶ πολλοὺς αὐτῶν κατα-
τιτρώσκοντες ἐποίησαν φυγεῖν εἰς τοὐπίσω. προ-
αγωνιζομένων δ' αὐτῶν ἐν τούτοις λαμπρῶς ἡ
πεζὴ δύναμις τῶν βαρβάρων ἅπασα συνῆψεν εἰς
3 χεῖρας. γενναίας δὲ μάχης γιγνομένης Ἄννων μὲν
ἔχων συναγωνιζόμενον τὸν ἱερὸν λόχον ἐπιλέκτων
ἀνδρῶν καὶ σπεύδων ποιῆσαι δι' αὑτοῦ τὴν νίκην
ἐνέκειτο βαρὺς τοῖς Ἕλλησι καὶ συχνοὺς ἀνῄρει.
φερομένων δ' ἐπ' αὐτὸν παντοδαπῶν βελῶν οὐκ
εἶκεν, ἀλλὰ καίπερ πολλοῖς τραύμασι περιπίπτων
ἐβιάζετο, μέχρις ὅτου καταπονηθεὶς ἐτελεύτησε.
4 τούτου δὲ πεσόντος οἱ μὲν ταύτῃ τεταγμένοι τῶν
Καρχηδονίων ἀνετράπησαν ταῖς ψυχαῖς, οἱ δὲ περὶ
τὸν Ἀγαθοκλέα μετεωρισθέντες πολὺ μᾶλλον ἐπερ-
5 ρώσθησαν. ἃ δὴ πυθόμενός τινων Βορμίλκας, ὁ
ἕτερος στρατηγός, καὶ νομίσας παρὰ θεῶν αὐτῷ
δεδόσθαι τὸν καιρὸν τοῦ λαβεῖν ἀφορμὰς πρὸς τὴν
ἐπίθεσιν τῆς τυραννίδος, διελογίζετο πρὸς αὑτόν,
εἰ μὲν ἡ μετὰ Ἀγαθοκλέους διαφθαρείη δύναμις,
μὴ δυνήσεσθαι τὴν ἐπίθεσιν ποιήσασθαι τῇ δυνα-
στείᾳ, τῶν πολιτῶν ἰσχυόντων, εἰ δὲ ἐκεῖνος νικήσας

for great successes. And so it happened on this _{310 B.C.} occasion also ; for when courage inspired the common soldiers and word was passed along that the deity was clearly foretelling victory for them, they awaited the battle with greater steadfastness.

12. Indeed, when the chariots charged against them, they shot down some, and allowed others to pass through, but most of them they forced to turn back against the line of their own infantry. In the same way they withstood also the charge of the cavalry ; and by bringing down many of them, they made them flee to the rear. While they were distinguishing themselves in these preliminary contests, the infantry force of the barbarians had all come to close quarters. A gallant battle developed, and Hanno, who had fighting under him the Sacred Band of selected men and was intent upon gaining the victory by himself, pressed heavily upon the Greeks and slew many of them. Even when all kinds of missiles were hurled against him, he would not yield but pushed on though suffering many wounds until he died from exhaustion. When he had fallen, the Carthaginians who were drawn up in that part of the line were disheartened, but Agathocles and his men were elated and became much bolder than before. When Bormilcar, the other general, heard of this from certain persons, thinking the gods had given him the opportunity for gaining a position from which to make a bid for the tyranny, he reasoned thus with himself : If the army of Agathocles should be destroyed, he himself would not be able to make his attempt at supremacy since the citizens would be strong ; but if the former should win the victory and

---

[1] ἱππέων Dindorf : ἵππων.

τὰ φρονήματα παρέλοιτο τῶν Καρχηδονίων, εὐ-
χειρώτους μὲν ἑαυτῷ τοὺς προηττημένους ἔσεσθαι,
τὸν δ' Ἀγαθοκλέα ῥᾳδίως καταπολεμήσειν, ὅταν
6 αὐτῷ δόξῃ. ταῦτα δὲ διανοηθεὶς ἀνεχώρησε μετὰ
τῶν πρωτοστατῶν, δοὺς τοῖς μὲν πολεμίοις ἄσημον
ἔκκλιμα, τοῖς δ' ἰδίοις δηλώσας τὸν Ἅννωνος
θάνατον καὶ παρακελευόμενος ἀναχωρεῖν ἐν τάξει
7 πρὸς τὸν γεώλοφον· τοῦτο γὰρ συμφέρειν. ἐπικειμένων δὲ τῶν πολεμίων καὶ τῆς ὅλης ὑποχωρήσεως
φυγῇ παραπλησίας γινομένης οἱ μὲν συνεχεῖς Λίβυες
ἀπὸ κράτους ἡττῆσθαι τοὺς πρωτοστάτας νομίσαντες πρὸς φυγὴν ὥρμησαν, οἱ δὲ τὸν ἱερὸν λόχον
ἔχοντες μετὰ τὸν Ἅννωνος τοῦ στρατηγοῦ θάνατον
τὸ μὲν πρῶτον ἀντεῖχον εὐρώστως καὶ τοὺς ἐξ
αὐτῶν[1] πίπτοντας ὑπερβαίνοντες ὑπέμενον πάντα
κίνδυνον, ἐπεὶ δὲ κατενόησαν τὸ πλεῖον μέρος τῆς
δυνάμεως πρὸς φυγὴν ὡρμημένον καὶ τοὺς πολεμίους περισταμένους κατὰ νώτου, συνηναγκάσθη-
8 σαν ἐκκλῖναι. διὸ καὶ τροπῆς γενομένης κατὰ πᾶν
τὸ τῶν Καρχηδονίων στρατόπεδον οἱ μὲν βάρβαροι
τὴν φυγὴν ἐποιοῦντο πρὸς τὴν Καρχηδόνα, Ἀγαθοκλῆς δὲ μέχρι τινὸς ἐπιδιώξας ἐπανῆλθε καὶ τὴν
στρατοπεδείαν τῶν Καρχηδονίων διήρπασεν.

13. Ἔπεσον δ' ἐν τῇ μάχῃ τῶν μὲν Ἑλλήνων εἰς
διακοσίους, τῶν δὲ Καρχηδονίων οὐ πλείους χιλίων,
ὡς δ' ἔνιοι γεγράφασιν, ὑπὲρ τοὺς ἑξακισχιλίους.
ἐν δὲ τῇ τῶν Καρχηδονίων παρεμβολῇ σὺν ταῖς
ἄλλαις ὠφελείαις εὑρέθησαν ἅμαξαι πλείους, ἐν αἷς
ἐκομίζετο ζεύγη χειροπεδῶν πλείω τῶν δισμυρίων·

quench the pride of the Carthaginians, the already 310 B.C. defeated people would be easy for him to manage, and he could defeat Agathocles readily whenever he wished. When he had reached this conclusion, he withdrew with the men of the front rank, presenting to the enemy an inexplicable retirement but making known to his own men the death of Hanno and ordering them to withdraw in formation to the high ground; for this, he said, was to their advantage. But as the enemy pressed on and the whole retreat was becoming like a rout, the Libyans of the next ranks, believing that the front rank was being defeated by sheer force, broke into flight; those, however, who were leading the Sacred Band after the death of its general Hanno, at first resisted stoutly and, stepping over the bodies of their own men as they fell, withstood every danger, but when they perceived that the greater part of the army had turned to flight and that the enemy was surrounding them in the rear, they were forced to withdraw. And so, when rout spread throughout the entire army of the Carthaginians, the barbarians kept fleeing toward Carthage; but Agathocles, after pursuing them to a certain point, turned back and plundered the camp of the enemy.

13. There fell in this battle Greeks to the number of two hundred, and of Carthaginians not more than a thousand, but as some have written, upwards of six thousand.[1] In the camp of the Carthaginians were found, along with other goods, many waggons, in which were being transported more than twenty

[1] Justin, 22. 6. 6, places the Greek losses at 2000 men, the Carthaginian at 3000. Orosius, 4. 6. 25, says that the Carthaginians lost 2000 and the Sicilians only 2.

[1] αὐτῶν editors : αὐτῶν.

2 ἐξ ἑτοίμου γὰρ οἱ βάρβαροι κρατήσειν ὑπειλη-
φότες τῶν Ἑλλήνων παρηγγέλκεισαν ἀλλήλοις
ζωγρεῖν ὡς πλείστους καὶ δήσαντες εἰς συνεργασίαν
3 ἐμβαλεῖν. ἀλλ', οἶμαι, τὸ δαιμόνιον ὥσπερ ἐπίτηδες
τοῖς ὑπερηφάνως διαλογιζομένοις τὸ τέλος τῶν
κατελπισθέντων εἰς τοὐναντίον μετατίθησιν. Ἀγαθοκλῆς μὲν οὖν Καρχηδονίους παραλόγως νικήσας
τειχήρεις συνεῖχεν, ἡ τύχη δὲ ἐναλλὰξ τὰ προτερήματα τοῖς ἐλαττώμασιν ἐπεισαγαγοῦσα τοὺς ὑπερ-
4 έχοντας ἴσον ἐταπείνωσε τοῖς ἡττωμένοις· ἐν Σικελίᾳ
μὲν γὰρ Καρχηδόνιοι μεγάλῃ νενικηκότες παρατάξει
Ἀγαθοκλέα τὰς Συρακούσσας ἐπολιόρκουν, ἐν
Λιβύῃ δὲ Ἀγαθοκλῆς τηλικαύτῃ μάχῃ προτερήσας
εἰς πολιορκίαν ἐνέκλεισε Καρχηδονίους, καὶ τὸ
θαυμασιώτατον, ὁ δυνάστης κατὰ μὲν τὴν νῆσον
ἀκεραίους ἔχων τὰς δυνάμεις ἐλείπετο τῶν βαρβάρων, ἐπὶ δὲ τῆς ἠπείρου τῷ μέρει τῆς προηττημένης στρατιᾶς περιεγένετο τῶν νενικηκότων.

14. Διόπερ οἱ Καρχηδόνιοι, νομίσαντες ἐκ θεῶν
αὐτοῖς γεγονέναι τὴν συμφοράν, ἐτράπησαν πρὸς
παντοίαν ἱκεσίαν τοῦ δαιμονίου καὶ νομίσαντες
μάλιστα μηνίειν αὐτοῖς τὸν Ἡρακλέα τὸν παρὰ
τοῖς ἀποικισταῖς[1] χρημάτων πλῆθος καὶ τῶν πολυ-
τελεστάτων ἀναθημάτων ἔπεμψαν εἰς τὴν Τύρον
2 οὐκ ὀλίγα. ἀποικισθέντες γὰρ ἐκ ταύτης εἰώθεισαν

---

[1] ἀποικισταῖς Wesseling : ἀποίκοις MSS., Fischer. Perhaps
one might read παρόντα τοῖς ἀποίκοις.

---

[1] So, too, the Spartans in a campaign against Tegea
carried fetters, and with the same result (Herodotus, 1. 66).

thousand pairs of manacles [1]; for the Carthaginians, 310 B.C
having expected to master the Greeks easily, had
passed the word along among themselves to take
alive as many as possible and, after shackling them,
to throw them into slave pens. But, I think, the
divinity of set purpose in the case of men who are
arrogant in their calculations, changes the outcome
of their confident expectations into its contrary.
Now Agathocles, having surprisingly defeated the
Carthaginians, was holding them shut up within
their walls ; but fortune, alternating victories with
defeats, humbled the victors equally with the vanquished. For in Sicily the Carthaginians, who had
defeated Agathocles in a great battle, were besieging
Syracuse, but in Libya Agathocles, having gained
the upper hand in a battle of such importance, had
brought the Carthaginians under siege ; and what
was most amazing, on the island the tyrant, though
his armaments were unscathed, had proved inferior
to the barbarians, but on the continent with a portion
of his once defeated army he got the better of those
who had been victorious.

14. Therefore the Carthaginians, believing that the
misfortune had come to them from the gods, betook
themselves to every manner of supplication of the
divine powers ; and, because they believed that Heracles, who was worshipped in their mother city,[2] was
exceedingly angry with them, they sent a large sum
of money and many of the most expensive offerings
to Tyre. Since they had come as colonists from
that city, it had been their custom in the earlier

---

[2] Or, reading τὸν παρόντα τοῖς ἀποίκοις, " who aids
colonists." The Greeks regularly identified the Tyrian god
Melkart with their Heracles.

ἐν τοῖς ἔμπροσθεν χρόνοις δεκάτην ἀποστέλλειν
τῷ θεῷ πάντων τῶν εἰς πρόσοδον πιπτόντων·
ὕστερον δὲ μεγάλους κτησάμενοι πλούτους καὶ
προσόδους ἀξιολογωτέρας λαμβάνοντες μικρὰ παντελῶς ἀπέστελλον, ὀλιγωροῦντες τοῦ δαιμονίου.
διὰ δὲ τὴν συμφορὰν ταύτην εἰς μεταμέλειαν
ἐλθόντες πάντων τῶν ἐν τῇ Τύρῳ θεῶν ἐμνημό-
3 νευον. ἔπεμψαν δὲ καὶ τοὺς ἐκ τῶν ἱερῶν χρυσοῦς
ναοὺς τοῖς¹ ἀφιδρύμασι πρὸς τὴν ἱκεσίαν, ἡγούμενοι
μᾶλλον ἐξιλάσεσθαι τὴν τοῦ θεοῦ μῆνιν τῶν ἀναθη-
4 μάτων πεμφθέντων ἐπὶ τὴν παραίτησιν. ᾐτιῶντο
δὲ καὶ τὸν Κρόνον αὐτοῖς ἐναντιοῦσθαι, καθ' ὅσον
ἐν τοῖς ἔμπροσθεν χρόνοις θύοντες τούτῳ τῷ θεῷ
τῶν υἱῶν τοὺς κρατίστους ὕστερον ὠνούμενοι
λάθρα παῖδας καὶ θρέψαντες ἔπεμπον ἐπὶ τὴν
θυσίαν· καὶ ζητήσεως γενομένης εὑρέθησάν τινες
τῶν καθιερουργημένων ὑποβολιμαῖοι γεγονότες.
5 τούτων δὲ λαβόντες ἔννοιαν καὶ τοὺς πολεμίους
πρὸς τοῖς τείχεσιν ὁρῶντες στρατοπεδεύοντας ἐδει-
σιδαιμόνουν ὡς καταλελυκότες τὰς πατρίους τῶν
θεῶν τιμάς. διορθώσασθαι δὲ τὰς ἀγνοίας σπεύδοντες διακοσίους μὲν τῶν ἐπιφανεστάτων παίδων
προκρίναντες ἔθυσαν δημοσίᾳ· ἄλλοι δ' ἐν διαβολαῖς
ὄντες ἑκουσίως ἑαυτοὺς ἔδοσαν, οὐκ ἐλάττους ὄντες
6 τριακοσίων. ἦν δὲ παρ' αὐτοῖς ἀνδριὰς Κρόνου
χαλκοῦς, ἐκτετακὼς τὰς χεῖρας ὑπτίας ἐγκεκλιμένας
ἐπὶ τὴν γῆν, ὥστε τὸν ἐπιτεθέντα τῶν παίδων

---

¹ ⟨αὐτοῖς⟩ τοῖς ἀφ. Fischer, ⟨αὐτοῖς⟩ ἀφ. Wesseling, ⟨σὺν⟩
τοῖς ἀφ. Madvig.

---

¹ These golden shrines containing images of the gods,
which are called offerings just below, seem to have been
dedications in the temples in Carthage. One may compare

period to send to the god a tenth of all that was paid 310 b.c. into the public revenue ; but later, when they had acquired great wealth and were receiving more considerable revenues, they sent very little indeed, holding the divinity of little account. But turning to repentance because of this misfortune, they bethought them of all the gods of Tyre. They even sent from their temples in supplication the golden shrines with their images,[1] believing that they would better appease the wrath of the god if the offerings were sent for the sake of winning forgiveness. They also alleged that Cronus [2] had turned against them inasmuch as in former times they had been accustomed to sacrifice to this god the noblest of their sons, but more recently, secretly buying and nurturing children, they had sent these to the sacrifice ; and when an investigation was made, some of those who had been sacrificed were discovered to have been supposititious. When they had given thought to these things and saw their enemy encamped before their walls, they were filled with superstitious dread, for they believed that they had neglected the honours of the gods that had been established by their fathers. In their zeal to make amends for their omission, they selected two hundred of the noblest children and sacrificed them publicly ; and others who were under suspicion sacrificed themselves voluntarily, in number not less than three hundred. There was in their city a bronze image of Cronus, extending its hands, palms up and sloping toward the ground, so that each of the children when placed

the silver shrines of Diana of Ephesus made and sold in large numbers in that city in the first century after Christ, Luke, *Acts of the Apostles*, 19. 24-27.   [2] *i.e.* Baal, or Moloch.

ἀποκυλίεσθαι καὶ πίπτειν εἴς τι χάσμα πλῆρες
πυρός. εἰκὸς δὲ καὶ τὸν Εὐριπίδην ἐντεῦθεν εἰληφέναι τὰ μυθολογούμενα παρ' αὐτῷ[1] περὶ τὴν ἐν
Ταύροις θυσίαν, ἐν οἷς εἰσάγει τὴν Ἰφιγένειαν ὑπὸ
Ὀρέστου διερωτωμένην

τάφος δὲ ποῖος δέξεταί μ', ὅταν θάνω;
πῦρ ἱερὸν ἔνδον χάσμα τ' εὐρωπὸν χθονός.[2]

7 καὶ ὁ παρὰ τοῖς Ἕλλησι δὲ μῦθος ἐκ παλαιᾶς φήμης
παραδεδομένος ὅτι Κρόνος ἠφάνιζε τοὺς ἰδίους
παῖδας παρὰ Καρχηδονίοις φαίνεται διὰ τούτου τοῦ
νομίμου τετηρημένος.

15. Οὐ μὴν ἀλλὰ τοιαύτης ἐν τῇ Λιβύῃ γεγενημένης μεταβολῆς οἱ μὲν Καρχηδόνιοι διεπέμποντο
πρὸς Ἀμίλκαν εἰς τὴν Σικελίαν, ἀξιοῦντες κατὰ
τάχος πέμψαι βοήθειαν, καὶ τὰ ληφθέντα χαλκώματα τῶν Ἀγαθοκλέους νεῶν ἀπέστειλαν αὐτῷ.
ὁ δὲ τοῖς καταπλεύσασι παρεκελεύσατο σιωπᾶν
μὲν τὴν γεγενημένην ἧτταν, διαδιδόναι δὲ λόγον εἰς
τοὺς στρατιώτας ὡς Ἀγαθοκλῆς ἄρδην ἀπώλεσε
2 καὶ τὰς ναῦς καὶ τὴν δύναμιν ἅπασαν. αὐτὸς δὲ
πέμψας τινὰς τῶν παρόντων ἐκ Καρχηδόνος εἰς
τὰς Συρακούσσας πρεσβευτὰς καὶ τὰ χαλκώματα
συναποστείλας ἠξίου παραδιδόναι τὴν πόλιν· τὴν
μὲν γὰρ δύναμιν τῶν Συρακοσίων ὑπὸ Καρχηδονίων
κατακεκόφθαι, τὰς δὲ ναῦς ἐμπεπυρίσθαι· τοῖς δ'
ἀπιστοῦσιν ἀπόδειξιν παρέχεσθαι τὴν τῶν ἐμβόλων
3 κομιδήν. τῶν δ' ἐν τῇ πόλει πυθομένων τὴν περὶ
τὸν Ἀγαθοκλέα προσηγγελμένην συμφορὰν οἱ πολλοὶ μὲν ἐπίστευσαν, οἱ προεστηκότες δὲ διστάζοντες

---

[1] αὐτῷ Rhodoman : αὐτοῖς.
[2] For χθονός the MSS. of Euripides give πέτρας.

thereon rolled down and fell into a sort of gaping pit 310 B.C. filled with fire. It is probable that it was from this that Euripides has drawn the mythical story found in his works about the sacrifice in Tauris, in which he presents Iphigeneia being asked by Orestes :

> But what tomb shall receive me when I die ?
> A sacred fire within, and earth's broad rift.[1]

Also the story passed down among the Greeks from ancient myth that Cronus did away with his own children appears to have been kept in mind among the Carthaginians through this observance.

15. However this may be, after such a reversal in Libya, the Carthaginians sent messengers into Sicily to Hamilcar, begging him to send aid as soon as possible ; and they dispatched to him the captured bronze beaks of Agathocles' ships. Hamilcar ordered those who had sailed across to keep silent about the defeat that had been sustained, but to spread abroad to the soldiers word that Agathocles had utterly lost his fleet and his whole army. Hamilcar himself, dispatching into Syracuse as envoys some of those who had come from Carthage and sending with them the beaks, demanded the surrender of the city ; for, he said, the army of the Syracusans had been cut to pieces by the Carthaginians and their ships had been burned, and the production of the beaks offered proof to those who disbelieved. When the inhabitants of the city heard the reported misfortune of Agathocles, the common people believed ; the magistrates,

---

[1] Euripides, *Iphigeneia among the Taurians*, 625-626. The second line is Iphigeneia's answer to Orestes ; and the sense seems to demand the insertion between the lines of some such phrase as " and answering."

διετήρησαν μὲν χάριν τοῦ μὴ γενέσθαι ταραχήν,
τοὺς πρεσβευτὰς δὲ ταχέως ἐξέπεμψαν, τοὺς δὲ
τῶν φυγάδων συγγενεῖς καὶ φίλους καὶ τῶν ἄλλων
τοὺς δυσχεραίνοντας τοῖς ὑπ' αὐτῶν πραττομένοις
ἐξέβαλον ἐκ τῆς πόλεως, ὄντας οὐκ ἐλάττους
4 ὀκτακισχιλίων. κἄπειτα τοσούτου πλήθους ἄφνω
συναναγκαζομένου τὴν πατρίδα φεύγειν ἔγεμεν ἡ
πόλις διαδρομῆς καὶ θορύβου καὶ γυναικείων κλαυ-
θμῶν· οὐδεμία γὰρ ἦν οἰκία πένθους ἀκοινώνητος
5 κατὰ τοῦτον τὸν καιρόν. οἱ μὲν γὰρ περὶ τὴν
τυραννίδα τοῦ Ἀγαθοκλέους καὶ τῶν τέκνων αὐτοῦ[1]
τὴν συμφορὰν ὠδύροντο, τῶν δ' ἰδιωτῶν οἱ μὲν
τοὺς ἀπολωλέναι δοκοῦντας κατὰ Λιβύην ἔκλαιον,
οἱ δὲ τοὺς ἐκπίπτοντας ἀφ' ἑστίας καὶ πατρῴων
θεῶν, οἷς οὔτε μένειν ἐξῆν οὔτ' ἐκτὸς τῶν τειχῶν
προάγειν, πολιορκούντων τῶν βαρβάρων, πρὸς δὲ
τοῖς εἰρημένοις κακοῖς τηλικούτοις οὖσιν ἠναγκάζοντο νηπίους παῖδας καὶ γυναῖκας συνεφέλκεσθαι
6 τῇ φυγῇ. ὁ δ' Ἀμίλκας, καταφυγόντων πρὸς
αὐτὸν τῶν φυγάδων, τούτοις μὲν τὴν ἀσφάλειαν
παρέσχετο, τὴν δὲ δύναμιν παρασκευάσας προῆγεν
ἐπὶ τὰς Συρακούσσας, ὡς αἱρήσων τὴν πόλιν διά
τε τὴν ἐρημίαν καὶ διὰ τὴν προσηγγελμένην τοῖς
ὑπολελειμμένοις συμφοράν.

16. Προαποστείλαντος δ' αὐτοῦ πρεσβείαν καὶ
διδόντος Ἀντάνδρῳ καὶ τοῖς μετ' αὐτοῦ, εἰ παρα-
διδόασι τὴν πόλιν, ἀσφάλειαν, συνήδρευσαν[2] τῶν
ἡγεμόνων οἱ μάλιστα ἀξίωμα δοκοῦντες ἔχειν.
ῥηθέντων οὖν πολλῶν λόγων Ἄντανδρος μὲν ᾤετο

however, being in doubt, watched closely that there might be no disorder, but they sent the envoys away at once ; and the relatives and friends of the exiles and any others who were displeased with the actions of the magistrates they cast out of the city, in number not less than eight thousand. Thereupon, when so great a multitude was suddenly forced to leave its native place, the city was filled with running to and fro and with uproar and the lamentation of women ; for there was no household that did not have its share of mourning at that time. Those who were of the party of the tyrant lamented at the misfortune of Agathocles and his sons ; and some of the private citizens wept for the men believed to have been lost in Libya, and others for those who were being driven from hearth and ancestral gods, who could neither remain nor yet go outside the walls since the barbarians were besieging the city, and who, in addition to the aforesaid evils, which were great enough, were being compelled to drag along with them in their flight infant children and women. But when the exiles took refuge with Hamilcar, he offered them safety ; and, making ready his army, he led it against Syracuse, expecting to take the city both because it was bereft of defenders and because of the disaster that had been reported to those who had been left there.

16. After Hamilcar had sent an embassy in advance and had offered safety to Antander and those with him if they surrendered the city, those of the leaders who were held in highest esteem came together in council. After prolonged discussion Antander thought

---

¹ αὐτοῦ Dindorf : αὐτῶν.
² συνήδρευσαν Stephanus : συνεδρευσάντων.

δεῖν παραδιδόναι τὴν πόλιν, ὣν ἄνανδρος φύσει καὶ
τῆς τἀδελφοῦ τόλμης καὶ πράξεως ἐναντίαν ἔχων
διάθεσιν· Ἐρύμνων δ' ὁ Αἰτωλός, παρακαθεστα-
μένος ὑπ' Ἀγαθοκλέους τἀδελφῷ σύνεδρος, τὴν
ἐναντίαν δοὺς γνώμην ἔπεισεν ἅπαντας διακαρτερεῖν
2 μέχρι ἂν πύθωνται τἀληθές. Ἀμίλκας δὲ μαθὼν
τὰ δόξαντα τοῖς ἐν τῇ πόλει συνεπήγνυε μηχανὰς
3 παντοίας, διεγνωκὼς προσβάλλειν. Ἀγαθοκλῆς δὲ
δύο τριακοντόρους μετὰ τὴν μάχην νεναυπηγημένος
τὴν ἑτέραν ἀπέστειλεν εἰς Συρακούσσας, ἐρέτας
ἐμβιβάσας τοὺς κρατίστους καὶ τῶν περὶ αὐτὸν
πιστευομένων φίλων ἕνα Νέαρχον, ἀπαγγελοῦντα
4 τοῖς ἰδίοις τὴν νίκην. ἔπειτ' εὐπλοίας γενομένης
πεμπταῖοι ταῖς Συρακούσσαις νύκτωρ προσεπέλα-
σαν καὶ στεφανωσάμενοι καὶ παιανίσαντες κατὰ
τὸν πλοῦν[1] ἅμ' ἡμέρᾳ κατέπλεον ἐπὶ τὴν πόλιν.
5 αἱ δὲ φυλακίδες τῶν Καρχηδονίων αἰσθόμεναι κατὰ
σπουδὴν ἐπεδίωκον καὶ οὐ πολὺ προειληφότων τῶν
ὑποφευγόντων ἀγὼν τῆς εἰρεσίας ἐγίνετο. ἅμα δὲ
τῇ τούτων φιλοτιμίᾳ συνέβη τούς τε ἐκ τῆς πόλεως
καὶ τοὺς πολιορκοῦντας αἰσθομένους συνδραμεῖν ἐπὶ
τὸν λιμένα καὶ τοῖς ἰδίοις ἑκάτεροι συναγωνιῶντας
6 ἀναβοᾶν θαρρεῖν. ἤδη δὲ τῆς τριακοντόρου κατα-
λαμβανομένης οἱ βάρβαροι μὲν ἐπηλάλαξαν, οἱ δ'
ἐκ τῆς πόλεως ἀδυνατοῦντες βοηθεῖν τοῖς θεοῖς
ηὔχοντο περὶ τῆς σωτηρίας τῶν καταπλεόντων.
τῆς πρῴρας δὲ τῶν διωκόντων εἰς ἐμβολὴν ἤδη
φερομένης οὐκ ἄπωθεν τῆς γῆς ἔφθασε τὸ διωκό-

---

[1] τὸν πλοῦν Hertlein : τὸ πλοῖον.

it necessary to surrender the city, since he was unmanly [1] by nature and of a disposition the direct opposite of the boldness and energy of his brother; but Erymnon the Aetolian, who had been set up by Agathocles as co-ruler with his brother, expressing the contrary opinion persuaded all of them to hold out until they should hear the truth. When Hamilcar learned the decision of those in the city, he constructed engines of all kinds, having determined to attack. But Agathocles, who had built two thirty-oared ships after the battle, sent one of them to Syracuse, placing on board his strongest oarsmen and Nearchus, one of his trusted friends, who was to report the victory to his own people. Having had a fair voyage, they approached Syracuse during the night of the fifth day, and wearing wreaths and singing paeans as they sailed they reached the city at daybreak. But the picket ships of the Carthaginians caught sight of them and pursued them vigorously, and since the pursued had no great start, there arose a contest in rowing. While they were vying with each other, the folk of the city and the besiegers, seeing what was happening, both ran to the port, and each group, sharing in the anxiety of its own men, encouraged them with shouts. When the dispatch boat was already at the point of being taken, the barbarians raised a shout of triumph, and the inhabitants of the city, since they could give no aid, prayed the gods for the safety of those who were sailing in. But when, not far from the shore, the ram of one of the pursuers was already bearing down to deliver its blow, the pursued ship succeeded in getting

[1] The play on words (Ἄντανδρος, ἄνανδρος) is probably intentional.

μενον σκάφος ἐντὸς βέλους γενόμενον καὶ τῶν Συρακοσίων προσβοηθησάντων ἐξέφυγε τὸν κίνδυνον.
7 Ἀμίλκας δ᾽ ὁρῶν τοὺς ἐκ τῆς πόλεως διὰ τὴν ἀγωνίαν καὶ τὸ παράδοξον τῆς προσδοκωμένης ἀγγελίας ἐπὶ τὸν λιμένα συνδεδραμηκότας, ὑπολαβὼν εἶναι μέρος τι τοῦ τείχους ἀφύλακτον, ἔπεμψε τῶν στρατιωτῶν τοὺς κρατίστους μετὰ κλιμάκων. οὗτοι δ᾽ εὑρόντες ἐκλελειμμένας τὰς φυλακὰς ἔλαθον προσαναβάντες· καὶ σχεδὸν αὐτῶν μεσοπύργιον ἤδη κατειληφότων ἡ κατὰ τὸ σύνηθες ἐφοδία παρα-
8 γενομένη κατενόησε. γενομένης δὲ μάχης οἱ μὲν ἐκ τῆς πόλεως συνέδραμον καὶ φθάσαντες τοὺς μέλλοντας τοῖς ἀναβεβηκόσι προσβοηθεῖν οὓς μὲν ἀπέκτειναν, οὓς δ᾽ ἀπὸ τῶν ἐπάλξεων κατεκρήμνι-
9 σαν. ἐφ᾽ οἷς Ἀμίλκας περιαλγὴς γενόμενος ἀπήγαγε τὴν δύναμιν ἀπὸ τῆς πόλεως καὶ τοῖς εἰς Καρχηδόνα βοήθειαν ἐξέπεμψε[1] μετὰ στρατιωτῶν πεντακισχιλίων.

17. Ἅμα δὲ τούτοις πραττομένοις ὁ μὲν Ἀγαθοκλῆς κρατῶν τῶν ὑπαίθρων τὰ περὶ τὴν Καρχηδόνα χωρία κατὰ κράτος ᾕρει καὶ τῶν πόλεων ἃς μὲν διὰ φόβον, ἃς δὲ διὰ τὸ πρὸς Καρχηδονίους μῖσος προσηγάγετο. παρεμβολὴν δὲ πλησίον τοῦ Τύνητος ὀχυρωσάμενος καὶ τὴν ἱκανὴν ἀπολιπὼν φυλακὴν ἀνέζευξε πρὸς τὰς ἐπὶ θαλάττῃ κειμένας πόλεις. καὶ πρώτην μὲν ἑλὼν Νέαν πόλιν κατὰ κράτος φιλανθρώπως ἐχρήσατο τοῖς χειρωθεῖσιν· εἶτα παρελθὼν ἐπ᾽ Ἀδρύμητα πρὸς μὲν ταύτην πολιορκίαν συνεστήσατο, Αἰλύμαν δὲ τὸν βασιλέα

inside of the range of missiles and, the Syracusans 310 B.C.
having come to its aid, escaped from the danger.
But when Hamilcar saw that the inhabitants of the
city, because of their anxiety and because of the sur-
prising nature of the message they now anticipated,
had run together to the port, surmising that some
portion of the wall was unguarded, he advanced his
strongest soldiers with scaling ladders. These, finding
that the guard-posts had been abandoned, ascended
without being discovered; but, when they had
almost taken the wall between two towers, the guard,
making its rounds according to custom, discovered
them. In the fighting that ensued the men of the
city ran together and arrived in advance of those
who were coming to reinforce the men who had scaled
the wall, of whom they killed some and hurled others
down from the battlements. Hamilcar, greatly dis-
tressed at this, withdrew his army from the city and
sent to those in Carthage a relief expedition of five
thousand men.

17. Meanwhile Agathocles, who had control of the
open country, was taking the strongholds about
Carthage by storm; and he prevailed on some of the
cities to come over to him because of fear, others
because of their hatred for the Carthaginians. After
fortifying a camp near Tunis [1] and leaving there
an adequate garrison, he moved against the cities
situated along the sea. Taking by storm the first,
Neapolis, he treated the captured people humanely;
then, marching against Hadrumetum, he began a
siege of that city, but received Aelymas, the king

[1] Cp. chap. 8. 7, and note.

---

[1] Fischer believes that either the number of ships or the
name of the leader has been lost.

2 τῶν Λιβύων εἰς συμμαχίαν προσελάβετο. ἃ δὴ
πυθόμενοι οἱ Καρχηδόνιοι πᾶσαν τὴν δύναμιν προ-
ήγαγον ἐπὶ τὸν Τύνητα καὶ τῆς μὲν Ἀγαθοκλέους
στρατοπεδείας ἐκυρίευσαν, τῇ πόλει δὲ μηχανὰς
3 προσαγαγόντες συνεχεῖς προσβολὰς ἐποιοῦντο. ὁ
δ᾽ Ἀγαθοκλῆς, ἀπαγγειλάντων τινῶν αὐτῷ τὰ περὶ
τοὺς ἰδίους ἐλαττώματα, τὸ μὲν πολὺ τῆς δυνάμεως
κατέλιπεν ἐπὶ τῆς πολιορκίας, τὴν δὲ θεραπείαν
καὶ τῶν στρατιωτῶν ὀλίγους ἀναλαβὼν λάθρᾳ
προσῆλθεν ἐπί τινα τόπον ὀρεινόν, ὅθεν ὁρᾶσθαι
δυνατὸν ἦν αὐτὸν ὑπό τε¹ τῶν Ἀδρυμητινῶν καὶ
τῶν Καρχηδονίων τῶν τὸν Τύνητα πολιορκούντων.
4 νυκτὸς δὲ συντάξας τοῖς στρατιώταις ἐπὶ πολὺν
τόπον πυρὰ κάειν, δόξαν ἐνεποίησε² τοῖς μὲν
Καρχηδονίοις ὡς μετὰ μεγάλης δυνάμεως ἐπ᾽
αὐτοὺς πορευόμενος, τοῖς δὲ πολιορκουμένοις ὡς
ἄλλης δυνάμεως ἁδρᾶς τοῖς πολεμίοις εἰς συμμα-
5 χίαν παραγεγενημένης. ἀμφότεροι δὲ τῷ ψεύδει
τοῦ στρατηγήματος παραλογισθέντες παραλόγως
ἠλαττώθησαν, οἱ μὲν τὸν Τύνητα πολιορκοῦντες
φυγόντες εἰς Καρχηδόνα καὶ τὰς μηχανὰς ἀπολιπόντες, οἱ δ᾽ Ἀδρυμητινοὶ διὰ τὸν φόβον παρα-
6 δόντες τὴν πατρίδα. Ἀγαθοκλῆς δὲ ταύτην δι᾽
ὁμολογίας παραλαβὼν Θάψον εἷλε κατὰ κράτος
καὶ τῶν ἄλλων τῶν ταύτῃ πόλεων ἃς μὲν ἐξεπολιόρκησεν, ἃς δὲ προσηγάγετο· τὰς ἁπάσας δὲ
πόλεις πλείους τῶν διακοσίων κεχειρωμένος εἰς
τοὺς ἄνω τόπους τῆς Λιβύης διενοεῖτο στρατεύειν.
18. Ἀναζεύξαντος οὖν αὐτοῦ καὶ πλείους ἡμέρας
ὁδοιπορῦντος Καρχηδόνιοι τὴν ἐκ Σικελίας δια-
κομισθεῖσαν δύναμιν καὶ τὴν ἄλλην στρατιὰν προ-
αγαγόντες πάλιν τὸν Τύνητα πολιορκεῖν ἐπεχείρησαν

of the Libyans, into alliance. On hearing of these
moves the Carthaginians brought their entire army
against Tunis and captured the encampment of
Agathocles ; then, after bringing siege engines up
to the city, they made unremitting attacks. But
Agathocles, when some had reported to him the
reverses suffered by his men, left the larger part of
his army for the siege, but with his retinue and a few
of the soldiers went secretly to a place in the mountains whence he could be seen both by the people
of Hadrumetum and by the Carthaginians who were
besieging Tunis. By instructing his soldiers to light
fires at night over a great area, he caused the Carthaginians to believe that he was coming against them
with a large army, while the besieged thought that
another strong force was at hand as an ally for their
enemy. Both of them, deceived by the deceptive
stratagem, suffered an unexpected defeat : those
who were besieging Tunis fled to Carthage abandoning their siege engines, and the people of Hadrumetum surrendered their home-land because of their
fright. After receiving this city on terms, Agathocles
took Thapsus by force ; and of the other cities of the
region some he took by storm and some he won by
persuasion. When he had gained control of all the
cities, which were more than two hundred in number,
he had in mind to lead his army into the inland
regions of Libya.

18. After Agathocles had set out and had marched
for a good many days, the Carthaginians, advancing
with the force that had been brought across from
Sicily and their other army, again undertook the siege

---

[1] τε Dindorf : τῆς.
[2] ἐνεποίησε Hertlein : ἐποίησε.

καὶ τῶν χωρίων οὐκ ὀλίγα τῶν ὑπὸ τοὺς πολεμίους
ὄντων ἀνεκτήσαντο. Ἀγαθοκλῆς δέ, βιβλιαφόρων
αὐτῷ παραγεγενημένων ἀπὸ τοῦ Τύνητος καὶ τὰ
πεπραγμένα τοῖς Φοίνιξι διασαφούντων, εὐθὺς ἀν-
2 έστρεψεν. ὡς δ' ἀπέσχε τῶν πολεμίων σταδίους
διακοσίους, κατεστρατοπέδευσε καὶ τοῖς στρατιώταις πυρὰ κάειν ἀπηγόρευσεν. χρησάμενος δὲ
νυκτοπορίᾳ προσέπεσεν ἅμ' ἡμέρᾳ τοῖς τε προνο-
μεύουσι τὴν χώραν καὶ τοῖς ἐκτὸς τῆς παρεμβολῆς
ἄνευ τάξεως πλανωμένοις καὶ φονεύσας μὲν ὑπὲρ
δισχιλίους, ζωγρήσας δ' οὐκ ὀλίγους πολλὰ πρὸς
3 τὸ μέλλον ἐπλεονέκτησεν. οἱ γὰρ Καρχηδόνιοι τῆς
ἐκ Σικελίας προσγενομένης βοηθείας καὶ τῶν κατὰ
Λιβύην συμμάχων συναγωνιζομένων ἐδόκουν ὑπερ-
έχειν τῶν περὶ τὸν Ἀγαθοκλέα· τούτου δὲ τοῦ[1]
προτερήματος γενομένου πάλιν συνεστάλη τὰ φρονήματα τῶν βαρβάρων. καὶ γὰρ Αἴλυμαν τὸν
βασιλέα τῶν Λιβύων ἀποστάτην γενόμενον ἐνίκησεν[2] μάχῃ καὶ τόν τε δυνάστην καὶ πολλοὺς τῶν
βαρβάρων ἀνεῖλεν.[3]

Καὶ τὰ μὲν περὶ Σικελίαν καὶ Λιβύην ἐν τούτοις
ἦν.

19. Κατὰ δὲ τὴν Μακεδονίαν Κάσανδρος μὲν
βοηθήσας Αὐδολέοντι τῷ Παιόνων βασιλεῖ διαπο-
λεμοῦντι πρὸς Αὐταριάτας, τοῦτον μὲν ἐκ τῶν
κινδύνων ἐρρύσατο, τοὺς δὲ Αὐταριάτας σὺν τοῖς
ἀκολουθοῦσι παισὶ καὶ γυναιξὶν ὄντας εἰς δισμυρίους κατῴκισεν παρὰ τὸ καλούμενον Ὀρβηλὸν[4]

---

[1] Fischer adds ἐπὶ before τοῦ προτερήματος, cp. Books 15. 35. 1 ; 16. 5. 2.

[2] ἐνίκησεν editors : ἐνίκησαν.

[3] ἀνεῖλεν editors : ἀνεῖλον.

[4] Ὀρβηλὸν Wesseling : Ὀρβηδὸν RX, Ὀρβίταον F.

of Tunis ; and they recaptured many of the positions 310 B.C. that were in the hands of the enemy. But Agathocles, since dispatch bearers had come to him from Tunis and disclosed what the Phoenicians had done, at once turned back. When he was at a distance of about two hundred stades [1] from the enemy, he pitched camp and forbade his soldiers to light fires. Then, making a night march, he fell at dawn upon those who were foraging in the country and those who were wandering outside their camp in disorder, and by killing over two thousand and taking captive no small number he greatly strengthened himself for the future. For the Carthaginians, now that their reinforcements from Sicily had arrived and that their Libyan allies were fighting along with them, seemed to be superior to Agathocles ; but as soon as he gained this success, the confidence of the barbarians again waned. In fact, he defeated in battle Aelymas, the king of the Libyans, who had deserted him, and slew the king and many of the barbarians.

This was the situation of affairs in Sicily and Libya.[2]

19. In Macedonia,[3] Cassander, going to the aid of Audoleon,[4] king of the Paeonians, who was fighting against the Autariatae,[5] freed the king from danger, but the Autariatae with the children and women who were following them, numbering in all twenty thousand, he settled beside the mountain called Orbelus.[6]

---

[1] About 23 miles.
[2] Continued in chap. 29. 2.
[3] Continued from Book 19. 105. 4.
[4] Cp. Justin, 15. 2. 1. One of Audoleon's daughters married Pyrrhus of Epirus (Plutarch, *Pyrrhus*, 9).
[5] A strong Illyrian people living in the Dalmatian mountains.
[6] On the border between Thrace and Macedonia.

2 ὅρος. τούτου δὲ περὶ ταῦτ' ὄντος κατὰ μὲν τὴν Πελοπόννησον Πτολεμαῖος ὁ στρατηγὸς Ἀντιγόνου δυνάμεις πεπιστευμένος καὶ τῷ δυνάστῃ προσκόψας ὡς οὐ κατὰ τὴν ἀξίαν τιμώμενος Ἀντιγόνου μὲν ἀπέστη, πρὸς δὲ Κάσανδρον συμμαχίαν ἐποιήσατο. καταλελοιπὼς δὲ τῆς ἐφ' Ἑλλησπόντῳ σατραπείας ἐπιστάτην Φοίνικα, ἕνα[1] τῶν πιστοτάτων φίλων, ἀπέστειλεν αὐτῷ στρατιώτας, ἀξιῶν διαφυλάττειν τὰ φρούρια καὶ τὰς πόλεις καὶ μὴ προσέχειν Ἀντιγόνῳ.

3 Τῶν δὲ κοινῶν συνθηκῶν τοῖς ἡγεμόσι περιεχουσῶν ἐλευθέρας ἀφεῖσθαι τὰς Ἑλληνίδας πόλεις, οἱ περὶ Πτολεμαῖον τὸν Αἰγύπτου δυνάστην, ἐγκαλέσαντες Ἀντιγόνῳ διότι φρουραῖς τινας διείληφε 4 τῶν πόλεων, πολεμεῖν παρεσκευάζοντο. καὶ τὴν μὲν δύναμιν ἐξαποστείλας Πτολεμαῖος καὶ στρατηγὸν Λεωνίδην τὰς ἐν τῇ τραχείᾳ Κιλικίᾳ πόλεις οὔσας ὑπ' Ἀντίγονον ἐχειρώσατο, διεπέμπετο δὲ καὶ εἰς[2] τὰς ὑπὸ Κάσανδρον καὶ Λυσίμαχον πόλεις, ἀξιῶν συμφρονεῖν ἑαυτῷ καὶ κωλύειν Ἀντίγονον 5 ἰσχυρὸν γίνεσθαι. ὁ δ' Ἀντίγονος τῶν υἱῶν Φίλιππον μὲν τὸν νεώτερον ἐξέπεμψεν ἐφ' Ἑλλήσποντον, διαπολεμήσοντα Φοίνικι καὶ τοῖς ἀφεστηκόσι, Δημήτριον δ' ἐπὶ Κιλικίαν, ὃς ἐνεργὸν ποιησάμενος τὴν στρατείαν ἐνίκησε τοὺς τοῦ Πτολεμαίου στρατηγοὺς καὶ τὰς πόλεις ἀνεκτήσατο.

20. Ἅμα δὲ τούτοις πραττομένοις Πολυπέρχων

---

[1] ἕνα added by Fischer.
[2] εἰς added by Fischer. πρὸς Rhodoman, κατὰ Dindorf.

---

[1] A nephew of Antigonus, cp. Book 19. 57. 4.
[2] But we find that two years earlier another nephew,

While he was thus engaged, in the Peloponnesus 310 B.C. Ptolemaeus,[1] the general of Antigonus, who had been entrusted with an army but had taken offence at the prince because, as he said, he was not being honoured according to his deserts,[2] revolted from Antigonus and made an alliance with Cassander. And having left as governor of the satrapy along the Hellespont one of his most faithful friends, Phoenix,[3] Ptolemaeus sent soldiers to him, bidding him garrison the strongholds and the cities and not to obey Antigonus.

Since the agreements common to the leaders provided for the liberation of the Greek cities,[4] Ptolemy, the ruler of Egypt, charged Antigonus with having occupied some of the cities with garrisons, and prepared to go to war. Sending his army and Leonides as its commander, Ptolemy subdued the cities in Cilicia Trachea which were subject to Antigonus; and he sent also to the cities that were controlled by Cassander and Lysimachus, asking them to co-operate with him and prevent Antigonus from becoming too powerful. But Antigonus sent Philip, the younger of his sons, to the Hellespont to fight it out with Phoenix and the rebels; and to Cilicia he sent Demetrius, who, carrying on the campaign with vigour, defeated the generals of Ptolemy and recovered the cities.

20. Meanwhile Polyperchon,[5] who was biding his

Telesphorus, had revolted because he thought that Ptolemaeus was being too highly honoured, Book 19. 87. 1.

[3] Probably the former follower and friend of Eumenes, Book 18. 40. 2.   [4] Cp. Book 19. 105. 1.

[5] Polyperchon seems to have remained inactive in the Peloponnesus from 315 B.C. (Book 19. 64. 1; 74. 2) down to this time.

περὶ Πελοπόννησον διατρίβων καὶ Κασάνδρῳ μὲν
ἐγκαλῶν, τῆς δὲ Μακεδόνων ἡγεμονίας πάλαι ὀρεγό-
μενος ἐκ Περγάμου μετεπέμψατο τὸν ἐκ Βαρσίνης
Ἡρακλέα, ὃς ἦν Ἀλεξάνδρου μὲν υἱός, τρεφόμενος
δὲ ἐν Περγάμῳ, τὴν δ' ἡλικίαν περὶ ἑπτακαίδεκα
2 ἔτη γεγονώς. ὁ δ' οὖν Πολυπέρχων διαπέμπων
πολλαχοῦ πρὸς τοὺς ἰδιοξένους καὶ τοὺς ἀλλοτρίως
διακειμένους πρὸς Κάσανδρον ἠξίου κατάγειν τὸ
3 μειράκιον ἐπὶ τὴν πατρῴαν βασιλείαν. ἔγραψε δὲ
καὶ πρὸς τὸ κοινὸν τῶν Αἰτωλῶν, ἀξιῶν δίοδόν τε
δοῦναι καὶ συστρατεύειν, ἐπαγγελλόμενος πολλαπλασίους χάριτας ἀποδώσειν, ἐὰν συγκατάγωσι τὸ
μειράκιον ἐπὶ τὴν πατρῴαν βασιλείαν. τῶν δὲ
πραγμάτων αὐτῷ κατὰ νοῦν γενομένων προθύμως
θ' ὑπακουόντων τῶν Αἰτωλῶν καὶ πολλῶν ἄλλων
συντρεχόντων ἐπὶ τὴν κάθοδον τοῦ βασιλέως, οἱ
σύμπαντες ἠθροίσθησαν πεζοὶ μὲν ὑπὲρ τοὺς δισμυ-
4 ρίους, ἱππεῖς δ' οὐκ ἐλάττους χιλίων. καὶ Πολυπέρχων μὲν περὶ τὰς εἰς τὸν πόλεμον παρασκευὰς
γινόμενος χρήματά τε συνῆγε καὶ πρὸς τοὺς οἰκείως
ἔχοντας τῶν Μακεδόνων διαπεμπόμενος ἠξίου
συνεργεῖν.

21. Πτολεμαῖος δὲ τῶν ἐν Κύπρῳ πόλεων κυριεύων, ἐπειδή τινων ἐπύθετο Νικοκλέα τὸν βασιλέα
τῶν Παφίων ἐν ἀπορρήτοις ἰδίᾳ πρὸς Ἀντίγονον

---

¹ This Barsinê was the daughter of Artabazus, a Persian
follower of Darius (Plutarch, *Alexander*, 21. 4; Justin,
11. 10. 2; 13. 2. 7), and must be distinguished from the
daughter of Darius whom Alexander married at Susa in
324 B.C., who is called Barsinê by Arrian (7. 4. 4) but Stateira
by our other sources (Book 17. 107. 6; Plutarch, *Alexander*,
70. 2; Justin, 12. 10. 9).

² It is probable that he was not a son of Alexander but a

time in the Peloponnesus, and who was nursing grievances against Cassander and had long craved the leadership of the Macedonians, summoned from Pergamon Barsinê's [1] son Heracles,[2] who was the son of Alexander but was being reared in Pergamon, being about seventeen years of age.[3] Moreover, Polyperchon, sending to his own friends in many places and to those who were at odds with Cassander, kept urging them to restore the youth to his ancestral throne. He also wrote to the governing body of the Aetolians, begging them to grant a safe conduct and to join forces with him and promising to repay the favour many times over if they would aid in placing the youth on his ancestral throne. Since the affair proceeded as he wished, the Aetolians being in hearty agreement and many others hurrying to aid in the restoration of the king, in all there were assembled more than twenty thousand infantry and at least one thousand horsemen. Meanwhile Polyperchon, intent on the preparations for the war, was gathering money ; and sending to those of the Macedonians who were friendly, he kept urging them to join in the undertaking.[4]

21. Ptolemy, however, who was master of the cities of Cyprus, on learning from certain persons that Nicocles,[5] the king of Paphos, had secretly and

pretender sponsored by Antigonus, cp. Tarn, *Journal of Hellenic Studies*, 14 (1921), 18 ff.

[3] Justin, 15. 2. 3, gives the age as fifteen years.

[4] Continued in chap. 28. 1.

[5] Nicocreon of Salamis (Book 19. 59. 1 ; 62. 5 ; 79. 5) is not identical with Nicocles of Paphos since Arrian (*FGrH*, 156. F 10. 6) clearly distinguishes them ; but it seems certain that in this passage Diodorus has confused them, and that the fate described is that of the former (Parian Marble for 311/10 B.C., *FGrH*, 239. B 17).

συντεθεῖσθαι φιλίαν, ἔπεμψε τῶν φίλων Ἀργαῖον
καὶ Καλλικράτην, προστάξας αὐτοῖς ἀνελεῖν τὸν
Νικοκλέα· πάνυ γὰρ εὐλαβεῖτο μὴ καὶ τῶν ἄλλων
τινὲς ὁρμήσωσι πρὸς μεταβολήν, ὁρῶντες ἀθῴους
γεγονότας τοὺς πρότερον ἀφεστηκότας. οὗτοι μὲν
οὖν πλεύσαντες εἰς τὴν νῆσον καὶ παρὰ Μενελάου
τοῦ στρατηγοῦ στρατιώτας λαβόντες περιέστησαν
τὴν οἰκίαν τοῦ Νικοκλέους καὶ τὰ δόξαντα τῷ
βασιλεῖ δηλώσαντες προσέταξαν ἑαυτὸν ἀπαλλάξαι
2 τοῦ ζῆν. ὁ δὲ τὸ μὲν πρῶτον πρὸς τὴν ἀπολογίαν
ἐτρέπετο τῶν ἐγκαλουμένων· ὡς δ' οὐδεὶς προσεῖχεν, ἑαυτὸν ἀπέκτεινεν. Ἀξιοθέα δὲ ἡ γυνὴ τοῦ
Νικοκλέους ἀκούσασα τὴν ἀνδρὸς τελευτὴν τὰς μὲν
θυγατέρας τὰς ἑαυτῆς παρθένους οὔσας ἀπέσφαξεν,
ὅπως μηδεὶς αὐτῶν πολέμιος κυριεύσῃ, τὰς δὲ τῶν
ἀδελφῶν τῶν Νικοκλέους γυναῖκας προετρέψατο
μεθ' αὑτῆς ἑλέσθαι τὸν θάνατον, οὐδὲν συντε-
ταχότος Πτολεμαίου περὶ τῶν γυναικῶν, ἀλλὰ
3 συγκεχωρηκότος αὐταῖς τὴν ἀσφάλειαν. τῶν δὲ
βασιλείων πεπληρωμένων φόνων καὶ συμπτωμάτων
ἀπροσδοκήτων οἱ τοῦ Νικοκλέους ἀδελφοὶ συγκλεί-
σαντες τὰς θύρας τὴν μὲν οἰκίαν ἐνέπρησαν ἑαυτοὺς
δ' ἀπέσφαξαν. ἡ μὲν οὖν τῶν ἐν Πάφῳ βασιλέων
οἰκία τραγικοῖς συγκυρήσασα πάθεσι τὸν εἰρημένον
τρόπον κατελύθη.

Ἡμεῖς δὲ τὴν ἀπαγγελίαν τῶν κατὰ τὴν Κύπρον[1]
γεγονότων διελθόντες ἐπὶ τὰς συνεχεῖς πράξεις
μεταβιβάσομεν τὸν λόγον.

22. Περὶ γὰρ τοὺς αὐτοὺς καιροὺς ἐν τῷ Πόντῳ
μετὰ τὴν Παρυσάδου τελευτήν, ὃς ἦν βασιλεὺς τοῦ
Κιμμερικοῦ Βοσπόρου, διετέλουν οἱ παῖδες αὐτοῦ

---

[1] κατὰ τὴν Κύπρον added by Reiske.

privately formed an alliance with Antigonus, dis- 310 B.C. patched two of his friends, Argaeus and Callicrates, ordering them to slay Nicocles; for he was taking all precautions lest any others also should hasten to shift allegiance when they saw that those were left unpunished who had previously rebelled. These two men, accordingly, after sailing to the island and obtaining soldiers from Menelaüs the general,[1] surrounded the house of Nicocles, informed him of the king's wishes and ordered him to take his own life. At first he tried to defend himself against the charges, but then, since no one heeded him, he slew himself. Axiothea, the wife of Nicocles, on learning of her husband's death, slew her daughters, who were unwed, in order that no enemy might possess them; and she urged the wives of Nicocles' brothers to choose death along with her, although Ptolemy had given no instructions in regard to the women but had agreed to their safety. When the palace had thus been filled full of death and unforeseen disaster, the brothers of Nicocles, after fastening the doors, set fire to the building and slew themselves. Thus the house of the kings of Paphos, after meeting such tragic suffering, was brought to its end in the way described.

Now that we have followed to its end the tale of what took place in Cyprus, we shall turn the course of our narrative toward the events which follow.

22. At about this same time in the region of the Pontus, after the death of Parysades, who was king of the Cimmerian Bosporus, his sons Eumelus, Satyrus,

---

[1] A brother of Ptolemy, cp. Book 19. 62. 4.

διαπολεμοῦντες πρὸς ἀλλήλους ὑπὲρ τῆς ἡγεμονίας,
2 Εὔμηλός τε καὶ Σάτυρος καὶ Πρύτανις. τούτων
δὲ ὁ μὲν Σάτυρος ὢν πρεσβύτατος[1] παρὰ τοῦ πατρὸς
παρειλήφει τὴν ἀρχήν, βεβασιλευκότος ἔτη τριάκοντα ὀκτώ· ὁ δ' Εὔμηλος φιλίαν συντεθειμένος
πρός τινας τῶν πλησιοχώρων βαρβάρων καὶ δύναμιν ἁδρὰν ἠθροικὼς ἠμφισβήτει τῆς βασιλείας.
3 ἃ δὴ πυθόμενος ὁ Σάτυρος ἀνέζευξεν ἐπ' αὐτὸν
μετὰ δυνάμεως ἁδρᾶς καὶ διαβὰς τὸν Θάτην ποταμόν, ἐπειδὴ πλησίον ἐγένετο τῶν πολεμίων, τὴν μὲν
παρεμβολὴν ταῖς ἁμάξαις περιλαβὼν αἷς ἦν κεκο-
μικὼς τὰς ἀγορὰς οὔσας παμπληθεῖς, τὴν δὲ δύναμιν
ἐκτάξας αὐτὸς κατὰ μέσην ὑπῆρχε τὴν φάλαγγα,
4 καθάπερ ἐστὶ Σκύθαις νόμιμον. συνεστρατεύοντο
δ' αὐτῷ μισθοφόροι μὲν Ἕλληνες οὐ πλείους δισχιλίων καὶ Θρᾷκες ἴσοι τούτοις, οἱ δὲ λοιποὶ πάντες
ὑπῆρχον σύμμαχοι Σκύθαι, πλείους τῶν δισμυρίων,
ἱππεῖς δὲ οὐκ ἐλάττους μυρίων. τῷ δ' Εὐμήλῳ
συνεμάχει[2] Ἀριφάρνης ὁ τῶν Σιρακῶν[3] βασιλεύς,
ἱππεῖς μὲν ἔχων δισμυρίους, πεζοὺς δὲ δισχιλίους
5 πρὸς τοῖς δισμυρίοις. γενομένης δὲ μάχης ἰσχυρᾶς
Σάτυρος μὲν ἔχων περὶ ἑαυτὸν ἐπιλέκτους ἄνδρας
ἱππομαχίαν συνεστήσατο πρὸς τοὺς περὶ Ἀριφάρνην
ἀνθεστηκότας κατὰ μέσην τὴν τάξιν καὶ πολλῶν
παρ' ἀμφοτέροις πεσόντων τέλος ἐκβιασάμενος
6 ἐτρέψατο τὸν βασιλέα τῶν βαρβάρων. καὶ τὸ μὲν
πρῶτον ἐπέκειτο φονεύων τοὺς ἀεὶ καταλαμβανο-
μένους· μετ' ὀλίγον δὲ πυθόμενος τὸν ἀδελφὸν

---

[1] πρεσβύτατος Dindorf : πρεσβύτερος.
[2] μὲν after συνεμάχει omitted by Fischer.

and Prytanis were engaged in a struggle against each 310 B.C.
other for the primacy. Of these, Satyrus, since he
was the eldest, had received the government from
his father, who had been king for thirty-eight years;
but Eumelus, after concluding a treaty of friendship
with some of the barbarians who lived near by and
collecting a strong army, set up a rival claim to the
throne. On learning this, Satyrus set out against
him with a strong army; and, after he had crossed
the river Thates [1] and drawn near the enemy, he
surrounded his camp with the waggons in which he
carried his abundant supplies, and drew up his army
for battle, taking his own place in the centre of the
phalanx as is the Scythian custom. Enrolled in his
army were not more than two thousand Greek mercenaries and an equal number of Thracians, but all
the rest were Scythian allies, more than twenty thousand foot-soldiers and not less than ten thousand
horse. Eumelus, however, had as ally Aripharnes,
the king of the Siraces,[2] with twenty thousand horse
and twenty-two thousand foot. In a stubborn battle
that took place, Satyrus with picked cavalry about
him charged against Aripharnes, who had stationed
himself in the middle of the line; and after many had
fallen on both sides, he finally forced back and routed
the king of the barbarians. At first he pushed on,
slaying the enemy as he overtook them; but after
a little, hearing that his brother Eumelus was gaining

---

[1] One of the streams flowing into the Maeotic Lake (the
Sea of Azov). The name is also given as Thapsis and
Psathis.

[2] A strong Sarmatian people living between Lake Maeotis
and the Caucasus Mountains (but cp. the critical note).

---

[3] Σιρακῶν Mueller : Θρᾳκῶν.

Εὔμηλον προτερεῖν περὶ τὸ δεξιὸν κέρας καὶ τοὺς παρ' αὐτῷ μισθοφόρους τετράφθαι τοῦ μὲν διώκειν ἀπέστη, παραβοηθήσας δὲ τοῖς ἡττημένοις καὶ τὸ δεύτερον αἴτιος γενόμενος τῆς νίκης ἅπαν ἐτρέψατο τῶν πολεμίων τὸ στρατόπεδον, ὥστε πᾶσι γενέσθαι φανερὸν ὅτι καὶ κατὰ γένος καὶ κατ' ἀρετὴν προσῆκον ἦν αὐτῷ διαδέχεσθαι τὴν πατρῴαν βασιλείαν.

23. Οἱ δὲ περὶ τὸν Ἀριφάρνην καὶ τὸν Εὔμηλον λειφθέντες ἐν τῇ μάχῃ συνέφυγον εἰς τὰ βασίλεια. ταῦτα δ' ἔκειτο μὲν παρὰ τὸν Θάτην ποταμόν, ὃς περιρρέων αὐτὰ καὶ βάθος ἔχων ἱκανὸν ἐποίει δυσπρόσιτα, περιείχετο δὲ κρημνοῖς μεγάλοις, ἔτι δ' ὕλης πλήθει, τὰς πάσας εἰσβολὰς δύο ἔχοντα[1] χειροποιήτους, ὧν ἡ μὲν ἦν ἐν αὐτοῖς τοῖς βασιλείοις, ὠχυρωμένη πύργοις ὑψηλοῖς καὶ προτειχίσμασιν, ἡ δ' ἐκ θατέρου[2] μέρους ἐν ἕλεσιν ὑπῆρχε, φρουρουμένη ξυλίνοις ἐρύμασι, διεστύλωτο δὲ δοκοῖς,[3] ὑπεράνω δὲ τῶν ὑδάτων εἶχε τὰς οἰκήσεις. τοιαύτης δ' οὔσης τῆς περὶ τὸν τόπον ὀχυρότητος τὸ μὲν πρῶτον ὁ Σάτυρος τήν τε χώραν τῶν πολεμίων ἐδῄωσε καὶ τὰς κώμας ἐνεπύρισεν, ἐξ ὧν αἰχμάλωτα σώματα καὶ λείας πλῆθος ἤθροισε.

2 μετὰ δὲ ταῦτα ἐγχειρήσας διὰ τῶν παρόδων βιάζεσθαι, κατὰ μὲν τὸ προτείχισμα καὶ τοὺς πύργους πολλοὺς ἀποβαλὼν τῶν στρατιωτῶν ἀπεχώρησε, κατὰ δὲ τὰ ἕλη βιασάμενος ἐκράτησε τῶν ξυλίνων

---

[1] ἔχοντα Dindorf : ἔχοντι.
[2] ἡ δ' ἐκ θατέρου Dindorf : ἡ δὲ καθ' ἑτέρου.
[3] δὲ δοκοῖς Reiske, Madvig, δ' ν' δοκοῖς Bekker : δ' οἴκοις RX, δ' εὖ κίοσιν 2nd hand in R. In F the passage reads as follows : . . . ὑπῆρχε φρουρουμένη· ξυλίνοις δὲ πείσμασι διεστύλωτο· ὑπεράνω . . .

the upper hand on the right wing and that his own 3;0 B.C
mercenaries had been turned to flight, he gave up
the pursuit. Going to the aid of those who had been
worsted and for the second time becoming the author
of victory, he routed the entire army of the enemy,
so that it became clear to all that, by reason both
of his birth and of his valour, it was proper that he
should succeed to the throne of his fathers.

23. Aripharnes and Eumelus, however, after having
been defeated in the battle, escaped to the capital
city.[1] This was situated on the Thates River, which
made the city rather difficult of access since the
river encircled it and was of considerable depth. The
city was surrounded also by great cliffs and thick
woods, and had only two entrances, both artificial,
of which one was within the royal castle itself and
was strengthened with high towers and outworks, and
the other was on the opposite side in swampy land,
fortified by wooden palisades, and it rested upon piles
at intervals and supported houses above the water.
Since the strength of the position was so great,
Satyrus at first plundered the country of the enemy
and fired the villages, from which he collected
prisoners and much booty. Afterwards, however,
he attempted to make his way by force through the
approaches. At the outworks and towers he lost
many of his soldiers and withdrew, but he forced a
passage through the swamp and captured the wooden

---

[1] *i.e.* the capital city of King Aripharnes.

3 φρουρίων. ταῦτα δὲ διαρπάσας καὶ διαβὰς τὸν ποταμὸν ἤρξατο κόπτειν τὴν ὕλην, δι' ἧς ἀναγκαῖον ἦν ἐλθεῖν ἐπὶ τὰ βασίλεια. τούτων δὲ ἐνεργῶς συντελουμένων Ἀριφάρνης ὁ βασιλεὺς ἀγωνιάσας μὴ κατὰ κράτος ἁλῶναι συμβῇ τὴν ἀκρόπολιν, διηγωνίζετο τολμηρότερον, ὡς ἐν μόνῳ τῷ νικᾶν

4 κειμένης τῆς σωτηρίας. διείλετο δὲ καὶ τοὺς τοξότας ἐπ' ἀμφότερα τὰ μέρη τῆς παρόδου, δι' ὧν ῥᾳδίως κατετίτρωσκε τοὺς τὴν ὕλην κόπτοντας, μὴ δυναμένους μήτε προορᾶσθαι τὰ βέλη μήτ' ἀμύνεσθαι τοὺς βάλλοντας διὰ τὴν πυκνότητα τῶν

5 δένδρων. οἱ δὲ περὶ τὸν Σάτυρον ἐπὶ τρεῖς μὲν ἡμέρας ἔτεμνον τὴν ὕλην, ὁδοποιούμενοι καὶ διακαρτεροῦντες ἐπιπόνως· τῇ δὲ τετάρτῃ συνήγγισαν μὲν τῷ τείχει, νικώμενοι δὲ τῷ πλήθει τῶν βελῶν καὶ τῇ τῶν τόπων στενοχωρίᾳ μεγάλοις ἐλαττώμασι

6 περιέπιπτον. Μενίσκος μὲν γὰρ ὁ τῶν μισθοφόρων ἡγεμών, ἀνὴρ καὶ συνέσει καὶ τόλμῃ διαφέρων, προσπεσὼν διὰ τῆς διόδου πρὸς τὸ τεῖχος καὶ μετὰ τῶν περὶ ἑαυτὸν λαμπρῶς ἀγωνισάμενος ἐξεβιάσθη,

7 πολλαπλασίων ἐπ' αὐτὸν ἐπεξελθόντων. ὃν ἰδὼν ὁ Σάτυρος κινδυνεύοντα ταχέως παρεβοήθει καὶ τὴν ἐπιφορὰν τῶν πολεμίων ὑποστὰς ἐτρώθη λόγχῃ διὰ τοῦ βραχίονος καὶ κακῶς ἀπαλλάττων ὑπὸ τοῦ τραύματος ἐπανῆλθεν εἰς τὴν παρεμβολὴν καὶ νυκτὸς ἐπιγενομένης ἐξέλιπε τὸν βίον, ἐννέα μόνον μῆνας βασιλεύσας μετὰ τὴν τοῦ πατρὸς τελευτὴν

8 Παρυσάδου. Μενίσκος δ' ὁ τῶν μισθοφόρων ἡγεμὼν λύσας τὴν πολιορκίαν ἀπήγαγε τὴν δύναμιν εἰς Γάργαζαν πόλιν κἀκεῖθεν τὸ τοῦ βασιλέως

barricades. After destroying these and crossing the 310 B.C.
river, he began to cut down the woods through which
it was necessary to advance to reach the palace.
While this was being energetically carried on, King
Aripharnes, alarmed lest his citadel should be taken
by storm, fought against him with great boldness
since he believed that in victory alone lay hope of
safety. He stationed archers on both sides of the
passage, by whose aid he easily inflicted mortal
wounds on the men who were cutting down the woods,
for because of the density of the trees they could
neither see the missiles in time nor strike back at the
archers. The men of Satyrus for three days went on
cutting down the woods and making a roadway, bearing up amid hardship ; on the fourth day they drew
near to the wall but they were overcome by the great
number of missiles and by the confined space, and
sustained great losses. Indeed, Meniscus, the leader
of the mercenaries, a man excelling in sagacity and
boldness, after pushing forward through the passage
to the wall and fighting brilliantly together with his
men, was forced to withdraw when a much stronger
force came out against him. Seeing him in danger,
Satyrus quickly came to his aid ; but, while with-
standing the onrush of the enemy, he was wounded
with a spear through the upper arm. Grievously
disabled because of the wound, he returned to the
camp and when night came on he died, having reigned
only nine months after the death of his father Parysades. But Meniscus, the leader of the mercenaries,
giving up the siege, led the army back to the city
Gargaza,[1] whence he conveyed the king's body by

---

[1] Probably the same as the city called Gerousa by Ptolemy, *Geography*, 5. 8. 2.

σῶμα διὰ τοῦ ποταμοῦ[1] διεκόμισεν εἰς Παντικάπαιον
πρὸς τὸν ἀδελφὸν Πρύτανιν.

24. Ὃς ταφὴν συντελέσας μεγαλοπρεπῆ καὶ
καταθέμενος εἰς τὰς βασιλικὰς θήκας τὸ σῶμα ταχέως ἧκεν εἰς Γάργαζαν καὶ τὴν δύναμιν ἅμα καὶ τὴν
δυναστείαν παρέλαβεν. Εὐμήλου δὲ διαπρεσβευομένου περὶ μέρους τῆς βασιλείας τούτῳ μὲν οὐ
προσεῖχεν, ἐν δὲ Γαργάζῃ φρουρὰν ἀπολιπὼν ἐπανῆλθεν εἰς Παντικάπαιον, ἀσφαλισόμενος τὰ κατὰ
τὴν βασιλείαν. καθ᾿ ὃν δὴ χρόνον Εὔμηλος, συν-
αγωνισαμένων αὐτῷ τῶν βαρβάρων, τήν τε Γάργαζαν κατελάβετο καὶ τῶν ἄλλων πολισμάτων καὶ
2 χωρίων οὐκ ὀλίγα. ἐπιστρατεύσαντος δὲ τοῦ Πρυ-
τάνιδος μάχῃ τε ἐνίκησε τὸν ἀδελφὸν καὶ συγκλεί-
σας εἰς τὸν ἰσθμὸν τὸν πλησίον τῆς Μαιώτιδος
λίμνης συνηνάγκασεν ὁμολογίας θέσθαι, καθ᾿ ἃς
τούς τε στρατιώτας παρέδωκε καὶ τῆς βασιλείας
ἐκχωρεῖν ὡμολόγησεν. ὡς δὲ παρεγένετο εἰς Παντικάπαιον, ἐν ᾧ τὸ βασίλειον ἦν ἀεὶ τῶν ἐν Βοσπόρῳ
βασιλευσάντων, ἐπεχείρησε μὲν πάλιν ἀνακτᾶσθαι
τὴν βασιλείαν, κατισχυθεὶς δὲ καὶ φυγὼν εἰς τοὺς
3 καλουμένους Κήπους ἀνῃρέθη. Εὔμηλος δὲ μετὰ
τὸν τῶν ἀδελφῶν θάνατον βουλόμενος ἀσφαλῶς
θέσθαι τὰ κατὰ τὴν ἀρχὴν ἀνεῖλε τούς τε φίλους
τῶν περὶ τὸν Σάτυρον καὶ Πρύτανιν, ἔτι δὲ τὰς
γυναῖκας καὶ τὰ τέκνα. μόνος δὲ διέφυγεν αὐτὸν
ὁ παῖς ὁ Σατύρου Παρυσάδης, νέος ὢν παντελῶς
τὴν ἡλικίαν· ἐξιππεύσας γὰρ ἐκ τῆς πόλεως κατ-
έφυγε πρὸς Ἄγαρον τὸν βασιλέα τῶν Σκυθῶν.

[1] For ποταμοῦ Fischer in apparatus suggests πορθμοῦ; cp.
Strabo, 9. 2. 6.

way of the river [1] to Panticapaeum to his brother, 310 B.C Prytanis.

24. Prytanis, after celebrating a magnificent funeral and placing the body in the royal tombs, came quickly to Gargaza and took over both the army and the royal power. When Eumelus sent envoys to discuss a partition of the kingdom, he did not heed him but he left a garrison in Gargaza and returned to Panticapaeum in order to secure the royal prerogatives for himself. During this time Eumelus with the co-operation of the barbarians captured Gargaza and several of the other cities and villages. When Prytanis took the field against him, Eumelus defeated his brother in battle ; and, after shutting him up in the isthmus [2] near the Maeotic Lake, he forced him to accept terms according to which he gave over his army and agreed to vacate his place as king. However, when Prytanis entered Panticapaeum, which had always been the capital of those who had ruled in Bosporus, he tried to recover his kingdom ; but he was overpowered and fled to the so-called Gardens,[3] where he was slain. After his brothers' death Eumelus, wishing to establish his power securely, slew the friends of Satyrus and Prytanis, and likewise their wives and children. The only one to escape him was Parysades, the son of Satyrus, who was very young ; he, riding out of the city on horseback, took refuge with Agarus,[4] the king of

[1] Or, reading πορθμοῦ : " through the straits."

[2] Probably the isthmus to the east of the Cimmerian Bosporus, separating the Maeotic Lake from the Euxine.

[3] Probably the modern Taman on the isthmus just referred to.

[4] King Agarus is otherwise unknown, but Appian, *Mithridatic War*, 88, mentions a Scythian people called the Agari.

4 ἀγανακτούντων δὲ τῶν πολιτῶν ἐπὶ τῷ φόνῳ τῶν
οἰκείων συναγαγὼν εἰς ἐκκλησίαν τὰ πλήθη περί
τε τούτων ἀπελογήσατο καὶ τὴν πάτριον πολιτείαν
ἀποκατέστησεν. συνεχώρησε δὲ καὶ τὴν ἀτέλειαν
ἔχειν τὴν ἐπὶ τῶν προγόνων οὖσαν τοῖς Παντι-
καπαιον οἰκοῦσι. προσεπηγγείλατο δὲ καὶ τῶν
εἰσφορῶν ἅπαντας ἀφήσειν καὶ πολλὰ διελέχθη
5 δημαγωγῶν τὰ πλήθη. ταχὺ δὲ πάντων εἰς τὴν
προϋπάρχουσαν εὔνοιαν ἀποκαταστάντων διὰ τὰς
εὐεργεσίας τὸ λοιπὸν ἐβασίλευεν ἄρχων νομίμως
τῶν ὑποτεταγμένων καὶ διὰ τὴν ἀρετὴν οὐ μετρίως
θαυμαζόμενος.

25. Βυζαντίους μὲν γὰρ καὶ Σινωπεῖς καὶ τῶν
ἄλλων Ἑλλήνων τῶν τὸν Πόντον περιοικούντων[1]
τοὺς πλείστους διετέλεσεν εὐεργετῶν· Καλλαντιανῶν
δὲ πολιορκουμένων ὑπὸ Λυσιμάχου καὶ πιεζουμένων
τῇ σπάνει τῶν ἀναγκαίων χιλίους ὑπεδέξατο τοὺς διὰ
τὴν σιτοδείαν ἐκχωρήσαντας. οἷς οὐ μόνον τῆς καταφυγῆς παρέσχετο τὴν ἀσφάλειαν, ἀλλὰ καὶ πόλιν
ἔδωκε κατοικεῖν, ἐπὶ δὲ τούτοις τὴν ὀνομαζομένην
2 Ψοανκαητικὴν[2] χώραν κατεκληρούχησεν. ὑπὲρ
δὲ τῶν πλεόντων τὸν Πόντον πόλεμον ἐξενέγκας
πρὸς τοὺς ληστεύειν εἰωθότας βαρβάρους Ἡνιόχους
καὶ Ταύρους, ἔτι δ' Ἀχαιοὺς καθαρὰν ληστῶν
ἀπέδειξε τὴν θάλασσαν, ὥστε μὴ μόνον κατὰ τὴν
βασιλείαν, ἀλλὰ καὶ κατὰ πᾶσαν σχεδὸν τὴν οἰκου-
μένην, διαγγελλόντων τῶν ἐμπόρων τὴν μεγα-

---

[1] περιοικούντων Fischer in apparatus : οἰκούντων.
[2] Ψοανκαητικὴν Madvig, approved by Fischer in apparatus :
Ψόαν καὶ τὴν.

---

[1] In 313 B.C. Lysimachus had begun a siege of Callantia

the Scythians. Since the citizens were angry at the 310 B.C.
slaughter of their kinsmen, Eumelus summoned the
people to an assembly in which he defended himself
in this matter and restored the constitution of their
fathers. He even granted to them the immunity
from taxation that those who lived in Panticapaeum
had enjoyed under his ancestors. He promised also
to free all of them from special levies, and he discussed many other measures as he sought the favour
of the people. When all had been promptly restored
to their former goodwill by his benevolence, from
that time on he continued to be king, ruling in a
constitutional way over his subjects and by his
excellence winning no little admiration.

25. For Eumelus continued to show kindness to
the people of Byzantium and to those of Sinopê and
to most of the other Greeks who lived on the Pontus ;
and when the people of Callantia were besieged by
Lysimachus and were hard pressed by lack of food,[1]
he took under his care a thousand who had left their
homes because of the famine. Not only did he grant
them a safe place of refuge, but he gave them a city
in which to live and allotted to them the region called
Psoancaëticê.[2] In the interests of those who sailed
on the Pontus he waged war against the barbarians
who were accustomed to engage in piracy, the
Heniochians, the Taurians, and the Achaeans ; and
he cleared the sea of pirates, with the result that,
not only throughout his own kingdom but even
throughout almost all the inhabited world, since the
merchants carried abroad the news of his nobility, he

concerning the outcome of which we have no information.
Cp. Book 19. 73.
  [2] The name is very doubtful. Cp. the critical note.

λοψυχίαν, ἀπολαμβάνειν τῆς εὐεργεσίας καρπὸν
3 κάλλιστον τὸν ἔπαινον. προσεκτήσατο δὲ καὶ τῆς
συνοριζούσης βαρβάρου πολλὴν καὶ τὴν βασιλείαν
ἐπιφανεστέραν ἐπὶ πολὺ κατεσκεύασε. καθόλου
δ' ἐπεχείρησε πάντα τὰ περὶ τὸν Πόντον ἔθνη
καταστρέφεσθαι καὶ τάχα ἂν ἐκράτησε τῆς ἐπιβολῆς εἰ μὴ σύντομον ἔσχε τὴν τοῦ βίου τελευτήν.
πέντε γὰρ ἔτη καὶ τοὺς ἴσους μῆνας βασιλεύσας
κατέστρεψε τὸν βίον, παραδόξῳ συμπτώματι χρη-
4 σάμενος. ἐκ γὰρ τῆς Σινδικῆς[1] ἐπανιὼν εἰς τὴν
οἰκείαν καὶ σπεύδων πρός τινα θυσίαν ἤλαυνε μὲν
ἐπί τινος τεθρίππου πρὸς τὰ βασίλεια, τοῦ δ'
ἅρματος ὄντος τετρακύκλου καὶ σκηνὴν ἔχοντος
συνέβη τοὺς ἵππους διαταραχθέντας ἐξενεγκεῖν αὐτόν. τοῦ γὰρ ἡνιόχου μὴ δυναμένου κρατῆσαι τῶν
ἡνιῶν, φοβηθεὶς μὴ κατενεχθῇ πρὸς τὰς φάραγγας,
ἐπεχείρησεν ἀφάλλεσθαι· ἐμπλακέντος δὲ τοῦ ξίφους
εἰς τὸν τροχὸν συνεφειλκύσθη τῇ φορᾷ καὶ παραχρῆμα ἐτελεύτησεν.

26. Περὶ δὲ τῆς τῶν ἀδελφῶν τελευτῆς Εὐμήλου
τέ καὶ Σατύρου παραδέδονται χρησμοί, μικρὸν μὲν
ἠλιθιώτεροι πιστευόμενοι δὲ παρὰ τοῖς ἐγχωρίοις.
τῷ μὲν γὰρ Σατύρῳ λέγουσι χρῆσαι τὸν θεὸν φυλάξασθαι τὸν μῦν μήποτ' αὐτὸν ἀνέλῃ. διόπερ
οὔτε δοῦλον οὔτ' ἐλεύθερον τῶν τεταγμένων ὑφ'
ἑαυτὸν εἴα τοῦτ' ἔχειν τοὔνομα· ἔπειτα δὲ τοὺς ἐν
ταῖς οἰκίαις καὶ ταῖς ἀρούραις ἐφοβεῖτο μῦς καὶ
τοῖς παισὶν ἀεὶ συνέταττε τούτους ἀποκτείνειν καὶ
τὰς κοίτας ἐμπλάττειν. πάντα δ' ἐνδεχομένως
αὐτοῦ ποιοῦντος οἷς ᾤετο κατισχύσειν τὸ πεπρω-
μένον, κατέστρεψε τὸν βίον πληγεὶς τοῦ βραχίονος

---

[1] Σινδικῆς Wesseling : Ἰνδικῆς RX, Σκυθικῆς F.

received that highest reward of well-doing—praise. He also gained possession of much of the adjacent region inhabited by the barbarians and made his kingdom far more famous. In sum, he undertook to subdue all the nations around the Pontus, and possibly he would have accomplished his purpose if his life had not been suddenly cut off. For, after he had been king for five years and an equal number of months, he died, suffering a very strange mishap. As he was returning home from Sindicê and was hurrying for a sacrifice, riding to his palace in a four-horse carriage which had four wheels and a canopy, it happened that the horses were frightened and ran away with him. Since the driver was unable to manage the reins, the king, fearing lest he be carried to the ravines, tried to jump out; but his sword caught in the wheel,[1] and he was dragged along by the motion of the carriage and died on the spot.

26. About the death of the brothers, Eumelus and Satyrus, prophecies have been handed down, rather silly yet accepted among the people of the land. They say that the god had told Satyrus to be on his guard against the mouse lest it sometime cause his death. For this reason he permitted neither slave nor freeman of those assigned to his service to have this name; and he also feared domestic and field mice and was always ordering his slaves to kill them and block up their holes. But, although he did everything possible by which he thought to ward off his doom, he died, struck in the upper arm through the

---

[1] Or possibly, "in the hoop that supported the canopy," cp. chap. 26. 2.

2 εἰς τὸν μῦν. τῷ δ' Εὐμήλῳ χρησμὸς ἦν τὴν
φερομένην οἰκίαν φυλάξασθαι. ὅθεν πάλιν οὗτος
εἰς οἰκίαν οὐκ εἰσῄει προχείρως μὴ προδιερευνη-
σάντων τῶν παίδων τὴν ὀροφὴν καὶ τὰ θεμέλια.
τελευτήσαντος δὲ αὐτοῦ διὰ τὴν ὀχουμένην ἐπὶ τοῦ
τεθρίππου σκηνὴν ἕκαστος ὑπελάμβανε τετελέσθαι
τὸν χρησμόν.

3 Καὶ περὶ μὲν τῶν ἐν τῷ Βοσπόρῳ πραχθέντων
ἅλις ἡμῖν ἐχέτω.

Κατὰ δὲ τὴν Ἰταλίαν οἱ τῶν Ῥωμαίων ὕπατοι
μετὰ δυνάμεως ἐμβαλόντες εἰς τὴν πολεμίαν[1] ἐνίκησαν μάχῃ Σαμνίτας περὶ τὸ καλούμενον Τάλιον.
τῶν δ' ἡττηθέντων καταλαμβανομένων τὸν Ἱερὸν
λόφον ὀνομαζόμενον τότε μὲν τῆς νυκτὸς ἐπιλαβούσης οἱ Ῥωμαῖοι πρὸς τὴν ἰδίαν στρατοπεδείαν
ἀπεχώρησαν, τῇ δ' ὑστεραίᾳ πάλιν μάχης γενομένης πολλοὶ μὲν ἀνῃρέθησαν τῶν Σαμνιτῶν,
αἰχμάλωτοι δ' ἐλήφθησαν ὑπὲρ τοὺς δισχιλίους
4 καὶ διακοσίους. τοιούτων δὲ προτερημάτων γενομένων τοῖς Ῥωμαίοις ἀδεῶς ἤδη τῶν ὑπαίθρων
συνέβαινε κυριεύειν τοὺς ὑπάτους καὶ τὰς ἀπειθού-
σας τῶν πόλεων χειροῦσθαι. Καταράκταν μὲν οὖν
καὶ Κεραυνιλίαν ἐκπολιορκήσαντες φρουροὺς ἐπέθη-
καν, τῶν δ' ἄλλων τινὰς πείσαντες προσηγάγοντο.

27. Ἐπ' ἄρχοντος δ' Ἀθήνῃσι Δημητρίου τοῦ
Φαληρέως τὴν ὕπατον ἀρχὴν ἐν Ῥώμῃ παρέλαβον
Κόιντος Φάβιος τὸ δεύτερον καὶ Γάιος Μάρκιος.

---

[1] πολεμίαν Burger, Ἀπουλίαν Kaerst, Καμπανίαν Binneboessel : Ἰταλίαν.

---

[1] The word μῦς is found in medical writers with the mean-

" mouse." [1] In the case of Eumelus the warning was 310 B.C.
that he should be on guard against the house that
is on the move.[2] Therefore he never afterward
entered a house freely unless his servants had previously examined the roof and the foundations. But
when he died because of the canopy that was carried
on the four-horse chariot, all agreed that the prophecy
had been fulfilled.

Concerning the events that took place in the Bosporus, let this suffice us.

In Italy the Roman consuls with an army invaded
the hostile territory [3] and defeated the Samnites in
battle at the place called Talium. When the defeated
had occupied the place named the Holy Mount, the
Romans for the moment withdrew to their own camp
since night was coming on ; but on the next day a
second battle was waged in which many of the Samnites were killed and more than twenty-two hundred
were taken prisoners. After such successes had been
won by the Romans, it came to pass that their consuls
from then on dominated the open country with impunity and overcame the cities which did not submit.
Taking Cataracta and Ceraunilia by siege, they im-
posed garrisons upon them, but some of the other
cities they won over by persuasion.[4]

27. When Demetrius of Phalerum was archon in 309 B.C.
Athens, in Rome Quintus Fabius received the consulship for the second time and Gaius Marcius for the

ing " muscle." Cp. the Latin *musculus*, literally " little
mouse."

[2] Literally, " the house that moves itself," or " the house
that is moved."

[3] The campaign that follows is not mentioned in other
sources and the places named are all unknown. The narrative
is continued from Book 19. 105. 5.

[4] Continued in chap. 35. 1.

ἐπὶ δὲ τούτων Πτολεμαῖος ὁ τῆς Αἰγύπτου βασιλεύων πυθόμενος τοὺς ἰδίους στρατηγοὺς ἀπο-
βεβληκέναι τὰς ἐν Κιλικίᾳ πόλεις, πλεύσας μετὰ
δυνάμεως ἐπὶ Φασήλιδα ταύτην μὲν ἐξεπολιόρκησεν,
εἰς δὲ τὴν Λυκίαν παρακομισθεὶς Ξάνθον φρουρου-
2 μένην ὑπ' Ἀντιγόνου κατὰ κράτος εἷλεν. εἶτα τῇ
Καύνῳ προσπλεύσας τὴν μὲν πόλιν παρέλαβε, τὰς
δὲ ἀκροπόλεις φρουρουμένας τῇ βίᾳ κατισχύσας
τὸ μὲν Ἡράκλειον ἐξεῖλε, τὸ δὲ Περσικὸν παρα-
δόντων τῶν στρατιωτῶν ὑποχείριον ἐποιήσατο.
3 μετὰ δὲ ταῦτα εἰς τὴν Κῶν πλεύσας μετεπέμψατο
Πτολεμαῖον, ὃς ὢν ἀδελφιδοῦς Ἀντιγόνου καὶ δύναμιν πεπιστευμένος τοῦτον μὲν κατέλιπε πρὸς δὲ
Πτολεμαῖον κοινοπραγίαν ἐτίθετο. πλεύσαντος δ'
ἐκ τῆς Χαλκίδος αὐτοῦ καὶ κομισθέντος εἰς Κῶν
τὸ μὲν πρῶτον ὁ Πτολεμαῖος φιλανθρώπως αὐτὸν
προσεδέξατο· εἶτα ὁρῶν πεφρονηματισμένον καὶ
τοὺς ἡγεμόνας ὁμιλίαις καὶ δωρεαῖς ἐξιδιοποιού-
μενον, φοβηθεὶς μή τινα ἐπιβουλὴν μηχανήσηται,
φθάσας αὐτὸν συνέλαβε καὶ πιεῖν κώνιον συνηνάγκασε. τοὺς δὲ συνηκολουθηκότας στρατιώτας
ἐπαγγελίαις δημαγωγήσας κατέμιξε τοῖς μεθ'
ἑαυτοῦ στρατευομένοις.

28. Ἅμα δὲ τούτοις πραττομένοις Πολυπέρχων
μὲν ἠθροικὼς ἁδρὰν δύναμιν κατήγαγεν ἐπὶ τὴν
πατρῴαν βασιλείαν Ἡρακλέα τὸν Ἀλεξάνδρου καὶ
Βαρσίνης, Κάσανδρος δὲ καταστρατοπεδεύσαντος
αὐτοῦ περὶ τὴν καλουμένην Στυμφαίαν[1] ἧκεν μετὰ

---

[1] Στυμφαίαν Palmer : Στυμφαλίαν.

---

[1] Demetrius was archon in 309/8 B.C. In the Fasti the
consuls for 310 B.C. are Q. Fabius Maximus Rullianus for

first.[1] While these were in office, Ptolemy, the king 309 B.C.
of Egypt, hearing that his own generals had lost the
cities of Cilicia, sailed with an army to Phaselis and
took this city. Then, crossing into Lycia, he took by
storm Xanthus, which was garrisoned by Antigonus.
Next he sailed to Caunus [2] and won the city ; and
violently attacking the citadels, which were held by
garrisons, he stormed the Heracleum, but he gained
possession of the Persicum when its soldiers delivered
it to him. Thereafter he sailed to Cos and sent for
Ptolemaeus, who, although he was the nephew of
Antigonus and had been entrusted by him with an
army, had deserted his uncle and was offering co-
operation to Ptolemy.[3] When Ptolemaeus had sailed
from Chalcis and had come to Cos, Ptolemy at first
received him graciously ; then, on discovering that
he had become presumptuous and was trying to win
over the leaders to himself by conversing with them
and giving them gifts, fearing lest he should devise
some plot, he forestalled this by arresting him and
compelled him to drink hemlock. As for the soldiers
who had followed Ptolemaeus, after Ptolemy had won
their favour through promises, he distributed them
among the men of his own army.

28. Meanwhile Polyperchon, who had collected a
strong army, brought back to his father's kingdom
Heracles, the son of Alexander and Barsinê [4] ; but
when he was in camp at the place called Stymphaeum,[5]

the second time and C. Marcius Rutilus, who was later called
Censorinus. Cp. Livy, 9. 33. The narrative is continued
from chap. 21.
  [2] Both Phaselis and Xanthus are in Lycia, the former on the
east, the latter on the west coast of the promontory. Caunus is
in Caria.   [3] Cp. chap. 19. 2.   [4] Cp. chap. 20, and note.
  [5] A region of Epirus, also called Tymphaeum.

τῆς δυνάμεως. οὐ μακρὰν δὲ τῶν παρεμβολῶν ἀπεχουσῶν ἀλλήλων καὶ τῶν Μακεδόνων οὐκ ἀηδῶς ὁρώντων τὴν κάθοδον τοῦ βασιλέως, δείσας ὁ Κάσανδρος μήποτε φύσει πρὸς μεταβολὴν ὄντες ὀξεῖς οἱ Μακεδόνες αὐτομολήσωσι πρὸς τὸν Ἡρα-

2 κλέα, διεπρεσβεύσατο πρὸς Πολυπέρχοντα. καὶ περὶ μὲν τοῦ βασιλέως ἐπειρᾶτο διδάσκειν αὐτὸν ὅτι γινομένης τῆς καθόδου ποιήσει τὸ προσταττό-μενον ὑφ᾽ ἑτέρων, συναγωνισάμενος δὲ αὐτῷ καὶ τὸν νεανίσκον ἀνελὼν παραχρῆμα μὲν ἀπολήψεται τὰς προγεγενημένας κατὰ Μακεδονίαν δωρεάς, εἶτα καὶ δύναμιν ἀναλαβὼν στρατηγὸς ἀποδειχθήσεται περὶ Πελοπόννησον καὶ πάντων τῶν ἐν τῇ δυνα-στείᾳ τῇ Κασάνδρου κοινωνὸς ἔσται, τιμώμενος διαφόρως. πέρας δὲ πολλαῖς καὶ μεγάλαις ἐπαγ-γελίαις πείσας τὸν Πολυπέρχοντα καὶ συνθήκας ἐν ἀπορρήτοις συνθέμενος προετρέψατο δολοφονῆσαι

3 τὸν βασιλέα. ὁ δὲ Πολυπέρχων ἀνελὼν τὸν νεα-νίσκον καὶ φανερῶς κοινοπραγῶν τοῖς περὶ τὸν Κάσανδρον τάς τ᾽ ἐν τῇ Μακεδονίᾳ δωρεὰς ἐκομί-σατο καὶ κατὰ τὰς ὁμολογίας παρέλαβε στρατιώτας πεζοὺς μὲν Μακεδόνας τετρακισχιλίους, ἱππεῖς δὲ

4 Θετταλοὺς πεντακοσίους. προσλαβόμενος δὲ καὶ τῶν ἄλλων τοὺς βουλομένους ἐπεχείρησε μὲν διὰ τῆς Βοιωτίας προάγειν εἰς Πελοπόννησον, ὑπὸ δὲ Βοιωτῶν καὶ Πελοποννησίων κωλυθεὶς ἀνέστρεψε καὶ προελθὼν εἰς Λοκροὺς ἐνταῦθα τὴν παραχει-μασίαν ἐποιεῖτο.

29. Ἅμα δὲ τούτοις πραττομένοις Λυσίμαχος

---

[1] For further details of the murder cp. Plutarch, *De falsa*

Cassander arrived with his army. As the camps were 309 B C.
not far distant from each other and the Macedonians
regarded the restoration of the king without dis-
favour, Cassander, since he feared lest the Macedonians, being by nature prone to change sides easily,
should sometime desert to Heracles, sent an embassy to
Polyperchon. As for the king, Cassander tried to show
Polyperchon that if the restoration should take place
he would do what was ordered by others ; but, he said,
if Polyperchon joined with him and slew the stripling,
he would at once recover what had formerly been
granted him throughout Macedonia, and then, after
receiving an army, he would be appointed general
in the Peloponnesus and would be partner in everything in Cassander's realm, being honoured above all.
Finally he won Polyperchon over by many great
promises, made a secret compact with him, and induced him to murder the king.[1] When Polyperchon
had slain the youth and was openly co-operating with
Cassander, he recovered the grants in Macedonia
and also, according to the agreement, received four
thousand Macedonian foot-soldiers and five hundred
Thessalian horse. Enrolling also those of the others
who wished, he attempted to lead them through
Boeotia into the Peloponnesus ; but, when he was
prevented by Boeotians and Peloponnesians, he
turned aside, advanced into Locris, and there passed
the winter.[2]

29. While these events were taking place, Lysi-

pudicitia, 4 (p. 530) ; Justin, 15. 2. 3. According to Justin,
15. 1. 1, Polyperchon was already dead at the time of the
murder.

[2] The winter of 309/8 B.C. Henceforth Polyperchon plays
a very minor part ; in 303 B.C. he is mentioned as a supporter
of Cassander (chap. 103. 6-7).

μὲν ἐν Χερρονήσῳ πόλιν ἔκτισεν ἀφ᾽ ἑαυτοῦ Λυσι-
μαχίαν καλέσας. Κλεομένης δ᾽ ὁ τῶν Λακεδαιμονίων βασιλεὺς ἐτελεύτησεν ἄρξας ἔτη ἑξήκοντα
καὶ μῆνας δέκα, τὴν δὲ βασιλείαν διαδεξάμενος ὁ
Ἀρεὺς . . . υἱὸς[1] ἦρξεν ἔτη τέσσαρα πρὸς τοῖς
τεσσαράκοντα.

2   Περὶ δὲ τοὺς αὐτοὺς καιροὺς Ἀμίλκας ὁ τῶν ἐν
Σικελίᾳ δυνάμεων στρατηγὸς τὰ λοιπὰ τῶν χωρίων
χειρωσάμενος προῆγεν μετὰ τῆς δυνάμεως ἐπὶ τὰς
Συρακούσσας, ὡς καὶ ταύτας αἱρήσων κατὰ κράτος.

3 τὴν μὲν οὖν σιτοπομπείαν διεκώλυε πολὺν ἤδη χρόνον θαλασσοκρατῶν, τοὺς δ᾽ ἐπὶ τῆς χώρας καρποὺς
καταφθείρας ἐπεβάλετο καταλαβέσθαι τοὺς περὶ τὸ
Ὀλυμπιεῖον[2] τόπους, κειμένους μὲν πρὸ τῆς πόλεως·
εὐθὺς δὲ καὶ προσβάλλειν ἐξ ἐφόδου τοῖς τείχεσι
διεγνώκει, τοῦ μάντεως εἰρηκότος αὐτῷ κατὰ τὴν
ἐπίσκεψιν τῶν ἱερῶν ὅτι τῇ μετὰ ταύτην ἡμέρᾳ
4 πάντως ἐν Συρακούσσαις δειπνήσει. οἱ δ᾽ ἐκ τῆς
πόλεως αἰσθόμενοι τὴν ἐπίνοιαν τῶν πολεμίων ἐξέπεμψαν τῶν μὲν πεζῶν νυκτὸς περὶ τρισχιλίους
καὶ τῶν ἱππέων περὶ τετρακοσίους, προστάξαντες
5 καταλαβέσθαι τὸν Εὐρύηλον. ταχὺ δὲ τούτων τὸ
παραγγελθὲν πραξάντων οἱ Καρχηδόνιοι νυκτὸς
οὔσης προσῆγον, νομίζοντες λήσεσθαι τοὺς πολε-

---

[1] ὁ Ἀρέτα υἱὸς RX, ὁ Ἀρέου υἱὸς F. Post suggests the loss of
a line, e.g., ὁ Ἀρεὺς ⟨υἱωνὸς ὢν Κλεωμένους, Ἀκροτάτου δὲ⟩
υἱός, cp. Plutarch, *Agis*, 3.
[2] Ὀλυμπιεῖον Post, cp. Book 16. 68. 1, 83. 2 : Ὀλύμπιον.

machus founded a city in the Chersonesus, calling it _{309 B.C.}
Lysimachea after himself.[1] Cleomenes, the king of
the Lacedaemonians, died after having ruled sixty
years and ten months[2] ; and Areus, grandson of
Cleomenes and son of Acrotatus,[3] succeeded to the
throne and ruled for forty-four years.

At about this time Hamilcar,[4] the general of the
armies in Sicily, after gaining possession of the remaining outposts, advanced with his army against
Syracuse, intending to take that city also by storm.
He prevented the importation of grain since he had
controlled the sea for a long time ; and after destroying the crops on the land he now undertook to capture
the region about the Olympieum,[5] which lies before
the city. Immediately on his arrival, however, he
also decided to attack the walls, since the soothsayer
had said to him at the inspection of the victims that
on the next day he would certainly dine in Syracuse.
But the people of the city, learning the intention of
their enemy, sent out at night about three thousand
of their infantry and about four hundred of their
cavalry, ordering them to occupy Euryelus.[6] These
quickly carried out the orders ; but the Carthaginians
advanced during the night, believing that they would

---

[1] The settlers came from the city of Cardia, which had been
destroyed by Lysimachus (Pausanias, 1. 9. 8).

[2] In Book 15. 60. 4 (370 B.C.) we are wrongly told that the
reign lasted for 34 years.

[3] The translation follows the reading suggested in the
critical note.

[4] Continued from chap. 18. 3.

[5] South of the city on the shore of the Great Harbour, near
the mouth of the Anapus River.

[6] The narrow entrance at the west end of the plateau,
Epipolae, which lies above the city on the west and overlooks
the valley of the Anapus River.

μίους. ἡγεῖτο μὲν οὖν Ἀμίλκας πάντων, ἔχων
τοὺς ἀεὶ περὶ ἑαυτὸν τεταγμένους, ἐπηκολούθει δὲ
Δεινοκράτης, τῶν ἱππέων εἰληφὼς τὴν ἡγεμονίαν.
6 τὸ δὲ τῶν πεζῶν στρατόπεδον εἰς δύο φάλαγγας
διῄρητο, τήν τε τῶν βαρβάρων καὶ τὴν τῶν συμ-
μαχούντων Ἑλλήνων. παρηκολούθει δὲ καὶ πλῆθος
ὄχλου παντοδαπὸν ἐκτὸς τῆς τάξεως ὠφελείας
ἕνεκα, χρείαν μὲν στρατιωτικὴν οὐδεμίαν παρεχό-
μενον, θορύβου δὲ καὶ ταραχῆς ἀλόγου γινόμενον
αἴτιον, ἐξ ὧν πολλάκις ὁλοσχερέστεροι συμβαίνουσι
7 κίνδυνοι. καὶ τότε δὲ τῶν ὁδῶν στενῶν οὐσῶν
καὶ τραχειῶν οἱ μὲν τὰ σκευοφόρα κομίζοντες καὶ
τῶν ἐκτὸς τῆς τάξεως συνακολουθούντων τινὲς
ἐβάδιζον πρὸς ἀλλήλους φιλοτιμούμενοι περὶ τῆς
ὁδοιπορίας· στενοχωρουμένου δὲ τοῦ πλήθους καὶ
διὰ τοῦτό τισιν ἐγγενομένης ἁψιμαχίας καὶ πολλῶν
ἑκατέροις παραβοηθούντων κραυγὴ καὶ πολὺς
θόρυβος κατεῖχε τὸ στρατόπεδον.
8 Καθ' ὃν δὴ χρόνον οἱ κατειληφότες τὸν Εὐρύηλον
Συρακόσιοι μετὰ θορύβου προσιόντας τοὺς πολεμίους αἰσθόμενοι καὶ τόπους ἔχοντες ὑπερδεξίους
9 ὥρμησαν ἐπὶ τοὺς πολεμίους. καὶ τινὲς μὲν ἐπὶ
τοῖς ὑψηλοῖς ἑστῶτες ἔβαλλον τοὺς ἐπιόντας, τινὲς
δὲ τοὺς εὐκαίρους τῶν τόπων καταλαβόντες ἀπέ-
κλειον τῆς ὁδοῦ τοὺς βαρβάρους, ἄλλοι δὲ κατὰ τῶν
κρημνῶν τοὺς φεύγοντας ῥίπτειν ἑαυτοὺς ἠνάγ-
καζον· διὰ γὰρ τὸ σκότος καὶ τὴν ἄγνοιαν ὑπ-
ελήφθησαν μεγάλῃ δυνάμει παραγεγονέναι πρὸς τὴν

not be seen by the enemy. Now Hamilcar was in the
foremost place with those who were regularly arrayed
about him, and he was followed by Deinocrates,[1] who
had received command of the cavalry. The main
body of the foot-soldiers was divided into two pha-
lanxes, one composed of the barbarians and one of
the Greek allies. Outside the ranks a mixed crowd
of rabble also followed along for the sake of booty,
men who are of no use whatever to an army, but
are the source of tumult and irrational confusion,
from which the most extreme dangers often arise.
And on this occasion, since the roads were narrow and
rough, the baggage train and some of the camp-
followers kept jostling each other as they competed
for the right of way ; and, since the crowd was
pressed into a narrow space and for this reason some
became involved in brawls and many tried to help
each side, great confusion and tumult prevailed in
the army.

At this point the Syracusans who had occupied
Euryelus, perceiving that the enemy were advancing
in confusion whereas they themselves occupied higher
positions, charged upon their opponents.[2] Some of
them stood on the heights and sent missiles at those
who were coming up, some by occupying advantageous positions blocked the barbarians from the passage,
and others forced the fleeing soldiers to cast themselves down the cliffs ; for on account of the darkness
and the lack of information the enemy supposed that
the Syracusans had arrived with a large force for the

---

[1] A Syracusan exile, cp. Book 19. 8. 6.

[2] In spite of the picturesque details that follow, the fighting
probably took place in the Anapus Valley, west and south
of Euryelus and Epipolae (Beloch, *Griechische Geschichte*[2],
4. 2. 192).

10 ἐπίθεσιν. οἱ δὲ Καρχηδόνιοι τὰ μὲν διὰ τὴν τῶν ἰδίων ταραχήν, τὰ δὲ διὰ τὴν τῶν πολεμίων ἐπιφάνειαν ἐλαττούμενοι, μάλιστα δὲ διὰ τὴν ἀπειρίαν τῶν τόπων καὶ στενοχωρίαν ἀπορούμενοι πρὸς φυγὴν ἐτράπησαν. οὐκ ἐχόντων δὲ τῶν τόπων εὐρυχωρῆ διέξοδον οἱ μὲν ὑπὸ τῶν ἰδίων ἱππέων συνεπατοῦντο πολλῶν ὄντων, οἱ δὲ πρὸς ἀλλήλους ὡς πολέμιοι διεμάχοντο, τῆς ἀγνοίας ἐπισχούσης

11 διὰ τὴν νύκτα. Ἀμίλκας δὲ τὸ μὲν πρῶτον ὑπέστη τοὺς πολεμίους εὐρώστως καὶ τοὺς περὶ αὐτὸν τεταγμένους ἠξίου συγκινδυνεύειν· μετὰ δὲ ταῦτα διὰ τὴν ταραχὴν καὶ τὸν φόβον ἐγκαταλιπόντων αὐτὸν τῶν στρατιωτῶν μονωθεὶς[1] ὑπὸ τῶν Συρακοσίων συνηρπάγη.

30. Εἰκότως δ' ἄν τις παρασημήναιτο τὴν ἀνωμαλίαν τῆς τύχης καὶ τὸ παράλογον τῶν παρὰ τὰς ὑπολήψεις συντελουμένων παρ' ἀνθρώποις. Ἀγαθοκλῆς μὲν γὰρ ἀνδρείᾳ διαφέρων καὶ πολλὴν δύναμιν ἐσχηκὼς τὴν συναγωνισαμένην περὶ τὸν Ἰμέραν οὐ μόνον ὑπὸ τῶν βαρβάρων ἡττήθη κατὰ κράτος, ἀλλὰ καὶ τῆς στρατιᾶς τὴν κρατίστην καὶ πλείστην ἀπέβαλεν· οἱ δὲ τειχήρεις ἀποληφθέντες ἐν ταῖς Συρακούσσαις μικρῷ μέρει τῶν προηττηθέντων οὐ μόνον τὴν πολιορκήσασαν δύναμιν ἐχειρώσαντο τῶν Καρχηδονίων, ἀλλὰ καὶ τὸν στρατηγὸν Ἀμίλκαν, ἐπιφανέστατον ὄντα τῶν πολιτῶν, ἐζώγρησαν· καὶ τὸ θαυμασιώτατον, δώδεκα μυριάδας πεζῶν καὶ πεντακισχιλίους ἱππεῖς ὀλίγος ἀριθμὸς

220

attack. The Carthaginians, being at a disadvantage partly because of the confusion in their own ranks and partly because of the sudden appearance of the enemy, and in particular at a loss because of their ignorance of the locality and their cramped position, were driven into flight. But since there was no broad passage through the place, some of them were trodden down by their own horsemen, who were numerous, and others fought among themselves as if enemies, ignorance prevailing because of the darkness. Hamilcar at first withstood the enemy stoutly and exhorted those drawn up near him to join with him in the fighting; but afterwards the soldiers abandoned him on account of the confusion and panic, and he, left alone, was pounced upon by the Syracusans.

30. One might with reason note the inconsistency of Fortune and the strange manner in which human events turn out contrary to expectation. For Agathocles, who was outstanding in courage and who had had a large army fighting in his support, not only was defeated decisively by the barbarians at the Himeras River, but he even lost the strongest and largest part of his army [1]; whereas the garrison troops left behind in Syracuse, with only a small part of those who had previously been defeated, not only got the better of the Carthaginian army that had besieged them, but even captured alive Hamilcar, the most famous of their citizens. And what was most amazing, one hundred and twenty thousand footsoldiers and five thousand horsemen were defeated

---

[1] Cp. Book 19. 108-109.

---

[1] μονωθείς Sintenis : μόγις σωθείς.

πολεμίων, προσλαβόμενος ἀπάτην καὶ τόπον, κατὰ
κράτος ἥττησεν, ὥστ' ἀληθὲς εἶναι τὸ λεγόμενον
ὅτι πολλὰ τὰ κενὰ τοῦ πολέμου.

2 Μετὰ δὲ τὴν τροπὴν οἱ μὲν Καρχηδόνιοι ἄλλοι[1]
κατ' ἄλλους τόπους διασπαρέντες μόγις εἰς τὴν
ὑστεραίαν ἠθροίσθησαν, οἱ δὲ Συρακόσιοι μετὰ
πολλῶν λαφύρων ἐπανελθόντες εἰς τὴν πόλιν τὸν
Ἀμίλκαν παρέδοσαν τοῖς βουλομένοις λαμβάνειν
παρ' αὐτοῦ τιμωρίαν· ἀνεμιμνήσκοντο δὲ καὶ τῆς
τοῦ μάντεως φωνῆς, ὃς ἔφησεν αὐτὸν εἰς τὴν ὑστεραίαν εἰς Συρακούσας δειπνήσειν, τοῦ δαιμονίου
3 παραγαγόντος τἀληθές. τὸν δ' οὖν Ἀμίλκαν οἱ
τῶν ἀπολωλότων συγγενεῖς δεδεμένον ἀγαγόντες
διὰ τῆς πόλεως καὶ δειναῖς αἰκίαις κατ' αὐτοῦ
χρησάμενοι μετὰ τῆς ἐσχάτης ὕβρεως ἀνεῖλον. εἶθ'
οἱ μὲν τῆς πόλεως προεστηκότες ἀποκόψαντες
αὐτοῦ τὴν κεφαλὴν ἀπέστειλαν τοὺς κομιοῦντας
εἰς τὴν Λιβύην πρὸς Ἀγαθοκλέα καὶ περὶ τῶν
γεγονότων εὐτυχημάτων ἀπαγγελοῦντας.

31. Ἡ δὲ τῶν Καρχηδονίων στρατιὰ μετὰ τὴν
γενομένην συμφορὰν μαθοῦσα τὴν αἰτίαν τῶν ἀτυχημάτων μόγις ἀπηλλάγη τῶν φόβων. ἀναρχίας
δ' οὔσης διέστησαν οἱ βάρβαροι πρὸς τοὺς Ἕλληνας.
2 οἱ μὲν οὖν φυγάδες μετὰ τῶν λοιπῶν Ἑλλήνων
Δεινοκράτην στρατηγὸν ἀπέδειξαν, οἱ δὲ Καρχηδόνιοι τοῖς δευτερεύουσι[2] μετὰ τὸν στρατηγὸν τιμῇ
τὴν ἡγεμονίαν ἐνεχείρισαν.

Καθ' ὃν δὴ χρόνον Ἀκραγαντῖνοι θεωροῦντες τὴν
ἐν Σικελίᾳ κατάστασιν εὐφυεστάτην οὖσαν πρὸς
ἐπίθεσιν ἠμφισβήτησαν τῆς κατὰ τὴν νῆσον ἡγε-

---

[1] ἄλλοι Hertlein : ἄλλος.
[2] τῇ after δευτερεύουσι omitted by Madvig.

in battle by a small number of the enemy who enlisted deception and terrain on their side ; so that
the saying is true that many are the empty alarms
of war.[1]

After the rout the Carthaginians, scattered some
here some there, were with difficulty gathered on
the next day ; and the Syracusans, returning to the
city with much plunder, delivered Hamilcar over to
those who wished to take vengeance upon him.
They recalled also the word of the soothsayer who
had said that Hamilcar would enter Syracuse and
dine there on the next day, the divinity having presented the truth in disguise. The kinsmen of the
slain, after leading Hamilcar through the city in
bonds and inflicting terrible tortures upon him, put
him to death with the utmost indignities. Then the
rulers of the city cut off his head and dispatched men
to carry it into Libya to Agathocles and report to
him the successes that had been gained.

31. When the Carthaginian army after the disaster
had taken place learned the cause of its misfortune,
it was with difficulty relieved from its fears. There
being no established commander, the barbarians
separated from the Greeks. Then the exiles along
with the other Greeks elected Deinocrates general,
and the Carthaginians gave the command to those
who had been second in rank to Hamilcar.

About this time the Acragantines, seeing that the
situation in Sicily was most favourable for an attempt,
made a bid for the leadership of the whole island ;

[1] Cp. Book 17. 86, 1 ; 20. 67. 4 ; Thucydides, 3. 30 ;
Aristotle, *Nicomachean Ethics*, 1116 b 7 ; Cicero, *Letters to
Atticus*, 5. 20. 3. In most of these passages the MSS. are
divided between κενά (empty) and καινά (strange) ; and Tyrrell
and Purser on the last passage suggest κοινά (common to all).

3 μονίας· ὑπελάμβανον γὰρ Καρχηδονίους μὲν μόγις
ἀνθέξειν τῷ πρὸς Ἀγαθοκλέα πολέμῳ, Δεινοκράτην
δ᾽ εὐκαταγώνιστον εἶναι συνηθροικότα φυγαδικὴν
στρατιάν, τοὺς δ᾽ ἐν ταῖς Συρακούσσαις θλιβο-
μένους τῇ σιτοδείᾳ μηδ᾽ ἐγχειρήσειν ἀμφισβητεῖν
τῶν πρωτείων, τὸ δὲ μέγιστον, τὴν στρατείαν
ἑαυτῶν ποιουμένων ἐπ᾽ ἐλευθερώσει τῶν πόλεων
ἀσμένως ἅπαντας ὑπακούσεσθαι διά τε τὸ πρὸς
τοὺς βαρβάρους μῖσος καὶ διὰ τὴν ἔμφυτον πᾶσιν
4 ἐπιθυμίαν τῆς αὐτονομίας. οὗτοι μὲν οὖν ἑλόμενοι
στρατηγὸν Ξενόδικον καὶ τὴν ἁρμόζουσαν δόντες
δύναμιν ἐξέπεμψαν ἐπὶ τὸν πόλεμον· ὁ δὲ παραχρῆμα ἐπὶ τὴν Γέλαν ὁρμήσας καὶ διά τινων ἰδιο-
ξένων νυκτὸς εἰσαχθεὶς ἐκυρίευσε τῆς πόλεως ἅμα
5 καὶ δυνάμεως ἁδρᾶς καὶ χρημάτων. ἐλευθερω-
θέντες οὖν οἱ Γελῷοι προθυμότατα πανδημεὶ συστρατεύοντες ἠλευθέρουν τὰς πόλεις. διαβοηθείσης
δὲ τῆς τῶν Ἀκραγαντίνων ἐπιβολῆς κατὰ πᾶσαν
τὴν νῆσον ἐνέπεσεν ὁρμὴ ταῖς πόλεσι πρὸς τὴν
ἐλευθερίαν. καὶ πρῶτοι μὲν Ἐνναῖοι πέμψαντες
τὴν πόλιν τοῖς Ἀκραγαντίνοις παρέδωκαν· οἱ δὲ
ταύτην ἐλευθερώσαντες παρῆλθον ἐπὶ τὸν Ἑρβησ-
σόν, φρουρᾶς ἐν αὐτῷ παραφυλαττούσης τὴν πόλιν.
γενομένης δὲ μάχης ἰσχυρᾶς καὶ τῶν πολιτικῶν
συνεργησάντων συνέβη τὴν φρουρὰν ἁλῶναι καὶ
πολλοὺς μὲν πεσεῖν τῶν βαρβάρων, εἰς πεντακοσίους
δὲ θεμένους τὰ ὅπλα παραδοῦναι σφᾶς αὐτούς.

32. Περὶ ταῦτα δ᾽ ὄντων τῶν Ἀκραγαντίνων
τῶν ἐν ταῖς Συρακούσσαις καταλελειμμένων στρα-

for they believed that the Carthaginians would 309 B.C. scarcely sustain the war against Agathocles; that Deinocrates was easy to conquer since he had collected an army of exiles; that the people of Syracuse, pinched by famine, would not even try to compete for the primacy; and, what was most important, that if they took the field to secure the independence of the cities, all would gladly answer the summons both through hatred for the barbarians and through the desire for self-government that is implanted in all men. They therefore elected Xenodicus [1] as general, gave him an army suitable for the undertaking, and sent him forth to the war. He at once set out against Gela, was admitted at night by certain personal friends, and became master of the city together with its strong army and its wealth. The people of Gela, having been thus freed, joined in his campaign very eagerly and unanimously, and set about freeing the cities. As news of the undertaking of the Acragantines spread throughout the whole island, an impulse toward liberty made itself manifest in the cities. And first the people of Enna sent to the Acragantines and delivered their city over to them; and when they had freed Enna, the Acragantines went on to Erbessus, although a garrison stationed there was keeping watch over the city. After a bitter battle had taken place in which the citizens aided the Acragantines, the garrison was captured and, although many of the barbarians fell, at least five hundred of them laid down their arms and surrendered.

32. While the Acragantines were thus engaged, some of the soldiers who had been left in Syracuse by

[1] Called Xenodocus in chaps. 56. 2; 62. 2.

τιωτῶν ὑπ' Ἀγαθοκλέους καταλαβόμενοί τινες τὴν
Ἐχέτλαν ἐπόρθουν τήν τε Λεοντίνην καὶ Καμαρι-
2 ναίαν. κακῶς οὖν πασχουσῶν τῶν πόλεων διὰ τὸ
τὴν χώραν δῃοῦσθαι καὶ τοὺς καρποὺς ἅπαντας
διαφθείρεσθαι ἐμβαλὼν εἰς τοὺς τόπους ὁ Ξενόδικος
Λεοντίνους μὲν καὶ Καμαριναίους ἀπήλλαξε τοῦ
πολέμου, τὴν δ' Ἐχέτλαν χωρίον ὀχυρὸν ἐκπολιορκήσας τοῖς μὲν πολίταις τὴν δημοκρατίαν
ἀποκατέστησε, τοὺς δὲ Συρακοσίους κατεπλήξατο·
καθόλου δ' ἐπιπορευόμενος τά τε φρούρια καὶ τὰς
πόλεις ἠλευθέρου τῆς τῶν Καρχηδονίων ἐπιστασίας.
3 Ἅμα δὲ τούτοις πραττομένοις Συρακόσιοι πιεζού-
μενοι τῇ σιτοδείᾳ καὶ πυνθανόμενοι σιτηγὰ πλοῖα
μέλλοντα ποιεῖσθαι πλοῦν ἐπὶ Συρακούσσας ἐπλή-
ρουν τριήρεις εἴκοσι, τηρήσαντες δὲ τοὺς ἐφορμεῖν
εἰωθότας βαρβάρους ἀφυλάκτους ὄντας ἔλαθον ἐκπλεύσαντες καὶ παρακομισθέντες εἰς τοὺς Μεγαρεῖς
4 ἐπετήρουν τὸν τῶν ἐμπόρων κατάπλουν. μετὰ δὲ
ταῦτα τῶν Καρχηδονίων τριάκοντα ναυσὶν ἐκπλευ-
σάντων ἐπ' αὐτοὺς τὸ μὲν πρῶτον ἐπεβάλοντο
ναυμαχεῖν, ταχὺ δὲ πρὸς τὴν γῆν ἐκδιωχθέντες
5 ἐξεκολύμβησαν πρός τινα ναὸν Ἥρας. γενομένης
οὖν μάχης περὶ τῶν σκαφῶν καὶ τῶν Καρχηδονίων
ἐπιβαλόντων σιδηρᾶς χεῖρας καὶ βιαιότερον ἀπο-
σπώντων ἀπὸ τῆς γῆς δέκα μὲν τριήρεις ἑάλωσαν,
τὰς δ' ἄλλας ἐκ τῆς πόλεως ἐπιβοηθήσαντές τινες
διέσωσαν.

Καὶ τὰ μὲν περὶ Σικελίαν ἐν τούτοις ἦν.

33. Περὶ δὲ τὴν Λιβύην Ἀγαθοκλῆς, ἐπειδὴ
κατέπλευσαν οἱ τὴν Ἀμίλκα κεφαλὴν κομίζοντες,
ἀναλαβὼν ταύτην καὶ παριππεύσας πλησίον τῆς

---

[1] This town is not definitely identified. Polybius, 1. 15. 10,

Agathocles, after seizing Echetla,[1] plundered Leon- 309 B.C.
tini and Camarina. Since the cities were suffering
from the plundering of their fields and the destruction
of all their crops, Xenodicus entered the region and
freed the peoples of Leontini and Camarina from
the war ; and after taking Echetla, a walled town,
by siege, he re-established democracy for its citizens
and struck fear into the Syracusans ; and, in general,
as he advanced he liberated the strongholds and the
cities from Carthaginian domination.

Meantime the Syracusans, hard pressed by famine
and hearing that grain ships were about to make the
voyage to Syracuse, manned twenty triremes and,
watching the barbarians who were accustomed to
lie at anchor off the harbour to catch them off guard,
sailed out unseen and coasted along to Megara,
where they waited for the approach of the traders.
Afterwards, however, when the Carthaginians sailed
out against them with thirty ships, they first tried
to fight at sea, but were quickly driven to land and
leapt from their ships at a certain shrine of Hera.
Then a battle took place for the ships ; and the Carthaginians, throwing grappling irons into the triremes
and with great force dragging them off from the
shore, captured ten [2] of them, but the others were
saved by men who came to the rescue from the
city.

And this was the condition of affairs in Sicily.

33. In Libya, when those who were carrying the
head of Hamilcar had come into port, Agathocles
took the head and, riding near the hostile camp to

mentions it as on the frontier between Syracusan and Carthaginian territory at the time of Hieron II.

[2] In the table of contents the number is given as twenty.

παρεμβολῆς τῶν πολεμίων εἰς φωνῆς ἀκοὴν ἔδειξε
τοῖς πολεμίοις καὶ τὴν τῶν στρατοπέδων ἧτταν
2 διεσάφησεν. οἱ δὲ Καρχηδόνιοι περιαλγεῖς γενόμενοι καὶ βαρβαρικῶς προσκυνήσαντες συμφορὰν
ἑαυτῶν ἐποιοῦντο τὸν τοῦ βασιλέως θάνατον καὶ
πρὸς τὸν ὅλον πόλεμον ἄθυμοι καθειστήκεισαν.
οἱ δὲ περὶ τὸν Ἀγαθοκλέα τοῖς περὶ Λιβύην προ-
τερήμασιν ἐπαρθέντες τηλικούτων εὐτυχημάτων
προσγενομένων μετέωροι ταῖς ἐλπίσιν ἐγενήθησαν,
3 ὡς ἀπηλλαγμένοι τῶν δεινῶν. οὐ μὴν ἡ τύχη γε
εἴασε τὴν εὔροιαν μένειν ἐπὶ τῆς αὐτῆς τάξεως, ἀλλ'
ἐκ τῶν ἰδίων στρατιωτῶν τῷ δυνάστῃ τοὺς μεγίστους ἐπήνεγκε κινδύνους. Λυκίσκος γάρ τις
τῶν ἐφ' ἡγεμονίᾳ τεταγμένων, παραληφθεὶς ὑπ'
Ἀγαθοκλέους ἐπὶ τὸ δεῖπνον, οἰνωθεὶς ἐβλασφήμει
4 τὸν δυνάστην. ὁ μὲν οὖν Ἀγαθοκλῆς διὰ τὰς ἐν
τῷ πολέμῳ χρείας ἀποδεχόμενος τὸν ἄνδρα τῇ
παιδιᾷ τὰ πρὸς πικρίαν λεγόμενα διέσυρεν· ὁ δ'
υἱὸς Ἀρχάγαθος χαλεπῶς φέρων ἐπετίμα τε καὶ
5 διηπειλεῖτο. διαλυθέντος δὲ τοῦ πότου καὶ πρὸς
τὴν σκηνὴν ἀπιόντων ἐλοιδόρησεν ὁ Λυκίσκος τὸν
Ἀρχάγαθον εἰς τὴν τῆς μητρυιᾶς μοιχείαν· ἐδόκει
γὰρ ἔχειν λάθρα τοῦ πατρὸς τὴν Ἀλκίαν· τοῦτο
6 γὰρ ἦν ὄνομα τῇ γυναικί. ὁ δ' Ἀρχάγαθος εἰς
ὀργὴν ὑπερβάλλουσαν προαχθεὶς καὶ παρά τινος
τῶν ὑπασπιστῶν ἁρπάσας σιβύνην διήλασε διὰ τῶν
πλευρῶν. τοῦτον μὲν οὖν παραχρῆμα τελευτήσαντα
πρὸς τὴν ἰδίαν ἀπήνεγκαν σκηνὴν οἷς ἦν ἐπιμελές·
ἅμα δ' ἡμέρᾳ συνελθόντες οἱ τοῦ φονευθέντος φίλοι
καὶ πολλοὶ τῶν ἄλλων στρατιωτῶν συνδραμόντες
ἠγανάκτουν ἐπὶ τοῖς πραχθεῖσι καὶ θορύβου τὴν
7 παρεμβολὴν ἐπλήρωσαν. πολλοὶ δὲ καὶ τῶν ἐφ'

within hearing distance, showed it to the enemy and 30ɔ B.C.
related to them the defeat of their expedition. The
Carthaginians, deeply grieved and prostrating themselves on the ground in barbarian fashion, regarded
the death of the king as their own misfortune, and
they fell into deep despair in regard to the whole
war. But Agathocles, who was already elated by his
successes in Libya, when such strokes of fortune were
now added, was borne aloft by soaring hopes, thinking
himself freed from all dangers. Fortune notwith-
standing did not permit success to remain long on
the same side but brought the greatest danger to
the prince from his own soldiers. For Lyciscus, one
of those who had been placed in command, invited
to dinner by Agathocles, became drunk and insulted
the prince. Now Agathocles, who valued the man
for his services in the war, turned aside with a joke
what had been said in bitterness ; but his son, Archagathus,[1] becoming angry, censured and threatened
Lyciscus. When the drinking was concluded and the
men were going away to their quarters, Lyciscus
taunted Archagathus on the score of his adultery
with his stepmother ; for he was supposed to possess
Alcia, for this was the woman's name, without his
father's knowledge. Archagathus, driven into an
overpowering rage, seized a spear from one of the
guard and thrust Lyciscus through his ribs. Now he
died at once and was carried away to his own tent
by those whose task it was ; but at daybreak the
friends of the murdered man came together, and
many of the other soldiers hastened to join them,
and all were indignant at what had happened and
filled the camp with uproar. Many, too, of those who

---

[1] For the form of this name cp. chap. 11. 1, and note.

ἡγεμονίαις τεταγμένων, ἐν ἐγκλήμασιν ὄντες καὶ
φοβούμενοι περὶ σφῶν αὐτῶν, συνεπιθέμενοι τῷ
καιρῷ στάσιν οὐ τὴν τυχοῦσαν ἐξέκαυσαν. παντὸς
δὲ τοῦ στρατεύματος μισοπονηροῦντος ἕκαστοι τὰς
πανοπλίας ἀνελάμβανον ἐπὶ τὴν τοῦ φονεύσαντος
τιμωρίαν· καὶ πέρας τὸ πλῆθος ᾤετο δεῖν Ἀρχάγαθον ἀναιρεῖσθαι, μὴ ἐκδιδόντος δὲ τὸν υἱὸν Ἀγαθοκλέους αὐτὸν ἀντ' ἐκείνου τὴν τιμωρίαν ὑπέχειν.
8 ἀπήτουν δὲ καὶ τοὺς μισθοὺς τοὺς ὀφειλομένους
καὶ στρατηγοὺς ἡροῦντο τοὺς ἀφηγησομένους τοῦ
στρατοπέδου καὶ τὸ τελευταῖον τὰ τείχη κατελαμ-
βάνοντό τινες τοῦ Τύνητος καὶ πανταχόθεν φυλακαῖς περιέλαβον τοὺς δυνάστας.

34. Οἱ δὲ Καρχηδόνιοι γνόντες τὴν παρὰ τοῖς
πολεμίοις στάσιν ἔπεμψάν τινας ἀξιοῦντες μετα-
βάλλεσθαι καὶ τούς τε μισθοὺς μείζους καὶ δωρεὰς
ἀξιολόγους δώσειν ἐπηγγέλλοντο. πολλοὶ μὲν οὖν
τῶν ἡγεμόνων ἀπάξειν πρὸς αὐτοὺς τὴν στρατιὰν
2 ἐπηγγείλαντο· ὁ δ' Ἀγαθοκλῆς ὁρῶν τὴν σωτηρίαν
ἐπὶ ῥοπῆς κειμένην καὶ φοβούμενος μὴ τοῖς πολεμίοις παραδοθεὶς μεθ' ὕβρεως καταστρέψῃ τὸν
βίον, ὑπέλαβε κρεῖττον εἶναι, κἂν δέῃ τι πάσχειν,
3 ὑπὸ τῶν στρατιωτῶν ἀποθανεῖν. διόπερ ἀποθέμενος τὴν πορφύραν καὶ μεταλαβὼν ἰδιωτικὴν καὶ
ταπεινὴν ἐσθῆτα παρῆλθεν εἰς τὸ μέσον. σιωπῆς
οὖν γενομένης διὰ τὸ παράδοξον καὶ πολλῶν γενομένων τῶν συνδραμόντων διεξῆλθε λόγους οἰκείους
τῆς περιστάσεως καὶ τῶν προκατεργασθεισῶν[1] αὐτῷ
πράξεων ἀναμνήσας ἔφησεν ἕτοιμος εἶναι τελευτᾶν
εἰ τοῦτο δόξει συμφέρειν τοῖς συστρατευομένοις·
4 οὐδέποτε γὰρ αὐτὸν δειλίᾳ συνεσχημένον ὑπομεῖναι

---

[1] προκατεργασθεισῶν Dindorf : προκατεργασθέντων.

had been placed in command, as they also were subject to accusation and feared for themselves, turned
the crisis to their own advantage and kindled no incon-
siderable sedition. When the whole army was full of
indignation, the troops severally donned full armour
to punish the murderer ; and finally the mob made
up its mind that Archagathus should be put to death,
and that, if Agathocles did not surrender his son,
he himself should pay the penalty in his place.
And they also kept demanding the pay that was due
them, and they elected generals to lead the army ;
and finally some of them seized the walls of Tunis
and surrounded the princes with guards on every
side.

34. The Carthaginians, on learning of the discord
among the enemy, sent men to them urging them
to change sides, and promised to give them greater
pay and noteworthy bonuses.[1] And indeed many
of the leaders did agree to take the army over to
them ; but Agathocles, seeing that his safety was
in the balance and fearing that, if he should be delivered to the enemy, he would end his life amid
insults, decided that it was better, if he had to suffer,
to die at the hands of his own men. Therefore,
putting aside the purple and donning the humble
garb of a private citizen, he came out into the middle
of the crowd. Silence fell because his action was
unexpected, and when a crowd had run together, he
delivered a speech suitable to the critical situation.
After recalling his earlier achievements, he said that
he was ready to die if that should seem best for his
fellow soldiers ; for never had he, constrained by

[1] Most of Agathocles' soldiers were mercenaries, cp. chaps.
11. 1 ; 33. 8.

τι παθεῖν ἄτοπον ἕνεκα τοῦ φιλοψυχεῖν. καὶ τούτου μάρτυρας ἐκείνους ὑπάρχειν ἀποφαινόμενος
ἐγύμνωσε τὸ ξίφος ὡς σφάξων ἑαυτόν. μέλλοντος
δ' ἐπιφέρειν πληγὴν ἀνεβόησε τὸ στρατόπεδον δια-
κωλῦον καὶ πανταχόθεν ἐγίνοντο φωναὶ τῶν ἐγκλη-
5 μάτων ἀπολύουσαι. προστάττοντος δὲ τοῦ πλήθους
ἀναλαβεῖν τὴν βασιλικὴν ἐσθῆτα δακρύων καὶ τοῖς
ὄχλοις εὐχαριστῶν ἐνεδύετο τὸν προσήκοντα κόσμον,
τοῦ πλήθους τὴν ἀποκατάστασιν κρότῳ παραμυ-
θησαμένου. τῶν δὲ Καρχηδονίων καραδοκούντων
ὡς αὐτίκα μάλα τῶν Ἑλλήνων πρὸς αὐτοὺς μεταθησομένων,[1] Ἀγαθοκλῆς οὐ παρεὶς τὸν καιρὸν ἐξή-
6 γαγεν ἐπ' αὐτοὺς τὴν δύναμιν. οἱ μὲν οὖν βάρβαροι
νομίζοντες τοὺς ἐναντίους ἀποχωρεῖν πρὸς αὐτούς,
οὐδεμίαν τῶν πρὸς ἀλήθειαν πεπραγμένων ἔννοιαν
ἐλάμβανον· ὁ δ' Ἀγαθοκλῆς ὡς ἐπλησίασε τοῖς
πολεμίοις, ἄφνω τὸ πολεμικὸν προσέταξε σημαίνειν
καὶ προσπεσὼν πολὺν ἐποίει φόνον. οἱ δὲ Καρχηδόνιοι παραδόξῳ συμπτώματι περιπεσόντες καὶ
πολλοὺς τῶν στρατιωτῶν ἀποβαλόντες συνέφυγον
7 εἰς τὴν παρεμβολήν. Ἀγαθοκλῆς μὲν οὖν διὰ τὸν
υἱὸν εἰς τοὺς ἐσχάτους ἐλθὼν κινδύνους διὰ τῆς
ἰδίας ἀρετῆς οὐ μόνον λύσιν εὗρε τῶν κακῶν, ἀλλὰ
καὶ τοὺς πολεμίους ἠλάττωσεν· οἱ δὲ τῆς στάσεως
μάλιστ' αἴτιοι γενόμενοι καὶ τῶν ἄλλων ὅσοι πρὸς
τὸν δυνάστην ἀλλοτρίως διέκειντο, ὑπὲρ τοὺς
διακοσίους ὄντες, ἐτόλμησαν πρὸς τοὺς Καρχηδονίους αὐτομολῆσαι.

Ἡμεῖς δὲ τὰ περὶ Λιβύην καὶ Σικελίαν διεληλυθότες μνησθησόμεθα καὶ τῶν ἐν Ἰταλίᾳ πραχθέντων.

cowardice, consented to endure any indignity through
love of life. And declaring that they themselves were
witnesses of this, he bared his sword as if to slay
himself. When he was on the point of striking the
blow, the army shouted bidding him stop, and from
every side came voices clearing him from the charges.
And when the crowd kept pressing him to resume
his royal garb, he put on the dress of his rank, weeping
and thanking the people, the crowd meanwhile ac-
claiming his restoration with a clash of arms. While
the Carthaginians were waiting intently, expecting
that the Greeks would very soon come over to them,
Agathocles, not missing the opportunity, led his army
against them. The barbarians, believing that their opponents were deserting to them, had no idea at all of
what had actually taken place ; and when Agathocles
had drawn near the enemy, he suddenly ordered the
signal for battle to be given, fell upon them, and
created great havoc. The Carthaginians, stunned by
the sudden reversal, lost many of their soldiers and
fled into their camp. Thus Agathocles, after having
fallen into the most extreme danger on account of his
son, through his own excellence not only found a way
out of his difficulties, but even defeated the enemy.
Those, however, who were chiefly responsible for the
sedition and any of the others who were hostile to
the prince, more than two hundred in number, found
the courage to desert to the Carthaginians.

Now that we have completed the account of events
in Libya and in Sicily,[1] we shall relate what took place
in Italy.

[1] Continued in chap. 38. 1.

---

[1] μεταθησομένων Dindorf : μετατεθησομένων RX, μεταβησο-
μένων F.

35. Τῶν γὰρ Τυρρηνῶν στρατευσάντων ἐπὶ πόλιν Σούτριον ἄποικον Ῥωμαίων οἱ μὲν ὕπατοι δυνάμεσιν ἁδραῖς ἐκβοηθήσαντες ἐνίκησαν μάχῃ τοὺς 2 Τυρρηνοὺς καὶ συνεδίωξαν εἰς τὴν παρεμβολήν, οἱ δὲ Σαυνῖται κατὰ τοῦτον τὸν χρόνον μακρὰν ἀπηρτημένης τῆς Ῥωμαίων δυνάμεως ἀδεῶς ἐπόρθουν τῶν Ἰαπύγων τοὺς τὰ Ῥωμαίων φρονοῦντας. διόπερ ἠναγκάσθησαν οἱ ὕπατοι διαιρεῖν τὰς δυνάμεις καὶ Φάβιος μὲν ἐν τῇ Τυρρηνίᾳ κατέμεινεν, Μάρκιος δὲ ἐπὶ τοὺς Σαυνίτας ἀναζεύξας Ἀλλίφας μὲν πόλιν εἷλεν κατὰ κράτος, τοὺς δὲ πολιορκουμένους τῶν συμμάχων ἐκ τῶν κινδύνων ἐρρύσατο. 3 ὁ δὲ Φάβιος Τυρρηνῶν πολλοῖς πλήθεσιν ἐπὶ τὸ Σούτριον συνδραμόντων ἔλαθε τοὺς πολεμίους διὰ τῆς τῶν ὁμόρων[1] χώρας ἐμβαλὼν[2] εἰς τὴν ἀνωτέρω Τυρρηνίαν, ἀπόρθητον γενομένην πολλῶν χρόνων· 4 ἐπιπεσὼν δὲ ἀνελπίστως τῆς τε χώρας πολλὴν ἐδῄωσε καὶ τοὺς ἐπελθόντας τῶν ἐγχωρίων νικήσας πολλοὺς μὲν ἀνεῖλεν, οὐκ ὀλίγους δὲ καὶ ζῶντας ὑποχειρίους ἔλαβεν. μετὰ δὲ ταῦτα περὶ τὴν καλουμένην Περυσίαν δευτέρᾳ μάχῃ τῶν Τυρρηνῶν κρατήσας, πολλοὺς ἀνελὼν κατεπλήξατο τὸ ἔθνος, πρῶτος Ῥωμαίων μετὰ δυνάμεως ἐμβεβληκὼς εἰς 5 τοὺς τόπους τούτους. καὶ πρὸς μὲν Ἀρρητίνους καὶ Κροτωνιάτας, ἔτι δὲ Περυσίνους ἀνοχὰς ἐποιήσατο· πόλιν δὲ τὴν ὀνομαζομένην Καστόλαν ἐκ-

[1] Ὀμβρικῶν Dindorf.

35. When the Etruscans [1] had taken the field against the city Sutrium, a Roman colony, the consuls, coming out to its aid with a strong army, defeated them in battle and drove them into their camp ; but the Samnites at this time, when the Roman army was far distant, were plundering with impunity those Iapyges who supported the Romans. The consuls, therefore, were forced to divide their armies ; Fabius remained in Etruria, but Marcius, setting out against the Samnites, took the city Allifae by storm and freed from danger those of the allies who were being besieged. Fabius, however, while the Etruscans in great numbers were gathering against Sutrium, marched without the knowledge of the enemy through the country of their neighbours [2] into upper Etruria, which had not been plundered for a long time. Falling upon it unexpectedly, he ravaged a large part of the country ; and in a victory over those of the inhabitants who came against him, he slew many of them and took no small number of them alive as prisoners. Thereafter, defeating the Etruscans in a second battle near the place called Perusia and destroying many of them, he overawed the nation since he was the first of the Romans to have invaded that region with an army. He also made truces with the peoples of Arretium and Crotona,[3] likewise with those of Perusia ; and, taking by siege the city called

[1] Continued from chap. 26. 4. For this campaign cp. Livy, 9. 35-40.

[2] Or, reading Ὀμβρικῶν : "through the country of the Umbrians."

[3] The Etruscan city, called Cortona by Livy, 9. 37. 12, and by Latin writers generally, but Κρότων by the Greeks except Polybius, 3. 82. 9, who has Κυρτώνιον.

---

[2] ἐμβαλών Dindorf : συνεμβαλών.

πολιορκήσας συνηνάγκασε τοὺς Τυρρηνοὺς λῦσαι
τὴν τοῦ Σουτρίου πολιορκίαν.

36. Ἐν δὲ τῇ Ῥώμῃ κατὰ τοῦτον τὸν ἐνιαυτὸν
τιμητὰς εἵλοντο καὶ τούτων ὁ ἕτερος Ἄππιος
Κλαύδιος ὑπήκοον ἔχων τὸν συνάρχοντα Λεύκιον
Πλαύτιον[1] πολλὰ τῶν πατρῴων νομίμων ἐκίνησε·
τῷ δήμῳ γὰρ τὸ κεχαρισμένον ποιῶν οὐδένα λόγον
ἐποιεῖτο τῆς συγκλήτου. καὶ πρῶτον μὲν τὸ καλούμενον Ἄππιον ὕδωρ ἀπὸ σταδίων ὀγδοήκοντα κατήγαγεν εἰς τὴν Ῥώμην καὶ πολλὰ τῶν δημοσίων
χρημάτων εἰς ταύτην τὴν κατασκευὴν ἀνήλωσεν
2 ἄνευ δόγματος τῆς συγκλήτου· μετὰ δὲ ταῦτα τῆς
ἀφ' ἑαυτοῦ κληθείσης Ἀππίας ὁδοῦ τὸ πλεῖον μέρος
λίθοις στερεοῖς κατέστρωσεν ἀπὸ Ῥώμης μέχρι
Καπύης, ὄντος τοῦ διαστήματος σταδίων πλειόνων
ἢ χιλίων, καὶ τῶν τόπων τοὺς μὲν ὑπερέχοντας
διασκάψας, τοὺς δὲ φαραγγώδεις ἢ κοίλους ἀνα-
λήμμασιν ἀξιολόγοις ἐξισώσας κατηνάλωσεν ἁπάσας τὰς δημοσίας προσόδους, αὑτοῦ δὲ μνημεῖον
ἀθάνατον κατέλιπεν, εἰς κοινὴν εὐχρηστίαν φιλο-
3 τιμηθείς. κατέμιξε δὲ καὶ τὴν σύγκλητον, οὐ τοὺς
εὐγενεῖς καὶ προέχοντας τοῖς ἀξιώμασι προσγράφων
μόνον, ὡς ἦν ἔθος, ἀλλὰ πολλοὺς καὶ τῶν ἀπελευθέρων υἱοὺς[2] ἀνέμιξεν· ἐφ' οἷς βαρέως ἔφερον οἱ
4 καυχώμενοι ταῖς εὐγενείαις. ἔδωκε δὲ τοῖς πολίταις καὶ τὴν ἐξουσίαν ἐν ὁποίᾳ τις βούλεται φυλῇ

---

[1] Πλαύτιον Rhodoman : Κλαύδιον.
[2] υἱοὺς Oudendorp : ἐνίους. πολλοὺς ⟨τῶν δυσγενῶν⟩ καὶ τῶν
ἀπελευθέρων ἐνίους Wesseling. Reiske would add τῶν πολλῶν
or τοῦ πλήθους.

Castola,[1] he forced the Etruscans to raise the siege 309 B.C. of Sutrium.

36. In Rome in this year censors were elected,[2] and one of them Appius Claudius, who had his colleague, Lucius Plautius, under his influence, changed many of the laws of the fathers ; for since he was following a course of action pleasing to the people, he considered the Senate of no importance. In the first place he built the Appian Aqueduct, as it is called, from a distance of eighty stades [3] to Rome, and spent a large sum of public money for this construction without a decree of the Senate. Next he paved with solid stone the greater part of the Appian Way, which was named for him, from Rome to Capua, the distance being more than a thousand stades.[4] And since he dug through elevated places and levelled with note-worthy fills the ravines and valleys, he expended the entire revenue of the state but left behind a deathless monument to himself, having been ambitious in the public interest. He also mixed the Senate, enrolling not merely those who were of noble birth and superior rank as was the custom, but also including many sons of freedmen.[5] For this reason those were incensed with him who boasted of their nobility. He also gave each citizen the right to be enrolled in whatever tribe

[1] Castola is unknown. Faesulae, Carsula, and Clusium have been suggested in its place.

[2] Livy, 9. 29. 5, places the beginning of this censorship in the consulship of M. Valerius and P. Decius, *i.e.* 311 B.C. according to Diodorus, 312 B.C. according to the conventional Roman system ; and in 9. 33-34 he has Appius retain the office contrary to law into the present year, 309 or 310 B.C.

[3] About 9 miles.

[4] About 115 miles.

[5] Or, adding τοῦ πλήθους after πολλούς : "adding many of the plebeians and sons of freedmen." Cp. Livy, 9. 46. 10-11.

τάττεσθαι καὶ ὅποι προαιροῖτο τιμήσασθαι.[1] τὸ
δ' ὅλον, ὁρῶν τεθησαυρισμένον κατ' αὐτοῦ παρὰ
τοῖς ἐπιφανεστάτοις τὸν φθόνον, ἐξέκλινε τὸ προσ-
κόπτειν τισὶ τῶν ἄλλων πολιτῶν, ἀντίταγμα κατα-
σκευάζων τῇ τῶν εὐγενῶν ἀλλοτριότητι τὴν παρὰ
5 τῶν πολλῶν εὔνοιαν. καὶ κατὰ μὲν τὴν τῶν
ἱππέων δοκιμασίαν οὐδενὸς ἀφείλετο τὸν ἵππον,
κατὰ δὲ τὴν τῶν συνέδρων καταγραφὴν οὐδένα
τῶν ἀδοξούντων συγκλητικῶν ἐξέβαλεν, ὅπερ ἦν
ἔθος ποιεῖν τοῖς τιμηταῖς. εἶθ' οἱ μὲν ὕπατοι διὰ
τὸν φθόνον καὶ διὰ τὸ βούλεσθαι τοῖς ἐπιφανεστάτοις χαρίζεσθαι συνῆγον τὴν σύγκλητον οὐ τὴν
ὑπὸ τούτου καταλεγεῖσαν, ἀλλὰ τὴν ὑπὸ τῶν προ-
6 γεγενημένων τιμητῶν καταγραφεῖσαν· ὁ δὲ δῆμος
τούτοις μὲν ἀντιπράττων τῷ δὲ Ἀππίῳ συμφιλο-
τιμούμενος καὶ τὴν τῶν συγγενῶν προαγωγὴν
βεβαιῶσαι βουλόμενος ἀγορανόμον εἵλετο τῆς ἐπι-
φανεστέρας ἀγορανομίας υἱὸν ἀπελευθέρου Γναῖον
Φλάυιον, ὃς πρῶτος Ῥωμαίων ἔτυχε ταύτης τῆς
ἀρχῆς πατρὸς ὢν δεδουλευκότος. ὁ δ' Ἄππιος
τῆς ἀρχῆς ἀπολυθεὶς καὶ τὸν ἀπὸ τῆς συγκλήτου
φθόνον εὐλαβηθεὶς προσεποιήθη τυφλὸς εἶναι καὶ
κατ' οἰκίαν ἔμενεν.

37. Ἐπ' ἄρχοντος δ' Ἀθήνησι Χαρίνου Ῥωμαῖοι μὲν τὴν ὕπατον ἀρχὴν παρέδοσαν Ποπλίῳ

---

[1] ἔδωκε δὲ . . . τιμήσασθαι Fischer, ἔδωκε δὲ καὶ τοῖς πολίταις
τὴν ἐξουσίαν ὅπου προαιροῖντο τιμήσασθαι Dindorf : ἔδωκε δὲ
τοῖς πολίταις ἐξουσίαν ἐν ὁποίᾳ τις βούλεται φυλῇ τάττεσθαι καὶ

he wished, and to be placed in the census class he preferred.[1] In short, seeing hatred toward himself treasured up by the most distinguished men, he avoided giving offence to any of the other citizens, securing as a counterpoise against the hostility of the nobles the goodwill of the many. At the inspection of the equestrian order he deprived no man of his horse, and in drawing up the album of the Senate he removed no one of the unworthy Senators, which it was the custom of the censors to do. Then the consuls, because of their hatred for him and their desire to please the most distinguished men, called together the Senate, not as it had been listed by him but as it had been entered in the album by the preceding censors ; and the people in opposition to the nobles and in support of Appius, wishing also to establish firmly the promotion of their own class, elected to the more distinguished of the aedileships the son of a freedman, Gnaeus Flavius, who was the first Roman whose father had been a slave to gain that office.[2] When Appius had completed his term of office, as a precaution against the ill will of the Senate, he professed to be blind and remained in his house.[3]

37. When Charinus was archon at Athens, the Romans gave the consulship to Publius Decius and

[1] Cp. Livy, 9. 46. 10-11. Dindorf, followed by Mommsen (*Römische Forschungen*, 1. 307), omits " to be enrolled in whatever tribe he wished, and."

[2] For the aedileship of Flavius cp. Livy, 9. 46, where it is placed five years later.

[3] Continued in chap. 44. 8.

τὴν ἐξουσίαν ὅποι προαιροῖτο τιμήσασθαι RX ; ἔδωκε δὲ καὶ τοῖς πολίταις ἐξουσίαν ὅποι προαιροῖντο τιμήσασθαι καὶ ἐν ὁποίᾳ τις βούλεται φυλῇ τάττεσθαι F.

Δεκίῳ καὶ Κοΐντῳ Φαβίῳ, παρὰ δὲ τοῖς Ἠλείοις ὀλυμπιὰς ἤχθη ὀγδόη πρὸς ταῖς ἑκατὸν δέκα, καθ' ἣν ἐνίκα στάδιον Ἀπολλωνίδης Τεγεάτης. κατὰ δὲ τούτους τοὺς χρόνους Πτολεμαῖος μὲν ἐκ τῆς Μύνδου πλεύσας ἁδρῷ στόλῳ διὰ νήσων ἐν παράπλῳ τὴν Ἄνδρον ἠλευθέρωσε καὶ τὴν φρουρὰν ἐξήγαγε. κομισθεὶς δ' ἐπὶ τὸν Ἰσθμὸν Σικυῶνα καὶ Κόρινθον παρέλαβεν παρὰ Κρατησιπόλεως. τὰς δὲ αἰτίας δι' ἃς ἐκυρίευσε πόλεων ἐπιφανῶν προδεδηλωκότες ἐν ταῖς πρὸ ταύτης βίβλοις τὸ διλο-
2 γεῖν ὑπὲρ τῶν αὐτῶν παρήσομεν. ἐπεβάλετο μὲν οὖν καὶ τὰς ἄλλας Ἑλληνίδας πόλεις Πτολεμαῖος ἐλευθεροῦν, μεγάλην προσθήκην ἡγούμενος ἔσεσθαι τοῖς ἰδίοις πράγμασι τὴν τῶν Ἑλλήνων εὔνοιαν· ἐπεὶ δὲ οἱ Πελοποννήσιοι συνταξάμενοι χορηγήσειν σῖτον καὶ χρήματα τῶν ὡμολογημένων οὐδὲν συνετέλουν, ἀγανακτήσας ὁ δυνάστης πρὸς μὲν Κάσανδρον εἰρήνην ἐποιήσατο, καθ' ἣν ἑκατέρους ἔδει κυριεύειν τῶν πόλεων ὧν εἶχον, τὴν δὲ Σικυῶνα καὶ Κόρινθον ἀσφαλισάμενος φρουρᾷ διῆρεν εἰς τὴν Αἴγυπτον.
3 Ἅμα δὲ τούτοις πραττομένοις Κλεοπάτρα τῷ μὲν Ἀντιγόνῳ προσκόπτουσα, τῇ δ' αἱρέσει πρὸς τὸν Πτολεμαῖον ἀποκλίνουσα προῆγεν ἐκ Σάρδεων, ὡς διακομισθησομένη πρὸς ἐκεῖνον. ἦν δὲ ἀδελφὴ μὲν Ἀλεξάνδρου τοῦ Πέρσας καταπολεμήσαντος, θυγάτηρ δὲ Φιλίππου τοῦ Ἀμύντου, γυνὴ δὲ γεγενημένη τοῦ εἰς Ἰταλίαν στρατεύσαντος Ἀλεξ-

---

[1] Charinus was archon in 308/7 B.C. In the Fasti the year 309 B.C. is a " dictator year " with L. Papirius Cursor as dictator and C. Junius Bubulcus Brutus as his master-of-horse. No consuls are given. For these dictator years,

Quintus Fabius [1]; and in Elis the Olympian Games 308 B.C.
were celebrated for the one hundred and eighteenth
time, at which celebration Apollonides of Tegea won
the foot race. At this time,[2] while Ptolemy was
sailing from Myndus with a strong fleet through the
islands, he liberated Andros as he passed by and drove
out the garrison. Moving on to the Isthmus, he took
Sicyon and Corinth from Cratesipolis. Since the
causes that explain her becoming ruler of famous
cities were made clear in the preceding Book,[3] we
shall refrain from again discussing the same subject.
Now Ptolemy planned to free the other Greek cities
also, thinking that the goodwill of the Greeks would
be a great gain for him in his own undertakings; but
when the Peloponnesians, having agreed to contribute
food and money, contributed nothing of what had
been promised, the prince in anger made peace with
Cassander, by the terms of which peace each prince
was to remain master of the cities that he was holding; and after securing Sicyon and Corinth with a
garrison, Ptolemy departed for Egypt.

Meanwhile Cleopatra quarrelled with Antigonus
and, inclining to cast her lot with Ptolemy, she
started from Sardis in order to cross over to him. She
was the sister of Alexander the conqueror of Persia
and daughter of Philip, son of Amyntas, and had been
the wife of the Alexander who made an expedition

probably invented to accommodate two systems of chronology, cp. Introduction to Vol. IX and H. Stuart Jones in
Cambridge Ancient History, 7. 321. This fictitious year is
omitted by both Livy and Diodorus, and from this point on
the Varronian chronology and that of Diodorus agree. The
consuls for 308 B.C. are given in the Fasti as P. Decius Mus
for the second time and Q. Fabius Maximus Rullianus for
the third, cp. Livy, 9. 40, 41.

[2] Continued from chap. 27. 3.   [3] Cp. Book 19. 67. 1.

4 ἀνδρου. διὰ τὴν ἐπιφάνειαν οὖν τοῦ γένους οἱ περὶ Κάσανδρον καὶ Λυσίμαχον, ἔτι δὲ Ἀντίγονον καὶ Πτολεμαῖον καὶ καθόλου πάντες οἱ μετὰ τὴν Ἀλεξάνδρου τελευτὴν ἀξιολογώτατοι τῶν ἡγεμόνων ταύτην ἐμνήστευον· ἕκαστος γὰρ τούτῳ τῷ γάμῳ συνακολουθήσειν Μακεδόνας ἐλπίζων ἀντείχετο τῆς βασιλικῆς οἰκίας, ὡς τὴν τῶν ὅλων ἀρχὴν

5 περιστήσων εἰς ἑαυτόν. ὁ δὲ ἐπιμελητὴς τῶν Σάρδεων ἔχων παράγγελμα παρ' Ἀντιγόνου τηρεῖν τὴν Κλεοπάτραν, διεκώλυεν αὐτῆς τὴν ἔξοδον· ὕστερον δὲ προστάξαντος τοῦ δυνάστου διά τινων γυναικῶν

6 ἐδολοφόνησεν. ὁ δ' Ἀντίγονος οὐ βουλόμενος λέγεσθαι κατ' αὐτοῦ περὶ τῆς ἀναιρέσεως, τῶν γυναικῶν τινας ἐκόλασεν ὡς ἐπιβεβουλευκυίας καὶ τὰ περὶ τὴν ἐκφορὰν βασιλικῶς ἐφιλοκάλησεν. Κλεοπάτρα μὲν οὖν περιμάχητος γενομένη παρὰ τοῖς ἐπιφανεστάτοις ἡγεμόσι πρὸ τοῦ συντελεσθῆναι τὸν γάμον τοιαύτης ἔτυχε καταστροφῆς.

7 Ἡμεῖς δὲ διεληλυθότες τὰ κατὰ τὴν Ἀσίαν καὶ τὴν Ἑλλάδα μεταβιβάσομεν τὸν λόγον ἐπὶ τὰ ἄλλα μέρη τῆς οἰκουμένης.

38. Κατὰ γὰρ τὴν Λιβύην Καρχηδονίων ἐκπεμψάντων δύναμιν τὴν προσαξομένην[1] τοὺς ἀφεστηκότας Νομάδας Ἀγαθοκλῆς ἐπὶ μὲν τοῦ Τύνητος ἀπέλιπεν Ἀρχάγαθον τὸν υἱὸν μετὰ μέρους τῆς στρατιᾶς, αὐτὸς δ' ἀναλαβὼν τοὺς κρατίστους, πεζοὺς μὲν ὀκτακισχιλίους, ἱππεῖς δὲ ὀκτακοσίους, ζεύγη δὲ Λιβύων πεντήκοντα, κατὰ σπουδὴν ἐπη-

2 κολούθει τοῖς πολεμίοις. οἱ δὲ Καρχηδόνιοι παρα-

---

[1] προσαξομένην Dindorf : προσδεξομένην.

---

[1] For the marriage of Cleopatra and Alexander, at which

into Italy.[1] Because of the distinction of her descent 308 B.C. Cassander and Lysimachus, as well as Antigonus and Ptolemy and in general all the leaders who were most important after Alexander's death, sought her hand ; for each of them, hoping that the Macedonians would follow the lead of this marriage, was seeking alliance with the royal house in order thus to gain supreme power for himself. The governor of Sardis, who had orders from Antigonus to watch Cleopatra, prevented her departure ; but later, as commanded by the prince, he treacherously brought about her death through the agency of certain women. But Antigonus, not wishing the murder to be laid at his door, punished some of the women for having plotted against her, and took care that the funeral should be conducted in royal fashion. Thus Cleopatra, after having been the prize in a contest among the most eminent leaders, met this fate before her marriage was brought to pass.

Now that we have related the events of Asia and of Greece, we shall turn our narrative to the other parts of the inhabited world.[2]

38. In Libya,[3] when the Carthaginians had sent out an army to win over the Nomads who had deserted, Agathocles left his son Archagathus before Tunis with part of the army, but he himself, selecting the strongest men—eight thousand foot, eight hundred horse, and fifty Libyan chariots—followed after the enemy at full speed. When the Carthaginians had

Philip was murdered, cp. Book 16. 91-94. After the death of Alexander of Epirus in 326 B.C., Cleopatra married Leonnatus (Plutarch, *Eumenes*, 3. 5), and on his death in 322 B.C., she took as her third husband Perdiccas (Arrian, *FGrH*, 156. 9. 26), who died in 321 B.C.   [2] Continued in chap. 45. 1.

[3] Continued from chap. 34. 7.

γενηθέντες εἰς τοὺς Νομάδας τοὺς καλουμένους
Ζούφωνας, πολλοὺς τῶν ἐγχωρίων προσηγάγοντο
καὶ τῶν ἀφεστηκότων ἐνίους εἰς τὴν προϋπάρχουσαν
ἀποκατέστησαν συμμαχίαν· ἐπεὶ δ' ἤκουσαν πλησίον εἶναι τοὺς πολεμίους, κατεστρατοπέδευσαν ἐπί
τινος γεωλόφου περιεχομένου ῥείθροις βαθέσι καὶ
3 δυσπεράτοις. καὶ πρὸς μὲν τὰς ἀπροσδοκήτους
ἐπιθέσεις τῶν ἐναντίων ταῦτα προεβάλοντο, τῶν
δὲ Νομάδων τοὺς μάλιστ' εὐθέτους προσέταξαν
ἐπακολουθεῖν τοῖς Ἕλλησιν καὶ παρενοχλοῦντας
κωλύειν αὐτῶν τὴν εἰς τοὔμπροσθεν πορείαν. ὧν
ποιησάντων τὸ προσταχθὲν Ἀγαθοκλῆς ἐπὶ μὲν
τούτους ἀπέστειλε τούς τε σφενδονήτας καὶ τοξότας,
αὐτὸς δὲ μετὰ τῆς ἄλλης δυνάμεως ὥρμησεν ἐπὶ
4 τὴν στρατοπεδείαν¹ τῶν πολεμίων. οἱ δὲ Καρχηδόνιοι τὴν ἐπίνοιαν αὐτοῦ κατανοήσαντες ἐξήγαγον
τὴν στρατιὰν ἐκ τῆς παρεμβολῆς καὶ παρατάξαντες
ἕτοιμοι πρὸς μάχην καθειστήκεισαν. ἐπεὶ δ' ἑώρων
τοὺς περὶ τὸν Ἀγαθοκλέα διαβαίνοντας ἤδη τὸν
ποταμόν, συντεταγμένοι ἐνέβαλον καὶ περὶ τὸ
ῥεῖθρον δυσπέρατον ὑπάρχον πολλοὺς τῶν ἐναντίων
5 ἀνῄρουν. προσβιαζομένων δὲ τῶν μετ' Ἀγαθοκλέους οἱ μὲν Ἕλληνες ταῖς ἀρεταῖς ὑπερεῖχον,
οἱ δὲ βάρβαροι τοῖς πλήθεσι περιεγίνοντο. ἔνθα
δὴ τῶν στρατοπέδων ἐπὶ πολὺν χρόνον φιλοτίμως
ἀγωνιζομένων οἱ παρ' ἀμφοτέροις Νομάδες τῆς
μὲν μάχης ἀφειστήκεισαν, ἐπετήρουν δὲ τὸ τέλος
τοῦ κινδύνου, διεγνωκότες τῶν ἡττημένων τὰς
6 ἀποσκευὰς διαρπάσαι. Ἀγαθοκλῆς δὲ τοὺς ἀρίστους ἔχων περὶ αὑτὸν πρῶτος ἐβιάσατο τοὺς
ἀνθεστηκότας καὶ τῇ τούτων τροπῇ τοὺς λοιποὺς
βαρβάρους φυγεῖν ἐποίησεν· μόνοι δὲ τῶν ἱππέων

come to the tribe of Nomads called the Zuphones, they won over many of the inhabitants and brought back some of the deserters to their former alliance, but on learning that the enemy were at hand, they camped on a certain hill, which was surrounded by streams that were deep and difficult to cross. These they used as protection against the unexpected attacks of their opponents, but they directed the fittest of the Nomads to follow the Greeks closely and by harassing them to prevent them from advancing. When these did as they had been directed, Agathocles sent against them his slingers and bowmen, but he himself with the rest of his army advanced against the camp of the enemy. The Carthaginians on discovering his intention led their army out from their camp, drew it up, and took their positions ready for battle. But when they saw that Agathocles was already crossing the river, they attacked in formation, and at the stream, which was difficult to ford, they slew many of their opponents. However, as Agathocles pressed forward, the Greeks were superior in valour, but the barbarians had the advantage of numbers. Then when the armies had been fighting gallantly for some time, the Nomads on both sides withdrew from the battle and awaited the outcome of the struggle, intending to plunder the baggage train of those who were defeated. But Agathocles, who had his best men about him, first forced back those opposite to him, and by their rout he caused the rest of the barbarians to flee. Of the cavalry only

---

1 ἄλλην before στρατοπεδείαν omitted by Dindorf.

οἱ συναγωνιζόμενοι τοῖς Καρχηδονίοις Ἕλληνες, ὧν Κλίνων ἡγεῖτο, τοὺς περὶ τὸν Ἀγαθοκλέα βαρεῖς ἐπικειμένους ὑπέστησαν. ἀγωνισαμένων δ' αὐτῶν λαμπρῶς οἱ πλεῖστοι μὲν ἀνῃρέθησαν μαχόμενοι γενναίως, οἱ δὲ περιλειφθέντες τύχῃ τινὶ διεσώθησαν.

39. Ὁ δ' Ἀγαθοκλῆς ἀφεὶς τὸ διώκειν τούτους ὥρμησεν ἐπὶ τοὺς καταφυγόντας βαρβάρους εἰς τὴν παρεμβολὴν καὶ προσβιαζόμενος τόποις προσάντεσι καὶ δυσπροσίτοις οὐχ ἧττον ἔπασχεν ἢ διετίθει τοὺς Καρχηδονίους. οὐ μὴν ἔληγε[1] τῆς τόλμης, ἀλλὰ τῇ νίκῃ μετεωριζόμενος ἐνέκειτο, διαλαμβάνων κατὰ κράτος αἱρήσειν τὴν στρατο-
2 πεδείαν. ἐν τοσούτῳ δὲ τὸ τέλος τῆς μάχης καραδοκοῦντες οἱ Νομάδες ταῖς μὲν τῶν Καρχηδονίων ἀποσκευαῖς οὐχ οἷοί τε ἦσαν ἐπιθέσθαι διὰ τὸ τὰς δυνάμεις ἀμφοτέρας πλησίον τῆς παρεμβολῆς ἀγωνίζεσθαι, ἐπὶ δὲ τὴν τῶν Ἑλλήνων στρατοπεδείαν ὥρμησαν, εἰδότες τὸν Ἀγαθοκλέα μακρὰν ἀπεσπασμένον. ἐρήμου δ' αὐτῆς οὔσης τῶν δυναμένων ἀμύνασθαι ῥᾳδίως ἐπιπεσόντες τοὺς μὲν ἀντιστάντας ὀλίγους ὄντας ἀπέκτειναν, αἰχμαλώτων δὲ
3 πλήθους καὶ τῆς ἄλλης ὠφελείας ἐκυρίευσαν. ἃ δὴ πυθόμενος ὁ Ἀγαθοκλῆς ἦγε κατὰ τάχος τὴν δύναμιν καὶ τινὰ μὲν τῶν ἀφῃρπασμένων ἀνέσωσε, τῶν δὲ πλείστων οἱ Νομάδες ἐκυρίευον καὶ νυκτὸς
4 ἐπιγενομένης μακρὰν ἑαυτοὺς ἐξετόπισαν. ὁ δὲ δυνάστης στήσας τρόπαιον τὰ μὲν λάφυρα διείλετο τοῖς στρατιώταις, ὅπως μηδεὶς ἀγανακτήσῃ περὶ τῶν ἀπολωλότων, τοὺς δ' αἰχμαλώτους Ἕλληνας τοὺς συστρατευσαμένους τοῖς Καρχηδονίοις εἴς τι[2]
5 φρούριον ἀπέθετο. οὗτοι[3] μὲν οὖν εὐλαβούμενοι

the Greeks who, led by Clinon, were assisting the 308 B.C.
Carthaginians withstood Agathocles' heavy armed
men as they advanced. Although they struggled
brilliantly, most of these Greeks were slain while
fighting gallantly, and those who survived were saved
by mere chance.

39. Agathocles, giving up the pursuit of the cavalry,
attacked the barbarians who had taken refuge in the
camp ; and, since he had to force his way over terrain
steep and difficult of access, he suffered losses no less
great than those he inflicted on the Carthaginians.
Nevertheless, he did not slacken his zeal, but rather,
made confident by his victory, pressed on, expecting
to take the camp by storm. At this the Nomads who
were awaiting the outcome of the battle, not being
able to fall on the baggage train of the Carthaginians
since both armies were fighting near the camp, made
an attack on the encampment of the Greeks, knowing
that Agathocles had been drawn off to a great distance. Since the camp was without defenders capable
of warding them off, they easily launched an attack,
killing the few who resisted them and gaining possession of a large number of prisoners and of booty as
well. On hearing this Agathocles led his army back
quickly and recovered some of the spoil, but most
of it the Nomads kept in their possession, and as night
came on they withdrew to a distance. The prince,
after setting up a trophy, divided the booty among
the soldiers so that no one might complain about his
losses ; but the captured Greeks, who had been
fighting for the Carthaginians, he put into a certain fortress. Now these men, dreading punishment

---

¹ ἐλήγέ γε Reiske.   ² εἴς τι Wesseling : εἰς τὸ,
³ οὗτοι Dindorf : αὐτοὶ,

τὴν ἀπὸ τοῦ δυνάστου τιμωρίαν νυκτὸς ἐπέθεντο
τοῖς ἐν τῷ φρουρίῳ καὶ τῇ μάχῃ κρατούμενοι
κατελάβοντο τόπον ἐρυμνόν, ὄντες οὐκ ἐλάττους τῶν
χιλίων, ὧν ἦσαν Συρακόσιοι πλείους τῶν πεντα-
6 κοσίων· Ἀγαθοκλῆς δὲ πυθόμενος τὸ πεπραγμένον
ἧκε μετὰ τῆς δυνάμεως καὶ καταβιβάσας ὑποσπόνδους τοὺς ἐπιθεμένους ἅπαντας ἀπέσφαξεν.

40. Ἀπὸ δὲ τῆς μάχης ταύτης γενόμενος καὶ
πάντα τῇ διανοίᾳ σκοπούμενος πρὸς τὸ λαβεῖν τοὺς
Καρχηδονίους ὑποχειρίους ἐξέπεμψε πρεσβευτὴν
Ὄρθωνα τὸν Συρακόσιον πρὸς Ὀφέλλαν εἰς Κυρήνην. οὗτος δ' ἦν μὲν τῶν φίλων τῶν συνεστρα-
τευμένων Ἀλεξάνδρῳ, κυριεύων δὲ τῶν περὶ
Κυρήνην πόλεων καὶ δυνάμεως ἁδρᾶς περιεβάλετο
2 ταῖς ἐλπίσι μείζονα δυναστείαν. τοιαύτην οὖν αὐτοῦ διάνοιαν ἔχοντος ἧκεν ὁ παρ' Ἀγαθοκλέους
πρεσβευτής, ἀξιῶν συγκαταπολεμῆσαι Καρχηδο-
νίους· ἀντὶ δὲ ταύτης τῆς χρείας ἐπηγγέλλετο τὸν
Ἀγαθοκλέα συγχωρήσειν αὐτῷ τῶν ἐν Λιβύῃ
3 πραγμάτων κυριεύειν. εἶναι γὰρ ἱκανὴν αὐτῷ τὴν
Σικελίαν, ἵν' ἐξῇ τῶν ἀπὸ τῆς Καρχηδόνος κινδύνων ἀπαλλαχθέντα μετ' ἀδείας κρατεῖν ἁπάσης τῆς
νήσου· παρακεῖσθαι δὲ καὶ τὴν Ἰταλίαν αὐτῷ πρὸς
ἐπαύξησιν τῆς ἀρχῆς, ἐὰν κρίνῃ μειζόνων ὀρέγεσθαι.
4 τὴν μὲν γὰρ Λιβύην διεζευγμένην μεγάλῳ καὶ
χαλεπῷ πελάγει μηδαμῶς ἁρμόζειν αὐτῷ, εἰς ἣν
καὶ νῦν οὐ κατ' ἐπιθυμίαν, ἀλλὰ κατ' ἀνάγκην
5 ἀφῖχθαι. ὁ δὲ Ὀφέλλας τῇ πάλαι βεβουλευμένῃ

---

[1] In 322 b.c. Ophellas as general of Ptolemy restored the
oligarchy in Cyrenê, which had been threatened by the mercenary leader Thibron in the service of the democrats (Book
18. 19-21). He seems to have remained in Cyrenê as Ptolemy's

from the prince, attacked those in the fortress at 308 B.C.
night and, although defeated in the battle, occupied
a strong position, being in number not less than a
thousand, of whom above five hundred were Syracusans. However, when Agathocles heard what had
happened, he came with his army, induced them to
leave their position under a truce, and slaughtered
all those who had made the attack.

40. After he had finished this battle, Agathocles,
examining in mind every device for bringing the
Carthaginians into subjection, sent Orthon the Syracusan as an envoy into Cyrenê to Ophellas.[1] The
latter was one of the companions who had made the
campaign with Alexander ; now, master of the cities
of Cyrenê and of a strong army, he was ambitious
for a greater realm. And so it was to a man in this
state of mind that there came the envoy from Agathocles inviting him to join him in subduing the
Carthaginians.[2] In return for this service Orthon
promised Ophellas that Agathocles would permit
him to exercise dominion over Libya. For, he said,
Sicily was enough for Agathocles, if only it should be
possible for him, relieved of danger from Carthage,
to rule over all the island without fear. Moreover,
Italy was close at his hand for increasing his realm
if he should decide to reach after greater things.
For Libya, separated by a wide and dangerous sea,
did not suit him at all, into which land he had even
now come through no desire but because of necessity.
Ophellas, now that to his long-considered judgement

governor, although he is not mentioned in connection with
the insurrection there put down by Ptolemy in 312 B.C. (Book
19. 79. 1-3).

[2] According to Justin, 22. 7. 4, Ophellas rather than
Agathocles first proposed the alliance.

κρίσει προστεθείσης τῆς γενομένης ἐλπίδος ἀσμένως
ὑπήκουσε καὶ πρὸς μὲν Ἀθηναίους περὶ συμμαχίας
διεπέμπετο, γεγαμηκὼς Εὐθυδίκην τὴν Μιλτιάδου
θυγατέρα τοῦ τὴν προσηγορίαν φέροντος εἰς τὸν
6 στρατηγήσαντα τῶν ἐν Μαραθῶνι νικησάντων. διὰ
δὴ ταύτην τὴν ἐπιγαμίαν καὶ τὴν ἄλλην σπουδήν,
ἣν¹ ὑπῆρχεν ἀποδεδειγμένος εἰς τὴν πόλιν, καὶ
πολλοὶ τῶν Ἀθηναίων προθύμως ὑπήκουσαν εἰς
τὴν στρατείαν. οὐκ ὀλίγοι δὲ καὶ τῶν ἄλλων
Ἑλλήνων ἔσπευδον κοινωνῆσαι τῆς ἐπιβολῆς, ἐλπί-
ζοντες τήν τε κρατίστην τῆς Λιβύης κατακληρου-
χήσειν καὶ τὸν ἐν Καρχηδόνι διαρπάσειν πλοῦτον.
7 τὰ μὲν γὰρ κατὰ τὴν Ἑλλάδα διὰ τοὺς συνεχεῖς
πολέμους καὶ τὰς τῶν δυναστῶν πρὸς ἀλλήλους
φιλοτιμίας ἀσθενῆ καὶ ταπεινὰ καθειστήκει· ὥσθ᾽
ὑπελάμβανον μὴ μόνον ἐγκρατεῖς ἔσεσθαι πολλῶν
ἀγαθῶν, ἀλλὰ καὶ τῶν παρόντων κακῶν ἀπαλλα-
γήσεσθαι.

41. Ὁ δ᾽ οὖν Ὀφέλλας, ἐπειδὴ πάντ᾽ αὐτῷ πρὸς
τὴν στρατείαν κατεσκεύαστο λαμπρῶς, ἐξώρμησε
μετὰ τῆς δυνάμεως, ἔχων πεζοὺς μὲν πλείους τῶν
μυρίων, ἱππεῖς δὲ ἑξακοσίους, ἅρματα δὲ ἑκατόν,
ἡνιόχους δὲ καὶ παραβάτας πλείους τῶν τριακοσίων.
ἠκολούθουν δὲ καὶ τῶν ἔξω τάξεως λεγομένων οὐκ
ἐλάττους μυρίων· πολλοὶ δὲ τούτων τέκνα καὶ
γυναῖκας καὶ τὴν ἄλλην παρασκευὴν ἦγον, ὥστε
2 ἐμφερῆ τὴν στρατιὰν ὑπάρχειν ἀποικίᾳ. ὀκτωκαίδεκα μὲν οὖν ἡμέρας ὁδοιπορήσαντες καὶ διελθόντες
σταδίους τρισχιλίους κατεσκήνωσαν περὶ Αὐτό-

¹ ἣν added by Dindorf.

was added this actual hope, gladly consented and sent to the Athenians an envoy to confer about an alliance, for Ophellas had married Euthydicê,[1] the daughter of a Miltiades who traced that name back to him who had commanded the victorious troops at Marathon. On account of this marriage and the other marks of favour which he had habitually displayed toward their city, a good many of the Athenians eagerly enlisted for the campaign. No small number also of the other Greeks were quick to join in the undertaking since they hoped to portion out for colonization the most fertile part of Libya and to plunder the wealth of Carthage. For conditions throughout Greece on account of the continuous wars and the mutual rivalries of the princes had become unstable and straitened, and they expected not only to gain many advantages, but also to rid themselves of their present evils.

41. And so Ophellas, when everything for his campaign had been prepared magnificently, set out with his army, having more than ten thousand foot-soldiers, six hundred horsemen, a hundred chariots, and more than three hundred charioteers and men to fight beside them. There followed also of those who are termed non-combatants not less than ten thousand; and many of these brought their children and wives and other possessions, so that the army was like a colonizing expedition. When they had marched for eighteen days and had traversed three thousand stades,[2] they encamped at Automala[3]; thence as

---

[1] After Ophellas' death she returned to Athens and became a wife of Demetrius Poliorcetes (Plutarch, *Demetrius*, 14. 1).

[2] About 345 miles.

[3] At the extreme western limit of Cyrenê, at the most southern point of the Greater Syrtis (Strabo, 2. 5. 20).

μαλα[1]· ἐντεῦθεν δὲ πορευομένοις ὑπῆρχεν ὄρος ἐξ ἀμφοτέρων τῶν μερῶν ἀπόκρημνον, ἐν μέσῳ δ' ἔχον φάραγγα βαθεῖαν, ἐξ ἧς ἀνέτεινε λισσὴ πέτρα
3 πρὸς ὀρθὸν ἀνατείνουσα σκόπελον· περὶ δὲ τὴν ῥίζαν αὐτῆς ἄντρον ἦν εὐμέγεθες, κιττῷ καὶ σμίλακι συνηρεφές, ἐν ᾧ μυθεύουσι γεγονέναι βασίλισσαν Λάμιαν τῷ κάλλει διαφέρουσαν· διὰ δὲ τὴν τῆς ψυχῆς ἀγριότητα διατυπῶσαι[2] φασι τὴν ὄψιν αὐτῆς τὸν μετὰ ταῦτα χρόνον θηριώδη. τῶν γὰρ γινομένων αὐτῇ παίδων ἁπάντων τελευτώντων βαρυθυμοῦσαν ἐπὶ τῷ πάθει καὶ φθονοῦσαν ταῖς τῶν ἄλλων γυναικῶν εὐτεκνίαις κελεύειν ἐκ τῶν ἀγκαλῶν ἐξαρπάζεσθαι τὰ βρέφη καὶ παραχρῆμα ἀπο-
4 κτέννειν. διὸ καὶ καθ' ἡμᾶς μέχρι τοῦ νῦν βίου παρὰ τοῖς νηπίοις διαμένειν τὴν περὶ τῆς γυναικὸς ταύτης φήμην καὶ φοβερωτάτην αὐτοῖς εἶναι τὴν
5 ταύτης προσηγορίαν. ὅτε δὲ μεθύσκοιτο, τὴν ἄδειαν διδόναι πᾶσιν ἃ βούλοιντο ποιεῖν ἀπαρατηρήτως. μὴ πολυπραγμονούσης οὖν αὐτῆς κατ' ἐκεῖνον τὸν χρόνον τὰ γινόμενα τοὺς[3] κατὰ τὴν χώραν ὑπολαμβάνειν μὴ βλέπειν αὐτήν· καὶ διὰ τοῦτ' ἐμυθολόγησάν τινες ὡς εἰς ἄρσιχον ἐμβάλοι τοὺς ὀφθαλμούς, τὴν ἐν οἴνῳ συντελουμένην ὀλιγωρίαν εἰς τὸ προειρημένον μέτρον μεταφέροντες,
6 ὡς τούτου παρῃρημένου τὴν ὅρασιν. ὅτι δὲ κατὰ

---

[1] Αὐτόμαλα Wesseling : Αὐτομόλας.
[2] διατετυπῶσθαί Madvig, Fischer.
[3] τοὺς added by Wesseling.

---

[1] The myth is also preserved in the scholia on Aristophanes, *Peace*, 758, and *Wasps*, 1035. In the latter place credit is

they advanced there was a mountain, precipitous on both sides but with a deep ravine in the centre, from which extended a smooth rock that rose up to a lofty peak. At the base of this rock was a large cave thickly covered with ivy and bryony, in which according to myth had been born Lamia, a queen of surpassing beauty.[1] But on account of the savagery of her heart they say that the time that has elapsed since has transformed her face to a bestial aspect. For when all the children born to her had died,[2] weighed down in her misfortune and envying the happiness of all other women in their children, she ordered that the new-born babies be snatched from their mothers' arms and straightway slain. Wherefore among us even down to the present generation, the story of this woman remains among the children and her name is most terrifying to them.[3] But whenever she drank freely, she gave to all the opportunity to do what they pleased unobserved. Therefore, since she did not trouble herself about what was taking place at such times, the people of the land assumed that she could not see. And for that reason some tell in the myth that she threw her eyes into a flask,[4] metaphorically turning the carelessness that is most complete amid wine into the aforesaid measure, since it was a measure of wine that took away her sight. One might also present Euripides

given to Duris (*FGrH*, 76. F 17), whom Diodorus is probably following here.

[2] This was because of the jealous wrath of Hera, the father of the children being Zeus.

[3] Strabo, 1. 2. 8, lists this myth among those used to frighten children. Cp. Horace, *Art of Poetry*, 340.

[4] Plutarch, *On Curiosity*, 2 (p. 516), says that she took her eyes out of her head when she wished to rest at home and replaced them when she went abroad.

τὴν Λιβύην γέγονεν αὕτη καὶ τὸν Εὐριπίδην δεῖξαι
τις ἂν μαρτυροῦντα· λέγει γὰρ

τίς τ᾽οὔνομα τὸ ἐπονείδιστον βροτοῖς[1]
οὐκ οἶδε Λαμίας τῆς Λιβυστικῆς γένος;

42. Ὁ δ᾽ οὖν[2] Ὀφέλλας ἀναλαβὼν τὴν δύναμιν
προῆγεν διὰ τῆς ἀνύδρου καὶ θηριώδους ἐπιπόνως·
οὐ μόνον γὰρ ὕδατος ἐσπάνιζεν, ἀλλὰ καὶ τῆς
ξηρᾶς τροφῆς ἀπολιπούσης ἐκινδύνευσεν ἅπαν ἀπ-
2 ολέσαι τὸ στρατόπεδον. δακέτων δὲ θηρίων παντοίων ἐπεχόντων τὰ περὶ τὰς Σύρτεις ἔρημα καὶ
τῶν πλείστων ὀλέθριον ἐχόντων τὸ δῆγμα πολλῇ
τῇ συμφορᾷ περιέπιπτον, ἀβοήθητον ἔχοντες τὴν
ἐκ τῶν ἰατρῶν καὶ φίλων ἐπικουρίαν. καὶ γὰρ
ἔνιοι τῶν ὄφεων ὁμοίαν ἔχοντες τὴν χρόαν τῇ κατ᾽
αὐτοὺς οὔσῃ χώρᾳ τὴν ἰδίαν φύσιν ἀπροόρατον
ἐποίουν· οἷς πολλοὶ διὰ τὴν ἄγνοιαν ἐπιβαίνοντες
δήγμασι θανατηφόροις περιέπιπτον. τέλος δὲ κατὰ
τὴν ὁδοιπορίαν πλεῖον ἢ δύο μῆνας κακοπαθήσαντες
μόγις διήνυσαν πρὸς τοὺς περὶ Ἀγαθοκλέα καὶ
βραχὺ διαχωρίσαντες ἀπ᾽ ἀλλήλων τὴν δύναμιν
κατεστρατοπέδευσαν.

3 Εἶθ᾽ οἱ μὲν Καρχηδόνιοι πυθόμενοι τὴν τούτων
παρουσίαν κατεπλάγησαν, ὁρῶντες τηλικαύτην δύναμιν κατ᾽ αὐτῶν ἥκουσαν· ὁ δ᾽ Ἀγαθοκλῆς ἀπαντήσας τοῖς περὶ τὸν Ὀφέλλαν καὶ φιλοφρόνως
ἅπαντα χορηγήσας τούτους μὲν ἠξίου τὴν στρατιὰν
ἀναλαμβάνειν ἐκ τῆς κακοπαθείας, αὐτὸς δὲ ἐπι-
μείνας ἡμέρας ὀλίγας καὶ κατασκεψάμενος ἕκαστα
τῶν πραττομένων ἐν τῇ παρεμβολῇ τῶν παρόντων,

---

[1] None of the attempts to heal this limping verse is con-
vincing.

as a witness that she was born in Libya, for he says :
" Who does not know the name of Lamia, Libyan in
race, a name of greatest reproach among mortals ? " [1]

42. Now Ophellas with his army was advancing
with great difficulty through a waterless land filled
with savage creatures ; for not only did he lack water,
but since dry food also gave out, he was in danger
of losing his entire army. Fanged monsters of all
kinds infest the desert near the Syrtis, and the bite
of most of these is fatal ; therefore it was a great
disaster into which they were fallen since they were
not helped by remedies supplied by physicians and
friends. For some of the serpents, since they had a
skin very like in appearance to the ground that was
beneath them, made their own forms invisible ; and
many of the men, treading upon these in ignorance,
received bites that were fatal. Finally, after suffering
great hardships on the march for more than two
months, they with difficulty completed the journey
to Agathocles and encamped, keeping the two forces
a short distance apart.

The Carthaginians, on hearing of their presence,
were panic stricken, seeing that so great a force had
arrived against them ; but Agathocles, going to meet
Ophellas and generously furnishing all needed supplies, begged him to relieve his army from its distress.[2]
He himself remained for some days and carefully
observed all that was being done in the camp of the

---

[1] The play from which this fragment comes is not known.
Cp. Nauck, *Trag. Gr. Frag.*, Euripides, 922.

[2] According to Justin, 22. 7. 5, Agathocles went so far in
showing his friendship as to have Ophellas adopt one of his
sons.

---

[2] δ' οὖν Dindorf : γοῦν R, γ' οὖν XF.

ἐπεὶ τὸ πλεῖον μέρος τῶν στρατιωτῶν ἐπὶ χορτάσματα καὶ σιτολογίαν ἐξεληλύθει, τὸν δὲ Ὀφέλλαν
ἑώρα μηδὲν τῶν ὑφ' ἑαυτοῦ βεβουλευμένων ὑπο-
νοοῦντα, συνήγαγεν ἐκκλησίαν τῶν ἰδίων στρατιωτῶν, κατηγορήσας δὲ τοῦ παρόντος ἐπὶ τὴν
συμμαχίαν ὡς ἐπιβουλεύοντος καὶ παροξύνας τὸ
πλῆθος εὐθὺς διεσκευασμένην τὴν δύναμιν ἦγεν
4 ἐπὶ τοὺς Κυρηναίους. εἶθ' ὁ μὲν Ὀφέλλας διὰ τὸ
παράδοξον καταπλαγεὶς ἐπεχείρησε μὲν ἀμύνασθαι,
καταταχούμενος δὲ καὶ τὴν ὑπολελειμμένην δύναμιν οὐκ ἔχων ἀξιόχρεων μαχόμενος ἐτελεύτησεν·
5 ὁ δ' Ἀγαθοκλῆς συναναγκάσας τὸ λοιπὸν πλῆθος
ἀποθέσθαι[1] τὰ ὅπλα καὶ φιλανθρώποις ἐπαγγελίαις
παραστησάμενος ἅπαντας κύριος ἐγένετο τῆς δυνάμεως πάσης. Ὀφέλλας μὲν οὖν ἐλπίσας μεγάλα
καὶ προχειρότερον αὐτὸν πιστεύσας τοιαύτης ἔτυχε
τῆς τοῦ βίου καταστροφῆς.

43. Ἐν δὲ τῇ Καρχηδόνι Βορμίλκας πάλαι δια-
νενοημένος ἐπιθέσθαι τυραννίδι καιρὸν ἐπεζήτει
ταῖς ἰδίαις ἐπιβολαῖς οἰκεῖον. πολλάκις δὲ διδόντος
τοῦ καιροῦ τὰς ἀφορμὰς τοῦ πράττειν τὸ βεβου-
λευμένον ἀεί τις αἰτία μικρὰ παρεμπίπτουσα διεκώ-
λυεν· δεισιδαίμονες γὰρ οἱ μέλλοντες ἐγχειρεῖν ταῖς
παρανόμοις καὶ μεγάλαις πράξεσι καὶ τὸ μέλλειν
ἀεὶ τοῦ πράττειν καὶ τὴν ὑπέρθεσιν τῆς συντελείας
προκρίνουσιν. ὃ καὶ τότε συνέβαινεν καὶ περὶ

---

[1] ἀποθέσθαι Dindorf : ἀποδόσθαι.

---

[1] The whole account, with its emphasis on the treachery

new arrivals. When the larger part of the soldiers
had scattered to find fodder and food, and when he
saw that Ophellas had no suspicion of what he himself
had planned, he summoned an assembly of his own
soldiers and, after accusing the man who had come
to join the alliance as if he were plotting against
himself and thus rousing the anger of his men,
straightway led his army in full array against the
Cyreneans. Then Ophellas, stunned by this unexpected action, attempted to defend himself; but,
pressed for time, the forces that he had remaining in
camp not being adequate, he died fighting. Agathocles forced the rest of the army to lay down its
arms, and by winning them all over with generous
promises, he became master of the whole army. Thus
Ophellas, who had cherished great hopes and had
rashly entrusted himself to another, met an end so
inglorious.[1]

43. In Carthage Bormilcar, who had long planned
to make an attempt at tyranny, was seeking a proper
occasion for his private schemes. Time and again
when circumstances put him in a position to carry out
what he had planned, some little cause intervened
to thwart him.[2] For those who are about to undertake
lawless and important enterprises are superstitious
and always choose delay rather than action, and post-
ponement rather than accomplishment. This happened also on this occasion and in regard to this man;

of Agathocles, is probably drawn from Duris, as a part of
it quite certainly is (cp. note on chap. 41. 3).

[2] For chaps. 43-44 cp. Justin, 22. 7. 6-11, who says that
Bormilcar, after Agathocles had inflicted severe losses on the
Carthaginians, wished to go over to Agathocles with his
army, was prevented by a sedition in the Sicilian camp, and
was put to death by his fellow citizens.

2 ἐκεῖνον· ἐξέπεμψε μὲν γὰρ τοὺς ἐπιφανεστάτους
τῶν πολιτῶν εἰς τὴν ἐπὶ τοὺς Νομάδας στρατείαν,
ἵνα μηδένα τῶν ἀξιολόγων ἔχῃ τὸν ἀντιστησόμενον,
οὐκ ἐτόλμα δὲ ἀποκαλύψασθαι πρὸς τὴν τυραννίδα,
3 μετακαλούμενος ὑπὸ τῆς εὐλαβείας. καθ᾽ ὃν δὲ
καιρὸν Ἀγαθοκλῆς ἐπέθετο τοῖς περὶ τὸν Ὀφέλλαν,
ὁρμῆσαι καὶ τοῦτον συνέβη πρὸς τὴν δυναστείαν,
ἀγνοούντων ἀμφοτέρων τὰ παρὰ τοῖς πολεμίοις
4 πραττόμενα. οὔτε γὰρ Ἀγαθοκλῆς ἔγνω τὴν ἐπίθεσιν τῆς τυραννίδος καὶ τὴν ἐν τῇ πόλει ταραχήν,
ἐπεὶ ῥαδίως ἂν ἐκράτησε τῆς Καρχηδόνος· εἵλετο
γὰρ ἂν Βορμίλκας ἐπ᾽ αὐτοφώρῳ γενόμενος συνεργεῖν Ἀγαθοκλεῖ μᾶλλον ἢ τοῖς πολίταις δοῦναι
τὴν ἐκ τοῦ σώματος τιμωρίαν· οὔτε πάλιν οἱ Καρχηδόνιοι τὴν ἐπίθεσιν τὴν Ἀγαθοκλέους ἐπύθοντο·
ῥαδίως γὰρ ἂν αὐτὸν ἐχειρώσαντο προσλαβόμενοι
5 τὴν μετ᾽ Ὀφέλλα δύναμιν. ἀλλ᾽, οἶμαι, παρ᾽
ἀμφοτέροις οὐκ ἀλογίστως συνέβη γενέσθαι ταύτην
τὴν ἄγνοιαν, καίπερ μεγάλων μὲν οὐσῶν τῶν
πράξεων, ἐγγὺς δ᾽ ἀλλήλων τῶν¹ ἐπικεχειρηκότων
6 τοῖς τηλικούτοις τολμήμασιν· ὅ τε γὰρ Ἀγαθοκλῆς
ἄνδρα φίλον μέλλων ἀναιρεῖν πρὸς οὐδὲν ἐπέβαλλε
τὴν διάνοιαν τῶν παρὰ τοῖς πολεμίοις συντελουμένων, ὅ τε Βορμίλκας τὴν τῆς πατρίδος ἐλευθερίαν
ἀφαιρούμενος οὐδὲν ὅλως ἐπολυπραγμόνει τῶν παρὰ
τοῖς ἀντιστρατοπεδεύουσιν, ὡς ἂν ἔχων προκεί-
μενον ἐν τῇ ψυχῇ τὸ μὴ τοὺς πολεμίους ἐπὶ τοῦ
παρόντος, ἀλλὰ τοὺς πολίτας καταπολεμῆσαι.

7 Ταύτῃ δ᾽ ἄν τις καὶ τὴν ἱστορίαν καταμέμψαιτο,
θεωρῶν ἐπὶ μὲν τοῦ βίου πολλὰς καὶ διαφόρους
πράξεις συντελουμένας κατὰ τὸν αὐτὸν καιρόν, τοῖς
δ᾽ ἀναγράφουσιν ἀναγκαῖον ὑπάρχον τὸ μεσολαβεῖν

for he sent out the most distinguished of the citizens to the campaign against the Nomads so that he might have no man of consequence to oppose him, but he did not venture to make an open bid for the tyranny, being held back by caution. But it happened that at the time when Agathocles attacked Ophellas, Bormilcar made his effort to gain the tyranny, each of the two being ignorant of what the enemy was doing. Agathocles did not know of the attempt at tyranny and of the confusion in the city when he might easily have become master of Carthage, for when Bormilcar was discovered in the act he would have preferred to co-operate with Agathocles rather than pay the penalty in his own person to the citizens. And again, the Carthaginians had not heard of Agathocles' attack, for they might easily have over-powered him with the aid of the army of Ophellas. But I suppose that not without reason did such ignor-ance prevail on both sides, although the actions were on a large scale and those who had undertaken deeds of such daring were near each other. For Agathocles, when about to kill a man who was his friend, paid attention to nothing that was happening among his enemies ; and Bormilcar, when depriving his father-land of its liberty, did not concern himself at all with events in the camp of the enemy, since he had as a fixed purpose in his mind to conquer at the time, not his enemies, but his fellow citizens.

At this point one might censure the art of history, when he observes that in life many different actions are consummated at the same time, but that it is necessary for those who record them to interrupt the

---

[1] τῶν added by Geer.

τὴν διήγησιν καὶ τοῖς ἅμα συντελουμένοις μερίζειν
τοὺς χρόνους παρὰ φύσιν, ὥστε τὴν μὲν ἀλήθειαν
τῶν πεπραγμένων τὸ πάθος ἔχειν, τὴν δ' ἀναγραφὴν
ἐστερημένην τῆς ὁμοίας ἐξουσίας μιμεῖσθαι μὲν
τὰ γεγενημένα, πολὺ δὲ λείπεσθαι τῆς ἀληθοῦς
διαθέσεως.

44. Ὁ δ' οὖν Βορμίλκας ἐξετασμὸν τῶν στρατιωτῶν ποιησάμενος ἐν τῇ καλουμένῃ Νέᾳ πόλει,
μικρὸν ἔξω τῆς ἀρχαίας Καρχηδόνος οὔσῃ, τοὺς
μὲν ἄλλους διαφῆκε, τοὺς δὲ συνειδότας περὶ τῆς
ἐπιθέσεως, ὄντας πολίτας μὲν πεντακοσίους, μισθοφόρους δὲ περὶ χιλίους ἀναλαβών,[1] ἀνέδειξεν ἑαυ-
2 τὸν τύραννον. εἰς πέντε δὲ μέρη τοὺς στρατιώτας
διελόμενος ἐπῄει πάντας τοὺς ἐν ταῖς ὁδοῖς ἀπαν-
τῶντας ἀποσφάττων. γενομένης δὲ κατὰ τὴν πόλιν
ταραχῆς ἐξαισίου τὸ μὲν πρῶτον οἱ Καρχηδόνιοι
τοὺς πολεμίους ὑπέλαβον παρεισπεπτωκέναι προ-
διδομένης τῆς πόλεως· ὡς δ' ἐπεγνώσθη τἀληθές,
συνέτρεχον οἱ νέοι καὶ εἰς τάξεις καταστάντες
3 ὥρμησαν ἐπὶ τὸν τύραννον. ὁ δὲ Βορμίλκας τοὺς
ἐν ταῖς ὁδοῖς ἀναιρῶν ὥρμησεν εἰς τὴν ἀγορὰν καὶ
πολλοὺς τῶν πολιτῶν ἀνόπλους καταλαβὼν ἀπ-
4 έκτεινε. τῶν δὲ Καρχηδονίων καταλαβομένων τὰς
περὶ τὴν ἀγορὰν οἰκίας ὑψηλὰς οὔσας καὶ τοῖς
βέλεσι πυκνοῖς χρωμένων οἱ μετέχοντες τῆς ἐπιθέσεως κατετραυματίζοντο, τοῦ τόπου παντὸς ἐμ-
5 βελοῦς ὄντος. διόπερ κακοπαθοῦντες συνέφραξαν
ἑαυτοὺς καὶ διὰ τῶν στενωπῶν συνεξέπεσαν εἰς
τὴν Νέαν πόλιν, βαλλόμενοι συνεχῶς ἀπὸ τῶν

narrative and to parcel out different times to simul- 308 B.C.
taneous events contrary to nature, with the result
that, although the actual experience of the events
contains the truth, yet the written record, deprived
of such power, while presenting copies of the events,
falls far short of arranging them as they really were.

44. Be that as it may, when Bormilcar had re-
viewed the soldiers in what was called the New City,
which is a short distance from Old Carthage, he dismissed the rest, but holding those who were his con-
federates in the plot, five hundred citizens and about
a thousand mercenaries, he declared himself tyrant.
Dividing his soldiers into five bands, he attacked,
slaughtering those who opposed him in the streets.
Since an extraordinary tumult broke out everywhere
in the city, the Carthaginians at first supposed that
the enemy had made his way in and that the city was
being betrayed ; when, however, the true situation
became known, the young men ran together, formed
companies, and advanced against the tyrant. But
Bormilcar, killing those in the streets, moved swiftly
into the market place ; and finding there many of
the citizens unarmed, he slaughtered them. The
Carthaginians, however, after occupying the buildings
about the market place, which were tall, hurled
missiles thick and fast, and the participants in the
uprising began to be struck down since the whole
place was within range. Therefore, since they were
suffering severely, they closed ranks and forced their
way out through the narrow streets into the New
City, being continuously struck with missiles from

---

¹ ἀναλαβών added by Rhodoman, who also suggests παρα-
καλεσάμενος, παρακελευσάμενος, and συναγαγών ; παρακατασχών
Reiske.

οἰκιῶν καθ' ἃς τυγχάνοιεν αἰεὶ γινόμενοι. καταλαβομένων δ' αὐτῶν ὑπερδέξιόν τινα τόπον οἱ
Καρχηδόνιοι τῶν πολιτῶν πάντων συνδραμόντων
ἐν τοῖς ὅπλοις ἀντεστρατοπέδευσαν τοῖς ἀφεστη-
6 κόσι. τέλος δὲ πρέσβεις πέμψαντες τῶν πρεσβυ-
τάτων τοὺς εὐθέτους καὶ τῶν ἐγκλημάτων δόντες
ἄφεσιν διελύθησαν· καὶ τοῖς μὲν ἄλλοις οὐδὲν ἐμνη-
σικάκησαν διὰ τοὺς περιεστῶτας τὴν πόλιν κινδύνους, αὐτὸν δὲ τὸν Βορμίλκαν αἰκισάμενοι δεινῶς
τοῦ ζῆν ἐστέρησαν, οὐδὲν φροντίσαντες τῶν δεδο-
μένων ὅρκων. Καρχηδόνιοι μὲν οὖν κινδυνεύσαντες
τοῖς ὅλοις σφαλῆναι τοῦτον τὸν τρόπον ἐκομίσαντο
τὴν πατρῴαν πολιτείαν.

7 Ἀγαθοκλῆς δὲ πλοῖα φορτηγὰ γεμίσας τῶν λα-
φύρων καὶ τοὺς ἀχρήστους εἰς πόλεμον τῶν ἐκ
Κυρήνης παραγενομένων ἐμβιβάσας ἀπέστειλεν εἰς
Συρακούσσας. χειμώνων δ' ἐπιγενομένων ἃ μὲν
διεφθάρη τῶν πλοίων, ἃ δ' ἐξέπεσε πρὸς τὰς κατ'
Ἰταλίαν Πιθηκούσσας νήσους, ὀλίγα δ' εἰς τὰς
Συρακούσσας διεσώθη.

8 Κατὰ δὲ τὴν Ἰταλίαν οἱ τῶν Ῥωμαίων ὕπατοι,
Μαρσοῖς πολεμουμένοις ὑπὸ Σαμνιτῶν βοηθήσαντες,
τῇ τε μάχῃ προετέρησαν καὶ συχνοὺς τῶν πολεμίων
9 ἀνεῖλον. εἶτα διὰ τῆς Ὀμβρίκων χώρας διελθόντες
ἐνέβαλον εἰς τὴν Τυρρηνίαν πολεμίαν οὖσαν καὶ
τὸ καλούμενον Καίριον φρούριον ἐξεπολιόρκησαν.
διαπρεσβευομένων δὲ τῶν ἐγχωρίων ὑπὲρ ἀνοχῶν
πρὸς μὲν Ταρκυνιήτας εἰς ἔτη τεσσαράκοντα, πρὸς
δὲ τοὺς ἄλλους Τυρρηνοὺς ἅπαντας εἰς ἐνιαυτὸν
ἀνοχὰς ἐποιήσαντο.

whatever houses they chanced at any time to be near. 308 B.C. After these had occupied a certain elevation, the Carthaginians, now that all the citizens had assembled in arms, drew up their forces against those who had taken part in the uprising. Finally, sending as envoys such of the oldest men as were qualified and offering amnesty, they came to terms. Against the rest they invoked no penalty on account of the dangers that surrounded the city, but they cruelly tortured Bormilcar himself and put him to death, paying no heed to the oaths which had been given. In this way, then, the Carthaginians, after having been in the gravest danger, preserved the constitution of their fathers.

Agathocles, loading cargo vessels with his spoil and embarking on them those of the men who had come from Cyrenê who were useless for war, sent them to Syracuse. But storms arose, and some of the ships were destroyed, some were driven to the Pithecusan Islands off the coast of Italy, and a few came safe to Syracuse.[1]

In Italy [2] the Roman consuls, going to the aid of the Marsi, against whom the Samnites were making war, were victorious in the battle and slew many of the enemy. Then, crossing the territory of the Umbrians, they invaded Etruria, which was hostile, and took by siege the fortress called Caerium.[3] When the people of the region sent envoys to ask a truce, the consuls made a truce for forty years with the Tarquinians but with all the other Etruscans for one year.[4]

[1] Continued in chap. 54. 1.
[2] Continued from chap. 36. 6. Cp. Livy, 9. 41. 5-7.
[3] Unknown. Caprium in Table of Contents, p. 138, and in *var. lect.* here.   [4] Continued in chap. 80. 1.

45. Τοῦ δ' ἐνιαυσίου χρόνου διεληλυθότος Ἀθήνησι μὲν ἦρχεν Ἀναξικράτης, ἐν Ῥώμῃ δὲ ὕπατοι κατέστησαν Ἄππιος Κλαύδιος καὶ Λεύκιος Οὐολόμνιος. ἐπὶ δὲ τούτων Δημήτριος μὲν ὁ Ἀντιγόνου παραλαβὼν παρὰ τοῦ πατρὸς δύναμιν ἁδρὰν πεζικήν τε καὶ ναυτικήν, ἔτι δὲ βελῶν καὶ τῶν ἄλλων τῶν εἰς πολιορκίαν χρησίμων τὴν ἁρμόζουσαν παρασκευὴν ἐξέπλευσεν ἐκ τῆς Ἐφέσου· παράγγελμα δ' εἶχεν ἐλευθεροῦν πάσας μὲν τὰς κατὰ τὴν Ἑλλάδα πόλεις, πρώτην δὲ τὴν Ἀθη-
2 ναίων, φρουρουμένην ὑπὸ Κασάνδρου. καταπλεύσαντος δ' αὐτοῦ μετὰ τῆς δυνάμεως εἰς τὸν Πειραιᾶ καὶ πανταχόθεν προσβαλόντος ἐξ ἐφόδου καὶ κήρυγμα ποιησαμένου,[1] Διονύσιος ὁ καθεσταμένος ἐπὶ τῆς Μουνυχίας φρούραρχος καὶ Δημήτριος ὁ Φαληρεὺς ἐπιμελητὴς τῆς πόλεως γεγενημένος ὑπὸ Κασάνδρου, πολλοὺς ἔχοντες στρατιώτας, ἀπὸ τῶν
3 τειχῶν ἠμύνοντο. τῶν δ' Ἀντιγόνου στρατιωτῶν τινες βιασάμενοι καὶ κατὰ τὴν ἀκτὴν ὑπερβάντες ἐντὸς τοῦ τείχους παρεδέξαντο πλείους τῶν συναγωνιζομένων. τὸν μὲν οὖν Πειραιᾶ τοῦτον τὸν τρόπον ἁλῶναι συνέβη, τῶν δ' ἔνδον Διονύσιος μὲν ὁ φρούραρχος εἰς τὴν Μουνυχίαν συνέφυγε, Δημή-
4 τριος δ' ὁ Φαληρεὺς ἀπεχώρησεν εἰς ἄστυ. τῇ δ' ὑστεραίᾳ πεμφθεὶς μεθ' ἑτέρων πρεσβευτὴς ὑπὸ τοῦ δήμου πρὸς Δημήτριον καὶ περὶ τῆς αὐτονομίας διαλεχθεὶς καὶ τῆς ἰδίας ἀσφαλείας ἔτυχε παρα-

[1] After ποιησαμένου Fischer in apparatus suggests the addition of ὅτι Δημήτριος τὰς Ἀθήνας ἐλευθεροῖ, cp. Plutarch, *Demetrius*, 8.

45. When that year had come to an end, Anaxi- 307 B.C.
crates was archon in Athens and in Rome Appius
Claudius and Lucius Volumnius became consuls.[1]
While these held office, Demetrius, the son of Antigonus, having received from his father strong land
and sea forces, also a suitable supply of missiles and
of the other things requisite for carrying on a siege,
set sail from Ephesus. He had instructions to free
all the cities throughout Greece, but first of all
Athens, which was held by a garrison of Cassander.[2]
Sailing into the Peiraeus with his forces, he at once
made an attack on all sides and issued a proclama-
tion.[3] Dionysius, who had been placed in command
of the garrison on Munychia, and Demetrius of
Phalerum, who had been made military governor
of the city [4] by Cassander, resisted him from the
walls with many soldiers. Some of Antigonus' men,
attacking with violence and effecting an entrance
along the coast, admitted many of their fellow
soldiers within the wall. The result was that in this
way the Peiraeus was taken ; and, of those within
it, Dionysius the commander fled to Munychia and
Demetrius of Phalerum withdrew into the city. On
the next day, when he had been sent with others as
envoys by the people to Demetrius and had discussed
the independence of the city and his own security,
he obtained a safe-conduct for himself and, giving

---

[1] Anaxicrates was archon in 307/6 B.C. In the Fasti the
consuls for 307 B.C. are Ap. Claudius Caecus and L. Volumnius Flamma Violens ; cp. Livy, 9. 42. 2. The narrative is
continued from chap. 37. 6.

[2] For this campaign cp. Plutarch, *Demetrius*, 8-9.

[3] If we accept Fischer's suggested supplement, we should
add " that Demetrius was freeing Athens."

[4] *i.e.* of Athens.

πομπῆς καὶ τὰ κατὰ τὰς Ἀθήνας ἀπογινώσκων
ἔφυγεν εἰς τὰς Θήβας, ὕστερον δὲ πρὸς Πτολεμαῖον
5 εἰς Αἴγυπτον. οὗτος μὲν οὖν ἔτη δέκα τῆς πόλεως
ἐπιστατήσας ἐξέπεσεν ἐκ τῆς πατρίδος τὸν εἰρημένον τρόπον. ὁ δὲ δῆμος τῶν Ἀθηναίων κομισάμενος τὴν ἐλευθερίαν ἐψηφίσατο τιμὰς τοῖς αἰτίοις
τῆς αὐτονομίας.

Δημήτριος δ' ἐπιστήσας τοὺς πετροβόλους καὶ
τὰς ἄλλας μηχανὰς καὶ τὰ βέλη προσέβαλλε τῇ
6 Μουνυχίᾳ καὶ κατὰ γῆν καὶ κατὰ θάλατταν. ἀμυνομένων δὲ τῶν ἔνδον ἀπὸ τῶν τειχῶν εὐρώστως
συνέβαινε τοὺς μὲν περὶ Διονύσιον προέχειν ταῖς
δυσχωρίαις καὶ ταῖς τῶν τόπων ὑπεροχαῖς, οὔσης
τῆς Μουνυχίας ὀχυρᾶς οὐ μόνον ἐκ φύσεως ἀλλὰ
καὶ ταῖς τῶν τειχῶν κατασκευαῖς, τοὺς δὲ περὶ τὸν
Δημήτριον τῷ τε πλήθει τῶν στρατιωτῶν πολλαπλασίους εἶναι καὶ ταῖς παρασκευαῖς πολλὰ πλεον-
7 εκτεῖν. τέλος δ' ἐπὶ δύο ἡμέρας συνεχῶς τῆς
πολιορκίας γινομένης οἱ μὲν φρουροὶ τοῖς καταπέλταις καὶ πετροβόλοις συντιτρωσκόμενοι καὶ
διαδόχους οὐκ ἔχοντες ἠλαττοῦντο, οἱ δὲ περὶ τὸν
Δημήτριον ἐκ διαδοχῆς κινδυνεύοντες καὶ νεαλεῖς
ἀεὶ γινόμενοι, διὰ τῶν πετροβόλων ἐρημωθέντος
τοῦ τείχους, ἐνέπεσον εἰς τὴν Μουνυχίαν καὶ τοὺς
μὲν φρουροὺς ἠνάγκασαν θέσθαι τὰ ὅπλα, τὸν δὲ
φρούραρχον Διονύσιον ἐζώγρησαν.

46. Τούτων δὲ ὀλίγαις ἡμέραις κατευτυχηθέντων
ὁ μὲν Δημήτριος κατασκάψας τὴν Μουνυχίαν ὁλό-
κληρον τῷ δήμῳ τὴν ἐλευθερίαν ἀποκατέστησεν καὶ
2 φιλίαν καὶ συμμαχίαν πρὸς αὐτοὺς συνέθετο, οἱ δὲ
Ἀθηναῖοι γράψαντος ψήφισμα Στρατοκλέους ἐψη-

up the direction of Athens, fled to Thebes and later 307 B.C. into Egypt to Ptolemy.[1] And so this man, after he had been director of the city for ten years, was driven from his fatherland in the way described. The Athenian people, having recovered their freedom, decreed honours to those responsible for their liberation.

Demetrius, however, bringing up ballistae and the other engines of war and missiles, assaulted Munychia both by land and by sea. When those within defended themselves stoutly from the walls, it turned out that Dionysius had the advantage of the difficult terrain and the greater height of his position, for Munychia was strong both by nature and by the fortifications which had been constructed, but that Demetrius was many times superior in the number of his soldiers and had a great advantage in his equipment. Finally, after the attack had continued unremittingly for two days, the defenders, severely wounded by the catapults and the ballistae and not having any men to relieve them, had the worst of it ; and the men of Demetrius, who were fighting in relays and were continually relieved, after the wall had been cleared by the ballistae, broke into Munychia, forced the garrison to lay down its arms, and took the commander Dionysius alive.[2]

46. After gaining these successes in a few days and razing Munychia completely, Demetrius restored to the people their freedom and established friendship and an alliance with them. The Athenians, Stratocles

[1] Cp. Diogenes Laertius, 5. 78 ; Strabo, 9. 1. 20 (p. 398).

[2] Plutarch, *Demetrius*, 9, places the capture of Megara (cp. chap. 46. 3) between the surrender of Athens and the taking of Munychia.

φίσαντο χρυσᾶς μὲν εἰκόνας ἐφ' ἅρματος στῆσαι τοῦ
τε Ἀντιγόνου καὶ Δημητρίου πλησίον Ἁρμοδίου
καὶ Ἀριστογείτονος, στεφανῶσαι δὲ ἀμφοτέρους
ἀπὸ ταλάντων διακοσίων καὶ βωμὸν ἱδρυσαμένους
προσαγορεῦσαι Σωτήρων, πρὸς δὲ τὰς δέκα φυλὰς
προσθεῖναι δύο, Δημητριάδα καὶ Ἀντιγονίδα, καὶ
συντελεῖν αὐτοῖς κατ' ἐνιαυτὸν ἀγῶνας καὶ πομπὴν
καὶ θυσίαν, ἐνυφαίνειν τε[1] αὐτοὺς εἰς τὸν τῆς
3 Ἀθηνᾶς πέπλον.[2] ὁ μὲν οὖν δῆμος ἐν τῷ Λαμιακῷ
πολέμῳ καταλυθεὶς ὑπ' Ἀντιπάτρου μετ' ἔτη
πεντεκαίδεκα παραδόξως ἐκομίσατο τὴν πάτριον
πολιτείαν· ὁ δὲ Δημήτριος, φρουρουμένης τῆς
Μεγαρέων πόλεως, ἐκπολιορκήσας αὐτὴν ἀπέδωκεν
τὴν αὐτονομίαν τῷ δήμῳ καὶ τιμῶν ἀξιολόγων
ἔτυχεν ὑπὸ τῶν εὖ παθόντων.
4 Ἀντίγονος δέ, παραγενομένων πρὸς αὐτὸν Ἀθή-
νηθεν πρεσβευτῶν καὶ τό τε περὶ τῶν τιμῶν ἀνα-
δόντων ψήφισμα καὶ περὶ σίτου καὶ ξύλων εἰς
ναυπηγίαν διαλεχθέντων, ἔδωκεν αὐτοῖς πυροῦ μὲν
μεδίμνων πεντεκαίδεκα μυριάδας, ὕλην δὲ τὴν
ἱκανὴν ναυσὶν ἑκατόν· ἐξ Ἴμβρου δὲ τὴν φρουρὰν
5 ἐξαγαγὼν ἀπέδωκεν αὐτοῖς τὴν πόλιν. πρὸς δὲ
τὸν υἱὸν Δημήτριον ἔγραψε κελεύων τῶν μὲν συμμαχίδων πόλεων συνέδρους συστήσασθαι τοὺς
βουλευσομένους κοινῇ περὶ τῶν τῇ Ἑλλάδι συμ-
φερόντων, αὐτὸν δὲ μετὰ τῆς δυνάμεως εἰς Κύπρον
πλεῦσαι καὶ διαπολεμῆσαι τὴν ταχίστην πρὸς τοὺς

---

[1] ἐνυφαίνειν τε Dindorf : ἐνυφαινόντων.
[2] κατ' ἐνιαυτόν after πέπλον omitted by Wesseling.

---

[1] For the honours conferred on Demetrius and Antigonus
cp. Plutarch, *Demetrius*, 10-12. For Stratocles, an old
political ally of Hypereides, who had acted as an accuser in

writing the decree,[1] voted to set up golden statues 307 B.C.
of Antigonus and Demetrius in a chariot near the
statues of Harmodius and Aristogeiton, to give them
both honorary crowns at a cost of two hundred talents,
to consecrate an altar to them and call it the altar
of the Saviours, to add to the ten tribes two more,
Demetrias and Antigonis, to hold annual games in
their honour with a procession and a sacrifice, and
to weave their portraits in the peplos of Athena.
Thus the common people, deprived of power in
the Lamian War by Antipater,[2] fifteen years afterwards unexpectedly recovered the constitution of the
fathers. Although Megara was held by a garrison,
Demetrius took it by siege, restored their autonomy
to its people, and received noteworthy honours from
those whom he had served.[3]

When an embassy had come to Antigonus from
Athens and had delivered to him the decree concerning the honours conferred upon him and discussed with
him the problem of grain and of timber for ships, he gave
to them one hundred and fifty thousand medimni [4]
of grain and timber sufficient for one hundred ships ;
he also withdrew his garrison from Imbros and gave
the city back to the Athenians. He wrote to his son
Demetrius ordering him to call together counsellors
from the allied cities who should consider in common
what was advantageous for Greece, and to sail himself with his army to Cyprus and finish the war with

the affair of Harpalus and had played an important rôle in
Athens during the Lamian War, cp. Plutarch, *Demetrius*,
11-12. A number of decrees which he introduced in the
Assembly in this period are extant, *e.g. IG*, 2. 240, 247.

[2] Cp. Book 18. 18.

[3] But cp. the note on chap. 45. 7.

[4] About 230,000 bushels.

6 Πτολεμαίου στρατηγούς. οὗτος μὲν οὖν συντόμως
πάντα πράξας κατὰ τὰς ἐντολὰς τοῦ πατρὸς καὶ
κομισθεὶς ἐπὶ Καρίας παρεκάλει τοὺς Ῥοδίους πρὸς
τὸν κατὰ Πτολεμαίου πόλεμον. οὐ προσεχόντων
δ' αὐτῶν, ἀλλὰ κοινὴν εἰρήνην αἱρουμένων ἄγειν
πρὸς ἅπαντας ταύτην ἀρχὴν συνέβη γενέσθαι τῷ
δήμῳ τῆς πρὸς Ἀντίγονον ἀλλοτριότητος.

47. Ὁ δὲ Δημήτριος παραπλεύσας εἰς Κιλικίαν
κἀκεῖθεν ναῦς καὶ στρατιώτας προσλαβόμενος δι-
έπλευσεν εἰς τὴν Κύπρον ἔχων πεζοὺς μὲν μυρίους
πεντακισχιλίους, ἱππεῖς δὲ τετρακοσίους, ναῦς δὲ
ταχυναυτούσας μὲν τριήρεις[1] πλείους τῶν ἑκατὸν
δέκα, τῶν δὲ βαρυτέρων στρατιωτίδων πεντήκοντα
καὶ τρεῖς καὶ πόρια τῶν παντοδαπῶν ἱκανὰ τῷ
2 πλήθει τῶν ἱππέων τε καὶ πεζῶν. καὶ τὸ μὲν
πρῶτον κατεστρατοπέδευσεν ἐν τῇ παραλίᾳ τῆς
Καρπασίας καὶ νεωλκήσας τὰ σκάφη χάρακι καὶ
τάφρῳ βαθείᾳ τὴν παρεμβολὴν ὠχύρωσεν· ἔπειτα
τοῖς πλησιοχώροις προσβολὰς ποιησάμενος εἷλε
κατὰ κράτος Οὐρανίαν καὶ Καρπασίαν, τῶν δὲ
νεῶν τὴν ἱκανὴν φυλακὴν ἀπολιπὼν ἀνέζευξε μετὰ
3 τῆς δυνάμεως ἐπὶ τὴν Σαλαμῖνα. ὁ δὲ τεταγμένος
ὑπὸ Πτολεμαίου τῆς νήσου στρατηγὸς Μενέλαος
συναγαγὼν τοὺς στρατιώτας ἐκ τῶν φρουρίων
διέτριβεν ἐν Σαλαμῖνι, ἀπεχόντων δὲ τεσσαράκοντα

---

[1] τριήρεις omitted by Hertlein. Cp. note on translation.

---

[1] Cp. chap. 27.
[2] So the text; but in chap. 50. 1-3 we find that Demetrius,
after leaving 10 quinqueremes at Salamis, had 10 quinqueremes, 10 sixes, and 7 sevens in his left wing alone. It

the generals of Ptolemy as soon as possible.[1] De- 307 B.C.
metrius, promptly doing all according to his father's
orders, moved toward Caria and summoned the
Rhodians for the war against Ptolemy. They did not
obey, preferring to maintain a common peace with
all, and this was the beginning of the hostility between
that people and Antigonus.

47. Demetrius, after coasting along to Cilicia and
there assembling additional ships and soldiers, sailed
to Cyprus with fifteen thousand foot-soldiers and
four hundred horsemen, more than one hundred
and ten swift triremes, fifty-three heavier transports,[2]
and freighters of every kind sufficient for the strength
of his cavalry and infantry. First he went into camp
on the coast of Carpasia,[3] and after beaching his ships,
strengthened his encampment with a palisade and
a deep moat ; then, making raids on the peoples who
lived near by, he took by storm Urania [4] and Carpasia ; then leaving an adequate guard for the ships,
he moved with his forces against Salamis. Menelaüs,[5]
who had been made general of the island by Ptolemy,
had gathered his soldiers from the outposts and was
waiting in Salamis ; but when the enemy was at a

seems certain, therefore, that the βαρύτεραι στρατιώτιδες are
not transports (which is the regular meaning of the term) but
heavy warships (quinqueremes and larger) carrying armed
men as well as oarsmen. Such ships would fight by boarding
rather than by ramming (cp. Tarn, *Hellenistic Military and
Naval Developments*, 144). It is quite certain also that among
the ταχυναυτοῦσαι ναῦς are the quadriremes mentioned in the
battle (chap. 50. 3), the τριήρεις of the text being an error
either of the copyists or of Diodorus himself. For this whole
passage cp. Beloch, *Griechische Geschichte*[2], 4. 1. 154, note 1.

[3] On the north coast of Cyprus, near the end of the cape
that projects to the north-east.

[4] The exact situation of this city is unknown.

[5] Cp. chap. 21. 1.

σταδίους τῶν πολεμίων ἐξῆλθεν ἔχων πεζοὺς μὲν
μυρίους καὶ δισχιλίους, ἱππεῖς δὲ περὶ ὀκτακοσίους.
γενομένης δὲ μάχης ἐπ᾽ ὀλίγον χρόνον οἱ μὲν περὶ
τὸν Μενέλαον ἐκβιασθέντες ἐτράπησαν, ὁ δὲ Δημήτριος συνδιώξας τοὺς πολεμίους εἰς τὴν πόλιν
αἰχμαλώτους μὲν ἔλαβεν οὐ πολὺ ἐλάττους τρισχι-
4 λίων, ἀνεῖλε δὲ περὶ χιλίους. τοὺς δ᾽ ἁλόντας τὸ
μὲν πρῶτον ἀπολύσας τῶν ἐγκλημάτων καταδιεῖλεν
εἰς τὰς τῶν ἰδίων στρατιωτῶν τάξεις· ἀποδιδρα-
σκόντων δ᾽ αὐτῶν πρὸς τοὺς περὶ τὸν Μενέλαον διὰ
τὸ τὰς ἀποσκευὰς ἐν Αἰγύπτῳ καταλελοιπέναι παρὰ
Πτολεμαίῳ, γνοὺς ἀμεταθέτους ὄντας ἐνεβίβασεν
εἰς τὰς ναῦς καὶ πρὸς Ἀντίγονον εἰς Συρίαν
ἀπέστειλεν.

5 Οὗτος δὲ τοῦτον τὸν χρόνον διέτριβε περὶ τὴν
ἄνω Συρίαν, πόλιν κτίζων περὶ τὸν Ὀρόντην ποταμὸν τὴν ὠνομασμένην Ἀντιγονίαν ἀφ᾽ ἑαυτοῦ.
κατεσκεύαζε δὲ πολυτελῶς, τὴν περίμετρον ὑπο-
στησάμενος σταδίων ἑβδομήκοντα· εὐφυὴς γὰρ ἦν
ὁ τόπος ἐφεδρεῦσαι τῇ τε Βαβυλῶνι καὶ ταῖς ἄνω
σατραπείαις καὶ πάλιν τῇ κάτω Συρίᾳ καὶ ταῖς
6 περὶ Αἰγύπτου σατραπείαις.[1] οὐ μὴν πολύν γε χρόνον συνέβη μεῖναι τὴν πόλιν, Σελεύκου καθελόν-
τος αὐτὴν καὶ μεταγαγόντος ἐπὶ τὴν κτισθεῖσαν
μὲν ὑπ᾽ αὐτοῦ, ἀπ᾽ ἐκείνου δὲ κληθεῖσαν Σελεύ-
κειαν.[2] ἀλλὰ περὶ μὲν τούτων ἀκριβῶς ἕκαστα
δηλώσομεν ἐπὶ τοὺς οἰκείους χρόνους παραγενη-

---

[1] ταῖς περὶ Αἰγύπτου σατραπείαις Reiske, ταῖς ἀπ᾽ Αἰ. στρατείαις Madvig, τοῖς περὶ Αἰ. πράγμασι Fischer in apparatus, cp.
chap. 104. 4 : ταῖς ἀπ᾽ Αἰ. σατραπείαις.

[2] ἀπὸ δὲ τοῦ πατρὸς ἐκείνου κληθεῖσαν Ἀντιόχειαν Dindorf.

distance of forty stades,[1] he came out with twelve thousand foot and about eight hundred horse. In a battle of short duration which occurred, the forces of Menelaüs were overwhelmed and routed; and Demetrius, pursuing the enemy into the city, took prisoners numbering not much less than three thousand and killed about a thousand. At first he freed the captives of all charges and distributed them among the units of his own soldiers; but when they ran off to Menelaüs because their baggage had been left behind in Egypt with Ptolemy, recognizing that they would not change sides, he forced them to embark on his ships and sent them off to Antigonus in Syria.

At this time Antigonus was tarrying in upper Syria, founding a city on the Orontes River, which he called Antigonia after himself. He laid it out on a lavish scale, making its perimeter seventy stades[2]; for the location was naturally well adapted for watching over Babylon and the upper satrapies, and again for keeping an eye upon lower Syria and the satrapies near Egypt.[3] It happened, however, that the city did not survive very long, for Seleucus dismantled it and transported it to the city which he founded and called Seleucea after himself.[4] But we shall make these matters clear in detail when we

---

[1] About 4½ miles.

[2] About 8 miles.

[3] Or, reading ταῖς ἀπ' Αἰγύπτου στρατείαις, " and expeditions from Egypt "; or again, reading τοῖς περὶ Αἰγύπτου πράγμασι, " and affairs in Egypt."

[4] So the text; but the city was actually called Antiochea after Seleucus' father. The error is probably Diodorus' rather than the copyist's. Antigonia was not completely abandoned; at least it is mentioned as if still in existence in 51 B.C. (Dio Cassius, 40. 29. 1. Cp. also Benziger, in Pauly-Wissowa, s.v. Antiocheia (1) and Antigoneia (1).)

7 θέντες· τῶν δὲ κατὰ τὴν Κύπρον οἱ περὶ τὸν Μενέλαον ἡττημένοι τῇ μάχῃ τὰ μὲν βέλη καὶ τὰς
μηχανὰς παρεκόμισαν ἐπὶ τὰ τείχη καὶ τοῖς στρατιώταις διαλαβόντες τὰς ἐπάλξεις παρεσκευάζοντο
πρὸς τὸν κίνδυνον, ὁρῶντες καὶ τὸν Δημήτριον πρὸς
8 πολιορκίαν ἑτοιμαζόμενον, πρὸς δὲ Πτολεμαῖον
ἀπέστειλαν εἰς Αἴγυπτον τοὺς δηλώσοντας περὶ
τῶν ἐλαττωμάτων καὶ ἀξιώσοντας βοηθεῖν, ὡς
κινδυνευόντων αὐτῷ τῶν ἐν τῇ νήσῳ πραγμάτων.

48. Δημήτριος δὲ τήν τε τῶν Σαλαμινίων ὁρῶν
πόλιν οὐκ εὐκαταφρόνητον οὖσαν καὶ στρατιωτῶν
πλῆθος ὑπάρχον ἐν αὐτῇ τῶν ἀμυνομένων ἔκρινε
μηχανάς τε τοῖς μεγέθεσιν ὑπεραιρούσας κατασκευάζειν καὶ καταπέλτας ὀξυβελεῖς καὶ λιθοβόλους
παντοίους καὶ τὴν ἄλλην κατασκευὴν καταπλη-
κτικήν. μετεπέμψατο δὲ καὶ τεχνίτας ἐκ τῆς Ἀσίας
καὶ σίδηρον, ἔτι δ' ὕλης πλῆθος καὶ τῆς ἄλλης χορη-
2 γίας τὴν ἐπιτήδειον κατασκευήν. ταχὺ δὲ πάντων
εὐτρεπῶν αὐτῷ γενομένων συνέπηξε μηχανὴν τὴν
ὀνομαζομένην ἑλέπολιν, τὸ πλάτος ἔχουσαν ἑκάστην
πλευρὰν τεσσαράκοντα καὶ πέντε πήχεις, τὸ δ'
ὕψος πηχῶν ἐννενήκοντα, διειλημμένην στέγαις
ἐννέα, ὑπότροχον δὲ πᾶσαν τροχοῖς στερεοῖς τέσ-
3 σαρσιν ὀκταπήχεσι τὸ ὕψος. κατεσκεύασε δὲ καὶ
κριοὺς ὑπερμεγέθεις καὶ χελώνας δύο κριοφόρους.
τῆς δ' ἑλεπόλεως εἰς μὲν τὰς κάτω στέγας εἰσή-
νεγκε πετροβόλους παντοίους, ὧν ἦσαν οἱ μέγιστοι
τριτάλαντοι, εἰς δὲ τὰς μέσας καταπέλτας ὀξυβελεῖς

---

[1] No further reference to this is found in the extant portions
of the history.
[2] For this campaign cp. Plutarch, *Demetrius*, 15-17.

come to the proper time.[1]   As to affairs in Cyprus, 307 B.C.
Menelaüs, after having been defeated in the battle,
had missiles and engines brought to the walls, assigned
positions on the battlements to his soldiers, and made
ready for the fight ; and since he saw that Demetrius
was also making preparations for siege, he sent messengers into Egypt to Ptolemy to inform him about
the defeat and to ask him to send aid as his interests
on the island were in danger.

48. Since Demetrius saw that the city of the Sala-
minians was not to be despised and that a large force
was in the city defending it, he determined to prepare
siege engines of very great size, catapults for shooting
bolts and ballistae of all kinds, and the other equipment that would strike terror.[2]   He sent for skilled
workmen from Asia, and for iron, likewise for a large
amount of wood and for the proper complement of
other supplies.   When everything was quickly made
ready for him, he constructed a device called the
" helepolis,"[3] which had a length of forty-five cubits
on each side and a height of ninety cubits.   It was
divided into nine storeys, and the whole was mounted
on four solid wheels each eight cubits high.   He also
constructed very large battering rams and two penthouses to carry them.   On the lower levels of the
helepolis he mounted all sorts of ballistae, the largest
of them capable of hurling missiles weighing three
talents[4] ; on the middle levels he placed the largest

[3] Literally, " city-taker." Cp. chap. 91. If the cubit used
is the standard Attic measure of about 1½ feet, the dimensions
given are about 68 feet on each side and 135 feet in height,
with wheels 12 feet in diameter ; but a shorter Macedonian
cubit, perhaps about one foot long, is possible (Tarn, *Hellenistic Military and Naval Developments*, 15-16).

[4] About 180 lbs.

μεγίστους, εἰς δὲ τὰς ἀνωτάτας ὀξυβελεῖς τε τοὺς
ἐλαχίστους καὶ πετροβόλων[1] πλῆθος, ἄνδρας τε τοὺς
χρησομένους τούτοις κατὰ τρόπον πλείους τῶν
διακοσίων.

4   Προσαγαγὼν δὲ τὰς μηχανὰς τῇ πόλει καὶ πυκνοῖς χρώμενος τοῖς βέλεσι τῇ μὲν τὰς ἐπάλξεις
ἀπέσυρε τοῖς πετροβόλοις, τῇ δὲ τὰ τείχη διέσεισε
5 τοῖς κριοῖς. ἀμυνομένων δὲ καὶ τῶν ἔνδον εὐρώστως καὶ τοῖς μηχανήμασιν ἑτέρας μηχανὰς ἀντι-
ταττόντων ἐφ᾽ ἡμέρας μέν τινας ἀμφίδοξος ἦν ὁ
κίνδυνος, ἀμφοτέρων κακοπαθούντων καὶ κατα-
τραυματιζομένων· τὸ δὲ τελευταῖον τοῦ τείχους
πίπτοντος καὶ τῆς πόλεως κινδυνευούσης ἁλῶναι
κατὰ κράτος νυκτὸς ἐπιγενομένης ἔληξε τὰ τῆς
6 τειχομαχίας. οἱ δὲ περὶ τὸν Μενέλαον ἀκριβῶς
εἰδότες ἁλωσομένην τὴν πόλιν, εἰ μή τι καινοτομεῖν
ἐπιχειρήσειαν, ἤθροισαν ὕλης ξηρᾶς πλῆθος, ταύτην
δὲ περὶ τὸ μεσονύκτιον ἐμβαλόντες ταῖς τῶν πολεμίων μηχαναῖς καὶ ἅμα πάντες οἰστοὺς[2] πυρ-
σοφόρους ἀπὸ τῶν τειχῶν ἀφέντες ἀνῆψαν τὰ
7 μέγιστα τῶν ἔργων. ἄφνω δὲ τῆς φλογὸς εἰς ὕψος
ἀρθείσης οἱ περὶ τὸν Δημήτριον ἐπεχείρησαν μὲν
βοηθεῖν, τοῦ δὲ πυρὸς καταταχήσαντος συνέβη τὰς
8 μηχανὰς κατακαυθῆναι καὶ πολλοὺς τῶν ἐν αὐταῖς
ὄντων διαφθαρῆναι. ὁ δὲ Δημήτριος ἀποσφαλεὶς
τῆς ἐλπίδος οὐδ᾽ ὣς ἔληγεν, ἀλλὰ προσεκαρτέρει τῇ
πολιορκίᾳ καὶ κατὰ γῆν καὶ κατὰ θάλατταν, νομίζων τῷ χρόνῳ καταπολεμήσειν τοὺς πολεμίους.

49. Πτολεμαῖος δὲ πυθόμενος τὴν τῶν ἰδίων
ἧτταν ἐξέπλευσεν ἐκ τῆς Αἰγύπτου δύναμιν ἔχων
ἀξιόλογον πεζικήν τε καὶ ναυτικήν. κατενεχθεὶς
δὲ τῆς Κύπρου πρὸς τὴν Πάφον ἔκ τε τῶν πόλεων

catapults, and on the highest his lightest catapults _{307 B.C.} and a large number of ballistae ; and he also stationed on the helepolis more than two hundred men to operate these engines in the proper manner.

Bringing the engines up to the city and hurling a shower of missiles, he cleared the battlements with the ballistae and shattered the walls with the rams. Since those within resisted boldly and opposed his engines of war with other devices, for some days the battle was doubtful, both sides suffering hardships and severe wounds ; and when finally the wall was falling and the city was in danger of being taken by storm, the assault was interrupted by the coming of night. Menelaüs, seeing clearly that the city would be taken unless he tried something new, gathered a large amount of dry wood, at about midnight threw this upon the siege engines of the enemy, and at the same time all shot down fire-bearing arrows from the walls and set on fire the largest of the siege engines. As the flames suddenly blazed high, Demetrius tried to come to the rescue ; but the flames got the start of him, with the result that the engines were completely destroyed and many of those who manned them were lost. Demetrius, although disappointed in his expectations, did not stop but pushed the siege persistently by both land and sea, believing that he would overcome the enemy in time.

49. When Ptolemy heard of the defeat of his men,[1] he sailed from Egypt with considerable land and sea forces. Reaching Cyprus at Paphos, he received

---

[1] The defeat described in chap. 47. 3.

---

[1] Fischer suggests the addition of ἐλαττόνων before πετρο-βόλων.

[2] πάντες οἰστοὺς Fischer, cp. Arrian, 2. 21. 3 ; πάντας τοὺς.

παρεδέξατο τὰ σκάφη καὶ παρέπλευσεν εἰς Κίτιον,
2 τῆς Σαλαμῖνος ἀπέχον σταδίους διακοσίους. εἶχε
δὲ τὰς πάσας ναῦς μακρὰς ἑκατὸν καὶ τεσσαρά-
κοντα· τούτων δ' ἦν ἡ μεγίστη πεντήρης, ἡ δ'
ἐλαχίστη τετρήρης· στρατιωτικὰ δὲ πόρια ταύταις
ἐπηκολούθει πλείω τῶν διακοσίων, ἄγοντα πεζοὺς
3 οὐκ ἐλάττους τῶν μυρίων. οὗτος μὲν οὖν πρὸς
τὸν Μενέλαον κατὰ γῆν ἔπεμψέ τινας, διακελευό-
μενος τὰς ναῦς, ἂν ᾖ δυνατόν, κατὰ τάχος ἐκ τῆς
Σαλαμῖνος πρὸς αὐτὸν ἀποστεῖλαι, οὔσας ἑξήκοντα·
ἤλπιζε γάρ, εἰ προσλάβοι ταύτας, ῥᾳδίως κρατήσειν
τῇ ναυμαχίᾳ, διακοσίοις σκάφεσιν ἀγωνιζόμενος.
4 ὁ δὲ Δημήτριος νοήσας αὐτοῦ τὴν ἐπιβολὴν ἐπὶ
μὲν τῆς πολιορκίας ἀπέλιπε μέρος τῆς δυνάμεως,
τὰς δὲ ναῦς ἁπάσας πληρώσας καὶ τῶν στρατιωτῶν
τοὺς κρατίστους ἐμβιβάσας βέλη καὶ πετροβόλους
ἐνέθετο καὶ τῶν τρισπιθάμων ὀξυβελῶν τοὺς ἱκα-
5 νοὺς ταῖς πρῴραις ἐπέστησε. κοσμήσας δὲ πολυτελῶς πρὸς ναυμαχίαν τὸν στόλον περιέπλευσε τὴν
πόλιν καὶ κατὰ τὸ στόμα τοῦ λιμένος μικρὸν ἔξω
βέλους ἀφεὶς τὰς ἀγκύρας διενυκτέρευσεν, ἅμα μὲν
τὰς ἐκ τῆς πόλεως ναῦς κωλύων συμμῖξαι ταῖς
ἄλλαις, ἅμα δὲ καραδοκῶν τὸν ἐπίπλουν τῶν πο-
6 λεμίων καὶ πρὸς ναυμαχίαν ὢν ἕτοιμος. τοῦ δὲ
Πτολεμαίου πλέοντος ἐπὶ τὴν Σαλαμῖνα καὶ τῶν
ὑπηρετικῶν πλοίων συνεπομένων πόρρωθεν κατα-
πληκτικὸν ὁρᾶσθαι συνέβαινε τὸν στόλον διὰ τὸ
πλῆθος.
50. Ὁ δὲ Δημήτριος κατανοήσας τὸν ἐπίπλουν
Ἀντισθένην μὲν τὸν ναύαρχον ἔχοντα ναῦς δέκα

---

[1] About 23 miles, which is approximately correct for the

ships from the cities and coasted along to Citium, _{307 B.C.} which was distant from Salamis two hundred stades.[1] He had in all one hundred and forty [2] ships of war, of which the largest were quinqueremes and the smallest quadriremes ; more than two hundred transports followed, which carried at least ten thousand foot-soldiers. Ptolemy sent certain men to Menelaüs by land, directing him, if possible, to send him quickly the ships from Salamis, which numbered sixty ; for he hoped that, if he received these as reinforcement, he would easily be superior in the naval engagement since he would have two hundred ships in the battle. Learning of his intention, Demetrius left a part of his forces for the siege ; and, manning all his ships and embarking upon them the best of his soldiers, he equipped them with missiles and ballistae and mounted on the prows a sufficient number of catapults for throwing bolts three spans [3] in length. After making the fleet ready in every way for a naval battle, he sailed around the city and, anchoring at the mouth of the harbour just out of range, spent the night, preventing the ships from the city from joining the others, and at the same time watching for the coming of the enemy and occupying a position ready for battle. When Ptolemy sailed up toward Salamis, the service vessels following at a distance, his fleet was awe-inspiring to behold because of the multitude of its ships.

50. When Demetrius observed Ptolemy's approach, he left the admiral Antisthenes with ten of the

distance by land ; but the distance by sea around Cape Pedalium is at least twice as great.

[2] Plutarch, *Demetrius*, 16. 1, gives the number as 150.

[3] About 21 inches. For this battle cp. Plutarch, *Demetrius*, 16 ; Polyaenus, 4. 7. 7.

τῶν πεντηρικῶν ἀπέλιπε κωλύσοντα τὰς ἐκ τῆς
πόλεως ναῦς ἐπεξιέναι πρὸς τὴν ναυμαχίαν, ἔχοντος
τοῦ λιμένος στενὸν τὸν ἔκπλουν, τοῖς δ' ἱππεῦσι
προσέταξε παράγειν παρὰ τὸν αἰγιαλόν, ἵν' ἐάν τι
γένηται πταῖσμα, διασώσειαν[1] τοὺς πρὸς τὴν γῆν
2 διανηξομένους. αὐτὸς δ' ἐκτάξας τὰς ναῦς ἀπήντα
τοῖς πολεμίοις, ἔχων τὰς ἁπάσας ὀκτὼ πλείους τῶν
ἑκατὸν[2] σὺν ταῖς πληρωθείσαις ἐκ τῶν χωρίων τῶν
ληφθέντων· τούτων δ' ἦσαν αἱ μέγισται μὲν ἑπτή-
3 ρεις, αἱ πλεῖσται δὲ πεντήρεις. καὶ τὸ μὲν εὐώνυμον κέρας ἐπεῖχον ἑπτήρεις ἑπτὰ Φοινίκων,
τετρήρεις δὲ τριάκοντα τῶν Ἀθηναίων, Μηδίου
τοῦ ναυάρχου τὴν ἡγεμονίαν ἔχοντος· ἐπίπλους δὲ
τούτοις ἔταξεν ἑξήρεις δέκα καὶ πεντήρεις ἄλλας
τοσαύτας, διεγνωκὼς[3] ἰσχυρὸν κατασκευάσαι τοῦτο
τὸ κέρας ἐφ' οὗ καὶ αὐτὸς ἤμελλε διαγωνίζεσθαι.
4 κατὰ μέσην δὲ τὴν τάξιν τὰ ἐλάχιστα τῶν σκαφῶν
ἔστησεν, ὧν ἡγοῦντο Θεμίσων τε ὁ Σάμιος καὶ
Μαρσύας ὁ τὰς Μακεδονικὰς πράξεις συνταξάμενος.
τὸ δὲ δεξιὸν εἶχε κέρας Ἡγήσιππός τε ὁ Ἁλικαρ-
νασσεὺς καὶ Πλειστίας ὁ Κῷος, ἀρχικυβερνήτης
ὢν τοῦ σύμπαντος στόλου.
5 Πτολεμαῖος δὲ τὸ μὲν πρῶτον ἔτι νυκτὸς ἐπέπλει
κατὰ σπουδὴν ἐπὶ τὴν Σαλαμῖνα, νομίζων φθάσειν[4]
τοὺς πολεμίους τὸν εἴσπλουν ποιησάμενος· ὡς δ'
ἡμέρας ἐπιγενομένης οὐ μακρὰν ὁ τῶν ἐναντίων

---

[1] διασώσειαν Dindorf, διασώσαιεν Fischer, F, διασώση μὲν RX.
[2] See note on translation.
[3] ἴσως after διεγνωκὼς omitted by Dindorf.
[4] φθάσειν Dindorf : φθάσαι Fischer, following the MSS.

---

[1] The number is probably corrupt; Plutarch (*Demetrius*,

280

quinqueremes to prevent the ships in the city from
going forth for the battle, since the harbour had a
narrow exit ; and he ordered the cavalry to patrol
the shore so that, if any wreck should occur, they
might rescue those who should swim across to the
land. He himself drew up the fleet and moved
against the enemy with one hundred and eight ships
in all,[1] including those that had been provided with
crews from the captured towns. The largest of the
ships were sevens and most of them were quinqueremes.[2] The left wing was composed of seven
Phoenician sevens and thirty Athenian quadriremes,
Medius the admiral having the command. Sailing
behind these he placed ten sixes and as many quinqueremes, for he had decided to make strong this
wing where he himself was going to fight the decisive
battle. In the middle of the line he stationed the
lightest of his ships, which Themison of Samos and
Marsyas,[3] who compiled the history of Macedonia,
commanded. The right wing was commanded by
Hegesippus of Halicarnassus and Pleistias of Cos,
who was the chief pilot of the whole fleet.

At first, while it was still night, Ptolemy made for
Salamis at top speed, believing that he could gain an
entrance before the enemy was ready ; but as day
broke, the fleet of the enemy in battle array was

16) gives the total as 180, Polyaenus (4. 7. 7) as 170. If we
were right in regard to the βαρύτεραι στρατιώτιδες (cp. chap.
47. 1, and note), Demetrius by Diodorus' own count should
have had in this battle 110 triremes and quadriremes and 43
heavier warships (10 having been left at Salamis) plus any
from the captured ports.

[2] This statement also appears to be false.

[3] According to Suidas he was a half-brother of Antigonus.
He wrote a history of Macedonia in 10 books, one of Attica
in 12 books, and a work on the education of Alexander.

στόλος ἐκτεταγμένος ἑωρᾶτο, καὶ αὐτὸς τὰ πρὸς
6 τὴν ναυμαχίαν παρεσκευάζετο. τὰ μὲν οὖν πόρια
πόρρωθεν ἐπακολουθεῖν παρήγγειλεν, τῶν δὲ ἄλλων
νεῶν τὴν ἁρμόζουσαν τάξιν ποιησάμενος αὐτὸς τὸ
λαιὸν κέρας διακατεῖχε, συναγωνιζομένων αὐτῷ
τῶν μεγίστων σκαφῶν. τοιαύτης δὲ τῆς διατάξεως
γενομένης εὐχὰς ἑκάτεροι τοῖς θεοῖς ἐποιοῦντο,
καθάπερ ἦν ἔθος, διὰ τῶν κελευστῶν, συνεπιλα-
βομένου καὶ τοῦ πλήθους τῇ φωνῇ.

51. Οἱ δὲ δυνάσται, ὡς ἂν περὶ τοῦ βίου καὶ τῶν
ὅλων μέλλοντες διακινδυνεύειν, ἐν ἀγωνίᾳ πολλῇ
καθειστήκεισαν. Δημήτριος μὲν οὖν τῶν ἐναντίων
ἀποσχὼν ὡς ἂν τρεῖς σταδίους ἦρεν τὸ συγκείμενον
πρὸς μάχην σύσσημον, ἀσπίδα κεχρυσωμένην, φα-
2 νερὰν πᾶσιν ἐκ διαδοχῆς· τὸ παραπλήσιον δὲ καὶ
τῶν περὶ Πτολεμαῖον ποιησάντων ταχὺ τὸ διεῖργον
διάστημα συνῃρέθη. ὡς δ᾽ αἵ τε σάλπιγγες τὸ
πολεμικὸν ἐσήμαινον καὶ συνηλάλαξαν αἱ δυνάμεις
ἀμφότεραι, φερομένων ἁπασῶν τῶν νεῶν εἰς ἐμβολὴν καταπληκτικῶς τὸ μὲν πρῶτον τοῖς τόξοις
καὶ τοῖς πετροβόλοις, ἔτι δὲ τοῖς ἀκοντίσμασι πυκνοῖς χρώμενοι κατετραυμάτιζον τοὺς ὑποπίπτοντας·
εἶτα συνεγγισάντων τῶν σκαφῶν καὶ μελλούσης
γίνεσθαι τῆς ἐμβολῆς βιαίου οἱ μὲν ἐπὶ τῶν κατα-
στρωμάτων συγκαθῆκαν, οἱ δ᾽ ἐρέται παρακλη-
θέντες ὑπὸ τῶν κελευστῶν ἐκθυμότερον ἐνέκειντο·
3 ἀπὸ κράτους δὲ καὶ βίας ἐλαθεισῶν τῶν νεῶν αἱ
μὲν παρέσυρον ἀλλήλων τοὺς ταρσούς, ὥστε πρὸς
φυγὴν καὶ διωγμὸν ἀχρήστους γίνεσθαι καὶ τοὺς
ἐπιβεβηκότας ἄνδρας ὡρμηκότας πρὸς ἀλκὴν κω-
λύεσθαι τῆς πρὸς τὸν κίνδυνον ὁρμῆς· αἱ δὲ κατὰ
πρῷραν τοῖς ἐμβόλοις συρράττουσαι πρύμναν ἀνε-

visible at no great distance, and Ptolemy also pre- 307 B.C.
pared for the battle. Ordering the supply ships to
follow at a distance and effecting a suitable formation
of the other ships, he himself took command of the left
wing with the largest of his warships fighting under
him. After the fleet had been disposed in this way,
both sides prayed to the gods as was the custom, the
signalmen [1] leading and the crews joining in the
response.

51. The princes, since they were about to fight for
their lives and their all, were in much anxiety. When
Demetrius was about three stades [2] distant from the
enemy, he raised the battle signal that had been
agreed upon, a gilded shield, and this sign was made
known to all by being repeated in relays. Since
Ptolemy also gave a similar signal, the distance between the fleets was rapidly reduced. When the
trumpets gave the signal for battle and both forces
raised the battle cry, all the ships rushed to the encounter in a terrifying manner ; using their bows and
their ballistae at first, then their javelins in a shower,
the men wounded those who were within range ;
then when the ships had come close together and the
encounter was about to take place with violence,
the soldiers on the decks crouched down and the oarsmen, spurred on by the signalmen, bent more desperately to their oars. As the ships drove together
with force and violence, in some cases they swept off
each other's oars so that the ships became useless for
flight or pursuit, and the men who were on board,
though eager for a fight, were prevented from joining
in the battle ; but where the ships had met prow to

---

[1] The men who kept time for the oarsmen.
[2] About ⅓ mile.

κρούοντο πρὸς ἄλλην ἐμβολὴν καὶ κατετραυμάτιζον
ἀλλήλους οἱ ταύταις ἐφεστῶτες, ἅτε τοῦ σκοποῦ
σύνεγγυς ἑκάστοις κειμένου. τινὲς δὲ τῶν τριηράρχων ἐκ πλαγίας τυπτόντων[1] καὶ τῶν ἐμβόλων
δυσαποσπάστως ἐχόντων ἐπεπήδων ἐπὶ τὰς τῶν
πολεμίων ναῦς, πολλὰ καὶ πάσχοντες δεινὰ καὶ
4 διατιθέντες· οἱ μὲν γὰρ τῶν ἐγγιζόντων τοίχων
ἐφαψάμενοι καὶ σφαλέντες τῆς βάσεως περιέπιπτον
εἰς θάλασσαν καὶ παραχρῆμα τοῖς δόρασιν ὑπὸ τῶν
ἐφεστώτων ἐφονεύοντο, οἱ δὲ κρατήσαντες τῆς ἐπιβολῆς τοὺς μὲν ἀνῇρουν, τοὺς δὲ κατὰ τὴν στενοχωρίαν ἐκβιαζόμενοι περιέτρεπον εἰς τὸ πέλαγος.
ὅλως δὲ ποικίλαι καὶ παράλογοι συνίσταντο μάχαι,
πολλάκις τῶν μὲν ἡττόνων ἐπικρατούντων διὰ τὴν
τῶν σκαφῶν ὑπεροχήν, τῶν δὲ κρειττόνων θλιβομένων διὰ τὸ περὶ τὴν στάσιν ἐλάττωμα καὶ τὴν
ἀνωμαλίαν τῶν συμβαινόντων ἐν τοῖς τοιούτοις
5 κινδύνοις. ἐπὶ μὲν γὰρ τῶν ἐπὶ τῆς γῆς ἀγώνων
διάδηλος ἡ ἀρετὴ γίνεται, δυναμένη τυγχάνειν τῶν
πρωτείων μηδενὸς ἔξωθεν αὐτομάτου παρενοχλοῦν-
τος· κατὰ δὲ τὰς ναυμαχίας πολλὰς καὶ ποικίλας
αἰτίας συμβαίνει παραλόγως ἐλαττοῦν τοὺς δι᾽
ἀνδρείαν δικαίως ἂν τυχόντας τῆς νίκης.

52. Λαμπρότατα δὲ πάντων Δημήτριος ἠγωνί-
σατο τῆς ἑπτήρους[2] ἐπιβεβηκὼς ἐπὶ τῇ πρύμνῃ.
ἀθρόων γὰρ αὐτῷ περιχυθέντων οὓς μὲν ταῖς λόγ-
χαις ἀκοντίζων, οὓς δὲ ἐκ χειρὸς τῷ δόρατι τύπτων
ἀνῄρει· πολλῶν δὲ καὶ παντοίων βελῶν ἐπ᾽ αὐτὸν
φερομένων ἃ μὲν προορώμενος ἐξέκλινεν, ἃ δὲ τοῖς

prow with their rams, they drew back for another 307 B.C. charge, and the soldiers on board shot at each other with effect since the mark was close at hand for each party. Some of the men, when their captains had delivered a broadside blow and the rams had become firmly fixed, leaped aboard the ships of the enemy, receiving and giving severe wounds ; for certain of them, after grasping the rail of a ship that was drawing near, missed their footing, fell into the sea, and at once were killed with spears by those who stood above them ; and others, making good their intent, slew some of the enemy and, forcing others along the narrow deck, drove them into the sea. As a whole the fighting was varied and full of surprises : many times those who were weaker got the upper hand because of the height of their ships, and those who were stronger were foiled by inferiority of position and by the irregularity with which things happen in fighting of this kind. For in contests on land, valour is made clearly evident, since it is able to gain the upper hand when nothing external and fortuitous interferes ; but in naval battles there are many causes of various kinds that, contrary to reason, defeat those who would properly gain the victory through prowess.

52. Demetrius fought most brilliantly of all, having taken his stand on the stern of his seven. A crowd of men rushed upon him, but by hurling his javelins at some of them and by striking others at close range with his spear, he slew them ; and although many missiles of all sorts were aimed at him, he avoided some that he saw in time and received others

---

[1] τυπτόντων Geer, ἔτυπτον.

[2] Reiske adds ἑαυτοῦ or ναυαρχίδος before ἑπτήρους. Fischer suggests τῆς ἰδίας ἑπτήρους.

2 σκεπαστηρίοις ὅπλοις ἐδέχετο. τριῶν δ᾽ ὑπερασπι-
ζόντων αὐτὸν εἷς μὲν λόγχῃ πληγεὶς ἔπεσεν, οἱ δὲ
δύο κατετραυματίσθησαν. τέλος δὲ τοὺς ἀντιστάντας ὁ Δημήτριος ἐκβιασάμενος καὶ τροπὴν τοῦ
δεξιοῦ κέρατος ποιήσας εὐθὺ καὶ τὰς συνεχεῖς
3 φυγεῖν ἠνάγκασεν. Πτολεμαῖος δὲ τὰ μέγιστα τῶν
σκαφῶν καὶ τοὺς κρατίστους ἄνδρας ἔχων μεθ᾽
αὑτοῦ ῥᾳδίως ἐτρέψατο τοὺς καθ᾽ αὑτὸν τεταγμένους καὶ τῶν νεῶν ἃς μὲν κατέδυσεν, ἃς δὲ αὐτάνδρους εἷλεν. ὑποστρέφων δ᾽ ἀπὸ τοῦ νικήματος
ἤλπιζε καὶ τὰς ἄλλας ῥᾳδίως χειρώσασθαι· θεωρή-
σας δὲ τό τε δεξιὸν[1] κέρας τῶν ἰδίων συντετριμμένον
καὶ τὰς συνεχεῖς ἁπάσας πρὸς φυγὴν ὡρμημένας,
ἔτι δὲ τοὺς περὶ τὸν Δημήτριον μετὰ βάρους ἐπιφερομένους ἀπέπλευσεν εἰς Κίτιον.

4 Δημήτριος δὲ νικήσας τῇ ναυμαχίᾳ τῷ μὲν Νέωνι
καὶ Βουρίχῳ παρέδωκε τὰ στρατιωτικὰ τῶν πλοίων,
προστάξας διώκειν καὶ τοὺς ἐν τῇ θαλάττῃ διανη-
χομένους ἀναλαμβάνειν· αὐτὸς δὲ τὰς ἰδίας ναῦς
κοσμήσας τοῖς ἀκροστολίοις καὶ τὰς ἁλούσας ἐφελ-
κόμενος τὸν πλοῦν ἐποιεῖτο πρὸς τὸ στρατόπεδον
5 καὶ τὸν οἰκεῖον λιμένα. κατὰ δὲ τὸν τῆς ναυμαχίας
καιρὸν Μενέλαος ὁ ἐν τῇ Σαλαμῖνι στρατηγὸς πληρώσας τὰς ἑξήκοντα ναῦς ἐξαπέστειλε πρὸς βοήθειαν
τῷ Πτολεμαίῳ, ναύαρχον ἐπιστήσας Μενοίτιον.
γενομένου δ᾽ ἀγῶνος περὶ τὸ στόμα τοῦ λιμένος πρὸς
τὰς ἐφορμούσας ναῦς καὶ τῶν ἐκ τῆς πόλεως βια-
σαμένων αἱ μὲν τοῦ Δημητρίου δέκα ναῦς ἔφυγον
πρὸς τὸ πεζὸν στρατόπεδον, οἱ δὲ περὶ τὸν Μενοίτιον ἀναπλεύσαντες καὶ τῶν καιρῶν μικρὸν ὑστερή-
σαντες ἀνέστρεψαν πάλιν εἰς τὴν Σαλαμῖνα.

6 Τῆς δὲ ναυμαχίας τοιοῦτον τέλος λαβούσης τῶν

upon his defensive armour. Of the three men who 307 B.C.
protected him with shields, one fell struck by a
lance and the other two were severely wounded.
Finally Demetrius drove back the forces confronting him, created a rout in the right wing, and forth-
with forced even the ships next to the wing to flee.
Ptolemy, who had with himself the heaviest of his
ships and the strongest men, easily routed those
stationed opposite him, sinking some of the ships
and capturing others with their crews. Turning back
from that victorious action, he expected easily to
subdue the others also ; but when he saw that the
right wing of his forces had been shattered and all
those next to that wing driven into flight, and further,
that Demetrius was pressing on with full force, he
sailed back to Citium.

Demetrius, after winning the victory, gave the
transports to Neon and Burichus, ordering them to
pursue and pick up those who were swimming in the
sea ; and he himself, decking his own ships with bow
and stern ornaments and towing the captured craft,
sailed to his camp and his home port. At the time
of the naval battle Menelaüs, the general in Salamis,
had manned his sixty ships and sent them as a reinforcement to Ptolemy, placing Menoetius in command. When a battle occurred at the harbour mouth
with the ships on guard there, and when the ships
from the city pressed forward vigorously, Demetrius'
ten ships fled to the camp of the army ; and Menoetius, after sailing out and arriving a little too late,
returned to Salamis.

In the naval battle, whose outcome was as stated,

---

¹ δεξιὸν Geer, cp. chaps. 50. 6 ; 52. 2 : εὐώνυμον.

μὲν πορίων ἥλω πλείω τῶν ἑκατόν, ἐν οἷς ἦσαν σχεδὸν στρατιῶται ὀκτακισχίλιοι· τῶν δὲ μακρῶν αὔτανδροι μὲν ἐλήφθησαν τεσσαράκοντα, διεφθάρησαν δὲ περὶ ὀγδοήκοντα, ἃς πλήρεις οὔσας θαλάττης κατήγαγον οἱ κρατήσαντες εἰς τὴν πρὸς τῇ πόλει στρατοπεδείαν. διεφθάρη δὲ καὶ τῶν Δημητρίου σκαφῶν εἴκοσι· πάντα δὲ τῆς προσηκούσης ἐπιμελείας τυχόντα παρείχετο τὰς ἁρμοζούσας χρείας.

53. Μετὰ δὲ ταῦτα Πτολεμαῖος ἀπογνοὺς τὰ κατὰ τὴν Κύπρον ἀπῆρεν εἰς Αἴγυπτον. Δημήτριος δὲ πάσας τὰς ἐν τῇ νήσῳ πόλεις παραλαβὼν καὶ τοὺς φρουροῦντας στρατιώτας, τούτους μὲν εἰς τάξεις κατεχώρισεν, ὄντας πεζοὺς μὲν μυρίους ἑξακισχιλίους συντεταγμένους, ἱππεῖς δὲ περὶ ἑξακοσίους, πρὸς δὲ τὸν πατέρα ταχέως ἐμβιβάσας εἰς τὴν μεγίστην ναῦν τοὺς δηλώσοντας περὶ τῶν κατ-
2 ορθωθέντων ἐξαπέστειλεν. ὁ δ' Ἀντίγονος πυθόμενος τὴν γεγενημένην νίκην καὶ μετεωρισθεὶς ἐπὶ τῷ μεγέθει τοῦ προτερήματος διάδημα περιέθετο καὶ τὸ λοιπὸν ἐχρημάτιζε βασιλεύς, συγχωρήσας καὶ τῷ Δημητρίῳ τῆς αὐτῆς τυγχάνειν προσηγορίας
3 καὶ τιμῆς. ὁ δὲ Πτολεμαῖος οὐδὲν τῇ ψυχῇ ταπεινωθεὶς διὰ τὴν ἧτταν καὶ αὐτὸς ὁμοίως ἀνέλαβε τὸ διάδημα καὶ πρὸς ἅπαντας ἀνέγραφεν ἑαυτὸν
4 βασιλέα. παραπλησίως δὲ τούτοις καὶ οἱ λοιποὶ δυνάσται ζηλοτυπήσαντες ἀνηγόρευον ἑαυτοὺς βασιλεῖς, Σέλευκος μὲν προσφάτως τὰς ἄνω σατραπείας προσκεκτημένος, Λυσίμαχος δὲ καὶ Κάσανδρος τὰς ἐξ ἀρχῆς δοθείσας μερίδας διατηροῦντες.

Ἡμεῖς δὲ περὶ τούτων ἱκανῶς εἰρηκότες ἐν μέρει διέξιμεν περὶ τῶν κατὰ Λιβύην καὶ Σικελίαν πραχθέντων.

more than a hundred of the supply ships were taken,
upon which were almost eight thousand soldiers, and
of the warships forty were captured with their crews
and about eighty were disabled, which the victors
towed, full of sea water, to the camp before the city.
Twenty of Demetrius' ships were disabled, but all of
these, after receiving proper care, continued to per-
form the services for which they were suited.

53. Thereafter Ptolemy gave up the fight in
Cyprus and returned to Egypt. Demetrius, after he
had taken over all the cities of the island and their
garrisons, enrolled the men in companies ; and when
they were organized they came to sixteen thousand
foot and about six hundred horse. He at once sent
messengers to his father to inform him of the successes, embarking them on his largest ship. And
when Antigonus heard of the victory that had been
gained, elated by the magnitude of his good fortune,
he assumed the diadem and from that time on he
used the style of king ; and he permitted Demetrius
also to assume this same title and rank. Ptolemy,
however, not at all humbled in spirit by his defeat,
also assumed the diadem and always signed himself
king.[1] And in a similar fashion in rivalry with them
the rest of the princes also called themselves kings :
Seleucus, who had recently gained the upper satrapies,
and Lysimachus and Cassander, who still retained the
territories originally allotted to them.[2]

Now that we have said enough about these matters,
we shall relate in their turn the events that took place
in Libya and in Sicily.

---

[1] Ptolemy's assumption of the diadem is placed in the year
305/4 by the Parian Marble, FGrH, 239. B 23.
[2] Continued in chap. 73.

54. Ἀγαθοκλῆς γὰρ πυθόμενος τοὺς προειρη-
μένους δυνάστας ἀνῃρημένους τὸ διάδημα[1] καὶ
νομίζων μήτε δυνάμεσι μήτε χώρᾳ μήτε τοῖς πραχθεῖσι λείπεσθαι τούτων ἑαυτὸν ἀνηγόρευσε βασιλέα.
καὶ διάδημα μὲν οὐκ ἔκρινεν ἔχειν· ἐφόρει γὰρ αἰεὶ
στέφανον, ὃν κατὰ τὴν ἐπίθεσιν τῆς τυραννίδος ἔκ
τινος ἱερωσύνης[2] περικείμενος οὐκ ἀπέθετο περὶ
τῆς δυναστείας ἀγωνιζόμενος· ἔνιοι δέ φασιν αὐτὸν
ἐπιτετηδεῦσθαι τοῦτον ἐξ ἀρχῆς φορεῖν διὰ τὸ μὴ
2 λίαν αὐτὸν εὐχαίτην εἶναι.[3] οὐ μὴν ἀλλὰ τῆς προσηγορίας ταύτης ἄξιόν τι σπεύδων πρᾶξαι ἐπὶ μὲν
Ἰτυκαίους ἐστράτευσεν ἀφεστηκότας· ἄφνω δ' αὐτῶν τῇ πόλει προσπεσὼν καὶ τῶν ἐπὶ τῆς χώρας
ἀπειλημμένων πολιτικῶν ζωγρήσας εἰς τριακοσίους
τὸ μὲν πρῶτον διδοὺς ἄφεσιν τῶν ἐγκλημάτων
ἠξίου παραδιδόναι τὴν πόλιν· οὐ προσεχόντων δὲ
τῶν ἔνδον συνεπήγνυε μηχανὴν καὶ κρεμάσας ἐπ'
αὐτῇ τοὺς αἰχμαλώτους προσήγαγε τοῖς τείχεσιν.
3 οἱ δ' Ἰτυκαῖοι τοὺς μὲν ἠτυχηκότας ἠλέουν, πλείονα
δὲ λόγον τῆς τῶν ἁπάντων ἐλευθερίας ἢ τῆς ἐκείνων
σωτηρίας ποιούμενοι διέλαβον τὰ τείχη τοῖς στρατιώταις καὶ τὴν πολιορκίαν εὐγενῶς ὑπέμενον.
4 εἶθ' ὁ μὲν Ἀγαθοκλῆς ἐπιστήσας τῇ μηχανῇ τούς
τε ὀξυβελεῖς καὶ σφενδονήτας καὶ τοξότας ἀπὸ
ταύτης ἀγωνιζόμενος ἤρχετο τῆς πολιορκίας καὶ
ταῖς ψυχαῖς τῶν ἔνδον ὥσπερ καυτήριά τινα προσ-

---

[1] τὸ διάδημα added by Rhodoman.
[2] ἱερωσύνης ὃν MSS., ὃν transferred by Dindorf.
[3] διὰ τὸ . . . εἶναι editors : διὰ τὸ μὴ τέλειον αὐτὸν εὐχαιτίαν
εἶναι F, ἐπὶ τῷ μὴ λίαν αὐ. εὐ. εἶ. Fischer.

---

[1] Cp. Aelian, Var. Hist. 11. 4. For a similar reason Julius

54. When Agathocles heard that the princes whom 307 B.C.
we have just mentioned had assumed the diadem,
since he thought that neither in power nor in territory
nor in deeds was he inferior to them, he called himself king. He decided not to take a diadem ; for
he habitually wore a chaplet, which at the time when
he seized the tyranny was his because of some priest-
hood and which he did not give up while he was
struggling to gain the supreme power. But some say
that he originally had made it his habit to wear this
because he did not have a good head of hair.[1] However this may be, in his desire to do something worthy
of this title, he made a campaign against the people
of Utica, who had deserted him.[2] Making a sudden
attack upon their city and taking prisoner those of
the citizens who were caught in the open country to
the number of three hundred, he at first offered a
free pardon and requested the surrender of the
city ; but when those in the city did not heed his
offer, he constructed a siege engine,[3] hung the
prisoners upon it, and brought it up to the walls. The
Uticans pitied the unfortunate men ; yet, holding
the liberty of all of more account than the safety of
these, they assigned posts on the walls to the soldiers
and bravely awaited the assault. Then Agathocles,
placing upon the engine his catapults, slingers, and
bowmen, and fighting from this, began the assault,
applying, as it were, branding-irons to the souls of

Caesar welcomed the right to wear a laurel wreath (Suetonius, *Divus Iulius*, 45. 2).

[2] But, according to Polybius, 1. 82. 8, Utica and Hippu
Acra (cp. chap. 55. 3) were the only cities that had remained
true to Carthage.

[3] Probably a movable tower like the " helepolis " of chap.
48. 2.

5 ἦγεν· οἱ δ' ἐπὶ τῶν τειχῶν ἑστῶτες τὸ μὲν πρῶτον
ὤκνουν τοῖς βέλεσι χρήσασθαι, προκειμένων αὐτοῖς
σκοπῶν πολιτικῶν ἀνδρῶν, ὧν ἦσάν τινες καὶ τῶν
ἐπιφανεστάτων· ἐπικειμένων δὲ τῶν πολεμίων βαρύ-
τερον ἠναγκάζοντο τοὺς ἐπὶ τῆς μηχανῆς ὄντας
6 ἀμύνεσθαι. ἔνθα δὴ συνέβαινε γίνεσθαι παράλογα
πάθη τοῖς Ἰτυκαίοις καὶ τύχης ἐπηρεασμὸν ἐν
ἀνάγκαις κειμένοις ἀνεκφεύκτοις[1]· προβεβλημένων
γὰρ τῶν Ἑλλήνων τοὺς ἡλωκότας τῶν ἐξ Ἰτύκης
ἀναγκαῖον ἦν ἢ τούτων φειδομένους περιορᾶν ὑποχείριον τοῖς πολεμίοις γινομένην τὴν πατρίδα ἢ τῇ
πόλει βοηθοῦντας ἀνηλεῶς φονεῦσαι πλῆθος πολι-
7 τῶν ἠτυχηκότων. ὅπερ καὶ συνέβη γενέσθαι· ἀμυ-
νόμενοι γὰρ τοὺς πολεμίους καὶ παντοίοις βέλεσι
χρώμενοι καί τινας τῶν ἐφεστηκότων τῇ μηχανῇ
κατηκόντισαν καὶ τὰ μὲν τῶν κρεμαμένων πολιτῶν
σώματα κατηκίσαντο, τὰ[2] δὲ τοῖς ὀξυβελέσι πρὸς
τῇ μηχανῇ προσκαθήλωσαν καθ' οὓς ποτε τύχοι
τοῦ σώματος τόπους, ὥστε σταυρῷ παραπλησίαν
εἶναι τὴν ὕβριν ἅμα καὶ τὴν τιμωρίαν. καὶ ταῦτ'
ἐγίνετό τισιν ὑπὸ συγγενῶν ἢ φίλων, εἰ τύχοι, τῆς
ἀνάγκης οὐ πολυπραγμονούσης τι τῶν παρ' ἀνθρώποις ὁσίων.

55. Ὁ δ' Ἀγαθοκλῆς, ὁρῶν αὐτοὺς ἀπαθῶς
ὡρμηκότας πρὸς τὸν κίνδυνον, περιστήσας πανταχόθεν τὴν δύναμιν καὶ κατά τινα τόπον φαύλως
ᾠκοδομημένον βιασάμενος εἰσέπεσεν εἰς τὴν πόλιν.
2 τῶν δ' Ἰτυκαίων τῶν μὲν εἰς τὰς οἰκίας, τῶν δ' εἰς

---

[1] κειμένοις ἀνεκφεύκτοις Reiske : κείμενον ἀνέκφευκτον.
[2] τινας τῶν ἐφ. τῇ μη. κατηκόντισαν καὶ τὰ μὲν τῶν κρ. πολ.
σώματα κατηκίσαντο, τὰ Geer : τὰ τῶν ἐφ. τῇ μη. σώματα κατηκίσαντο καὶ τινὰς μὲν τῶν κρ. πολ. κατηκόντισαν, τινὰς.

those within the city. Those standing on the walls
at first hesitated to use their missiles since the targets
presented to them were their own fellow-countrymen,
of whom some were indeed the most distinguished
of their citizens ; but when the enemy pressed on
more heavily, they were forced to defend themselves
against those who manned the engine. As a result
there came unparalleled suffering and despiteful
treatment of fortune to the men of Utica, placed as
they were in dire straits from which there was no
escape ; for since the Greeks had set up before them
as shields the men of Utica who had been captured,
it was necessary either to spare these and idly watch
the fatherland fall into the hands of the enemy or,
in protecting the city, to slaughter mercilessly a large
number of unfortunate fellow citizens. And this,
indeed, is what took place ; for as they resisted the
enemy and employed missiles of every kind, they
shot down some of the men who were stationed on
the engine, and they also mangled some of their
fellow citizens who were hanging there, and others
they nailed to the engine with their bolts at whatever
places on the body the missiles chanced to strike, so
that the wanton violence and the punishment almost
amounted to crucifixion. And this fate befell some
at the hands of kinsmen and friends, if so it chanced,
since necessity is not curiously concerned for what
is holy among men.

55. But when Agathocles saw that they were cold-
bloodedly intent on fighting, he put his army in
position to attack from every side and, forcing an
entrance at a point where the wall had been poorly
constructed, broke into the city. As some of the
Uticans fled into their houses, others into temples,

293

ἱερὰ καταφευγόντων δι' ὀργῆς αὐτοὺς ἔχων φόνου
τὴν πόλιν ἐπλήρωσε. τοὺς μὲν γὰρ ἐν χειρῶν νόμῳ
διέφθειρε, τοὺς δ' ἁλόντας ἐκρέμασε, τοὺς δ' ἐπὶ
θεῶν ἱερὰ καὶ βωμοὺς καταφυγόντας διαψευσθῆναι
3 τῆς ἐλπίδος ἐποίησεν. διαφορήσας δὲ τὰς κτήσεις
καὶ φυλακὴν ἀπολιπὼν ἐπὶ τῆς πόλεως ἐστρατοπέδευσεν ἐπὶ τὴν Ἵππου καλουμένην ἄκραν,
ὠχυρωμένην φυσικῶς τῇ παρακειμένῃ λίμνῃ. πολιορκήσας δὲ αὐτὴν ἐνεργῶς καὶ τῶν ἐγχωρίων
ναυμαχίᾳ περιγενόμενος κατὰ κράτος εἷλε. τούτῳ
δὲ τῷ τρόπῳ τὰς πόλεις χειρωσάμενος τῶν τε ἐπὶ
θαλάττῃ τόπων τῶν πλείστων ἐκυρίευσεν καὶ τῶν
τὴν μεσόγειον οἰκούντων πλὴν τῶν Νομάδων· ὧν
τινὲς μὲν φιλίαν πρὸς αὐτὸν ἐποιήσαντο, τινὲς δ'
4 ἐκαραδόκουν τὴν τῶν ὅλων κρίσιν. τέτταρα γὰρ
τὴν Λιβύην διείληφε γένη, Φοίνικες μὲν οἱ τὴν
Καρχηδόνα τότε κατοικοῦντες, Λιβυφοίνικες δὲ
πολλὰς ἔχοντες πόλεις ἐπιθαλαττίους καὶ κοινω-
νοῦντες τοῖς Καρχηδονίοις ἐπιγαμίας, οἷς ἀπὸ τῆς
συμπεπλεγμένης συγγενείας συνέβη τυχεῖν ταύτης
τῆς προσηγορίας· ὁ δὲ πολὺς λαὸς τῶν ἐγχωρίων,
ἀρχαιότατος ὤν, Λίβυς ὠνομάζετο, μισῶν διαφερόντως τοὺς Καρχηδονίους διὰ τὸ βάρος τῆς
ἐπιστασίας· οἱ δὲ τελευταῖοι Νομάδες ὑπῆρχον,
πολλὴν τῆς Λιβύης νεμόμενοι μέχρι τῆς ἐρήμου.
5 Ἀγαθοκλῆς δὲ τοῖς μὲν κατὰ Λιβύην συμμάχοις
καὶ ταῖς δυνάμεσιν ὑπερέχων τῶν Καρχηδονίων,
περὶ δὲ τῶν ἐν Σικελίᾳ πραγμάτων ἀγωνιῶν
ἄφρακτα καὶ πεντηκοντόρους ναυπηγησάμενος ἐν-

---

¹ Literally, " The citadel of the horse " or " The cape of
the horse," identified with Hippos Diarrhytus, the modern
294

Agathocles, enraged as he was against them, filled 307 B.C. the city with slaughter. Some he killed in hand-to-hand fighting ; those who were captured he hanged, and those who had fled to temples and altars of the gods he cheated of their hopes. When he had sacked the movable property, he left a garrison in possession of the city, and led his army into position against the place called Hippu Acra,¹ which was made naturally strong by the marsh that lay before it. After laying siege to this with vigour and getting the better of its people in a naval battle, he took it by storm. When he had conquered the cities in this way, he became master both of most of the places along the sea and of the peoples dwelling in the interior except the Nomads, of whom some arrived at terms of friendship with him and some awaited the final issue. For four stocks have divided Libya : the Phoenicians, who at that time occupied Carthage ; the Libyphoenicians, who have many cities along the sea and intermarry with the Carthaginians, and who received this name as a result of the interwoven ties of kinship. Of the inhabitants the race that was most numerous and oldest was called Libyan, and they hated the Carthaginians with a special bitterness because of the weight of their overlordship ; and last were the Nomads, who pastured their herds over a large part of Libya as far as the desert.

Now that Agathocles was superior to the Carthaginians by reason of his Libyan allies and his own armies but was much troubled about the situation in Sicily, he constructed light ships and penteconters

Bisertê ; cp. Beloch, *Griechische Geschichte*², 4. 1. 195, note 2. Here Agathocles gathered material for the construction of his fleet, Appian, *African Wars*, 110.

ἐβίβασε στρατιώτας δισχιλίους. καταλιπὼν δὲ τῶν
ἐν τῇ Λιβύῃ πραγμάτων στρατηγὸν Ἀγάθαρχον
τὸν υἱὸν ἀνήχθη ταῖς ναυσίν, ἐπὶ Σικελίαν τὸν
πλοῦν ποιούμενος.

56. Ἅμα δὲ τούτοις πραττομένοις Ξενόδοκος ὁ
τῶν Ἀκραγαντίνων στρατηγὸς πολλὰς μὲν τῶν πόλεων ἠλευθερωκώς, ἐλπίδας δὲ μεγάλας παρεσχηκὼς
τοῖς Σικελιώταις τῆς καθ᾽ ὅλην τὴν νῆσον αὐτονομίας ἐξήγαγε τὴν δύναμιν ἐπὶ τοὺς Ἀγαθοκλέους
στρατηγούς, οὖσαν πεζῶν μὲν πλειόνων ἢ μυρίων,
2 ἱππέων δὲ σχεδὸν χιλίων. οἱ δὲ περὶ Λεπτίνην καὶ
Δημόφιλον ἐκ τῶν Συρακουσσῶν καὶ τῶν φρουρίων
ἐπιλέξαντες ὅσους ἠδύναντο πλείστους[1] ἀντεστρατοπέδευσαν πεζοῖς μὲν ὀκτακισχιλίοις καὶ διακοσίοις, ἱππεῦσι δὲ χιλίοις καὶ διακοσίοις. γενομένης
οὖν παρατάξεως ἰσχυρᾶς ἡττηθεὶς ὁ Ξενόδοκος
ἔφυγεν εἰς τὸν Ἀκράγαντα καὶ τῶν στρατιωτῶν
ἀπέβαλεν οὐκ ἐλάττους τῶν χιλίων καὶ πεντακο-
3 σίων. οἱ μὲν οὖν Ἀκραγαντῖνοι ταύτῃ τῇ συμφορᾷ
περιπεσόντες διέλυσαν ἑαυτῶν μὲν τὴν καλλίστην
ἐπιβολήν, τῶν δὲ συμμάχων τὰς τῆς ἐλευθερίας
ἐλπίδας· Ἀγαθοκλῆς δὲ τῆς μάχης ἄρτι γεγενημένης καταπλεύσας τῆς Σικελίας εἰς Σελινοῦντα
Ἡρακλεώτας μὲν ἠλευθερωκότας τὴν πόλιν ἠνάγκασε πάλιν ὑποτάττεσθαι, παρελθὼν δὲ ἐπὶ θάτερον
μέρος τῆς νήσου Θερμίτας μὲν προσαγαγόμενος
ὑποσπόνδους ἀφῆκε τῶν Καρχηδονίων τοὺς φρουροῦντας[2] ταύτην τὴν πόλιν, Κεφαλοίδιον δὲ ἐκπολιορκήσας Λεπτίνην μὲν ταύτης ἐπιμελητὴν

---

[1] ὅσους ἠδύναντο πλείστους Dindorf : οὓς ἠδύναντο πλείους.

and placed upon them two thousand soldiers.[1] Leaving 307 B.C. his son Agatharchus[2] in command of affairs in Libya, he put out with his ships and made the voyage to Sicily.

56. While this was happening, Xenodocus,[3] the general of the Acragantines, having freed many of the cities and roused in the Sicilians great hopes of autonomy throughout the whole island, led his army against the generals of Agathocles. It consisted of more than ten thousand foot-soldiers and nearly a thousand horsemen. Leptines and Demophilus, assembling from Syracuse and the fortresses as many men as they could, took up a position opposite him with eighty-two hundred foot-soldiers and twelve hundred horse. In a bitter fight that ensued, Xenodocus was defeated and fled to Acragas, losing not less than fifteen hundred of his soldiers. The people of Acragas after meeting with this reverse put an end to their own most noble enterprise and, at the same time, to their allies' hopes of freedom. Shortly after this battle had taken place, Agathocles put in at Selinus in Sicily and forced the people of Heraclea, who had made their city free, to submit to him once more. Having crossed to the other side of the island, he attached to himself by a treaty the people of Therma, granting safe conduct to the Carthaginian garrison. Then, after taking Cephaloedium and leaving Leptines as its governor, he himself marched

---

[1] The fleet was constructed at Hippu Acra, cp. Appian, *African Wars*, 110.
[2] Usually called Archagathus, cp. chap. 11. 1, and note.
[3] Cp. chap. 31. 4.

---

[2] τοὺς φρουροῦντας Reiske, Madvig ; approved by Fischer in apparatus : φρουρούντων.

ἀπέλιπεν, αὐτὸς δὲ διὰ τῆς μεσογείου ποιούμενος
τὴν πορείαν ἐπεβάλετο μὲν νυκτὸς εἰς τὰ Κεντόριπα
παρεισπεσεῖν εἰσδεχομένων αὐτόν τινων πολιτικῶν
ἀνδρῶν, καταφανοῦς δὲ τῆς ἐπιβουλῆς γενομένης
καὶ τῶν φρουρῶν παραβοηθησάντων ἐξέπεσεν ἐκ
τῆς πόλεως, ἀποβαλὼν τῶν στρατιωτῶν πλείους
4 πεντακοσίων. μετὰ δὲ ταῦτα τινων ἐκ τῆς Ἀπολλωνίας μεταπεμπομένων αὐτὸν καὶ τὴν πατρίδα
προδώσειν ἐπαγγελλομένων ἧκε πρὸς τὴν πόλιν·
τῶν δὲ προδοτῶν καταφανῶν γενομένων καὶ κολα-
σθέντων κατὰ μὲν πρώτην ἡμέραν πολιορκήσας
ἄπρακτος ἐγένετο, τῇ δ' ὑστεραίᾳ πολλὰ κακοπαθήσας καὶ συχνοὺς ἀποβαλὼν μόλις εἷλε τὴν
πόλιν καὶ τῶν Ἀπολλωνιατῶν τοὺς πλείστους
ἀποσφάξας διήρπασε τὰς κτήσεις.

57. Τούτου δὲ περὶ ταῦτ' ὄντος Δεινοκράτης ὁ
τῶν φυγάδων ἡγούμενος ἀναλαβὼν τὴν Ἀκραγαντίνων προαίρεσιν καὶ προστάτην αὐτὸν ἀναδείξας
τῆς κοινῆς ἐλευθερίας ἐποίησε πολλοὺς ἀπανταχόθεν
2 συνδραμεῖν πρὸς αὐτόν· οἱ μὲν γὰρ διὰ τὴν ἔμφυτον
πᾶσιν ἐπιθυμίαν τῆς αὐτονομίας, οἱ δὲ διὰ τὸν
Ἀγαθοκλέους φόβον προθύμως ὑπήκουον τοῖς παρ-
αγγελλομένοις. ἠθροισμένων δ' αὐτῷ[1] πεζῶν μὲν
οὐ πολὺ ἐλάττων δισμυρίων, ἱππέων δὲ χιλίων καὶ
πεντακοσίων καὶ πάντων τούτων ἐν φυγαῖς καὶ
μελέταις τοῦ πονεῖν συνεχῶς γεγονότων κατεστρατοπέδευσεν ἐν ὑπαίθρῳ, προκαλούμενος τῇ μάχῃ
3 τὸν δυνάστην. τοῦ δ' Ἀγαθοκλέους λειπομένου
πολὺ ταῖς δυνάμεσι καὶ φυγομαχοῦντος ἐκ ποδὸς
ἠκολούθει συνεχῶς, ἀκονητὶ περιπεποιημένος τὴν
νίκην.

Ἀπὸ δὲ τούτων τῶν καιρῶν τοῖς περὶ τὸν Ἀγα-

through the interior and attempted to slip by night 307 B.C.
into Centoripa, where some of the citizens were to
admit him. When their plan was discovered, however, and the guard came to the defence, he was
thrown out of the city, losing more than five hundred
of his soldiers. Thereupon, men from Apollonia
having invited him and promised to betray their
fatherland, he came to that city. As the traitors had
become known and had been punished, he attacked
the city but without effect for the first day, and on
the next, after suffering heavily and losing a large
number of men, he barely succeeded in taking it.
After slaughtering most of the Apolloniates, he
plundered their possessions.

57. While Agathocles was engaged on these
matters, Deinocrates, the leader of the exiles, taking
over the policy of the Acragantines and proclaiming
himself champion of the common liberty, caused many
to flock to him from all sides ; for some eagerly gave
ear to his appeals because of the desire for independence inborn in all men, and others because of their
fear of Agathocles. When Deinocrates had collected
almost twenty thousand foot-soldiers and fifteen
hundred mounted men, all of them men who had had
uninterrupted experience of exile and hardship, he
camped in the open, challenging the tyrant to battle.
However, when Agathocles, who was far inferior in
strength, avoided battle, he steadily followed on his
heels, having secured his victory without a struggle.
From this time on the fortunes of Agathocles, not

---

¹ αὐτῷ Dindorf : αὐτῶν.

θοκλέα συνέβαινε πρὸς τὸ χεῖρον μεταβάλλειν οὐ
μόνον τὰ κατὰ Σικελίαν, ἀλλὰ καὶ τὰ κατὰ Λιβύην
4 πράγματα. Ἀρχάγαθος γὰρ ὁ καταλειφθεὶς ὑπ'
αὐτοῦ στρατηγὸς μετὰ τὴν ἀναγωγὴν τοῦ πατρὸς τὸ
μὲν πρῶτον ἐπλεονέκτει, πέμψας εἰς τοὺς ἄνω τόπους μέρος τι τῆς δυνάμεως, ἧς ἦν ἡγεμὼν Εὔμαχος.
οὗτος γὰρ Τώκας πόλιν εὐμεγέθη χειρωσάμενος
πολλοὺς προσηγάγετο τῶν πλησίον κατοικούντων
5 Νομάδων. εἶθ' ἑτέραν ἐκπολιορκήσας, τὴν ὀνομαζομένην Φελλίνην, ἠνάγκασε πειθαρχεῖν τοὺς τὴν
ἑξῆς χώραν νεμομένους, τοὺς καλουμένους Ἀσφο-
δελώδεις, ὄντας τῷ χρώματι παραπλησίους τοῖς
6 Αἰθίοψι. τρίτην δ' εἷλε Μεσχέλαν, μεγίστην οὖσαν,
ᾠκισμένην δὲ τὸ παλαιὸν ὑπὸ τῶν ἐκ Τροίας ἀνα-
κομιζομένων Ἑλλήνων, περὶ ὧν ἐν τῇ τρίτῃ βίβλῳ
προειρήκαμεν, ἑξῆς δὲ τὴν ὀνομαζομένην ἄκραν
Ἵππου τὴν ὁμώνυμον τῇ χειρωθείσῃ κατὰ κράτος
ὑπ' Ἀγαθοκλέους καὶ τελευταίαν τὴν προσαγορευο-
μένην Ἀκρίδα πόλιν αὐτόνομον, ἣν ἐξανδραποδι-
σάμενος ἐξέδωκε τοῖς στρατιώταις διαρπάσαι.

58. Ἐμπλήσας δ' ὠφελείας τὸ στρατόπεδον κατ-
έβη πρὸς τοὺς περὶ τὸν Ἀρχάγαθον καὶ δόξας
ἀγαθὸς ἀνὴρ γεγονέναι πάλιν ἐστράτευσεν εἰς τοὺς
ἄνω τῆς Λιβύης τόπους. ὑπερβαλὼν δὲ τὰς πόλεις
ὧν πρότερον ἐγεγόνει κύριος, παρεισέπεσεν εἰς τὴν
καλουμένην Μιλτινὴν πόλιν, ἀπροσδοκήτως ἐπι-
2 φανείς· συστραφέντων δ' ἐπ' αὐτὸν τῶν βαρβάρων
καὶ κρατησάντων ἐν ταῖς ὁδοῖς ἐξεβλήθη παραλόγως
καὶ πολλοὺς τῶν στρατιωτῶν ἀπέβαλεν. ἐντεῦθεν

---

[1] The name means " like the asphodel.'
[2] There is nothing about this incident in Book 3 ; and

only in Sicily but also in Libya, suffered a change for 307 B.C. the worse. Archagathus, who had been left by him as general, after the departure of his father at first gained some advantage by sending into the inland regions a part of the army under the command of Eumachus. This leader, after taking the rather large city of Tocae, won over many of the Nomads who dwelt near by. Then, capturing another city called Phellinê, he forced the submission of those who used the adjacent country as pasture, men called the Asphodelodes,[1] who are similar to the Ethiopians in colour. The third city that he took was Meschela, which was very large and had been founded long ago by the Greeks who were returning from Troy, about whom we have already spoken in the third Book.[2] Next he took the place called Hippu Acra, which has the same name as that captured by storm by Agathocles,[3] and finally the free city called Acris, which he gave to his soldiers for plundering after he had enslaved the people.[4]

58. After sating his army with booty, he returned to Archagathus ; and since he had gained a name for good service, he again led an army into the inland regions of Libya. Passing by the cities that he had previously mastered, he gained an entrance into the city called Miltinê, having appeared before it without warning ; but when the barbarians gathered together against him and overpowered him in the streets, he was, to his great surprise, driven out and lost many of his men. Departing thence, he marched through

chronologically it belongs in Book 7, of which only fragments are extant ; cp. Vol. III, pp. 358-359.

[3] Cp. chap. 55. 3.

[4] None of the cities or peoples mentioned in this paragraph can be identified with certainty.

δ' ἀναζεύξας προῆγεν δι' ὅρους ὑψηλοῦ παρήκοντος
ἐπὶ σταδίους διακοσίους, πλήρους δ' ὄντος αἰλούρων,
ἐν ᾧ συνέβαινε μηδὲν ὅλως πτηνὸν νεοττεύειν μήτε
ἐπὶ τοῖς δένδρεσι μήτε ἐν[1] ταῖς φάραγξι διὰ τὴν
3 ἀλλοτριότητα τῶν προειρημένων ζῴων. διελθὼν
δὲ τὴν ὀρεινὴν ταύτην ἐνέβαλεν εἰς χώραν ἔχουσαν
πλῆθος πιθήκων καὶ πόλεις τρεῖς τὰς ἀπὸ τούτων
τῶν ζῴων ὀνομαζομένας εἰς τὸν Ἑλληνικὸν τρόπον
4 τῆς διαλέκτου μεθερμηνευομένας Πιθηκούσσας. ἐν
δὲ ταύταις οὐκ ὀλίγα τῶν νομίμων πολὺ παρήλ-
λαττε τῶν παρ' ἡμῖν. τάς τε γὰρ αὐτὰς οἰκίας οἱ
πίθηκοι κατῴκουν τοῖς ἀνθρώποις, θεοὶ παρ' αὐτοῖς νομιζόμενοι καθάπερ παρ' Αἰγυπτίοις οἱ κύνες,
ἔκ τε τῶν παρεσκευασμένων ἐν τοῖς ταμιείοις τὰ
ζῷα τὰς τροφὰς ἐλάμβανον ἀκωλύτως ὁπότε βούλοιντο. καὶ τὰς προσηγορίας δ' ἐτίθεσαν οἱ γονεῖς
τοῖς παισὶ κατὰ τὸ πλεῖστον ἀπὸ τῶν πιθήκων,
5 ὥσπερ παρ' ἡμῖν ἀπὸ τῶν θεῶν. τοῖς δ' ἀποκτεί-
νασι τοῦτο τὸ ζῷον ὡς ἠσεβηκόσι τὰ μέγιστα
θάνατος ὥριστο πρόστιμον· διὸ δὴ καὶ παρά τισιν
ἐνίσχυσεν ἐν παροιμίας μέρει λεγόμενον ἐπὶ τῶν
ἀνατεὶ κτεινομένων ὅτι πιθήκου αἷμ' ἀποτίσειαν.
6 ὁ δ' οὖν Εὔμαχος μίαν μὲν τούτων τῶν πόλεων
ἑλὼν κατὰ κράτος διήρπασε, τὰς δὲ δύο προσηγάγετο. πυνθανόμενος δὲ τοὺς περιοικοῦντας βαρβάρους ἀθροίζειν ἐπ' αὐτὸν μεγάλας δυνάμεις
προῆγε συντονώτερον, διεγνωκὼς ἐπανιέναι πρὸς
τοὺς ἐπὶ θαλάττῃ τόπους.

59. Μέχρι μὲν δὴ τούτων τῶν καιρῶν ἐν τῇ

---

[1] ἐν Reiske : ἐπὶ.

a high mountain range that extended for about two _{307 b.c.} hundred stades[1] and was full of wildcats,[2] in which, accordingly, no birds whatever nested either among the trees or the ravines because of the rapacity of the aforementioned beasts. Crossing this range, he came out into a country containing a large number of apes and to three cities called from these beasts Pithecusae,[3] if the name is translated into the Greek language. In these cities many of the customs were very different from those current among us. For the apes lived in the same houses as the men, being regarded among them as gods, just as the dogs are among the Egyptians,[4] and from the provisions laid up in the storerooms the beasts took their food without hindrance whenever they wished. Parents usually gave their children names taken from the apes, just as we do from the gods. For any who killed this animal, as if he had committed the greatest sacrilege, death was established as the penalty. For this reason, among some there was current a proverbial saying about those slain with impunity that they were paying the penalty for a monkey's blood. However this may be, Eumachus, after taking one of these cities by storm, destroyed it, but the other two he won over by persuasion. When, however, he heard that the neighbouring barbarians were collecting great forces against him, he pushed on more vigorously, having decided to go back to the regions by the sea.

59. Up to this time all the campaign in Libya had

---

[1] About 23 miles.

[2] Or " weasels."

[3] " Ape-cities " ; cp. the Πιθηκοῦσαι νῆσοι, " Ape Islands," off the coast of Campania (chap. 44. 7).

[4] Cp. Book 1, chap. 83. 1.

Λιβύῃ κατὰ νοῦν ἅπαντα τὰ πράγματα τοῖς περὶ
τὸν Ἀρχάγαθον ἦν. μετὰ δὲ ταῦτα τῆς γερουσίας
ἐν Καρχηδόνι βουλευσαμένης περὶ τοῦ πολέμου
καλῶς ἔδοξε τοῖς συνέδροις τρία στρατόπεδα ποιή-
σαντας ἐκ τῆς πόλεως ἐκπέμψαι, τὸ μὲν ἐπὶ τὰς
παραθαλαττίους πόλεις, τὸ δ' εἰς τὴν μεσόγειον,
2 τὸ δ' εἰς τοὺς ἄνω τόπους. ἐνόμιζον γὰρ τοῦτο
πράξαντες πρῶτον μὲν τὴν πόλιν ἀπαλλάξειν τῆς
πολιορκίας ἅμα δὲ καὶ τῆς σιτοδείας· πολλῶν γὰρ
καὶ παντοδαπῶν ὄχλων συμπεφευγότων εἰς τὴν
Καρχηδόνα συνέβαινε πάντων γεγονέναι σπάνιν,
ἐξανηλωμένων ἤδη τῶν ἐπιτηδείων· ἀπὸ[1] δὲ τῆς
πολιορκίας οὐκ ἦν κίνδυνος, ἀπροσίτου τῆς πόλεως
οὔσης διὰ τὴν ἀπὸ τῶν τειχῶν καὶ τῆς θαλάττης
3 ὀχυρότητα· ἔπειθ' ὑπελάμβανον καὶ τοὺς συμμάχους διαμένειν μᾶλλον πλειόνων στρατοπέδων ὄντων
ἐν ὑπαίθρῳ τῶν παραβοηθούντων· τὸ δὲ μέγιστον,
ἤλπιζον καὶ τοὺς πολεμίους ἀναγκασθήσεσθαι μερίζειν τὰς δυνάμεις καὶ μακρὰν ἀποσπᾶσθαι τῆς
Καρχηδόνος. ἅπερ ἅπαντα κατὰ τὴν ἐπίνοιαν αὐ-
4 τῶν συνετελέσθη· τρισμυρίων μὲν γὰρ στρατιωτῶν
ἐκ τῆς πόλεως ἐκπεμφθέντων οἱ καταλειπόμενοι
ἔμφρουροι[2] οὐχ οἷον ἱκανὰ πρὸς αὐτάρκειαν εἶχον,
ἀλλ' ἐκ περιουσίας ἐχρῶντο δαψιλέσι πᾶσιν, οἵ τε
σύμμαχοι τὸ πρὸ τοῦ διὰ τὸν ἀπὸ τῶν πολεμίων
φόβον ἀναγκαζόμενοι προστίθεσθαι τοῖς πολεμίοις
τότε πάλιν θαρρήσαντες ἀνέτρεχον εἰς τὴν προ-
υπάρχουσαν φιλίαν.

60. Ὁ δ' Ἀρχάγαθος ὁρῶν διειλημμένην ἅπασαν
τὴν Λιβύην πολεμίοις στρατοπέδοις καὶ αὐτὸς διεῖλε τὴν δύναμιν καὶ μέρος μὲν ἐξέπεμψεν εἰς τὴν

been satisfactory to Archagathus. But after this the 307 B.C. senate in Carthage took good counsel about the war and the senators decided to form three armies and send them forth from the city, one against the cities of the coast, one into the midland regions, and one into the interior. They thought that if they did this they would in the first place relieve the city of the siege and at the same time of the scarcity of food ; for since many people from all parts had taken refuge in Carthage, there had resulted a general scarcity, the supply of provisions being already exhausted, but there was no danger from the siege since the city was inaccessible because of the protection afforded by the walls and the sea. In the second place, they assumed that the allies would continue more loyal if there were more armies in the field aiding them. And, what was most important, they hoped that the enemy would be forced to divide his forces and to withdraw to a distance from Carthage. All of these aims were accomplished according to their purpose ; for when thirty thousand soldiers had been sent out from the city, the men who were left behind as a garrison not only had enough to maintain themselves, but out of their abundance they enjoyed everything in profusion ; and the allies, who hitherto, because of their fear of the enemy, were compelled to make terms with him, again gained courage and hastened to return to the formerly existing friendship.

60. When Archagathus saw that all Libya was being occupied in sections by hostile armies, he himself also divided his army ; part he sent into the

---

¹ ἀπὸ Fischer : ὁ.
² ἔμφρουροι Madvig ; ἐν τῇ πόλει Dindorf ; εὐπόρως Post : ἔμποροι.

παραθαλάττιον, τῆς δ' ἄλλης στρατιᾶς ἦν μὲν Αἰ-
σχρίωνι παραδοὺς ἐξέπεμψεν, ἧς δ' αὐτὸς ἡγεῖτο,
καταλιπὼν τὴν ἱκανὴν φυλακὴν ἐπὶ τοῦ Τύνητος.
2 τοσούτων δὲ στρατοπέδων ἐπὶ τῆς χώρας πανταχῇ
πλαζομένων καὶ προσδοκωμένης ἔσεσθαι πραγμάτων ὁλοσχεροῦς[1] μεταβολῆς ἅπαντες ἠγωνίων,
3 καραδοκοῦντες τὸ τέλος τῶν ἀποβησομένων. "Αν-
νων μὲν οὖν ἡγούμενος τοῦ κατὰ τὴν μεσόγειον
στρατοπέδου θεὶς ἐνέδραν τοῖς περὶ τὸν Αἰσχρίωνα
καὶ παραδόξως ἐπιθέμενος ἀνεῖλε πεζοὺς μὲν
πλείους τῶν τετρακισχιλίων, ἱππεῖς δὲ περὶ διακοσίους, ἐν οἷς ἦν καὶ αὐτὸς ὁ στρατηγός· τῶν δ'
ἄλλων οἱ μὲν ἥλωσαν οἱ δὲ διεσώθησαν πρὸς
Ἀρχάγαθον, ἀπέχοντα σταδίους πεντακοσίους.
4 Ἰμίλκων δ' ἐπὶ τοὺς ἄνω τόπους στρατεύειν ἀπο-
δειχθεὶς τὸ μὲν πρῶτον ἐφήδρευε ἔν τινι[2] πόλει
προσδεχόμενος[3] τὸν Εὔμαχον, ἐφελκόμενον βαρὺ
τὸ στρατόπεδον διὰ τὰς ἐκ τῶν ἁλουσῶν πόλεων
5 ὠφελείας. μετὰ δὲ ταῦτα τῶν Ἑλλήνων ἐκταξάντων τὴν δύναμιν καὶ προκαλουμένων εἰς μάχην
Ἰμίλκων μέρος μὲν τῆς στρατιᾶς κατέλιπε δι-
εσκευασμένον ἐν τῇ πόλει, διακελευσάμενος, ὅταν
αὐτὸς ἀναχωρῇ προσποιούμενος φεύγειν, ἐπεξελθεῖν
τοῖς ἐπιδιώκουσιν· αὐτὸς δὲ προαγαγὼν τοὺς ἡμί-
σεις τῶν στρατιωτῶν καὶ μικρὸν πρὸ τῆς παρεμβολῆς συνάψας μάχην εὐθὺς ἔφευγεν ὡς καταπε-
6 πληγμένος. οἱ δὲ περὶ τὸν Εὔμαχον ἐπαρθέντες τῇ
νίκῃ καὶ τῆς τάξεως οὐδὲν φροντίσαντες ἐδίωκον
καὶ τεθορυβημένως τῶν ὑποχωρούντων ἐξήπτοντο·

---

[1] ὁλοσχεροῦς Dindorf : ὁλοσχερῶν.

coastal region, and of the rest of his forces he gave
part to Aeschrion and sent him forth, and part he
led himself, leaving an adequate garrison in Tunis.
When so many armies were wandering everywhere
in the country and when a decisive crisis in the
campaign was expected, all anxiously awaited the
final outcome. Now Hanno,[1] who commanded the
army of the midland region, laid an ambush for Aeschrion and fell on him suddenly, slaying more than
four thousand foot-soldiers and about two hundred
mounted troops, among whom was the general himself; of the others some were captured and some
escaped in safety to Archagathus, who was about
five hundred stades distant.[2] As for Himilco, who
had been appointed to conduct the campaign into the
interior, at first he rested in a certain city lying in
wait for Eumachus, who was dragging along his army
heavily loaded with the spoils from the captured
cities. Then when the Greeks drew up their forces
and challenged him to battle, Himilco left part of
his army under arms in the city, giving them orders
that, when he retired in pretended flight, they should
burst out upon the pursuers. He himself, leading
out half of his soldiers and joining battle a little
distance in front of the encampment, at once took
to flight as if panic-stricken. Eumachus' men, elated
by their victory and giving no thought at all to
their formation, followed, and in confusion pressed
hard upon those who were withdrawing; but when

[1] To be distinguished from the Hanno of chaps. 10. 1. and
12. 3, who is now dead. Nothing further is known of this
Hanno. [2] About 57 miles.

---

[2] ἔν τινι Holm : τῇ MSS., Fischer.
[3] προσδεχόμενος Reiske : πρὸς MSS., Fischer.

ἄφνω δὲ καθ᾽ ἕτερον μέρος τῆς πόλεως ἐκχυθείσης
τῆς δυνάμεως κατεσκευασμένης καὶ πλήθους ἱκανοῦ
πρὸς ἓν παρακέλευσμα συναλαλάξαντος κατεπλά-
7 γησαν. ἐμβαλόντων οὖν τῶν βαρβάρων εἰς ἀσυν-
τάκτους καὶ πεφοβημένους διὰ τὸ παράδοξον, ταχὺ
τροπὴν συνέβη γενέσθαι τῶν Ἑλλήνων. ὑποτεμο-
μένων δὲ τῶν Καρχηδονίων τὴν εἰς τὴν στρατοπεδείαν ἀποχώρησιν τῶν πολεμίων ἠναγκάσθησαν
οἱ περὶ τὸν Εὔμαχον καταφυγεῖν ἐπὶ τὸν πλησίον
8 λόφον ὕδατος σπανίζοντα. περιστρατοπεδευσάντων
δὲ τὸν τόπον τῶν Φοινίκων ἅμα μὲν ὑπὸ τοῦ δίψους
καταπονηθέντες, ἅμα δ᾽ ὑπὸ τῶν πολεμίων κρατούμενοι σχεδὸν ἅπαντες ἀνῃρέθησαν· ἀπὸ μὲν γὰρ
πεζῶν ὀκτακισχιλίων τριάκοντα μόνον διεσώθησαν,
ἀπὸ δ᾽ ἱππέων ὀκτακοσίων τετταράκοντα διέφυγον
τὸν κίνδυνον.

61. Ὁ δ᾽ Ἀρχάγαθος τηλικαύτῃ συμφορᾷ περιπεσὼν ἐπανῆλθεν εἰς Τύνητα. καὶ τῶν μὲν ἐκπεμφθέντων στρατιωτῶν τοὺς περιλειπομένους
μετεπέμπετο πανταχόθεν, εἰς δὲ τὴν Σικελίαν
ἐξέπεμψε τοὺς δηλώσοντας τῷ πατρὶ τὰ συμβεβη-
κότα καὶ παρακαλέσοντας βοηθεῖν τὴν ταχίστην.
2 τοῖς δὲ προγεγονόσιν ἀτυχήμασιν ἕτερα τοῖς Ἕλλησιν ἐλάττωσις ἐπεγένετο· ἀπέστησαν μὲν γὰρ
ἀπ᾽ αὐτῶν πλὴν ὀλίγων ἅπαντες οἱ σύμμαχοι, συν-
εστράφησαν δὲ αἱ τῶν πολεμίων δυνάμεις καὶ
3 πλησίον ποιησάμενοι παρεμβολὰς ἐφήδρευον. Ἰμίλκων μὲν γὰρ κατελάβετο τὰ στενὰ καὶ τῶν ἀπὸ
τῆς χώρας ἐκβολῶν[1] ἀπέκλεισε τοὺς ἐναντίους,
ἀπέχοντας σταδίους ἑκατόν· ἐκ δὲ θατέρου μέρους
ἐστρατοπέδευσεν Ἀτάρβας ἀπὸ τεσσαράκοντα στα-
4 δίων τοῦ Τύνητος. διόπερ τῶν πολεμίων οὐ μόνον

suddenly from another part of the city there poured
forth the army all ready for battle and when a great
host shouted at a single command, they became
panic-stricken.   Accordingly, when the barbarians
fell upon an enemy who had been thrown into disorder and frightened by the sudden onslaught, the
immediate result was the rout of the Greeks.   Since
the Carthaginians cut off the enemy's return to his
camp, Eumachus was forced to withdraw to the near-
by hill, which was ill supplied with water.   When the
Phoenicians invested the place, the Greeks, who had
become weak from thirst and were being overpowered
by the enemy, were almost all killed.   In fact, of
eight thousand foot-soldiers only thirty were saved,
and of eight hundred horsemen forty escaped from
the battle.

61. After meeting with so great a disaster Archagathus returned to Tunis.   He summoned from all
sides the survivors of the soldiers who had been sent
out ; and he sent messengers to Sicily to report to
his father what had happened and to urge him to
come to his aid with all possible speed.   In addition
to the preceding disasters, another loss befell the
Greeks ; for all their allies except a few deserted
them, and the armies of the enemy gathered together
and, pitching camp near by, lay in wait for them.
Himilco occupied the passes and shut off his opponents, who were at a distance of a hundred stades,[1]
from the routes leading from the region ; and on the
other side Atarbas camped at a distance of forty
stades [2] from Tunis.   Therefore, since the enemy

---

[1] About 11½ miles.
[2] About 4½ miles.

---

[1] ἐκβολῶν Post : εἰσβολῶν.

τῆς θαλάττης ἀλλὰ καὶ τῆς χώρας κυριευόντων,
σιτοδείᾳ τε συνέβαινε συνέχεσθαι τοὺς Ἕλληνας
καὶ τῷ φόβῳ πάντοθεν κατείχοντο.

5 Ἐν ἀθυμίᾳ δὲ δεινῇ πάντων ὄντων Ἀγαθοκλῆς
ὡς ἐπύθετο τὰ κατὰ τὴν Λιβύην ἐλαττώματα, παρ-
εσκευάσατο ναῦς[1] μακρὰς ἑπτακαίδεκα, διανοούμενος βοηθεῖν τοῖς περὶ τὸν Ἀρχάγαθον. καὶ τῶν
κατὰ Σικελίαν δὲ πραγμάτων ἐπὶ τὸ χεῖρον αὐτῷ
μεταβεβληκότων διὰ τὸ τοὺς περὶ Δεινοκράτην
φυγάδας ηὐξῆσθαι ἐπὶ πλεῖον, τὸν μὲν ἐν τῇ νήσῳ
πόλεμον τοῖς περὶ Λεπτίνην στρατηγοῖς ἐνεχείρισεν,
αὐτὸς δὲ πληρώσας τὰς ναῦς ἐπετήρει τὸν τοῦ πλοῦ
καιρόν, ἐφορμούντων τῶν Καρχηδονίων τριάκοντα
6 ναυσί. καθ᾽ ὃν δὴ χρόνον ἐκ Τυρρηνίας αὐτῷ
κατέπλευσαν ὀκτωκαίδεκα ναῦς ἐπὶ βοήθειαν, αἳ
διὰ νυκτὸς εἰς τὸν λιμένα εἰσπεσοῦσαι τοὺς Καρχηδονίους ἔλαθον. ὁ δ᾽ Ἀγαθοκλῆς ταύτης τυχὼν
τῆς ἀφορμῆς κατεστρατήγησε τοὺς πολεμίους, τοῖς
μὲν συμμάχοις μένειν παραγγείλας μέχρι ἂν αὐτὸς
ἐκπλεύσας ἐπισπάσηται τοὺς Φοίνικας πρὸς τὸν
διωγμόν, αὐτὸς δέ, καθάπερ ἦν συντεθειμένος, ἐκ
τοῦ λιμένος ἀνήχθη κατὰ σπουδὴν τοῖς ἑπτακαίδεκα
7 σκάφεσιν. εἶθ᾽ οἱ μὲν ἐφορμοῦντες ἐδίωκον, οἱ δὲ
περὶ τὸν Ἀγαθοκλέα κατανοήσαντες τοὺς Τυρρηνοὺς παραφαινομένους ἐκ τοῦ λιμένος ἄφνω τὰς
ναῦς ἐπέστρεψαν καὶ καταστάντες εἰς ἐμβολὴν δι-
εναυμάχουν τοῖς βαρβάροις. οἱ δὲ Καρχηδόνιοι
διά τε τὸ παράδοξον καὶ διὰ τὸ τῶν πολεμίων εἰς
μέσον ἀπολαμβάνεσθαι τὰς ἰδίας τριήρεις κατα-
8 πλαγέντες ἔφυγον. εἶθ᾽ οἱ μὲν Ἕλληνες πέντε
νεῶν αὐτάνδρων ἐκυρίευσαν, ὁ δὲ τῶν Καρχηδονίων
στρατηγὸς ἁλισκομένης ἤδη τῆς ναυαρχίδος ἀπ-

controlled not only the sea but also the land, the 307 B.C.
Greeks both suffered from famine and were beset by
fear on every side.

While all were in deep despair, Agathocles, when
he learned of the reverses in Libya, made ready
seventeen warships intending to go to the aid of
Archagathus. Although affairs in Sicily had also
shifted to his disadvantage because of the increase
in the strength of the exiles who followed Deinocrates, he entrusted the war on the island to Leptines
as general; and he himself, manning his ships,
watched for a chance to set sail, since the Carthaginians were blockading the harbour with thirty
ships. Now at this very time eighteen ships arrived
from Etruria as a reinforcement for him, slipping into
the harbour at night without the knowledge of the
Carthaginians. Gaining this resource, Agathocles
outgeneralled his enemies; ordering the allies to
remain until he should have sailed out and drawn the
Carthaginians into the chase, he himself, just as he
had planned, put to sea from the harbour at top speed
with his seventeen ships. The ships on guard pursued, but Agathocles, on seeing the Etruscans appearing from the harbour, suddenly turned his ships, took
position for ramming, and pitted his ships against
the barbarians. The Carthaginians, terror-stricken by
the surprise and because their own triremes were
cut off between the enemy fleets, fled. Thereupon
the Greeks captured five ships with their crews;
and the commander of the Carthaginians, when his
flagship was on the point of being captured, killed

---

¹ τε after ναῦς omitted by Dindorf.

ἔσφαξεν ἑαυτόν, προκρίνας τὸν θάνατον τῆς προσ-
δοκηθείσης αἰχμαλωσίας. οὐ μὴν ἐφάνη γε εὖ
βεβουλευμένος· ἡ γὰρ ναῦς φοροῦ πνεύματος ἐπι-
λαβομένη τοῦ δόλωνος ἀρθέντος ἐξέφυγε τὸν
κίνδυνον.

62. Ἀγαθοκλῆς μὲν οὖν οὐδ' ἐλπίδας ἔχων τοῦ
κατὰ θάλατταν περιέσεσθαί ποτε Καρχηδονίων
ἐνίκησε ναυμαχίᾳ παραδόξως καὶ τὸ λοιπὸν θαλασσοκρατῶν παρείχετο τοῖς ἐμπόροις τὴν ἀσφάλειαν.
διόπερ οἱ Συρακόσιοι, πάντοθεν πρὸς αὐτοὺς κομι-
ζομένης ἀγορᾶς, ἀντὶ τῆς τῶν ἐπιτηδείων σπάνεως
2 ταχέως πάντων ἔσχον δαψίλειαν. ὁ δὲ δυνάστης
μετεωρισθεὶς τῷ γεγονότι προτερήματι Λεπτίνην
ἐξαπέστειλε λεηλατήσοντα τὴν πολεμίαν καὶ μάλιστα τὴν Ἀκραγαντίνην. ὁ γὰρ Ξενόδοκος διὰ
τὴν γεγενημένην ἧτταν βλασφημούμενος ὑπὸ τῶν
3 ἀντιπολιτευομένων ἐστασίαζε πρὸς αὐτούς. παρήγγειλε μὲν οὖν τῷ Λεπτίνῃ πειρᾶσθαι προκαλέσασθαι
τὸν ἄνδρα πρὸς μάχην[1]· ῥᾳδίως γὰρ προτερήσειν
ὡς στασιαζούσης δυνάμεως καὶ προηττημένης.
4 ὅπερ καὶ συνετελέσθη· ὁ μὲν γὰρ Λεπτίνης ἐμβαλὼν
εἰς τὴν Ἀκραγαντίνην τὴν χώραν ἐδῄου, ὁ δὲ Ξενόδοκος τὸ μὲν πρῶτον ἡσυχίαν εἶχεν, οὐ νομίζων
αὑτὸν ἀξιόμαχον εἶναι, ὀνειδιζόμενος δὲ ὑπὸ τῶν
πολιτῶν εἰς δειλίαν προήγαγε τὴν στρατιάν, τῷ
μὲν ἀριθμῷ βραχὺ λειπομένην τῶν ἐναντίων, τῇ δ'
ἀρετῇ πολὺ καταδεεστέραν οὖσαν, ὡς ἂν τῆς μὲν

---

[1] τὴν before μάχην omitted by Hertlein.

---

[1] The δόλων was either a light spar that could be rigged at

himself, preferring death to the anticipated captivity.
But in truth he was shown by the event to have
judged unwisely ; for his ship caught a favouring
wind, raised its jury mast [1] and fled from the battle.

62. Agathocles, who had no hope of ever getting
the better of the Carthaginians on the sea, unexpectedly defeated them in a naval battle, and
thereafter he ruled the sea and gave security to his
merchants. For this reason the people of Syracuse,
goods being brought to them from all sides, in place
of scarcity of provisions soon enjoyed an abundance
of everything. The tyrant, encouraged by the success that had been won, dispatched Leptines to
plunder the country of the enemy and, in particular,
that of Acragas. For Xenodocus, vilified by his
political opponents because of the defeat he had
suffered,[2] was at strife with them. Agathocles therefore ordered Leptines to try to entice the man out
to a battle ; for, he said, it would be easy to defeat
him since his army was seditious and had already been
overcome. And indeed this was accomplished ; for
when Leptines entered the territory of Acragas and
began plundering the land, Xenodocus at first kept
quiet, not believing himself strong enough for battle ;
but when he was reproached by the citizens for
cowardice, he led out his army, which in number fell
little short of that of his opponents but in morale was
far inferior since the citizen army had been formed

the prow of the warship, extending forward like a high bow-
sprit, or a square sail hung on a crossarm at the end of such
a spar. We hear of this rig only on Phoenician and Roman
craft. Since it could be set up more quickly than the ordinary
mast, which was stowed before battle, it seems often to have
been used as here. Cp. Livy, 36. 44. 3, 45. 1 ; 37. 30. 7 ;
Polybius, 16. 15. 2.   [2] Cp. chap. 56. 2.

πολιτικῆς ἐν ἀνέσει καὶ σκιατροφίᾳ γεγενημένης,
τῆς δ' ἐν ἀγραυλίᾳ καὶ συνεχέσι στρατείαις γε-
5 γυμνασμένης. διὸ καὶ μάχης γενομένης οἱ περὶ
τὸν Λεπτίνην ταχὺ τοὺς Ἀκραγαντίνους τρεψάμενοι
συνεδίωξαν εἰς τὴν πόλιν· ἔπεσον δ' ἐπὶ τῆς παρατάξεως τῶν ἡττηθέντων πεζοὶ μὲν περὶ πεντακοσίους, ἱππεῖς δὲ πλείω τῶν πεντήκοντα. εἶθ' οἱ
μὲν Ἀκραγαντῖνοι δυσφοροῦντες ἐπὶ τοῖς ἐλαττώμασιν ἐν αἰτίαις εἶχον τὸν Ξενόδοκον, ὡς δι' ἐκεῖνον
δὶς ἡττημένοι· ὁ δὲ φοβηθεὶς τὰς ἐπιφερομένας
εὐθύνας καὶ κρίσεις ἀπεχώρησεν εἰς τὴν Γέλαν.

63. Ἀγαθοκλῆς δὲ ἐν ἡμέραις ὀλίγαις καὶ πεζῇ
καὶ κατὰ θάλατταν νενικηκὼς τοὺς πολεμίους ἔθυε
τοῖς θεοῖς καὶ λαμπρὰς ὑποδοχὰς τῶν φίλων ἐποιεῖτο. ἀπετίθετο δ' ἐν τοῖς πότοις τὸ τῆς τυραννίδος
ἀξίωμα καὶ τῶν τυχόντων ἰδιωτῶν ταπεινότερον
ἑαυτὸν ἀπεδείκνυεν, ἅμα μὲν διὰ τῆς τοιαύτης
πολιτείας θηρώμενος τὴν παρὰ τῶν πολλῶν εὔνοιαν
ἅμα δὲ διδοὺς ἐν τῇ μέθῃ καθ' αὑτοῦ παρρησίαν,
ἀκριβῶς κατενόει τὴν ἑκάστου διάνοιαν, τῆς ἀληθείας ἐκφερομένης ἀπαρακαλύπτως διὰ τὸν οἶνον.
2 ὑπάρχων δὲ καὶ φύσει γελωτοποιὸς καὶ μῖμος οὐδ'
ἐν ταῖς ἐκκλησίαις ἀπείχετο τοῦ σκώπτειν τοὺς
καθημένους καί τινας αὐτῶν εἰκάζειν, ὥστε τὸ
πλῆθος πολλάκις εἰς γέλωτα ἐκτρέπεσθαι καθάπερ
τινὰ τῶν ἠθολόγων ἢ θαυματοποιῶν θεωροῦντας.
3 δορυφορούμενος δὲ ὑπὸ πλήθους εἰς τὰς ἐκκλησίας
εἰσῄει μόνος, οὐχ ὁμοίως Διονυσίῳ τῷ τυράννῳ·
οὗτος γὰρ ἐπὶ τοσοῦτον ἀπίστως διέκειτο πρὸς
ἅπαντας ὥστε κατὰ μὲν τὸ πλεῖστον κομᾶν καὶ
πωγωνοτροφεῖν, ὅπως μὴ συναναγκασθῇ τῷ τοῦ
κουρέως σιδήρῳ παραβαλεῖν τὰ κυριώτατα μέρη

amid indulgence and a sheltered way of life and the 307 B.C. other had been trained in military service in the field and in constant campaigns. Therefore when battle was joined, Leptines quickly routed the men of Acragas and pursued them into the city ; and there fell in the battle on the side of the vanquished about five hundred foot soldiers and more than fifty horsemen. Then the people of Acragas, vexed over their disasters, brought charges against Xenodocus, saying that because of him they had twice been defeated ; but he, fearing the impending investigation and trial, departed to Gela.

63. Agathocles, having within a few days defeated his enemies both on land and on sea, sacrificed to the gods and gave lavish entertainments for his friends. In his drinking bouts he used to put off the pomp of tyranny and to show himself more humble than the ordinary citizens ; and by seeking through a policy of this sort the goodwill of the multitude and at the same time giving men licence to speak against him in their cups he used to discover exactly the opinion of each, since through wine the truth is brought to light without concealment. Being by nature also a buffoon and a mimic, not even in the meetings of the assembly did he abstain from jeering at those who were present and from portraying certain of them, so that the common people would often break out into laughter as if they were watching one of the impersonators or conjurors. With a crowd serving as his bodyguard he used to enter the assembly unattended, unlike Dionysius the tyrant. For the latter was so distrustful of one and all that as a rule he let his hair and beard grow long so that he need not submit the most vital parts of his body to the

τοῦ σώματος· εἰ δὲ καί ποτε χρεία γένοιτο τὴν
κεφαλὴν ἀποκείρασθαι, περιέκαε τὰς τρίχας, μίαν
ἀσφάλειαν τυραννίδος ἀποφαινόμενος τὴν ἀπιστίαν.
4 ὁ δ' οὖν Ἀγαθοκλῆς παρὰ τὸν πότον λαβὼν ῥυτὸν
μέγαν χρυσοῦν εἶπεν ὡς οὐ πρότερον ἀπέστη τῆς
κεραμευτικῆς τέχνης ἕως τοιαῦτα ἐκπωμάτων
πλάσματα φιλοτεχνῶν ἐκεραμεύσατο. οὐ γὰρ
ἀπηρνεῖτο τὴν ἐπιστήμην, ἀλλὰ καὶ τοὐναντίον
ἐκαυχᾶτο, διὰ τῆς ἰδίας ἀρετῆς ἀποφαινόμενος ἀντὶ
τοῦ ταπεινοτάτου βίου τὸν ἐπιφανέστατον μετειλη-
5 φέναι. καί ποτε πολιορκοῦντος αὐτοῦ τινα τῶν
οὐκ ἀδόξων πόλεων καὶ τῶν ἀπὸ τοῦ τείχους βοών-
των '' Κεραμεῦ καὶ καμινεῦ, πότε τοὺς μισθοὺς
ἀποδώσεις τοῖς στρατιώταις; '' ὑπολαβὼν εἶπεν
6 '' Ὅταν ταύτην ἐξέλω.'' οὐ μὴν ἀλλὰ διὰ τὴν ἐν
τοῖς πότοις εὐτραπελίαν κατανοήσας τῶν μεθυόντων
τοὺς ἀλλοτρίως τὰ πρὸς τὴν δυναστείαν ἔχοντας
παρέλαβεν αὐτούς ποτε κατ' ἰδίαν πάλιν ἐπὶ τὴν
ἑστίασιν καὶ τῶν ἄλλων Συρακοσίων τοὺς μάλιστα
πεφρονηματισμένους, τὸν ἀριθμὸν πεντακοσίους
ὄντας· οἷς περιστήσας τῶν μισθοφόρων τοὺς εὐ-
7 θέτους ἅπαντας ἀπέσφαξεν. σφόδρα γὰρ εὐλαβεῖτο μὴ χωρισθέντος αὐτοῦ εἰς Λιβύην καταλύσωσι
τὴν δυναστείαν, ἐπικαλεσάμενοι τοὺς μετὰ Δεινοκράτους φυγάδας. τοῦτον δὲ τὸν τρόπον ἀσφαλισάμενος τὰ κατὰ τὴν ἀρχὴν ἐξέπλευσεν ἐκ τῶν
Συρακουσσῶν.

64. Καὶ κομισθεὶς εἰς Λιβύην κατέλαβε τὸ στρατόπεδον ἐν ἀθυμίᾳ καὶ σπάνει πολλῇ· διόπερ κρίνων

steel of the barber ; and if ever it became necessary 307 B.C.
for him to have his head trimmed, he singed off the
locks, declaring that the only safety of a tyrant was
distrust.[1]   Now Agathocles at the drinking bout,
taking a great golden cup, said that he had not given
up the potters' craft [2] until in his pursuit of art he had
produced in pottery beakers of such workmanship as
this. For he did not deny his trade but on the contrary used to boast of it, claiming that it was by his
own ability that in place of the most lowly position
in life he had secured the most exalted one. Once
when he was besieging a certain not inglorious city
and people from the wall shouted, " Potter and
furnace-man, when will you pay your soldiers ? " he
said in answer, " When I have taken this city." [3]
None the less, however, when through the jesting at
drinking bouts he had discovered which of those who
were flushed with wine were hostile to his tyranny
he invited them individually on another occasion to
a banquet, and also those of the other Syracusans
who had become particularly presumptuous, in number about five hundred ; and surrounding them with
suitable men from his mercenaries he slaughtered
them all. For he was taking very careful precautions
lest, while he was absent in Libya, they should overthrow the tyranny and recall Deinocrates and the
exiles. After he had made his rule secure in this
way, he sailed from Syracuse.

64. When he arrived in Libya [4] he found the army
discouraged and in great want : deciding, therefore,

---

[1] Cp. Cicero, *Tusculan Disputations*, 5. 20. 58.
[2] Cp. Book 19. 2. 7.
[3] Cp. Plutarch, *Apophthegmata*, p. 176. For the character
of Agathocles cp. Book 19. 9 ; Polybius, 9. 23. 2 ; 15. 35.
[4] For this second Libyan campaign cp. Justin, 22. 8. 4-15.

συμφέρειν διαγωνίζεσθαι παρεκάλεσε τοὺς στρατιώτας εἰς τὸν κίνδυνον καὶ προαγαγὼν τὴν δύναμιν
ἐκτεταγμένην προεκαλεῖτο τοὺς βαρβάρους εἰς
2 μάχην. εἶχε δὲ πεζοὺς μὲν τοὺς ἅπαντας ὑπολει-
πομένους Ἕλληνας ἑξακισχιλίους, Κελτοὺς δὲ καὶ
Σαυνίτας καὶ Τυρρηνοὺς τούτων οὐκ ἐλάττους,
Λίβυας δὲ μικρὸν ἀπολείποντας τῶν μυρίων, οὓς
ἐφέδρους εἶναι συνέβαινε, συμμεταβαλλομένους ἀεὶ
3 τοῖς καιροῖς· χωρὶς δὲ τούτων ἠκολούθουν ἱππεῖς
χίλιοι πεντακόσιοι, ζεύγη δὲ Λιβύων πλείω τῶν
ἑξακισχιλίων. οἱ δὲ Καρχηδόνιοι κατεστρατοπε-
δευκότες ἐπὶ τῶν ὑπερδεξίων καὶ δυσπροσίτων διακινδυνεύειν μὲν πρὸς ἀνθρώπους ἀπογινώσκοντας
τὴν σωτηρίαν οὐκ ἔκρινον, μένοντες δ᾽ ἐν τῇ παρεμβολῇ καὶ πάντων εὐποροῦντες τῇ σπάνει καὶ
τῷ χρόνῳ καταπολεμήσειν τοὺς ἐναντίους ἤλπιζον.
4 ὁ δ᾽ Ἀγαθοκλῆς οὐ δυνάμενος μὲν αὐτοὺς εἰς τὰ
πεδία προάγεσθαι, τῶν δὲ καιρῶν ἀναγκαζόντων
τολμᾶν τι καὶ παραβάλλεσθαι τὴν δύναμιν ἤγαγεν
ἐπὶ τὴν τῶν βαρβάρων στρατοπεδείαν. ἐπεξελθόντων οὖν τῶν Καρχηδονίων καὶ πολὺ τῷ πλήθει καὶ
ταῖς δυσχωρίαις ὑπερεχόντων ἐπὶ μέν τινα χρόνον
οἱ περὶ τὸν Ἀγαθοκλέα διεκαρτέρουν πάντοθεν
ἐκθλιβόμενοι, μετὰ δὲ ταῦτ᾽ ἐνδόντων τῶν μισθοφόρων καὶ τῶν ἄλλων ἠναγκάσθησαν ἀναχωρῆσαι
5 πρὸς τὴν στρατοπεδείαν. οἱ δὲ βάρβαροι βαρέως
ἐπικείμενοι τοὺς μὲν Λίβυας παρήλλαττον οὐδὲν
ἐνοχλοῦντες, ἵνα τὴν εὔνοιαν αὐτῶν ἐκκαλέσωνται,
τοὺς δ᾽ Ἕλληνας καὶ μισθοφόρους γνωρίζοντες
διὰ τῶν ὅπλων ἐφόνευον, μέχρις ὅτου συνεδίωξαν
εἰς τὴν παρεμβολήν.

Τότε μὲν οὖν ἀνῃρέθησαν Ἀγαθοκλέους εἰς τρισ-

that it was best to fight a battle, he encouraged the 307 B.C.
soldiers for the fray and, after leading forth the army
in battle array, challenged the barbarians to combat.
As infantry he had all the surviving Greeks, six
thousand in number, at least as many Celts, Samnites,
and Etruscans, and almost ten thousand Libyans,
who, as it turned out, only sat and looked on, being
always ready to change with changing conditions.
In addition to these there followed him fifteen
hundred horsemen and more than six thousand
Libyan chariots. The Carthaginians, since they were
encamped in high and inaccessible positions, decided
not to risk a battle against men who had no thought
of safety ; but they hoped that, by remaining in their
camp where they were plentifully supplied with
everything, they would defeat their enemy by
famine and the passage of time. But Agathocles,
since he could not lure them down to the plain and
since his own situation forced him to do something
daring and chance the result, led his army against
the encampment of the barbarians. Then when the
Carthaginians came out against him, even though
they were far superior in number and had the advantage of the rough terrain, Agathocles held out for
some time although hard pressed on every side ; but
afterwards, when his mercenaries and the others began to give way, he was forced to withdraw toward his
camp. The barbarians, as they pressed forward stoutly,
passed by the Libyans without molesting them in
order to elicit their goodwill ; but recognizing the
Greeks and the mercenaries by their weapons, they
continued to slay them until they had driven them
into their own camp.

Now on this occasion about three thousand of

χιλίους· κατὰ δὲ τὴν ἐπιοῦσαν νύκτα τὰς δυνάμεις ἀμφοτέρας συνέβη περιπεσεῖν παραλόγῳ τινὶ συμφορᾷ καὶ πᾶσιν ἀνελπίστῳ.

65. Τῶν γὰρ Καρχηδονίων μετὰ τὴν νίκην τοὺς καλλίστους τῶν αἰχμαλώτων θυόντων χαριστήρια νυκτὸς τοῖς θεοῖς καὶ πολλοῦ πυρὸς τοὺς ἱεροκαυτουμένους ἄνδρας κατέχοντος ἐξαίφνης πνεύματος ἐπιπεσόντος συνέβη τὴν ἱερὰν σκηνὴν ἀναφθῆναι, πλησίον οὖσαν τοῦ βωμοῦ, ἀπὸ δὲ ταύτης τὴν στρατηγικὴν καὶ τὰς¹ κατὰ τὸ συνεχὲς οὔσας τῶν ἡγεμόνων, ὥστε πολλὴν ἔκπληξιν γενέσθαι καὶ φόβον κατὰ πᾶν τὸ στρατόπεδον. τινὲς μὲν γὰρ τὸ πῦρ ἐπιχειροῦντες σβέσαι, τινὲς δὲ τὰς πανοπλίας καὶ τὰ πολυτελέστατα τῶν παρεσκευασμένων ἐκκομίζοντες ὑπὸ τῆς φλογὸς ἀπελαμβάνοντο· τῶν γὰρ σκηνῶν ἐκ καλάμου καὶ χόρτου συγκειμένων καὶ τοῦ πυρὸς ὑπὸ τοῦ πνεύματος βιαιότερον ἐκριπισθέντος ἡ παρὰ τῶν στρατιωτῶν βοήθεια κατ-
2 εταχεῖτο. διὸ καὶ τῆς παρεμβολῆς ταχὺ πάσης φλεγομένης πολλοὶ μὲν ἐν στεναῖς ταῖς διόδοις ἀποληφθέντες ζῶντες κατεκαύθησαν καὶ τῆς εἰς τοὺς αἰχμαλώτους ὠμότητος παραχρῆμα τὴν κόλασιν ὑπέσχον, αὐτῆς τῆς ἀσεβείας ἴσην τὴν τιμωρίαν πορισαμένης· τοῖς δ' ἐκ τῆς παρεμβολῆς ἐκπίπτουσι μετὰ θορύβου καὶ κραυγῆς ἕτερος μείζων ἐπηκολούθησε κίνδυνος.

66. Τῶν μὲν γὰρ Ἀγαθοκλεῖ συντεταγμένων Λιβύων εἰς πεντακισχιλίους ἀποστάντες τῶν Ἑλλήνων νυκτὸς ηὐτομόλουν πρὸς τοὺς βαρβάρους. τούτους δὲ οἱ πρὸς τὴν κατασκοπὴν ἐκπεμφθέντες ὡς ἴδον ἐπὶ τὴν παρεμβολὴν τῶν Καρχηδονίων προσάγοντας, νομίσαντες τὴν τῶν Ἑλλήνων δύναμιν ἅπασαν

Agathocles' men were killed ; but on the following 307 B.C.
night it so happened that each army was visited by
a strange and totally unexpected mishap.

65. While the Carthaginians after their victory
were sacrificing the fairest of their captives as thank-
offerings to the gods by night, and while a great blaze
enveloped the men who were being offered as victims,
a sudden blast of wind struck them, with the result
that the sacred hut, which was near the altar, caught
fire, and from this the hut of the general caught and
then the huts of the leaders, which were in line with
it, so that great consternation and fear sprang up
throughout the whole camp. Some were trapped
by the conflagration while trying to put out the fire
and others while carrying out their armour and the
most valued of their possessions ; for, since the huts
were made of reeds and straw and the fire was forcibly
fanned by the breeze, the aid brought by the soldiers
came too late. Thus when almost the entire camp
was in flames, many, caught in the passages which were
narrow, were burned alive and suffered due punishment on the spot for their cruelty to the captives, the
impious act itself having brought about a punishment
to match it ; and as for those who dashed from the
camp amid tumult and shouting, another greater
danger awaited them.

66. As many as five thousand of the Libyans who
had been taken into Agathocles' army had deserted
the Greeks and were going over by night to the barbarians. When those who had been sent out as
scouts saw these men coming toward the Carthaginian
camp, believing that the whole army of the Greeks

---

¹ τὰς added by Reiske.

διεσκευασμένην ἐπιέναι,[1] ταχὺ τοῖς στρατιώταις
2 ἐδήλωσαν τὴν προσιοῦσαν δύναμιν. διαδοθέντος οὖν
πρὸς ἅπαντας τοῦ λόγου θόρυβος ἐνέπιπτε καὶ
προσδοκία τῆς τῶν πολεμίων ἐφόδου. ἑκάστου
δὲ τὴν σωτηρίαν ἐν τῇ φυγῇ τιθεμένου, καὶ μήτε
παραγγέλματος δοθέντος ὑπὸ τῶν στρατηγῶν μήτε
τάξεως οὔσης μηδεμιᾶς οἱ φεύγοντες ἐνέπιπτον
ἀλλήλοις· ὧν οἱ μὲν διὰ τὸ σκότος, οἱ δὲ διὰ τὴν
ἔκπληξιν ἀγνοοῦντες τοὺς οἰκείους ὡς πολεμίους
3 ἠμύνοντο. πολλοῦ δὲ φόνου γινομένου καὶ τῆς
ἀγνοίας ἐπικρατούσης οἱ μὲν ἐν χειρῶν νόμῳ διεφθάρησαν, οἱ δ' ἐκπεπηδηκότες ἄνοπλοι καὶ τὴν
φυγὴν ποιούμενοι διὰ τῶν δυσχωριῶν κατεκρημνί-
ζοντο, τῆς ψυχῆς ἐπτοημένης διὰ τὸν ἀπροσδόκητον
φόβον. τὸ δὲ τέλος πλειόνων ἢ πεντακισχιλίων
ἀπολομένων τὸ λοιπὸν πλῆθος διεσώθη πρὸς τὴν
4 Καρχηδόνα. οἱ δ' ἐν τῇ πόλει τότε μὲν συνεξ-
απατηθέντες τῇ φήμῃ τῶν ἰδίων ὑπέλαβον ἡττῆσθαι
μάχῃ καὶ τῆς δυνάμεως τὸ πλεῖστον διεφθάρθαι.
διόπερ ἀγωνιῶντες ἀνέῳξαν τὰς πύλας καὶ μετὰ
θορύβου καὶ πτοήσεως ἐδέχοντο τοὺς στρατιώτας,
φοβούμενοι μὴ τοῖς ἐσχάτοις οἱ πολέμιοι συνεισ-
πέσωσιν· ἡμέρας δὲ γενομένης μαθόντες τἀληθὲς
μόλις ἀπελύθησαν τῆς τῶν δεινῶν προσδοκίας.

67. Οἱ δὲ περὶ τὸν Ἀγαθοκλέα κατὰ τὸν αὐτὸν χρόνον δι' ἀπάτην καὶ προσδοκίαν ψευδῆ ταῖς
ὁμοίαις περιέπεσον συμφοραῖς. τῶν γὰρ ἀποστα-
τῶν Λιβύων μετὰ τὸν ἐμπυρισμὸν τῆς παρεμβολῆς
καὶ τὸν γενόμενον θόρυβον οὐ τολμησάντων προάγειν, ἀλλ' εἰς τοὐπίσω πάλιν ἐπανιόντων, τῶν

was advancing ready for battle, they quickly reported the approaching force to their fellow soldiers. When the report had been spread through the whole force, there arose tumult and dread of the enemy's attack. Each man placed his hope of safety in flight; and since no order had been given by the commanders nor was there any formation, the fugitives kept running into each other. When some of them failed to recognize their friends because of the darkness and others because of fright, they fought against them as if they were enemies. A general slaughter took place; and while the misunderstanding still prevailed, some were slain in hand to hand fighting and others, who had sped away unarmed and were fleeing through the rough country, fell from cliffs, distraught in mind by the sudden panic. Finally after more than five thousand had perished, the rest of the multitude came safe to Carthage. But those in the city, who had also been deceived at that time by the report of their own people, supposed that they had been conquered in a battle and that the largest part of the army had been destroyed. Therefore in great anxiety they opened the city gates and with tumult and excitement received their soldiers, fearing lest with the last of them the enemy should burst in. When day broke, however, they learned the truth and were with difficulty freed from their expectation of disaster.

67. At this same time, however, Agathocles by reason of deceit and mistaken expectation met with similar disaster. For the Libyans who had deserted did not dare go on after the burning of the camp and the tumult that had arisen, but turned back again;

---

[1] ἐπιέναι Fischer : εἶναι.

Ἑλλήνων τινὲς αἰσθόμενοι προσιόντας αὐτοὺς καὶ δόξαντες τὴν τῶν Καρχηδονίων δύναμιν ἥκειν ἀπήγγειλαν τοῖς περὶ τὸν Ἀγαθοκλέα πλησίον ὑπάρχειν
2 τὸ τῶν πολεμίων στρατόπεδον. τοῦ δυνάστου δὲ παραγγείλαντος εἰς ὅπλα χωρεῖν, ἐξέπιπτον ἐκ τῆς στρατοπεδείας οἱ στρατιῶται μετὰ πολλοῦ θορύβου. ἅμα δὲ τῆς τε κατὰ τὴν παρεμβολὴν φλογὸς εἰς ὕψος ἀρθείσης καὶ τῆς τῶν Καχηδονίων κραυγῆς ἐξακούστου γινομένης ὑπέλαβον πρὸς ἀλήθειαν τοὺς βαρβάρους ἁπάσῃ τῇ δυνάμει προσάγειν ἐπ᾽ αὐτούς.
3 τῆς δ᾽ ἐκπλήξεως τὸ βουλεύεσθαι παραιρουμένης ἐνέπεσε φόβος εἰς τὸ στρατόπεδον καὶ πάντες πρὸς φυγὴν ὥρμησαν. εἶτα προσμιξάντων αὐτοῖς τῶν Λιβύων καὶ τῆς νυκτὸς μείζονα τὴν ἄγνοιαν φυλαττούσης οἱ περιτυγχάνοντες ἀλλήλους ὡς πολεμίους
4 ἠμύνοντο. ὅλην δὲ τὴν νύκτα πανταχῇ διασπειρομένων αὐτῶν καὶ πανικῷ θορύβῳ συνεχομένων συνέβη πλείους τῶν τετρακισχιλίων ἀναιρεθῆναι. ἐπιγνωσθείσης δὲ μόγις τῆς ἀληθείας οἱ διασωθέντες ἐπανῆλθον εἰς τὴν παρεμβολήν. αἱ μὲν οὖν δυνάμεις ἀμφότεραι τὸν εἰρημένον τρόπον ἠτύχησαν, ἐξαπατηθεῖσαι κατὰ τὴν παροιμίαν τοῖς κενοῖς τοῦ πολέμου.

68. Ἀγαθοκλῆς δέ, μετὰ τὴν γενομένην ἀτυχίαν τῶν μὲν Λιβύων ἁπάντων ἀποστάντων ἀπ᾽ αὐτοῦ, τῆς δὲ ὑπολειπομένης δυνάμεως ἀδυνατούσης διαπολεμεῖν πρὸς τοὺς Καρχηδονίους διέγνω τὴν Λιβύην ἐκλιπεῖν. διακομίσαι δὲ τοὺς στρατιώτας οὐχ ὑπελάμβανεν δυνήσεσθαι διὰ τὸ μήτε πόρια παρεσκευάσθαι μήτε τοὺς Καρχηδονίους ἐπιτρέψαι ποτ᾽
2 ἂν θαλασσοκρατοῦντας. διαλύσεις δ᾽ οὐκ ἐνόμιζε ποιήσεσθαι τοὺς βαρβάρους, πολὺ προέχοντας ταῖς

and some of the Greeks, seeing them advancing and 307 B.C. believing that the army of the Carthaginians had come, reported to Agathocles that the enemy's forces were near at hand. The dynast gave the order to take up arms, and the soldiers rushed from the camp with great tumult. Since at the same time the fire in the Carthaginian camp blazed high and the shouting of the Carthaginians became audible, the Greeks believed that the barbarians were in very truth advancing against them with their whole army. Since their consternation prevented deliberation, panic fell upon the camp and all began to flee. Then as the Libyans mingled with them and the darkness fostered and increased their uncertainty, those who happened to meet fought each other as if they were enemies. They were scattered about everywhere throughout the whole night and were in the grip of panic fear, with the result that more than four thousand were killed. When the truth was at long last discovered, those who survived returned to their camp. Thus both armies met with disaster in the way described, being tricked, according to the proverb, by the empty alarms of war.[1]

68. Since after this misfortune the Libyans all deserted him and the army which remained was not strong enough to wage battle against the Carthaginians, Agathocles decided to leave Libya. But he did not believe that he would be able to transport his soldiers since he had not prepared any transports and the Carthaginians would never permit it while they controlled the sea. He did not expect that the barbarians would agree to a truce because they were

---

[1] Cp. chap. 30. 1, and note.

δυνάμεσι καὶ διαβεβαιουμένους ταῖς τῶν πρῶτον
διαβάντων ἀπωλείαις ἀποτρέψαι τοὺς ἄλλους ἐπι-
3 τίθεσθαι τῇ Λιβύῃ. ἔκρινεν οὖν μετ' ὀλίγων λάθρα
ποιήσασθαι τὴν ἀναγωγὴν καὶ συνενεβίβασε[1] τὸν
νεώτερον τῶν υἱῶν Ἡρακλείδην· τὸν γὰρ Ἀρχάγαθον εὐλαβεῖτο μήποτε συνὼν τῇ μητρυιᾷ καὶ
φύσει τολμηρὸς ὢν ἐπιβουλὴν κατ' αὐτοῦ συστήσῃ.
ὁ δ' Ἀρχάγαθος ὑποπτεύσας αὐτοῦ τὴν ἐπίνοιαν
παρετήρει τὸν ἔκπλουν, διανοούμενος μηνῦσαι τῶν
ἡγεμόνων τοῖς διακωλύσουσι τὴν ἐπιβολήν· ἡγεῖτο
γὰρ δεινὸν εἶναι τὸ τῶν μὲν κινδύνων ἑαυτὸν προθύμως μετεσχηκέναι, προαγωνιζόμενον τοῦ πατρὸς
καὶ τἀδελφοῦ, τῆς δὲ σωτηρίας μόνον ἀποστε-
ρεῖσθαι, καταλειπόμενον ἔκδοτον τοῖς πολεμίοις.
4 διὸ δὴ τοὺς περὶ τὸν Ἀγαθοκλέα μέλλοντας λάθρα
τὸν ἀπόπλουν ποιεῖσθαι νυκτὸς ἐμήνυσέ τισι τῶν
ἡγεμόνων. οἱ δὲ συνδραμόντες οὐ μόνον διεκώ-
λυσαν, ἀλλὰ καὶ τῷ πλήθει τὴν ῥᾳδιουργίαν ἐξ-
έθηκαν· ἐφ' οἷς οἱ στρατιῶται περιαλγεῖς γενόμενοι
συνελάβοντο τὸν δυνάστην καὶ δήσαντες παρέδωκαν
εἰς φυλακήν.

69. Ἀναρχίας οὖν γενομένης ἐν τῷ στρατοπέδῳ
θόρυβος ἦν καὶ ταραχὴ καὶ τῆς νυκτὸς ἐπιλαβούσης διεδόθη λόγος ὡς πλησίον εἰσὶν οἱ πολέμιοι.
ἐμπεσούσης[2] δὲ πτόης καὶ φόβου πανικοῦ διεσκευα-
σμένος ἕκαστος προῆγεν ἐκ τῆς παρεμβολῆς οὐδε-
2 νὸς παραγγέλλοντος. καθ' ὃν δὴ χρόνον οἱ τὸν
δυνάστην παραφυλάττοντες οὐχ ἧττον τῶν ἄλλων
ἐκπεπληγμένοι καὶ δόξαντες ὑπό τινων καλεῖσθαι

far superior in their armies and were determined by the destruction of those who had first come across to prevent others from attacking Libya. He decided, therefore, to make the return voyage with a few in secret, and he took on board with him the younger of his sons, Heracleides; for he was on his guard against Archagathus, lest at some time this son, who was on intimate terms with his step-mother and was bold by nature, should form a conspiracy against himself. Archagathus, however, suspecting his purpose watched for the sailing with care, being determined to reveal the plot to such of the leaders as would prevent the attempt; for he thought it monstrous that, although he had shared willingly in the battles, fighting in behalf of his father and brother, yet he alone should be deprived of a safe return and left behind as a victim to the enemy. He therefore disclosed to some of the leaders that Agathocles was about to sail away in secret by night. These coming quickly together not only prevented this, but also revealed Agathocles' knavery to the rank and file; and the soldiers, becoming furious at this, seized the tyrant, bound him, and put him in custody.

69. Consequently, when discipline disappeared in the camp, there was tumult and confusion, and as night came on word was spread abroad that the enemy was near. When fright and panic fear fell upon them, each man armed himself and rushed forth from the encampment, no man giving orders. At this very time those who were guarding the tyrant, being no less frightened than the others and imagining that they were being summoned by somebody, hastily

---

1 συνενεβίβασε Dindorf : συνεβίβασε.
2 ἐμπεσούσης Rhodoman : ἐκπεσούσης.

ταχέως ἐξῆγον τὸν Ἀγαθοκλέα διειλημμένον δε-
3 σμοῖς. τὸ δὲ πλῆθος ὡς ἴδεν, εἰς ἔλεον ἐτράπη
καὶ πάντες ἐπεβόων ἀφεῖναι. ὁ δὲ λυθεὶς καὶ μετ᾽
ὀλίγων ἐμβὰς εἰς τὸ πορθμεῖον ἔλαθεν ἐκπλεύσας
κατὰ τὴν δύσιν τῆς Πλειάδος χειμῶνος ὄντος.
οὗτος μὲν οὖν τῆς ἰδίας σωτηρίας φροντίσας ἐγκατ-
έλιπε τοὺς υἱούς, οὓς οἱ στρατιῶται τὸν δρασμὸν
ἀκούσαντες εὐθὺς ἀπέσφαξαν, καὶ στρατηγοὺς ἐξ
ἑαυτῶν ἑλόμενοι διελύθησαν πρὸς Καρχηδονίους,
ὥστε τὰς πόλεις ἃς εἶχον παραδοῦναι καὶ λαβεῖν
τάλαντα τριακόσια καὶ τοὺς μὲν αἱρουμένους μετὰ
Καρχηδονίων στρατεύειν κομίζεσθαι τοὺς ἀεὶ δι-
δομένους μισθούς, τοὺς δ᾽ ἄλλους εἰς Σικελίαν
4 διακομισθέντας λαβεῖν οἰκητήριον Σολοῦντα. τῶν
μὲν οὖν στρατιωτῶν οἱ πλείους ἐμμείναντες ταῖς
συνθήκαις ἔτυχον τῶν ὁμολογηθέντων· ὅσοι δὲ τὰς
πόλεις διακατέχοντες ἀντεῖχον ταῖς παρ᾽ Ἀγαθο-
5 κλέους ἐλπίσιν, ἐξεπολιορκήθησαν κατὰ κράτος. ὧν
οἱ Καρχηδόνιοι τοὺς μὲν ἡγεμόνας ἀνεσταύρωσαν,
τοὺς δ᾽ ἄλλους δήσαντες πέδαις, ἣν διὰ τὸν πόλεμον ἐξηγρίωσαν χώραν, ἐξηνάγκαζον τοῖς ἰδίοις
πόνοις πάλιν ἐξημεροῦν.

Καρχηδόνιοι μὲν οὖν ἔτος τέταρτον πολεμούμενοι
τοῦτον τὸν τρόπον ἐκομίσαντο τὴν ἐλευθερίαν.

70. Τῆς δ᾽ Ἀγαθοκλέους στρατείας εἰς Λιβύην
ἐπισημήναιτ᾽ ἄν τις τό τε παράδοξον καὶ τὴν εἰς
τὰ τέκνα γενομένην τιμωρίαν οἷον τῇ θείᾳ προνοίᾳ.
ἐπὶ μὲν γὰρ τῆς Σικελίας ἡττηθεὶς καὶ τὴν πλείστην

---

[1] About November 1, 307 B.C.
[2] Cp. Polybius, 7. 2. 4.

brought out Agathocles bound with chains. When 307 B.C. the common soldiers saw him they were moved to pity and all shouted to let him go. When released, he embarked on the transport with a few followers and secretly sailed away, although this was in the winter at the season of the setting of the Pleiades.[1] This man, then, concerned about his own safety, abandoned his sons, whom the soldiers at once slew when they learned of his escape [2]; and the soldiers selected generals from their own number and made peace with the Carthaginians on these terms: they were to give back the cities which they held and to receive three hundred talents, and those who chose to serve with the Carthaginians were to receive pay at the regular rates, and the others, when transported to Sicily, were to receive Solus [3] as a dwelling-place. Now, most of the soldiers abided by the terms and received what had been agreed upon; but all those who continued to occupy the cities because they still clung to hopes of Agathocles were attacked and taken by storm. Their leaders the Carthaginians crucified; the others they bound with fetters and forced them by their own labour to bring back again into cultivation the country they had laid waste during the war.

In this way, then, the Carthaginians recovered their liberty in the fourth year of the war.

70. One might well draw attention both to the almost incredible elements in Agathocles' expedition to Libya and to the punishment that befell his children as if by divine providence. For although in Sicily he had been defeated and had lost the largest

---

[3] A Carthaginian city on the north coast of Sicily about 12 miles east of Panormus.

τῆς δυνάμεως ἀπολέσας ἐπὶ τῆς Λιβύης μικρῷ
2 μέρει τοὺς προνενικηκότας κατεπολέμησεν. καὶ
τὰς μὲν ἐν τῇ Σικελίᾳ πόλεις ἁπάσας ἀποβαλὼν
πρὸς Συρακούσσαις ἐπολιορκεῖτο, κατὰ δὲ τὴν
Λιβύην πασῶν τῶν ἄλλων πόλεων ἐγκρατὴς γενόμενος εἰς πολιορκίαν κατέκλεισε τοὺς Καρχηδονίους,
τῆς τύχης ὥσπερ ἐπίτηδες ἐπιδεικνυμένης τὴν
3 ἰδίαν δύναμιν ἐπὶ τῶν ἀπηλπισμένων. εἰς τηλικαύτην δ᾿ ὑπεροχὴν ἐλθόντος αὐτοῦ καὶ τὸν Ὀφέλλαν
φονεύσαντος, ὄντα φίλον καὶ ξένον, φανερῶς ἐπε-
σημήνατο τὸ δαιμόνιον ὡς διὰ τὴν εἰς τοῦτον παρα-
νομίαν τῶν ὕστερον αὐτῷ γεγενημένων τὸ θεῖον[1]
ἐπιστῆσαι· τοῦ γὰρ αὐτοῦ μηνὸς καὶ τῆς αὐτῆς
ἡμέρας Ὀφέλλαν ἀνελὼν παρέλαβε τὴν δύναμιν
καὶ πάλιν τοὺς υἱοὺς ἀπολέσας ἀπέβαλε τὸ στρα-
4 τόπεδον. καὶ τὸ πάντων ἰδιώτατον, ὁ θεὸς ὥσπερ
ἀγαθὸς νομοθέτης διπλῆν ἔλαβε παρ᾿ αὐτοῦ τὴν
κόλασιν· ἕνα γὰρ φίλον ἀδίκως φονεύσας δυεῖν υἱῶν
ἐστερήθη, τῶν μετ᾿ Ὀφέλλα παραγενομένων προσ-
ενεγκάντων τὰς χεῖρας τοῖς νεανίσκοις. ταῦτα μὲν
οὖν ἡμῖν εἰρήσθω πρὸς τοὺς καταφρονοῦντας τῶν
τοιούτων.

71. Ὁ δ᾿ Ἀγαθοκλῆς ἐπειδὴ διεκομίσθη ταχέως
ἐκ τῆς Λιβύης εἰς τὴν Σικελίαν, μεταπεμψάμενος
μέρος τῆς δυνάμεως παρῆλθεν εἰς τὴν τῶν Αἰγε-
σταίων πόλιν οὖσαν σύμμαχον. ἀπορούμενος δὲ
χρημάτων εἰσφέρειν ἠνάγκαζε τοὺς εὐπόρους τὸ
πλεῖον μέρος τῆς ὑπάρξεως, οὔσης τῆς πόλεως τότε
2 μυριάνδρου. πολλῶν δ᾿ ἐπὶ τούτοις ἀγανακτούντων
καὶ συντρεχόντων αἰτιασάμενος τοὺς Αἰγεσταίους

part of his army, in Libya with a small portion of
his forces he defeated those who had previously been
victorious.   And after he had lost all the cities in
Sicily, he was besieged at Syracuse ; but in Libya,
after becoming master of all the other cities, he confined the Carthaginians by a siege, Fortune, as if
of set purpose, displaying her peculiar power when
a situation has become hopeless. After he had come
to such a position of superiority and had murdered
Ophellas [1] although he was a friend and a guest, the
divine power clearly showed that it established
through his impious acts against Ophellas a portent
of that which later befell him ; for in the same
month and on the same day on which he murdered
Ophellas and took his army, he caused the death
of his own sons and lost his own army.   And
what is most peculiar of all, the god like a good
lawgiver exacted a double punishment from him ;
for when he had unjustly slain one friend, he was
deprived of two sons, those who had been with
Ophellas laying violent hands upon the young men.
Let these things, then, be said as our answer to those
who scorn such matters.

71. When with all speed Agathocles had crossed
from Libya into Sicily, he summoned a part of his
army and went to the city of Segesta, which was an
ally.   Because he was in need of money, he forced
the well-to-do to deliver to him the greater part of
their property, the city at that time having a population of about ten thousand.   Since many were angry
at this and were holding meetings, he charged the

[1] Cp. chap. 42.

[1] τὴν θωὴν Fischer.

ἐπιβουλεύειν αὐτῷ δειναῖς περιέβαλε συμφοραῖς τὴν
πόλιν· τοὺς μὲν γὰρ ἀπορωτάτους προαγαγὼν ἐκτὸς τῆς πόλεως παρὰ τὸν Σκάμανδρον ποταμὸν
ἀπέσφαξεν, τοὺς δὲ δοκοῦντας οὐσίαν κεκτῆσθαι
μείζονα βασανίζων ἠνάγκαζε λέγειν ὁπόσα ἔχων
τις τυγχάνει χρήματα, καὶ τοὺς μὲν αὐτῶν ἐτρόχιζε
τοὺς δὲ εἰς τοὺς καταπέλτας ἐνδεσμεύων κατ-
ετόξευεν, ἐνίοις δ' ἀστραγάλους προστιθεὶς βιαιότε-
3 ρον δειναῖς ἀλγηδόσι περιέβαλλεν. ἐξεῦρε δὲ καὶ
ἑτέραν τιμωρίαν ἐμφερῆ τῷ Φαλάριδος ταύρῳ· κατεσκεύασε γὰρ κλίνην χαλκῆν ἀνθρωπίνου σώματος
τύπον ἔχουσαν καὶ καθ' ἕκαστον μέρος κλεισὶ διειλημμένην, εἰς ταύτην δ' ἐναρμόζων τοὺς βασανι-
ζομένους ὑπέκαιε ζῶντας, τούτῳ διαφερούσης τῆς
κατασκευῆς ταύτης παρὰ τὸν ταῦρον, τῷ καὶ θεω-
4 ρεῖσθαι τοὺς ἐν ταῖς ἀνάγκαις ἀπολλυμένους. τῶν
δὲ γυναικῶν τῶν εὐπόρων τινῶν μὲν καρκίνοις
σιδηροῖς τὰ σφυρὰ πιέζων συνέτεινε, τινῶν δὲ τοὺς
τιτθοὺς ἀπέτεμνεν, ταῖς δ' ἐγκύοις πλίνθους ἐπὶ
τὴν ὀσφὺν ἐπιτιθεὶς τὸ ἔμβρυον ἀπὸ τοῦ βάρους
ἐξέθλιβεν. τούτῳ δὲ τῷ τρόπῳ τὰ χρήματα πάντα
τοῦ τυράννου ζητοῦντος καὶ μεγάλου φόβου τὴν
πόλιν ἐπέχοντος τινὲς μὲν αὐτοὺς συγκατέκαυσαν
5 ταῖς οἰκίαις, τινὲς δὲ ἀγχόνῃ τὸ ζῆν ἐξέλιπον. ἡ
μὲν οὖν Αἴγεστα τυχοῦσα μιᾶς ἡμέρας ἀτυχοῦς ἡβη-
δὸν ἐθανατώθη. ὁ δ' Ἀγαθοκλῆς παρθένους μὲν
καὶ παῖδας εἰς τὴν Ἰταλίαν διακομίσας ἀπέδοτο τοῖς
Βρεττίοις, τῆς δὲ πόλεως οὐδὲ τὴν προσηγορίαν

people of Segesta with conspiring against him and ^{307 B.C.} visited the city with terrible disasters. For instance, the poorest of the people he brought to a place outside the city beside the river Scamander and slaughtered them; but those who were believed to have more property he examined under torture and compelled each to tell him how much wealth he had; and some of them he broke on the wheel, others he placed bound in the catapults and shot forth, and by applying knucklebones with violence to some, he caused them severe pain.[1] He also invented another torture similar to the bull of Phalaris: that is, he prepared a brazen bed that had the form of a human body and was surrounded on every side by bars; on this he fixed those who were being tortured and roasted them alive, the contrivance being superior to the bull in this respect, that those who were perishing in anguish were visible. As for the wealthy women, he tortured some of them by crushing their ankles with iron pincers, he cut off the breasts of others, and by placing bricks on the lower part of the backs of those who were pregnant, he forced the expulsion of the foetus by the pressure. While the tyrant in this way was seeking all the wealth, great panic prevailed throughout the city, some burning themselves up along with their houses, and others gaining release from life by hanging. Thus Segesta, encountering a single day of disaster, suffered the loss of all her men from youth upward. Agathocles then took the maidens and children across to Italy and sold them to the Bruttians, leaving not even the name

---

[1] It is possible that the ἀστράγαλοι are whips studded with bits of bone. Cp. Lucian, *Ass*, 38; Plutarch, *Moralia*, 1127 c.

ἀπολιπών, ἀλλὰ Δικαιόπολιν μετονομάσας ἔδωκεν
οἰκητήριον τοῖς αὐτομόλοις.

72. Ἀκούσας γὰρ τὴν τῶν υἱῶν ἀναίρεσιν καὶ
δι' ὀργῆς ἔχων ἅπαντας τοὺς ἀπολελειμμένους κατὰ
Λιβύην ἔπεμψε τῶν φίλων τινὰς εἰς Συρακούσσας
πρὸς Ἄντανδρον τὸν ἀδελφόν, διακελευσάμενος
τοὺς τῶν συστρατευσάντων ἐπὶ Καρχηδόνα συγ-
2 γενεῖς ἅπαντας ἀποσφάξαι. ταχὺ δὲ τούτου τὸ
προσταχθὲν ποιήσαντος ποικιλώτατον γενέσθαι
συνέβη φόνον τῶν προγεγονότων· οὐ γὰρ μόνον
τοὺς ἀκμάζοντας ταῖς ἡλικίαις ἀδελφοὺς ἢ πατέρας
ἢ παῖδας ἐξῆγεν ἐπὶ τὸν θάνατον, ἀλλὰ καὶ
πάππους καὶ τούτων, εἰ τύχοι, καὶ πατέρας περιόν-
τας ἐσχατογήρους καὶ ταῖς ὅλαις αἰσθήσεσι διὰ
τὸν χρόνον ἤδη παραλελυμένους, ἔτι δὲ νηπίους παῖδας ἐν ἀγκάλαις φερομένους καὶ τῆς ἐπιφερομένης
αὐτοῖς συμφορᾶς οὐδεμίαν αἴσθησιν λαμβάνοντας.
ἤγοντο¹ δὲ καὶ γυναῖκες ὅσαι μετεῖχον οἰκειότητος ἢ
συγγενείας καὶ καθόλου πᾶς ὁ μέλλων τῇ καθ'
αὑτὸν τιμωρίᾳ λύπην ἐμποιῆσαι τοῖς ἐπὶ τῆς Λι-
3 βύης ἀπολειφθεῖσι. πολλοῦ δὲ πλήθους καὶ παντοίου
πρὸς τὴν θάλατταν ἀχθέντος ἐπὶ τὴν τιμωρίαν καὶ
τῶν σφαγέων ἐφεστώτων δάκρυα καὶ δεήσεις καὶ
θρῆνος ἐγίνετο συμφορητός, ὧν μὲν ἀνηλεῶς
φονευομένων, ὧν δὲ ἐπὶ ταῖς τῶν πλησίον συμφοραῖς ἐκπληττομένων καὶ διὰ τὸ προσδοκώμενον
οὐδὲν διαφερόντων ταῖς ψυχαῖς τῶν προαποθνη-

---

¹ ἤγοντο Dindorf : ἦγον.

---

¹ The name (lit. " Just City ") is not found elsewhere.

of the city ; but he changed the name to Dicaeopolis
and gave it as dwelling to the deserters.[1]

72. On hearing of the murder of his sons Agathocles became enraged at all those who had been
left behind in Libya, and sent some of his friends
into Syracuse to Antander his brother, ordering him
to put to death all the relatives of those who had
taken part in the campaign against Carthage.[2] As
Antander promptly carried out the order, there
occurred the most elaborately devised massacre that
had taken place up to this time ; for not only did
they drag out to death the brothers, fathers, and sons
who were in the prime of manhood, but also the
grandfathers, and even the fathers of these if such
survived, men who lingered on in extreme old age
and were already bereft of all their senses by lapse
of time, as well as infant children borne in arms who
had no consciousness whatever of the fate that was
bearing down upon them. They also led away any
women who were related by marriage or kinship, and
in sum, every person whose punishment would bring
grief to those who had been left in Libya. When a
crowd, large and composed of all kinds of people, had
been driven to the sea for punishment and when
the executioners had taken their places beside them,
weeping and prayers and wailing arose mingled together, as some of them were mercilessly slaughtered
and others were stunned by the misfortunes of their
neighbours and because of their own imminent fate
were no better in spirit than those who were being

Segesta certainly recovered its name and became again a
Carthaginian ally (Book 22. 10. 2), probably in 306 B.C.,
when all cities formerly belonging to Carthage were restored
by Agathocles (chap. 79. 5).
  [2] Cp. chap. 4. 3.

4 σκόντων. τὸ δὲ πάντων χαλεπώτατον, πολλῶν ἀν-
αιρεθέντων καὶ παρὰ τὸν αἰγιαλὸν ἐρριμμένων τῶν
σωμάτων οὔτε συγγενὴς οὐδεὶς οὔτε φίλος ἐτόλμα
τινὰ κηδεύειν, φοβούμενος μὴ δόξῃ προσαγγέλ-
λειν ἑαυτὸν μετέχοντα τῆς ἐκείνων οἰκειότητος.
5 διὰ δὲ τὸ πλῆθος τῶν φονευθέντων ἐπὶ τοῦ κύματος συνέβη τὴν θάλατταν ἐφ' ἱκανὸν τόπον αἵματι
κραθεῖσαν πόρρωθεν διαφαίνειν τὴν ὑπερβολὴν
τῆς τοῦ πάθους ὠμότητος.

73. Τοῦ δ' ἐνιαυσίου χρόνου διεληλυθότος Ἀθήνησι μὲν ἦρχε Κόροιβος, ἐν Ῥώμῃ δὲ τὴν ὕπατον
ἀρχὴν παρέλαβον Κόιντος Μάρκιος καὶ Πόπλιος
Κορνήλιος. ἐπὶ δὲ τούτων Ἀντίγονος ὁ βασιλεύς,
τελευτήσαντος αὐτῷ τοῦ νεωτέρου τῶν υἱῶν Φοίνικος, τοῦτον μὲν βασιλικῶς ἔθαψε, τὸν δὲ Δημήτριον ἐκ τῆς Κύπρου μεταπεμψάμενος ἤθροιζε
τὰς δυνάμεις εἰς τὴν Ἀντιγονίαν. ἔκρινε δὲ στρα-
2 τεύειν ἐπὶ τὴν Αἴγυπτον. αὐτὸς μὲν οὖν τοῦ πεζοῦ
στρατεύματος ἀφηγούμενος προῆγε διὰ τῆς Κοίλης
Συρίας, ἔχων πεζοὺς μὲν πλείους τῶν ὀκτακισ-
μυρίων, ἱππεῖς δὲ περὶ ὀκτακισχιλίους, ἐλέφαντας
δὲ τρισὶ πλείους τῶν ὀγδοήκοντα· τῷ δὲ Δημητρίῳ παραδοὺς τὸν στόλον συνέταξε συμπαραπλεῖν
ἅμα πορευομένῃ τῇ δυνάμει, παρεσκευασμένων νεῶν
τῶν ἁπασῶν μακρῶν μὲν ἑκατὸν πεντήκοντα, πορίων δὲ στρατιωτικῶν ἑκατόν, ἐν οἷς ἐκομίζετο
3 βελῶν πλῆθος. τῶν δὲ κυβερνητῶν οἰομένων δεῖν

---

[1] Continued in chap. 77.
[2] Coroebus was archon in 306/5. Livy, 9. 42. 10, gives the

put to death before them. And what was most 307 B.C.
cruel of all, when many had been slain and their
bodies had been cast out along the shore, neither
kinsmen nor friend dared pay the last rites to any,
fearing lest he should seem to inform on himself as
one who enjoyed intimacy with those who were dead.
And because of the multitude of those who had been
slain beside its waves, the sea, stained with blood
over a great expanse, proclaimed afar the unequalled
savagery of this outrage.[1]

73. When this year had passed, Coroebus became 306 B.C.
archon in Athens, and in Rome Quintus Marcius
and Publius Cornelius succeeded to the consulship.[2]
While these held office King Antigonus, the younger
of whose sons, Phoenix,[3] had died, buried this son with
royal honours ; and, after summoning Demetrius
from Cyprus, he collected his forces in Antigonia.[4]
He had decided to make a campaign against Egypt.
So he himself took command of the land army and
advanced through Coelê Syria with more than eighty
thousand foot soldiers, about eight thousand horsemen, and eighty-three elephants. Giving the fleet
to Demetrius, he ordered him to follow along the
coast in contact with the army as it advanced. In
all there had been made ready a hundred and fifty
warships and a hundred transports in which a large
stock of ordnance was being conveyed. When the
pilots thought it necessary to heed the setting of the

consuls for 306 B.C. as P. Cornelius Arvina and Q. Marcius
Tremulus. The Capitoline Fasti are fragmentary for a period
of some 40 years beginning at this point.

[3] An error by Diodorus or a copyist for Philip ; cp. chap.
19. 5 ; Plutarch, *Demetrius*, 2. 1.

[4] Continued from chap. 53. For the following campaign
cp. Plutarch, *Demetrius*, 19, 1-2 ; Pausanias, 1. 6. 6.

ἀπομένειν[1] τὴν τῆς Πλειάδος δύσιν δοκοῦσαν ἔσεσθαι μεθ' ἡμέρας ὀκτώ, τούτοις μὲν ἐπετίμησεν
ὡς κατορρωδοῦσι τοὺς κινδύνους, αὐτὸς δὲ στρα-
τοπεδεύων περὶ Γάζαν καὶ σπεύδων φθάσαι τὴν
τοῦ Πτολεμαίου παρασκευὴν τοῖς μὲν στρατιώταις
παρήγγειλε δέχ' ἡμερῶν ἔχειν ἐπισίτισιν, ἐπὶ δὲ
ταῖς καμήλοις ταῖς ἀθροισθείσαις ὑπὸ τῶν Ἀράβων ἐπέθηκε σίτου μυριάδας μεδίμνων τρισκαίδεκα
καὶ χόρτου πλῆθος τοῖς τετράποσι· τά τε βέλη κομίζων τοῖς ζεύγεσι προῆγε διὰ τῆς ἐρήμου μετὰ
κακοπαθείας διὰ τὸ πολλοὺς εἶναι τῶν τόπων τελ-
ματώδεις καὶ μάλιστα περὶ τὰ καλούμενα Βάραθρα.

74. Οἱ δὲ περὶ τὸν Δημήτριον ἐκ τῆς Γάζης
ἐκπλεύσαντες περὶ μέσας νύκτας τὸ μὲν πρῶτον
εὐδίας οὔσης ἐφ' ἡμέρας τινὰς ταῖς ταχυναυτούσαις
ναυσὶν ἐρυμούλκουν τὰ στρατιωτικὰ πόρια· ἔπειτα
τῆς Πλειάδος περικαταλαμβανούσης αὐτοὺς καὶ
πνεύματος ἐπιγενομένου βορίου συνέβη πολλὰ τῶν
τετρηρικῶν σκαφῶν ὑπὸ τοῦ χειμῶνος κατενεχθῆ-
ναι παραβόλως ἐπὶ πόλιν Ῥαφίαν, οὖσαν δυσ-
2 προσόρμιστον καὶ τεναγώδη. τῶν δὲ πλοίων τῶν
κομιζόντων τὰ βέλη τὰ μὲν ὑπὸ τοῦ χειμῶνος συγ-
κλυσθέντα διεφθάρη, τὰ δ' ἐπαλινδρόμησεν εἰς τὴν
Γάζαν· τοῖς δὲ κρατίστοις τῶν σκαφῶν βιασάμενοι
3 διέτειναν μέχρι τοῦ Κασίου. τοῦτο δὲ τοῦ μὲν Νείλου διέστηκεν οὐ μακράν, ἀλίμενον δέ ἐστι καὶ κατὰ
τὰς χειμερίους περιστάσεις ἀπροσόρμιστον. διόπερ
ἠναγκάζοντο τὰς ἀγκύρας ἀφέντες ὡς ἂν ἐν δυσὶ

---

[1] ἀπομένειν Fischer : ἀπιδεῖν.

---

[1] About November 1.
[2] Literally " Pits," a region of quicksands between the

Pleiades,[1] which was expected to take place after eight days, Antigonus censured them as men afraid of danger ; but he himself, since he was encamped at Gaza and was eager to forestall the preparations of Ptolemy, ordered his soldiers to provide themselves with ten days' rations, and loaded on the camels, which had been gathered together by the Arabs, one hundred and thirty thousand measures of grain and a good stock of fodder for the beasts ; and, carrying his ordnance in waggons, he advanced through the wilderness with great hardship because many places in the region were swampy, particularly near the spot called Barathra.[2]

74. As for Demetrius, after setting sail from Gaza about midnight, since the weather at first was calm for several days, he had his transports towed by the swifter ships ; then the setting of the Pleiades overtook them and a north wind arose, so that many of the quadriremes were driven dangerously by the storm to Raphia,[3] a city which affords no anchorage and is surrounded by shoals. Of the ships that were carrying his ordnance, some were overwhelmed by the storm and destroyed, and others ran back to Gaza ; but pressing on with the strongest of the ships he held his course as far as Casium.[4] This place is not very distant from the Nile, but it has no harbour and in the stormy season it is impossible to make a landing here. They were therefore compelled to cast their anchors and ride the waves at a distance

Sirbonian Lake and the Mediterranean. Cp. Books 1. 30. 4-9, and 16. 46. 4-5, for accounts of the dangers of this region.

[3] A day's march south of Gaza.

[4] Probably at the western end of the Sirbonian Lake. For the dangers from storms on this coast cp. Strabo, 16. 2. 26 (p. 758).

σταδίοις ἀπὸ τῆς γῆς ἀποσαλεύειν, ἅμα πολλοῖς
περιεχόμενοι δεινοῖς· τοῦ μὲν γὰρ κλύδωνος ῥηγνυ-
μένου τραχύτερον[1] ἐκινδύνευον αὔτανδρα τὰ σκάφη
συγκλυσθῆναι, τῆς δὲ γῆς οὔσης ἀπροσορμίστου
καὶ πολεμίας οὔτε ναῦς ἀκινδύνως ἦν προσπλεῖν
οὔτε τοὺς ἄνδρας προσνήξασθαι, τὸ δὲ μέγιστον,
ἐλελοίπει τὸ εἰς πότον αὐτοῖς ὕδωρ, εἰς τοιαύτην
τε σπάνιν κατεκλείσθησαν ὥστε εἰ μίαν ἡμέραν ὁ
χειμὼν ἐπέμεινεν, πάντες ἂν τῷ δίψει διεφθάρησαν.
4 ἐν ἀθυμίᾳ δ' ὄντων ἁπάντων καὶ προσδοκωμένης
ἤδη τῆς ἀπωλείας τὸ μὲν πνεῦμα κατέπαυσεν, ἡ
δὲ μετ' Ἀντιγόνου δύναμις καταντήσασα πλησίον
5 τοῦ στόλου κατεστρατοπέδευσεν. ἐκβάντες οὖν ἐκ
τῶν σκαφῶν καὶ προσαναλαβόντες ἑαυτοὺς ἐν τῇ
στρατοπεδείᾳ προσέμενον τῶν νεῶν τὰς ἀποσπα-
σθείσας. διεφθάρη δ' ἐν τούτῳ τῷ σάλῳ τρία σκάφη
τῶν πεντηρικῶν, ἐξ ὧν ἔνιοι τῶν ἀνδρῶν διενήξαντο
πρὸς τὴν γῆν. ἔπειτα Ἀντίγονος μὲν προαγαγὼν
τὴν δύναμιν πλησίον τοῦ Νείλου κατεστρατοπέδευσεν, ἀπέχων δύο σταδίους τοῦ ποταμοῦ.

75. Πτολεμαῖος δὲ προκατειληφὼς τοὺς εὐκαι-
ροτάτους τόπους ἀσφαλέσι φυλακαῖς ἀπέστειλέν
τινας ἐν τοῖς κοντωτοῖς, παρακελευσάμενος προσπλεῖν πλησίον τῆς ἐκβάσεως καὶ κηρύττειν ὅτι
δώσει τοῖς μεταβαλομένοις ἀπ' Ἀντιγόνου, τῶν
μὲν ἰδιωτῶν ἑκάστοις δύο μνᾶς, τοῖς δ' ἐφ' ἡγε-
2 μονίας τεταγμένοις τάλαντον. γενομένων οὖν τῶν
κηρυγμάτων τοιούτων ἐνέπεσέ τις ὁρμὴ πρὸς μετάθεσιν τοῖς μετ' Ἀντιγόνου μισθοφόροις, ἐν οἷς καὶ
τῶν ἡγεμόνων πλείους ῥέπειν[2] συνέβαινε δι' αἰτίας

of about two stades [1] from the land, where they were at once encompassed by many dangers; for since the surf was breaking rather heavily, there was danger that the ships would founder with their crews, and since the shore was harbourless and in enemy hands, the ships could neither approach without danger, nor could the men swim ashore, and what was worst of all, the water for drinking had given out and they were reduced to such straits that, if the storm had continued for a single day more, all would have perished of thirst. When all were in despair and already expecting death, the wind fell, and the army of Antigonus came up and camped near the fleet. They therefore left the ships and recuperated in the camp while waiting for those vessels that had become separated. In this exposure to the waves three of the quinqueremes were lost, but some of the men from these swam to the shore. Then Antigonus led his army nearer to the Nile and camped at a distance of two stades [1] from the river.

75. Ptolemy, who had occupied in advance the most strategic points with trustworthy garrisons, sent men in small boats, ordering them to approach the landing-place and proclaim that he would pay a premium to any who deserted Antigonus, two minae to each of the ordinary soldiers and one talent to each man who had been assigned to a position of command. When proclamations to that effect had been made, an urge to change sides fell upon the mercenaries of Antigonus, and it transpired that many even of their officers were inclined for one reason or another

---

[1] A little less than ¼ mile.

---

[1] τραχύτερον Rhodoman : ταχύτερον.
[2] ῥέπειν Capps, ⟨προθύμους⟩ εἶναι Fischer : εἶναι.

3 τινὰς εἰς τὸ μεταβολῆς ἐπιθυμεῖν. πολλῶν δὲ πρὸς
αὐτὸν αὐτομολούντων ὁ μὲν Ἀντίγονος ἐπιστήσας
τῷ χείλει τοῦ ποταμοῦ τοξότας καὶ σφενδονήτας
καὶ πολλὰ τῶν ὀξυβελικῶν τοὺς προσπλέοντας ἐν
τοῖς κοντωτοῖς ἀνέστελλε· τῶν δ' αὐτομολούντων
συλλαβών τινας δεινῶς ᾐκίσατο, βουλόμενος κατα-
πλήξασθαι τοὺς τῆς ὁμοίας ὁρμῆς ἀντεχομένους.
4 καὶ προσλαβών τὰ καθυστεροῦντα τῶν σκαφῶν
προσέπλευσεν ἐπὶ τὸ καλούμενον Ψευδόστομον, νομίζων ἐνταῦθα δυνήσεσθαί τινας τῶν στρατιωτῶν
ἀποβιβάσαι. εὑρὼν δὲ πρὸς αὐτῷ φυλακὴν ἰσχυρὰν
καὶ τοῖς τε ὀξυβελέσι καὶ τοῖς ἄλλοις παντοίοις
βέλεσιν ἀνειργόμενος ἀπέπλευσε περικαταλαμβα-
5 νούσης νυκτός. ἔπειτα παραγγείλας τοῖς κυβερνή-
ταις ἀκολουθεῖν τῇ στρατηγίδι νηὶ προσέχοντας τῷ
λαμπτῆρι προσέπλευσεν ἐπὶ τὸ στόμα τοῦ Νείλου
τὸ καλούμενον Φατνιτικόν[1]· ἡμέρας δὲ γενομένης,
ἐπειδὴ πολλαὶ τῶν νεῶν ἀπεπλανήθησαν, ἠναγκάσθη
ταύτας περιμένειν καὶ τὰς μάλιστα ταχυναυτούσας
τῶν ἠκολουθηκυιῶν[2] ἐξαποστέλλειν ἐπὶ τὴν τούτων
ζήτησιν.

76. Διόπερ χρόνου γενομένου πλείονος οἱ μὲν
περὶ τὸν Πτολεμαῖον πυθόμενοι τὸν κατάπλουν τῶν
πολεμίων ἧκον ὀξέως βοηθήσοντες καὶ τὴν δύναμιν
διασκευάσαντες ἔστησαν παρὰ τὸν αἰγιαλόν· ὁ δὲ
Δημήτριος ἀποτυχὼν καὶ ταύτης τῆς ἐκβάσεως
καὶ τὴν συνάπτουσαν παραλίαν ἀκούων ἕλεσι καὶ
λίμναις ὠχυρῶσθαι φυσικῶς ἐπαλινδρόμει παντὶ
2 τῷ στόλῳ. εἶτ' ἐμπεσόντος βορέου λαμπροῦ καὶ
τοῦ κλύδωνος εἰς ὕψος αἰρομένου τρία μὲν σκάφη
τῶν τετρηρικῶν καὶ τῶν στρατιωτικῶν πορίων τινὰ[3]
κατὰ τὸ αὐτὸ βιαιότερον ὑπὸ τοῦ κύματος ἐπὶ τὴν

to desire a change. But when many were going over 306 B.C. to Ptolemy, Antigonus, stationing bowmen, slingers, and many of his catapults on the edge of the river, drove back those who were drawing near in their punts ; and he captured some of the deserters and tortured them frightfully, wishing to intimidate any who were contemplating such an attempt as this. After adding to his force the ships that were late in arriving, he sailed to the place called Pseudostomon,[1] believing that he would be able to disembark some of the soldiers there. But when he found at that place a strong garrison and was held in check by bolts and other missiles of every kind, he sailed away as night was closing in. Then giving orders to the pilots to follow the ship of the general, keeping their eyes fixed on its light, he sailed to the mouth of the Nile called Phatniticum ; but when day came, since many of the ships had missed the course, he was forced to wait for these and to send out the swiftest of those that had followed him to search for them.

76. Since this caused considerable delay, Ptolemy, hearing of the arrival of the enemy, came quickly to reinforce his men and after drawing up his army, stationed it along the shore ; but Demetrius, having failed to make this landing also and hearing that the adjacent coast was naturally fortified by swamps and marshes, retraced his course with his whole fleet. Then a strong north wind burst upon them and the billows rose high ; and three of his quadriremes and in the same way some of the transports were cast

[1] Literally, " False Mouth."

---

[1] Φατνιτικόν Stephanus : Φαγνιτικὸν RX, Φαγνητικόν F.
[2] ἠκολουθηκυιῶν Schaefer : ἠκολουθηκότων.
[3] τινὰ Rhodoman, ἔνια Madvig : ἅμα.

γῆν ἐξεβράσθη καὶ τοῖς περὶ τὸν Πτολεμαῖον ὑποχείρια κατέστη· αἱ δ' ἄλλαι ἐκβιασαμένων τῶν
πληρωμάτων διεσώθησαν πρὸς τὴν Ἀντιγόνου
3 στρατοπεδείαν. τῶν δὲ περὶ τὸν Πτολεμαῖον διειληφότων πᾶσαν τὴν περὶ τὸν ποταμὸν ἔκβασιν
φυλακαῖς ἰσχυραῖς καὶ πολλῶν μὲν σκαφῶν πο-
ταμίων αὐτῷ παρεσκευασμένων, πάντων δὲ τούτων
ἐχόντων βέλη παντοῖα καὶ τοὺς χρησομένους αὐτοῖς ἄνδρας οἱ περὶ τὸν Ἀντίγονον οὐ μετρίως ἠπο-
4 ροῦντο· ἡ γὰρ ναυτικὴ δύναμις ἄχρηστος ἦν αὐτοῖς
προκατειλημμένου τοῦ Πηλουσιακοῦ στόματος ὑπὸ
τῶν πολεμίων, τό τε πεζὸν στράτευμα τὴν ὁρμὴν
ἄπρακτον εἶχε τῷ μεγέθει τοῦ ποταμοῦ διειργό-
μενον, τὸ δὲ μέγιστον, ἡμερῶν ἤδη συχνῶν διεληλυ-
θυιῶν ὑπολείπειν ἤδη συνέβαινε τόν τε σῖτον καὶ
5 τὰ χορτάσματα τοῖς κτήνεσι. διὰ δὴ ταῦτα τῆς
δυνάμεως ἀθυμούσης παρακαλῶν[1] τὸ στρατόπεδον
καὶ τοὺς ἡγεμόνας Ἀντίγονος προέθηκε βουλὴν
πότερον συμφέρει μένειν καὶ διαπολεμεῖν, ἢ νῦν
μὲν ἐπανελθεῖν εἰς Συρίαν, ὕστερον δὲ κάλλιον
παρασκευασαμένους στρατεῦσαι καθ' ὃν ἂν χρόνον
6 ἐλάχιστος ὁ Νεῖλος εἶναι δόξῃ. πάντων δὲ κατεν-
εχθέντων ἐπὶ τὸ τὴν ταχίστην ἀπιέναι παρήγγειλε
τοῖς στρατιώταις ἀναζευγνύειν καὶ ταχὺ πάλιν
ἐπανῆλθεν εἰς τὴν Συρίαν, συμπαραπλέοντος αὐτῷ
καὶ τοῦ στόλου παντός. Πτολεμαῖος δὲ μετὰ τὴν
ἀπαλλαγὴν τῶν πολεμίων περιχαρὴς γενόμενος καὶ
θύσας τοῖς θεοῖς χαριστήρια τοὺς φίλους εἱστία
7 λαμπρῶς. καὶ πρὸς μὲν τοὺς περὶ Σέλευκον καὶ
Λυσίμαχον καὶ Κάσανδρον ἔγραψε περὶ τῶν εὐτυχημάτων καὶ περὶ τοῦ πλήθους τῶν πρὸς αὐτὸν αὐτο-

violently upon the land by the waves and came into 306 B.C.
the possession of Ptolemy; but the other ships,
whose crews had kept them from the shore by main
force, reached the camp of Antigonus in safety.
Since Ptolemy, however, had already occupied every
landing-place along the river with strong guards,
since many river boats had been made ready for him,
and since all of these were equipped with ordnance
of every kind and with men to use it, Antigonus was
in no little difficulty; for his naval force was of no
use to him since the Pelusiac mouth of the Nile had
been occupied in advance by the enemy, and his land
forces found their advance thwarted since they were
checked by the width of the river, and what was of
greatest importance, as many days had passed, food
for the men and fodder for the beasts were falling
short. Since, then, his forces for these reasons were
disheartened, Antigonus called together the army
and its leaders and laid before them the question
whether it was better to remain and continue the
war or to return for the present to Syria and later
make a campaign with more complete preparation
and at the time at which the Nile was supposed to
be lowest. When all inclined toward the quickest
possible withdrawal, he commanded the soldiers to
break camp and speedily returned to Syria, the whole
fleet coasting along beside him. After the departure
of the enemy Ptolemy rejoiced greatly; and, when
he had made a thank-offering to the gods, he entertained his friends lavishly. He also wrote to Seleucus,
Lysimachus, and Cassander about his successes and
about the large number of men who had deserted to

---

[1] παρακαλῶν Capps : παραλαβών. Fischer in apparatus suggests παραλαβὼν κατὰ τὸ σ. τοὺς ἡ.

μολησάντων, αὐτὸς δὲ τὸ δεύτερον ἠγωνισμένος
ὑπὲρ τῆς Αἰγύπτου καὶ νομίσας δορίκτητον ἔχειν
τὴν χώραν ἐπανῆλθεν εἰς τὴν Ἀλεξάνδρειαν.

77. Ἅμα δὲ τούτοις πραττομένοις Διονύσιος ὁ
τῆς Ἡρακλείας τῆς ἐν τῷ Πόντῳ τύραννος ἐτελεύτησεν ἄρξας ἔτη τριάκοντα δύο, τὴν δὲ δυναστείαν
διαδεξάμενοι οἱ υἱοὶ Ὀξάθρας[1] καὶ Κλέαρχος ἦρξαν
ἔτη ἑπτακαίδεκα.

Κατὰ δὲ τὴν Σικελίαν Ἀγαθοκλῆς ἐπῄει τὰς
ὑπ' αὐτὸν πόλεις ἀσφαλιζόμενος φρουραῖς καὶ χρήματα πραττόμενος· σφόδρα γὰρ εὐλαβεῖτο μήποτε
διὰ τὰς γεγενημένας περὶ αὐτὸν ἀτυχίας ὁρμήσωσιν
2 οἱ Σικελιῶται πρὸς τὴν αὐτονομίαν. καθ' ὃν δὴ
χρόνον Πασίφιλος ὁ στρατηγός, ἀκούσας τὴν τῶν
Ἀγαθοκλέους υἱῶν ἀναίρεσιν καὶ τὰ περὶ τὴν Λιβύην ἐλαττώματα, τοῦ μὲν δυνάστου κατεφρόνησε,
πρὸς δὲ Δεινοκράτην ἀποστὰς καὶ φιλίαν αὐτῷ
συνθέμενος τάς τε πόλεις ἃς ἦν πεπιστευμένος δια-
κατέσχεν καὶ τὴν μετ' αὐτοῦ δύναμιν ἐλπίσι ψυχ-
3 αγωγήσας ἀλλοτρίαν κατεσκεύασε τοῦ τυράννου. ὁ
δ' Ἀγαθοκλῆς πανταχόθεν τῶν ἐλπίδων περικοπτο-
μένων οὕτως ἐταπεινώθη τὴν ψυχὴν ὥστε διαπρε-
σβεύσασθαι πρὸς Δεινοκράτην καὶ παρακαλεῖν ἐπὶ
τοῖσδε συνθήκας ποιήσασθαι, ἐκχωρῆσαι μὲν τῆς
δυναστείας Ἀγαθοκλέα, παραδοῦναι δὲ τὰς Συρακούσσας τοῖς πολίταις καὶ μηκέτι εἶναι φυγάδα
Δεινοκράτην, ἐξαίρετα δὲ δοθῆναι τῶν ἐρυμάτων

---

[1] Ὀξάθρας Wesseling (cp. Book 17. 34. 2 Ὀξάθρης): ζαθρας.

him ; and he himself, having finished the second 306 B.C.
struggle for Egypt [1] and convinced that the country
was his as a prize of war, returned to Alexandria.[2]

77. While these events were taking place, Dionysius, the tyrant of Heraclea Pontica, died after having
ruled for thirty-two years [3] ; and his sons, Oxathras
and Clearchus, succeeding to his tyranny, ruled for
seventeen years.

In Sicily [4] Agathocles visited the cities that were
subject to him, making them secure with garrisons
and exacting money from them ; for he was taking
extreme precautions lest, because of the misfortunes
that had befallen him, the Sicilian Greeks should
make an effort to gain their independence. Indeed
at that very time Pasiphilus the general, having heard
of the murder of Agathocles' sons and of his reverses
in Libya, regarded the tyrant with contempt ; and,
deserting to Deinocrates and establishing friendship
with him, he both kept a firm grip on the cities which
had been entrusted to him and by alluring the minds
of his soldiers with hopes alienated them from the
tyrant. Agathocles, now that his hopes were being
curtailed in every quarter, was so cast down in spirit
that he sent an embassy to Deinocrates and invited
him to make a treaty on these terms : that, on the
one hand, Agathocles should withdraw from his
position as tyrant and restore Syracuse to its citizens,
and Deinocrates should no longer be an exile, and
that, on the other hand, there should be given to

[1] Cp. Book 18. 33-35.
[2] It is probably in the winter after this campaign that
Ptolemy assumed the diadem and the royal title ; cp. chap.
53. 3, and note. The narrative is continued in chap. 81.
[3] Cp. Book 16. 88. 5.
[4] Continued from chap. 72. 5.

᾿Αγαθοκλεῖ δύο, Θέρμα καὶ Κεφαλοίδιον καὶ τὴν χώραν τὴν τούτων.

78. Θαυμάσαι δ' ἄν τις εἰκότως ἐν τούτοις πῶς ᾿Αγαθοκλῆς, ὑποστατικὸς ἐν τοῖς ἄλλοις πᾶσι γενόμενος καὶ μηδέποθ' ἑαυτὸν ἐν ταῖς ἐσχάταις προσδοκίαις ἀπελπίσας, τότε δειλωθεὶς ἀκονιτὶ παρεχώρησε τοῖς πολεμίοις τῆς τυραννίδος, ὑπὲρ ἧς πολλοὺς καὶ μεγάλους κινδύνους προηγωνίσατο, καὶ τὸ πάντων παραλογώτατον, Συρακουσσῶν τε κυριεύσας καὶ τῶν ἄλλων πόλεων καὶ ναῦς καὶ χρήματα κεκτημένος καὶ δύναμιν σύμμετρον, ἐξησθένησε τοῖς λογισμοῖς, οὐδὲν τῶν γενομένων περὶ 2 Διονύσιον τὸν τύραννον μνησθείς. τούτου γάρ ποτε συνδιωχθέντος εἰς περίστασιν ὁμολογουμένως ἀπεγνωσμένην καὶ διὰ τὸ μέγεθος τῶν ἐπηρτημένων κινδύνων ἀπελπίσαντος μὲν τὰ κατὰ τὴν δυναστείαν, μέλλοντος δ' ἐκ τῶν Συρακουσσῶν ἐξιππεύειν πρὸς ἑκούσιον φυγήν, ῞Ελωρις ὁ πρεσβύτατος τῶν φίλων ἐπιλαβόμενος τῆς ὁρμῆς " Διονύσιε," φησίν, " καλὸν 3 ἐντάφιον ἡ τυραννίς." παραπλησίως δὲ τούτῳ καὶ ὁ κηδεστὴς Μεγακλῆς ἀπεφήνατο πρὸς αὐτόν, εἰπὼν ὅτι δεῖ τὸν ἐκ τυραννίδος ἐκπίπτοντα τοῦ σκέλους ἑλκόμενον ἀπιέναι καὶ μὴ κατὰ προαίρεσιν ἀπαλλάττεσθαι. ὑπὸ δὲ τούτων τῶν παρακλήσεων ὁ Διονύσιος μετεωρισθεὶς ἐνεκαρτέρησε πᾶσι τοῖς δοκοῦσιν εἶναι δεινοῖς καὶ τὴν μὲν ἀρχὴν μείζονα κατεσκεύασεν, αὐτὸς δὲ ἐν τοῖς ταύτης καλοῖς ἐγγηράσας ἀπέλιπε τοῖς ἐκγόνοις μεγίστην τῶν κατὰ τὴν Εὐρώπην δυναστείαν.

79. ᾿Αγαθοκλῆς δ' ἐπ' οὐδενὶ τούτων μετεω-

---

[1] In Book 14. 8. 4-6 the words of Heloris are given as here ;

Agathocles two designated fortresses, Therma and 306 B.C. Cephaloedium, together with their territories.

78. One might with good reason express wonder at this point that Agathocles, who had shown himself resolute in every other situation and had never lost confidence in himself when his prospects were at their lowest, at this time became a coward and without a fight abandoned to his enemies the tyranny for the sake of which he had previously fought many great battles, and what was the most unaccountable of all, that while he was master of Syracuse and of the other cities and had possession of ships and wealth and an army commensurate with these, he lost all power of calculating chances, recalling not one of the experiences of the tyrant Dionysius. For instance, when that tyrant had been driven into a situation that was confessedly desperate and when, because of the greatness of the impending dangers, he had given up hope of retaining his throne and was about to ride out from Syracuse into voluntary exile, Heloris, the eldest of his friends, opposing his impulse, said, "Dionysius, tyranny is a good winding-sheet." And similarly his brother-in-law, Megacles, spoke his mind to Dionysius, saying that the man who was being expelled from a tyranny ought to make his exit dragged by the leg and not to depart of his own free choice.[1] Encouraged by these exhortations, Dionysius firmly faced all the emergencies that seemed formidable, and not only made his dominion greater, but when he himself had grown old amid its blessings, he left to his sons the greatest empire of Europe.

79. Agathocles, however, buoyed up by no such

but the advice here assigned to Megacles is there put in the mouth of the historian Philistus.

ρισθεὶς οὐδὲ τὰς ἀνθρωπίνας ἐλπίδας ἐξελέγξας τῇ πείρᾳ τηλικαύτην ἀρχὴν ἔκδοτον ἐποίει ταύταις[1] ταῖς ὁμολογίαις. ταύτας δ' ἀσυντελέστους συνέβη γενέσθαι τῇ μὲν Ἀγαθοκλέους προαιρέσει κυρωθείσαις, διὰ δὲ τὴν Δεινοκράτους πλεονεξίαν μὴ προσδεχθεί-

2 σας. οὗτος γὰρ μοναρχίας ὢν ἐπιθυμητὴς τῆς μὲν ἐν ταῖς Συρακούσσαις δημοκρατίας ἀλλότριος ἦν, τῇ δὲ ἡγεμονίᾳ τῇ τότε οὔσῃ περὶ αὐτὸν εὐαρεστεῖτο· ἀφηγεῖτο γὰρ πεζῶν μὲν πλειόνων ἢ δισμυρίων, ἱππέων δὲ τρισχιλίων, πόλεων δὲ πολλῶν καὶ μεγάλων, ὥστε αὐτὸν μὲν καλεῖσθαι τῶν φυγάδων στρατηγόν, τῇ δ' ἀληθείᾳ βασιλικὴν ἔχειν ὑπεροχήν,

3 τῆς ἐξουσίας οὔσης περὶ αὐτὸν αὐτοκράτορος. εἰ κατέλθοι δ' εἰς τὰς Συρακούσσας, πάντως ἀναγκαῖον ἂν ἦν ἰδιώτην ὑπάρχειν καὶ ἕνα τῶν πολλῶν ἀριθμεῖσθαι, τῆς αὐτονομίας ἀγαπώσης τὴν ἰσότητα, ἔν τε ταῖς χειροτονίαις ὑπὸ τοῦ τυχόντος δημαγωγοῦ παρευημερεῖσθαι, τοῦ πλήθους ἀντικειμένου ταῖς ὑπεροχαῖς τῶν ἀνδρῶν τῶν ἀγόντων παρρησίαν. διόπερ Ἀγαθοκλῆς μὲν δικαίως ἂν λέγοιτο λελοιπέναι τὴν τῆς τυραννίδος τάξιν, Δεινοκράτης δ' αἴτιος εἶναι νομίζοιτο τῶν ὕστερον τῷ

4 δυνάστῃ κατορθωθέντων. οὗτος γάρ, συνεχῶς Ἀγαθοκλέους διαπρεσβευομένου περὶ τῶν ὁμολογιῶν καὶ δεομένου συγχωρῆσαι τὰ δύο φρούρια πρὸς καταβίωσιν, ἀεὶ προφάσεις εὐλόγους κατεσκεύαζε δι' ὧν διέκοπτε τὰς ἐλπίδας τῶν ὁμολογιῶν, ποτὲ μὲν ἀποφαινόμενος ἐκ Σικελίας αὐτὸν ἀπαλλάττεσθαι, ποτὲ δὲ τὰ τέκνα πρὸς ὁμηρίαν

5 αἰτῶν. ὁ δ' Ἀγαθοκλῆς γνοὺς αὐτοῦ τὴν ἐπίνοιαν πρὸς μὲν τοὺς φυγάδας διεπέμπετο κατηγορῶν τοῦ

---

[1] ἐποίει ταύταις Post, ἐποιεῖτο Dindorf : πεποίηται.

consideration and failing to test his mortal hopes by 306 B.C. experience, was on the point of abandoning his empire, great as it was, on these terms. But as it happened, the treaty never went into effect, ratified indeed by the policy of Agathocles, but not accepted because of the ambition of Deinocrates. The latter, having set his heart upon sole rule, was hostile to the democracy in Syracuse and was well pleased with the position of leadership that he himself then had ; for he commanded more than twenty thousand foot soldiers, three thousand horsemen, and many great cities, so that, although he was called general of the exiles, he really possessed the authority of a king, his power being absolute. But if he should return to Syracuse, it would inevitably be his lot to be a private citizen and be numbered as one of the many, since independence loves equality ; and in the elections he might be defeated by any chance demagogue, since the crowd is opposed to the supremacy of men who are outspoken. Thus Agathocles might justly be said to have deserted his post as tyrant, and Deino- crates might be regarded as responsible for the later successes of the dynast. For Deinocrates, when Agathocles kept sending embassies to discuss the terms of peace and begging him to grant the two fortresses in which he might end his days, always trumped up specious excuses by which he cut off any hope of a treaty, now insisting that Agathocles should leave Sicily, and now demanding his children as hostages. When Agathocles discovered his pur- pose, he sent to the exiles and accused Deinocrates

Δεινοκράτους ὡς διακωλύοντος αὐτοῦ τυχεῖν αὐτοὺς
τῆς αὐτονομίας, πρὸς δὲ Καρχηδονίους πρεσβευτὰς
ἀποστείλας συνέθετο τὴν εἰρήνην ἐφ' οἷς τὰς πόλεις
κομίσασθαι τοὺς Φοίνικας πάσας τὰς πρότερον ὑπ'
αὐτοὺς γεγενημένας· ἀντὶ δὲ τούτων ἔλαβε παρὰ
Καρχηδονίων χρυσίον μὲν εἰς ἀργυρίου λόγον ἀν-
αγόμενον¹ τριακοσίων ταλάντων, ὡς δὲ Τίμαιός
φησιν, ἑκατὸν πεντήκοντα, σίτου δὲ μεδίμνων εἴκοσι μυριάδας.

Καὶ τὰ μὲν περὶ Σικελίαν ἐν τούτοις ἦν.

80. Κατὰ δὲ τὴν Ἰταλίαν Σαμνῖται μὲν Σώραν
καὶ Καλατίαν² πόλεις Ῥωμαίοις συμμαχούσας
ἐκπολιορκήσαντες ἐξηνδραποδίσαντο· οἱ δ' ὕπατοι
δυνάμεσιν ἁδραῖς εἰς τὴν Ἰαπυγίαν ἐμβαλόντες πλη-
2 σίον Σιλβίου πόλεως κατεστρατοπέδευσαν. φρουρουμένης δὲ αὐτῆς ὑπὸ Σαμνιτῶν συνεστήσαντο
πολιορκίαν ἐφ' ἱκανὰς ἡμέρας καὶ κατὰ κράτος
ἑλόντες αἰχμάλωτα σώματα πλείω τῶν πεντακισχιλίων ἔλαβον καὶ τῶν ἄλλων λαφύρων ἱκανόν τι
3 πλῆθος. ἀπὸ δὲ τούτων γενόμενοι³ τὴν τῶν Σαμνιτῶν χώραν ἐπῆλθον δενδροτομοῦντες καὶ πάντα
τόπον καταφθείροντες· πολλὰ γὰρ ἔτη τῆς Ῥώμης
πρὸς τοῦτο τὸ ἔθνος διαπολεμούσης ὑπὲρ τῆς ἡγεμονίας ἤλπιζον τῶν ἐπὶ τῆς χώρας κτήσεων στε-
ρήσαντες τοὺς πολεμίους ἀναγκάσειν εἶξαι τοῖς
4 ὑπερέχουσιν. διὸ καὶ πέντε μῆνας καταναλώσαν-

_____
¹ ἀναγόμενον added by Fischer, cp. Books 16. 56. 6;
17. 71. 1.

of hindering them from gaining their independence, 306 B.C. and to the Carthaginians he sent envoys and made peace with them on terms such that the Phoenicians should regain all the cities which had formerly been subject to them, and in return for them he received from the Carthaginians gold to the value of three hundred talents of silver (or, as Timaeus says, one hundred and fifty), and two hundred thousand measures of grain.[1]

And affairs in Sicily were in this condition.

80. In Italy the Samnites took Sora and Calatia, cities that were allied to the Romans, and enslaved the inhabitants [2]; and the consuls with strong armies invaded Iapygia and camped near Silvium.[3] This city was garrisoned by the Samnites, and the Romans began a siege which lasted a considerable number of days. Capturing the city by storm, they took prisoner more than five thousand persons and collected a considerable amount of booty besides. When they had finished with this, they invaded the country of the Samnites, cutting down the trees and destroying every district. For the Romans, who had for many years been fighting the Samnites for the primacy, hoped that if they deprived the enemy of their property in the country, it would force them to submit to the stronger. For this reason they devoted

[1] Cp. Justin, 22. 8. 15. The narrative is continued in chap. 89.
[2] Cp. Livy 9. 43. 1. The narrative is continued from chap. 44. 9.
[3] Strabo, 6. 3. 8 (p. 283), places Silvium on the frontier between Apulia and Iapygia.

---

[2] καὶ Καλατίαν Wesseling, καὶ Καιατίαν or καὶ ᾿Ατίναν Mommsen: καὶ ᾿Ατίαν RX, καὶ ᾿Αττίαν F.
[3] γενόμενοι added by Kallenberg.

τες εἰς τὴν τῆς πολεμίας γῆς καταφθορὰν τάς τε
ἐπαύλεις σχεδὸν ἁπάσας ἐπυρπόλησαν καὶ τὴν
χώραν ἐξηγρίωσαν, ἀφανίσαντες πᾶν τὸ δυνάμενον
ἐνεγκεῖν ἥμερον καρπόν. μετὰ δὲ ταῦτα τοῖς μὲν
Ἀναγνίταις[1] ἀδικήματα ποιοῦσι πόλεμον κατήγγει-
λαν, Φρουσίνωνα δὲ ἐκπολιορκήσαντες ἀπέδοντο τὴν
χώραν.

81. Τοῦ δ' ἐνιαυσίου χρόνου διεληλυθότος Ἀθήνησι μὲν ἦρχεν Εὐξένιππος, ἐν Ῥώμῃ δ' ὑπῆρχον
ὕπατοι Λεύκιος Ποστούμιος καὶ Τιβέριος Μινού-
κιος. ἐπὶ δὲ τούτων Ῥοδίοις ἐνέστη πόλεμος πρὸς
2 Ἀντίγονον διὰ τοιαύτας τινὰς αἰτίας. ἡ πόλις ἡ
τῶν Ῥοδίων ἰσχύουσα ναυτικαῖς δυνάμεσι καὶ πολι-
τευομένη κάλλιστα τῶν Ἑλλήνων περιμάχητος τοῖς
δυνάσταις καὶ βασιλεῦσιν ἦν, ἑκάστου σπεύδοντος
εἰς τὴν αὑτοῦ[2] φιλίαν προσλαμβάνεσθαι. προορω-
μένη δὲ πόρρωθεν τὸ συμφέρον καὶ πρὸς ἅπαντας
κατ' ἰδίαν συντιθεμένη τὴν φιλίαν τῶν πρὸς ἀλλή-
3 λους τοῖς δυνάσταις πολέμων οὐ μετεῖχεν. διόπερ
συνέβαινεν αὐτὴν τιμᾶσθαι μὲν ὑφ' ἑκάστου βασιλι-
καῖς δωρεαῖς, ἄγουσαν δὲ πολὺν χρόνον εἰρήνην
μεγάλην ἐπίδοσιν λαβεῖν πρὸς αὔξησιν· ἐπὶ τοσοῦτον γὰρ προεληλύθει δυνάμεως ὥσθ' ὑπὲρ μὲν τῶν
Ἑλλήνων ἰδίᾳ τὸν πρὸς τοὺς πειρατὰς πόλεμον
ἐπαναιρεῖσθαι καὶ καθαρὰν παρέχεσθαι τῶν κακ-
ούργων τὴν θάλατταν, τὸν δὲ πλεῖστον ἰσχύσαντα
τῶν μνημονευομένων Ἀλέξανδρον προτιμήσαντ' αὐτὴν μάλιστα τῶν πόλεων καὶ τὴν ὑπὲρ ὅλης τῆς

---

[1] Ἀναγνίταις Rhodoman, cp. Livy, 9. 43 : Αἰγινήταις RX,
Αἰγινίταις F.   [2] αὑτοῦ Post : αὐτοῦ.

five months to the ruining of the enemy's land ; and they burned nearly all the farm-buildings and laid waste the land, destroying everything that could produce cultivated fruit. Thereafter they declared war on the Anagnitae, who were acting unjustly, and taking Frusino they distributed the land.[1]

81. When this year had passed, Euxenippus be- came archon in Athens, and in Rome Lucius Postumius and Tiberius Minucius were consuls.[2] While these held office war arose between the Rhodians and Antigonus for some such reasons as these.[3] The city of the Rhodians, which was strong in sea power and was the best governed city of the Greeks, was a prize eagerly sought after by the dynasts and kings, each of them striving to add her to his alliance. Seeing far in advance what was advantageous and establishing friendship with each of the dynasts separately, Rhodes took no part in their wars with each other. As a result she was honoured by each of them with regal gifts and, while enjoying peace for a long time, made great steps forward. In fact she advanced to such strength that in behalf of the Greeks she by herself undertook her war against the pirates and purged the seas of these evil-doers ; and Alexander, the most powerful of men known to memory, honouring Rhodes above all cities, both deposited there the

---

[1] Anagnia was the chief city of the Hernici. Livy, 9. 43, places the victory over the Hernici in this year but the confiscation of the land of Frusino three years later (10. 1. 3). The narrative is continued in chap. 90. 3.

[2] Euxenippus was archon in 305/4 B.C. Livy, 9. 44. 2, gives as the consuls of 305 B.C., L. Postumius and T. Minucius; but a fragment of the Fasti Capitolini supports Diodorus in the praenomen of the last-named.

[3] The narrative is continued from chap. 76. For the Rhodian campaign cp. Plutarch, *Demetrius*, 21-22.

βασιλείας διαθήκην ἐκεῖ θέσθαι καὶ τἄλλα θαυ-
4 μάζειν καὶ προάγειν εἰς ὑπεροχήν. οἱ δ' οὖν
Ῥόδιοι πρὸς πάντας τοὺς δυνάστας συντεθειμένοι
τὴν φιλίαν διετήρουν μὲν ἑαυτοὺς ἐκτὸς ἐγκλήμα-
τος δικαίου, ταῖς δ' εὐνοίαις ἔρεπον μάλιστα πρὸς
Πτολεμαῖον· συνέβαινε γὰρ αὐτοῖς τῶν τε προσόδων
τὰς πλείστας εἶναι διὰ τοὺς εἰς Αἴγυπτον πλέοντας
ἐμπόρους καὶ τὸ σύνολον τρέφεσθαι τὴν πόλιν ἀπὸ
ταύτης τῆς βασιλείας.

82. Ὁ δὴ συνορῶν ὁ Ἀντίγονος καὶ σπεύδων
αὐτοὺς ἀποσπάσαι τῆς πρὸς ἐκεῖνον ἐπιπλοκῆς τὸ
μὲν πρῶτον πρεσβευτὰς ἀπέστειλε καθ' ὃν καιρὸν
ὑπὲρ τῆς Κύπρου διεπολέμει πρὸς Πτολεμαῖον,
ἀξιῶν αὐτῷ συμμαχεῖν καὶ ναῦς συναποστεῖλαι τῷ
2 Δημητρίῳ· οὐ προσεχόντων δ' αὐτῶν ἀπέστειλέ
τινα τῶν στρατηγῶν μετὰ νεῶν, συντάξας τοὺς
πλέοντας εἰς Αἴγυπτον ἐκ τῆς Ῥόδου κατάγειν καὶ
περιαιρεῖσθαι τὰ φορτία. τούτου δ' ἐκβληθέντος
ὑπὸ τῶν Ῥοδίων φήσας αὐτοὺς ἀδίκου κατῆρχ-
θαι πολέμου διηπειλήσατο πολιορκήσειν δυνάμεσιν
ἁδραῖς τὴν πόλιν. οἱ δὲ Ῥόδιοι τὸ μὲν πρῶτον
ἐψηφίσαντο μεγάλας αὐτῷ τιμὰς καὶ πέμψαντες
πρέσβεις ἠξίουν μὴ βιάσασθαι τὴν πόλιν προπεσεῖν[1]
παρὰ τὰς συνθήκας εἰς τὸν πόλεμον πρὸς Πτολε-
3 μαῖον. τραχύτερον δὲ τοῦ βασιλέως ἀπαντῶντος
καὶ τὸν υἱὸν Δημήτριον ἐκπέμψαντος μετὰ δυνάμεως καὶ πολιορκητικῶν ὀργάνων φοβηθέντες τὴν

---

[1] προπεσεῖν Dindorf : προσπεσεῖν.

[1] Alexander entrusted certain memoranda to Craterus
(Book 18. 4. 1), but these were not a will, and Diodorus'

testament [1] disposing of his whole realm and in other 305 B.C. ways showed admiration for her and promoted her to a commanding position. At any rate, the Rhodians, having established pacts of friendship with all the rulers, carefully avoided giving legitimate grounds for complaint ; but in displaying goodwill they inclined chiefly toward Ptolemy, for it happened that most of their revenues were due to the merchants who sailed to Egypt, and that in general the city drew its food supply from that kingdom.

82. Because Antigonus knew this and was intent on separating the Rhodians from their connection with Ptolemy, he first sent out envoys to them at the time when he was fighting with Ptolemy for Cyprus and asked them to ally themselves with him and to dispatch ships in company with Demetrius [2] ; and when they did not consent, he dispatched one of his generals with ships, ordering him to bring to land any merchants sailing to Egypt from Rhodes and to seize their cargoes. When this general was driven off by the Rhodians, Antigonus, declaring that they were authors of an unjust war, threatened to lay siege to the city with strong forces. The Rhodians, however, first voted great honours for him ; and, sending envoys, they begged him not to force the city to rush into the war against Ptolemy contrary to their treaties. But then, when the king answered rather harshly and sent his son Demetrius with an army and siege equipment, they were so

narrative of the events following Alexander's death assumes that no will existed.

[2] Cp. chap. 46. 6. In 315 B.C. Rhodes had built warships for Antigonus from timber that he furnished (Book 19. 57. 4 ; 58. 5) ; and in 313 B.C. she had furnished 10 ships for the campaign to free Greece (Book 19. 77. 2).

ὑπεροχὴν τοῦ βασιλέως τὸ μὲν πρῶτον ἀπέστειλαν πρὸς τὸν Δημήτριον, φήσαντες συμπολεμήσειν
Ἀντιγόνῳ πρὸς Πτολεμαῖον· ὡς δ' ἐκεῖνος ὁμήρους
ἑκατὸν ᾔτει τοὺς ἐπιφανεστάτους καὶ τοῖς λιμέσι
δέχεσθαι τὸν στόλον προσέταττεν, ὑπολαβόντες
ἐπιβουλεύειν αὐτὸν τῇ πόλει, τὰ πρὸς πόλεμον
4 παρεσκευάζοντο. Δημήτριος δὲ πᾶσαν τὴν δύναμιν
ἀθροίσας εἰς τὸν ἐν Λωρύμοις¹ λιμένα στόλον ἐξ-
ήρτυε πρὸς τὸν ἐπίπλουν τὸν ἐπὶ τὴν Ῥόδον. εἶχε
δὲ ναῦς μακρὰς μὲν παντοίας μεγέθει διακοσίας,
ὑπηρετικὰ δὲ πλείω τῶν ἑκατὸν ἑβδομήκοντα· ἐν
δὲ τούτοις ἐκομίζοντο στρατιῶται βραχὺ λειπόμενοι
τῶν τετρακισμυρίων σὺν ἱππεῦσι καὶ τοῖς συμμα-
χοῦσι πειραταῖς. ὑπῆρχε δὲ καὶ βελῶν παντοίων
πλῆθος καὶ πάντων τῶν πρὸς πολιορκίαν χρησίμων
5 μεγάλη παρασκευή. χωρὶς δὲ τούτων ἰδιωτικὰ
πόρια συνηκολούθει τῶν ταῖς ἀγοραῖς χρωμένων
βραχὺ λειπόμενα τῶν χιλίων· πολλὰ γὰρ ἔτη τῆς
χώρας τῆς Ῥοδίων ἀπορθήτου γεγενημένης συν-
έρρει πανταχόθεν πλῆθος τῶν εἰωθότων ὠφελείας
ἰδίας ἡγεῖσθαι τὰ τῶν πολεμουμένων ἀτυχήματα.

83. Ὁ μὲν οὖν Δημήτριος ὥσπερ εἴς τινα ναυμαχίαν ἐκτάξας τὸν στόλον καταπληκτικῶς προ-
ηγεῖσθαι μὲν ἐποίησε τὰς μακρὰς ναῦς, ἐχούσας
ἐπὶ ταῖς πρῴραις τοὺς τρισπιθάμους τῶν ὀξυβελῶν,
ἐπακολουθεῖν δὲ τὰς στρατιωτικὰς καὶ τὰς ἱππη-
γοὺς ῥυμουλκουμένας ὑπὸ τῶν ταῖς εἰρεσίαις χρω-

frightened by the superior power of the king that at 305 B.C. first they sent to Demetrius, saying that they would join Antigonus in the war with Ptolemy, but when Demetrius demanded as hostages a hundred of the noblest citizens and ordered also that his fleet should be received in their harbours, concluding that he was plotting against the city, they made ready for war. Demetrius, gathering all his forces in the harbour at Loryma,[1] made his fleet ready for the attack on Rhodes. He had two hundred warships of all sizes and more than one hundred and seventy auxiliary vessels ; on these were transported not quite forty thousand soldiers besides the cavalry and the pirates who were his allies. There was also an ample supply of ordnance of all sorts and a large provision of all the things necessary for a siege. In addition there accompanied him almost a thousand privately owned ships, which belonged to those who were engaged in trade ; for since the land of the Rhodians had been un-plundered for many years, there had gathered together from all quarters a host of those who were accustomed to consider the misfortunes of men at war a means of enriching themselves.

83. And so Demetrius, having drawn up his fleet as if for a naval battle in a way to inspire panic, sent forward his warships, which had on their prows the catapults for bolts three spans in length [2] ; and he had the transports for men and horses follow, towed by the ships that used oarsmen ; and last of all came

---

[1] Loryma is in Caria about twenty miles distant from Rhodes.

[2] For the use of catapults on ships cp. Tarn, *Hellenistic Military and Naval Developments*, 120-121.

---

[1] Λωρύμοις Palmer, cp. Book 17. 83. 7 : Ἐλωρύμνοις.

μένων, ἐπὶ πᾶσι δὲ καὶ τὰ τῶν πειρατῶν πόρια
καὶ τὰ τῶν ἐμπόρων καὶ ἀγοραίων, ὑπεράγοντα
τῷ πλήθει, καθάπερ προείρηται, ὥστε πάντα τὸν
ἀνὰ μέσον τόπον τῆς τε νήσου καὶ τῆς ἀντικειμένης
παραλίας συμπεπληρωμένον φαίνεσθαι τοῖς πλοίοις
καὶ πολὺν φόβον καὶ κατάπληξιν παρέχεσθαι τοῖς
2 ἀπὸ τῆς πόλεως θεωροῦσιν. οἱ μὲν γὰρ στρατιῶται
τῶν Ῥοδίων διειληφότες τὰ τείχη τὸν ἐπίπλουν
ἐκαραδόκουν τῶν πολεμίων, πρεσβῦται δὲ καὶ γυναῖκες ἀπὸ τῶν οἰκιῶν ἀφεώρων, οὔσης[1] τῆς πόλεως
θεατροειδοῦς, πάντες δὲ[2] τό τε μέγεθος τοῦ στόλου
καὶ τὴν αὐγὴν τῶν ἀποστιλβόντων ὅπλων κατα-
πληττόμενοι περὶ τῶν ὅλων οὐ μετρίως ἠγωνίων.
3 εἶθ' ὁ μὲν Δημήτριος κατέπλευσεν εἰς τὴν νῆσον,
ἀποβιβάσας δὲ τὴν δύναμιν κατεστρατοπέδευσεν
πλησίον τῆς πόλεως, ἐκτὸς βέλους ποιησάμενος τὴν
παρεμβολήν. εὐθὺς δὲ τῶν πειρατῶν καὶ τῶν ἄλλων τοὺς εὐθέτους ἐξέπεμψε πορθήσοντας τὴν νῆσον
4 καὶ κατὰ γῆν καὶ κατὰ θάλατταν. ἐδενδροτό-
μησε δὲ καὶ τὴν πλησίον χώραν καὶ καθεῖλε τὰς
ἐπαύλεις, ἐξ ὧν ὠχύρωσε τὴν στρατοπεδείαν, περιλαβὼν τριπλῷ χάρακι καὶ σταυρώμασι πυκνοῖς καὶ
μεγάλοις, ὥστε τὴν τῶν πολεμίων βλάβην γίνεσθαι
τῶν ἰδίων ἀσφάλειαν. μετὰ δὲ ταῦτα πάσῃ τῇ
δυνάμει καὶ τοῖς πληρώμασιν ἔχωσεν ἐν ὀλίγαις
ἡμέραις τὸ μεταξὺ τῆς πόλεως διαλεῖπον πρὸς τὴν
ἔκβασιν καὶ κατεσκεύασε λιμένα ταῖς ναυσὶν
ἀρκοῦντα.

84. Οἱ δὲ Ῥόδιοι μέχρι μέν τινος πρέσβεις ἐκ-
πέμποντες ἠξίουν μηδὲν πρᾶξαι κατὰ τῆς πόλεως

---

[1] δὲ after οὔσης omitted by Dindorf.
[2] δὲ added by Dindorf.

also the cargo-ships of the pirates and of the mer- chants and traders, which as we have already said, were exceedingly numerous, so that the whole space between the island and the opposite shore was seen to be filled with his vessels, which brought great fear and panic to those who were watching from the city. For the soldiers of the Rhodians, occupying their several positions on the walls, were awaiting the approach of the hostile fleet, and the old men and women were looking on from their homes, since the city is shaped like a theatre [1] ; and all, being terror-stricken at the magnitude of the fleet and the gleam of the shining armour, were not a little anxious about the final outcome. Then Demetrius sailed to the island ; and after disembarking his army, he took position near the city, setting up his camp out of range of missiles. He at once sent out fit and proper men from the pirates and others to plunder the island both by land and by sea. He also cut down the trees in the region near by and destroyed the farm buildings, and with this material he fortified the camp, surrounding it with a triple palisade and with great, close-set stockades, so that the loss suffered by the enemy became a protection for his own men. After this, using the whole army and the crews, he in a few days closed with a mole the space between the city and the exit, and made a port large enough for his ships.

84. For a time the Rhodians kept sending envoys and asking him to do nothing irreparable against the

[1] Cp. Book 19. 45. 3.

ἀνήκεστον· ὡς δ' οὐδεὶς αὐτοῖς προσεῖχεν, ἀπογνόν-
τες τὰς διαλύσεις ἐξέπεμψαν πρεσβευτὰς πρὸς
Πτολεμαῖον καὶ Λυσίμαχον καὶ Κάσανδρον, ἀξιοῦντες βοηθεῖν, ὡς τῆς πόλεως προπολεμούσης[1]
2 ὑπὲρ αὐτῶν. τῶν δ' ἐν τῇ πόλει κατοικούντων
παροίκων καὶ ξένων δόντες ἐξουσίαν τοῖς βουλομένοις συναγωνίζεσθαι, τοὺς λοιποὺς ἀχρήστους
ἐκ τῆς πόλεως ἐξέπεμψαν, ἅμα μὲν τῆς τῶν ἀναγκαίων ἐνδείας προνοηθέντες, ἅμα δὲ καὶ τοῦ μηδένα
τῇ καταστάσει δυσχεραίνοντα γίνεσθαι τῆς πόλεως
προδότην. ἀριθμὸν δὲ ποιησάμενοι τῶν δυναμένων
ἀγωνίζεσθαι πολιτῶν μὲν εὗρον περὶ ἑξακισχιλίους,
3 τῶν δὲ παροίκων καὶ ξένων εἰς χιλίους. ἐψηφίσαντο δὲ καὶ τῶν δούλων τοὺς ἄνδρας ἀγαθοὺς
γενομένους ἐν τοῖς κινδύνοις ἀγοράσαντας παρὰ
τῶν δεσποτῶν ἐλευθέρους[2] καὶ πολίτας εἶναι· ἔγραψαν δὲ καὶ τῶν τελευτησάντων ἐν τῷ πολέμῳ τὰ
μὲν σώματα δημοσίᾳ θάπτεσθαι, τοὺς δὲ γονεῖς[3]
καὶ παῖδας τρέφεσθαι λαμβάνοντας τὴν χορηγίαν
ἀπὸ τοῦ κοινοῦ ταμιείου, καὶ τὰς μὲν παρθένους
δημοσίᾳ προικίζεσθαι, τοὺς δ' υἱοὺς ἐν ἡλικίᾳ
γενομένους ἐν τῷ θεάτρῳ στεφανῶσαι τοῖς Διονυ-
4 σίοις πανοπλίᾳ. διὰ δὲ τούτων ἐκκαλεσάμενοι τὰς
ἁπάντων προθυμίας εἰς τὸ τοὺς κινδύνους ὑπομένειν
εὐψύχως, ἐποιήσαντο καὶ τῶν ἄλλων τὴν ἐνδεχο-
μένην παρασκευήν. ὁμονοοῦντος γὰρ τοῦ πλήθους
οἱ μὲν εὔποροι χρήματ' εἰσέφερον, οἱ δὲ τεχνῖται
τὰς αὐτῶν ἐπιστήμας παρεῖχοντο πρὸς τὴν τῶν

[1] προπολεμούσης Wesseling : προσπολεμούσης.

city ; but as no one paid any heed to these, they gave 305 B.C. up hope of a truce and sent envoys to Ptolemy, Lysimachus, and Cassander, begging them to give aid and saying that the city was fighting the war on their behalf. As to the metics and aliens who dwelt in the city, to those who wished they gave permission to join them in the fighting, and the others who were of no service they sent forth from the city, partly as a precaution against scarcity of supplies, and partly that there might be no one to become dissatisfied with the situation and try to betray the city. When they made a count of those who were able to fight, they found that there were about six thousand citizens and as many as a thousand metics and aliens. They voted also to buy from their masters any slaves who proved themselves brave men in the battle, and to emancipate and enfranchise them. And they also wrote another decree, that the bodies of those who fell in the war should be given public burial and, further, that their parents and children should be maintained, receiving their support from the public treasury, that their unmarried daughters should be given dowries at the public cost, and that their sons on reaching manhood should be crowned in the theatre at the Dionysia and given a full suit of armour. When by these measures they had roused the spirits of all to endure the battles with courage, they also made what preparation was possible in regard to other matters. Since the whole people was of one mind, the rich contributed money, the craftsmen gave their skilled services for the preparation of the arms, and

---

² ἐλευθέρους Capps : ἐλευθεροῦν.
³ Fischer suggests the addition of καὶ γυναῖκας after γονεῖς, cp. Book 17. 11. 5.

ὅπλων κατασκευήν, ἅπας δ' ἦν ἐνεργός, τῇ φιλο-
5 τιμίᾳ τοὺς ἄλλους ὑπερθέσθαι σπεύδων. διόπερ οἱ
μὲν ἐγίνοντο περὶ τοὺς ὀξυβελεῖς καὶ πετροβόλους,
οἱ δὲ περὶ τὴν τῶν ἄλλων κατασκευήν, τινὲς δὲ τὰ
πεπονηκότα τῶν τειχῶν ἐπεσκεύαζον, πλεῖστοι δὲ
λίθους πρὸς τὰ τείχη φέροντες ἐσώρευον. ἐξέπεμψαν δὲ καὶ τῶν ἄριστα πλεουσῶν νεῶν τρεῖς
ἐπὶ τοὺς πολεμίους καὶ τοὺς παρακομίζοντας αὐτοῖς
6 ἀγορὰς ἐμπόρους. αὗται δὲ παραδόξως ἐπιφανεῖσαι
πολλὰ μὲν πλοῖα τῶν ἐπὶ τὴν προνομὴν τῆς χώρας
ὠφελείας χάριν πλεόντων ἐμπόρων κατεπόντισαν,
οὐκ ὀλίγα δὲ καὶ πρὸς τὸν αἰγιαλὸν κατασπῶσαι
συνέκαυσαν, καὶ τῶν αἰχμαλώτων τὰ δυνάμενα
δοῦναι λύτρον παρεκόμιζον εἰς τὴν πόλιν· συνέθεντο
γὰρ οἱ Ῥόδιοι πρὸς τὸν Δημήτριον ὥστε ἀλλήλοις
διδόναι λύτρον ἐλευθέρου μὲν χιλίας δραχμάς, δού-
λου δὲ πεντακοσίας.

85. Πρὸς τὰς θέσεις τῶν ὀργάνων δὲ ὁ Δημήτριος ἄφθονον ἔχων ἁπάντων χορηγίαν ἤρξατο
κατασκευάζειν δύο χελώνας, τὴν μὲν πρὸς τοὺς πετροβόλους, τὴν δὲ πρὸς τοὺς ὀξυβελεῖς, ἀμφοτέρας
δὲ ταύτας ἐπὶ δύο πλοίων φορτηγῶν διαβεβηκυίας κατεζευγμένων,[1] δύο δὲ πύργους τετραστέ-
γους ὑπερέχοντας τοῖς ὕψεσι τῶν ἐπὶ τοῦ λιμένος
πύργων, ἑκάτερον δὲ τούτων ἐπὶ δύο πλοίων ἴσων[2]
βεβηκότα καὶ κατειλημμένον ὅπως ἐν τῷ προσάγειν ἡ στάσις ἑκατέρα τῶν πλευρῶν ἰσόρροπον
2 ἔχῃ τὸ βάρος. κατεσκεύασε δὲ καὶ χάρακα πλωτὸν

every man was active, each striving in a spirit of 305 P.C.
rivalry to surpass the others. Consequently, some
were busy with the catapults and ballistae, others
with the preparation of other equipment, some were
repairing any ruined portions of the walls, and very
many were carrying stones to the walls and stacking
them. They even sent out three of their swiftest
ships against the enemy and the merchant ships
which brought provisions to him. These ships on
appearing unexpectedly sank many vessels belonging
to merchants who had sailed for the purpose of
plundering the land for their own profit, and even
hauled not a few of the ships up on the beach and
burned them. As for the prisoners, those who could
pay a ransom they took into the city, for the Rhodians
had made an agreement with Demetrius that each
should pay the other a thousand drachmae as ransom
for a free man and five hundred for a slave.

85. Demetrius, who had an ample supply of everything required for setting up his engines of war, began
to prepare two penthouses, one for the ballistae, the
other for the catapults, each of them firmly mounted
on two cargo vessels fastened together,[1] and two
towers of four storeys, exceeding in height the
towers of the harbour, each of them mounted upon
two ships of the same size and fastened there in such
a way that as the towers advanced the support on
each side upheld an equal weight. He also prepared

---

[1] Or, reading καὶ κατεζευγμένας : " mounted on two cargo
vessels and fastened securely."

---

[1] διαβεβηκυίας κατεζευγμένων Geer, διαβεβηκυίας καὶ κατεζευγμένας Fischer : διαβεβηκότων καὶ κατεζευγμένων.
[2] ἴσον Madvig, Fischer.

τετραπέδων ξύλων ἐπικαθηλωμένων,[1] ὅπως προπλέων[2] οὗτος κωλύῃ τοὺς πολεμίους ἐπιπλέοντας
ἐμβολὰς διδόναι τοῖς φέρουσι τὰς μηχανὰς πλοίοις.
3 ἐν ὅσῳ δὲ ταῦτα τὴν συντέλειαν ἐλάμβανεν, ἀθροίσας
τοὺς ἀδροτάτους τῶν λέμβων καὶ τούτους κατα-
φράξας σανίσι καὶ θυρίδας κλειστὰς κατασκευάσας
ἐνέθετο μὲν τῶν τρισπιθάμων ὀξυβελῶν τοὺς πορ-
ρωτάτω βάλλοντας καὶ τοὺς τούτοις κατὰ τρόπον
χρησομένους, ἔτι δὲ τοξότας Κρῆτας, τὰς δὲ ναῦς
προσαγαγὼν ἐντὸς βέλους κατετίτρωσκε τοὺς κατὰ
τὴν πόλιν ὑψηλότερα τὰ παρὰ τὸν λιμένα τείχη
κατασκευάζοντας.
4 Οἱ δὲ Ῥόδιοι θεωροῦντες τοῦ Δημητρίου τὴν
πᾶσαν ἐπιβολὴν οὖσαν ἐπὶ τὸν λιμένα καὶ αὐτοὶ τὰ
πρὸς τὴν ἀσφάλειαν τούτου παρεσκευάζοντο. δύο
μὲν οὖν ἔστησαν μηχανὰς ἐπὶ τοῦ χώματος, τρεῖς
δ' ἐπὶ φορτηγῶν πλοίων πλησίον τῶν κλείθρων
τοῦ μικροῦ λιμένος· ἐν δὲ ταύταις ἔθηκαν πλῆθος
ὀξυβελῶν καὶ πετροβόλων παντοίων τοῖς μεγέθεσιν, ὅπως, ἐάν τε ἀποβιβάζωσιν οἱ πολέμιοι πρὸς
τὸ χῶμα στρατιώτας ἄν τε τὰς μηχανὰς προσ-
άγωσι, διὰ τούτων αὐτοὺς εἴργεσθαι τῆς ἐπιβολῆς. ἐπέστησαν δὲ καὶ τοῖς ὁρμοῦσι τῶν φορτηγῶν
πλοίων ἐν τῷ λιμένι βελοστάσεις οἰκείας τοῖς
ἐπιτίθεσθαι μέλλουσι καταπέλταις.[3]
86. Ἀμφοτέρων δὲ τοῦτον τὸν τρόπον παρεσκευασμένων ὁ Δημήτριος τὸ μὲν πρῶτον ἐπι-
βαλόμενος προσάγειν τὰς μηχανὰς τοῖς λιμέσιν
ἐκωλύθη κλύδωνος ἐπιγενομένου τραχυτέρου· μετὰ

---

[1] τετραπέδων ξύλων ἐπικαθηλωμένων Geer, ἐπὶ τετρ. ξύ.
καθηλωμένον Fischer : ἐπὶ τετρ. ξύ. καθηλωμένων.
[2] προπλέων Dindorf : προσπλέων.

a floating boom of squared logs studded with spikes,[1] in order that as this was floated forward it might prevent the enemy from sailing up and ramming the ships that were carrying the engines of war. In the interval while these were receiving their finishing touches, he collected the strongest of the light craft, fortified them with planks, provided them with ports that could be closed, and placed upon them those of the catapults for bolts three palms long which had the longest range and the men to work them properly, and also Cretan archers; then, sending the boats within range, he shot down the men of the city who were building higher the walls along the harbour.

When the Rhodians saw that the entire attack of Demetrius was aimed against the harbour, they themselves also took measures for its security. They placed two machines [2] on the mole and three upon freighters near the boom of the small harbour; in these they mounted a large number of catapults and ballistae of all sizes, in order that if the enemy should disembark soldiers on the mole or should advance his machines, he might be thwarted in his design by this means. They also placed on such cargo ships as were at anchor in the harbour platforms suitable for the catapults that were to be mounted on them.

86. After both sides had made their preparations in this way, Demetrius at first endeavoured to bring his engines of war against the harbour, but he was prevented when too rough a sea arose; later on,

---

[1] Or, reading ἐπὶ τετράπεδον ξύλον καθηλωμένον: "a floating palisade fastened with spikes to squared logs."

[2] Probably penthouses or sheds.

---

[3] καταπέλταις Rhodoman: καταπέλτας.

δὲ ταῦτα νυκτὸς εὐδίας λαβόμενος ἔλαθε παραπλεύσας καὶ καταλαβόμενος ἄκρον τὸ χῶμα τοῦ μεγάλου
λιμένος εὐθὺς περιεχαράκωσε τὸν τόπον καὶ δι-
έφραξε θυρώμασι καὶ πέτροις, ἐξεβίβασε δ' εἰς
αὐτὸν στρατιώτας τετρακοσίους καὶ βελῶν πλῆθος
παντοδαπῶν, ἀπέχοντος ἀπὸ τῶν τειχῶν τοῦ τόπου
2 τούτου πέντε πλέθρα. ἔπειθ' ἡμέρας γενομένης
παρεκόμισε[1] τὰς μηχανὰς εἰς τὸν λιμένα μετὰ
σάλπιγγος καὶ κραυγῆς· καὶ τοῖς μὲν ἐλάττοσιν
ὀξυβελέσι μακρὰν φερομένοις ἀνεῖργε τοὺς ἐργαζομένους τὸ παρὰ τὸν λιμένα τεῖχος, τοῖς δὲ πετροβόλοις τάς τε μηχανὰς τῶν πολεμίων καὶ τὸ διὰ
τοῦ χώματος τεῖχος τῇ μὲν διέσεισε, τῇ δὲ κατ-
έβαλεν, ἀσθενὲς ὑπάρχον καὶ ταπεινὸν ἐκείνοις τοῖς
3 καιροῖς. ἀμυνομένων δὲ καὶ τῶν ἐκ τῆς πόλεως
εὐρώστως τότε μὲν ὅλην τὴν ἡμέραν διετέλεσαν
ἀμφότεροι πολλὰ κακὰ καὶ δρῶντες καὶ πάσχοντες·
τῆς δὲ νυκτὸς ἤδη καταλαμβανούσης ὁ μὲν Δημήτριος ταῖς ῥυμουλκούσαις ναυσὶν ἀπήγαγε τὰς μηχανὰς πάλιν ἔξω βέλους· οἱ δὲ Ῥόδιοι ξηρᾶς ὕλης
καὶ δαδὸς ἀκάτια πληρώσαντες καὶ πῦρ ἐνθέμενοι
τὸ μὲν πρῶτον ἐπιδιώξαντες προσέπλεον ταῖς μηχαναῖς ταῖς τῶν πολεμίων καὶ τὴν ὕλην ὑφῆψαν,
μετὰ δὲ ταῦτα τῷ πλωτῷ χάρακι καὶ τοῖς βέλεσιν
ἀνειρχθέντες συνηναγκάσθησαν χωρεῖν εἰς τοὐπίσω.
4 τῆς δὲ φλογὸς ἐπισχυούσης ὀλίγοι μὲν κατασβέ-
σαντες ἐπανῆλθον σὺν τοῖς σκάφεσιν, οἱ πλεῖστοι
δὲ καιομένων τῶν ἀκατίων ἐξεκολύμβησαν. τῇ δ'
ὑστεραίᾳ κατὰ μὲν θάλατταν ὁ Δημήτριος παραπλησίαν ἐποιήσατο τὴν ἐπίθεσιν, κατὰ δὲ τὴν γῆν
προσέταξεν ἅμα πανταχόθεν προσβάλλειν μετ' ἀλα-
λαγμοῦ καὶ σάλπιγγος, ὅπως εἰς ἀγωνίαν καὶ

however, taking advantage of calm weather at night, 305 B.C.
he sailed in secretly, and after seizing the end of the
mole of the great harbour he at once fortified the
place, cutting it off with walls of planks and stones,
and landed there four hundred soldiers and a supply
of ordnance of all kinds. This point was five plethra [1]
distant from the city walls. Then at daybreak he
brought his engines into the harbour with the sound
of trumpets and with shouts ; and with the lighter
catapults, which had a long range, he drove back
those who were constructing the wall along the harbour, and with the ballistae he shook or destroyed
the engines of the enemy and the wall across the
mole, for it was weak and low at this time. But since
those from the city also fought stoutly, during that
whole day both sides continued to inflict and suffer
severe losses ; and when night was already closing
in, Demetrius by means of towboats drew his engines
back out of range. The Rhodians, however, filled
light boats with dry pitchy wood and placed fire in
them ; at first they went in pursuit and, drawing near
to the engines of the enemy, lighted the wood, but
afterwards, repelled by the floating boom and by the
missiles, they were forced to withdraw. As the fire
gained force a few put it out and sailed back with
their boats, but most of them plunged into the sea
as their boats were consumed. On the following day
Demetrius made a similar attack by sea, but he also
gave orders to assail the city at the same time by
land from all sides with shouts and sound of trumpet

[1] About 500 feet.

---

[1] παρεκόμισε Wesseling : παρεκόμισαν.

φόβον ἀγάγῃ τοὺς Ῥοδίους, πολλῶν τῶν ἀντισπασμάτων ὄντων.

87. Τοιαύτην δὲ τὴν πολιορκίαν ποιησάμενος ἐφ᾽ ἡμέρας ὀκτὼ τὰς μὲν μηχανὰς τὰς ἐπὶ τοῦ χώματος τοῖς ταλαντιαίοις πετροβόλοις συνέτριψε, τοῦ δὲ διατειχίσματος τὸ μεσοπύργιον σὺν αὐτοῖς τοῖς πύργοις διέσεισεν. κατελάβοντο δὲ καὶ τῶν στρατιωτῶν τινες μέρος τοῦ παρὰ τὸν λιμένα διατειχίσματος· ἐφ᾽ οὓς[1] συστραφέντες οἱ Ῥόδιοι μάχην συνῆψαν καὶ πολλαπλάσιοι γενόμενοι τοὺς μὲν ἀνεῖλον, τοὺς δ᾽ ἐπανελθεῖν εἰς τοὐπίσω συνηνάγκασαν· συνήργει δὲ τοῖς ἐκ τῆς πόλεως ἡ τοῦ παρὰ τὸ τεῖχος τόπου τραχύτης, πολλῶν καὶ μεγάλων πετρῶν κατὰ τὸ συνεχὲς κειμένων παρὰ τὴν 2 οἰκοδομὴν ἔξω τοῦ τείχους. τῶν δὲ τοὺς στρατιώτας τούτους κομισάντων σκαφῶν οὐκ ὀλίγων διὰ τὴν ἄγνοιαν[2] ἐποκειλάντων οἱ Ῥόδιοι ταχέως τὰ μὲν ἀκροστόλια περιέσπασαν, ὕλην δὲ ξηρὰν καὶ δᾷδας ταῖς ναυσὶν ἐνέντες ἐνέπρησαν. τούτων δὲ περὶ ταῦτ᾽ ὄντων οἱ μὲν τοῦ Δημητρίου στρατιῶται πανταχοῦ περιπλέοντες κλίμακας προσέφερον τοῖς τείχεσι καὶ βιαιότερον ἐνέκειντο, συναγωνιζομένων καὶ τῶν ἀπὸ τῆς γῆς πανταχόθεν καὶ συναλαλαζόν 3 των. ἔνθα δὴ πολλῶν παραβόλως κινδυνευσάντων καὶ συχνῶν ἀναβάντων ἐπὶ τὰ τείχη συνίστατο καρτερὰ μάχη, τῶν μὲν ἔξωθεν βιαζομένων, τῶν δ᾽ ἐκ τῆς πόλεως ἀθρόων παραβοηθούντων. τέλος δὲ τῶν Ῥοδίων ἐκθύμως ἀγωνιζομένων οἱ μὲν ἔπεσον τῶν προσαναβάντων, οἱ δὲ κατατραυματισθέντες ἑάλωσαν, ἐν οἷς ἦσάν τινες καὶ τῶν ἐπιφανεστά 4 των ἡγεμόνων. τοιούτων δὲ γενομένων τοῖς ἔξωθεν

---

[1] ἐφ᾽ οὓς Fischer : ἐφ᾽ οὖ.

in order to throw the Rhodians into an agony of ^{305 B.C.} terror because of the many distractions.

87. After carrying on this kind of siege warfare for eight days, Demetrius shattered the engines of war upon the mole by means of his heavy ballistae and weakened the curtain of the cross-wall together with the towers themselves. Some of his soldiers also occupied a part of the fortifications along the harbour ; the Rhodians rallying their forces joined battle against these, and now that they outnumbered the enemy, they killed some and forced the rest to withdraw. The men of the city were aided by the ruggedness of the shore along the wall, for many large rocks lay close together beside the structure outside of the wall. Of the ships which had conveyed these soldiers no small number ran aground in their ignorance ; and the Rhodians at once, after stripping off the beaks, threw dry pitchy wood into the ships and burned them. While the Rhodians were so occupied, the soldiers of Demetrius sailing up on every side placed ladders against the walls and pressed on more strongly, and the troops who were attacking from the land also joined in the struggle from every side and raised the battle cry in unison. Then indeed, since many had recklessly risked their lives, and a good number had mounted the walls, a mighty battle arose, those on the outside trying to force their way in and those in the city coming to the defence with one accord. Finally, as the Rhodians contended furiously, some of the men who had mounted were thrown down and others were wounded and captured, among whom were some of their most distinguished leaders. Since such losses had befallen those who

---

² ἄγνοιαν Geer : ἀγωνίαν.

ἐλαττωμάτων ὁ μὲν Δημήτριος ἀπεκόμισε τὰς
μηχανὰς εἰς τὸν ἴδιον λιμένα καὶ τὰ πεπονηκότα
τῶν πλοίων καὶ μηχανῶν ἐπεσκεύασεν, οἱ δὲ Ῥόδιοι τοὺς μὲν τελευτήσαντας τῶν πολιτῶν ἔθαψαν,
τὰ δὲ ὅπλα τῶν πολεμίων καὶ τὰ ἀκροστόλια τοῖς
θεοῖς ἀνέθηκαν, τὰ δὲ διὰ τῶν πετροβόλων πεπτωκότα τῶν τειχῶν ἀνῳκοδόμουν.

88. Δημήτριος δὲ περὶ τὴν ἐπισκευὴν τῶν μηχανῶν καὶ τῶν πλοίων ἡμέρας ἑπτὰ γενόμενος καὶ
πάντα τὰ πρὸς τὴν πολιορκίαν παρασκευασάμενος
πάλιν ἐπέπλευσε τῷ λιμένι· πᾶσα γὰρ ἦν ἡ σπουδὴ
περὶ τὸ κρατῆσαι τούτου καὶ τῆς σιτοπομπείας
2 ἀποκλεῖσαι τοὺς κατὰ τὴν πόλιν. γενόμενος δ'
ἐντὸς βέλους τοῖς μὲν πυρφόροις πολλοῖς οὖσιν εἰς
τὰ διωρμισμένα¹ πλοῖα τῶν Ῥοδίων ἐνέβαλε, τοῖς
δὲ πετροβόλοις τὰ τείχη διέσεισε, τοῖς δ' ὀξυβελέσι τὰ φαινόμενα τῶν σωμάτων κατετίτρωσκε.
3 συνεχοῦς οὖν καὶ καταπληκτικῆς γενομένης τῆς
προσβολῆς οἱ μὲν παρὰ τοῖς Ῥοδίοις ναύκληροι
διαγωνιάσαντες περὶ τῶν πλοίων κατέσβεσαν τοὺς
πυρφόρους, οἱ δὲ πρυτάνεις κινδυνεύοντος ἁλῶναι τοῦ λιμένος παρεκάλεσαν τοὺς ἀρίστους τῶν
πολιτῶν τὸν ὑπὲρ τῆς κοινῆς σωτηρίας ὑπομεῖ-
4 ναι κίνδυνον. πολλῶν οὖν προθύμως ὑπακουόντων
τρεῖς ναῦς τὰς κρατίστας ἐπλήρωσαν ἐπιλέκτων
ἀνδρῶν, οἷς παρήγγειλαν πειρᾶσθαι τοῖς ἐμβόλοις
βυθίσαι τὰ πλοῖα τὰ τὰς μηχανὰς κομίζοντα τῶν
5 πολεμίων. οὗτοι μὲν οὖν, καίπερ πολλῶν ἐπ'
αὐτοὺς φερομένων βελῶν, ὠσάμενοι τὸ μὲν πρῶτον
τὸν σεσιδηρωμένον χάρακα διέσπασαν, τοῖς δὲ

fought from the outside, Demetrius withdrew his 305 B.C.
engines of war to his own harbour [1] and repaired the
ships and engines that had been damaged; and the
Rhodians buried those of their citizens who had
perished, dedicated to the gods the arms of the
enemy and the beaks of the ships, and rebuilt the
parts of the wall that had been overthrown by
the ballistae.

88. After Demetrius had spent seven days on the
repair of his engines and ships and had made all his
preparations for the siege, he again attacked the
harbour; for his whole effort centred upon capturing
this and shutting off the people of the city from their
grain supplies. When he was within range, with
the fire-arrows, of which he had many, he made an
attack on the ships of the Rhodians that lay at anchor,
with his ballistae he shook the walls, and with his
catapults he cut down any who showed themselves.
Then when the attack had become continuous and
terrifying, the Rhodian ship-captains, after a fierce
struggle to save their ships, put out the fire-arrows,
and the magistrates, since the harbour was in danger
of being taken, summoned the noblest citizens to
undergo the perils of war for the sake of the common
safety. When many responded with alacrity, they
manned the three staunchest ships with picked men,
whom they instructed to try to sink with their rams
the ships that carried the engines of the enemy.
These men, accordingly, pushed forward although missiles in large numbers were speeding against them;
and at first they broke through the iron studded
boom, and then by delivering repeated blows with

[1] Cp. chap. 83. 4.

---

[1] διωρμισμένα Fischer : διωρισμένα.

πλοίοις πολλὰς ἐμβολὰς δόντες καὶ θαλάττης αὐτὰ
πληρώσαντες δύο μὲν τῶν μηχανῶν κατέβαλον,
τῆς δὲ τρίτης ὑπὸ τῶν περὶ τὸν Δημήτριον εἰς
τοὐπίσω τοῖς ῥύμασιν ἑλκομένης οἱ μὲν Ῥόδιοι
θαρρήσαντες τοῖς κατωρθωμένοις θρασύτερον τοῦ
6 καθήκοντος προέπιπτον εἰς τὸν κίνδυνον. διὸ πολλῶν αὐτοῖς καὶ μεγάλων νεῶν περιχυθεισῶν καὶ τοῖς
ἐμβόλοις πολλὰ μέρη τῶν τοίχων ἀναρρηττουσῶν[1]
ὁ μὲν ναύαρχος Ἐξήκεστος καὶ ὁ τριήραρχος καὶ
τινες ἄλλοι κατατραυματισθέντες ἥλωσαν, τοῦ δ'
ἄλλου πλήθους ἐκκολυμβήσαντος καὶ διανηξαμένου
πρὸς τοὺς ἰδίους μία μὲν τῶν νεῶν ὑποχείριος
ἐγένετο τοῖς περὶ τὸν Δημήτριον, αἱ δ' ἄλλαι δι-
7 έφυγον τὸν κίνδυνον. τοιαύτης οὖν γενομένης τῆς
ναυμαχίας ὁ μὲν Δημήτριος ἄλλην μηχανὴν κατεσκεύασε τριπλασίαν τῷ ὕψει καὶ πλάτει τῆς πρότερον, προσάγοντος δ' αὐτὴν πρὸς τὸν λιμένα νότος
ἐκνεφίας ἐπιγενόμενος τὰ μὲν ὁρμοῦντα τῶν πλοίων
συνέκλυσε, τὴν δὲ μηχανὴν κατέβαλε. καθ' ὃν δὴ
χρόνον οἱ Ῥόδιοι τῷ καιρῷ δεξιῶς χρησάμενοι
πύλην ἀνοίξαντες ἐπέθεντο τοῖς τὸ χῶμα κατειλη-
8 φόσι. γενομένης δὲ μάχης ἐπὶ πολὺν χρόνον ἰσχυρᾶς καὶ τοῦ μὲν Δημητρίου διὰ τὸν χειμῶνα μὴ
δυναμένου βοηθῆσαι, τῶν δὲ Ῥοδίων ἐκ διαδοχῆς
ἀγωνιζομένων ἠναγκάσθησαν οἱ τοῦ βασιλέως ἀπο-
θέμενοι τὰ ὅπλα παραδοῦναι σφᾶς αὐτούς, ὄντες
9 σχεδὸν τετρακόσιοι. τούτων δὲ τῶν προτερημάτων
γενομένων τοῖς Ῥοδίοις κατέπλευσαν τῇ πόλει
σύμμαχοι παρὰ μὲν Κνωσσίων ἑκατὸν πεντήκοντα,
παρὰ δὲ Πτολεμαίου πλείους τῶν πεντακοσίων,

---

[1] ἀναρρηττουσῶν Dindorf: ἀναρρηττόντων RX, ἀνορυττόν-
των F.

their rams upon the ships and filling them with 305 b.c. water, they overthrew two of the engines; but when the third was drawn back with ropes by the men of Demetrius, the Rhodians, encouraged by their successes, pressed on into the battle more boldly than was prudent. And so, when many large ships crowded around them and the sides of their own ships had been shattered in many places by the rams, the admiral Execestus, the trierarch, and some others were disabled by wounds and captured; and as the rest of its crew jumped into the sea and swam to their own fellows, one of the ships came into the possession of Demetrius; but the other ships escaped from the battle. When the naval battle had turned out in this way, Demetrius constructed another machine three times the size of the former in height and width; but while he was bringing this up to the harbour, a violent storm from the south sprang up, which swept over the ships that were anchored and overthrew the engine. And at this very time the Rhodians, shrewdly availing themselves of the situation, opened a gate and sallied out upon those who had occupied the mole. A severe battle ensued lasting for a long time; and since Demetrius could not send reinforcements because of the storm, and the Rhodians, on the other hand, were fighting in relays, the king's men were forced to lay down their arms and surrender, in number about four hundred. After the Rhodians had gained these advantages there sailed in as allies for the city one hundred and fifty soldiers from the Cnossians and more than five hundred from Ptolemy,

ὧν ἦσάν τινες Ῥόδιοι μισθοφοροῦντες παρὰ τῷ βασιλεῖ.

Καὶ τὰ μὲν περὶ τὴν ἐν Ῥόδῳ πολιορκίαν ἐν τούτοις ἦν.

89. Κατὰ δὲ τὴν Σικελίαν Ἀγαθοκλῆς οὐ δυνάμενος διαλύσασθαι πρὸς τοὺς περὶ Δεινοκράτην φυγάδας ἀνέζευξεν ἐπ' αὐτοὺς μεθ' ἧς εἶχε δυνάμεως, νομίζων ἀναγκαῖον ὑπάρχειν αὐτῷ διακινδυνεύειν καὶ παραβάλλεσθαι περὶ τῶν ὅλων. συνηκολούθουν δ' αὐτῷ πεζοὶ μὲν οὐ πλείους τῶν 2 πεντακισχιλίων, ἱππεῖς δὲ εἰς ὀκτακοσίους. οἱ δὲ περὶ Δεινοκράτην φυγάδες ὁρῶντες τὴν τῶν πολεμίων ὁρμὴν ἄσμενοι κατήντησαν εἰς τὴν μάχην, ὄντες πολλαπλάσιοι· πεζοὶ μὲν γὰρ ὑπῆρχον πλείους τῶν δισμυρίων καὶ πεντακισχιλίων, ἱππεῖς δ' οὐκ ἐλάττους τρισχιλίων. ἀντιστρατοπεδευσάντων δ' αὐτῶν περὶ τὸ καλούμενον Τόργιον[1] καὶ μετὰ ταῦτα παραταξαμένων ἐπ' ὀλίγον μὲν χρόνον συνέστη καρτερὰ μάχη διὰ τὰς ἀμφοτέρων προθυμίας· μετὰ δὲ ταῦτα τῶν πρὸς τὸν Δεινοκράτην διαφερομένων τινές, ὄντες πλείους τῶν δισχιλίων, μετεβάλοντο πρὸς τὸν τύραννον καὶ τοῖς φυγάσιν αἴτιοι κατ- 3 έστησαν τῆς ἥττης. οἱ μὲν γὰρ μετ' Ἀγαθοκλέους ὄντες πολὺ μᾶλλον ἐθάρρησαν, οἱ δὲ Δεινοκράτει συναγωνιζόμενοι κατεπλάγησαν καὶ νομίσαντες πλείους εἶναι τοὺς ἀφισταμένους πρὸς φυγὴν ὥρμησαν. εἶθ' ὁ μὲν Ἀγαθοκλῆς διώξας αὐτοὺς μέχρι τινὸς καὶ τοῦ φονεύειν ἀποσχόμενος διεπέμψατο πρὸς τοὺς ἡττημένους, ἀξιῶν παύσασθαι μὲν τῆς

some of whom were Rhodians serving as mercenaries 305 B.C. in the king's army.

This was the state of the siege of Rhodes.[1]

89. In Sicily Agathocles,[2] since he had been unable to make terms with Deinocrates and the exiles, took the field against them with what forces he had, believing that it was necessary for him to fight a battle with them and stake everything on the result. Not more than five thousand foot soldiers followed him and horsemen to the number of eight hundred. Deinocrates and the exiles, when they saw the move made by the enemy, gladly came out to meet him in battle, being many times as strong ; for their foot soldiers came to more than twenty-five thousand and their cavalry to not less than three thousand. When the armies had encamped opposite each other near the place called Torgium,[3] and then were drawn up against each other in battle array, for a short time there was a stubborn battle because of the eagerness of both sides ; but then some of those who were at odds with Deinocrates, more than two thousand in number, went over to the tyrant and were responsible for the defeat of the exiles. For those who were with Agathocles gained much more confidence, and those who were fighting on the side of Deinocrates were dismayed and, overestimating the number of the deserters, broke into flight. Then Agathocles, after pursuing them for a certain distance and refraining from slaughter, sent envoys to the defeated and asked them to put an end to the quarrel and return

[1] Continued in chap. 91. [2] Continued from chap. 79.
[3] The exact position is unknown.

---

[1] Τόργιον Ortelius and Cluverius from Hesychius : Γόργιον RX, Γοργόνιον F.

διαφορᾶς, καταπορευθῆναι δ' εἰς τὰς πατρίδας·
εἰληφέναι γὰρ αὐτοὺς πεῖραν τοῦ μηδέποτ' ἂν δύνασθαι περιγενέσθαι τοὺς φυγάδας ἀγωνιζομένους
πρὸς αὐτόν, ὅτε καὶ νῦν πολλαπλασίους ὄντας
4 αὐτοὺς ἡττῆσθαι. τῶν δὲ φυγάδων οἱ μὲν ἱππεῖς
ἅπαντες ἀπὸ τῆς φυγῆς διεσώθησαν εἰς Ἄμβικας
χωρίον, τῶν δὲ πεζῶν ἔνιοι μὲν νυκτὸς ἐπιγενομένης διέδρασαν, οἱ δὲ πλείους καταλαβόμενοι
λόφον καὶ τὴν μὲν ἐκ τοῦ διαγωνίζεσθαι νίκην
ἀπελπίσαντες, ἐπιθυμοῦντες δὲ συγγενῶν καὶ
φίλων καὶ πατρίδος καὶ τῶν ἐν ταύτῃ καλῶν διελύ-
5 σαντο πρὸς Ἀγαθοκλέα. λαβόντων οὖν αὐτῶν πί-
στεις καὶ καταβάντων ἀπό τινος ἐρυμνοῦ λόφου τὰ
μὲν ὅπλα παρείλετο, τὴν δὲ δύναμιν περιστήσας
ἅπαντας κατηκόντισεν, ὄντας περὶ ἑπτακισχιλίους,
ὡς Τίμαιός φησιν, ὡς δ' ἔνιοι γράφουσιν, εἰς τετρα-
κισχιλίους· ἀεὶ γὰρ ὁ τύραννος οὗτος πίστεως μὲν
καὶ τῶν ὅρκων κατεφρόνει, τὴν δ' ἰδίαν ἰσχὺν οὐκ
ἐκ τῆς περὶ αὐτὸν δυνάμεως, ἀλλ' ἐκ τῆς τῶν ὑποτεταγμένων ἀσθενείας περιεποιεῖτο, πλεῖον δεδοικὼς
τοὺς συμμάχους ἢ τοὺς πολεμίους.

90. Τὴν δὲ ἀντιτεταγμένην δύναμιν οὕτω δια-
φθείρας προσεδέξατο τοὺς ὑπολελειμμένους τῶν φυγάδων καὶ πρὸς Δεινοκράτην διαλυθεὶς στρατηγὸν
αὐτὸν μέρους τῆς δυνάμεως ἀπέδειξε καὶ διετέλεσε
πιστεύων τὰ μέγιστα. θαυμάσειε δ' ἄν τις ἐν τούτοις τὸν Ἀγαθοκλέα, πῶς πρὸς ἅπαντας ὑπόπτως
ἔχων καὶ μηδέποτε μηδενὶ βεβαίως πιστεύσας πρὸς
μόνον Δεινοκράτην διετήρησε τὴν φιλίαν μέχρι τε-
2 λευτῆς. ὁ δὲ Δεινοκράτης προδοὺς τοὺς συμμάχους
τὸν μὲν Πασίφιλον ἐν τῇ Γέλᾳ συναρπάσας ἀπ-

to their native cities ; for, he said, they had found by 305 B.C.
experience that the exiles would never be able to
prevail in a battle with him, seeing that even on
this occasion, although they were many times more
numerous, they had been defeated. Of the exiles,
all the horsemen survived the flight and came safe
into Ambicae [1] ; but as for the foot soldiers, although
some escaped when night came on, most of them after
occupying a hill made terms with Agathocles, for
they had lost hope of victory by fighting and longed
for their relatives and friends and for their fatherland and its comforts. Now when they had received
pledges of good faith and had come down from the
hill-fort, such as it was, Agathocles took their arms ;
and then, stationing his army about them, he shot
them all down, their number being about seven thousand, as Timaeus says, but as some have written, about
four thousand. Indeed, this tyrant always scorned
faith and his oaths ; and he maintained his own
power, not by the strength of his armed forces but by
the weakness of his subjects, fearing his allies more
than his enemies.

90. When he had destroyed in this manner the
army that had been arrayed against him, Agathocles
received any exiles who survived and, making terms
with Deinocrates, appointed him general over part of
his army and continued to entrust the most important matters to him. In this connection one might
well wonder why Agathocles, who was suspicious of
everyone and never completely trusted anybody, continued his friendship toward Deinocrates alone until
death. But Deinocrates, after betraying his allies,
seized and slew Pasiphilus in Gela and handed the

[1] Or Ambycae. The place is unknown.

ἔκτεινεν, τὰ δὲ φρούρια καὶ τὰς πόλεις ἐνεχείρισεν
Ἀγαθοκλεῖ, διετῆ χρόνον ἀναλώσας εἰς τὴν τῶν
πολεμίων παράθεσιν.

3   Κατὰ δὲ τὴν Ἰταλίαν Ῥωμαῖοι μὲν Παιλιγνοὺς[1]
καταπολεμήσαντες τὴν χώραν ἀφείλοντο καί τισι
τῶν δοξάντων τὰ Ῥωμαίων πεφρονηκέναι μετέδω-
καν τῆς πολιτείας. μετὰ δὲ ταῦτα Σαμνιτῶν τὴν
Φαλερῖτιν πορθούντων ἀνέζευξαν ἐπ' αὐτοὺς οἱ
ὕπατοι καὶ γενομένης παρατάξεως προετέρησαν οἱ
4 Ῥωμαῖοι. σημείας μὲν οὖν εἷλον εἴκοσι, στρατιώτας δ' ἐζώγρησαν ὑπὲρ τοὺς δισχιλίους. τῶν δ'
ὑπάτων εὐθὺς ἑλόντων πόλιν Βῶλαν, Γέλλιος Γάιος
ὁ τῶν Σαμνιτῶν ἡγεμὼν ἐφάνη μετὰ στρατιωτῶν
ἑξακισχιλίων. γενομένης δὲ μάχης ἰσχυρᾶς αὐτός
τε ὁ Γέλλιος ἑάλω καὶ τῶν ἄλλων Σαμνιτῶν οἱ
πλεῖστοι μὲν κατεκόπησαν, τινὲς δὲ καὶ ζῶντες συν-
ελήφθησαν. οἱ δ' ὕπατοι τοιούτοις προτερήμασι
χρησάμενοι τῶν συμμαχίδων πόλεων τὰς ἁλούσας
ἀνεκτήσαντο Σώραν, Ἀρπίναν καὶ Σερεννίαν.

91.   Τοῦ δ' ἐνιαυσίου χρόνου διεληλυθότος Ἀθήνησι μὲν ἦρχε Φερεκλῆς, ἐν Ῥώμῃ δὲ τὴν ὑπατικὴν
ἀρχὴν διεδέξαντο Πόπλιος Σεμπρώνιος καὶ Πόπλιος
Σολπίκιος, ὀλυμπιὰς δ' ἤχθη παρὰ τοῖς Ἠλείοις
ἐνάτη πρὸς ταῖς ἑκατὸν δέκα, καθ' ἣν ἐνίκα στάδιον
Ἀνδρομένης Κορίνθιος. ἐπὶ δὲ τούτων Δημήτριος

---

[1] Παιλιγνοὺς Fischer in apparatus (cp. Ptolemaeus, *Geography*, 3. 1. 16. 55): Παλινίους RX, Παληνίους F.

---

[1] Continued in chap. 101.
[2] Continued from chap. 80. Cp. Livy, 9. 44.
[3] The Ager Falernus is in northern Campania, a little to
the west of the Ager Stellatinus where Livy places these
Samnite raids.

strongholds and the cities to Agathocles, spending 305 B.C.
two years in the delivery of the enemy.[1]

In Italy[2] the Romans defeated the Paeligni and
took their land, and to some of those who seemed
well disposed toward Rome, they granted citizenship.
Thereafter, since the Samnites were plundering Fa-
lernitis,[3] the consuls took the field against them, and
in the battle that followed the Romans were victorious. They took twenty standards and made prisoners
of more than two thousand soldiers. The consuls
at once took the city of Bola, but Gellius Gaius, the
leader of the Samnites, appeared with six thousand
soldiers. A hard fought battle took place in which
Gellius himself was made prisoner, and of the other
Samnites most were cut down but some were captured alive. The consuls, taking advantage of such
victories, recovered those allied cities that had been
captured : Sora, Harpina, and Serennia.[4]

91. When that year had passed, Pherecles became 304 B.C.
archon in Athens and in Rome Publius Sempronius
and Publius Sulpicius received the consulship[5] ; and
in Elis the Olympian Games were celebrated for the
one hundred and nineteenth time, at which celebration Andromenes of Corinth won the footrace. While

---

[4] Livy (9. 44) places three battles in this year, the first
indecisive, the other two decisive Roman victories with 21
standards captured in one and 26 in the other. According
to him Bovianum (not Bola, which is unknown) was captured
after the second battle (not between them), the Samnite
leader is named Statius Gellius (not Gellius Gaius), and the
three cities recovered are Sora, Arpinum, and Cesennia
(or Censennia). Diodorus returns to Italian affairs in chap.
101. 5.

[5] Pherecles was archon in 304/3 B.C. Livy, 9. 45. 1, gives
the consuls of 304 B.C. as P. Sulpicius Saverrio and P. Sempronius Sophus.

μὲν Ῥόδον πολιορκῶν, ἐπὶ ταῖς κατὰ θάλατταν προσβολαῖς ἀποτυγχάνων, ἀπὸ τῆς γῆς διέγνω τὰς 2 ἐπιθέσεις ποιεῖσθαι. παρασκευασάμενος οὖν ὕλης παντοίας πλῆθος κατεσκεύασε μηχανὴν τὴν καλουμένην ἑλέπολιν, ὑπεραίρουσαν πολὺ τῷ μεγέθει τῶν πρὸ αὐτῆς γενομένων. ἐσχαρίου γὰρ ὄντος τετραγώνου τὴν μὲν πλευρὰν ἑκάστην ὑπεστήσατο πηχῶν σχεδὸν πεντήκοντα, συμπεπηγυῖαν ἐκ τετραγώνων ξύλων σιδήρῳ δεδεμένων· τὴν δὲ ἀνὰ μέσον χώραν διέλαβε δοκοῖς ἀλλήλων ἀπεχούσαις ὡσανεὶ πῆχυν, ὅπως παράστασις ᾖ τοῖς προωθεῖν[1] τὴν μηχανὴν 3 μέλλουσιν. τὸ δὲ πᾶν βάρος ἦν ὑπότροχον, στερεοῖς καὶ μεγάλοις ὀκτὼ τροχοῖς ὑπειλημμένον· τὰ γὰρ πάχη τῶν ἀψίδων ὑπῆρχε πηχῶν δυεῖν, σεσιδηρωμένα λεπίσιν ἰσχυραῖς. πρὸς δὲ τὴν ἐκ πλαγίας μετάθεσιν[2] ἦσαν ἀντίστρεπτα πεπραγματευμένα, δι' ὧν ἡ πᾶσα μηχανὴ ῥᾳδίως παντοίαν ὑπελάμβανε 4 κίνησιν. ἐκ δὲ τῶν γωνιῶν ὑπῆρχον κίονες ἴσοι τῷ μήκει, βραχὺ λείποντες τῶν ἑκατὸν πηχῶν, οὕτως συννενευκότες εἰς ἀλλήλους ὡς τοῦ παντὸς κατασκευάσματος ὄντος ἐννεαστέγου τὴν μὲν πρώτην στέγην ὑπάρχειν ἀκαινῶν[3] τεσσαράκοντα τριῶν,

---

[1] προωθεῖν Reiske : παρωθεῖν.
[2] τὴν ἐκ πλαγίας μετάθεσιν Reiske : ταῖς ἐκ πλαγίας μεταθέσεσιν RX, ταῖς πλαγίαις μεταθέσεσιν F.
[3] ἀκαινῶν Fischer : κλινῶν.

---

[1] Continued from chap. 88. For the siege of Rhodes cp. Plutarch, *Demetrius*, 21–22.
[2] Literally, " taker of cities." Cp. the helepolis described in chap. 48. 2. According to Vitruvius, 10. 16. 4, this helepolis was built by Epimachus of Athens. Cp. Plutarch, *Demetrius*, 21. 1, and Athenaeus in Wescher, *Poliorcétique*, pp. 27 ff.
[3] About 75 feet. Tarn (*Hellenistic Military and Naval*

these held office, Demetrius,[1] who was besieging 304 B.C. Rhodes, failing in his assaults by sea, decided to make his attacks by land. Having provided therefore a large quantity of material of all kinds, he built an engine called the helepolis,[2] which far surpassed in size those which had been constructed before it. Each side of the square platform he made almost fifty cubits in length,[3] framed together from squared timber and fastened with iron ; the space within he divided by bars set about a cubit [4] from each other so that there might be standing space for those who were to push the machine forward. The whole structure was movable, mounted on eight great solid wheels ; the width of their rims was two cubits and these were overlaid with heavy iron plates. To permit motion to the side, pivots had been constructed,[5] by means of which the whole device was easily moved in any direction. From each corner there extended upward beams equal in length and little short of a hundred cubits long, inclining toward each other in such a way that, the whole structure being nine storeys high, the first storey had an area of forty-three hundred square feet and the topmost

Developments, pp. 15-16) suggests that there was a shorter Macedonian cubit of about 13 inches. This would reduce all the figures given in the notes by about 30 per cent, which seems probable in most cases, but impossible in the spacing of the crossbeams, see next note.

[4] About 18 inches. Probably these crossbars or beams were below the platform, which would protect the men who stood on the ground and moved the tower by pushing on the bars. It is possible, however, that the " platform " was simply an open frame of cross timbers, between which the men stood.

[5] *i.e.* the axles were connected to the frame by vertical pivots, castor fashion.

5 τὴν δ' ἀνωτάτω ἐννέα. τὰς δὲ τρεῖς ἐπιφανεῖς[1]
πλευρὰς τῆς μηχανῆς ἔξωθεν συνεκάλυψε λεπίσι
σιδηραῖς καθηλωμέναις, ἵνα μηδὲν ὑπὸ τῶν πυρφόρων βλάπτηται. θυρίδας δ' εἶχον αἱ στέγαι κατὰ
πρόσωπον, τοῖς μεγέθεσι καὶ τοῖς σχήμασι πρὸς
τὰς ἰδιότητας τῶν μελλόντων ἀφίεσθαι βελῶν ἁρμο-
6 ζούσας. αὗται δὲ εἶχον καλύμματα διὰ μηχανῆς
ἀνασπώμενα, δι' ὧν ἀσφάλειαν ἐλάμβανον οἱ κατὰ
τὰς στέγας περὶ τὴν ἄφεσιν τῶν βελῶν ἀναστρεφό-
μενοι· ἦσαν μὲν γὰρ ἐκ βυρσῶν περιερραμμένα,
πλήρη δὲ ἐρίων, εἰς τὸ τῇ πληγῇ[2] ἐνδιδόναι τῶν
7 λιθοβόλων. ἑκάστη δὲ τῶν στεγῶν εἶχε δύο κλίμακας πλατείας, ὧν τῇ μὲν πρὸς τὴν ἀνακομιδὴν
τῶν χρησίμων, τῇ δὲ πρὸς τὴν κατάβασιν ἐχρῶντο
πρὸς τὸ χωρὶς θορύβου πᾶν ὑπηρετεῖσθαι. οἱ δὲ
μέλλοντες κινήσειν τὴν μηχανὴν ἐξελέχθησαν ἐξ
ἁπάσης τῆς δυνάμεως οἱ ταῖς ῥώμαις διαφέροντες
8 ἄνδρες τρισχίλιοι καὶ τετρακόσιοι· τούτων δ' οἱ
μὲν ἐντὸς ἀποληφθέντες, οἱ δ' ἐκ τῶν ὄπισθεν
μερῶν παριστάμενοι προεώθουν,[3] πολλὰ τῆς τέχνης
συνεργούσης εἰς τὴν κίνησιν. κατεσκεύασε δὲ καὶ
χελώνας τὰς μὲν χωστρίδας, τὰς δὲ κριοφόρους καὶ
στοὰς δι' ὧν ἔμελλον οἱ τοῖς ἔργοις προσιόντες
ἐλεύσεσθαι καὶ πάλιν ἐπιστρέψειν ἀσφαλῶς. τοῖς
δ' ἐκ τῶν νεῶν πληρώμασιν ἀνεκάθαρε[4] τὸν τόπον
ἐπὶ σταδίους τέτταρας, δι' ὧν ἔμελλεν προσάξειν

---

[1] ἐπιφανεῖς added by Fischer, cp. Pol. 8. 4. 8.
[2] τῇ πληγῇ Dindorf: τὴν πληγὴν.
[3] προεώθουν Wesseling: προσώθουν.
[4] ἀνεκάθαρε Fischer: ἀνεκάθαιρε RX, ἀνεκάθηρε F.

---

[1] The tower then would be nearly 150 feet high, about
30 feet square at the top and 65½ feet square at the base. If

384

storey of nine hundred.[1] The three exposed sides 304 B.C
of the machine he covered externally with iron plates
nailed on so that it should receive no injury from
fire carriers. On each storey there were ports on
the front, in size and shape fitted to the individual
characteristics of the missiles that were to be shot
forth. These ports had shutters, which were lifted
by a mechanical device and which secured the safety
of the men on the platforms who were busy serving
the artillery ; for the shutters were of hides stitched
together and were filled with wool so that they would
yield to the blows of the stones from the ballistae.
Each of the storeys had two wide stairways, one of
which they used for bringing up what was needed
and the other for descending, in order that all might
be taken care of without confusion. Those who were
to move the machine were selected from the whole
army, three thousand four hundred [2] men excelling
in strength ; some of them were enclosed within the
machine while others were stationed in its rear, and
they pushed it forward, the skilful design aiding
greatly in its motion. He also constructed penthouses—some to protect the men who were filling
the moat, others to carry rams—and covered passages
through which those who were going to their labours
might go and return safely. Using the crews of the
ships, he cleared a space four stades wide through
which he planned to advance the siege engines he

the platform was 75 feet square, a ledge about 5 feet wide
would be left about the base of the tower.
  [2] Either they worked in relays or this figure includes all
the men employed for moving the various machines, towers,
and penthouses. Allowing five square feet to the man, a
minimum if they were to work effectively, 3400 men would
occupy 17,000 sq. ft., three times the area of the helopolis.

τὰς κατασκευασθείσας μηχανάς, ὥστε γίνεσθαι τὸ
ἔργον ἐπὶ μῆκος μεσοπυργίων ἓξ καὶ πύργων ἑπτά.
τὸ δ' ἠθροισμένον πλῆθος τῶν τεχνιτῶν καὶ τῶν
τοῖς ἔργοις προσιόντων οὐ πολὺ ἐλείπετο τῶν τρισμυρίων.

92. Διόπερ τῇ πολυχειρίᾳ τάχιον τῆς προσδοκίας
ἁπάντων ἐπιτελουμένων φοβερὸς ἦν ὁ Δημήτριος
τοῖς Ῥοδίοις. οὐ μόνον γὰρ τὰ μεγέθη τῶν μηχανῶν καὶ τὸ πλῆθος τῆς ἠθροισμένης δυνάμεως
ἐξέπληττεν αὐτούς, ἀλλὰ καὶ τὸ τοῦ βασιλέως βίαιον
2 καὶ φιλότεχνον ἐν ταῖς πολιορκίαις. εὐμήχανος γὰρ
ὢν καθ' ὑπερβολὴν ἐν ταῖς ἐπινοίαις καὶ πολλὰ
παρὰ τὴν τῶν ἀρχιτεκτόνων τέχνην παρευρίσκων
ὠνομάσθη μὲν πολιορκητής, τὴν δ' ἐν ταῖς προσβολαῖς ὑπεροχὴν καὶ βίαν τοιαύτην εἶχεν ὥστε
δόξαι μηδὲν οὕτως ὀχυρὸν εἶναι τεῖχος ὃ δύναιτ'
ἂν τὴν ἀπ' ἐκείνου τοῖς πολιορκουμένοις ἀσφά-
3 λειαν παρέχεσθαι. ἦν δὲ καὶ κατὰ τὸ μέγεθος τοῦ
σώματος καὶ κατὰ τὸ κάλλος ἡρωικὸν ἀποφαίνων
ἀξίωμα, ὥστε καὶ τοὺς ἀφικνουμένους τῶν ξένων
θεωροῦντας εὐπρέπειαν κεκοσμημένην ὑπεροχῇ βα-
σιλικῇ θαυμάζειν καὶ παρακολουθεῖν ἐν ταῖς ἐξόδοις
4 ἕνεκεν τῆς θέας. ἐπὶ δὲ τούτοις ὑπῆρχε καὶ τῇ
ψυχῇ μετέωρος καὶ μεγαλοπρεπὴς καὶ καταφρονῶν
οὐ τῶν πολλῶν μόνον, ἀλλὰ καὶ τῶν ἐν ταῖς δυ-
ναστείαις ὄντων, καὶ τὸ πάντων ἰδιώτατον, κατὰ
μὲν τὴν εἰρήνην ἐν μέθαις διέτριβε καὶ συμποσίοις
ἔχουσιν ὀρχήσεις καὶ κώμους καὶ τὸ σύνολον ἐζήλου
τὴν μυθολογουμένην ποτὲ γενέσθαι κατ' ἀνθρώπους
τοῦ Διονύσου διάθεσιν, κατὰ δὲ τοὺς πολέμους
ἐνεργὸς ἦν καὶ νήφων, ὥστε παρὰ πάντας τοὺς
ἐργατευομένους ἐναγώνιον παρέχεσθαι τὸ σῶμα καὶ

had prepared, wide enough so that it covered a front 304 B.C. of six curtains and seven towers. The number of craftsmen and labourers collected was not much less than thirty thousand.

92. As everything, therefore, because of the many hands was finished sooner than was expected, Demetrius was regarded with alarm by the Rhodians; for not only did the size of the siege engines and the number of the army which had been gathered stun them, but also the king's energy and ingenuity in conducting sieges. For, being exceedingly ready in invention and devising many things beyond the art of the master builders, he was called Poliorcetes [1]; and he displayed such superiority and force in his attacks that it seemed that no wall was strong enough to furnish safety from him for the besieged. Both in stature and in beauty he displayed the dignity of a hero, so that even those strangers who had come from a distance, when they beheld his comeliness arrayed in royal splendour, marvelled at him and followed him as he went abroad in order to gaze at him. Furthermore, he was haughty in spirit and proud and looked down not only upon common men but also upon those of royal estate; and what was most peculiar to him, in time of peace he devoted his time to winebibbing and to drinking bouts accompanied by dancing and revels, and in general he emulated the conduct said by mythology to have been that of Dionysus among men; but in his wars he was active and sober, so that beyond all others who practised this profession he devoted both body

[1] *i.e.* "stormer of cities." Cp. Plutarch, *Demetrius*, 2-4, for his character.

5 τὴν ψυχήν. ἐπὶ γὰρ τούτου βέλη τὰ μέγιστα συνετελέσθη καὶ μηχαναὶ παντοῖαι πολὺ τὰς παρὰ τοῖς ἄλλοις γενομένας ὑπεραίρουσαι· καὶ σκάφη δὲ μέγιστα καθείλκυσεν οὗτος μετὰ τὴν πολιορκίαν ταύτην καὶ τὴν τοῦ πατρὸς τελευτήν.

93. Οἱ δὲ Ῥόδιοι θεωροῦντες τὴν προκοπὴν τῶν παρὰ τοῖς πολεμίοις ἔργων κατεσκεύασαν ἐντὸς ἕτερον τεῖχος παράλληλον τῷ μέλλοντι πονεῖν κατὰ τὰς προσβολάς. ἐχρῶντο δὲ λίθοις καθαιροῦντες τοῦ θεάτρου τὸν περίβολον καὶ τὰς πλησίον οἰκίας, ἔτι δὲ τῶν ἱερῶν ἔνια, τοῖς θεοῖς εὐξάμενοι καλ-
2 λίονα κατασκευάσειν σωθείσης τῆς πόλεως. ἐξ-έπεμψαν δὲ καὶ τῶν νεῶν ἐννέα, διακελευσάμενοι τοὺς ἀφηγουμένους πανταχῇ πλεῖν καὶ παραδόξως ἐπιφαινομένους ἃ μὲν βυθίζειν τῶν ἁλισκομένων πλοίων, ἃ δὲ κατάγειν εἰς τὴν πόλιν. ἐκπλευσάν-των δὲ τούτων καὶ τριχῇ διαιρεθέντων Δαμόφιλος μὲν ἔχων ναῦς τὰς καλουμένας παρὰ Ῥοδίοις φυλα-κίδας ἔπλευσεν εἰς Κάρπαθον καὶ πολλὰ μὲν πλοῖα τῶν Δημητρίου καταλαβών, ἃ μὲν τοῖς ἐμβόλοις θραύων κατεπόντιζεν, ἃ δ' ἐπὶ τὸν αἰγιαλὸν κομίζων ἐνεπύριζεν, ἐκλεγόμενος τῶν σωμάτων τὰ χρη-σιμώτατα, οὐκ ὀλίγα δὲ τῶν κομιζόντων τοὺς ἐκ τῆς νήσου καρποὺς κατήγαγεν εἰς τὴν πατρίδα.
3 Μενέδημος δὲ τριῶν ἀφηγούμενος τριημιολιῶν πλεύ-σας τῆς Λυκίας ἐπὶ τὰ Πάταρα καὶ καταλαβὼν ὁρμοῦσαν ναῦν τοῦ πληρώματος ἐπὶ γῆς ὄντος ἐνεπύρισε τὸ σκάφος, πολλὰ δὲ πλοῖα τῶν κομι-ζόντων τὴν ἀγορὰν ἐπὶ τὸ στρατόπεδον ὑποχείρια

and mind to the task. For it was in his time that the 304 B.C.
greatest weapons were perfected and engines of all
kinds far surpassing those that had existed among
others ; and this man launched the greatest ships
after this siege [1] and after the death of his father.

93. When the Rhodians saw the progress of the
enemy's siege works, they built a second wall inside
parallel to the one that was on the point of failing
under the attacks. They used stones obtained by
tearing down the theatre's outer wall and the adjacent
houses, and also some of the temples, vowing to the
gods that they would build finer ones when the city
had been saved. They also sent out nine of their
ships, giving the commanders orders to sail in every
direction and, appearing unexpectedly, to sink some
of the ships they intercepted and bring others to the
city. After these had sailed out and had been
divided into three groups, Damophilus, who had
ships of the kind called by the Rhodians " guard-
ships," sailed to Carpathos [2] ; and finding there many
of Demetrius' ships, he sank some, shattering them
with his rams, and some he beached and burnt after
selecting the most useful men from their crews, and
not a few of those that were transporting the grain
from the island, he brought back to Rhodes. Mene-
demus, who commanded three light undecked ships,[3]
sailed to Patara in Lycia ; and finding at anchor
there a ship whose crew was on shore, he set the hull
on fire ; and he took many of the freighters that were
carrying provisions to the army and dispatched them

---

[1] Cp. Plutarch, *Demetrius*, 31. 1, 32. 2, 43. 3-5.
[2] An island between Rhodes and Crete.
[3] Literally, three " one and a halves," perhaps ships with
one and one half banks of oars ; or more probably, with half
the oars manned by two men, half by one.

4 λαβὼν ἐξαπέστειλεν εἰς τὴν Ῥόδον. εἷλε δὲ καὶ
τετρήρη πλέουσαν μὲν ἐκ Κιλικίας, ἔχουσαν δ'
ἐσθῆτα βασιλικὴν καὶ τὴν ἄλλην ἀποσκευὴν ἣν ἡ
γυνὴ Δημητρίου Φίλα παρασκευασαμένη φιλοτιμό-
τερον ἀπεστάλκει τἀνδρί. τὸν μὲν οὖν ἱματισμὸν
ἀπέστειλεν εἰς Αἴγυπτον, οὐσῶν τῶν στολῶν ἁλουρ-
γῶν καὶ βασιλεῖ φορεῖν πρεπουσῶν, τὴν δὲ ναῦν
ἐνεώλκησεν καὶ τοὺς ναύτας ἀπέδοτο τούς τ' ἐκ τῆς
τετρήρους καὶ τοὺς ἐκ τῶν ἄλλων πλοίων τῶν
5 ἁλόντων. τῶν δ' ὑπολοίπων νεῶν τριῶν Ἀμύντας
ἡγούμενος ἔπλευσεν ἐπὶ νήσων καὶ πολλοῖς πλοίοις
περιτυχὼν κομίζουσι τὰ πρὸς τὰς μηχανὰς ἁρμό-
ζοντα τοῖς πολεμίοις ἃ μὲν αὐτῶν κατέδυσεν, ἃ δὲ
κατήγαγεν εἰς τὴν πόλιν, ἐν οἷς ἑάλωσαν καὶ
τεχνῖται τῶν ἀξιολόγων καὶ πρὸς βέλη καὶ καταπέλτας ἐμπειρίᾳ διαφέροντες ἕνδεκα.

6 Μετὰ δὲ ταῦτα ἐκκλησίας συναχθείσης συνεβού-
λευόν τινες τὰς εἰκόνας τὰς Ἀντιγόνου καὶ Δημητρίου κατασπάσαι, δεινὸν εἶναι λέγοντες ἐν ἴσῳ
τιμᾶσθαι τοὺς πολιορκοῦντας τοῖς εὐεργέταις· ἐφ'
οἷς ὁ δῆμος ἀγανακτήσας τούτοις μὲν ὡς ἁμαρ-
τάνουσιν ἐπετίμησεν, τῶν δὲ περὶ Ἀντίγονον τιμῶν
οὐδεμίαν μετεκίνησεν, καλῶς πρός τε δόξαν[1] καὶ τὸ
7 συμφέρον βουλευσάμενος. ἥ τε γὰρ μεγαλοψυχία
καὶ τὸ βέβαιον τῆς ἐν δημοκρατίᾳ κρίσεως παρὰ
μὲν τοῖς ἄλλοις ἐπαίνων ἐτύγχανε, παρὰ δὲ τοῖς
πολιορκοῦσι μεταμελείας· τὰς γὰρ κατὰ τὴν Ἑλλάδα πόλεις οὐδεμίαν ἐνδεδειγμένας εὔνοιαν εἰς
τοὺς εὐεργέτας ἐλευθεροῦντες τὴν διὰ τῆς πείρας
φανεῖσαν βεβαιοτάτην εἰς ἀμοιβὴν χάριτος ἐφαί-

[1] πρός τε δόξαν Reiske, πρὸς τὴν δόξαν Wesseling : πρὸς τὸ
δόξαν.

to Rhodes. He also captured a quadrireme that was 304 B.C. sailing from Cilicia and had on board royal robes and the rest of the outfit that Demetrius' wife Phila had with great pains made ready and sent off for her husband.[1] The clothing Damophilus sent to Egypt since the garments were purple and proper for a king to wear ; but the ship he hauled up on land, and he sold the sailors, both those from the quadrireme and those from the other captured ships. Amyntas, who was in command of the three remaining ships, made for islands where he fell in with many freighters carrying to the enemy materials useful for the engines of war ; he sank some of these and some he brought to the city. On these ships were also captured eleven famous engineers, man of outstanding skill in making missiles and catapults.

Thereafter, when an assembly had been convened, some advised that the statues of Antigonus and Demetrius should be pulled down, saying that it was absurd to honour equally their besiegers and their benefactors. At this the people were angry and censured these men as erring, and they altered none of the honours awarded to Antigonus, having made a wise decision with a view both to fame and to self interest. For the magnanimity and the soundness of this action in a democracy won plaudits from all others and repentance from the besiegers ; for while the latter were setting free the cities throughout Greece, which had displayed no goodwill at all toward their benefactors, they were manifestly trying to enslave the city that in practice showed itself most

[1] Cp. chap. 53.

νοντο καταδουλούμενοι· πρός τε τὸ παράδοξον τῆς
τύχης, εἰ συμβαίη τὴν πόλιν ἁλῶναι, κατελείπετ'
αὐτοῖς πρὸς παραίτησιν τῆς τηρηθείσης ὑπ' αὐτῶν
φιλίας ἀνάμνησις. ταῦτα μὲν οὖν τοῖς Ῥοδίοις
ἐπράχθη συνετῶς.

94. Δημητρίου δὲ διὰ τῶν μεταλλέων ὑπορύ-
ξαντος τὸ τεῖχος τῶν αὐτομόλων τις ἐμήνυσε τοῖς
πολιορκουμένοις ὡς οἱ ταῖς ὑπονομαῖς χρώμενοι
2 σχεδὸν ἐντός εἰσι τοῦ τείχους. διόπερ οἱ Ῥόδιοι
τάφρον ὀρύξαντες βαθεῖαν, παράλληλον τῷ δοκοῦντι
πεσεῖσθαι τείχει, ταχὺ καὶ αὐτοὶ ταῖς μεταλλείαις
χρώμενοι συνῆψαν ὑπὸ γῆν τοῖς ἐναντίοις καὶ δι-
3 εκώλυσαν τῆς εἰς τοὔμπροσθεν πορείας. τῶν δὲ
διορυγμάτων παρ' ἀμφοτέροις τηρουμένων ἐπεχεί-
ρησάν τινες τῶν παρὰ τοῦ Δημητρίου διαφθείρειν
χρήμασι τὸν τεταγμένον ἐπὶ τῆς φυλακῆς ὑπὸ τῶν
Ῥοδίων Ἀθηναγόραν· οὗτος δ' ἦν Μιλήσιος μὲν τὸ
γένος, ὑπὸ Πτολεμαίου δ' ἐξαπεσταλμένος ἡγεμὼν
4 τῶν μισθοφόρων. ἐπαγγειλάμενος δὲ προδώσειν
συνετάξαθ' ἡμέραν καθ' ἣν ἔδει παρὰ Δημητρίου
πεμφθῆναί τινα τῶν ἀξιολόγων ἡγεμόνων τὸν νυκτὸς ἀναβησόμενον διὰ τοῦ ὀρύγματος εἰς τὴν
πόλιν, ὅπως κατασκέψηται τὸν τόπον τὸν μέλλοντα
5 δέξασθαι τοὺς στρατιώτας. εἰς ἐλπίδας δὲ μεγάλας
ἀγαγὼν τοὺς περὶ Δημήτριον ἐμήνυσε τῇ βουλῇ·
καὶ πέμψαντος τοῦ βασιλέως τῶν περὶ αὐτὸν φίλων
Ἀλέξανδρον τὸν Μακεδόνα τοῦτον μὲν ἀναβάντα
διὰ τῆς διώρυχος συνέλαβον οἱ Ῥόδιοι, τὸν δ'
Ἀθηναγόραν ἐστεφάνωσαν χρυσῷ στεφάνῳ καὶ δωρεὰν ἔδωκαν ἀργυρίου τάλαντα πέντε, σπεύδοντες
καὶ τῶν ἄλλων μισθοφόρων καὶ ξένων ἐκκαλεῖσθαι
τὴν πρὸς τὸν δῆμον εὔνοιαν.

constant in repaying favours; and as protection against the sudden shift of fortune if the war should result in the capture of Rhodes, the Rhodians retained as a means of gaining mercy the memory of the friendship that they had preserved. These things, then, were done prudently by the Rhodians.

94. When Demetrius had undermined the wall by using his sappers, one of the deserters informed the besieged that those who were working underground were almost within the walls. Therefore the Rhodians by digging a deep trench parallel to the wall which was expected to collapse and by quickly undertaking mining operations themselves, made contact with their opponents underground and prevented them from advancing farther. Now the mines were closely watched by both sides, and some of Demetrius' men tried to bribe Athenagoras, who had been given command of the guard by the Rhodians. This man was a Milesian by descent, sent by Ptolemy as commander of the mercenaries.[1] Promising to turn traitor he set a day on which one of the ranking leaders should be sent from Demetrius to go by night through the mine up into the city in order to inspect the position where the soldiers would assemble. But after leading Demetrius on to great hopes, he disclosed the matter to the council; and when the king sent one of his friends, Alexander the Macedonian, the Rhodians captured him as he came up through the mine. They crowned Athenagoras with a golden crown and gave him a gift of five talents of silver, their object being to stimulate loyalty to the city on the part of the other men who were mercenaries and foreigners.

[1] Cp. chap. 88. 9.

95. Δημήτριος δὲ τῶν τε μηχανῶν αὐτῷ τέλος
ἐχουσῶν καὶ τοῦ πρὸς τὸ τεῖχος τόπου παντὸς
ἀνακαθαρθέντος τὴν μὲν ἑλέπολιν μέσην ἔστησε, τὰς
δὲ χωστρίδας χελώνας ἐπιδιεῖλεν, οὔσας¹ ὀκτώ·
κατέστησεν δ' εἰς ἑκάτερον μέρος τῆς μηχανῆς
τέτταρας καὶ τούτων ἑκάστῃ συνῆψεν στοὰν μίαν
εἰς τὸ δύνασθαι μετ' ἀσφαλείας ἐπιτελεῖν τὸ προσ-
ταττόμενον τοὺς εἰσιόντας τε καὶ πάλιν ἐξιόντας,
κριοφόρους δὲ δύο πολλαπλασίας τοῖς μεγέθεσιν·
εἶχε γὰρ ἑκάτερα δοκὸν² πηχῶν ἑκατὸν εἴκοσι,
σεσιδηρωμένην καὶ τὴν ἐμβολὴν ἔχουσαν παραπλησίαν νεὼς ἐμβόλῳ, καὶ προωθουμένην μὲν εὐκινή-
τως, ὑπότροχον δὲ καὶ τὴν ἐναγώνιον ἐνέργειαν
λαμβάνουσαν δι' ἀνδρῶν οὐκ ἐλαττόνων ἢ χιλίων.
2 μέλλων δὲ προσάγειν τὰς μηχανὰς τοῖς τείχεσι τοὺς
μὲν πετροβόλους καὶ τοὺς ὀξυβελεῖς παρήνεγκε τῆς
ἑλεπόλεως εἰς ἑκάστην στέγην τοὺς ἁρμόζοντας,
3 ἐπὶ δὲ τοὺς λιμένας καὶ τοὺς πλησίον τόπους
ἀπέστειλε τὴν ναυτικὴν δύναμιν, πρὸς δὲ τὸ λοιπὸν
τεῖχος τὸ δυνάμενον προσβολὰς δέξασθαι τὸ πεζὸν
4 στρατόπεδον ἐπιδιεῖλεν. ἔπειτα δὲ πρὸς ἓν παρακέλευσμα καὶ σημεῖον πάντων συναλαλαξάντων
πανταχόθεν τῇ πόλει προσβολὰς ἐποιεῖτο. δια-
σείοντος δ' αὐτοῦ τοῖς κριοῖς καὶ τοῖς πετροβόλοις
τὰ τείχη παρεγενήθησαν Κνιδίων πρέσβεις, ἀξιοῦντες ἐπισχεῖν καὶ πείσειν ἐπαγγελλόμενοι τοὺς
Ῥοδίους δέχεσθαι τὰ δυνατώτατα τῶν προσ-
5 ταγμάτων. ἀνέντος δὲ τοῦ βασιλέως καὶ τῶν

---

¹ εἰς after οὔσας omitted by Hertlein.
² ἑκατέρα δοκὸν Reiske : ἑκατέραν.

95. Demetrius, when his engines of war were completed and all the space before the walls was cleared,
stationed the helepolis in the centre, and assigned
positions to the penthouses, eight in number, which
were to protect the sappers. He placed four of these
on each side of the helepolis and connected with each
of them one covered passage so that the men who
were going in and out might accomplish their assigned
tasks in safety ; and he brought up also two enormous
penthouses in which battering rams were mounted.
For each shed held a ram with a length of one hundred
and twenty cubits, sheathed with iron and striking a
blow like that of a ship's ram ; and the ram was moved
with ease, being mounted on wheels and receiving
its motive power in battle from not less than a thousand men.[1] When he was ready to advance the
engines against the walls, he placed on each storey
of the helepolis ballistae and catapults of appropriate
size,[2] stationed his fleet in position to attack the
harbours and the adjacent areas, and distributed his
infantry along such parts of the wall as could be
attacked. Then, when all at a single command and
signal had raised the battle cry together, he launched
attacks on the city from every side. While he was
shaking the walls with the rams and the ballistae,
Cnidian envoys arrived, asking him to withhold his
attack and promising to persuade the Rhodians to
accept the most feasible of his demands. The king
broke off the attack, and the envoys carried on

[1] A ram 180 feet long would probably buckle in use in
spite of the iron reinforcement ; but see the footnote on chap.
91. 2 for the possibility that the cubit used here is shorter
than the Attic standard. Cp. the rams used by the Romans
before Carthage in 149 B.C., Appian, *Punic Wars*, 98.

[2] Cp. chap. 48. 3.

πρέσβεων δεῦρο κἀκεῖσε πολλὰ διαλεχθέντων πέρας
οὐ δυναμένων συμφωνῆσαι πάλιν ἐνηργεῖτο τὰ τῆς
πολιορκίας. καὶ Δημήτριος μὲν κατέβαλε τὸν
στερεώτατον τῶν πύργων, ᾠκοδομημένον ἐκ λίθων
τετραπέδων, καὶ μεσοπύργιον ὅλον διέσεισεν, ὥστε
μὴ δύνασθαι τοὺς ἐν τῇ πόλει πάροδον ἔχειν ἐπὶ
τὰς ἐπάλξεις κατὰ τοῦτον τὸν τόπον.

96. Ἐν δὲ ταῖς αὐταῖς ἡμέραις Πτολεμαῖος ὁ
βασιλεὺς ἀπέστειλε τοῖς Ῥοδίοις πλοίων πλῆθος
τῶν τὴν ἀγορὰν κομιζόντων, ἐν οἷς ἦσαν σίτου
τριάκοντα μυριάδες ἀρταβῶν σὺν τοῖς ὀσπρίοις.
2 προσφερομένων δ' αὐτῶν πρὸς τὴν πόλιν ἐπεχείρησε
Δημήτριος ἀποστέλλειν σκάφη τὰ κατάξοντα πρὸς
τὴν αὑτοῦ στρατοπεδείαν. φοροῦ δὲ πνεύματος
αὐτοῖς ἐπιγενομένου ταῦτα μὲν πλήρεσι τοῖς ἱστίοις
φερόμενα κατηνέχθη πρὸς τοὺς οἰκείους λιμένας, οἱ
δ' ὑπὸ Δημητρίου πεμφθέντες ἐπανῆλθον ἄπρακτοι.
3 ἔπεμψε δὲ τοῖς Ῥοδίοις καὶ Κάσανδρος κριθῶν
μεδίμνους μυρίους καὶ Λυσίμαχος πυρῶν μεδίμνους
τετρακισμυρίους καὶ κριθῶν τοὺς ἴσους. τηλικαύ-
της οὖν χορηγίας τοῖς κατὰ τὴν πόλιν γενομένης
ἤδη κάμνοντες ταῖς ψυχαῖς οἱ πολιορκούμενοι πάλιν
ἀνεθάρρησαν καὶ κρίναντες συμφέρειν ἐπιθέσθαι ταῖς
μηχαναῖς τῶν πολεμίων πυρφόρων τε πλῆθος παρ-
εσκευάσαντο καὶ τοὺς πετροβόλους καὶ τοὺς ὀξυ-
4 βελεῖς ἔστησαν ἅπαντας ἐπὶ τοῦ τείχους. νυκτὸς
δ' ἐπιγενομένης περὶ δευτέραν φυλακὴν ἄφνω τοῖς
μὲν πυρφόροις συνεχῶς τὴν ἑλέπολιν ἔβαλλον,[1] τοῖς
δ' ἄλλοις βέλεσι παντοίοις χρώμενοι τοὺς ἐκεῖ

---

[1] τὴν ἑλέπολιν ἔβαλλον Reiske : τὴν φυλακὴν ἔβαλον.

---

[1] This Egyptian measure, like the Greek medimnus (the

negotiations back and forth at great length ; but in _{304 B.C.} the end they were not able to reach any agreement, and the siege was actively resumed. Demetrius also overthrew the strongest of the towers, which was built of squared stones, and shattered the entire curtain, so that the forces in the city were not able to maintain a thoroughfare on the battlements at this point.

96. At this same period King Ptolemy dispatched to the Rhodians a large number of supply ships in which were three hundred thousand measures [1] of grain and legumes. While these ships were on their way to the city, Demetrius attempted to dispatch ships to bring them to his own camp. But a wind favourable to the Egyptians sprang up, and they were carried along with full sails and brought into the friendly harbours, but those sent out by Demetrius returned with their mission unaccomplished. Cassander also sent to the Rhodians ten thousand measures of barley, and Lysimachus sent them forty thousand measures of wheat and the same amount of barley. Consequently, when those in the city obtained such large supplies, the besieged, who were already disheartened, regained their courage. Deciding that it would be advantageous to attack the siege engines of the enemy, they made ready a large supply of fire-bearing missiles and placed all their ballistae and catapults upon the wall. When night had fallen, at about the second watch, they suddenly began to strike the helepolis with an unremitting shower of the fire missiles, and by using other missiles of all kinds, they shot down any who rushed to the

measure referred to below), was somewhat more than a bushel.

5 συντρέχοντας κατετίτρωσκον. οἱ δὲ περὶ τὸν
Δημήτριον, ἀνελπίστου τῆς ἐπιθέσεως γενομένης,
ἀγωνιάσαντες περὶ τῶν κατασκευασθέντων ἔργων
6 συνέτρεχον ἐπὶ τὴν βοήθειαν. ἀσελήνου δὲ τῆς
νυκτὸς οὔσης οἱ μὲν πυρφόροι διέλαμπον φερόμενοι
βιαίως, οἱ δ᾽ ὀξυβελεῖς καὶ πετροβόλοι τὴν φορὰν
ἀπροόρατον ἔχοντες πολλοὺς διέφθειρον τῶν μὴ
7 δυναμένων συνιδεῖν τὴν ἐπιφερομένην πληγήν. ἔτυχον δὲ καὶ τῶν ἀπὸ τῆς μηχανῆς λεπίδων τινὲς
ἀποπεσοῦσαι, καταψιλωθέντος δὲ[1] τοῦ τόπου προσ-
έπιπτον οἱ πυρφόροι τῷ ξυλοφανεῖ τοῦ κατασκευάσματος. διόπερ ἀγωνιάσας ὁ Δημήτριος μήποτε
τοῦ πυρὸς ἐπινεμηθέντος ἅπασαν συμβῇ τὴν μηχανὴν λυμανθῆναι, κατὰ τάχος ἐβοήθει καὶ τῷ
παρασκευασθέντι ὕδατι ἐν ταῖς στέγαις ἐπειρᾶτο
σβεννύναι τὴν ἐπιφερομένην φλόγα. τὸ δὲ τελευταῖον ἀθροίσας τῇ σάλπιγγι τοὺς τεταγμένους ἐπὶ
τῆς κινήσεως τῶν ἔργων διὰ τούτων ἀπήγαγε τὰς
μηχανὰς ἐκτὸς βέλους.

97. Ἔπειτα γενομένης ἡμέρας προσέταξε τοῖς
ὑπηρέταις ἀθροῖσαι τὰ βέλη τὰ πεσόντα παρὰ τῶν
Ῥοδίων, ἐκ τούτων βουλόμενος συλλογίσασθαι τῶν
2 ἐν τῇ πόλει τὴν παρασκευήν. ὧν ταχὺ τὸ προσταχθὲν ποιησάντων ἠριθμήθησαν πυρφόροι μὲν τοῖς
μεγέθεσι παντοῖοι πλείους τῶν ὀκτακοσίων, ὀξυβελεῖς δὲ οὐκ ἐλάττους τῶν χιλίων πεντακοσίων.
τοσούτων δὲ βελῶν ἐνεχθέντων ἐν βραχεῖ χρόνῳ
νυκτὸς ἐθαύμαζε τὴν χορηγίαν τῆς πόλεως καὶ τὴν
ἐν τούτοις δαψίλειαν.

3 Τότε μὲν οὖν ὁ Δημήτριος κατεσκεύασε[2] τὰ πεπο-

---

[1] δὲ added by editors.
[2] ἐπεσκεύασε Dindorf, cp. § 7 below.

spot. Since the attack was unforeseen, Demetrius, 304 B.C. alarmed for the siege works that had been constructed, hurried to the rescue. The night was moonless ; and the fire missiles shone bright as they hurtled violently through the air ; but the catapults and ballistae, since their missiles were invisible, destroyed many who were not able to see the impending stroke. It also happened that some of the iron plates of the helepolis were dislodged, and where the place was laid bare the fire missiles rained upon the exposed wood of the structure. Therefore Demetrius, fearing that the fire would spread and the whole machine be ruined, came quickly to the rescue, and with the water that had been placed in readiness on the platforms he tried to put out the spreading fire. He finally assembled by a trumpet signal the men who were assigned to move the apparatus and by their efforts dragged the machine beyond range.

97. Then when day had dawned he ordered the camp followers to collect the missiles that had been hurled by the Rhodians, since he wished to estimate from these the armament of the forces within the city. Quickly carrying out his orders, they counted more than eight hundred fire missiles of various sizes and not less than fifteen hundred catapult bolts. Since so many missiles had been hurled in a short time at night, he marvelled at the resources possessed by the city and at their prodigality in the use of these weapons.

Next Demetrius repaired such of his works as had

νηκότα τῶν ἔργων καὶ περί τε τὴν ταφὴν τῶν τελευτησάντων καὶ τὴν θεραπείαν τῶν τραυματιῶν
4 ἐγίνετο. καθ' ὃν δὴ χρόνον οἱ κατὰ τὴν πόλιν
ἄνεσιν λαβόντες τῆς ἀπὸ τῶν μηχανῶν βίας ᾠκο-
δόμησαν τρίτον τεῖχος μηνοειδές, περιλαμβάνοντες
τῇ μὲν περιφερείᾳ πάντα τὸν κινδυνεύοντα τόπον
τοῦ τείχους· οὐδὲν δ' ἧττον καὶ τάφρῳ βαθείᾳ περιέλαβον τὸ πεπτωκὸς τοῦ τείχους, ὅπως μὴ δύνηται
ῥᾳδίως ὁ βασιλεὺς ἐξ ἐφόδου μετὰ βάρους εἰσπεσεῖν
5 εἰς τὴν πόλιν. ἐξέπεμψαν δὲ καὶ ναῦς τῶν ἄριστα
πλεουσῶν, Ἀμύνταν ἐπιστήσαντες ἡγεμόνα, ὃς ἐκπλεύσας πρὸς τὴν Περαίαν τῆς Ἀσίας ἐπεφάνη
παραδόξως πειραταῖς τισιν ἀπεσταλμένοις ὑπὸ Δημητρίου. οὗτοι δ' εἶχον ἄφρακτα τρία, κράτιστοι
δοκοῦντες εἶναι τῶν τῷ βασιλεῖ συστρατευόντων.
γενομένης δ' ἐπ' ὀλίγον χρόνον ναυμαχίας οἱ Ῥόδιοι
βιασάμενοι τῶν νεῶν αὐτάνδρων ἐκυρίευσαν, ἐν οἷς
6 ἦν καὶ Τιμοκλῆς ὁ ἀρχιπειρατής. ἐπέπλευσαν δὲ
καὶ τῶν ἐμπόρων τισὶ καὶ παρελόμενοι κέλητας
οὐκ ὀλίγους γέμοντας σίτου τούτους τε καὶ τὰ τῶν
πειρατῶν ἄφρακτα κατήγαγον εἰς τὴν Ῥόδον νυ-
7 κτός, λαθόντες τοὺς πολεμίους. ὁ δὲ Δημήτριος
ἐπισκευάσας τὰ πεπονηκότα τῶν ἔργων προσέβαλλε
τῷ τείχει τὰς μηχανὰς καὶ πᾶσι τοῖς βέλεσιν ἀφει-
δῶς χρώμενος τοὺς μὲν ἐπὶ ταῖς ἐπάλξεσιν ἐφεστῶ-
τας ἀνεῖρξε, τοῖς δὲ κριοῖς τύπτων τὸ συνεχὲς τοῦ
τόπου δύο μὲν μεσοπύργια κατέβαλε, περὶ δὲ τὸν
πύργον τὸν ἀνὰ μέσον τούτων φιλοτιμουμένοις τοῖς
ἐκ τῆς πόλεως ἰσχυροὶ καὶ συνεχεῖς ἐκ διαδοχῆς
ἀγῶνες ἐγίνοντο, ὥστε καὶ τὸν στρατηγὸν αὐτῶν

been damaged, and devoted himself to the burial 304 B.C. of the dead and the care of the wounded. Meanwhile the people of the city, having gained a respite from the violent attacks of the siege engines, constructed a third crescent-shaped wall and included in its circuit every part of the wall that was in a dangerous condition; but none the less they dug a deep moat around the fallen portion of the wall so that the king should not be able to break into the city easily by an assault with a heavily armed force. They also sent out some of their fastest ships, installing Amyntas as commander; he, sailing to Peraea [1] in Asia, suddenly confronted some pirates who had been sent out by Demetrius. These had three deckless ships and were supposed to be the strongest of the pirates who were fighting as allies of the king. In the brief naval battle that ensued, the Rhodians overpowered the foe and took the ships with their crews, among whom was Timocles, the chief pirate. They also encountered some of the merchants and, seizing a fair number of light craft loaded with grain, they sent these and the undecked ships of the pirates to harbour in Rhodes by night, escaping the notice of the enemy. Demetrius, after he had repaired such of his equipment as was damaged, brought his siege engines up to the wall. By using all his missiles without stint, he drove back those who were stationed on the battlements, and striking with his rams a continuous portion of the wall, he overthrew two curtains; but as the city's forces fought obstinately for the tower that was between them, there were bitter and continuous encounters, one after another, with the

---

[1] Literally, "the opposite land," the Rhodian territory in Caria directly opposite the island.

'Ανανίαν ἐκθύμως ἀγωνισάμενον ἀναιρεθῆναι καὶ συχνοὺς τῶν ἄλλων στρατιωτῶν ἀποθανεῖν.

98. Ἅμα δὲ τούτοις πραττομένοις Πτολεμαῖος μὲν ὁ βασιλεὺς ἀπέστειλε τοῖς Ῥοδίοις σῖτον καὶ τὴν ἄλλην ἀγορὰν οὐκ ἐλάττονα τῆς πρότερον ἐκπεμφθείσης καὶ στρατιώτας χιλίους καὶ πεντακοσίους, ὧν ἦν ἡγεμὼν Ἀντίγονος ὁ Μακεδών. 2 καθ' ὃν δὴ χρόνον ἧκον πρὸς τὸν Δημήτριον πρέσβεις παρά τε Ἀθηναίων καὶ τῶν ἄλλων Ἑλληνίδων πόλεων, τὸν ἀριθμὸν μὲν ὄντες ὑπὲρ τοὺς πεντήκοντα, πάντες δὲ ἀξιοῦντες διαλύσασθαι τὸν βασιλέα 3 πρὸς τοὺς Ῥοδίους. γενομένων οὖν ἀνοχῶν καὶ πολλῶν καὶ παντοδαπῶν ῥηθέντων λόγων πρός τε τὸν δῆμον καὶ πρὸς τοὺς περὶ τὸν Δημήτριον οὐδαμῶς ἐδυνήθησαν συμφωνῆσαι· διόπερ οἱ πρέσβεις ἀπῆλθον ἄπρακτοι.

4 Δημήτριος δὲ διανοηθεὶς νυκτὸς ἐπιθέσθαι τῇ πόλει κατὰ τὸ πεπτωκὸς τοῦ τείχους ἐπέλεξε τῶν τε μαχίμων τοὺς κρατίστους καὶ τῶν ἄλλων τοὺς 5 εὐθέτους εἰς χιλίους καὶ πεντακοσίους. τούτους μὲν οὖν προσέταξεν ἡσυχῇ προσελθεῖν τῷ τείχει περὶ δευτέραν φυλακήν, αὐτὸς δὲ διασκευάσας παρήγγειλε τοῖς ἐφ' ἑκάστῳ μέρει τεταγμένοις, ὅταν σημήνῃ, συναλαλάξαι καὶ προσβολὰς ποιεῖσθαι 6 καὶ κατὰ γῆν καὶ κατὰ θάλατταν. πάντων δὲ τὸ παραγγελθὲν ποιούντων οἱ μὲν ἐπὶ τὰ πεπτωκότα τῶν τειχῶν ὁρμήσαντες τοὺς προφυλάττοντας ἐπὶ τῆς τάφρου κατασφάξαντες παρεισέπεσον εἰς τὴν πόλιν καὶ τοὺς περὶ τὸ θέατρον τόπους κατελαμβά- 7 νοντο· οἱ δὲ τῶν Ῥοδίων πρυτάνεις[1] πυθόμενοι τὸ

---

[1] πρυτάνεις added by Dindorf, cp. chap. 88. 3.

[1] Cp. chap. 96. 1.

result that their leader Ananias was killed fighting
desperately and many of the soldiers were slain also.

98. While these events were taking place, King
Ptolemy sent to the Rhodians grain and other supplies in no less quantity than those formerly sent,[1]
and fifteen hundred soldiers, whose leader was Antigonus, the Macedonian. At this very time there
came to Demetrius more than fifty envoys from the
Athenians and the other Greek cities, all of them
asking the king to come to terms with the Rhodians.
A truce, therefore, was made ; but although many
arguments of all sorts were presented to the city
and to Demetrius, they could in no way agree ; and
so the envoys returned without accomplishing their
aim.[2]

Demetrius, having determined to attack the city
at night through the breach in the wall, selected the
strongest of his fighting men and of the rest those
fitted for his purpose to the number of fifteen hundred.
These, then, he ordered to advance to the wall in
silence during the second watch ; as for himself,
when he had made his preparations, he gave orders
to those stationed on each side that when he gave
the signal they should raise the battle cry and make
attacks both by land and sea. When they all carried
out the order, those who had advanced against
breaches in the walls, after dispatching the advance
guards at the moat, charged past into the city and
occupied the region of the theatre ; but the magistrates of the Rhodians, learning what had happened

[2] According to Plutarch, *Demetrius*, 22. 4, Demetrius, who
was looking for a pretext to end the siege, was induced by the
Athenians to make terms on condition that the Rhodians
should be allies of Antigonus and Demetrius except in a war
with Ptolemy. Cp. chap. 99. 3.

συμβεβηκὸς καὶ τὴν πόλιν ὁρῶντες ἅπασαν τεθορυ-
βημένην τοῖς μὲν ἐπὶ τοῦ λιμένος καὶ τῶν τειχῶν
παρήγγειλαν μένειν ἐπὶ τῆς ἰδίας τάξεως καὶ τοὺς
ἔξωθεν, ἂν προσβάλωσιν, ἀμύνασθαι, αὐτοὶ δ᾽
ἔχοντες τὸ τῶν ἐπιλέκτων σύστημα καὶ τοὺς ἀπὸ
τῆς Ἀλεξανδρείας προσφάτως καταπεπλευκότας
στρατιώτας ὥρμησαν ἐπὶ τοὺς ἐντὸς τοῦ τείχους
8 παρεισπεπτωκότας. περικαταλαβούσης δ᾽ ἡμέρας
καὶ τοῦ Δημητρίου τὸ σύσσημον ἄραντος οἱ μὲν τῷ
λιμένι προσβαλόντες καὶ τὸ τεῖχος πάντοθεν περι-
εστρατοπεδευκότες συνηλάλαξαν, εὐθαρσεῖς ποιοῦντες τοὺς κατειληφότας μέρος τοῦ περὶ τὸ θέατρον
τόπου, ὁ δὲ κατὰ τὴν πόλιν ὄχλος παίδων καὶ
γυναικῶν ἐν φόβοις ἦν καὶ δάκρυσιν, ὡς τῆς πατρί-
9 δος κατὰ κράτος ἁλισκομένης. οὐ μὴν ἀλλὰ τοῖς
παρεισπεσοῦσιν ἐντὸς τοῦ τείχους γενομένης μάχης
πρὸς τοὺς Ῥοδίους καὶ πολλῶν παρ᾽ ἀμφοτέροις
πεσόντων τὸ μὲν πρῶτον οὐδέτεροι τῆς ἰδίας τάξεως
ἐξεχώρουν, μετὰ δὲ ταῦτα τῶν μὲν Ῥοδίων ἀεὶ
πλειόνων γινομένων καὶ τὸν κίνδυνον ἑτοίμως ὑπο-
μενόντων, ὡς ἂν ὑπὲρ πατρίδος καὶ τῶν μεγίστων
ἀγωνιζομένων, τῶν δὲ τοῦ βασιλέως θλιβομένων,
Ἄλκιμος μὲν καὶ Μαντίας οἱ τὴν ἡγεμονίαν ἔχοντες
πολλοῖς περιπεσόντες τραύμασιν ἐτελεύτησαν, τῶν
δ᾽ ἄλλων οἱ πλεῖστοι οἱ μὲν ἐν χειρῶν νόμῳ διεφθάρησαν, οἱ δ᾽ ἥλωσαν, ὀλίγοι δὲ πρὸς τὸν βασιλέα
φυγόντες διεσώθησαν. πολλοὶ δὲ καὶ τῶν Ῥοδίων
ἀνῃρέθησαν, ἐν οἷς ἦν καὶ ὁ πρύτανις Δαμοτέλης
ἐπ᾽ ἀρετῇ γενόμενος περίβλεπτος.

99. Δημήτριος δὲ τὴν τῆς πόλεως ἅλωσιν ὑπολαβὼν ἐκ τῶν χειρῶν αὐτοῦ τὴν τύχην ἀφῃρῆσθαι
πάλιν παρεσκευάζετο πρὸς τὴν πολιορκίαν. εἶτα

and seeing that the whole city had been thrown into confusion, sent orders to those at the harbour and the walls to remain at their own posts and oppose the enemy outside if he should attack ; and they themselves, with their contingent of selected men and the soldiers who had recently sailed in from Alexandria, attacked the troops who had got within the walls. When day returned and Demetrius raised the ensign, those who were attacking the port and those who had been stationed about the wall on all sides shouted the battle cry, giving encouragement to the men who had occupied part of the region of the theatre ; but in the city the throng of children and women were in fear and tears, thinking that their native city was being taken by storm. Nevertheless, fighting began between those who had made their way within the wall and the Rhodians, and many fell on both sides. At first neither side withdrew from its position ; but afterwards, as the Rhodians constantly added to their numbers and were prompt to face danger—as is the way with men fighting for their native land and their most precious things,—and on the other hand the king's men were in distress, Alcimus and Mantias, their commanders, expired after receiving many wounds, most of the others were killed in hand-to-hand fighting or were captured, and only a few escaped to the king and survived. Many also of the Rhodians were slain, among whom was the president Damoteles, who had won great acclaim for his valour.

99. When Demetrius realized that Fortune had snatched from his hand the capture of the city, he made new preparations for the siege. When his

τοῦ πατρὸς αὐτῷ γράψαντος διαλύσασθαι πρὸς
Ῥοδίους ὡς ἄν ποτε δύνηται, τὸν κάλλιστον ἐπετήρει καιρόν, δώσοντα προφάσεις εὐλόγους τῆς
2 συνθέσεως. Πτολεμαίου δὲ γράψαντος τοῖς Ῥοδίοις τὸ μὲν πρῶτον ὅτι πέμψει σίτου πλῆθος
αὐτοῖς καὶ στρατιώτας τρισχιλίους, μετὰ δὲ ταῦτα
συμβουλεύοντος, ἐὰν ᾖ δυνατόν, μετρίως διαλύσασθαι πρὸς Ἀντίγονον, ἅπαντες ἔρεπον πρὸς τὴν
3 εἰρήνην. καθ᾽ ὃν δὴ χρόνον τοῦ κοινοῦ τῶν Αἰτωλῶν ἀποστείλαντος πρεσβευτὰς περὶ διαλύσεων οἱ
Ῥόδιοι συνέθεντο πρὸς Δημήτριον ἐπὶ τοῖσδε, αὐτόνομον καὶ ἀφρούρητον εἶναι τὴν πόλιν καὶ ἔχειν
τὰς ἰδίας προσόδους, συμμαχεῖν δὲ Ῥοδίους Ἀντιγόνῳ πλὴν ἐὰν ἐπὶ Πτολεμαῖον στρατεύηται, καὶ
δοῦναι τῶν πολιτῶν ὁμήρους ἑκατὸν οὓς ἂν ἀπο-
γράψηται Δημήτριος πλὴν τῶν ἀρχὰς ἐχόντων.

100. Οἱ μὲν οὖν Ῥόδιοι πολιορκηθέντες ἐνιαύσιον
χρόνον τούτῳ τῷ τρόπῳ κατελύσαντο τὸν πόλεμον.
τοὺς δ᾽ ἐν τοῖς κινδύνοις ἄνδρας ἀγαθοὺς γενομένους ἐτίμησαν ταῖς ἀξίαις δωρεαῖς καὶ τῶν
δούλων τοὺς ἀνδραγαθήσαντας ἐλευθερίας καὶ πολι-
2 τείας ἠξίωσαν. ἔστησαν δὲ καὶ τῶν βασιλέων
εἰκόνας Κασάνδρου καὶ Λυσιμάχου[1] τῶν δευτε-
ρευόντων μὲν ταῖς δόξαις, συμβεβλημένων δὲ
3 μεγάλα πρὸς τὴν τῆς πόλεως σωτηρίαν. τὸν δὲ
Πτολεμαῖον ἐν ἀνταποδόσει μείζονος χάριτος ὑπερ-
βάλλεσθαι βουλόμενοι θεωροὺς ἀπέστειλαν εἰς Λιβύην τοὺς ἐπερωτήσοντας τὸ παρ᾽ Ἄμμωνι μαντεῖον

father thereafter wrote to him to come to terms with 304 B.C.
the Rhodians as best he could, he awaited a favourable opportunity that would provide a specious excuse
for the settlement. Since Ptolemy had written to
the Rhodians, first saying that he would send them
a great quantity of grain and three thousand soldiers,
but then advising them, if it should be possible, to
make equitable terms with Antigonus, everyone inclined toward peace. At just this time the Aetolian
League sent envoys to urge a settlement, and the
Rhodians came to terms with Demetrius on these
conditions : that the city should be autonomous and
ungarrisoned and should enjoy its own revenue ; that
the Rhodians should be allies of Antigonus unless
he should be at war with Ptolemy ; and that they
should give as hostages a hundred of their citizens
whom Demetrius should select, those holding office
being exempt.[1]

100. In this way, then, the Rhodians, after they
had been besieged for a year, brought the war to
an end. Those who had proved themselves brave
men in the battles they honoured with the prizes
that were their due, and they granted freedom and
citizenship to such slaves as had shown themselves
courageous. They also set up statues of King Cassander and King Lysimachus, who though they held
second place in general opinion, yet had made great
contributions to the salvation of the city. In the case
of Ptolemy, since they wanted to surpass his record
by repaying his kindness with a greater one, they
sent a sacred mission into Libya to ask the oracle at

---

[1] Cp. Plutarch, *Demetrius*, 22. 4.

---

[1] καὶ after Λυσιμάχου omitted by Wesseling.

εἰ συμβουλεύει Ῥοδίοις Πτολεμαῖον ὡς θεὸν τιμῆ-
4 σαι. συγκατατιθεμένου δὲ τοῦ χρηστηρίου τέμενος
ἀνῆκαν ἐν τῇ πόλει τετράγωνον, οἰκοδομήσαντες
παρ᾽ ἑκάστην πλευρὰν στοὰν¹ σταδιαίαν, ὃ προσ-
ηγόρευσαν Πτολεμαῖον. ἀνῳκοδόμησαν δὲ καὶ τὸ
θέατρον καὶ τὰ πεπτωκότα τῶν τειχῶν καὶ τῶν
ἄλλων τόπων τοὺς καθῃρημένους πολλῷ κάλλιον
ἢ προϋπῆρχον.
5 Δημήτριος δὲ κατὰ τὰς ἐντολὰς τοῦ πατρὸς
διαλυσάμενος πρὸς Ῥοδίους ἐξέπλευσε μετὰ πάσης
τῆς δυνάμεως καὶ κομισθεὶς διὰ νήσων κατέπλευσε
6 τῆς Βοιωτίας εἰς Αὐλιν. σπεύδων δ᾽ ἐλευθερῶσαι
τοὺς Ἕλληνας (οἱ γὰρ περὶ Κάσανδρον καὶ Πολυπέρχοντα τὸν ἔμπροσθεν χρόνον ἄδειαν ἐσχηκότες
ἐπόρθουν τὰ πλεῖστα μέρη τῆς Ἑλλάδος) πρῶτον
μὲν τὴν Χαλκιδέων πόλιν ἠλευθέρωσε, φρουρουμένην ὑπὸ Βοιωτῶν, καὶ τοὺς κατὰ τὴν Βοιωτίαν
καταπληξάμενος ἠνάγκασεν ἀποστῆναι τῆς Κασάνδρου φιλίας, μετὰ δὲ ταῦτα πρὸς μὲν Αἰτωλοὺς
συμμαχίαν ἐποιήσατο, πρὸς δὲ τοὺς περὶ Πολυπέρχοντα καὶ Κάσανδρον διαπολεμεῖν παρεσκευάζετο.
7 Ἅμα δὲ τούτοις πραττομένοις Εὔμηλος μὲν ὁ
Βοσπόρου βασιλεὺς βασιλεύων ἕκτον ἔτος ἐτελεύτησε, τὴν δὲ βασιλείαν διαδεξάμενος Σπάρτακος
ὁ υἱὸς ἦρξεν ἔτη εἴκοσιν.
101. Ἡμεῖς δὲ τὰ περὶ τὴν Ἑλλάδα καὶ τὴν
Ἀσίαν διευκρινηκότες μεταβιβάσομεν τὸν λόγον ἐπὶ
θάτερα μέρη τῆς οἰκουμένης.

¹ πλευρὰν στοὰν Rhodoman : στοὰν πλευρὰν.

¹ 600 feet.　　² Continued in chap. 102. 1.

Ammon if it advised the Rhodians to honour Ptolemy 304 B.C. as a god. Since the oracle approved, they dedicated in the city a square precinct, building on each of its sides a portico a stade [1] long, and this they called the Ptolemaeum. They also rebuilt the theatre, the fallen portions of the walls, and the buildings that had been destroyed in the other quarters in a manner more beautiful than before.

Now that Demetrius, in accordance with injunctions of his father, had made peace with the Rhodians, he sailed out with his whole force ; and after passing through the islands, he put in at Aulis in Boeotia. Since he was intent on freeing the Greeks (for Cassander and Polyperchon having up to this time enjoyed impunity were engaged in plundering the greater part of Greece), he first freed the city of the Chalcidians, which was garrisoned by Boeotians, and by striking fear into the Boeotians, he forced them to renounce their friendship with Cassander ; and after this he made an alliance with the Aetolians and began his preparations for carrying on war against Polyperchon and Cassander.[2]

While these events were taking place, Eumelus, the king of Bosporus, died in the sixth year of his reign,[3] and his son Spartacus [4] succeeded to the throne and reigned for twenty years.

101. Now that we have carefully passed in review the happenings in Greece and Asia, we shall turn our narrative toward the other parts of the inhabited world.

[3] For the reign of Eumelus cp. chaps. 22. 1—26. 2.
[4] The name is spelled Σπάρτοκος on coins and inscriptions, *e.g.* the Athenian inscription of 289/8 honouring this king for a gift of grain to the city (*IG*, 2². 653 = Dittenberger, *Syll.*³ 370).

Κατὰ μὲν γὰρ τὴν Σικελίαν Ἀγαθοκλῆς, εἰρήνην ἀγόντων τῶν Λιπαραίων, ἐπιπλεύσας αὐτοῖς ἀπροσδοκήτως εἰσεπράξατο τοὺς μηδ' ὁτιοῦν προαδική-
2 σαντας ἀργυρίου τάλαντα πεντήκοντα. ὅτε δὴ πολλοῖς ἔδοξε θεῖον εἶναι τὸ ῥηθησόμενον, τῆς παρανομίας τυχούσης ἐπισημασίας παρὰ τοῦ δαιμονίου. ἀξιούντων γὰρ τῶν Λιπαραίων εἰς τὰ προσελλείποντα τῶν χρημάτων δοῦναι χρόνον καὶ λεγόντων μηδέποτε τοῖς ἱεροῖς ἀναθήμασι κατακεχρῆσθαι, ὁ Ἀγαθοκλῆς βιασάμενος αὐτοὺς δοῦναι τὰ κατὰ τὸ πρυτανεῖον, ὧν εἶχον ἐπιγραφὴν τὰ μὲν Αἰόλου, τὰ δ' Ἡφαίστου, λαβὼν παραχρῆμα ἐξέπλευσεν. πνεύματος δ' ἐπιγενομένου τῶν νεῶν ἕνδεκα συνετρίβησαν αἱ τὰ χρήματα κομίζουσαι.
3 διόπερ ἔδοξε πολλοῖς ὁ μὲν λεγόμενος περὶ τοὺς τόπους ἐκείνους εἶναι κύριος τῶν ἀνέμων εὐθὺς κατὰ τὸν πρῶτον πλοῦν λαβεῖν παρ' αὐτοῦ τιμωρίαν, ὁ δὲ Ἥφαιστος ἐπὶ τῆς τελευτῆς, οἰκείως τῆς ἀσεβείας κολάσαι[1] τὸν τύραννον ἐν τῇ πατρίδι, συνωνύμως ἐπὶ θερμοῖς τοῖς ἄνθραξι κατακαύσας ζῶντα· τῆς γὰρ αὐτῆς προαιρέσεως ἦν καὶ δικαιοσύνης τὸ τῶν περὶ τὴν Αἴτνην σωζόντων τοὺς ἑαυτῶν γονεῖς ἀποσχέσθαι καὶ τὸ τοὺς ἀσεβοῦντας εἰς τὸ θεῖον διὰ τῆς ἰδίας δυνάμεως μετελθεῖν.
4 Οὐ μὴν ἀλλ' ὑπὲρ μὲν τῆς καταστροφῆς Ἀγαθοκλέους, ὅταν πρὸς τοὺς οἰκείους χρόνους ἔλθωμεν, αὐτὸ[2] τὸ γενόμενον βεβαιώσει τὸ νῦν εἰρημένον·

---

[1] κολάσαι Madvig : κολάσας.
[2] ἔλθωμεν, αὐτὸ Post : ἔλθωμεν αὐτοῦ.

---

[1] Continued from chap. 90. 2.

In Sicily,[1] although the inhabitants of the Lipa-
raean Islands were at peace with him, Agathocles
sailed against them without warning and exacted
from men who had done him no prior injury whatever,
fifty talents of silver. To many, indeed, what I am
about to relate seemed the work of a god, since his
crime received its brand from the divinity. When
the Liparaeans begged him to grant them time for
what was lacking in the payment and said that they
had never turned the sacred offerings to profane uses,
Agathocles forced them to give him the dedications
in the Prytaneum, of which some bore inscriptions
to Aeolus and some to Hephaestus ; and taking these
he at once sailed away. But a wind came up and the
eleven of his ships that were carrying the money were
sunk. And so it seemed to many that the god who
was said in that region to be master of the winds at
once on his first voyage exacted punishment from
him, and that at the end Hephaestus punished him
in his own country in a way that matched the tyrant's
impious actions and the god's own name by burning
him alive on hot coals [2] ; for it belonged to the same
character and the same justice to refrain from touch-
ing those who were saving their own parents on
Aetna,[3] and with his proper power to search after
those who had been guilty of impiety toward his
shrine.

However, as regards the disaster that befell Agathocles, when we come to the proper time, the action
itself will confirm what we now have said ; but we

---

[2] For the death of Agathocles cp. Book 21, frag. 16.

[3] The reference is to Amphinomus and Anapia. While
they were rescuing their parents from a irruption of Aetna,
the volcanic fires opened and made a way for them to pass.
Cp., *e.g.*, Seneca, *de Beneficiis*, 3. 37. 2 ; Pausanias, 10. 28. 4.

ἐφεξῆς δὲ ῥητέον ἡμῖν τὰ πραχθέντα κατὰ τοὺς
συνεχεῖς τῆς Ἰταλίας τόπους.

5 Ῥωμαῖοι μὲν καὶ Σαμνῖται διαπρεσβευσάμενοι
πρὸς ἀλλήλους εἰρήνην συνέθεντο, πολεμήσαντες
ἔτη εἴκοσι δύο καὶ μῆνας ἕξ· τῶν δ' ὑπάτων
Πόπλιος Σεμπρώνιος μετὰ δυνάμεως ἐμβαλὼν εἰς
τὴν τῶν Αἰκλῶν χώραν ἐχειρώσατο τετταράκοντα
πόλεις ἐν ἡμέραις ταῖς πάσαις πεντήκοντα, ἀναγ-
κάσας δὲ πᾶν τὸ ἔθνος ὑποτάττεσθαι Ῥωμαίοις
ἐπανῆλθε καὶ θρίαμβον κατήγαγεν ἐπαινούμενον.
ὁ δὲ δῆμος ὁ Ῥωμαίων πρός τε Μαρσοὺς καὶ
Παλιγνούς,[1] ἔτι δὲ Μαρρουκίνους, συμμαχίαν
ἐποιήσατο.

102. Τοῦ δ' ἐνιαυσίου χρόνου διεληλυθότος Ἀθήνησι μὲν ἦρχε Λεώστρατος, ἐν Ῥώμῃ δ' ὑπῆρχον
ὕπατοι Σερούιος Κορνήλιος καὶ Λεύκιος Γενούκιος.
ἐπὶ δὲ τούτων Δημήτριος εἶχε πρόθεσιν πρὸς μὲν
τοὺς περὶ Κάσανδρον διαπολεμεῖν, τοὺς δ' Ἕλληνας
ἐλευθεροῦν· καὶ πρῶτον τὰ κατὰ τὴν Ἑλλάδα
διοικεῖν, ἅμα μὲν νομίζων δόξαν οἴσειν αὐτῷ μεγάλην τὴν τῶν Ἑλλήνων αὐτονομίαν, ἅμα δὲ καὶ
τοὺς περὶ Πρεπέλαον ἡγεμόνας τοῦ Κασάνδρου
πρότερον συντρῖψαι καὶ τότε προσάγειν δεῖν[2] ἐπ'
αὐτὴν τὴν Μακεδονίαν,[3] εἰ μὴ ἐπ' αὐτὸν πορεύοιτο
2 ὁ Κάσανδρος.[4] τῆς δὲ τῶν Σικυωνίων πόλεως

---

[1] Παλιγνούς Rhodoman: Παλλινοὺς R, Παλλίνους X, Πελη-
νοὺς F.
[2] δεῖν added by Post.
[3] Μακεδονίαν Reiske: ἡγεμονίαν.
[4] εἰ μὴ . . . ὁ Κάσανδρος Post: ἢ . . . τὸν Κάσανδρον.

must now tell of events in the adjacent parts of Italy.[1]

The Romans and the Samnites interchanged envoys and made peace after having fought for twenty-two years and six months[2]; and one of the consuls, Publius Sempronius, invading the country of the Aecli[3] with an army, captured forty cities in a total of fifty days, and after forcing the entire tribe to submit to Rome, returned home and celebrated a triumph with great applause. The Roman people made alliances with the Marsi, the Paligni, and the Marrucini.[4]

102. When the year had come to its end, Leo- stratus was archon in Athens, and in Rome the consuls were Servius Cornelius and Lucius Genucius.[5] While these held office Demetrius proposed to carry on his war with Cassander and to free the Greeks; and first he planned to establish order in the affairs of Greece, for he believed that the freeing of the Greeks would bring him great honour, and at the same time he thought it necessary to wipe out Prepelaüs[6] and the other leaders before attacking Cassander, and then to go on against Macedonia itself if Cassander did not march against him. Now

---

[1] The next reference to Sicilian affairs is in Book 21. 2. 1.

[2] Cp. Livy, 9. 45. 1-4; the narrative is continued from chap. 90. 4.

[3] The Aequi or Aequiculi in Latin writers; usually called the Aikoi or Aikanoi by the Greek historians. Cp. Livy, 9. 45. 5-18.   [4] Continued in chap. 104. 1.

[5] Leostratus was archon in 303/2. Livy, 10. 1. 1, gives as consuls for 303 B.C. L. Genucius and Ser. Cornelius. In the Fasti Capitolini only Lentulus, the cognomen of Cornelius, can be read. The narrative is continued from chap. 100. 6. Cp. Plutarch, *Demetrius*, 25.

[6] Cp. Book 19. 64. 3.

φρουρουμένης ὑπὸ τῶν Πτολεμαίου τοῦ βασιλέως
στρατιωτῶν, ὧν ἦν ἐπιφανέστατος στρατηγὸς Φίλιππος, νυκτὸς ἐπιθέμενος ἀπροσδοκήτως παρεισέπεσεν ἐντὸς τοῦ τείχους. εἶτα οἱ μὲν φρουροὶ
συνέφυγον[1] εἰς τὴν ἀκρόπολιν, ὁ δὲ Δημήτριος τῆς
πόλεως κυριεύσας τὸν μεταξὺ τόπον τῶν οἰκιῶν καὶ
τῆς ἄκρας κατεῖχε. μέλλοντος δ' αὐτοῦ μηχανὰς
προσάγειν καταπλαγέντες τὴν μὲν ἀκρόπολιν δι'
ὁμολογίας παρέδοσαν, αὐτοὶ δ' ἀπέπλευσαν εἰς
Αἴγυπτον. ὁ δὲ Δημήτριος τοὺς Σικυωνίους εἰς τὴν
ἀκρόπολιν μετοικίσας τὸ μὲν τῷ λιμένι συνάπτον
μέρος τῆς πόλεως κατέσκαψεν, ἀνοχύρου[2] παντελῶς
ὄντος τοῦ τόπου, τῷ δὲ πολιτικῷ πλήθει συνεπιλα-
βόμενος τῆς οἰκοδομίας καὶ τὴν ἐλευθερίαν ἀπο-
καταστήσας τιμῶν ἰσοθέων ἔτυχε παρὰ τοῖς εὖ
3 παθοῦσι· Δημητριάδα μὲν γὰρ τὴν πόλιν ὠνόμασαν,
θυσίας δὲ καὶ πανηγύρεις, ἔτι δ' ἀγῶνας ἐψηφίσαντο
συντελεῖν αὐτῷ κατ' ἐνιαυτὸν καὶ τὰς ἄλλας ἀπο-
νέμειν τιμὰς ὡς κτίστῃ. ἀλλὰ ταῦτα μὲν ὁ χρόνος
διαληφθεὶς πραγμάτων μεταβολαῖς ἠκύρωσεν, οἱ δὲ
Σικυώνιοι πολλῷ κρείττονα μεταλαβόντες τόπον
διετέλεσαν ἐν αὐτῷ μέχρι τῶν καθ' ἡμᾶς χρόνων
4 ἐνοικοῦντες. ὁ γὰρ τῆς ἀκροπόλεως περίβολος ἐπί-
πεδος ὢν καὶ μέγας κρημνοῖς δυσπροσίτοις περι-
έχεται πανταχόθεν, ὥστε μηδαμῇ δύνασθαι μηχανὰς
προσάγειν· ἔχει δὲ καὶ πλῆθος ὑδάτων, ἐξ οὗ κη-
πείας δαψιλεῖς κατεσκεύασαν, ὥστε τὴν ἐπίνοιαν
τοῦ βασιλέως καὶ πρὸς ἀπόλαυσιν εἰρηνικὴν καὶ
πρὸς ἀσφάλειαν πολέμου δόξαι καλῶς προεωρᾶσθαι.
103. Ὁ δὲ Δημήτριος διοικήσας τὰ περὶ τοὺς

---

[1] συνέφυγον Bekker : συνεισέπεσον RX, συνέπεσον F.
[2] ἀνοχύρου Dindorf : ὀχυροῦ.

the city of Sicyon was garrisoned by King Ptolemy's 303 B.C.
soldiers, commanded by a very distinguished general,
Philip.   Attacking this city suddenly by night,
Demetrius broke his way inside the walls.   Then the
garrison fled to the acropolis, but Demetrius took
possession of the city and occupied the region between
the houses and the acropolis.   While he hesitated
to bring up his siege engines, the garrison in panic
surrendered the acropolis on terms and the men
themselves sailed off to Egypt.   After Demetrius had
moved the people of Sicyon into their acropolis, he
destroyed the part of the city adjacent to the harbour,
since its site was quite insecure ; then, after he had
assisted the common people of the city in building
their houses and had re-established free government
for them, he received divine honours from those whom
he had benefited ; for they called the city Demetrias,
and they voted to celebrate sacrifices and public
festivals and also games in his honour every year and
to grant him the other honours of a founder.   Time,
however, whose continuity has been broken by
changes of conditions, has invalidated these honours ;
but the people of Sicyon, having thus obtained a much
better location, continue to live there down to our
times.[1]   For the enclosed area of the acropolis is level
and of ample size, and it is surrounded on all sides by
cliffs difficult to scale, so that on no side can engines
of war be brought near ; moreover, it has plenty of
water by the aid of which they developed rich gardens,
so that the king in his design seems to have made
excellent provision both for comfort in time of peace
and for safety in time of war.

103. After Demetrius had settled the affairs of the

[1] Cp. Pausanias, 2. 7. 1 ; Strabo 8. 6. 25.

Σικυωνίους ἀνέζευξε μετὰ πάσης τῆς δυνάμεως
ἐπὶ τὴν Κόρινθον, ἣν ἐφρούρει Πρεπέλαος Κασάνδρου στρατηγός. τὸ μὲν οὖν πρῶτον νυκτὸς ὑπό
τινων πολιτῶν εἰσαχθεὶς διά τινος πυλίδος ἐκράτησε
2 τῆς πόλεως καὶ τῶν λιμένων. τῶν δὲ φρουρῶν
καταφυγόντων τῶν μὲν εἰς τὸ καλούμενον Σισύφιον,
τῶν δ' εἰς τὸν Ἀκροκόρινθον, προσαγαγὼν μηχανὰς
τοῖς ὀχυρώμασι καὶ πολλὰ κακοπαθήσας εἷλε τὸ
Σισύφιον κατὰ κράτος. εἶτα τῶν ἐνταῦθα[1] συμ-
φυγόντων πρὸς τοὺς κατειληφότας τὸν Ἀκροκόρινθον καὶ τούτους καταπληξάμενος ἠνάγκασε
3 παραδοῦναι τὴν ἄκραν· σφόδρα γὰρ ἦν ἀνυπόστατος
οὗτος ὁ βασιλεὺς ἐν ταῖς προσβολαῖς, εὐμήχανος
ὑπάρχων περὶ τὴν κατασκευὴν τῶν πολιορκητικῶν
ἔργων. οὐ μὴν ἀλλὰ τοὺς Κορινθίους ἐλευθερώσας
παρεισήγαγε φυλακὴν εἰς τὸν Ἀκροκόρινθον, βου-
λομένων τῶν πολιτῶν διὰ τοῦ βασιλέως τηρεῖσθαι
τὴν πόλιν μέχρι ἂν ὁ πρὸς Κάσανδρον καταλυθῇ
4 πόλεμος. καὶ Πρεπέλαος μὲν αἰσχρῶς ἐκπεσὼν ἐκ
τῆς Κορίνθου πρὸς Κάσανδρον ἀπεχώρησεν, Δημήτριος δὲ παρελθὼν εἰς τὴν Ἀχαΐαν Βοῦραν μὲν κατὰ
κράτος εἷλε καὶ τοῖς πολίταις ἀπέδωκε τὴν αὐτονομίαν, Σκῦρον[2] δ' ἐν ὀλίγαις ἡμέραις παραλαβὼν
5 ἐξέβαλε τὴν φρουράν. μετὰ δὲ ταῦτ' ἐπ' Ὀρχο-
μενὸν τῆς Ἀρκαδίας στρατεύσας ἐκέλευσε τῷ τῆς
φρουρᾶς ἀφηγουμένῳ Στρομβίχῳ παραδοῦναι τὴν
πόλιν. οὐ προσέχοντος δ' αὐτοῦ τοῖς λόγοις ἀλλὰ
καὶ πολλὰ λοιδοροῦντος ἀπὸ τοῦ τείχους βλασφήμως
προσαγαγὼν μηχανὰς ὁ βασιλεὺς καὶ καταβαλὼν
6 τὰ τείχη κατὰ κράτος εἷλε τὴν πόλιν. τὸν μὲν οὖν
Στρόμβιχον τὸν ὑπὸ Πολυπέρχοντος καθεσταμένον

---

[1] ἐνταῦθα Hertlein : ἐν ταύτῃ.

people of Sicyon, he set out with his whole army for 303 B.C. Corinth, which was held by Prepelaüs, a general of Cassander. At first, after he had been admitted at night by certain citizens through a postern gate, Demetrius gained possession of the city and its harbours. The garrison, however, fled, some to the place called Sisyphium,[1] some to Acrocorinth ; but he brought up engines of war to the fortifications and took Sisyphium by storm after suffering heavy losses. Then, when the men there fled to those who had occupied Acrocorinth, he intimidated them also and forced them to surrender the citadel ; for this king was exceedingly irresistible in his assaults, being particularly skilled in the construction of siege equipment. Be that as it may, when once he had freed the Corinthians he brought a garrison into Acrocorinth, since the citizens wished the city to be protected by the king until the war with Cassander should be brought to an end. Prepelaüs, ignominiously driven out of Corinth, withdrew to Cassander, but Demetrius, advancing into Achaia, took Bura by storm and restored autonomy to its citizens ; then, capturing Scyrus in a few days, he cast out its garrison. After this, making a campaign against Arcadian Orchomenus, he ordered the garrison commander, Strombichus, to surrender the city. When he paid no attention to the orders but even poured much abuse upon him from the wall in an insulting manner, the king brought up engines of war, overthrew the walls, and took the city by storm. As for Strombichus, who had been made garrison-commander by Polyperchon,

---

[1] Sisyphium is on the slope of Acrocorinth below Peirenê, Strabo, 8. 6. 21.

---

[2] Σκίρον Wesseling.

φρούραρχον καὶ τῶν ἄλλων τῶν ἀλλοτρίως δια-
τεθέντων πρὸς αὐτὸν εἰς ὀγδοήκοντα πρὸ τῆς πόλεως ἀνεσταύρωσε, τῶν δ' ἄλλων μισθοφόρων ἑλὼν
εἰς δισχιλίους κατέμιξε τοῖς ἰδίοις στρατιώταις.
7 μετὰ δὲ τὴν ἅλωσιν ταύτης τῆς πόλεως οἱ σύνεγγυς
τὰ φρούρια κατέχοντες, ὑπολαμβάνοντες ἀδύνατον
ὑπάρχειν τὸ διαφυγεῖν τὴν βίαν τοῦ βασιλέως, παρέδωκαν αὐτῷ τὰ χωρία. ὁμοίως δὲ τούτοις καὶ οἱ
τὰς πόλεις φρουροῦντες, τῶν μὲν περὶ Κάσανδρον
καὶ Πρεπέλαον καὶ Πολυπέρχοντα μὴ βοηθούντων
τοῦ δὲ Δημητρίου μετὰ μεγάλης δυνάμεως καὶ
μηχανῶν ὑπεραγουσῶν προσιόντος, ἑκουσίως ἐξεχώρουν.

Καὶ τὰ μὲν περὶ Δημήτριον ἐν τούτοις ἦν.

104. Κατὰ δὲ τὴν Ἰταλίαν Ταραντῖνοι πόλεμον
ἔχοντες πρὸς Λευκανοὺς καὶ Ῥωμαίους ἐξέπεμψαν
πρεσβευτὰς εἰς τὴν Σπάρτην, αἰτούμενοι βοήθειαν
2 καὶ στρατηγὸν Κλεώνυμον. τῶν δὲ Λακεδαιμονίων
προθύμως ἡγεμόνα δόντων τὸν αἰτούμενον καὶ τῶν
Ταραντίνων χρήματα καὶ ναῦς ἀποστειλάντων ὁ
μὲν Κλεώνυμος ἐπὶ Ταινάρῳ τῆς Λακωνικῆς ξενο-
λογήσας στρατιώτας πεντακισχιλίους συντόμως
κατέπλευσεν εἰς Τάραντα. ἐνταῦθα δὲ μισθοφόρους
ἀθροίσας ἄλλους οὐκ ἐλάττους τῶν προτέρων κατέγραφε καὶ τοὺς πολιτικοὺς πεζοὺς μὲν πλείους
τῶν δισμυρίων, ἱππεῖς δὲ δισχιλίους. προσελάβετο
δὲ τῶν τε κατ' Ἰταλίαν Ἑλλήνων τοὺς πλείστους
3 καὶ τὸ τῶν Μεσσαπίων ἔθνος. ἁδρᾶς οὖν δυνάμεως

---

[1] Continued in chap. 106. 1.
[2] Continued from chap. 101. 5.
[3] Son of King Cleomenes II, but passed over in favour of
Areus I because of his violent and tyrannical character. Cp.

and at least eighty of the others who were hostile to 303 B.C.
him, Demetrius crucified them in front of the city, but
having captured at least two thousand of the other
mercenaries, he incorporated them with his own
men. After the capture of this city, those who commanded the forts in the vicinity, assuming that it
was impossible to escape the might of the king, surrendered the strongholds to him. In like fashion
those also who guarded the cities withdrew of their
own accord, since Cassander, Prepelaüs, and Polyperchon failed to come to their aid but Demetrius
was approaching with a great army and with over-
whelming engines of war.

This was the situation of Demetrius.[1]

104. In Italy [2] the people of Tarentum were waging
war with the Lucanians and the Romans ; and they
sent envoys to Sparta asking for assistance and for
Cleonymus as general.[3] When the Lacedaemonians
willingly granted them the leader whom they requested and the Tarentines sent money and ships,
Cleonymus enrolled five thousand mercenaries at
Taenarum in Laconia [4] and sailed at once to Tarentum.
After collecting there other mercenaries no less in
number than those previously enrolled, he also enlisted more than twenty thousand citizens as foot-
soldiers and two thousand as mounted troops. He
won the support also of most of the Greeks in Italy
and of the tribe of the Messapians.[5] Then, since

Plutarch, *Pyrrhus*, 26. 8 ; Pausanias, 3. 6. 2. Originally
Tarentum was a colony of Sparta.

[4] For Taenarum as a recruiting ground for mercenaries cp.
Book 18. 21. 1-3.

[5] The Messapians, an Italic tribe occupying the heel of the
Italian peninsula, were the closest neighbours of the Tarentines.

περὶ αὐτὸν οὔσης οἱ μὲν Λευκανοὶ καταπλαγέντες
φιλίαν ἐποιήσαντο πρὸς τοὺς Ταραντίνους, τῶν δὲ
Μεταποντίνων οὐ προσεχόντων αὐτῷ τοὺς Λευκανοὺς ἔπεισεν ἐμβαλεῖν εἰς τὴν χώραν καὶ τῷ
καιρῷ συνεπιθέμενος κατεπλήξατο τοὺς Μεταποντί-
νους. παρελθὼν δ' εἰς τὴν πόλιν ὡς φίλος ἐπράξατο
μὲν ἀργυρίου τάλαντα πλείω τῶν ἑξακοσίων, διακοσίας δὲ παρθένους τὰς ἐπιφανεστάτας ἔλαβεν εἰς
ὁμηρίαν, οὐχ οὕτω τῆς περὶ τὴν πίστιν ἀσφαλείας
4 χάριν, ὡς τῆς ἰδίας ἕνεκεν λαγνείας. ἀποθέμενος
γὰρ τὴν Λακωνικὴν ἐσθῆτα διετέλει τρυφῶν καὶ
τοὺς πιστεύσαντας αὐτῷ καταδουλούμενος· τηλι-
καύτας γὰρ ἔχων δυνάμεις καὶ χορηγίας οὐδὲν τῆς
Σπάρτης ἄξιον ἔπραξεν. ἐπεβάλετο μὲν γὰρ ἐπὶ
τὴν Σικελίαν στρατεύειν, ὡς τὴν τυραννίδα μὲν
καταλύσων τὴν Ἀγαθοκλέους, τὴν δ' αὐτονομίαν
τοῖς Σικελιώταις ἀποκαταστήσων, ὑπερθέμενος δὲ
ἐπὶ τοῦ παρόντος ταύτην τὴν στρατείαν ἔπλευσεν
εἰς Κόρκυραν καὶ κρατήσας τῆς πόλεως χρημάτων
τε πλῆθος εἰσεπράξατο καὶ φρουρὰν ἐγκατέστησε,
διανοούμενος ὁρμητηρίῳ τούτῳ τῷ τόπῳ χρήσασθαι καὶ τοῖς περὶ τὴν Ἑλλάδα πράγμασιν ἐφεδρεύειν.

105. Εὐθὺ δὲ καὶ πρεσβειῶν πρὸς αὐτὸν παραγενομένων παρά τε Δημητρίου τοῦ πολιορκητοῦ
καὶ Κασάνδρου περὶ συμμαχίας τούτων μὲν οὐδε-
τέρῳ προσέθετο, τοὺς δὲ Ταραντίνους καὶ τῶν
ἄλλων τινὰς πυθόμενος ἀφεστηκέναι τῆς μὲν Κορ-
κύρας τὴν ἱκανὴν φυλακὴν ἀπέλιπεν, μετὰ δὲ τῆς
ἄλλης δυνάμεως ἔπλει κατὰ σπουδὴν ἐπὶ τὴν
Ἰταλίαν, ὡς κολάσων τοὺς ἀπειθοῦντας. προσσχὼν
δὲ τῇ χώρᾳ καθ' ὃν τόπον ἐφύλασσον οἱ βάρβαροι,

he had a strong army under his command, the 303 B.C. Lucanians in alarm established friendship with the Tarentines ; and when the people of Metapontum did not come over to him, he persuaded the Lucanians to invade the territory of the Metapontines and, by making a simultaneous attack himself, intimidated them. Then, entering their city as a friend, he exacted more than six hundred talents of silver ; and he took two hundred maidens of the best families as hostages, not so much as a guarantee of the city's faith as to satisfy his own lust.[1] Indeed, having discarded the Spartan garb, he lived in continued luxury and made slaves of those who had trusted in him ; for although he had so strong an army and such ample supplies, he did nothing worthy of Sparta. He planned to invade Sicily as if to overthrow the tyranny of Agathocles and restore their independence to the Siciliots ; but postponing this campaign for the present, he sailed to Corcyra, and after getting possession of the city exacted a great sum of money and installed a garrison, intending to use this place as a base and to await a chance to take part in the affairs in Greece.

105. But soon, when envoys did come to him both from Demetrius Poliorcetes and from Cassander proposing alliances, he joined with neither of them ; but when he learned that the Tarentines and some of the others were in revolt, he left an adequate garrison in Corcyra, and with the rest of his army sailed at top speed to Italy in order to punish those who defied his commands. Putting in to land in the district that was defended by the barbarians, he took

[1] Cp. Duris, *FGrH*, 76. 18 ; Athenaeus, 13. 84 (p. 605 e).

τὴν μὲν πόλιν[1] ἑλὼν ἐξηνδραποδίσατο, τὴν δὲ χώραν
2 ἐλεηλάτησεν. ὁμοίως δὲ τὸ καλούμενον Τριόπιον
ἐκπολιορκήσας εἰς τρισχιλίους ἔλαβεν αἰχμαλώτους.
καθ' ὃν δὴ χρόνον οἱ μὲν ἀπὸ τῆς χώρας βάρβαροι
συνδραμόντες ἐπέθεντο νυκτὸς τῇ στρατοπεδείᾳ καὶ
μάχης γενομένης ἀνεῖλον τῶν μετὰ Κλεωνύμου
πλείους τῶν διακοσίων, ἐζώγρησαν δὲ περὶ χιλίους.
3 ἅμα δὲ τῷ κινδύνῳ τούτῳ χειμὼν ἐπιγενόμενος
εἴκοσι τῶν νεῶν διέφθειρε πλησίον ὁρμουσῶν τῆς
παρεμβολῆς. ὁ δὲ Κλεώνυμος δυσὶν ἐλαττώμασι
τηλικούτοις περιπεσὼν ἀπέπλευσε μετὰ τῆς δυνάμεως εἰς τὴν Κόρκυραν.

106. Τοῦ δ' ἐνιαυσίου χρόνου διεληλυθότος Ἀθήνησι μὲν ἦν ἄρχων Νικοκλῆς, ἐν Ῥώμῃ δὲ τὴν
ὕπατον ἀρχὴν διεδέξαντο Μάρκος Λίβιος καὶ
Μάρκος Αἰμίλιος. ἐπὶ δὲ τούτων Κάσανδρος ὁ
Μακεδόνων βασιλεὺς ὁρῶν τὴν δύναμιν τῶν Ἑλλήνων αὐξομένην καὶ πάντα τὸν πόλεμον ἐπὶ τὴν
Μακεδονίαν συνιστάμενον περίφοβος ἦν ὑπὲρ τοῦ
2 μέλλοντος. διόπερ ἐξέπεμψε πρεσβευτὰς πρὸς
Ἀντίγονον εἰς τὴν Ἀσίαν, ἀξιῶν διαλύσασθαι πρὸς
αὐτόν. ἀποκριναμένου δ' ἐκείνου διότι μίαν γι-
νώσκει διάλυσιν, ἐὰν ὁ Κάσανδρος ἐπιτρέπῃ τὰ
καθ' αὑτόν, καταπλαγεὶς Λυσίμαχον ἐκ τῆς Θρᾴκης

---

[1] The name of the city seems to have been lost.

---

[1] The context (if, indeed, Tarentines above is right) suggests that the city is Tarentum ; but no enslavement of its
population is known, and it is most probable that some city
name has fallen out. Cleonymus' raid upon Thuriae (Livy,

the city,[1] sold its people into slavery, and plundered 303 B.C.
the countryside. He likewise took by siege the city
called Triopium,[2] capturing about three thousand
prisoners. But at this very time the barbarians
throughout the region came together and attacked
his camp by night, and in the battle that took place
they slew more than two hundred of Cleonymus' men
and made prisoners about a thousand. A storm
rising at the time of the battle destroyed twenty of
the ships that lay at anchor near his encampment.
Having met with two such disasters, Cleonymus
sailed away to Corcyra with his army.[3]

106. When this year had passed, Nicocles was 302 B.C.
archon in Athens, and in Rome Marcus Livius and
Marcus Aemilius received the consulship.[4] While
these held office, Cassander, the king of the Macedonians, on seeing that the power of the Greeks [5] was
increasing and that the whole war was directed
against Macedonia, became much alarmed about
the future. He therefore sent envoys into Asia to
Antigonus, asking him to come to terms with him.
But when Antigonus replied that he recognized only
one basis for a settlement—Cassander's surrender
of whatever he possessed,—Cassander was alarmed
and summoned Lysimachus from Thrace to take con-

10. 2. 1), an otherwise unknown city on the east coast of
the Bay of Tarentum, belongs in the next year.
    [2] The exact site is not known.
    [3] There is nothing more about Cleonymus in what remains
of Diodorus. For his further adventures cp. Livy 10. 2.
    [4] Nicocles was archon in 302/1. Livy, 10. 1. 7, gives the
consuls of 302 B.C. as M. Livius Denter and Aemilius (without
praenomen).
    [5] *i.e.* the alliance under Demetrius Poliorcetes. The
narrative is continued from chap. 103. 7. Cp. Justin, 15. 2. 15;
Orosius, 3. 23. 41.

μετεπέμψατο πρὸς τὴν τῶν ὅλων κοινοπραγίαν·
3 ἀεὶ γὰρ εἰώθει τοῦτον κατὰ τοὺς μεγίστους φόβους
εἰς τὴν βοήθειαν προσλαμβάνεσθαι διά τε τὴν
τἀνδρὸς ἀρετὴν καὶ διὰ τὸ τὴν βασιλείαν αὐτοῦ
ὅμορον εἶναι τῇ Μακεδονίᾳ. συνεδρεύσαντες οὖν
οἱ βασιλεῖς οὗτοι περὶ τοῦ κοινοῦ συμφέροντος
ἐξέπεμψαν πρεσβευτὰς πρός τε Πτολεμαῖον τὸν
Αἰγύπτου βασιλέα καὶ πρὸς Σέλευκον τὸν τῶν ἄνω
σατραπειῶν κυριεύοντα, περί τε τῆς ὑπερηφανίας
τῆς ἐν ταῖς ἀποκρίσεσιν ἐμφανίζοντες καὶ τὸν ἐκ
τοῦ πολέμου κίνδυνον κοινὸν εἶναι πάντων διδά-
4 σκοντες. τῆς γὰρ Μακεδονίας κρατήσαντα τὸν
Ἀντίγονον εὐθὺς ἀφελεῖσθαι καὶ τῶν ἄλλων τὰς
βασιλείας· δεδωκέναι γὰρ αὐτὸν πεῖραν πλεονάκις
ὅτι πλεονέκτης ἐστὶ καὶ πᾶσαν ἀρχὴν ἀκοινώνητον
ποιεῖ. συμφέρειν οὖν ἅπαντας συμφρονῆσαι καὶ
5 κοινῇ πρὸς Ἀντίγονον ἐπανελέσθαι πόλεμον. οἱ
μὲν οὖν περὶ Πτολεμαῖον καὶ Σέλευκον δόξαντες
ἀληθῆ λέγειν[1] προθύμως ὑπήκουσαν καὶ συνετά-
ξαντο πρὸς ἀλλήλους[2] βοηθεῖν ἁδραῖς δυνάμεσι.

107. Τοῖς δὲ περὶ Κάσανδρον ἔδοξε μὴ περιμένειν τὴν τῶν πολεμίων ἔφοδον, ἀλλὰ καὶ αὐτοὺς
φθάσαντας ἐπιστρατεύειν καὶ προλαμβάνειν τὸ
χρήσιμον. διόπερ ὁ Κάσανδρος Λυσιμάχῳ μὲν
παρέδωκε μέρος τοῦ στρατοπέδου καὶ στρατηγὸν
Πρεπέλαον[3] συνεξέπεμψεν, αὐτὸς δὲ ἀνέζευξε μετὰ
τῆς λοιπῆς δυνάμεως εἰς Θετταλίαν, διαπολεμήσων
2 Δημητρίῳ καὶ τοῖς Ἕλλησι. Λυσίμαχος δὲ μετὰ

---

[1] πρὸς ἀλλήλους after λέγειν omitted by Bekker.
[2] πρὸς ἀλλήλους added by Bekker.
[3] Πρεπέλαον added by Beloch (Griechische Geschichte², 4. 1. 162, note 3).

certed action in regard to their highest interests ;
for it was his invariable custom when facing the most
alarming situations to call on Lysimachus for assistance, both because of his personal character and
because his kingdom lay next to Macedonia. When
these kings had taken counsel together about their
common interest, they sent envoys to Ptolemy, the
king of Egypt, and to Seleucus, who was ruler of the
upper satrapies, revealing the arrogance of Antigonus'
answer and showing that the danger arising from the
war was common to all. For they said, if Antigonus
should gain control of Macedonia, he would at once
take their kingdoms from the others also ; indeed
he had given proof many times that he was grasping
and regarded any command as a possession not to
be shared. It would therefore, they said, be advantageous for all to make plans in common and jointly
undertake a war against Antigonus. Now Ptolemy
and Seleucus, believing that the statements were true,
eagerly agreed and arranged with Cassander to
assist one another with strong forces.

107. Cassander, however, thought it best not to
await the attack of his enemies but to get the start
of them by opening the campaign himself and seizing
what he could use to advantage. Therefore Cassander gave to Lysimachus a part of his army and
sent with it Prepelaüs as general,[1] while he himself
moved with the rest of the army into Thessaly to
carry on the war with Demetrius and the Greeks.

[1] But cp. critical note.

στρατοπέδου διαβὰς ἐκ τῆς Εὐρώπης εἰς τὴν Ἀσίαν
Λαμψακηνοὺς μὲν καὶ Παριανοὺς ἑκουσίως προσ-
θεμένους ἀφῆκεν ἐλευθέρους, Σίγειον δὲ ἐκπολιορκήσας φρουρὰν παρεισήγαγε. μετὰ δὲ ταῦτα
Πρεπελάῳ μὲν τῷ στρατηγῷ δοὺς πεζοὺς ἑξακισχιλίους, ἱππεῖς δὲ χιλίους ἐξέπεμψε προσαξόμενον
τὰς πόλεις τάς τε κατὰ τὴν Αἰολίδα καὶ τὴν Ἰωνίαν,
αὐτὸς δὲ τὸ μὲν πρῶτον ἐπεχείρησε πολιορκεῖν τὴν
Ἄβυδον καὶ βέλη καὶ μηχανὰς καὶ τἄλλα παρ-
3 εσκευάζετο· ἐπεὶ δὲ κατὰ θάλατταν ἦλθε τοῖς
πολιορκουμένοις στρατιωτῶν πλῆθος παρὰ Δημητρίου τὸ δυνάμενον τὴν ἀσφάλειαν παρέχεσθαι τῇ
πόλει, ταύτης μὲν τῆς ἐπιβολῆς ἀπέστη, τὴν δ' ἐφ'
Ἑλλησπόντῳ Φρυγίαν προσαγαγόμενος καὶ Σύνναδα[1] πόλιν ἔχουσαν ἀποσκευὰς μεγάλας βασιλικὰς
4 ἐπολιόρκησεν. ὅτε δὴ καὶ Δόκιμον τὸν Ἀντιγόνου
στρατηγὸν πείσας κοινοπραγεῖν τά τε Σύνναδα
παρέλαβε διὰ τούτου καὶ τῶν ὀχυρωμάτων ἔνια
τῶν ἐχόντων τὰ βασιλικὰ χρήματα. ὁ δ' ἐπὶ τῆς
Αἰολίδος καὶ τῆς Ἰωνίας πεμφθεὶς ὑπὸ Λυσιμάχου
στρατηγὸς Πρεπέλαος Ἀδραμυττίου μὲν ἐκυρίευσεν
ἐν παρόδῳ, τὴν δ' Ἔφεσον πολιορκήσας καὶ καταπληξάμενος τοὺς ἔνδον παρέλαβε τὴν πόλιν. καὶ
τοὺς μὲν ἐγκαταληφθέντας τῶν Ῥοδίων ἑκατὸν
ὁμήρους ἀπέστειλεν εἰς τὴν πατρίδα, τοὺς δ' Ἐφε-
σίους ἀφῆκε,[2] τὰς δὲ ναῦς τὰς ἐν τῷ λιμένι πάσας
ἐνέπρησε διὰ τὸ θαλασσοκρατεῖν τοὺς πολεμίους

---

[1] Fischer in apparatus suggests reading καὶ <ἐπὶ τὴν ἄνω
Φρυγίαν προάγων> Σύνναδα, . . . Cp. note on translation.

Lysimachus with his army crossed from Europe to 302 B.C.
Asia, and since the inhabitants of Lampsacus and
Parium came over to him willingly, he left them free,
but when he took Sigeum by force, he installed a
garrison there. Next, giving his general Prepelaüs
six thousand foot-soldiers and a thousand horse, he
sent him to win over the cities throughout Aeolis and
Ionia ; as for himself, he first attempted to invest
Abydus and set about preparing missiles and engines
and the other equipment ; but when there arrived
by sea to assist the besieged a large body of soldiers
sent by Demetrius, a force sufficient to secure the
safety of the city, he gave up this attempt and won
over Hellespontine Phrygia, and also laid siege to
the city of Synnada,[1] which possessed a great royal
treasure. It was at this very time that he even persuaded Docimus, the general of Antigonus, to make
common cause with him, and by his aid he took
Synnada and also some of the strongholds that held
the royal wealth. Prepelaüs, the general who had
been sent by Lysimachus to Aeolis and Ionia, mastered Adramyttium as he passed by, and then, laying
siege to Ephesus and frightening its inhabitants, he
took the city. The hundred Rhodian hostages [2] whom
he found there he sent back to their native land ;
and he left the Ephesians free but burned all the ships
in the harbour, since the enemy controlled the sea

---

[1] Since Synnada is not in Hellespontine Phrygia, we may
suppose either an error on Diodorus' part or the loss of some
such words as those suggested by Fischer : " and then
advancing into Upper Phrygia, he laid siege to Synnada."
[2] Cp. chap. 99. 3.

---

[2] ⟨ἐλευθέρους⟩ ἀφῆκε Reiske ; ⟨ὑποσπόνδους⟩ ἀφῆκε Hertlein,
Fischer.

καὶ τὴν ὅλην κρίσιν τοῦ πολέμου ἄδηλον ὑπάρχειν.
5 μετὰ δὲ ταῦτα Τηίους μὲν καὶ Κολοφωνίους προσ
ηγάγετο, Ἐρυθραίοις δὲ καὶ Κλαζομενίοις ἐλθούσης
κατὰ θάλατταν βοηθείας τὰς μὲν πόλεις ἑλεῖν οὐκ
ἠδυνήθη, τὴν δὲ χώραν αὐτῶν πορθήσας ἀνέζευξεν
ἐπὶ Σάρδεις. ἐνταῦθα δὴ τὸν Ἀντιγόνου στρα
τηγὸν Φοίνικα[1] πείσας ἀποστῆναι τοῦ βασιλέως
παρέλαβε τὴν πόλιν πλὴν τῆς ἄκρας· ταύτην γὰρ
φυλάττων Φίλιππος εἷς τῶν Ἀντιγόνου φίλων
βεβαίαν ἐτήρει τὴν εὔνοιαν τὴν πρὸς τὸν πεπι
στευκότα.

Τὰ μὲν οὖν περὶ Λυσίμαχον ἐν τούτοις ἦν.

108. Ἀντίγονος δὲ προκεχειρισμένος ἀγῶνα μέ
γαν καὶ πανήγυριν ἐν Ἀντιγονίᾳ συντελεῖν πάντο
θεν ἀθλητάς τε καὶ τεχνίτας τοὺς ἐπιφανεστάτους
ἐπὶ μεγάλοις ἄθλοις καὶ μισθοῖς ἠθροίκει. ὡς δ᾽
ἤκουσε τὴν Λυσιμάχου διάβασιν καὶ τῶν στρατηγῶν
τὴν ἀπόστασιν, τὸν μὲν ἀγῶνα διέλυσε, τοῖς δ᾽
ἀθληταῖς καὶ τοῖς τεχνίταις ἀπέδωκε μισθοὺς οὐκ
2 ἐλάττους διακοσίων ταλάντων. αὐτὸς δὲ τὴν δύ
ναμιν ἀναλαβὼν ὥρμησεν ἐκ τῆς Συρίας σύντομον
τὴν πορείαν ποιούμενος ἐπὶ τοὺς πολεμίους. εἰς
δὲ Ταρσὸν τῆς Κιλικίας ἀφικόμενος ἐξ ὧν κατεκό
μισε χρημάτων ἐκ τῶν Κυΐνδων[2] τὸ στρατόπεδον
3 εἰς τρεῖς μῆνας ἐμισθοδότησεν. χωρὶς δὲ τούτων
τρισχίλια τάλαντα μετὰ τῆς δυνάμεως ἐκόμιζεν,
ὅπως τοιαύτην ἔχῃ τὴν χορηγίαν, ὅταν αὐτῷ χρεία
γένηται χρημάτων. ἔπειτα τὸν Ταῦρον ὑπερβαλὼν

[1] καὶ Δόκιμον after Φοίνικα omitted by Wesseling.

and the whole outcome of the war was uncertain.
After this he secured the adherence of the people of
Teos and of Colophon, but since reinforcements came
by sea to Erythrae and Clazomenae, he could not
capture these cities ; however, he plundered their
territory and then set out for Sardis. There, by persuading Antigonus' general Phoenix to desert the
king, he gained control of the city except the acropolis ; for Philip,[1] one of the friends of Antigonus,
who was guarding the citadel, held firm his loyalty
toward the man who had placed trust in him.

The affairs of Lysimachus were in this position.

108. Antigonus, who had made preparations to
celebrate great games and a festival in Antigonia,
had collected from all sides the most famous athletes
and artists to compete for great prizes and fees. But
when he heard of the crossing of Lysimachus and the
desertion of his own generals, he abandoned the
games but distributed to the athletes and artists not
less than two hundred talents as compensation. He
himself taking his army set out from Syria and made
a rapid march against the enemy. Arriving at Tarsus
in Cilicia, he paid the army for three months from
the money he had brought down from Cyinda.[2]
Apart from this fund, he was carrying three thousand
talents with the army in order that he might have
this provision whenever he had need of money.
Then, crossing the Taurus Range, he marched toward

---

[1] This is probably the same Philip as the adviser given to
Demetrius by Antigonus in 314 B.C., Book 19. 69. 1.
[2] For the treasury of Alexander at Cyinda cp. Book 18.
62. 2 ; 19. 56. 5.

---

[2] Κυΐνδων, cp. Books 18. 62. 2 ; 19. 56. 5 ; Κουΐνδων RF,
Κουΐνδῶν X.

προῆγεν ἐπὶ Καππαδοκίας καὶ τοὺς ἀφεστηκότας
περὶ τὴν ἄνω Φρυγίαν καὶ Λυκαονίαν ἐπιπορευόμενος πάλιν εἰς τὴν προϋπάρχουσαν συμμαχίαν
4 ἀποκατέστησεν. καθ' ὃν δὴ χρόνον οἱ περὶ τὸν
Λυσίμαχον πυθόμενοι τὴν τῶν πολεμίων παρουσίαν
συνήδρευον, βουλευόμενοι πῶς χρηστέον εἴη τοῖς
5 ἐπιφερομένοις κινδύνοις. ἔδοξεν οὖν αὐτοῖς εἰς μὲν
μάχην μὴ συγκαταβαίνειν, ἕως ἂν οἱ περὶ Σέλευκον
ἐκ τῶν ἄνω σατραπειῶν καταβῶσι, τόπους δ'[1]
ὀχυροὺς καταλαβέσθαι καὶ χάρακι καὶ τάφρῳ τὴν
στρατοπεδείαν ἀσφαλισαμένους ὑπομένειν τῶν πολεμίων τὴν ἔφοδον. οὗτοι μὲν οὖν τὸ δοχθὲν αὐτοῖς
ἐπετέλουν κατὰ σπουδήν· ὁ δ' Ἀντίγονος ἐπεὶ
πλησίον ἐγένετο τῶν πολεμίων, ἐκτάξας τὴν δύ-
6 ναμιν προεκαλεῖτο εἰς μάχην. οὐδενὸς δ' ἐπεξιέναι
τολμῶντος αὐτὸς μὲν κατελάβετο τόπους τινάς, δι'
ὧν ἀναγκαῖον ἦν τὰς τροφὰς τοῖς ἐναντίοις παρα-
κομίζεσθαι· οἱ δὲ περὶ τὸν Λυσίμαχον φοβηθέντες
μήποτε τῆς ἀγορᾶς ἀποκοπείσης ὑποχείριοι γένωνται τοῖς πολεμίοις, νυκτὸς ἀνέζευξαν καὶ διατείναντες σταδίους τετρακοσίους κατεστρατοπέδευσαν
7 περὶ Δορύλαιον· εἶχε γὰρ τὸ χωρίον σίτου τε καὶ
τῆς ἄλλης χορηγίας πλῆθος καὶ ποταμὸν παραρ-
ρέοντα δυνάμενον ἀσφάλειαν παρέχεσθαι τοῖς παρ'
αὐτὸν στρατοπεδεύουσι. βαλόμενοι δὲ στρατοπεδείαν ὠχύρωσαν τὴν παρεμβολὴν βαθείᾳ τάφρῳ
καὶ τριπλῷ χάρακι.

109. Ἀντίγονος δὲ πυθόμενος τὴν τῶν πολεμίων
ἀποχώρησιν εὐθὺς ἐπεδίωκεν αὐτοὺς καὶ πλησίον
γενόμενος τῆς παρεμβολῆς, ἐπεὶ πρὸς παράταξιν οὐ
συγκατέβαινον, ἤρξατο περιταφρεύειν τὴν στρατοπεδείαν καὶ καταπέλτας καὶ βέλη μετεπέμψατο,

Cappadocia ; and, advancing upon those who had 302 B.C.
deserted him in upper Phrygia and Lycaonia, he
restored them again to the former alliance. At this
very time Lysimachus, on hearing of the presence
of the enemy, held a council considering how he
ought to meet the approaching dangers. They
decided not to join in battle until Seleucus should
come down from the upper satrapies, but to occupy
strong positions and, after making their encampment
safe with palisade and ditch, to await the onslaught
of the enemy. They therefore carried out their
decision with vigour ; but Antigonus, when he came
near the enemy, drew up his army and challenged
them to battle. When no one dared to issue forth,
he himself occupied certain places through which it
was necessary that the provisions for his opponents
should be transported ; and Lysimachus, fearing that
if their food supply should be cut off, they would then
be at the mercy of the enemy, broke camp at night,
made a forced march of four hundred stades,[1] and
camped near Dorylaeum ; for the stronghold had an
ample store of grain and other supplies, and a river ran
by it that could give protection to those who camped
beside it. Pitching camp, they strengthened their
encampment with a deep ditch and a triple stockade.

109. When Antigonus learned of the departure
of the enemy he at once pursued them ; and, after
he had approached their encampment, since they
did not come out for battle, he began to surround
their camp with a trench, and he sent for catapults

------

[1] About 44 miles.

------

[1] δ' Geer : δέ.

βουλόμενος αὐτὴν πολιορκῆσαι. συντελουμένων δ᾽
ἀκροβολισμῶν περὶ τὴν ταφρείαν καὶ τῶν περὶ τὸν
Λυσίμαχον πειρωμένων ἀνείργειν τοῖς βέλεσι τοὺς
ἐργαζομένους ἐν πᾶσιν προετέρουν οἱ περὶ τὸν
2 Ἀντίγονον. ἔπειτα χρόνου γενομένου καὶ τῶν ἔργων ἤδη συντέλειαν λαμβανόντων, τῆς δὲ τροφῆς
ὑπολιπούσης τοὺς πολιορκουμένους οἱ περὶ Λυσίμαχον, τηρήσαντες νύκτα χειμέριον, ἀναζεύξαντες
ἐκ τῆς παρεμβολῆς διὰ τῶν ὑπερδεξίων τόπων
ἀπεχώρησαν εἰς παραχειμασίαν. ὁ δ᾽ Ἀντίγονος
ἡμέρας γενομένης ὡς εἶδε τὴν τῶν πολεμίων ἀπαλ-
3 λαγήν, ἀντιπαρῆγεν αὐτὸς διὰ τῶν πεδίων. ἐπιγενομένων δὲ ὄμβρων μεγάλων καὶ τῆς χώρας
οὔσης βαθυγείου καὶ πηλώδους τῶν τε ὑποζυγίων
οὐκ ὀλίγα συνέβη καὶ τῶν σωμάτων τινὰ διαφθαρῆναι καὶ τὸ σύνολον ἐπιπόνως ἅπασαν τὴν δύναμιν
4 διατεθῆναι. διόπερ ὁ βασιλεὺς ἅμα μὲν ἀναλαβεῖν
βουλόμενος ἐκ τῆς κακοπαθίας τοὺς στρατιώτας,
ἅμα δὲ τὴν χειμερινὴν ὥραν ὁρῶν περιλαμβάνουσαν
τοῦ μὲν καταδιώκειν ἀπέστη, πρὸς δὲ τὴν χειμασίαν
ἐπιλεξάμενος τοὺς εὐθετωτάτους τόπους διεῖλε κατὰ
5 μέρη τὴν δύναμιν. πυνθανόμενος δὲ Σέλευκον κατα-
βαίνειν ἐκ τῶν ἄνω σατραπειῶν μετὰ μεγάλης
δυνάμεως, ἔπεμψέ τινας τῶν φίλων εἰς τὴν Ἑλλάδα πρὸς Δημήτριον, παρακελευόμενος ἥκειν πρὸς
αὐτὸν μετὰ τῆς δυνάμεως τὴν ταχίστην· σφόδρα
γὰρ εὐλαβεῖτο μὴ πάντων τῶν βασιλέων ἐπ᾽ αὐτὸν
συνδραμόντων ἀναγκασθῇ παρατάξει κρῖναι τὸν
ὅλον πόλεμον πρὶν ἢ συνελθεῖν εἰς ταὐτὸν τὴν ἐκ
6 τῆς Εὐρώπης δύναμιν. παραπλησίως δὲ καὶ Λυσίμαχος διεῖλε τὴν δύναμιν εἰς χειμασίαν ἐν τῷ καλου-
μένῳ Σαλωνίας[1] πεδίῳ. ἀγορὰν δὲ πολλὴν ἐξ

and missiles, intending to storm it. When shots were 302 B.C.
exchanged about the excavation and Lysimachus'
men tried to drive away with missiles those who were
working, in every case Antigonus had the better of
it. Then as time passed and the work was already
nearing completion, since food was growing scarce
for the besieged, Lysimachus, after waiting for a
stormy night, set out from the camp and departed
through the higher land to go into winter quarters.
But when at daybreak Antigonus saw the departure
of the enemy, he himself marched parallel with them
through the plains. Great rainstorms occurred, with
the result that, as the country had deep soil and
became very muddy, he lost a considerable number
of his pack animals and a few of his men, and
in general the whole army was in serious difficulty.
Therefore the king, both because he wished to restore his soldiers after their sufferings and because
he saw that the winter season was at hand, gave up
the pursuit ; and selecting the places best suited for
wintering, he divided his army into sections. But
when he learned that Seleucus was coming down
from the upper satrapies with a great force, he sent
some of his friends into Greece to Demetrius, bidding
him come to him with his army as soon as possible ;
for, since all the kings had united against him, he was
taking every precaution not to be forced to decide
the whole war in battle before the army in Europe
came to join him. Similarly Lysimachus also divided
his army in order to go into winter quarters in the
plain called that of Salonia. He obtained ample

---

¹ Σαλωνίας Wesseling (cp. Strabo, 12. 5. 7) : Σαλμωνίας.

Ἡρακλείας μετεπέμπετο, ποιησάμενος ἐπιγαμίαν
7 πρὸς τοὺς Ἡρακλεώτας· ἔγημε γὰρ Ἄμηστριν τὴν
Ὀξυάρτου μὲν θυγατέρα, Δαρείου δὲ τοῦ βασιλέως ἀδελφιδῆν, Κρατεροῦ δὲ γυναῖκα γενομένην
ὑπ᾽ Ἀλεξάνδρου δοθεῖσαν, τότε δυναστεύουσαν τῆς
πόλεως.

Καὶ τὰ μὲν περὶ τὴν Ἀσίαν ἐν τούτοις ἦν.

110. Κατὰ δὲ τὴν Ἑλλάδα Δημήτριος διατρίβων
ἐν ταῖς Ἀθήναις ἔσπευδε μυηθῆναι καὶ παραλαβεῖν[1]
τὴν ἐν Ἐλευσῖνι τελετήν. ἀπεχούσης δὲ χρόνον
ἱκανὸν τῆς κατὰ νόμους ἡμέρας, καθ᾽ ἣν εἰώθεισαν
Ἀθηναῖοι συντελεῖν τὴν τελετήν, ἔπεισε τὸν δῆμον
διὰ τὰς εὐεργεσίας κινῆσαι τὸ πάτριον ἔθος. παραδοὺς οὖν αὐτὸν ἄνοπλον τοῖς ἱερεῦσι καὶ πρὸ τῆς
ὡρισμένης ἡμέρας μυηθεὶς ἀνέζευξεν ἐκ τῶν Ἀθη-
2 νῶν. καὶ τὸ μὲν πρῶτον εἰς Χαλκίδα τῆς Εὐβοίας
ἤθροισε τὸν στόλον καὶ τὴν πεζὴν δύναμιν· μετὰ δὲ
ταῦτα πυθόμενος τοὺς περὶ Κάσανδρον προκατει-
λῆφθαι τὰς παρόδους, πεζῇ μὲν ἀπέγνω τὴν εἰς
Θετταλίαν ποιεῖσθαι πορείαν, παραπλεύσας δὲ μετὰ
τῆς δυνάμεως εἰς τὸν ἐν Λαρίσῃ λιμένα καὶ τὴν δύναμιν ἐκβιβάσας τὴν μὲν πόλιν ἐξ ἐφόδου παρέλαβε,
τὴν δ᾽ ἄκραν ἐκπολιορκήσας τοὺς μὲν φρουροὺς
δήσας παρέδωκεν εἰς φυλακήν, τοῖς δὲ Λαρισαίοις
3 τὴν αὐτονομίαν ἀποκατέστησεν. μετὰ δὲ ταῦτα
Ἀντρῶνας[2] μὲν καὶ Πτελεὸν προσηγάγετο, Δίον δὲ

---

[1] παραλαβεῖν Fischer (in apparatus) : καταλαβεῖν.

[2] Ἀντρῶνας Unger, Fischer, Ἄντρωνας Madvig, Ἄντρωνα
Wesseling : Πρώνας.

---

[1] After Craterus deserted Amestris (or Amastris) in order
to marry Phila (Book 18. 18. 7), she married Dionysius, the

434

supplies from Heraclea, having made a marriage 302 B.C. alliance with the Heracleotes ; for he had married Amestris, the daughter of Oxyartes and niece of King Darius. She had been wife of Craterus, given him by Alexander, and at the time in question was ruler of the city.[1]

Such was the situation in Asia.

110. In Greece Demetrius, who was tarrying in Athens, was eager to be initiated and to participate in the mysteries at Eleusis.[2] Since it was a considerable time before the legally established day on which the Athenians were accustomed to celebrate the mysteries, he persuaded the people because of his benefactions to change the custom of their fathers. And so, giving himself over unarmed to the priests, he was initiated before the regular day and departed from Athens. And first he gathered together his fleet and his land army in Chalcis of Euboea ; then, learning that Cassander had already occupied the passes in advance, he gave up the attempt to advance into Thessaly by land, but sailed along the coast with the army into the port of Larisa.[3] Disembarking the army, he captured the city at once ; and taking the acropolis, he imprisoned the garrison and put them under guard, but he restored their autonomy to the people of Larisa. Thereafter he won over Antrones and Pteleum,[4] and when Cassander would have trans-

---

ruler of Heraclea. On his death she continued to rule that city for their minor children until her marriage with Lysimachus (Strabo, 12. 3. 10). Lysimachus in his turn soon deserted her to marry Arsinoë.

[2] Cp. Plutarch, *Demetrius*, 26.

[3] This is Larisa Cremastê in Phthiotis.

[4] Antron (or Antrones) and Pteleum are also in Phthiotis, a little north-east of Larisa.

καὶ Ὀρχομενὸν¹ μετοικίζοντος εἰς Θήβας Κασάνδρου διεκώλυσε μετοικισθῆναι τὰς πόλεις. Κάσανδρος δὲ θεωρῶν τὰ πράγματα τῷ Δημητρίῳ
κατὰ νοῦν χωροῦντα Φερὰς μὲν καὶ Θήβας ἁδρο-
τέραις φρουραῖς παρεφύλαττε, τὴν δὲ δύναμιν πᾶσαν εἰς ἕνα τόπον ἀθροίσας ἀντεστρατοπέδευσε τοῖς
4 περὶ τὸν Δημήτριον. εἶχε δὲ τοὺς σύμπαντας
πεζοὺς μὲν εἰς δισμυρίους ἐννακισχιλίους, ἱππεῖς
δὲ δισχιλίους. τῷ δὲ Δημητρίῳ συνηκολούθουν
ἱππεῖς μὲν χίλιοι καὶ πεντακόσιοι, πεζοὶ δὲ Μακεδόνες οὐκ ἐλάττους τῶν ὀκτακισχιλίων, μισθοφόροι
δ᾽ εἰς μυρίους καὶ πεντακισχιλίους, ἐκ δὲ τῶν κατὰ
τὴν Ἑλλάδα πόλεων δισμύριοι καὶ πεντακισχίλιοι,
ψιλικὰ δὲ τάγματα καὶ πειρατῶν παντοδαπῶν τῶν
συντρεχόντων ἐπὶ τοὺς πολέμους² καὶ τὰς ἁρπαγὰς
οὐκ ἐλάττους τῶν ὀκτακισχιλίων, ὥστ᾽ εἶναι τοὺς
ἅπαντας πεζοὺς περὶ τοὺς πεντακισμυρίους ἑξακισ-
5 χιλίους. ἀντικαθημένων δὲ τῶν στρατοπέδων
ἀλλήλοις ἐπὶ πολλὰς ἡμέρας ἐκτάξεις μὲν ἐγίνοντο
παρ᾽ ἀμφοτέροις, εἰς μάχην δὲ οὐδέτερος συγ-
κατέβαινε, καραδοκῶν τὴν ἐπὶ τῆς Ἀσίας ἐσομένην
6 τῶν ὅλων κρίσιν. Δημήτριος δέ, τῶν Φεραίων
ἐπικαλεσαμένων αὐτόν, παρεισπεσὼν εἰς τὴν πόλιν
μετὰ μέρους τῆς δυνάμεως τὴν μὲν ἄκραν ἐκπολιορκήσας ὑποσπόνδους ἀφῆκε τοὺς παρὰ Κασάνδρου
στρατιώτας, τοῖς δὲ Φεραίοις τὴν ἐλευθερίαν ἀποκατέστησεν.

111. Ἐν τούτοις δ᾽ ὄντων τῶν περὶ Θεσσαλίαν
ἧκον πρὸς τὸν Δημήτριον οἱ πεμφθέντες ὑπ᾽ Ἀντιγόνου, διασαφοῦντες τὰς παρὰ τοῦ πατρὸς ἐντολὰς

---

¹ Fischer in apparatus suggests Νηλίαν and Ὀρμένιον from
Strabo, 9. 5. 15.

ported the people of Dium and Orchomenus [1] into Thebes, he prevented the transplanting of the cities. But when Cassander saw that Demetrius' undertakings were prospering, he first protected Pherae and Thebes with stronger garrisons ; and then, after collecting his whole army into one place, he encamped over against Demetrius. He had in all twenty-nine thousand foot-soldiers and two thousand horsemen. Demetrius was followed by fifteen hundred horsemen, not less than eight thousand Macedonian foot-soldiers, mercenaries to the number of fifteen thousand, twenty-five thousand from the cities throughout Greece, and at least eight thousand of the light armed troops and of the freebooters of all sorts who had gathered for the fighting and the plundering ; so that there were in all about fifty-six thousand foot-soldiers. For many days the camps were pitched opposite each other, and the battle lines were drawn up on both sides, but neither came forward into battle since each was awaiting the decision of the whole matter that would take place in Asia. Demetrius, however, when the people of Pherae called upon him, entering their city with part of his army and taking the citadel, dismissed the soldiers of Cassander on terms and restored their liberty to the people of Pherae.

111. While affairs in Thessaly were in this state, there came to Demetrius the messengers sent by Antigonus, accurately detailing the orders of his

[1] Dium and Orchomenus in this region are unknown ; but since the Thebes in question must be Thebae Phthiotides (cp. Pherae and Thebes below), Demetrius can hardly have returned to Boeotia.

---

[2] πολέμους Dindorf : πολεμίους.

καὶ παρακελευόμενοι τὴν ταχίστην διαβιβάζειν τὰς
2 δυνάμεις εἰς τὴν Ἀσίαν. διόπερ ἀναγκαῖον ἡγησά-
μενος ὑπάρχειν ὁ βασιλεὺς τὸ πείθεσθαι τῷ πατρί,
πρὸς μὲν Κάσανδρον διαλύσεις ἐποιήσατο, συνθέμενος εἶναι κυρίας τὰς συνθήκας, ἐὰν ὦσιν εὐάρεστοι
τῷ πατρί, ἀκριβῶς μὲν εἰδὼς οὐ προσδεξόμενον
αὐτὸν διὰ τὸ κεκρικέναι πάντως διὰ τῶν ὅπλων
ἐπιθεῖναι τέλος τῷ συμβάντι πολέμῳ, βουλόμενος
δὲ τὴν ἐκ τῆς Ἑλλάδος ἀποχώρησιν εὐσχήμονα
ποιήσασθαι καὶ μὴ φυγῇ παραπλησίαν· ἐγέγραπτο
γὰρ ἐν ταῖς συνθήκαις πρὸς τοῖς ἄλλοις καὶ τὸ τὰς
Ἑλληνίδας πόλεις ἐλευθέρας ὑπάρχειν, οὐ τὰς κατὰ
τὴν Ἑλλάδα μόνον, ἀλλὰ καὶ τὰς κατὰ τὴν Ἀσίαν.
3 μετὰ δὲ ταῦθ' ὁ Δημήτριος παρασκευασάμενος
πόρια πρὸς τὴν παρακομιδὴν τῶν τε στρατιωτῶν
καὶ τῆς ἀποσκευῆς ἀνήχθη παντὶ τῷ στόλῳ καὶ
κομισθεὶς διὰ νήσων κατέπλευσεν εἰς Ἔφεσον.
ἐκβιβάσας δὲ τὴν δύναμιν καὶ στρατοπεδεύσας
πλησίον τῶν τειχῶν ἠνάγκασε τὴν πόλιν εἰς τὴν
προϋπάρχουσαν ἀποκαταστῆναι τάξιν καὶ τὴν μὲν
ὑπὸ Πρεπελάου τοῦ Λυσιμάχου στρατηγοῦ παρεισ-
αχθεῖσαν φρουρὰν ἀφῆκεν ὑπόσπονδον, ἰδίαν δὲ
φυλακὴν εἰς τὴν ἄκραν καταστήσας παρῆλθεν εἰς
Ἑλλήσποντον. καὶ Λαμψακηνοὺς μὲν καὶ Παρια-
νούς, ἔτι δὲ τῶν ἄλλων τῶν μεταβεβλημένων
πόλεών τινας ἀνεκτήσατο, ἐπὶ δὲ τὸ στόμα τοῦ
Πόντου παραγενόμενος πρὸς τῷ Χαλκηδονίων[1] ἱερῷ
στρατοπεδείαν περιεβάλετο καὶ τοὺς φυλάξοντας
τὸν τόπον ἀπέλιπε στρατιώτας πεζοὺς μὲν τρισχιλίους, ναῦς δὲ μακρὰς τριάκοντα· τὴν δ' ἄλλην

father and bidding him take his army across into Asia 302 B.C. as swiftly as possible. Since he regarded obedience to his father's orders as obligatory, the king came to terms with Cassander, making the condition that the agreements should be valid only if they were acceptable to his father ; for although he very well knew that his father would not accept them since he had definitely made up his mind to bring to an end by force of arms the war which had set in, yet Demetrius wished to make his withdrawal from Greece appear respectable and not like a flight. Indeed, it was written among other conditions in the agreement that the Greek cities were to be free, not only those of Greece but also those of Asia. Then Demetrius, after preparing ships for the transportation of the soldiers and the equipment, set sail with his whole fleet and, going through the islands, put in at Ephesus. Disembarking his army and camping near the walls, he forced the city to return to its former status ; then he dismissed on terms the garrison that had been introduced by Prepelaüs, the general of Lysimachus, and after stationing his own garrison on the acropolis, he went on to the Hellespont. He also recovered Lampsacus and Parium, likewise some of the other cities that had changed sides ; and when he arrived at the entrance of the Pontus, he constructed a camp beside the shrine of the Chalcedonians [1] and left to guard the region three thousand foot-soldiers and thirty warships. Then he sent the rest of the

---

[1] The shrine of the Chalcedonians may be identical with the place on the shore of the Pontus called Hieron, Book 19. 73. 6.

---

[1] Χαλκηδονίων Fischer (in apparatus ; cp. Books 18. 72, 4 ; 19. 60. 3) : Καλχηδονίων RX, Καρχηδονίων F.

δύναμιν διελόμενος κατὰ πόλεις διέδωκεν εἰς χειμασίαν.

4 Περὶ δὲ τούτους τοὺς χρόνους καὶ Μιθριδάτης, ὑπήκοος ὢν Ἀντιγόνῳ καὶ δόξας ἀφίστασθαι πρὸς τοὺς περὶ Κάσανδρον, ἀνῃρέθη περὶ Κίον τῆς Μυσίας, ἄρξας αὐτῆς καὶ Μυρλείας[1] ἔτη τριάκοντα καὶ πέντε· τὴν δὲ δυναστείαν διαδεξάμενος Μιθριδάτης πολλοὺς προσεκτήσατο, τῆς δὲ Καππαδοκίας καὶ Παφλαγονίας ἦρξεν ἔτη τριάκοντα ἕξ.

112. Ἐν δὲ ταῖς αὐταῖς ἡμέραις Κάσανδρος μετὰ τὴν ἀπαλλαγὴν τὴν Δημητρίου τὰς μὲν κατὰ τὴν Θετταλίαν πόλεις ἀνεκτήσατο, Πλείσταρχον δὲ μετὰ δυνάμεως ἐξέπεμψεν εἰς τὴν Ἀσίαν βοηθήσοντα τοῖς περὶ Λυσίμαχον. οἱ δὲ συναποσταλέντες ἦσαν πεζοὶ μὲν μύριοι δισχίλιοι, ἱππεῖς δὲ

2 πεντακόσιοι. ὁ δὲ Πλείσταρχος ἐπειδὴ παραγενόμενος ἐπὶ τὸ στόμα τοῦ Πόντου κατέλαβε τοὺς τόπους προκατεχομένους ὑπὸ τῶν πολεμίων, ἀπογνοὺς τὴν διάβασιν παρῆλθεν εἰς Ὀδησσόν, ἣ κεῖται μεταξὺ μὲν τῆς τε Ἀπολλωνίας καὶ Καλλαντίας,[2] κατ' ἀντικρὺ δὲ τῆς ἐν τῷ πέραν Ἡρακλείας,

3 ἐχούσης τι μέρος τῆς Λυσιμάχου δυνάμεως. οὐκ ἔχων δ' ἱκανὰ πόρια πρὸς τὴν τῶν στρατιωτῶν διάβασιν τριχῇ διεμέρισε τὴν δύναμιν. τὴν μὲν οὖν πρώτην ἀποστολὴν συνέβη διασωθῆναι πρὸς τὴν Ἡράκλειαν, τὴν δὲ δευτέραν ὑπὸ τῶν περὶ τὸ στόμα τοῦ Πόντου φυλακίδων νεῶν ἁλῶναι. κατὰ τὴν

---

[1] Μυρλείας Post: Ἀρρήνης RX, Μαρίνης F.
[2] Καλλαντίας Palmer: Γαλατίας.

army into winter quarters, dividing it among the cities.

At about this time Mithridates,[1] who was subject to Antigonus but appeared to be shifting his allegiance to Cassander, was slain at Cius in Mysia after having ruled that city and Myrlea[2] for thirty-five years; and Mithridates,[3] inheriting the kingdom, added many new subjects and was king of Cappadocia and Paphlagonia for thirty-six years.

112. In these same days Cassander, after the departure of Demetrius, took possession of the cities of Thessaly and sent Pleistarchus with an army into Asia to aid Lysimachus. Those sent with him were twelve thousand foot-soldiers and five hundred horsemen. But when Pleistarchus came to the entrance of the Pontus, he found that the region had already been taken over by the enemy and, abandoning the crossing, he turned aside to Odessus, which lies between Apollonia and Callantia, directly opposite to Heraclea on the opposite shore, where a part of the army of Lysimachus was quartered. Since he did not have ships enough for transporting his soldiers, he divided his army into three contingents. Now the first force sent out came safe to Heraclea, but the second was captured by the guard-ships at the entrance to the Pontus. When Pleistarchus himself

---

[1] Mithridates II of Cius in Bithynia, son of Ariobarzanes, cp. Book 16. 90. 2.

[2] Myrlea, later called Apamea, was an important port near Cius; but see critical note.

[3] Mithridates III of Cius and I of Pontus, if identical with the Mithridates of Book 19. 40. 2, and Plutarch, *Demetrius*, 4, is son of an Ariobarzanes who is probably the brother of Mithridates II. In our passage, then, the nephew succeeds his uncle.

τρίτην δὲ αὐτοῦ συνδιαβαίνοντος τοῦ Πλειστάρχου
χειμὼν ἐπεγενήθη τηλικοῦτος ὥστε τὰ πλεῖστα τῶν
4 σκαφῶν καὶ τῶν σωμάτων διαφθαρῆναι· καὶ γὰρ
ἡ κομίζουσα ναῦς ἑξήρης τὸν στρατηγὸν συνεκλύ-
σθη καὶ τῶν ἐν αὐτῇ πλεόντων οὐκ ἐλαττόνων
ἢ πεντακοσίων τρεῖς πρὸς τοῖς τριάκοντα μόνον
διεσώθησαν. ἐν δὲ τούτοις ἦν καὶ ὁ Πλείσταρχος,
ναυαγίου μὲν ἐπειλημμένος, εἰς δὲ τὴν γῆν ἡμιθανὴς
ἐκβεβρασμένος. οὗτος μὲν οὖν ἀποκομισθεὶς εἰς
Ἡράκλειαν καὶ προσαναλαβὼν ἐκ τῆς ἀτυχίας τὸ
σῶμα πρὸς Λυσίμαχον εἰς τὴν χειμασίαν ἀνέζευξε,
ἀποβεβληκὼς τὸ πλεῖον τῆς δυνάμεως.

113. Ἐν δὲ ταῖς αὐταῖς ἡμέραις καὶ Πτολεμαῖος
ὁ βασιλεὺς ἀναζεύξας ἐξ Αἰγύπτου μετὰ δυνάμεως
ἀξιολόγου τὰς μὲν ἐν τῇ Κοίλῃ Συρίᾳ πόλεις ἁπάσας
ὑποχειρίους ἐποιήσατο· Σιδῶνα δὲ πολιορκοῦντος
αὐτοῦ τινες παρῆσαν ἀπαγγέλλοντες ψευδῶς ὅτι
παρατάξεως γενομένης τοῖς βασιλεῦσιν οἱ μὲν περὶ
Λυσίμαχον καὶ Σέλευκον ἡττηθέντες ἀποκεχωρή-
κασιν εἰς τὴν Ἡράκλειαν, Ἀντίγονος δὲ νενικηκὼς
2 προσάγει μετὰ δυνάμεως ἐπὶ Συρίας. παραλο-
γισθεὶς οὖν ὑπὸ τούτων καὶ πεισθεὶς ἀληθῆ τὴν
προσαγγελίαν εἶναι, πρὸς μὲν τοὺς Σιδωνίους εἰς
τέτταρας μῆνας ἀνοχὰς ἐποιήσατο, τὰς δὲ χειρω-
θείσας πόλεις φρουραῖς ἀσφαλισάμενος ἐπανῆλθε
3 μετὰ τῆς δυνάμεως εἰς Αἴγυπτον. ἅμα δὲ τούτοις
πραττομένοις ἔνιοι[1] τῶν παρὰ Λυσιμάχῳ στρατιωτῶν αὐτομολήσαντες ἦλθον[2] ἐκ τῆς χειμασίας παρ'
Ἀντίγονον, Αὐταριάται μὲν δισχίλιοι, Λύκιοι δὲ
καὶ Παμφύλιοι περὶ ὀκτακοσίους. τούτοις μὲν οὖν
Ἀντίγονος φιλανθρώπως προσενεχθεὶς τούς τε μι-

[1] ἔνιοι Capps : οἱ.

set sail with the third group, so great a tempest rose that most of the vessels and the men on them were lost ; and indeed the large warship [1] that carried the general sank, and of the not less than five hundred men who sailed in her, only thirty-three were saved. Among these was Pleistarchus who, holding to a piece of wreckage, was cast ashore half dead. He was carried to Heraclea and after recovering from the misfortune went to Lysimachus at winter quarters, having lost the larger part of his army.

113. During these same days King Ptolemy, setting out from Egypt with an army of considerable size, subjugated all the cities of Coelê-Syria ; but while he was besieging Sidon certain men came to him with the false report that a battle had taken place between the kings in which Lysimachus and Seleucus had been defeated, that they had withdrawn to Heraclea, and that Antigonus, after winning the victory, was advancing with an army against Syria. Consequently Ptolemy, deceived by them and believing that their report was true, made a four-month's truce with the Sidonians, secured with garrisons the cities that he had captured, and went back to Egypt with his army. At the same time as this was taking place, some of the soldiers of Lysimachus, having left their winter quarters as deserters, went over to Antigonus, namely two thousand Autariatae and about eight hundred Lycians and Pamphylians. Now Antigonus, receiving these men

---

[1] The *hexeres* was probably a ship with a single row of oars on each side, each oar manned by six men, rather than a ship with six superimposed banks of oars on each side. Cp. Tarn, *Hellenistic and Naval Developments*, 122-141.

---

[2] ἦλθον added by Rhodoman.

σθοὺς ἔδωκεν, οὓς ἔφασαν ὀφείλεσθαι παρὰ Λυσι-
4 μάχου, καὶ δωρεαῖς ἐτίμησε. καθ' ὃν δὴ χρόνον
ἦλθε καὶ Σέλευκος ἐκ τῶν ἄνω σατραπειῶν δια-
βεβηκὼς εἰς Καππαδοκίαν μετὰ πολλῆς δυνάμεως
καὶ κατασκευάσας στεγνὰ τοῖς στρατιώταις παρεχείμαζεν.[1] εἶχε δὲ πεζοὺς μὲν εἰς δισμυρίους,
ἱππεῖς δὲ σὺν τοῖς ἱπποτοξόταις περὶ μυρίους
δισχιλίους, ἐλέφαντας δὲ ὀγδοήκοντα πρὸς τοῖς
τετρακοσίοις, ἅρματα δὲ δρεπανηφόρα πλείω τῶν
ἑκατόν.
5 Αἱ μὲν οὖν τῶν βασιλέων δυνάμεις τοῦτον τὸν
τρόπον ἠθροίζοντο, κεκρικότων ἁπάντων κατὰ τὴν
ἐπιοῦσαν θερίαν διὰ τῶν ὅπλων κρῖναι τὸν πόλεμον.
ἡμεῖς δέ, καθάπερ ἐν ἀρχῇ προεθέμεθα, τὸν γενόμενον τούτοις τοῖς βασιλεῦσι πρὸς ἀλλήλους πόλεμον περὶ τῶν ὅλων πράξεων ἀρχὴν ποιησόμεθα
τῆς ἑπομένης βίβλου.

---

[1] παρεχείμαζεν Dindorf : παραχειμάζειν.

in kindly fashion, not only gave them the pay which 302 B.C. they said was due them from Lysimachus but also honoured them with gifts. At this time Seleucus also arrived, having crossed over from the upper satrapies into Cappadocia with a large army, and after making huts for the soldiers he went into winter quarters near by. He had foot-soldiers to the number of about twenty thousand, about twelve thousand horsemen including his mounted archers, four hundred and eighty elephants, and more than a hundred scythed chariots.

In this way, then, the forces of the kings were being gathered together, since they all had determined to decide the war by force of arms during the coming summer. But, as we proposed in the beginning, we shall make the war that these kings waged against each other for supreme rule the beginning of the following book.

INDEX OF NAMES

447

INDEX OF NAMES

448

INDEX OF NAMES

INDEX OF NAMES

INDEX OF NAMES

INDEX OF NAMES

452

INDEX OF NAMES

453

INDEX OF NAMES

Printed in Great Britain by R. & R. CLARK, LIMITED, *Edinburgh*

THE LOEB CLASSICAL LIBRARY

VOLUMES ALREADY PUBLISHED

LATIN AUTHORS

AMMIANUS MARCELLINUS. J. C. Rolfe. 3 Vols. (*2nd Imp. revised.*)

APULEIUS: THE GOLDEN ASS (METAMORPHOSES). W. Adlington (1566). Revised by S. Gaselee. (*7th Imp.*)

ST. AUGUSTINE, CONFESSIONS OF. W. Watts (1631). 2 Vols. (Vol. I *7th Imp.*, Vol. II *6th Imp.*)

ST. AUGUSTINE, SELECT LETTERS. J. H. Baxter. (*2nd Imp.*)

AUSONIUS. H. G. Evelyn White. 2 Vols. (*2nd Imp.*)

BEDE. J. E. King. 2 Vols. (*2nd Imp.*)

BOETHIUS: TRACTS AND DE CONSOLATIONE PHILOSOPHIAE. Rev. H. F. Stewart and E. K. Rand. (*6th Imp.*)

CAESAR: CIVIL WARS. A. G. Peskett. (*5th Imp.*)

CAESAR: GALLIC WAR. H. J. Edwards. (*10th Imp.*)

CATO AND VARRO: DE RE RUSTICA. H. B. Ash and W. D. Hooper. (*2nd Imp.*)

CATULLUS. F. W. Cornish: TIBULLUS. J. B. Postgate; and PERVIGILIUM VENERIS. J. W. Mackail. (*12th Imp.*)

CELSUS: DE MEDICINA. W. G. Spencer. 3 Vols. (Vol. I *3rd Imp. revised*, Vols. II and III *2nd Imp.*)

CICERO: BRUTUS AND ORATOR. G. L. Hendrickson and H. M. Hubbell. (*3rd Imp.*)

CICERO: DE FATO; PARADOXA STOICORUM; DE PARTITIONE ORATORIA. H. Rackham. (With De Oratore, Vol. II.) (*2nd Imp.*)

CICERO: DE FINIBUS. H. Rackham. (*4th Imp. revised.*)

1

CICERO : DE INVENTIONE, etc. H. M. Hubbell.
CICERO : DE NATURA DEORUM AND ACADEMICA. H. Rackham. (2nd Imp.)
CICERO : DE OFFICIIS. Walter Miller. (6th Imp.)
CICERO : DE ORATORE. E. W. Sutton and H. Rackham. 2 Vols. (2nd Imp.)
CICERO : DE REPUBLICA AND DE LEGIBUS. Clinton W. Keyes. (4th Imp.)
CICERO : DE SENECTUTE, DE AMICITIA, DE DIVINATIONE. W. A. Falconer. (6th Imp.)
CICERO : IN CATILINAM, PRO MURENA, PRO SULLA, PRO FLACCO. Louis E. Lord. (3rd Imp. revised.)
CICERO : LETTERS TO ATTICUS. E. O. Winstedt. 3 Vols. (Vol. I 6th Imp., Vols. II and III 4th Imp.)
CICERO : LETTERS TO HIS FRIENDS. W. Glynn Williams. 3 Vols. (Vols. I and II 3rd Imp., Vol. III 2nd Imp. revised and enlarged.)
CICERO : PHILIPPICS. W. C. A. Ker. (3rd Imp.)
CICERO : PRO ARCHIA, POST REDITUM, DE DOMO, DE HARUSPICUM RESPONSIS, PRO PLANCIO. N. H. Watts. (2nd Imp.)
CICERO : PRO CAECINA, PRO LEGE MANILIA, PRO CLUENTIO, PRO RABIRIO. H. Grose Hodge. (3rd Imp.)
CICERO : PRO MILONE, IN PISONEM, PRO SCAURO, PRO FONTEIO, PRO RABIRIO POSTUMO, PRO MARCELLO, PRO LIGARIO, PRO REGE DEIOTARO. N. H. Watts. (2nd Imp.)
CICERO : PRO QUINCTIO, PRO ROSCIO AMERINO, PRO ROSCIO COMOEDO, CONTRA RULLUM. J. H. Freese. (2nd Imp.)
CICERO : TUSCULAN DISPUTATIONS. J. E. King. (4th Imp.)
CICERO : VERRINE ORATIONS. L. H. G. Greenwood. 2 Vols. (Vol. I 3rd Imp., Vol. II 2nd Imp.)
CLAUDIAN. M. Platnauer. 2 Vols.
COLUMELLA : DE RE RUSTICA. H. B. Ash. 2 Vols. Vol. I. Books I-IV. (2nd Imp.)
CURTIUS, Q. : HISTORY OF ALEXANDER. J. C. Rolfe. 2 Vols.
FLORUS. E. S. Forster ; and CORNELIUS NEPOS. J. C. Rolfe. (2nd Imp.)
FRONTINUS : STRATAGEMS AND AQUEDUCTS. C. E. Bennett and M. B. McElwain. (2nd Imp.)
FRONTO : CORRESPONDENCE. C. R. Haines. 2 Vols. (2nd Imp.)
GELLIUS. J. C. Rolfe. 3 Vols. (2nd Imp.)
HORACE : ODES AND EPODES. C. E. Bennett. (14th Imp. revised.)

THE LOEB CLASSICAL LIBRARY

HORACE: SATIRES, EPISTLES, ARS POETICA. H. R. Fairclough. (8th Imp. revised.)

JEROME: SELECT LETTERS. F. A. Wright. (2nd Imp.)

JUVENAL AND PERSIUS. G. G. Ramsay. (7th Imp.)

LIVY. B. O. Foster, F. G. Moore, Evan T. Sage and A. C. Schlesinger. 14 Vols. Vols. I-XIII. (Vol. I 4th Imp., Vols. II, III and IX 3rd Imp., Vols. IV-VII, X-XII 2nd Imp. revised.)

LUCAN. J. D. Duff. (3rd Imp.)

LUCRETIUS. W. H. D. Rouse. (7th Imp. revised.)

MARTIAL. W. C. A. Ker. 2 Vols. (Vol. I 5th Imp., Vol. II 4th Imp. revised.)

MINOR LATIN POETS: from PUBLILIUS SYRUS to RUTILIUS NAMATIANUS, including GRATTIUS, CALPURNIUS SICULUS, NEMESIANUS, AVIANUS, with "Aetna," "Phoenix" and other poems. J. Wight Duff and Arnold M. Duff. (2nd Imp.)

OVID: THE ART OF LOVE AND OTHER POEMS. J. H. Mozley. (3rd Imp.)

OVID: FASTI. Sir James G. Frazer. (2nd Imp.)

OVID: HEROIDES AND AMORES. Grant Showerman. (4th Imp.)

OVID: METAMORPHOSES. F. J. Miller. 2 Vols. (Vol. I 10th Imp., Vol. II 8th Imp.)

OVID: TRISTIA AND EX PONTO. A. L. Wheeler. (3rd Imp.)

PETRONIUS. M. Heseltine; SENECA: APOCOLOCYNTOSIS. W. H. D. Rouse. (8th Imp. revised.)

PLAUTUS. Paul Nixon. 5 Vols. (Vols. I and II 5th Imp., Vol. III 3rd Imp., Vols. IV-V 2nd Imp.)

PLINY: LETTERS. Melmoth's translation revised by W. M. L. Hutchinson. 2 Vols. (Vol. I 6th Imp., Vol. II 4th Imp.)

PLINY: NATURAL HISTORY. H. Rackham and W. H. S. Jones. 10 Vols. Vols. I-VI and IX. (Vol. I 3rd Imp., Vols. II-IV 2nd Imp.)

PROPERTIUS. H. E. Butler. (7th Imp.)

PRUDENTIUS. H. J. Thomson. 2 Vols.

QUINTILIAN. H. E. Butler. 4 Vols. (3rd Imp.)

REMAINS OF OLD LATIN. E. H. Warmington. 4 Vols. Vol. I (Ennius and Caecilius). Vol. II (Livius, Naevius, Pacuvius, Accius). Vol. III (Lucilius, Laws of the XII Tables). Vol. IV (Archaic Inscriptions). (Vol. IV 2nd Imp.)

3

SALLUST. J. C. Rolfe. (*3rd Imp. revised.*)

SCRIPTORES HISTORIAE AUGUSTAE. D. Magie. 3 Vols. (Vol. I *3rd Imp.*, Vol. II *2nd Imp. revised.*)

SENECA: APOCOLOCYNTOSIS. *Cf.* PETRONIUS.

SENECA: EPISTULAE MORALES. R. M. Gummere. 3 Vols. (Vol. I *4th Imp.*, Vols. II and III *3rd Imp. revised.*)

SENECA: MORAL ESSAYS. J. W. Basore. 3 Vols. (Vol. II *3rd Imp. revised*, Vols. I and III *2nd Imp. revised.*)

SENECA: TRAGEDIES. F. J. Miller. 2 Vols. (Vol. I *4th Imp.*, Vol. II *3rd Imp. revised.*)

SIDONIUS: POEMS AND LETTERS. W. B. Anderson. 2 Vols. Vol. I.

SILIUS ITALICUS. J. D. Duff. 2 Vols. (Vol. I *2nd Imp.*, Vol. II *3rd Imp.*)

STATIUS. J. H. Mozley. 2 Vols. (*2nd Imp.*)

SUETONIUS. J. C. Rolfe. 2 Vols. (Vol. I *7th Imp.*, Vol. II *6th Imp.*)

TACITUS: DIALOGUS. Sir Wm. Peterson; and AGRICOLA AND GERMANIA. Maurice Hutton. (*6th Imp.*)

TACITUS: HISTORIES AND ANNALS. C. H. Moore and J. Jackson. 4 Vols. (Vols. I and II *3rd Imp.*, Vols. III and IV *2nd Imp.*)

TERENCE. John Sargeaunt. 2 Vols. (Vol. I *6th Imp.*, Vol. II *5th Imp.*)

TERTULLIAN: APOLOGIA AND DE SPECTACULIS. T. R. Glover; MINUCIUS FELIX. G. H. Rendall. (*2nd Imp.*)

VALERIUS FLACCUS. J. H. Mozley. (*2nd Imp. revised.*)

VARRO: DE LINGUA LATINA. R. G. Kent. 2 Vols. (*2nd Imp. revised.*)

VELLEIUS PATERCULUS AND RES GESTAE DIVI AUGUSTI. F. W. Shipley.

VIRGIL. H. R. Fairclough. 2 Vols. (Vol. I *17th Imp.*, Vol. II *13th Imp. revised.*)

VITRUVIUS: DE ARCHITECTURA. F. Granger. 2 Vols. (Vol. I *2nd Imp.*)

GREEK AUTHORS

ACHILLES TATIUS. S. Gaselee. (*2nd Imp.*)

AENEAS TACTICUS, ASCLEPIODOTUS AND ONASANDER. The Illinois Greek Club. (*2nd Imp.*)

AESCHINES. C. D. Adams. (*2nd Imp.*)

THE LOEB CLASSICAL LIBRARY

AESCHYLUS. H. Weir Smyth. 2 Vols. (Vol. I *6th Imp.*, Vol. II *5th Imp.*)

ALCIPHRON, AELIAN AND PHILOSTRATUS: LETTERS. A. R. Benner and F. H. Fobes.

APOLLODORUS. Sir James G. Frazer. 2 Vols. (*2nd Imp.*)

APOLLONIUS RHODIUS. R. C. Seaton. (*4th Imp.*)

THE APOSTOLIC FATHERS. Kirsopp Lake. 2 Vols. (Vol. I *8th Imp.*, Vol. II *6th Imp.*)

APPIAN'S ROMAN HISTORY. Horace White. 4 Vols. (Vol. I *3rd Imp.*, Vols. II, III and IV *2nd Imp.*)

ARATUS. *Cf.* CALLIMACHUS.

ARISTOPHANES. Benjamin Bickley Rogers. 3 Vols. (Vols. I and II *5th Imp.*, Vol. III *4th Imp.*) Verse trans.

ARISTOTLE: ART OF RHETORIC. J. H. Freese. (*3rd Imp.*)

ARISTOTLE: ATHENIAN CONSTITUTION, EUDEMIAN ETHICS, VIRTUES AND VICES. H. Rackham. (*3rd Imp.*)

ARISTOTLE: GENERATION OF ANIMALS. A. L. Peck. (*2nd Imp.*)

ARISTOTLE: METAPHYSICS. H. Tredennick. 2 Vols. (*3rd Imp.*)

ARISTOTLE: METEOROLOGICA. H. D. P. Lee.

ARISTOTLE: MINOR WORKS. W. S. Hett. " On Colours," " On Things Heard," " Physiognomics," " On Plants," " On Marvellous Things Heard," " Mechanical Problems," " On Indivisible Lines," " Situations and Names of Winds," " On Melissus, Xenophanes, and Gorgias." (*2nd Imp.*)

ARISTOTLE: NICOMACHEAN ETHICS. H. Rackham. (*5th Imp. revised.*)

ARISTOTLE: OECONOMICA AND MAGNA MORALIA. G. C. Armstrong. (With Metaphysics, Vol. II.) (*3rd Imp.*)

ARISTOTLE: ON THE HEAVENS. W. K. C. Guthrie. (*3rd Imp.*)

ARISTOTLE: ON THE SOUL, PARVA NATURALIA, ON BREATH. W. S. Hett. (*2nd Imp. revised.*)

ARISTOTLE: ORGANON. H. P. Cooke and H. Tredennick. 3 Vols. Vol. I. (*2nd Imp.*)

ARISTOTLE: PARTS OF ANIMALS. A. L. Peck; MOTION AND PROGRESSION OF ANIMALS. E. S. Forster. (*3rd Imp.*)

ARISTOTLE: PHYSICS. Rev. P. Wicksteed and F. M. Cornford. 2 Vols. (Vol. I *2nd Imp.*, Vol. II *3rd Imp.*)

ARISTOTLE: POETICS and LONGINUS. W. Hamilton Fyfe; DEMETRIUS ON STYLE. W. Rhys Roberts. (*5th Imp. revised.*)

THE LOEB CLASSICAL LIBRARY

ARISTOTLE: POLITICS. H. Rackham. (*4th Imp.*)

ARISTOTLE: PROBLEMS. W. S. Hett. 2 Vols. (Vol. I *2nd Imp. revised.*)

ARISTOTLE: RHETORICA AD ALEXANDRUM. H. Rackham. (With Problems, Vol. II.)

ARRIAN: HISTORY OF ALEXANDER AND INDICA. Rev. E. Iliffe Robson. 2 Vols. (*2nd Imp.*)

ATHENAEUS: DEIPNOSOPHISTAE. C. B. Gulick. 7 Vols. (Vols. I, V and VI *2nd Imp.*)

ST. BASIL: LETTERS. R. J. Deferrari. 4 Vols. (*2nd Imp.*)

CALLIMACHUS AND LYCOPHRON. A. W. Mair; ARATUS. G. R. Mair. (*2nd Imp.*)

CLEMENT OF ALEXANDRIA. Rev. G. W. Butterworth. (*3rd Imp.*)

COLLUTHUS. *Cf.* OPPIAN.

DAPHNIS AND CHLOE. *Cf.* LONGUS.

DEMOSTHENES I: OLYNTHIACS, PHILIPPICS AND MINOR ORATIONS: I-XVII AND XX. J. H. Vince. (*2nd Imp.*)

DEMOSTHENES II: DE CORONA AND DE FALSA LEGATIONE. C. A. Vince and J. H. Vince. (*3rd Imp. revised.*)

DEMOSTHENES III: MEIDIAS, ANDROTION, ARISTOCRATES, TIMOCRATES, ARISTOGEITON. J. H. Vince.

DEMOSTHENES IV-VI: PRIVATE ORATIONS AND IN NEAERAM. A. T. Murray. (Vol. IV *2nd Imp.*)

DEMOSTHENES VII: FUNERAL SPEECH, EROTIC ESSAY, EXORDIA AND LETTERS. N. W. and N. J. DeWitt.

DIO CASSIUS: ROMAN HISTORY. E. Cary. 9 Vols. (Vols. I and II *2nd Imp.*)

DIO CHRYSOSTOM. 5 Vols. Vols I and II. J. W. Cohoon. Vol. III. J. W. Cohoon and H. Lamar Crosby. Vols IV and V. H. Lamar Crosby. (Vols. I-III *2nd Imp.*)

DIODORUS SICULUS. 12 Vols. Vols. I-VI. C. H. Oldfather. Vol. VII. C. L. Sherman. Vols. IX and X. Russel M. Geer. (Vols. I-III *2nd Imp.*)

DIOGENES LAERTIUS. R. D. Hicks. 2 Vols. (Vol. I *4th Imp.*, Vol. II *3rd Imp.*)

DIONYSIUS OF HALICARNASSUS: ROMAN ANTIQUITIES. Spelman's translation revised by E. Cary. 7 Vols. (Vols. I-IV *2nd Imp.*)

EPICTETUS. W. A. Oldfather. 2 Vols. (*2nd Imp.*)

EURIPIDES. A. S. Way. 4 Vols. (Vols. I and II *7th Imp.*, Vol. III *6th Imp.*, Vol. IV *5th Imp.*) Verse trans.

THE LOEB CLASSICAL LIBRARY

THE LOEB CLASSICAL LIBRARY

ARISTOTLE: POLITICS. H. Rackham. (*4th Imp.*)
ARISTOTLE: PROBLEMS. W. S. Hett. 2 Vols. (Vol. I *2nd Imp. revised.*)
ARISTOTLE: RHETORICA AD ALEXANDRUM. H. Rackham. (With Problems, Vol. II.)
ARRIAN: HISTORY OF ALEXANDER AND INDICA. Rev. E. Iliffe Robson. 2 Vols. (*2nd Imp.*)
ATHENAEUS: DEIPNOSOPHISTAE. C. B. Gulick. 7 Vols. (Vols. I, V and VI *2nd Imp.*)
ST. BASIL: LETTERS. R. J. Deferrari. 4 Vols. (*2nd Imp.*)
CALLIMACHUS AND LYCOPHRON. A. W. Mair; ARATUS. G. R. Mair. (*2nd Imp.*)
CLEMENT OF ALEXANDRIA. Rev. G. W. Butterworth. (*3rd Imp.*)
COLLUTHUS. *Cf.* OPPIAN.
DAPHNIS AND CHLOE. *Cf.* LONGUS.
DEMOSTHENES I: OLYNTHIACS, PHILIPPICS AND MINOR ORATIONS: I–XVII AND XX. J. H. Vince. (*2nd Imp.*)
DEMOSTHENES II: DE CORONA AND DE FALSA LEGATIONE. C. A. Vince and J. H. Vince. (*3rd Imp. revised.*)
DEMOSTHENES III: MEIDIAS, ANDROTION, ARISTOCRATES, TIMOCRATES, ARISTOGEITON. J. H. Vince.
DEMOSTHENES IV–VI: PRIVATE ORATIONS AND IN NEAERAM. A. T. Murray. (Vol. IV *2nd Imp.*)
DEMOSTHENES VII: FUNERAL SPEECH, EROTIC ESSAY, EXORDIA AND LETTERS. N. W. and N. J. DeWitt.
DIO CASSIUS: ROMAN HISTORY. E. Cary. 9 Vols. (Vols. I and II *2nd Imp.*)
DIO CHRYSOSTOM. 5 Vols. Vols I and II. J. W. Cohoon. Vol. III. J. W. Cohoon and H. Lamar Crosby. Vols IV and V. H. Lamar Crosby. (Vols. I–III *2nd Imp.*)
DIODORUS SICULUS. 12 Vols. Vols. I–VI. C. H. Oldfather. Vol. VII. C. L. Sherman. Vols. IX and X. Russel M. Geer. (Vols. I–III *2nd Imp.*)
DIOGENES LAERTIUS. R. D. Hicks. 2 Vols. (Vol. I *4th Imp.*, Vol. II *3rd Imp.*)
DIONYSIUS OF HALICARNASSUS: ROMAN ANTIQUITIES. Spelman's translation revised by E. Cary. 7 Vols. (Vols. I–IV *2nd Imp.*)
EPICTETUS. W. A. Oldfather. 2 Vols. (*2nd Imp.*)
EURIPIDES. A. S. Way. 4 Vols. (Vols. I and II *7th Imp.*, Vol. III *6th Imp.*, Vol. IV *5th Imp.*) Verse trans.

THE LOEB CLASSICAL LIBRARY

EUSEBIUS: ECCLESIASTICAL HISTORY. Kirsopp Lake and J. E. L. Oulton. 2 Vols. (Vol. I *3rd Imp.*, Vol. II *4th Imp.*)

GALEN: ON THE NATURAL FACULTIES. A. J. Brock. (*4th Imp.*)

THE GREEK ANTHOLOGY. W. R. Paton. 5 Vols. (Vols. I and II *5th Imp.*, Vol. III *4th Imp.*, Vols. IV and V *3rd Imp.*)

THE GREEK BUCOLIC POETS (THEOCRITUS, BION, MOSCHUS). J. M. Edmonds. (*7th Imp. revised.*)

GREEK ELEGY AND IAMBUS WITH THE ANACREONTEA. J. M. Edmonds. 2 Vols. (Vol. I *3rd Imp.*, Vol. II *2nd Imp.*)

GREEK MATHEMATICAL WORKS. Ivor Thomas. 2 Vols. (*2nd Imp.*)

HERODES. *Cf.* THEOPHRASTUS: CHARACTERS.

HERODOTUS. A. D. Godley. 4 Vols. (Vols. I-III *4th Imp.*, Vol. IV *3rd Imp.*)

HESIOD AND THE HOMERIC HYMNS. H. G. Evelyn White. (*7th Imp. revised and enlarged.*)

HIPPOCRATES AND THE FRAGMENTS OF HERACLEITUS. W. H. S. Jones and E. T. Withington. 4 Vols. (Vols. I, II and IV *3rd Imp.*, Vol. III *2nd Imp.*)

HOMER: ILIAD. A. T. Murray. 2 Vols. (*6th Imp.*)

HOMER: ODYSSEY. A. T. Murray. 2 Vols. (*7th Imp.*)

ISAEUS. E. S. Forster. (*2nd Imp.*)

ISOCRATES. George Norlin and LaRue Van Hook. 3 Vols. (Vols. I and III *2nd Imp.*)

ST. JOHN DAMASCENE: BARLAAM AND IOASAPH. Rev. G. R. Woodward and Harold Mattingly. (*2nd Imp. revised.*)

JOSEPHUS. H. St. J. Thackeray and Ralph Marcus. 9 Vols. Vols. I-VII. (Vol. V *3rd Imp.*, Vols. I and VI *2nd Imp.*)

JULIAN. Wilmer Cave Wright. 3 Vols. (Vol. I *2nd Imp.*, Vol. II *3rd Imp.*)

LONGUS: DAPHNIS AND CHLOE. Thornley's translation revised by J. M. Edmonds; and PARTHENIUS. S. Gaselee. (*3rd Imp.*)

LUCIAN. A. M. Harmon. 8 Vols. Vols. I-V. (Vols. I, II and III *3rd Imp.*, Vol. IV *2nd Imp.*)

LYCOPHRON. *Cf.* CALLIMACHUS.

LYRA GRAECA. J. M. Edmonds. 3 Vols. (Vol. I *4th Imp.*, Vols. II and III *3rd Imp.*)

LYSIAS. W. R. M. Lamb. (*2nd Imp.*)

MANETHO. W. G. Waddell; PTOLEMY: TETRABIBLOS. F. E. Robbins. (*2nd Imp.*)

7

THE LOEB CLASSICAL LIBRARY

Marcus Aurelius. C. R. Haines. (*4th Imp. revised.*)

Menander. F. G. Allinson. (*3rd Imp. revised.*)

Minor Attic Orators. 2 Vols. K. J. Maidment and J. O. Burtt. (Vol. I *2nd Imp.*)

Nonnos: Dionysiaca. W. H. D. Rouse. 3 Vols. (Vol. III *2nd Imp.*)

Oppian, Colluthus, Tryphiodorus. A. W. Mair.

Papyri. Non-Literary Selections. A. S. Hunt and C. C. Edgar. 2 Vols. (Vol. I *2nd Imp.*) Literary Selections. Vol. I (Poetry). D. L. Page. (*3rd Imp.*)

Parthenius. *Cf.* Longus.

Pausanias: Description of Greece. W. H. S. Jones. 5 Vols. and Companion Vol. arranged by R. E. Wycherley. (Vols. I and III *2nd Imp.*)

Philo. 10 Vols. Vols. I-V. F. H. Colson and Rev. G. H. Whitaker; Vols. VI-IX. F. H. Colson. (Vols. I-III, V-IX *2nd Imp.*, Vol. IV *3rd Imp.*)
Two Supplementary Vols. from the Armenian Text. Ralph Marcus.

Philostratus: The Life of Apollonius of Tyana. F. C. Conybeare. 2 Vols. (Vol. I *4th Imp.*, Vol. II *3rd Imp.*)

Philostratus: Imagines; Callistratus: Descriptions. A. Fairbanks.

Philostratus and Eunapius: Lives of the Sophists. Wilmer Cave Wright. (*2nd Imp.*)

Pindar. Sir J. E. Sandys. (*7th Imp. revised.*)

Plato I: Euthyphro, Apology, Crito, Phaedo, Phaedrus. H. N. Fowler. (*9th Imp.*)

Plato II: Theaetetus and Sophist. H. N. Fowler. (*4th Imp.*)

Plato III: Statesman, Philebus. H. N. Fowler; Ion. W. R. M. Lamb. (*4th Imp.*)

Plato IV: Laches, Protagoras, Meno, Euthydemus. W. R. M. Lamb. (*3rd Imp. revised.*)

Plato V: Lysis, Symposium, Gorgias. W. R. M. Lamb. (*4th Imp. revised.*)

Plato VI: Cratylus, Parmenides, Greater Hippias, Lesser Hippias. H. N. Fowler. (*3rd Imp.*)

Plato VII: Timaeus, Critias, Clitopho, Menexenus, Epistulae. Rev. R. G. Bury. (*3rd Imp.*)

Plato VIII: Charmides, Alcibiades, Hipparchus, The

THE LOEB CLASSICAL LIBRARY

LOVERS, THEAGES, MINOS AND EPINOMIS. W. R. M. Lamb. (2nd Imp.)

PLATO: LAWS. Rev. R. G. Bury. 2 Vols. (3rd Imp.)

PLATO: REPUBLIC. Paul Shorey. 2 Vols. (Vol. I 4th Imp., Vol. II 3rd Imp.)

PLUTARCH: MORALIA. 14 Vols. Vols. I-V. F. C. Babbitt; Vol. VI. W. C. Helmbold; Vol. X. H. N. Fowler. (Vols. I, III and X 2nd Imp.)

PLUTARCH: THE PARALLEL LIVES. B. Perrin. 11 Vols. (Vols. I, II, III and VII 3rd Imp., Vols. IV, VI, VIII-XI 2nd Imp.)

POLYBIUS. W. R. Paton. 6 Vols.

PROCOPIUS: HISTORY OF THE WARS. H. B. Dewing. 7 Vols. (Vol. I 2nd Imp.)

PTOLEMY: TETRABIBLOS. Cf. MANETHO.

QUINTUS SMYRNAEUS. A. S. Way. (2nd Imp.) Verse trans.

SEXTUS EMPIRICUS. Rev. R. G. Bury. 4 Vols. (Vols. I and III 2nd Imp.)

SOPHOCLES. F. Storr. 2 Vols. (Vol. I 9th Imp., Vol. II 6th Imp.) Verse trans.

STRABO: GEOGRAPHY. Horace L. Jones. 8 Vols. (Vols. I and VIII 3rd Imp., Vols. II, V and VI 2nd Imp.)

THEOPHRASTUS: CHARACTERS. J. M. Edmonds; HERODES, etc. A. D. Knox. (3rd Imp.)

THEOPHRASTUS: ENQUIRY INTO PLANTS. Sir Arthur Hort. 2 Vols. (2nd Imp.)

THUCYDIDES. C. F. Smith. 4 Vols. (3rd Imp.)

TRYPHIODORUS. Cf. OPPIAN.

XENOPHON: CYROPAEDIA. Walter Miller. 2 Vols. (Vol. I 3rd Imp., Vol. II 4th Imp.)

XENOPHON: HELLENICA, ANABASIS, APOLOGY, AND SYMPOSIUM. C. L. Brownson and O. J. Todd. 3 Vols. (Vols. I and III 3rd Imp., Vol. II 4th Imp.)

XENOPHON: MEMORABILIA AND OECONOMICUS. E. C. Marchant. (3rd Imp.)

XENOPHON: SCRIPTA MINORA. E. C. Marchant. (2nd Imp)

(For Volumes in Preparation see next page.)

THE LOEB CLASSICAL LIBRARY

VOLUMES IN PREPARATION

GREEK AUTHORS

ARISTOTLE: DE MUNDO, etc. D. Furley and E. S. Forster.
ARISTOTLE: HISTORY OF ANIMALS. A. L. Peck.
PLOTINUS. A. H. Armstrong.

LATIN AUTHORS

ST. AUGUSTINE: CITY OF GOD.
CAESAR: AFRICAN, ALEXANDRINE AND SPANISH WARS. A. S. Way.
[CICERO:] AD HERENNIUM. H. Caplan.
CICERO: PRO SESTIO, IN VATINIUM, PRO CAELIO, DE PROVINCIIS CONSULARIBUS, PRO BALBO. J. H. Freese and R. Gardner.
PHAEDRUS AND OTHER FABULISTS. B. E. Perry.

DESCRIPTIVE PROSPECTUS ON APPLICATION

CAMBRIDGE, MASS.	LONDON
HARVARD UNIV. PRESS	WILLIAM HEINEMANN LTD
Cloth $2.50	Cloth 15s.